The Rites of Eastern Christendom

The Rites of Eastern Christendom

ARCHDALE KING

VOLUME 1

GORGIAS PRESS
2007

This edition is a facsimile reprint of the
original edition published by the Catholic Book Agency, Rome, 1948

Set ISBN 978-1-59333-390-4

ISBN 978-1-59333-391-1 (Volume 1)

ISBN 978-1-59333-392-8 (Volume 2)

GORGIAS PRESS
46 Orris Ave., Piscataway, NJ 08854 USA
www.gorgiaspress.com

The paper used in this publication meets the minimum requirements of the
American National Standards.

Printed in the United States of America

CONTENTS

FOREWORD

The present state of human affairs should urge us ever more to strive for that unity of which Our Lord spoke when He said: "There shall be one fold and one Shepherd." In the light of such a prophecy, he who thinks that: "East is East and West is West and never the twain shall meet" is wrong in his reckoning, at least in matters of Church unity. For the day of union shall surely dawn.

The liturgy is the language of our Holy Mother the Church, and beneath the varying outward forms of Catholic ritual there is heard the common voice, recognisable by her children the world over. Yet outside the Catholic fold also there are liturgies in which the voice of truth is able to be recognised, however much it may have been dimmed, mingled as it is with discordant sounds that are not the voice of the one Shepherd, Jesus Christ.

The author of this book has set himself the task of instructing the ordinary folk in the Rites of Eastern Christendom. Many will be grateful to him for setting forth such instruction in so readable a form. The separated Eastern Churches find a place in the volume, and that is a great gain for those who wish to know more of the manner of worship of those who, whilst faithfully following Jesus

Christ according to the light of their conscience, have unfortunately become separated from the Apostolic See. It is satisfactory in these pages to see Christian worship in all its Eastern forms, and to be led to pray more earnestly for that oneness in Christ which must be the striving and goal of all Christian men.

London, May 1946.

† W. GODFREY
Archbishop of Cius
Apostolic Delegate in Great Britain

PREFACE

The aim of this book, which it has taken twenty years to write, is to provide a manual for those who wish to know something about the rites of Eastern Christendom.

Three of the chapters were published sixteen years ago, but they have been entirely rewritten and enlarged.

The book is emphatically not one for the expert liturgical scholar, but he is seldom to be found in this island.

In the first place, it may be remarked that The Rites of Eastern Christendom *is a Catholic publication, and therefore presupposes that communion* [1] *with the Apostolic See of Rome is a* sine qua non *of Catholic fellowship. As Mar Theophilus, a bishop of the Syro-Malankara rite in South India, said in 1931: "Communion with the Roman Pontiff is a certain sign that one is a member of the true Church. To be separated from the Roman Pontiff is schism."*

The separated Eastern churches, however, have not been excluded, and much information has been given in regard to their history, rites and ceremonies.

Within the framework of Catholic teaching, the writer has been at pains to say nothing offensive concerning those dissident Christians, who have kept the lamp of Christianity burning through many centuries of slavery and persecution.

There is of course the difficulty of nomenclature.

The term "schismatic" has been avoided, as it seems to imply a personal guilt to those who for reasons largely beyond

---

[1] "Whoever is not in the peace and unity of the Church will not be able to possess God." Pope Pelagius II (578-590). *Epist. ad episcopos Istriae, Acta Conc. Oecum.,* II, 107.

their control are members of churches out of communion with the see of Peter.

In respect to the faithful of the Byzantine and Armenian rites, the task is comparatively easy. For the former, the title "Orthodox" can be applied, as they alone of the separated Christians of the East accept the ecumenical council of Chalcedon (451). There is, however, the problem of whether to speak of "Ruthenian" or "Ukrainian" Catholics. The former term is used by the Holy Father in his recent encyclical letter[2] and by the Sacred Congregation for the Oriental Church. It would seem therefore to be the official title. On the other hand, the faithful of the rite insist on calling themselves "Ukrainians," and strongly resent the use of the word "Ruthenians." As this book is entirely devoid of any political or controversial aim the use of both terms has been retained.

The Armenian dissidents may be classed as "Gregorians" to distinguish them from their Catholic countrymen, notwithstanding the fact that St. Gregory the Illuminator, the apostle of Armenia, lived and died in communion with Rome.

The members of the other Eastern rites have been styled "Dissidents," a not very satisfactory term, but denoting those Orientals, who, since they are out of communion with the Pope, are not Catholics.

Sometimes, also, they have been described as either "Nestorians" or "Monophysites," although such labels are not intended to imply more than the fact that they are members of those churches which ostensibly came into being as a result of one or other of those heresies. The Catholics of the Eastern rites are never referred to as "Uniates," since the word is offensive to Catholic ears, although it is often used in all

---

[2] *Orientales Omnes Ecclesias,* December 23, 1945.

good faith by many Latin Catholics. "Uniates" and "Uniatism" imply liturgical hybridism, that is a violation of oriental liturgical integrity by the interpolation of Western customs, usages or ceremonial: a practice condemned by Rome. Alternatively, the words may suggest that the Roman rite is in some way superior to those of the East: a fallacy now equally reprobated by Rome.

One purpose for the publication of the book is that English Catholics may be helped to follow the directive of the Holy Father, when by the encyclical Rerum Orientalium *(1928) he urged upon* all *Catholics the importance of studying the Eastern Churches. A not unimportant result of such a study is a better knowledge of the Roman rite itself.*

Western Catholics, for the most part, are deplorably ignorant of the rites of the East, and seem sometimes even to glory in their "shame," although there is happily no reputable writer to-day, who would refer to the Byzantine liturgy as having "an awkward immobility which makes it impervious to all progress." [3]

The intolerable misunderstanding, injustice and persecution meted out to Ruthenian Catholics by their coreligionists of the Latin rite between the two world wars were incontrovertible proofs of the necessity for the carrying out of the papal instructions.

English Catholics are sometimes heard to speak slightingly and disparagingly of the Eastern rites, in spite of the repeated teaching of Rome to the contrary. Thus, the writer

---

[3] *Ce caractère, opposé à la marche de toute véritable orthodoxie, est une immobilité brute qui la rend inaccessible à tout progrès.* Dom Prosper GUÉRANGER, *Institutions liturgiques,* 2nd edit., t. I, chap. IX, p. 226.

The same writer (*Ibid.,* p. 228) gave it as his considered opinion that the four Eastern patriarchates would be Catholic to-day, if it had been possible to compel these churches to adopt the Latin rite and language.

once heard a priest describe a Syrian "low Mass" celebrated in his church as "little better than a dog fight," while it is a common occurrence to hear the liturgies that were used by doctors of the Universal Church spoken of as "fossilised" or failing to "march with the times."

Remarks such as these probably come from an inherent dislike of the unknown and the unusual, but they are not very helpful to the cause of unity, and it is ungenerous and unchivalrous to sneer at the worship of those who for centuries, in spite of Islamic ferocity and persecution, have remained faithful to Christ.

In describing the nine rites of Eastern Christendom, the writer has endeavoured to give the historical background and setting of the church to which each rite belongs; some account of the hierarchical organisations; the architecture of the ecclesiastical buildings; liturgical furnishings and books; and, finally, the texts of the various liturgies themselves.

The order of the chapters follows that found in the Annuario Pontificio.

In a work of this size it is well nigh impossible not to make mistakes, although the greatest pains have been taken to avoid or eliminate them.

Three very kind friends, all well known liturgical scholars, have examined each chapter, and given valuable advice. Most heartfelt thanks are due to them for their laborious and painstaking work—Dom Benedict Steuart, a monk of Prinknash Abbey; Fr. Ronald Pilkington, a priest formerly of the archdiocese of Florence, and now incardinated in that of Westminster; and Mr. Donald Attwater. The chapter on the Syrian rite has been examined by Mgr. Paul Hindo, Chorepiscopus and Procurator of the Syrian Patriarch to the Holy See; the Ethiopic rite by Fr. J. M. Hanssens, S. J., Consultor of the Sacred Congregation for the Oriental Church; the

Byzantine rite by Fr. Schwiegl, S. J., a priest of the Slav-Byzantine rite at the Russicum; the Chaldean rite by Fr. Garmo, a Chaldean priest of the eparchy of Mosul; and the Armenian rite by Fr. Kaftandjian, Vardaped and Vice Rector of the Armenian College. Priests, also, of the Rumanian and Ruthenian colleges have read the parts of the chapter on the Byzantine rite relating to their respective variants. Grateful thanks are owing to all the above for the trouble that they have taken to make the book more accurate.

General acknowledgements for assistance in the several rites will be found after the bibliography at the end of each chapter. His Eminence Cardinal Tisserant, Bishop of the suburbicarian diocese of Porto and Santa Rufina, and Secretary of the Sacred Congregation for the Oriental Church, has been graciously pleased to permit this book to be dedicated to him, and his Eminence has been so kind as to read the preface.

The faithful of the Eastern rites have in his Eminence a wise and learned adviser, in whom there is no shadow of "uniatism."

A debt of gratitude is owing also to Mgr. William Godfrey, Archbishop of Cius and Apostolic Delegate to Great Britain, who has been good enough to write a foreword.

The photographs of the Holy Father, Cardinal Tisserant, and the Byzantine liturgy in the Basilica of St. Peter have been reproduced through the courtesy of Signor Felici, photographer to the Holy See. Permission also has been kindly given by Mgr. Hindo for some photographs illustrative of the Syrian rite; by Fr. Kaftandjian, Vice Rector of the Armenian College, for those of the Patriarch Arpiarian and Cardinal Agagianian; by Fr. Bidawid for that of the Chaldean patriarch; by Fr. Jerome Leussink, a Benedictine of the Byzantine rite, for photographs of his paintings in the oriental chapel of the Eastern Congregation; by a priest of the Pontifical Ruthenian College (Rome) for several illustrations of his rite; by the "Universe" for a photograph of three bishops from Malabar; and by Mr. Claude Fisher of Walsingham for a reproduction of the Coptic eucharistic bread. Other photographs were taken by the author.

The writer himself professes no outstanding ability for his task beyond a profound interest in liturgical matters, combined with an intense love of Eastern rites, which has been fostered and encouraged by the patience, trouble and courtesy shown to him by Oriental bishops and clergy, Catholic and dissident alike.

In many instances, the manuscript dealing with a particular rite has been submitted to a priest of that rite.

The writer has had the good fortune to assist at every Catholic Eastern liturgy, with the exception of those celebrated in Malabar; and to attend all the liturgies of the dissidents, except those of the Malabar Jacobites, Nestorians and Ethiopians.

Mr. Alfred Butler [4] *has pointed out that "the rendering of Arabic names and words in English characters is a problem which no writer on oriental subjects has yet solved satisfactorily," and it is difficult to show consistency, when almost every book has some variation in spelling.*

This difficulty, also, is increased when, as is generally the case with Europeans, a writer is himself ignorant of Eastern languages, with the possible exception of Greek.

The statistics and condition of the several Oriental churches date for the most part from before the second world war (1939-1944), and consequently some of them have been materially altered by the appalling events of recent years.

---

[4] *The Ancient Coptic Churches of Egypt,* vol. I, Preface, p. XI.

This is especially the case with the Ruthenian Catholic church, which save for the diaspora *in Western Europe and the New World, may in a few years be a thing of the past— martyrdom, Siberia, and apostasy will have done their work in the alleged interest of that religious "freedom" and "democracy" which the allied nations have been fighting for!*

In 1931, the Sacred Congregation for the Eastern Church estimated the Oriental Catholics at 8,177,522, [5] *while the dissidents numbered about 157 millions—"et illas oportet* me adducere, et vocem meam audient, et fiet unum ovile, et unus pastor." [6]

Reconciliation, however, is only possible with integrity of rite. The Oriental Congregation, carrying out the wishes of the Pope, insists upon a liturgy free from latinisation. [7]

Changes may be small and comparatively unimportant, such as a slight variation in dress or the omission of some ceremonial adjunct, but it is nevertheless a violation of pledges, even if such a "uniatism" should come from the Easterns themselves, suffering from a liturgical inferiority complex— "Inimici hominis, domestici ejus." [8]

In conclusion, the author submits all that he has written to the magisterium *of the Catholic Apostolic and Roman Church.*

Walsingham, in fest. SS. Petri et Pauli, 1946.

Rome, in fest. S. Josaphat, 1946.

---

[5] It is estimated that there are about 26 non-Latin Catholics to every 1000 Latin Catholics: about 56 Catholic Easterns to every 1000 non-Catholic Easterns.

[6] Joann. X, 16.

[7] This is the policy of the present day. In the past, while Rome has always upheld integrity of rite in theory, certain minor changes were sometimes permitted.

[8] Matt. X, 36.

CHAPTER I

INTRODUCTION

" Liturgy is the first and indispensable
source of the true Christian spirit."
Pius X, *Motu proprio*, Nov. 23, 1903.

The Catholic religion is devotion to the person of Jesus
Christ, true God and true man, and the yearly cycle of the
liturgy venerates and honours, with a marvellous variety of
expression, our divine Lord, the author and founder of the
Church, as "King and Lord, and as King of kings." "In this
continuous praise of the Christ-King," the Sovereign Pontiff
in the encyclical letter instituting the feast of the Kingship
of Christ (*Quas primas*, December 11, 1925) says: "one can
easily discern the wonderful harmony between our rites and
those of the East, so that once again the adage holds good: [1]
'The rule of prayer establishes that of faith.' "

Evolution of the Liturgy

From the foundation of Christianity, the substance of the
liturgy or eucharistic service has been the reproduction of
what our Lord did in the upper room "on the day before he

---

[1] *Legem credendi statuat lex supplicandi.* St. Celestine I (422-432),
De gratia Dei Indiculus (cap. 8), joined to *Epist.* 21 (to the bishops
of Gaul against Pelagianism), *Apostolici verba praecepti.* DENZINGER,
Enchiridion Symbolorum (edit. 21-23, 1937), p. 66. Bossuet (*Défense
de la Tradition et des saints Pères*, p. 551), commenting on this adage,
says: " C'est le principal argument dont saint Augustin appuie sa
doctrine."

1 - A. A. KING. *The Rites of Eastern Christendom* - 1st Vol.

suffered," and this has always formed the basis of the Mass of the faithful.

The taking of bread and wine, mingled with a little water, the giving of thanks, the blessing of the elements and breaking of the bread, after repeating the words of institution, and finally the feeding upon these sacred species in holy communion have found a place in every Catholic liturgy from the days of the apostles, who in obedience to their master did these things "in remembrance of him."

In the *Acts of the Apostles* we also find the beginnings of the Mass of the catechumens, in lessons from the Old Testament, psalm-singing and preaching.   These aids to divine worship seem to have been taken from the use of the synagogue, [2] where we find the offering up of prayer by a recognised official minister.   The prayer called "Great Love" (*'Ahabah Rabbah*) was said before the reading from the Law, and the lessons were followed by a further prayer known as "Prayer" (*Tephilla*) or the "Eighteen Benedictions" (*Shemoneh 'Esreh*).   The later development in the Christian liturgy of offering intercessions after the gospel (prayer of the faithful) also appears to owe its origin to the synagogue service, which had a long series of prayers and blessings.

In early days, this first part was often divorced from the eucharist, although it sometimes preceded the holy sacrifice, especially when it formed the vigil service of Sunday (*pannuchis*), which was held in commemoration of the resurrection, and in a widely spread belief that our Lord would shortly come again as judge (*parousia*).

The celebrant in the first two centuries of the Christian

---

[1] W. O. E. OESTERLEY, *Psalms in the Jewish Church*, chap. VIII, pp. 144-145. London; Skeffington, 1910; cf. Morning prayer for Saturday, *Schacharit.*

era appears to have improvised at will, and within the limits set down above much of the service was extempore.

Several things, however, tended to stereotype liturgies, thus bringing to an end the necessarily temporary period of freedom in the order and wording of the eucharist.

In the first place, a constant repetition of prayer, praise, thanksgiving and intercession round a central theme inevitably produced a set form of words, at least in a given district.

Secondly, the service came to be attended by concelebrating presbyters, as well as by the faithful laity, and it became increasingly necessary to have a more or less fixed order, so that each section of the worshippers might take its share in the liturgy. This custom of concelebration, [*] the presbyters with the bishop, grew up "during the 2nd century, between Clement (ab. 99) and Hippolytus (235)."

Finally, the liturgical expressions used in an important church or by a well known bishop were copied by others. Thus, in course of time, the great sees, especially those of patriarchal rank, developed stereotyped liturgies, which their daughter churches were required to adopt, although even here we find additions and amendments in later centuries. This grouping of liturgies round a patriarchal or metropolitan see developed in the 4th and 5th centuries, producing distinct types in respect to the arrangement of some of the prayers.

The so-called *Apostolic Tradition of Hippolytus*, written about the year 225 and showing signs of an earlier work, has a short liturgy, beginning with the kiss of peace and ending with the doxology of the eucharistic prayer. An Ethiopic form of this rite underlies an anaphora which is still in use in the Ethiopic Church.

[*] Gregory Dix, *Shape of the Liturgy*, chap. II, p. 34.

The *Testament of the Lord* [4] is an expanded version in Syriac of the work of Hippolytus, but it is not now considered to be of a date earlier than the 4th century. The absence of the *sanctus* is explained as either a local custom or an intentional omission designed to give it a more ancient appearance.

The *Didache*, which probably originated in Egypt or Syria, is so entirely *sui generis* that it may possibly have been the production of a local sect. Dom Leclercq [5] considers its composition to have been before the end of the 1st century of our era, perhaps about the year 80 or 90, but modern scholarship tends to treat the document as descriptive of the Eastern agape in pre-Nicene times, and representative of 2nd century ideas about the liturgical eucharist.

The *Apostolic Constitutions* (VIII), which Dr. Neale and others have called the *Liturgy of St. Clement,* appear to have been a purely "literary" work, and never in actual use. Dom Guéranger [7] maintains that it was already completed by the time of the council of Nicea (325), but it would seem more likely to have been written between the year 370, when St. Basil wrote, and 390, when public penance was abolished, and also that at the time of its appearance the *disciplina arcani* was still in existence. The intercessions, however, are *in* the anaphora, which would seem to point to a later date.

The first liturgy which has come down to us is that of *St. James,* emanating from the patriarchal see of Antioch in the 4th century, and strongly influenced by Jerusalem. With

[4] S. SALAVILLE, *Liturgia,* XXIII, chap. III, p. 880.
[5] *Dict. d'Archéol. Chrét. et de Lit.,* art. *Didache.*
[6] Gregory DIX, *loc. cit.,* chap. IV, p. 93.
[7] *Institutions Liturgique,* t. III, pp. 26-27.
[8] LE BRUN, *Explication de la Messe,* t. II, pp. 19-25.

additions and alterations, it is used to-day in Greek by the Orthodox, [9] on two days in the year and in two places, and in Syriac by the Syrians, [10] Catholic as well as dissident, and by the Jacobites of Malabar and the Malankarese Catholic converts.

Tradition has ascribed the abridgement and rearrangement of this liturgy to St. Basil (ab. 329-379), who produced that which is known to-day as the *Liturgy of St. Basil*. This was introduced at Constantinople, where it became the normal Byzantine rite. Soon, however, another and still shorter liturgy was formulated, called after the name of *St. John Chrysostom* (ab. 347-407), but in general of later date. This succeeded in relegating the Basilian service book to certain days in the year, which the Orthodox church to-day has retained. Thus, the ordinary Byzantine liturgy is St. John Chrysostom, with St. Basil ten times annually.

Two more Antiochene liturgies came into being in the 5th century. One, the *East Syrian* rite, which was in use in the church of Edessa, and is found to-day among the Nestorians, as well as the Chaldean and Malabarese Catholics, and the other, the *Armenian* rite, which is a form of the Byzantine liturgy, received from Caesarea, and used by the whole nation, Gregorian and Catholic alike.

A second oriental parent rite is that of Alexandria, existing to-day in the *Coptic* and *Ethiopic* liturgies, which have been built up on the *Liturgy of St. Mark*.

The history of these several extant rites will be considered in the chapters which follow, but the liturgical developments

---

[9] Zakynthos (island of Zante) on the feast of St. James (October 23), since 1886, and Jerusalem, since 1900, on December 31. In recent years this liturgy has also been celebrated in Athens and Cyprus.

[10] A form of the liturgy of St. James is used in Syria by the Jacobites, and also by the Catholics of the Syrian and Maronite rites.

in the West, centring round the Apostolic See of Rome must be left to another volume.

With the evolution of the great patriarchates [11] came the custom of "rite following patriarchate," [12] although, as we shall see, the imperial ambition of New Rome reduced a more or less rigid uniformity on all those churches which remained in communion with Constantinople. The christological heresies of the Nestorians and Monophysites alone saved the rites of the East from a total Byzantinisation.

Schism

1054 has been the generally accepted date of the final schism between Rome and Constantinople, but historians are beginning to find that the separation between East and West was a gradual process, later in some countries than in others. Thus, Professor Dvornik [13] says: "One thing is sure: in spite of what happened in 1054, the faithful of both churches remained long unaware of any change in their relations and acts of intercommunion were so numerous that 1054 as the date of the schism becomes inadmissable .... These and other circumstances converge on the Crusades as the first starting

---

[11] From the 5th century, the liturgies seem to have grouped themselves round the patriarchates and some of the more important metropolitan sees, but the patriarchal division of Christendom was not a primitive feature in the Church. The council of Nicea (canon 6; 325) certainly recognised Rome, Alexandria and Antioch as sees of outstanding importance, but St. Gregory Nazianzen († ab. 390) wrote (*Orat.* 42, 23) of the "older bishops" generally as " patriarchs", and as late as the 6th century, we find Celidonius, bishop of Besançon, called "the venerable patriarch" (*Acta SS. Febr.*, III, 742 - *Vita Romani*, 2).

[12] The Italo-Greek-Albanian rite of *Magna Graecia* is an exception to this general rule.

[13] *Eastern Churches Quarterly. Church History and Christian Reunion*, pp. 29-30. January-March 1945.

point of the schism, or more correctly, of the estrangement that arose between East and West. Some historians date the schism from the failure of the emperor Manuel (1143-1180) to regain his possessions in the West and so to restore relations between the five patriarchates."

Reunion

Several groups, which are Catholic to-day, have claimed perpetual orthodoxy, maintaining that their spiritual forbears were never out of communion with Rome, but it seems highly improbable that there is any historical justification for such an assertion. All the separated churches of the East have in the course of centuries yielded many converts, who have been received with their own specific service books, hieratic languages and customs. Matters of faith, however, admitted of no compromise, whether the believers were European, Asiatic or African, white, brown or black. The Church of God is "One" and "Catholic," all holding the creed in exactly the same way, in peace and communion with the Apostolic See, and at the same time sweeping over all national boundaries, extending throughout the whole earth.

These *Orientales uniti sanctae sedi* are sometimes called "Uniates" but the term, which was coined by the opponents of the Ukrainian synod of Brest, is generally used in an offensive sense by non-Catholics, and is never found in the ecclesiastical acts of Rome or in such publications as the *Annuario Pontificio*. The word is derived through the Polish *unia*, [14] but the more respectful term for "union" is *jednosc*. [15] "Uniatism" implies hybridism or latinisation.

---

[14] Russian, *unija*; Greek, *ounia*.
[15] Russian, *soedinenie*; Greek, *enosis*.

Thus, Fr. Cyril Korolewskji, [16] one of the consultors of the Sacred Oriental Congregation, says: "Uniatism is evil in itself: it is to sound orientalism what individualistic piety, the forsaking of liturgical offices, the love of *devotionettes* and small chapels, rose water piety is to strong and healthy Western Christianity."

The importance of the Eastern Catholics is out of all proportion to their numbers, for out of 330 millions of Catholics less than 9 millions are of the oriental rites. Yet, despite their minority, "this variety of rites ... declares the divine unity of the Catholic faith," [17] "for they adorn the common Mother Church with a royal garment of many colours." [18]

All these "are to be held in equal esteem and equal honour," [19] since "the Church of Christ is neither Latin, nor Greek, nor Slav, but Catholic, it does not make any distinction between its sons, be they Greeks, Latins, Slavs or members of other national groups, all hold the same position before this Apostolic See." [20]

In the face of these pronouncements on the part of recent popes it would be manifestly disloyal as well as ignorant for Western Catholics to assume an ecclesiastical superiority complex in their regard. St. John Chrysostom, St. Athanasius and St. Ephrem were not semi-orthodox or semi-Catholic, and a Ukrainian, Syrian or Armenian in communion with Rome is a Catholic exactly in the same degree as an Englishman or Italian who belongs to the Church.

There are 9 Eastern rites, as well as a number of By-

---

[16] *L'Uniatisme.*   Prieuré d'Amay-sur-Meuse.
[17] Leo XIII in the encyclical *Orientalium dignitas* (1894).
[18] Pius XII in the encyclical *Orientalis Ecclesiae* (1944).
[19] Leo XIII in the encyclical *Orientalium dignitas* (1894).
[20] Benedict XV in the "motu proprio" *Dei providentis* (1917).

zantine variants, used by different national groups converted at different times and under different circumstances.

As we have seen, each group of converts from heresy or schism retained the rite to which it had been accustomed; and there was for example no idea of putting a member of the West Syrian rite under the jurisdiction of the Melkite patriarch of Antioch, although many of the Melkites would consider this to be right and proper. Thus it has come about that there are three Catholic patriarchs of Alexandria [21] and four of Antioch, [22] while Aleppo has two archbishops [23] and an apostolic administrator. [24]

In ancient times, a plurality of prelates in a city was strictly forbidden, and we find the East Syrian synod, convened in 410 by Mar Isaac, prohibiting the "confusion" of having two or three bishops in the same town. The 4th council of the Lateran (1215) made a similar enactment: "We forbid altogether that one and the same city or diocese should have several pontiffs, like one body with several heads, which would be a monster." This regulation was explained and defended by Pope Benedict XIV (1740-1758).

The actual situation to-day, however, works well, and there is neither serious rivalry nor cross-jurisdiction, although there are those [25] who look forward to the day when Syria

[21] Latin (non resident), Melkite (a personal title still retained) and Coptic (now in abeyance).

[22] Latin (non resident), Melkite, Syrian and Maronite.

[23] Armenian and Syrian.

[24] Maronite (bishop of Cyprus).

[25] e. g. Philip Assemrany, in an article in *Al-Manâra,* the official publication of the Maronite patriarchate (January 1939), in which the author claims that Christian unity will only be found in the East when the " pure Antiochene rite, proper to Syria" is restored to all. Guglielmo DE VRIES, *Cattolicismo e Problemi Religiosi nel Prossimo Oriente* (Rome 1944), II, p. 44.

will have "one rite, one patriarch and one episcopal authority."

Canon [26] law protects the Eastern Catholics from proselytising on the part of the Latins, and without a serious reason and special permission from Rome no change [27] of rite is permitted.

Attendance, [28] however, at the Mass of another rite to one's own fulfills the Sunday obligation for all Catholics, and holy communion may be received in any church, even when the custom is to receive under both kinds.

Eastern Catholics are under the care of the Sacred Congregation for the Oriental Church, of which the Pope himself is prefect.

A more detailed description of the action of Rome throughout the centuries in respect to the East will be found later in the chapter.

Many of the proposals for union were made with the Eastern Orthodox church, and the majority of oriental Catholics come from one or other of its national churches, but it is a serious mistake to suppose that the Byzantine church is the only and exclusive witness of the ancient and authentic eastern tradition.

During the octave of the Epiphany in the church of S. Andrea della Valle, Rome, Mass is said or sung on each of the eight days in a Western rite and an Eastern rite, while a sermon is preached every day in a different language. The custom was started in 1836 by the Venerable Vincent Pallotti (1798-1850), founder of the Pious Society of Missions, as an affirmation of the unity and universality of

[26] Canon 98, 2.
[27] Canon 98, 3.
[28] Code of canon law, 866.

the Catholic Church, and at the same time to afford an opportunity for prayer that they "all may be one" in one fold and under one shepherd.

Legitimacy of the Liturgies

The *legitimacy* of the liturgies rests on the consent and approbation of the Church, which can be readily given since they all, at least in substance, date from before the days of schism. Some of the Syrian anaphoras seem to have been composed after the separation from Rome, but they have little in their composition which is heterodox.

After secession, each of the several churches seems to have hated liturgical novelty and clung to antiquity, recalling the dictum [29] of the council of Nicea (325)—"Let ancient customs prevail."

Thus the eastern rites were substantially preserved from heterodox interpolations, and on the return to unity of groups of their members but little was required in the way of alteration or amendment.

Authenticity of the Liturgies

The *authenticity* of the liturgies is derived from the constant and living use of the Church, rather than from the names [30] of the alleged authors, [31] many of which are manifestly false. In a certain sense, however, we may allow

---

[29] τὰ ἀρχαῖα ἔθη κρατείτω.

[30] "*Tales porro sunt Liturgiae, de quibus huc usque diximus, et quarum commendatio praecipua, non tam a nominibus eorum tribuuntur, quam a communi usu Ecclesiarum, quae a multis saeculis ad altaria iis utuntur, petenda est.*" RENAUDOT, *Lit. Orient*, t. I, p. XLIX.

[31] e. g. Twelve Apostles in the Syrian and Ethiopic rites; St. John the Evangelist in the Syrian rite.

St. Basil and St. John Chrysostom; while in regard to St. James it may be affirmed that the liturgy originated at Jerusalem, and seems to have been known to St. Cyril, if we may judge from the *Catecheses mystagogicae*.[32] St. Mark as the author of the liturgy of Alexandria was repudiated by Theodore IV Balsamon, patriarch of Antioch (1186-1203), but his intention was to force all those in communion with Constantinople to use her service books and none other, and a study of the liturgies of Egypt points to a very remote antiquity for the Alexandrine type.

Antiquity, Origin and Integrity of the Liturgies

The *antiquity* and *origin* of the liturgies have been already referred to, and it will be shown how careful Rome has been to maintain their *integrity*, sometimes ordering the removal of some latinism perpetrated by an ill advised oriental.

It has often been said, for the most part by non-Catholics, that Rome is the bitter foe [33] of "national liturgies." One of the outstanding supporters of this mendacious statement [34] was Dr. Neale, [35] who after recounting the fate of the Gallican, Mozarabic and Neo-Gallican liturgies said that Rome "would have, had it lain in her power, destroyed, with equal readiness, the venerable liturgies of the East." Speaking of the rite of Malabar, the same writer [36] says of Menezes, archbishop of Goa, that he "so completely extirpated the

---

[32] *Catech.* XXIII; written ab. 347.

[33] The statement can be more truly applied to Constantinople.

[34] The question of Western liturgies is not under discussion in this volume, which deals solely with those of the East.

[35] *Essays on Liturgiology and Church History*, chap. IX, *Prospects of the Oriental Church*, p. 279. London 1867.

[36] *Ibid.*, p. 279.

rites of one of the most ancient churches in the world—the Christians of St. Thomas—that they are now absolutely unknown." It will be seen from chapter VIII of this book how ludicrous and false is such a perversion of the facts. "Everyone knows," continues Neale, "and no one complains more bitterly than Renaudot—that the Roman revisions of Eastern liturgies make them absolutely worthless; and that the changes wrought in the Syrian and Armenian offices have rendered them utterly unlike their original selves!" Certainly some revisions and alterations have been needless and unnecessary, and scholars like Renaudot have been at pains to point them out, but deliberate "uniatism" has been the work of ill-advised Latins *against* the wishes of the Apostolic See or of the Eastern Catholics themselves—*et inimici hominis, domestici ejus.* [37] In any case, despite the alterations, *all* the Oriental rites have retained their integrity. The restoration of the pope's name to the diptychs, necessarily demanded on a return to Catholic unity, was of the nature of a revival of the *status quo ante.*

Liturgical Texts

The *Liturgical texts* in some of the rites used by Catholics are better and more accurately produced than in the corresponding books of the dissidents, but in 1928 the writer saw a *euchologion* of the Orthodox on the altar of a Rumanian Catholic church.

In 1937, however, Pope Pius XI expressed a wish that, wherever possible, a Catholic edition of the liturgy might be used.

The liturgies were in manuscript until the 16th century,

[37] Matt. X, 36.

at which time many of them were virtually unknown in the West.

Pope Clement XI (1700-1721) established a congregation for the correction of the oriental liturgical books, and Pius IX (1846-1878) in 1862 requested the Eastern patriarchs and bishops to send to Propaganda all the books that might need revision or amendment. At an audience on February 8, 1930, Pope Pius XI approved the setting up of a liturgical commission within the Congregation for the Eastern Church for the liturgical publications of the different rites.

Liturgical Languages

The language of the liturgy depends upon authority, and in the case of the Catholic rites upon that of the Apostolic See.

In the first centuries of the Church, the spread of the gospel was facilitated by the universality of Greek in the civilised world, and the Septuagint version of the Bible and the earliest liturgies were written in that language.

The Aramaic spoken at the Last Supper in the Upper Room at Jerusalem appears to have soon given place to Greek. By the year 50 Greek was used in the liturgy at Antioch, and it is probable that the whole Bible was translated into Greek before *A. D.* 200. It has been thought that Greek persisted at Antioch till the 13th or 14th century.

To-day, *Greek* is used by the Byzantine Catholics [38] of Greece and Constantinople, the Italo-Greek-Albanians of Italy and Sicily, the Melkites (occasionally), and in the Hungarian eparchy of Hajdudorog.

---

[38] It seems hardly necessary to point out that the Orthodox equally use Greek for the liturgy.

At a solemn papal Mass, the epistle and gospel are sung in Greek, as well as in Latin, while the evangelical lesson is preceded by the exclamation σοφία with the Greek choir responding Δόξα συ, Κύριε, δόξα συ at its conclusion. The custom of using the two languages was mentioned in 1286 by Durandus, [39] bishop of Mende.

On great feasts at Constantinople, the gospel of the liturgy was at one time preceded by the recitation of the gospel in Latin. A letter [40] of Pope Leo IX to the patriarch Michael Caerularius shows that this was still the custom in the 11th century.

The epistle and gospel were sung in Hebrew, Greek and Latin at the coronation [41] of Pope Alexander V (1409) during the council of Pisa.

In the 10th century at Monte Cassino, [42] the chants on Easter Tuesday, until after the gospel, were alternately Latin and Greek, while until the revolution the abbey of St. Denis near Paris had the entire Roman Mass sung in Greek on the octave day of St. Denis (October 16).

A copy of the rule [43] of the monastery of St. Sabbas (Palestine), made in the 12th or 13th century, speaks of Greek, Syrian, Georgian and "Frankish" monks, who said their offices and sang the first part of the liturgy in their own languages at their own churches, but came together in the great church of the Greeks for the liturgy of the faithful.

---

[39] *Ration. div. Offic.*, lib. III, n. 36, fol. 92.
[40] *Epist. I ad Michaelem patriarcham*, Labb. t. IX, p. 963.
[41] Luke D'ACHERY, *Spicilegium*, t. VI, p. 334.
[42] D. Edmond MARTÈNE, *De Antiquis Ecclesiae Ritibus*, t. I, p. 281.
[43] Prosper GUÉRANGER, *Instit. lit.*, t. III, chap. III, p. 148.
[44] The copy of the rule is now preserved on Sinai. *Cod. Sinai.* 1096, cited by George EVERY, *Eastern Churches Quarterly* (July-September, 1946), p. 364.

Among the Italo-Albanians, the chief responses are sung in some places in *Albanian,* and certain formulas are recited in the same language.

Greek is the official hieratic tongue in the eparchy of Hajdudorog, but from ignorance of that speech many priests use *Magyar,* although they lack the formal authority of Rome.

In 1939, the Holy See authorised Fr. Bourgeois, a Jesuit of the Byzantine rite, to recite the liturgy in *Esthonian* at Esna near Talinn.

Vernacular *Rumanian* has been used since the 17th century in Rumania by Catholics and Orthodox alike.

Church Slavonic or *Staroslav* is the liturgical language of the Ruthenian, Russian, Jugoslav [15] and Bulgarian Catholics, while *Georgian* is found in a monastery at Constantinople and among the missionaries in Georgia.

The Melkites of the united patriarchates of Antioch, Jerusalem and Alexandria finally substituted *Arabic* for *Syriac* in the 17th century.

The Orthodox church allows more than 14 languages for the liturgy, and in the United States English is used by a group of Ukrainians who have fallen into schism.

Syriac, an idiom of Hebrew, is said to have been spoken by our Lord himself, and in looking at the title of the cross it is of interest to consider that the inscription on it was written in the three great liturgical languages of the world: Latin, Greek and Syriac. At the present day there are two forms of Syriac used in the liturgy: West Syrian of

[15] This applies only to the eparchy of the Byzantine rite, and the majority of the Catholics in the country are of the Roman rite, although some churches of Dalmatia and of the Franciscan third order of regulars are permitted to celebrate in old Slavonic, with missals printed in Glagolitic characters.

Palace of the Sacred Congregation for the Oriental Church, Rome

Chapel of the Byzantine Rite.
Palace of the Sacred Congregation for the Oriental Church, Rome

the Syrian, Maronite and Malankarese rites, and East Syrian of the Chaldean and Malabarese rites. The normal and every day language of the Syrians and Maronites is Arabic, and the lessons are now read in that tongue for the benefit of the people. The Maronite synod of 1736 [46] forbade priests to translate the Syriac text into Arabic during the liturgy itself, and the synod of Sharfeh (1888) issued a similar prohibition for the Syrians. The objection, however, was not to the use of Arabic, but lest an inadequate translation might lead to error. Official interpreters who made a running translation of the scriptural passages for the benefit of those who only understood Syriac [47] were referred to by Etheria in Jerusalem (end of the 4th century) and Procopius († 303) in Scythopolis. [48]

The classical *Armenian* of the liturgy is said to be akin to Persian, and to have words which bear a resemblance to German.

The rites of the ancient patriarchate of Alexandria have two obsolete languages—*Coptic* in Egypt and *Geez* in Ethiopia.

At the beginning of the 14th century, we read of the Franciscan missionary, John of Montecorvino [49] (1305), who, during the life-time of a Tartar king (George), was permitted by Pope Clement V (1305-1314) to say Mass in *Tartar*.

Le Brun [50] says that Paul V in 1611 authorised the use of *Chinese—non tamen vulgarem*—by the Jesuit missionaries, but that the permission was never carried out in

[46] Part. II, chap. 13, n. 11.
[47] The liturgy was celebrated in Greek.
[48] The modern Beisan.
[49] LE BRUN, *Explication de la Messe*, t. IV, pp. 211-212.
[50] *Ibid.*, t. IV, pp. 239-243.

practice, whereas Guéranger [51] alleges that the Jesuits applied three times (1615, 1667, 1671) for this authorisation, and it was never accorded.

The great abbot of Solesmes, however, looked upon a liturgical language other than Latin as a definite aid to schism. "If the Roman pontiffs," says Dom Guéranger, [52] "had been able to establish liturgical unity and the Latin language in the East as in the West the schism of Photius and Michael Caerularius would not so easily have gained the victory, and the destinies of half the world, compromised by this revolt, would have taken another course." In another place, the Benedictine liturgist [53] looks forward to a time when "the language of Rome, like her faith, will be for the East, as well as for the West, the sole means of unity and regeneration." The forcing into schism [54] of millions of Ukrainians was made possible, says Dom Guéranger, [55] by *l'indulgence désastreuse de Jean VIII. La Ruthénie* [56] *reconquise, est de nouveau perdue, faute d'être unie à Rome par la langue sacrée.*

Rome, however, has thought otherwise. It is not her policy to do evil that good may come, even if, as Dom Guéranger, [57] supposes: *Une même langue liturgique avec Rome eût sauvé du schisme.*

The insistence of certain Western heretics at the time of

[51] *Institutions Liturgiques,* t. III, pp. 126-128.
[52] *Ibid.,* t. I, chap. IX, pp. 227-229.
[53] *Ibid.,* t. I, p. 142.
[54] Dom Guéranger considers that the work of the tsars in the 18th and 19th centuries was made possible by the permission to use the Slavonic language accorded to the south Slavs by Pope John VIII in 880. *Instit. Lit.,* t. III, p. 489.
[55] *Inst. Lit.,* t. III, p. 110.
[56] *Ibid.,* p. 109.
[57] *Ibid.,* p. 74.

the Reformation that they should have a liturgy in a "language understanded of the people" has caused the use of a living tongue to sound offensive to many Catholic ears, although there is nothing inherently sacred about a dead language. The council of Trent[58] was rightly suspicious of a vernacular rite, and "for several (churches), the vulgar tongue in divine service would even seem to have been the direct instrument of separation."[59]

Times, however, have changed, and Rome has sanctioned for the eastern rites both the obsolete and the vernacular.

For Catholics, it is a question of what is permitted by the Apostolic See—nothing more.

The ecclesiastical training of students demands a perfect knowledge of the liturgical language necessary to the rite. Thus, Pope Benedict XIV in 1751 enjoined the Melkite Basilian monks of St. Saviour to acquire a very exact knowledge of Greek: "You may understand how necessary it is for you to acquire an exact knowledge of Greek, not an ordinary superficial knowledge, but a really thorough and finished knowledge, such as is indispensable for a complete appreciation of the authors' thought."

Celibacy and Marriage

The ordination of married men to the priesthood still continues in some of the Eastern Catholic churches, but, although there is a saying that "a priest's wife is the most precious of possessions, for if she dies she can never be replaced," the practice is not encouraged, and the number

[58] Sess. XXII, cap. VIII.
[59] GUÉRANGER, loc. cit., t. III, p. 140.

of married priests is decreasing. Dom Guéranger, [60] however, exaggerates when he says that "the marriage of priests is the sole cause for the daily celebration of Mass not being able to be established in the church of the East."

Dissident clergy who are converted to the Catholic Church are normally permitted to retain their wives and continue their ministry.

The Diaspora

Persecution and economic hardships have diffused the Eastern rites throughout the New World, but care is taken that the emigrants may not be drawn into the Latin rite.

Devotional Borrowings

Roman devotions have been adopted by nearly all the Catholic groups, but integrity of rite is not necessarily interfered with by elements of universal piety or the common manifestation of devotions approved by the Holy See for all Catholics. This is especially true of Benediction, which in some form or other is found in all the groups except the Russian.

"Of course," writes Dom Benedict Morrison, [61] "exposition of the blessed Sacrament remains an anomaly in an oriental rite; for according to Eastern mentality holy things are to be hidden and not exposed. The only exceptions, so far as we know, are the elevation of the sacred species at the τὰ ἅγια τοῖς ἁγίοις, and their uncovering again for the

---

[60] "Assurément, il ne faut pas être bien profond, ni bien clairvoyant, pour avoir compris que les mariages des prêtres est la cause unique pour laquelle la célébration journalière de la Messe n'a pu s'établir dans l'Eglise d'Orient."—Institutions liturgiques, t. II, chap. XXIV, p. 643.

[61] Eastern Churches Quarterly, vol. III, No. 8 (October 1939), pp. 480-481, n.

distribution of holy communion. In the Antiochene liturgy, the priest blesses the people with the holy gifts veiled before the communion of the faithful. The blessed Sacrament, also, is veiled in the procession from the table of the prothesis to the altar during the Liturgy of the Presanctified in the Byzantine rite. In the Pontifical Greek and Russian Colleges in Rome they have neither Exposition and Benediction of the blessed Sacrament nor the feast of Corpus Christi." The foregoing quotation shows therefore that Western devotional practices borrowed by Eastern Catholics are contrary to their tradition and foreign to oriental mentality.

Catholic Faith expressed in the Eastern Liturgies

The Eastern rites are of outstanding value for their dogmatic witness, and show clearly that the faith of the East is one with the West—the *lex credendi*[62] is found in the *lex orandi*.

In fact, this is more noticeable in the oriental liturgies than in the Roman Mass, which is terse and austere in comparison.

The members of the Eastern churches have had an innate love of theology, and it was said that in the 5th century an Alexandrine workman was certain to bring up the subject of the natures of our Lord in any conversation. It was the theological emperors who caused the endless troubles of the Church in the East, while St. Gregory of Nyssa († ab. 395) said: "the city is full of workmen and slaves who are all theologians, if you ask a man to change money, he will tell you how the Son differs from the Father;

---

[62] Pope St. Celestine, *Legem credendi statuat lex supplicandi* (422-432). *Epist. XXI*, apud *Constant.*

if you ask the price of a loaf, he will argue that the Son is less than the Father; you want to know if the bath be ready, and you are told that the Son was made out of nothing."

From the East came all the great christological heresies and the battle for sacred images (pictures). Ecclesiastical hymns provided the street cries for orthodox and heterodox alike; while the liturgy was the centre of life and culture for all classes.

The doctrine of the Holy Trinity is succinctly expressed in the Byzantine odes and theotokion, the Syrian anaphora of St. Xystus and in the liturgy of the East Syrians.

The Byzantine church bore the brunt of the attacks against the right belief in the *Incarnation,* and the liturgical books of that church are filled with a perfect exposition of the orthodox doctrine. Nestorians and Monophysites, in an attempt to support their respective heresies, have introduced phrases into their liturgies which appear to give credence to their errors, but they are surprisingly few in number and can be easily expunged or altered for the use of Catholics.

The *Redemptive work* and *Resurrection of our Lord* are acknowledged in every liturgy; while the *Sacrifice of the Mass* and *Transubstantiation* [63] are clearly admitted in all the rites.

In fact, no liturgy has such forceful language on the presence of Christ in the blessed eucharist as the Coptic, in the prayer said by the priest before communion. The exact moment of consecration, which has become a ubject of

[63] The earliest use of the Greek equivalent for transubstantiation (μετουσίωσις) seems to date from a translation of the profession of faith made by Michael VIII Paleologus, a profession which had been imposed in a Latin text, containing the use of the word *transubstantiatio,* by Clement IV (1265-1268) and approved by Gregory X (1268-1276) in 1274.

controversy with the dissidents, in no way affects the doctrine expressed.

The *divine and supernatural character of the Church* is declared in the communion chant of the Armenians, where the church is apostrophized as "mother of faith, ark of the holy espousals, celestial couch, habitation of thy immortal spouse, who has adorned thee for ever." No less definite is the East Syrian liturgy, and the *kudra* for the 3rd Sunday of the Sanctification guarantees the perpetuity of the Church of Christ on the testimony of the Apostolic See: "*Rome* says that the church shall continue from generation to generation, and shall not be overcome by kings or emperors." The *Primacy of Peter* is clearly expressed in the liturgy and office of his feast in all the rites, and we are very far from that "Roman spiritual Caesarism," which the Russian Kolemin invented to support the schismatic position of his church. The Byzantine church says of St. Peter: "Thou art worthily called the Rock, on which the Lord built the inviolate faith of the Church, constituting thee chief pastor of the reasoning sheep." And again: "the foundation of the Church and rock of the faith" (*menaion*, January 16 for St. Peter's Chains at vespers); "Immoveable basis of dogmas;" "Throne of the faith;" "sitting on the first throne of the apostles."

On June 29, the same church sings: "Let the protector of Rome, the steward of the kingdom, rock of the faith, firm foundation stone of the Catholic church, be celebrated in sacred hymns;" and on the following day, the Commemoration of all the Apostles (*menaion*): "Summit and foundation of the apostles, you left all things and followed your master, saying: May I die with you, so as to live the life of the blessed. You became the first bishop of Rome; you were the glory and honour of the greatest of all cities and fulcrum of the Church, O Peter, against which the gates of hell shall never prevail." The April commemoration of St. Martin [64] in the *menaion* says: "By what name shall I call thee, O Martin! Shall I call thee the glorious ruler of the Orthodox faith for all? Or the sacred chief of divine dogmas, unstained by error? ... or the most true reprover of heresy? ... We know that thou wast the foundation of bishops, pillar of the Orthodox faith, teacher of religion ... Thou didst adorn the divine see of Peter, and since thou from this divine rock didst guard the Church unmoved, so now with him (St. Peter) art thou glorified."

In equally clear terms a Byzantine hymn honours St. Gregory Dialogus (St. Gregory the Great): "Most sacred pastor, thou art the successor of the see and also of the zeal of the chief (St. Peter), cleansing the people and bringing them to God, successor of the throne of the prince of the choir of disciples, whence thou dost by thy teaching as with a torch enlighten the faithful, O Gregory! When the first of churches embraced thee, she watered all the earth that is beneath the sun with divine teaching. Hail, torch of religion, who dost light up all the world with the glory of thy words! Lighthouse, who dost call back to the shore those who are tossed among the waves of error! Instrument sounded by the breath of the holy Ghost." On the feast of St. Leo the Great (February 18) the Byzantine office bears witness to the supremacy of the pope: "He himself, who now is the venerable successor of Peter and has acquired his presidency as riches."

Although an "understanding of the Roman primate and of a real and effective primacy forms part of the religious

---

[64] The feast of Pope St. Martin is observed in the West on November 12, and in the East on April 13 and September 20.

psychology of the Byzantine," [65] some passages in the liturgy have been deliberately deleted from Greek Orthodox books [66] of the 19th century. Thus, the phrase "Rock of the faith" has been removed from the editions of the *Menaion* since 1843, although it has been kept in the Russian books. A Greek edition published at Venice in 1895 has taken away the title "chief bishop of Rome," and altered all the passages in the office of St. Peter and St. Paul (June 29) that referred to their sojourn at Rome.

The other Eastern churches have been no less insistent on the Roman primacy, and the Syrian anaphora of the most blessed apostle St. Peter says: "Thou art he, who before time was, God foresaw from eternity and predestined, O most fortunate Peter, as the governor and ruler of the Church." Some of the Syrian anaphoras have been ascribed to papal authorship, which is significant of the ancient reputation of Rome in the Christian East. Renaudot, [67] in writing of the anaphora of St. Xystus, says that it might be considered the work of a Maronite anxious to emphasize union with Rome, but the conjecture would be false. On November 24 (St. Clement), the Catholic Syrians sing in the office: "This is he who sits on the throne of Peter, head of the apostles, in the Roman capital and became like him (St. Peter) even in power, common pastor of the whole flock of Christ and of the whole world after Pope Cletus, who again reigned after Linus, first bishop of Rome after Peter the apostle."

The Coptic formula of absolution contains the words: "Thou art Peter etc." The Nestorian, as well as the Chal-

[65] *Incontro ai fratelli separati di Oriente*, p. 214; Fr. Venantius GRUMEL, *Echos d'Orient*, t. XXX (1931), p. 430.
[66] *Incontro ai Fratelli separati di Oriente*, p. 215.
[67] *Liturgiarum Orientalium collectio*, t. II, pp. 142-143, n. 1.

dean office, has the following praise of St. Peter on his feast: "Peter, prince of the apostles, on whose strength the Saviour built his faithful Church. Simon Peter who holds the keys of heaven (the heights) and hell (the depths). Simon Cephas, to whom the master said: 'Feed my sheep and my lambs; for to thee I will give the keys of the spiritual treasures, so that you may bind and loose all things which are on earth, and all things which are in heaven,' betook himself to Rome in order to root out error and sow the doctrine of life in that city. Wise architect, builder of churches, demand from thy *magisterium* the salvation of our souls."

The same office says: "Head and first-born of the disciples ... I (Christ) have appointed thee steward of the kingdom of heaven: govern and administer wisely as a prudent majordomo, distribute faithfully my spiritual treasure;" and, in another place: "Blessed art thou, Simon, steward and possessor of the keys of the kingdom: holy Church has been built upon thee, as thou art the rock of strength! Thy master has placed thee in the midst of the Church as a foundation."

The Formula of Hormisdas (514-523), which the Greeks and Latins accepted at the 4th council of Constantinople in 869, contained the following words: "Because in the Apostolic See the Catholic religion is always kept immaculate ... in which communion is the whole, real and perfect solidity of the Christian religion ... I promise that in future I will not say in the holy mysteries (i. e. in the diptychs) the names of those who are banished from the communion of the Catholic church, that is, who do not agree with the Apostolic See." [68]

[68] The formula was confirmed at the councils of Lyons (1274) and Florence (1439), and played a part in the Vatican council of 1870.

The dogmatic authority of the pope was maintained by St. Nicephorus († 828) in his *Apologeticum* [69] *pro sacris imaginibus*, and in the panegyric of St. Peter by Nicetas of Paphlagonia, the disciple of Photius, we have the "swan song" [70] of that faith which the Byzantines held for ten centuries.

In short, the Eastern fathers taught and the Eastern liturgies expressed the belief that *a*) Peter was the Prince of the Apostles and the "Rock;" *b*) the Roman pontiffs succeed him in this office; *c*) therefore the Roman bishop has jurisdiction over the whole Church of Christ; and *d*) the faith of his Church is the standard of orthodoxy for all Christians. These four points, as Dr. Adrian Fortescue [71] says, make up exactly what Catholics believe about the pope.

Before leaving this subject of the primacy of Peter and his successors one very significant fact may be noted. In 529 years, that is from the year 323 to the usurpation of Photius in 852, 203 years were spent by Constantinople out of communion with Rome, but in every single case the Eastern

---

[69] "... *quia illi (romani pontifices) sacerdotii principatum sortiti sunt, eamque dignitatem a duobus coryphaeis apostolis traditam habent.*" MI-GNE, *Pat. Graec.*, t. C., col. 597.

[70] "*Haec verba ad nostras perveniunt aures tamquam suprema ac iucundissima echus, tamquam verus cygnorum cantus, illius fidei quam per decem saecula Byzantini professi sunt.*" A. Vogt, *Deux discours inédits de Nicétas de Paphlagonie, disciple de Photius*, in *Orientalia Christiana*, No. LXXI (1931), p. 20.

[71] *The Orthodox Eastern Church*, chap. II, p. 61. Writing to Pope St. Paschal I from his prison at Bonita (Asia Minor), St. Theodore the Studite († 826) says: "Listen, O apostolic bishop, shepherd appointed by God over the flock of Jesus Christ. You have received the keys of the kingdom of Heaven: you are the rock on which the Church is built: you are Peter, since you fill his see. Help us." Donald Attwater, *Golden Book of Eastern Saints*, p. 51.

church was on the wrong or heretical side, and to-day the Orthodox [72] themselves would agree that on all these occasions Rome was right!

The *ecumenical councils* are declared to be divinely inspired, but the Byzantine church acknowledges their number to be seven, whereas the Monophysite churches admit three, and the Nestorian only two.

The Sunday after the Ascension is kept by the Orthodox as the Feast of the 318 Fathers of Nicea (325); while the absolution in the Coptic liturgy is said to come from the mouths of the 318 Nicene Fathers, the 150 from Constantinople (381) and the 100 from Ephesus (431).

The *cult of our Lady and the Saints* is more developed in the Eastern liturgies than in the Western, and feasts in honour of the *Theotokos* were celebrated some centuries earlier in the orient. The Greeks thus earned the title of ὑποφιλοπάρθενοι, and Photius charged the Latins with insufficient reverence towards her, since they spoke of the "God-bearing" as "holy Mary." A convert Russian [73] has expressed the belief that "Mary is the link that will unite the two churches."

One Byzantine chant declares: "Those who do not kiss thy sacred image, O God-bearing Virgin, reckon them as atheists and hand them over to hell fire;" while the fourth strophe in every hymn is in honour of the blessed Virgin under the title of *Theotokion.* One prayer seems to anticipate the litany of Loreto: "Help of the meek, hope of the hopeless, consolation of the sad, food of the hungry, cure of the sick, safeguard of sinners, aid and refuge of all Christians."

---

[72] Adrian FORTESCUE, *op. cit.,* chap. II, pp. 96-97.
[73] SCHUVALOFF, ap. *Incontro ai fratelli separati di Oriente,* p. 247.

The Armenians, in a hymn sung over a child on the
fortieth day after baptism, salute the Mother of God as the
"door of heaven." The Copts and Ethiopians, encouraged
by the example of their hero, St. Cyril, show a very marked
devotion to our Lady in their liturgies. The former celebrate
32 feasts in her honour, and they have a form of the "Hail
Mary" in the prayer of the 11th hour: "Hail thou who hast
found grace, holy Mary, Mother of God: blessed art thou
amongst women, and blessed is the fruit of thy womb. Thou
hast borne to us the Saviour of our souls."

The Ethiopian dissidents are said to exaggerate this
devotion to a point of superstition. Protestants are sometimes
known as "enemies of Mary" (zerré Mariam), but the term
was first applied to the Catholic Portuguese, [74] for, as Fr. Tel-
lez said, the Ethiopians did not find them intense enough
in their devotion to the Mother of God!

The Nestorians deny the title of "Mother of God" to
the blessed Virgin, but they nevertheless hail her as "the
Mother of the Lord of heaven and earth" and as the "chaste,
pure, holy, sanctified .... ever Virgin, sanctified from the
womb and chosen from the beginning as a refuge, home,
dwelling, temple, place of rest, tomb, palace and throne
for the ever-living God."

It is, indeed, true to say that East Syrian dissidents
are as fervent in their praise of our Lady as the members of
the other Eastern rites. In the Warda, [75] appointed to be
recited on all feasts of our Lady, she is spoken of as: one
"in whom God dwelt, and from whom sprang the Son of
God .... Her infancy was spotless and her youth immaculate

---

[74] Incontro ai fratelli separati di Oriente (Roma, 1945), p. 256.
[75] The Warda derives its name from George Warda, a writer of the
13th century.

.... the sick and afflicted called upon her name and were
healed, and when she rested (died) her prayers were a tower
of help to all the distressed."

The burial office for priests in the same rite says: "O
Mary .... plead and supplicate for mercy upon the sinners
who flee to thy prayers, that they may not be lost. Let thy
prayers be to us a wall of defence in this world, and in that
which is to come."

The *Assumption of our Lady* [76] is almost the only feast
of our Lady which is observed in every Eastern rite without exception.

Among the Syrians, the most common name for the
feast, "Transmigration of the Mother of God" (*'îdo d'šunô-
yoh d'Yoldat Aloho*), implies the *corporal* Assumption. Thus
the West Syrians, Jacobite as well as Catholic, chant: "The
heaven of heavens received the throne of thy *body*, O Mother
of light, and so thou sittest in glory with thy Son amidst the
supernal beings and with them thou chantest in glory." In
the *Warda* of the East Syrian rite on feasts of our Lady, after
narrating the legend of how the Jews attempted to burn the
body of the blessed Virgin, we read: "But the Virgin came
forth and fled away in a cloud, and with her choirs of angels,
playing on their trumpets and horns, saying: 'Blessed art
thou, O Mary.' "

The corporal Assumption is admitted by the Armenians [77]
in a canticle of Gregory of Nareg (ab. 951) and in an authentic declaration of the synod of Sis [78] (1342).

The Sunday *Theotokion* [79] of the Copts says: "Who is

---

[76] Greek, κοίμησις "falling asleep."
[77] *Incontro ai fratelli separati di Oriente*, p. 251.
[78] MANSI, t. XXV, col. 1218.
[79] Tertiary paraphrase to section VI. De Lacy O'LEARY, *Daily
Office and Theotokia of the Coptic Church*, p. 139.

that in heaven except the Virgin, the body that bore Jesus Christ." In a book [80] published at Cairo in 1913, it is stated that although sacred Scripture does not teach the Assumption no one would dare to doubt it, as it is a truth that the Fathers have received from the Apostles.

The *Immaculate Conception* is latent and implicit in the Eastern liturgies, but the definition of the doctrine (1854) has had the effect of the Catholics expressing the dogma more clearly, and the dissidents tending to deny any such belief in their church.

Thus, Anthimos VII, [81] Orthodox patriarch of Constantinople, in 1895 declared that the "Church of the Seven Councils" had defined that there is only one immaculate conception, that of Christ, and that the "Papic Church" defines in opposition the immaculate conception of his blessed Mother as well. This is an absolutely false statement, and the Catholic Church down to the year 787 had defined nothing on this subject at all.

In keeping a feast of the Conception distinct from the Nativity it shows, however, that the separated East looks upon the conception itself as something especially holy and worshipful. The feast was probably not in the Roman calendar before the 14th century, but the marble calendar of Naples, so early as the 9th century, has a commemoration of the *Conceptio Sanctae Mariae Virginis*. Part of the object of the feast was certainly the announcement of the miraculous conception by St. Anne, as related in the proto-evangelion [82] of St. James, but the passive conception of our Lady was also

---

[80] *Incontro* etc., p. 251.

[81] Synod of Constantinople (1895): DUCHESNE, *Eglises séparées*, p. 110.

[82] Chap. II.

commemorated. The first authentic mention of the feast [83] in the Byzantine church comes from the end of the 7th or the beginning of the 8th century, and the earliest homily extant is that of John, bishop of Eubea, a contemporary of St. John Damascene († 749). From the 8th to the 10th century some Byzantine eparchies observed December 9 as one of the greatest feasts, and it was so ordered in 1166 by a constitution of the emperor Manuel I.

Among the Syrians, we find St. Ephrem (373), writing in a hymn about the year 370: "Thou and thy mother are the only ones who under every aspect are entirely beautiful, since in thee, O Lord, there is no stain nor any blemish in thy mother." Severus of Antioch (518), Denys bar Salibi (1171) and other writers [84] speak of a certain purification on the day of the Annunciation. In the 17th century a Jacobite patriarch [85] declared to Fr. Besson, S. J., his full adhesion to the doctrine.

The observance of the feast was referred to by St. Andrew of Crete (675), St. John Damascene (749) and St. Theodore the Studite (ab. 826). A Byzantine chant for "the child-begetting mother of the Mother of God, Anne" (Dec. 9), says: "For it was fitting that thou also in that should have a privilege as Mother of God, so that in the things of nature

---

[83] It is probable that the feast began at the end of the 6th or the beginning of the 7th century, and that it was observed on December 9. GORDILLO, *Compendium Theologiae Orientalis*, chap. V, art. II, pp. 150-151.

[84] *Incontro ai Fratelli separati di Oriente*, p. 252.

[85] "*Ego pauper Ignatius Andreas, Patriarcha Antiochenus nationis Syrorum, confirmo hanc sententiam orthodoxam, quam explanavit P. Joseph e S. J. dominam nostram Virginem purissimam sanctam Mariam, semper liberam exstitisse et immunem a peccato originali, ut explicuerunt antiqui sancti Patres longe plurimi, magistri Orentalis Ecclesiae.*"

(*Left to right*) St. John Rilski - St. Antony the Hermit - St. Vladimir - St. Sergius Radonetski - St. Ephrem - St. Nina

(*Left to right*) St. Maro - St. Onophrius - St. Moses - St. Constantine - St. Helena - St. John Damascene

Paintings in the Byzantine Chapel
Palace of the Sacred Congregation for the Oriental Church, Rome

Greek Pontifical College, Rome

you may be above nature and in human affairs above man, but intercede, we beseech thee, O spouse of God, for us, who in faith celebrate thy venerable conception." Photius (897) [86] acknowledged the blessed Virgin to have been conceived without sin, as also did Nicholas Cabasilas (1371) and Gregory Palamas (1452). Most writers, says Gordillo, [87] from the 12th to the 14th century taught the doctrine of the Immaculate Conception. Isidore Glabas, [88] metropolitan of Thessalonika († ab. 1393) said: "The all-pure Virgin, as is right, alone can refuse to apply to herself the words of the royal prophet, she alone can say: My mother did not conceive me in sin; this privilege is contained in the great things done to me by him who is mighty." In the 17th and early 18th century, Kiev in the Ukraine seems to have been a centre of devotion to the doctrine. [89] A confraternity for students was established in 1689 in two sections—for elder boys under the patronage of the Annunciation, and for younger under the Conception. A sodality of Orthodox youth at Polotsk in White Russia was also dedicated to the Conception, receiving the official approbation of the bishop. These Ukrainian movements were undoubtedly influenced by the Polono-Latin environment, but they were at the same time fiercely anti-Catholic. In 1695 a public thesis [90] expounded at Kiev maintained the conclusion that "This most blessed spouse, both before childbirth, in childbirth and after childbirth, is the Virgin conceived without original sin."

[86] GORDILLO, *Compendium Theologiae Orientalis*, chap. V, art. II, p. 146.
[87] *Compendium Theologiae Orientalis*, chap. V, art. II, p. 146.
[88] MIGNE, *Patr. Graec.*, CXXXXIX, 52.
[89] Devotion to the Conception of our Lady was especially marked during the years 1730-1735.
[90] GORDILLO, *op. cit.*, p. 150.

The first person in the East who seems to have formally denied the Immaculate Conception was Metrophanes Kritopulos († 1641), a friend of the Calvinistic Cyril Lukaris. In 1668, in answer to an enquiry from the Russians, Methodius III,[91] patriarch of Constantinople, said that his church did not believe in the doctrine, and since that time there has been an ever increasing number of Orthodox theologians who, largely on the strength of its being a dogma taught by the Catholic Church, have denied it.

The Orthodox bishop of Kernitza and Kalabryta in the Peloponnesus, Elias Meniates († 1714), definitely maintained the doctrine in his sermons, but when these came to be edited in 1849 by Anthimos Mazarakes, all the passages relating to the Immaculate Conception were deleted. Anthimos IV, patriarch of Constantinople, was party to the fraud, which the editor excused on the ground of "the youth of the author,"—"contamination from the West," and "interpolations by a foreign hand!"

The contest for *holy images,* known as the Iconoclastic controversy, was won in the Byzantine church, although oriental tradition has rejected the use of statues. The first Sunday in Lent is observed as the feast of Orthodoxy, commemorating the return of the images to Constantinople (February 19, 842). The Eastern liturgies express great devotion to the *holy angels,* and the Byzantines keep several feasts of St. Michael and two of St. Gabriel; while the Ethiopians honour St. Michael on the 12th day of each month. *Old Testament prophets* are held in veneration in the liturgies, and many days are observed in their honour. *Prayers* and *Masses for the dead* exist in all the rites, together with a virtual belief in *Purgatory,* although many Easterns tend to

⁹¹ GORDILLO, *op. cit.,* chap. V, art. I, p. 138.

deny the doctrine. St. John Chrysostom [92] said: "At the moment when all the people stand around, their hands lifted up, and the company of priests as well, and when that sacred victim is offered, how should we not appease God for them by our prayers?" The Syrians use the word *schiul* [93] to denote the place where the souls of those for whom they pray are resting. In the East Syrian burial office for priests, after the officiant has thrown earth into the grave, the people are directed to say: "Give rest to the soul of this thy servant in the place where the righteous dwell" (repeated thrice). The *seven sacraments* are administered in theory in all the rites, although in practice some of the dissident churches have allowed penance and extreme unction to fall into desuetude. Consequently, every oriental church has valid orders, but the carelessness with which abunas in Ethiopia have been known to ordain priests gives rise to uncertainty in that country. In the Eastern rites it is the ordination [94] of a bishop rather than the consecration, for, except among the Armenians and Maronites, the ceremony is performed with the imposition of hands only, without anointing with chrism. It is clear from this short dogmatic survey that the doctrines expressed in the Oriental liturgies are one and the same as the holy Roman church believes and teaches.

Defects and Imperfections

The simplicity and directness of the Roman service books make certain features of the eastern rites appear as *defects*. In the first place, the *florid and figurative style* in the prayers

---

[92] *In Phil. hom. III*, 4.

[93] Hebrew, *sheol.*

[94] *Statistica con cenni storici della Gerarchia e dei Fedeli di Rito Orientali*, p. 34, n. 1, 1932. The Armenian synod of Sis (1342) mentions the anointing conferred in the consecration of a bishop.

sometimes seems to overload the liturgy unnecessarily. The
great doctors of the Church were never unduly verbose or
given to extravagant metaphor, whereas later writers, in
adopting a Byzantine style, often abandoned directness and
precision, even to the point of playing in the liturgy with
the name of a saint. The Byzantines have compared our
Lady to "tongs," as the seraphim used these to take the
coal, which is Christ, from the altar. In the Armenian liturgy
St. Joachim and St. Anne are called "sheep," because it
was from them that the "divine fleece" (our Lady) was
prepared. The West Syrians, on the feast of our Lady of
Corn Ears (May 15), compare the blessed Virgin to a
"blessed field," whose womb carried Jesus, the heavenly
"ear of corn;" while the East Syrians call the cherubim and
seraphim "spiritual elephants," "horses," and "mules," since
they are likened to baggage animals carrying their loads. The
Friday *theotokion* in the Coptic rite says of the Virgin:
"Thou wast the 'spiritual hook' catching Christians, teaching them adoration of the life-giving Trinity;" while on
Saturday "Mary is the 'true ladder' which Jacob saw exalted
in truth to the heavens, the Lord was at the top of it."

A second criticism is the too easy reception of *apocryphal
and dubious matter*, spurious gospels and legends appearing
in the liturgies side by side with the authentic and the true.
Thus, we read in the Byzantine rite that our Lady lived in
the holy of holies in the Temple without human food, and
was fed by the archangel Gabriel. The Armenians say that
the blessed Virgin was foretold of her death by the same
angelic messenger; while the East Syrians assert that the
pharisees, wishing to burn the body of the Virgin as she lay
in the tomb, were themselves destroyed by the flames which
came from her.

The names of *heretics and unworthy characters in the*

calendars have been rectified in the Catholic rites, but in those of the dissidents there are still examples of "saints" who seem to be included for upholding error and opposing the "horns of Roman pride." Thus Mark of Ephesus (January 19), Photius (February 6), Gregory Palamos (second Sunday in Lent) and the Empress Theodora (November 15) are commemorated in the Byzantine rite. The Monophysite Copts honour Dioscorus, the virtual founder of the heresy in Egypt, on September 4, Barsuma († 458), whose "fame [95] rests largely on his opposition to the council of Chalcedon," on February 3, and no less than 40 patriarchs who have governed the National Church of Egypt since the schism. The name of Pontius Pilate finds a place in the calendar of Ethiopia on June 25.

Many *Jewish customs* have been retained by the Eastern churches. Saturday has assumed a quasi-festal character, and the Latin fast on that day was looked upon by the Greeks as an error of the first magnitude. The Ethiopians regard Saturday as a sabbath, claiming to possess the original tablets of Moses and the ark of the covenant.

The *length of the Eastern offices* is sometimes brought forward as a defect, especially in these days of hurry and stress. Until the authorisation for the oriental Catholics of a form of "low Mass" the liturgy was often too long for the faithful to stay the whole time, and, except in large churches and monasteries, it was the custom to confine its celebration to Saturdays, Sundays and festivals.

As an example of length, we may note that the Byzantine hymn for the "burial of Christ" has no less than 176 strophes.

[95] De Lacy O'LEARY, *The Saints of Egypt* (London, S. P. C. K. 1937), p. 99

A shortened form of the liturgy and divine office was sanctioned in 1755 by Pope Benedict XIV (*Quem religionis*) for the Italo-Greek Basilians, but the religious of Mezzojuso (Sicily) were expressly excepted, and the secular clergy were refused a like privilege. In the dissident churches, the recitation of the divine office is practically confined to religious, but Catholic priests of the various rites are now generally expected, even out of choir, to imitate their Western brethren.

A complaint sometimes heard about the oriental liturgies is the frequent *repetition*. Thus, the entrance chant (*lba-itokh*)—"O God, I have entered into thy house, etc."—in the Maronite rite is repeated several times; also the admonitions introducing the divisions of the Ethiopic liturgy; and "Sir, give the blessing" (*Orhnia Der*) in the Armenian Mass.

Separation from the Catholic Church has had its stultifying effect on the dissidents, but the complaint of Cardinal Schuster [96] is unduly severe: "Now the East has become like a kind of Egyptian mummy, that, shut up in its beautiful house with ancient hierogliphics, has well preserved the dessicated form of the body, but has no longer the throbbing of life." Dom Guéranger, who in his zeal for the Roman rite tended to depreciate those of other churches, grossly exaggerated when he wrote: "dans l'Eglise orientale .... dès le IXe siècle, tout s'apprête à finir pour la Liturgie, comme pour l'unité et la dignité du Christianisme." [97] And again, "Ce caractère, opposé à la marche de toute véritable orthodoxie, est une immobilité brute qui la rend inaccessible à tout progrès." [98] In another place, the Roman protagonist says:

[96] Ildefonso Card. SCHUSTER, *Roma e l'Oriente Cristiano*. G. Smit, Rome, 1944, pp. 62-63.
[97] *Inst. Lit.*, t. I, chap. IX, p. 214.
[98] *Ibid.*, p. 226.

"quelle triste immobilité ces mêmes Liturgies ont été frappées, impuissantes qu'elles sont, depuis huit siècles, à tout développement."[99] The abbot even suggests that the oriental liturgies are a permanent obstacle to a lasting reunion with Rome,[100] and considers that a "modification"[101] of them in a latinising direction would be necessary for a permanent settlement of differences.

The popes, in considering the venerable rites of Eastern Christendom, may well exclaim: *non tali auxilio et istis defensoribus!*

"People do not realise," said Pope Pius XI in an audience given in January 1927 to Italian university students, "how much faith, goodness and Christianity there is in these bodies now separated from the age-long Catholic truth. Pieces broken from gold-bearing rock themselves bear gold. The ancient Christian bodies of the East keep so venerable a holiness that they deserve not merely respect but complete sympathy."

There are, however, serious defects in the dissident churches. In the first place, there is so often a *false* traditionalism based on polemics against the Catholic church, which is reinforced by an equally false nationalism.

The original root of the schism between East and West was the idea of making the Church follow the vagaries of civil politics, and the inordinate love of one's race in ecclesiastical matters, which has come to be known as the heresy of *Philetism.*[102]

Dom Guéranger[103] was only exaggerating a very real

[99] *Ibid.,* t. II, chap. XXIV, p. 657.
[100] *Ibid.*
[101] *Ibid.,* pp. 657-658.
[102] φυλή." tribe;" φυλέτης, " tribesmen."
[103] *Inst. Lit.,* t. II, chap. XXIV, p. 671.

danger when he said that "every liturgy which is not Roman infallibly becomes national ...., falling under the power and the administration of the ruler or his agents."

Secondly, an undue stress on ceremonial actions sometimes leads to a lack of interior life in the priesthood, and all too many of the country clergy lack proper ecclesiastical formation, so that their standard of education often rises little, if at all, above the level of their people. The result that follows is a state of general mediocrity.

The Catholic Eastern churches, in consequence of their union with Rome, have attained a higher standard of piety and culture.

Their defects are rather in the category of ill-advised and slavish copyings of the Latin rite, such as a marked predilection for laced albs and the introduction into their churches of Western accessories of worship.

It would seem to be the aim of many Maronite and Armenian clergy to make their liturgies appear as much like a Roman Mass as possible.

A German proverb says: *Hinter dem berge sind auch leute,* "Behind the mountains there are people to be found," and we have seen that there are Catholics in the East with varying rites, ceremonies and organisations, who are identical in faith with the Latins, Teutons and Celts of the Roman rite.

Rome and the Christian East

There is, however, a further illusion that needs to be dispelled. It is sometimes said that the pope tolerates these variations on sufferance, and, given the opportunity, he will reduce the Eastern churches to pale copies of the Latin. In fact, the apparent zeal of the papacy for the venerable oriental liturgies is little more than an example of *reculer pour sauter le mieux.*

Pontifical words and actions throughout the centuries give the lie to this calumny—*In una fide nil officit sanctae Ecclesiae consuetudo diversa.* [104] Rome has never forbidden the Oriental way of doing things, and the "Imagers" who fled to Italy in the 8th and 9th centuries were received with their rite as confessors. Constantinople, on the other hand, has lost no opportunity of condemning the ceremonies of the West.

Many of the popes themselves have been orientals, both in the first centuries [105] and also between the years 642 and 752. [106]

The Roman rite itself has been influenced by the East. [107] "By wise eclecticism the Apostolic See has given the world a further proof of her truly cosmopolitan character .... has caused her to adopt all that is good and beautiful wherever she finds it, without needing to shut herself up within a

---

[104] St. Gregory the Great (590-604). *Reg. Pat.* I, t. XLI. Many centuries later, Cardinal Bona (1609-1674) wrote: "Debet unaquaeque ecclesia custodire ritus suos, sed receptos a maioribus, longoque usu praescriptos, et legitima auctoritate approbatos." *De Reb. Lit.,* lib. VI, n. 3.

[105] *Greeks:* Cletus († 91); Telesphorus († 139); Hyginus († 142); Eleutherius († 192); Anterus († 235); Sixtus II († 258); Eusebius († 310); Zosimus († 418).

Syrians: Evaristus († ab. 107); Anicetus († 168).

Africans: Victor I († 201); Melchiades († 313).

[106] *Greeks:* Theodore I († 649); Agatho († 681); Leo II († 683), John VI († 705); John VII († 707); Zacharias († 752).

Syrians: John V († 687); Sergius I († 701); Sisinnius († 708); Constantine († 715); Gregory III († 732).

The last Greek pope was a Cretan, Alexander V (Peter Philargios, 1409-1410), set up by the council of Pisa, but he was really an anti-pope, and Gregory XII (1405-1415) was the legitimate pope.

[107] Ildefonso SCHUSTER, *The Sacramentary,* vol. III, p. 13.

barrier of narrow and exclusive nationalism, as so many lesser churches have done." Thus, the artistic and dramatic character of the liturgy of Holy Week in Jerusalem, so well described by Etheria,[108] has been reproduced by Rome. The vestments of the pope, also, appear to have been influenced by Constantinople, and the Syrian pope, Constantine I (708-715), may well have been the first to wear the tiara.[109]

East and West retained visible unity until the 9th century, but ecclesiastical separatism had its germs in the division of the Empire consequent upon the death of Theodosius (394). Constantinople began to chafe at the primacy of Rome, seizing upon any and every excuse for a rupture.

In 862, Pope Nicholas I[110] (858-867) wrote to Photius, patriarch of Constantinople, assuring him that there was no objection to a variety of rites, so long as nothing was done contrary to the holy canons. Michael Caerularius, after the final schism in 1053, shut up the Latin churches in Constantinople, even including the chapel of the papal legate (apocrisarius), but there was no retaliation on the part of the pope (Leo IX, 1048-1054), who said: "Since both in and outside Rome many monasteries and churches of the Greeks are found, none of them has been disturbed or hindered in the tradition of their fathers, or their customs; but rather they are advised and encouraged to keep these." In the following year (1054), Dominic, bishop of Grado and Aquileia, wrote to Peter, patriarch of Antioch, on the question of the eucharistic bread, as the Greeks were not only denying the validity of azymes, but also referring to them as "dry mud:"—"Because

---

[108] The *Peregrinatio Egeriae* probably dates from the year 393.

[109] The tiara is first mentioned in the *Vita* of Pope Constantine, contained in the *Liber Pontificalis*. It is here called *camelaucum.*— *Cath. Encyclop.*, art. *Tiara*.

[110] *Epist. ad Phot.*, XII.

we know that the sacred mixture of fermented bread is used and lawfully observed by the most holy and orthodox fathers of the Eastern churches, we faithfully approve of both customs and confirm both by a spiritual explanation—leavened bread shows the substance of the Incarnate Word, and unleavened the purity of the human flesh which it hath pleased the divinity to unite with itself. If then our offering of azyme bread is not the body of Christ, we are all of us cut off from the source of life."

The council of Bari (1098) concerned itself with the reunion of East and West; and the 4th council of the Lateran (1215) assured the Greeks that Rome intended to "cherish and honour them, maintaining their customs and rites, as much as, with the help of the Lord, we are able." Pope Honorius III (1216-1227) spoke in the same strain to Henry I, king of Cyprus (1218-1253), regarding the Greeks who had been reconciled. In 1247, Innocent IV (1243-1254) said to Basilicus, king of Lodomeria: "We admit that the bishops and priests of Russia shall be allowed to consecrate in leavened bread, according to their use, and that they shall observe their other rites which are not opposed to the Catholic faith, which the Roman church holds." Union with Constantinople was temporarily effected in the council of Lyons (1274), and in 1278 Pope Nicholas III (1277-1280) wrote to his legate, Bartholomew, bishop of Grosseto, that the Greeks must recite the *filioque*, [111] but that otherwise they might retain their own rites, "concerning which it appears to the Apostolic See that the Catholic faith is not offended, nor the laws of the sacred canons disobeyed." The council of Florence (1439) enacted: "So also, whether in azyme or in leavened

[111] Most of the Catholic Eastern rites to-day say the *filioque* in the creed, but it is not said in the Greek college, Rome, or by the Catholic Russians.

bread, the body of Christ is truly present; and priests may consecrate the body of the Lord in either, each according to the use of the church, whether Western or Eastern."

Many examples of the solicitude of the popes for the rites of the Oriental churches will be found in the succeeding chapters. The Medici popes of the Renaissance, Leo X (1513-1521) and Clement VII (1523-1534), both reprimanded those Latins who openly despised the Eastern rite, while Gregory XIII (1572-1585) in 1576 founded the Greek college in Rome. Other popes,[112] also, defended the Ruthenians against the latinising tendencies of the Polish government, and Benedict XIII (1724-1730), in approving the synod of Zamosc (1720), declared that nothing could be allowed which would injure the rite.

In 1573, Gregory XIII, at the instigation of Cardinal Santoro, erected the *Congregatio de rebus Graecorum*, which was superseded by Clement VIII (1591-1605) in 1605, when a more general congregation was founded—*Congregatio super negotiis fidei et religionis catholicae*. This, in its turn, by the bull *Inscrutabili* of Gregory XV (1621-1623) gave birth (1622) to the *Congregatio de Propaganda Fide*, in which Urban VIII (1623-1644) in 1622 instituted two Eastern commissions, one for discipline and the other for the revision of liturgical books. The second of these was constituted as a separate congregation (*Congregatio super correctione librorum Ecclesiae Orientalis*) in 1717 by Clement XI (1700-1721).

The sovereign pontiffs were described in the *Monita ad Missionarios in partibus Orientalibus*, issued by Propaganda in 1669, as the champions of the Eastern rites "in all their integrity and purity."

---

[112] Clement VIII (1591-1605); Paul V (1605-1621).

The encyclical *Demandatum coelitus,* sent in 1743 by Benedict XIV (1740-1758) to Cyril VI, Melkite patriarch of Antioch, emphasised this "integrity and purity": "Concerning the rites and customs of the Greek church in general, we decree in the first place that no one, whatever his rank may be, even patriarchal or episcopal, may innovate or introduce anything that diminishes their complete and exact observance .... Moreover, we expressly forbid all and each of the Catholic Melkites who use the Greek rite to pass over to the Latin rite. We command severely that all missionaries, under pains named below, and under others to be inflicted according to our pleasure, shall not dare to persuade any of these to pass from the Greek to the Latin rite, or shall even allow them to do so, if they wish it, without they have first consulted the Apostolic See." The aforesaid "pains" included deprivation of both active and passive voice in elections, as well as inability to hold any office or degree in an order or congregation. These decisions were followed up in 1755 by the encyclical *Allatae sunt,* which was addressed to all missionaries in the "East." This was published so that "errors opposed to the Catholic faith might be rooted out, but it has never been attempted to do any injury to the venerable Eastern rite." Oriental Catholics, celebrating the liturgy in Latin churches, were to use their own rite. "We desire vehemently," [113] says the pope, "that their various nations should be preserved, not destroyed; that, to say all in one word, they should be Catholics, not that they should become Latins."

A similar view had been expressed to the Italo-Greeks in 1742 in the constitution *Etsi pastoralis:* "Our predecessors, the Roman pontiffs, considered it more proper to approve

[113] *Exoptans vehementer... ut omnes Catholici sint, non ut omnes Latini fiant.*

and permit these rites, which are in no way opposed to the
Catholic faith, nor cause danger to souls, nor diminish the
honour of the Church, rather than to bring them to the
standard of the Roman ceremonial .... Nor do we allow any
Latin ordinary to molest or disturb these or any of them,
and we inhibit all and any prelates or persons from blasphem-
ing, reproving or blaming the rites of the Greeks, which were
approved in the council of Florence or elsewhere."

Pope Benedict XIV necessarily required of the Italo-
Greeks a belief in the double procession of the Holy Spirit,
but it was expressly permitted to omit the *filioque* in the
creed.

It was not, however, until recent times that the perfect
equality of all rites was maintained, and in this same constitution the pope said: "The Latin rite rejoices in the pre-
eminence of a true primacy, because it is the rite of the
Roman Church, mother and mistress of all the churches, and
especially in Italy and its neighbouring isles." The encyclical
Etsi persuasum (1751) strictly prohibited the celebration of
a Latin Mass by the superior of an Italo-Greek monastery.

In this same century also, two constitutions were issued
for the Catholic Copts—*Eo quamvis tempore* (1745) and
Anno vertente (1750).

The Pope and the Eastern Churches
in Modern Times

From the days of Gregory XVI (1831-1846), the popes
have been increasingly concerned, not merely with the preservation of the oriental rites, but also with the idea that
each one has its own especial contribution to make in the
liturgical crown of the Universal Church.

Pius IX

The first encyclical of Pius IX (1846-1878), *In suprema Petri Apostoli* (1848), paternally invited the dissident Eastern bishops to return to unity: "We will preserve your Catholic liturgies intact, those you so rightly honour, although they differ in certain particulars from that of the Latin church. These liturgies have been equally honoured by our predecessors, as recommended by their venerable antiquity, as well as written in languages spoken by the apostles and the fathers, and containing ceremonies of incomparable pomp and magnificence, suitable for maintaining and nourishing the veneration of the faithful towards the divine mysteries."

The appeal remained unanswered. It was, however, followed in 1853 by an allocution, in which the pope said: "These rites must be kept and reverenced, being worthy of all respect by the antiquity of their origin, coming as they do, in great part, from the holy fathers. Particular constitutions have forbidden those who follow these rites to abandon them without the special permission of the supreme pontiff. Our predecessors knew that the spotless bride of Christ presents in these external notes an admirable variety, which in no way alters her unity. The Church, spreading beyond the frontiers of states, embraces all peoples and all nations, which she unites in the profession of the same faith, in spite of diversities of customs, language and rites; these differences being approved by the Roman church, mother and chief of all."

In 1862, the apostolic constitution *Romani Pontifices* divided the Congregation of *Propaganda Fide* into two branches. One of these, the *Congregatio pro negotiis Ritus Orientalis*, which had its own secretary, officials, consultors, etc., prepared the *schema* [114] of the Eastern rite to be discussed at the council of the Vatican. Invitations for this council were sent to all the dissident bishops, to participate "as your ancestors had come to the councils of Lyons and Florence," attending "with equal rights to those of the Latins."

The commission of prelates, appointed in 1867 to settle the controversy between the Melkite and Maronite patriarchs as to precedence at the centenary celebrations for St. Peter and St. Paul, admitted no preeminence for the Roman rite as such.

Leo XIII

Leo XIII (1878-1903) said in the consistory held on December 13, 1880: "At the beginning of our pontificate we hastened to occupy ourselves with the people of the East. There, indeed, was the cradle of the salvation of the whole human race and the first fruits of Christianity; thence, as a mighty river, all the blessings of the gospel came to the West."

Solicitude for the oriental rites was stimulated by the international eucharistic congress at Jerusalem (1893), and, in the following year, the pope issued two encyclicals bearing on the subject.

The first, *Praeclara gratulationis* (June 29, 1894), contained the following pertinent passages: "First we turn with a look of great affection to the East, whence came salvation to the world"; "For the defence of Catholic doctrines we take arguments and examples from the rites, the teaching and the practices of the Eastern Christians"; "For all their

---

[114] The adjournment of the council prevented the matter being brought up.

Ruthenian Pontifical College of St. Josaphat, Rome

Chapel of St. Josaphat, Ruthenian Pontifical College, Rome

Pontifical Institute for Oriental Studies and Russian Catholic Church of St. Antony the Hermit, Rome

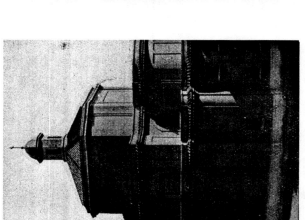

Chapel of the Annunciation. Rumanian Pontifical College, Rome

rites and practices we will provide without narrowness." In
the same encyclical, also, the pope solemnly affirmed that
he never wished to suppress the rites and usages of the East,
nor to suppress the privileges of their patriarchs. *Orientalium dignitas* (November 30, 1894) pointed out that the
eastern liturgies witness to the divine unity and apostolicity
of the Catholic faith, adding to it both dignity and honour.
They are "the reflection of that homage given to the new-
born Christ, divine founder of the Church, when the royal
Magi from different parts of the East came to adore him."
It is more than ever the duty of the pope "to watch carefully
lest any injury should be done to them by the imprudence
of ministers of the gospel from Western lands, whom zeal
for the teaching of Christ sends towards the Eastern nations."
Any Latin missionary, whether regular or secular, who by his
advice or influence shall have persuaded an Eastern Christian
to adopt the Latin rite, shall incur *ipso facto* suspension *a
divinis*, and all other pains threatened in the constitution
Demandatum coelitus. This penalty must be displayed in
all the Latin sacristies of the East. An Eastern, also, who
conforms to the Latin rite on account of the temporary
absence of his own clergy must return to his own rite when
the cause of "turning Latin" is removed; while a woman of
an oriental rite who marries a Latin husband may, on
becoming a widow, return to the rite of her birth. Even if
an Eastern Catholic has gone over to the Latin rite by virtue
of a papal rescript, he may at any time return to his old
church. In places where Oriental and Western students are
working together, the pope ordered special provision to be
made for those who belong to an Eastern rite. The motu-
proprio *Auspicia rerum secunda* (1896) enforced the regulations of this encyclical, and at the same time fixed the relations between the Eastern patriarchs and the Latin apost-

olic delegates.   In the same year, an encyclical on unity
(*Satis cognitum,* 1896) approved the new congregation of
the Augustinians of the Assumption, and praised the Jesuit
university, lately opened at Beirut.

Leo XIII nominated a commission of cardinals for pro-
moting the union of the dissident churches, presiding over
it personally until his death.

Pius X

Pius X (1903-1914) presided on the occasion of the 13th
centenary of the death of St. John Chrysostom (February 12,
1908), when the Byzantine liturgy was solemnly sung in the
Hall of Benedictions in the Vatican by the Melkite patriarch, [115] Cyril VIII.   The Holy Father chanted blessings
in Greek.   By the constitution *Tradita est ab antiquis*
(September 14, 1912) members of Eastern rites may receive
holy communion in Latin churches, and westerns in oriental
churches: "so that the holy eucharist as the centre of unity
and love may produce abundantly the fruit of reconciliation."

In 1922, a Roman document expressly stated that Eastern
Catholics must perform their Easter duties in churches of
their own rite, but in 1925, on examination by a special
commission of cardinals, as well as by the Sacred Congregation for the Oriental rite, this restriction was happily re-
pealed.

Benedict XV

Benedict XV (1914-1922) put an end even to an appearance of disparity between rites, for as the "Church of
Christ is neither Latin, nor Greek, nor Slav, but Catholic, it
does not make any distinction between its sons, be they

[115] The Syrian Catholic patriarch of Antioch, Ignatius Ephrem II,
also assisted at the liturgy.

Greeks, Latins, Slavs or members of other national groups, all hold the same position before this Apostolic See." With these words, the motu proprio *Dei providentis* (May 1, 1917) established the *Congregatio pro Ecclesia orientali*, and the Holy Father reserved to himself the office of prefect. In the same year, another motu proprio, *Orientis Catholici* (October 15, 1917), founded the Pontifical Oriental Institute, as a means to "mutual understanding," which was opened in 1918, and attached to the new Oriental Congregation in the old hospice *dei convertendi* in the Piazza Scossacavalli. The Institute [116] in 1922 was put in charge of the Jesuits, who, four years later, moved it to a building adjoining the Russian Catholic church of St. Antony of Egypt, near the basilica of S. Maria Maggiore. A new building, on the site of the old, was erected for the Oriental Congregation, which was ready for use in 1941. A chapel of the Byzantine rite has been fitted up (1946), and decorated with good frescoes by Dom Jerome Leussink, a Dutch Benedictine from the Greek College.

Benedict XV in 1920 created the Syrian deacon St. Ephrem a doctor of the universal Church, and in the same year, in a letter (*Il dolore*) to the Ukrainian metropolitan of Lviv (Lemberg), he spoke of the Ruthenian rite as *Il palladio della .... nazionalità.* Rome is no enemy of nationality, but only of that nationalism which seeks to deny the title of "children of God" to another race.

Pius XI

Pius XI (1922-1930) deserves the name of the "Pope of Unity." The encyclical *Ecclesiam Dei*, published on the 3rd centenary of the martyrdom of St. Josaphat (November

---

[116] The library of the Pontifical Institute has more than 50.000 books.

12, 1923), accentuated the equality between the rites. The importance of national clergy was strongly emphasized in *Rerum Ecclesiae* (February 28, 1926), an encyclical on foreign missions to non-Christians, but, in this respect, equally applicable to the Eastern churches. In the 19th century, a number of Latin priests had been permitted by the Holy See to change their rite, in order to facilitate the union of the dissidents, and Pius XI extended this privilege by asking certain Western religious orders [117] to establish Eastern branches. The idea was not without precedent, as something similar had been attempted in the 14th century in Armenia. The extension of Christ's mystical body by priests in a rite other than that of their birth was, however, not unknown in earlier days, and Pope Vitalian (657-672) appointed St. Theodore, [118] a native of Tarsus and a monk of a Greek monastery near Naples, to the metropolitan throne of Canterbury in 668. The first to advocate change of rite for priests who were working in Poland appears to have been Peter Skarga († 1612), although the suggestion bore no immediate fruit.

A project for the return to unity of the separated Russians (in particular), undertaken in 1924 by the Benedictines (*moines de l'Union*) at Amay [119] in Belgium, was warmly commended by Pius XI, to whom the Christians of that unhappy country were a source of constant solicitude. In 1929, the Leonine prayers, said after low Mass, were or-

---

[117] e. g. Redemptorists; Jesuits.
[118] Western prejudice showed itself in that Adrian, the abbot of the monastery, accompanied Theodore "lest he introduce into his church anything contrary to the Faith," to which St. Bede comments "as the Greeks have a habit of doing." Ven. BEDE, *Ecclesiastical History*, Bk. IV, chap. I, p. 171. London: Henry G. Bohn, York Street, Covent Garden. 1847.
[119] The house has since been moved to Chevtogne.

dered to be said for Russia, and the ejaculatory prayer: *Salvator mundi, salva Russiam* was provided with an indulgence. A commission for Russia was appointed in 1930 by the motu proprio *Inde ab initio,* which, four years later, was transformed by a further motu proprio, *Quam sollicita.* A Russian college at Rome [120] was opened in 1932 under Slav Jesuits of the Byzantine rite.

Many colleges for students of the oriental rites were built in this pontificate, and the Holy Father inserted a new petition into the litany of the saints: *Ut omnes errantes ad unitatem Ecclesiae revocare et infideles universos ad Evangelii lumen perducere digneris, te rogamus, audi nos.*

Two encyclicals relating to unity were published in 1928, *Mortalium animos* and *Rerum orientalium.* The latter invited the dissidents to return to communion with Rome, and, at the same time, urged upon all Catholics the importance of studying the Eastern churches. The pope went on to say that he wished all universities to have a chair of oriental science, and every seminary to teach the elements of Eastern theology.

These projects were furthered by the constitution *Deus scientiarum Dominus* (May 24, 1931). In 1935, all the seminaries were instructed to have an annual day *Pro Oriente Christiano.* A commission for the codification of Oriental canon law was set up in 1929, and a similar body in 1934 for the publication of the Slav liturgical books.

The year before the death of the pope, there was a modification of the administration, as well as of the territory, subject to the Congregation for the Oriental Church, where the majority of the Catholics were of the Eastern rite.

---

[120] The *Russicum,* as it is called, was founded on August 15, 1929 (*Quam curam*).

Pius XII

Pius XII (1939-19...) in October 1940 received in audience the members of the inter-eparchial synod of Italo-Greek-Albanians, which had been held at Grottaferrata, and of the alumni of the Greek colleges both there and at Rome. The Holy Father spoke of *gli usi legittimi del rito e le prescrizioni della liturgia vengano osservati nella loro integrale purezza.*

In the same year, the Sacred Congregation for the Oriental Church founded a residence in the Russicum under the patronage of St. John Damascene for priests of the various rites who wished to study in Rome. A solemn concelebration of the Byzantine liturgy in Staroslav was celebrated by the Russians and Ruthenians on May 21, 1942, at the altar of the Chair in the basilica of St. Peter, to commemorate the 950th anniversary of the baptism of St. Vladimir.

We may cite, also, the encyclical *Orientalis Ecclesiae,* published on April 9, 1944, on the occasion of the 15th centenary of the death of St. Cyril: "Each and every nation of Oriental rite must have its own rightful freedom in all that is bound up with its own history and its own genius and character, saving always the truth and integrity of the doctrine of Jesus Christ .... they will never be forced to abandon their own legitimate rites or to exchange their own venerable or traditional customs for Latin rites and customs. All these are *to be held in equal esteem and equal honour,* for they adorn the common Mother Church with a royal garment of many colours. Indeed this variety of rites and customs, preserving inviolate what is most ancient and most valuable in each, presents no obstacle to a true and genuine unity." St. Cyril exemplifies the triple bond of unity established by Jesus Christ to bind the Church together:

—defender of the faith, promoter of charity, and champion of the Holy See.

The pope stresses in this encyclical that an oriental rite stands not merely for ritual, but for a whole cultural tradition.

Eastern mentality is as necessary for the Universal Church as Western. *Roma locuta est: causa finita est.*

On December 23, 1945, the Holy Father in the encyclical *Orientales Omnes Ecclesias* brought home the reality of the persecution of the Ruthenian Catholic Church by Soviet Russia. The occasion was the 350th anniversary of the union of that church with Rome.

Finally, we may recall the departure from precedent on the 7th anniversary of the coronation of the pope (March 12, 1946), when, at the express wish of the Supreme Pontiff, the first cardinal created by Pius XII, Peter XV Agagianian, patriarch of *Cilicia Armenorum,* celebrated the Armenian liturgy in the Sistine Chapel of the Vatican in the presence of the Holy Father and twenty-three cardinals. The pope blessed the faithful in Armenian—*Chahahutiun amenetzum* ("peace be to all")—both before the gospel and the last gospel.

"The liturgy [121] is eternal; schisms and wars are the work of man. These will perish, but the liturgy will endure in this world in the various forms in which God has been pleased to let it develop."

[121] *The Cult of the Mother of God in the Byzantine Liturgy.* Cuthbert Gumbinger. *Franciscan Studies.* September 1941.

BIBLIOGRAPHY

1. *L'Anaphore Apostolique et ses témoins.* Dom Paul CAGIN. Paris: P. Lethielleux.

2. *Annuaire Pontifical Catholique* — 1914, 1928, 1929, 1930. E. Chardavoine. Paris: 5 Rue Bayard.

3. *Catholic Eastern Churches* Donald ATTWATER. The Bruce Publishing Company: Milwaukee, Wisconsin. 1935.

4. *Catholic Encyclopedia.* New York: The Encyclopedic Press. Inc.

5. *Catholic Encyclopedic Dictionary.* General Editor, Donald ATTWATER. Cassells & Co., Ltd. 1931.

6. *Cattolicismo e Problemi Religiosi nel Prossimo Oriente.* Guglielmo DE VRIES. Edizioni "La Civiltà Cattolica". Roma, 1944.

7. *Christian Worship:* its origin and evolution. A study of the Latin Liturgy up to the time of Charlemagne. Mgr. L. DUCHESNE. 4th English edition. London: S. P. C. K. 1912.

8. *Le Clergé Occidental et l'Apostolat dans l'Orient Asiatique et Gréco-Slav.* Cyrille KOROLEWSKJI. Paris: Gabriel Beauchesne, 1923.

9. *Commentary on the New Code of Canon Law.* Charles AUGUSTINE. 8 vols. B. Herder Book Co. London. 1918-1922.

10. *Compendium Theologiae Orientalis.* Mauricius GORDILLO. Romae: Pont. Institutum Orientalium Studiorum. 1939.

11. *Congrès des Œuvres Eucharistiques* tenu à *Jérusalem* les 28, 29, et 30 Juin, 1893. Paris: Imprimerie Paul Feron-Vrau, 1906.

12. *Dictionnaire d'Archéologie Chrétienne et de Liturgie.* Dom Fernand CABROL et Dom Henri LECLERCQ. Paris: Letouzey, 1924, seq.

13. *Dictionnaire de Théologie Catholique.* Sous la direction de A. VACANT et E. MANGENOT. Paris: Letouzey, 1932, seq.

14. *Dissident Eastern Churches.* Donald ATTWATER. The Bruce Publishing Company: Milwaukee, Wisconsin. 1937.

15. *East and West in the Unity of Christ.* Mgr. D'HERBIGNY. Translated from the French. London: Catholic Truth Society.

16. *Eastern Catholics.* W. L. SCOTT, Ottawa. London: Catholic Truth Society.

17. *Eastern Churches Quarterly.* Continuation of Eastern Churches Number of "Pax," founded 1931. St. Augustine's Abbey, Ramsgate.

18. *Echos d'Orient.* Revue Trimestrielle. Maison de la Bonne Presse, Paris VIII.

19. *Les Eglises Orientales et les Rites Orientaux.* Raymond JANIN. 2ᵉ édition. 5 Rue Bayard, Paris. 1926.

20. *Les Eglises Séparées d'Orient.* Raymond JANIN. Paris: Bloud et Gay. 1930.

21. *Enchiridion Symbolorum,* Definitionum et Declarationum de Rebus Fidei et Morum. Henricus DENZINGER. Editio 21-23. Friburg Brisgoviae: B. Herder. 1937.

22. *Essays on Liturgiology and Church History.* J. M. NEALE. London: Saunders, Otley, and Co. 1867.

23. *Explication* littérale, historique et dogmatique des prières et des cérémonies *de la Messe.* Pierre LE BRUN. T. I-IV. Paris: chez la Veuve Delaulne, rue Saint-Jacques à l'Empereur. 1726.

24. *Heortology.* A History of the Christian Festivals from their origin to the present day. K. A. Heinrich KELLNER. London: Kegan Paul, Trench, Trubner & Co., Ltd. 1908.

25. *The History of the Christian Church* from the Earliest Times to the Death of St. Leo the Great, A. D. 461. F. J. FOAKES JACKSON. 5th edition. Cambridge: J. Hall & Son. 1909.

26. *Incontro ai Fratelli Separati di Oriente.* Roma. Unione Missionaria del Clero. 1945.

27. *Institutiones Liturgicae de Ritibus Orientalibus.* T. II. *De Missa Rituum Orientalium.* Pars I. J. M. HANSSENS. Romae, Apud Aedes Pontificis Universitatis Gregorianae. 1930.

28. *Institutiones* etc. T. III. *De Missa Orientalium.* Pars altera. J. M. HANSSENS. 1932.

29. *Institutiones* etc. *Appendix* ad T. II, III. Indices et versiones. J. M. HANSSENS. 1932.

30. *Institutions Liturgiques.* Dom Prosper GUÉRANGER. 2ᵉ édition. T. I-III. Paris: Société Générale de Librairie Catholique. 1878-1883.

31. *An Introduction to the Study of Eastern Liturgies.* P. Sévérien SALAVILLE. London: Sands & Co. 1938.

32. *Irénikon*. Bulletin Mensuel des Moines de l'Union des Eglises. Amay-Schootenhof: Amay, Chevetogne.

33. *Jésuites Missionnaires: Syrie Proche Orient*. H. CHARLES. Gabriel Beauchesne, Editeur: Paris. 1923.

34. *Kalendarium Manuale Utriusque Ecclesiae Orientalis et Occidentalis*. Nicolaus NILLES. T. I (1896), T. II (1897). Oeniponte. Felician Rauch (K. Pustet).

35. The *Lay Folks' History of the Liturgy*. E. CREWDSON THOMAS. Rivingtons, 34 King Street, Covent Garden, London. 1929.

36. *The Lesser Eastern Churches*. Adrian FORTESQUE. London: Catholic Truth Society. 1913.

37. *Liturgia*. Encyclopédie Populaire des Connaissances Liturgiques. Publiée sous la direction de l'Abbé R. AIGRAIN. Paris: Librairie Bloud et Gay. 1930.

38. *Liturgiarum Orientalium Collectio*. Eusebii RENAUDOTII Parisini T. I, II. Francofurti ad Moenum sumptibus Josephi Baer, bibliopoli, Londini: Apud Joannem Leslie, bibliopolam. 1847.

39. *Liturgies Eastern and Western*. F. E. BRIGHTMAN. Vol. I. *Eastern Liturgies*. Oxford: At the Clarendon Press. 1896.

40. *Les Liturgies Eucharistiques*. Notes sur leur origine et leur développement. F. J. MOREAU. Vromant et Cie, Bruxelles. 1924.

41. Les *Liturgies Orientales et Occidentales*. Ignace Ephrem II RAHMANI, Patriarche Syrien d'Antioche. Beyrouth; Imprimerie Patriarcale Syrienne. 1929.

42. *The Liturgies of SS. Mark, James, Clement, Chrysostom and Basil, and the Church of Malabar*. Translated with Introduction and Appendices. J. M. NEALE & R. F. LITTLEDALE. 2nd edition. London: J. T. Hayes. 1869.

43. *The Liturgy in Rome*. M. A. R. TUKER. London: A. & C. Black. 1925.

44. *Manuel du Catéchiste en Orient. Les Eglises Orientales. Un ancien Missionnaire d'Egypte*. C. E. ALBERTIRI. Le Caire. 1939.

45. *The Mass*. A study of the Roman Liturgy. Adrian FORTESCUE. London. Longmans Green & Co. 1912.

46. *L'Oriente Cattolico*. Roma: Pont. Institutum Orientalium Studiorum. 1934.

47. *A Popular Handbook of the Origin, History and Structure of Liturgies*. Part. I. J. COMPER. Edinburgh: R. Grant & Son. 1891.

48. *Praelectiones de Liturgiis Orientalibus* habitae in Univer-

sitate Friburgensi Helvetiae a MAXIMILIANO PRINCIPE SAXONIAE. T. I,
1908; T. II, 1913. B. Herder, Friburgi Brisgoviae.

49. *I Riti e le Chiese Orientali.* C. GATTI-C. KOROLEWSKJI.
Vol. I. Genova-Sampierdarena. Libreria Salesiana. 1942.

50. *I Riti Orientali.* Rinaldo PILKINGTON. R. Berruti, Torino.
1939.

51. *Roma e l'Oriente Cristiano.* Giovanni SMIT. Roma: Fratelli Palombi. 1944.

52. *The Sacramentary.* Historical and Liturgical Notes on the
Roman Missal. Ildefonso SCHUSTER. From the Italian by A. L.
Marke. Vol. I, 1924; vol. II, 1925; vol. III, 1927; vol. IV, 1929;
vol. V, 1930. London: Burns, Oates & Washbourne.

53. *La Sainte Messe selon les Rites Orientaux.* Robert LESAGE.
Avignon: Librairie Aubanal Fils Aîné. 1930.

54. *The Shape of the Liturgy.* Gregory DIX. Dacre Press,
Westminster. 1943.

55. *Statistica* con cenni storici della Gerarchia e dei Fedeli *di
Rito Orientale.* Sacra Congregazione Orientale. Tipografia Poliglotta Vaticana. 1932.

56. *Studia Orientalia Liturgico-Theologica.* S. SALAVILLE. Ephemerides Liturgicæ. Roma 1940.

57. *Twenty-five Consecration Prayers.* Arthur LINTON. S. P.
C. K., 1921.

58. *L'Uniatisme. Irénikon Collection,* Nos. 5-6. Prieuré d'Amay-sur-Meuse. Cyrille KOROLEWSKJI. 1927.

59. *The Uniats and their Rites.* No. 16, *Alcuin Club Tracts.*
Stephen GASELEE. London: A. R. Mowbray & Co.

CHAPTER II

SYRIAN RITE

The Syrian rite, although originating in Jerusalem and referred to by St. Cyril († 387) in the *Catecheses,* is essentially connected with Antioch, the traditional residence of St. Peter before his departure for Rome.

History

Antioch (Antakieh) was founded about three hundred years before the Christian era by Seleucus Nikator, a general of Alexander the Great, and it remained under the Seleucides until the Roman conquest. Then, as the capital of Syria and the residence of the imperial legate, the city earned the name of the "Queen of the East." The three languages on the title of the cross were spoken by its inhabitants—Latin for administrative purposes, Greek for literature and culture, and Syriac by the natives of the suburbs and country districts.

The Christian community of Antioch was the most ancient after that of "holy Sion, the mother of all the churches," and it was here that the followers of Jesus were first called "Christians." [1]

According to Eusebius († ab. 340), [2] St. Peter became ἐπίσμοπος of Antioch in the fourth year after the Ascen-

[1] "ita ut cognominarentur primum Antiochiae discipuli, Christiani." *Actus Apost.* XI, 26.
[2] *Hist. Eccl.,* III, 36; cf. ORIGEN († 254), *Hom. VI in Lucam.*

sion of our Lord. "Antioch," says Pope St. Innocent I (ab. 402-417), "was the first see of the first Apostle," although St. Ignatius († ab. 107), the successor of St. Evodius, who was appointed by St. Peter himself, in a letter to the Romans writes "Bishop of Syria," not "Bishop of Antioch."

With the destruction of Jerusalem (70), the city was without a rival as the metropolis of Christianity in the East, and later, when Antioch had become a patriarchate, claimed jurisdiction over Syria, Phoenicia, Arabia, Palestine, Cilicia, Cyprus and Mesopotamia. The council of Nicea (325)[3] agreed that the privileges of the church of Antioch should be maintained; while the first council of Constantinople (381)[4] declared the jurisdiction of its bishop to be coterminous with the civil province of the Orient, the easternmost outpost of the Roman Empire. In the 5th century, Antioch, although still next in rank to Rome and Alexandria, suffered an eclipse. The council of Ephesus (431) acknowledged the church of Cyprus to be autocephalous, and the council of Chalcedon (451) sanctioned a patriarchate of Jerusalem.

Schism

A more serious blow, however, was to fall upon the church of Antioch than any curtailment of privileges, and the heresies of Nestorius and Eutyches, or rather of James Baradaeus, changed the one great Church in peace and communion with the Apostolic See into three mutually hostile religions,—Orthodox (Melkite), Nestorian and Monophysite (Jacobite). The Orthodox Church remained a constituent part of the Catholic Church of Christ until the schism of

[3] Canon 6.
[4] Canon 2.

Constantinople and the vicissitudes of the Nestorians will be considered in another place, but a word is necessary in explanation of Monophysism, which, after disturbing the peace and harmony of the Eastern Empire for two centuries, finally became the instrument for the formation of four national churches. [5]

The Catholics of the Syrian rite are converts from the Jacobites or their descendents.

Nestorianism [6] was condemned by the council of Ephesus, but, as a revulsion against this heresy, certain of the clergy fell into the opposite error, maintaining that the sacred humanity of our Lord was as a drop of wine in an ocean of water, so that in all things—personality and nature—he was inseparably one. Monophysites and Nestorians admitted the same false premise, that person ($\dot{v}\pi\acute{o}\sigma\tau\alpha\sigma\iota\varsigma$) and nature ($\phi\acute{v}\sigma\iota\varsigma$) were identical. The name $Mo\nu o\phi\upsilon\sigma\acute{\iota}\tau\eta\varsigma$ [7] or $Mo\nu o\phi\upsilon\sigma\iota\sigma\mu\acute{o}\varsigma$ thus came to be given to those who denied the two natures in Christ.

The first home of the heresy was Egypt, where Dioscorus of Alexandria came to be recognised as the leader. The influence of Eutyches, however, was small, as he had ventured to attack St. Cyril, the Coptic hero, for his agreement with John of Antioch,—"because Jesus Christ is one, although the difference of natures, indelibly united, may not be ignored."

Christology afforded a convenient excuse for both Egypt and Syria in their quarrels with the emperor, and politics came to be as much a cause of schism [8] as an erroneous

---

[5] Coptic; Ethiopic; Jacobite; Armenian.
[6] Chapter VIII.
[7] $\mu o\nu\grave{\eta}$ $\phi\acute{v}\sigma\iota\varsigma$, " one nature."
[8] Imperial politicians perverted national feeling into religious dissension.

belief touching the Incarnation, although Monophysism in Syria never developed into a national cause of the whole country, such as we find in Egypt.

A crisis was reached about the year 448, when Domnus, patriarch of Antioch, accused Eutyches of teaching Apollinarianism. [9]   The heretical archimandrite was deposed in synod and excommunicated; while a document to that effect was signed by about thirty bishops, including Julian of Cos, the representative of the pope at the court of Theodosius. The matter was brought before the Robber council of Ephesus, [10] which acquitted the defendant, and also before the council of Chalcedon.   Eutyches appealed to the pope (St. Leo) [11] in apparent filial humility: "I requested that this might be made known to your holiness, and that you might judge as you should think fit, declaring that in every way I should follow that which you approve."   St. Leo charitably put forward the plea that ignorance had been the cause of the heresy, but the offending monk remained intractable.

An appeal for support was also sent by Eutyches to St. Peter Chrysologus, [12] bishop of Ravenna († ab. 450), who, however, declined to give an opinion in what was the concern of the pope.   Pope St. Leo (440-461) had already

---

[9] Apollinaris, bishop of Laodicea († ab. 392), taught that our Lord had no human intellect and that his flesh was of one substance with his divinity, brought with him from heaven, so that God the Son actually died on the cross.   In effect the heresy deprived our Lord both of humanity and divinity.

[10] σύνοδος ληστρική; *Latrocinium Ephesinum.*

[11] *Epist.* XXI.

[12] "*Quoniam beatus Petrus qui in propria sede et vivit et praesidet, praestat quaerentibus fidei veritatem; nos enim pro studio pacis et fidei, extra consensum Romanae civitatis episcopi, causas fidei audire non possumus.*"

sent his dogmatic tome to Flavian, orthodox archbishop of Constantinople (447-449), a document which had defined the faith of the Church on the disputed points, and one which had called forth the famous affirmation at Chalcedon: "Peter has spoken by Leo." Submission, however, was by no means general, and Dioscorus of Alexandria presided at the heterodox gathering at Ephesus, where Flavian was so maltreated by the heretical soldiery that he died a few days later. The legates of the pope, who held a "watching brief" at the assembly, cried out their protest of *Contradicitur*, and left in disgust.

Dioscorus had the temerity to "excommunicate" the pope, a proceeding which the bishops at Chalcedon referred to in a letter to St. Leo: "the enemy like a beast roaring to himself outside the fold .... had stretched his madness even towards you, to whom the care of the vineyard was given by the Saviour, that is, as we say, against your holiness, and has conceived an excommunication against you, who hasten to unite the body of the Church."

The council of Chalcedon (451) was made possible by the accession to the imperial throne in the previous year of the orthodox Pulcheria and her consort Marcian, who endeavoured by every means in their power to reverse the heretical policy of Theodosius II, their predecessor (408-450). The papal legate, Paschasinus, bishop of Lilybaeum (Sicily), acted as president, and in opening the council declared that "the instructions of the most blessed and apostolic bishop of Rome forbid us to sit here in company with Dioscorus, archbishop of Alexandria."

St. Anatolius of Constantinople occupied the place of honour after the Roman delegates, although the patriarchs of Alexandria and Antioch should have been preferred before the patriarch of New Rome.[13]   The Tome of St. Leo was declared to express the true doctrine, that in Christ there are two natures, "without confusion, without change, without division, and without separation."[14]

Thus, the faith was safeguarded against Monophysism on the one hand and Nestorianism on the other.

An apologetic treatise, written in the 9th century by Elias, Jacobite patriarch of Antioch, shows clearly that the teaching[15] of the Monophysites was in opposition to that of Chalcedon, although they say that our Lord is perfect God and perfect man, and condemn Eutyches. They refuse, however, to admit the expression: "One person *in two natures*.[16]   Gregory Bar Hebraeus[17] says that "one nature is double and not simple."   Theirs is the verbal Monophysism of Severus of Antioch, which a recent book[18] has claimed as "substantially not to be distinguished from orthodox doctrine."

Monophysism originated in Egypt, Syria and Palestine as a party within the Church, and one finds an orthodox bishop succeeded by a heretic and vice versa. It was only after some years that definite schismatic churches were established.

The history of the Monophysites in Syria is beyond the scope of the book, but some reference must be made to

---

[13] Canon 28 of Chalcedon conferred the second place in Christendom on Constantinople, but, since the legates of the pope were absent, this canon forms no part of that which was enacted *conciliariter*.

[14] ἐν δύο φύσεσιν ἀσυγχύτως, ἀτρέπτως, ἀδιαιρέτως, ἀχωρίστως γνωριζόμενον.

[15] *Unam Dei Verbi incarnati naturam in Christo post unionem, salvis proprietatibus, profitentur.*

[16] μία ὑπόστασις ἐν δύο φύσεσιν

[17] ASSEMANI, *Bibliotheca Orientalis*, II, 297.

[18] *Incontro ai Fratelli Separati di Oriente* (Roma, 1945), p. 82.

Severus, patriarch of Antioch (512-518), whom the *Catholic Encyclopedia* [19] calls "the most famous and the most fertile of all the Monophysite writers."

He was acclaimed [20] "the excellent, clothed with light, occupant of the see of Antioch, who became a horn of salvation to the Orthodox (Monophysite) Church, and who sat upon the throne of the great Ignatius." Bar Hebraeus, the 13th century canonist, spoke of him as "the holy Severus, scorning life and despising glory." In 538 Severus died in exile in Egypt. External pressure and interior schism seemed to point to the end of the heresy, but an unexpected champion arose in James Baradaeus, the virtual founder of the Jacobite church. [21]

About this time, Pope Vigilius (537-555) showed a weakness unbecoming in one whose duty was to feed the sheep and the lambs of Christ. It would appear that he largely owed his position as Supreme Pontiff to the empress Theodora, who had been given to understand that her "protégé" would make concessions in favour of Monophysism. There is, of course, no question that Vigilius compromised the faith of the Church, but his spirit of vacillation estranged many of his flock. On November 20, 545, as he was saying Mass in the Transtiberian basilica of St. Cecilia, Vigilius, on the order of the emperor Justinian, was dragged from the altar and transported to Constantino-

[19] Art. *Monophysites*, vol. X, p. 490.
[20] Severus of AL-USHMUNAIN, *History of the Patriarchs of the Coptic of Alexandria*, ed. B. Evetts (*Patrol. Orient.* I, 449); *ap.* Adrian FORTESCUE, *Lesser Eastern Churches*, chap. X, p. 325, n. 6.
[21] Since about the 8th century, the term " Jacobite" has been applied to the West Syrian church, by reason of the prominent position occupied by James Baradaeus. Bar Hebraeus knows and admits this name (*Chron. Eccl.* I, 218).
Jacobite, *Ya'kuby*, (plural) *Ya'akyba*.

ple. Later, he was permitted to return to Rome, but, worn out with his trials, the pope died at Syracuse (June 555).

The Syrian church as a distinctive and schismatic entity may be said to date from the consecration in prison of two bishops by Theodosius, the imprisoned Monophysite patriarch of Alexandria, who had been instigated by the empress Theodora, probably in 543. The new prelates were Theodore for Bosra and the South and James Baradaeus for Edessa and the East. At the time of the consecration, says John of Ephesus, there were only two or three other Monophysite bishops who were out of prison, but James, [22] who had been a disciple of Severus, infused new life into the flagging heresy, and for nearly 40 years he journeyed the length and breadth of Syria.

James is said to have made two patriarchs of Antioch, [23] from whom the present Jacobite hierarchy is descended; twenty-seven bishops; and over two thousand priests and deacons. The name Baradaeus [24] was derived from the ragged cloak in which this apostle of heresy was wont to travel. He died in 578 as the undisputed leader of the Monophysite church, but he has left little in the way of writing beyond a liturgy and a few letters.

The Coming of the Arabs

When in 633 Syria was overrun by Moslem Arabs, the Jacobites, partly on the score of their hostility to the Greeks and partly by reason of their usefulness to the conquerors,

---

[22] *Ya'kub Burd'ôyô; Burd'ônô.*

[23] The first of the line of the Jacobite patriarchs was Paul of Beith Ukamin, who was consecrated by James Baradai in 543 or 544.

[24] *Barda'thô,* "coarse horse-cloth;" *bardūnâ,* "mule;" Greek, Ἰάκβος τζάντζαλος.

received preferential treatment. Under the Sofianid Omayyad dynasty from Medina, Syria for the first and only time became a great nation.

Christianity was free, and the architecture of the Syrians flourished under the name of "Arabesque;" while the Monophysites filled all the civil posts of importance.

Change of dynasty, however, brought disaster to the church of Syria, and by the 9th century the Christians, irrespective of race or belief, were ill-treated and persecuted.

In the face of the common enemy, the emperor Nicephorus Phocas (913-969) proposed a union of the churches, and John Sarighta, the Jacobite patriarch, went for discussions to Constantinople. The scheme, however, came to nothing, and John was imprisoned by the Byzantines!

Relations with Rome in the Middle Ages

At the time of the Crusades, the Jacobites assisted the Christian cause, and from about the year 1140 there was a resident bishop in Jerusalem. [25] It has been suggested [26] that the Jacobite colony was originally composed of immigrants who came to the Holy City with King Baldwin, Count of Edessa, from 1098-1100. In 1169, Denys bar Salibi [27] sent an explanation of the Syrian liturgy to the Jacobite bishop of Jerusalem, in order that he might be well equipped to defend its authenticity and integrity against the criticisms of the Franks.

Philip, prior of the Dominicans in Palestine, wrote a letter to Pope Gregory IX (1227-1241) in 1237, in which

[25] The title has since been merged in that of mafrian.
[26] George EVERY, *Syrian Christians in Palestine in the early Middle Ages. Eastern Churches Quarterly* (July-September, 1946), p. 365.
[27] ASSEMANI, *Bibliotheca Orientalis*, t. II, p. 156.

he informed him that the Jacobite patriarch [28] with a number of bishops and monks had arrived in Jerusalem, where they had abjured their heresy and promised obedience to the pope. The rejoicing, however, was premature, as the reconciliations had been prompted by fear of a Tartar invasion, and they later returned to heresy.

About the year 1247, the patriarch Ignatius III admitted the supremacy of the Apostolic See, and the mafrian bar Ma'dan spoke of Rome as the "mother and head of all the churches."

Unfortunately, the declarations were again neither sincere nor lasting.

Bar Hebraeus, [29] in the same century, drew attention to the presence in Jerusalem of seventy Jacobite monks.

From 1292-1495, the Jacobites seem to have been a prey to internal schisms, and despite the relative unimportance of their church [30] there were no less than three distinct jurisdictions. [31]

Hopes of the return of the Jacobites to Catholic unity were again entertained at the time of the council of Florence (1438-1445), and a decree (*Cantate Domino*) was promulgated on February 4, 1441, with a view to enlightening the dissident Syrians in the matter of Catholic christology.

Three years later, the patriarch Ignatius V sent Abdallah, archbishop of Edessa, as delegate to Rome, where in a congregation of cardinals and theologians named by the

[28] Ignatius III David Khaĭšĭimĭ (1237-1247) in the synod of Jerusalem.

[29] *Chron. Eccles.*, II, c. 653-4.

[30] The brother of the canonist described his coreligionists as "the small and weak people of the Jacobites."

[31] Four rival patriarchs. A. FORTESCUE, *Lesser Eastern Churches*, chap. X, p. 333.

pope agreement was arrived at on the three disputed points —the procession of the Holy Spirit, the two natures in our Lord, and the two wills in our Lord. The Syrian delegate submitted to the decree of union (*Multa et admirabilia*) and made solemn declarations of orthodoxy, but in spite of this no practical consequences seem to have resulted.

In 1555, the patriarch Jacob IV sent a priest named Mussa to Rome, in order that he might get some books printed in Syriac. Mussa, on behalf of his people, made a profession of Catholic faith before Pope Julius III, but the reconciliation was repudiated by the Jacobite patriarch.

Bishop John Qacha, at the request of the patriarch Nehemetallah, went to Rome in 1560, and established union with the Apostolic See. The patriarch, however, got into difficulties both with his own people and the Turkish authorities. He became a Moslem, but filled with remorse at his apostasy he fled to Rome, where he died a good Catholic.

In 1583, Nehemetallah sent the envoy of the apostolic delegate to his brother and successor in the patriarchate, David, in the hope that he might be influenced in the matter of union, but the mission was without result.

The 17th century

The 17th century was more propitious for the cause of Catholicism in Syria. The Capuchins reconciled the majority of the Jacobites in Aleppo, and also the patriarch.

A Catholic bishop was appointed to Aleppo in 1656, in the person of Andrew Akhidjan, an alumnus of the college of Propaganda, and six years later (1662) he was nominated patriarch. [32] A profession of faith was sent to Rome in 1665.

---

[32] 1662-1677.

The dissidents, furious at the success of Catholicism, persuaded the Turkish government to adopt a hostile attitude, and the church at Aleppo was given to the Jacobites.

Mar Andrew, anxious for the Catholic succession, asked Peter, bishop of Jerusalem, who was known to have aspirations towards unity, to become patriarch. Unfortunately, Peter delayed going to Aleppo, and the Jacobites elected Abd-ul-Massih. The Catholic claimant, however, obtained the firman from Constantinople, as well as a confirmation of his appointment from Rome. Two bishops were consecrated, in order to make the succession certain, but opposition on the part of the Jacobites persisted. Peter was twice deposed, and finally went to Rome to obtain the help of the pope.

The 18th century

In 1700, a treaty between the emperor and the Turks brought about the reinstatement of the Catholic patriarch.

Further opposition was not long delayed, and some months later the patriarch Stephen, an archbishop and ten priests were imprisoned at Adana. The lower clergy were released in 1704, but two years later (1706) the bishops died in prison. [33]

The 18th century was a difficult time for the Catholic Syrians, and the line of patriarchs was interrupted until 1783, in which year the patriarch adopted the title of Antioch in place of Aleppo. Some years previously, at an episcopal synod called by the Jacobite patriarch Gregory III, the archbishop of Aleppo, who had been secretly reconciled to the Catholic church, took the opportunity to make propaganda in favour of union. The bishop of Mosul returned

---

[33] The patriarch and three bishops are said to have died in prison. *Dict. de Théol. Cath.*, t. I, col. 1431.

to his diocese determined to work in the cause of unity, but only two priests and a handful of the laity responded to the appeal. At Aleppo the results were more encouraging.

Before the death of the patriarch, Gregory III nominated Michael Garweh, the Catholic archbishop of Aleppo, to succeed him. Mar Michael hastened to Mardin, the residence of the Jacobite patriarch, where he won over to the cause of unity the clergy of the city and many of the laity, in addition to four bishops and the metropolitan of Jerusalem.

The dissidents, however, taking advantage of the delay in obtaining the berat of investiture from the Porte, elected Matthew, bishop of Mosul, as patriarch. Mar Matthew hastened to Constantinople, where he received the necessary powers.

The Catholic patriarch, who was protected by Simon of Amida, Chaldean bishop of Mardin, fled first to Bagdad and then to the Maronites in the Lebanon, where he established his residence in the monastery of Sharfeh.

The 19th century

In the patriarchate of Mar Michael († 1801) the Syrian church was reconstituted and the number of Catholics increased, but from this time there came to be two separate and distinct hierarchies, the Catholic and the Jacobite. Persecution, however, continued and in 1819 the patriarch, Simon Zora, was put to death.

In 1830, the Catholic Syrians received a firman from the Turkish government, enabling them to be independent of the dissidents in civil matters, although it was not before 1843 that the Catholic patriarch was officially recognised as the civil head of his people.

The patriarch Peter Garweh (1820-1853), nephew of

Mar Michael and former metropolitan of Jerusalem, moved the patriarchal residence in 1831 from Sharfeh to Aleppo, but his successor, in the interest of unity, transferred it to Mardin (1854).

The patriarchate of Mar Garweh was very fruitful in respect to conversions, and between 1825 and 1830 nearly all the Jacobites in Damascus and southern Lebanon had, under the leadership of abu-Hamad and the bishop James al-Haliani, been reconciled to the Catholic Church. The Jacobite patriarch, ibn-Sayar, infuriated at the progress of the Catholics sent Mar Matthew Gregory Nakkar, metropolitan of Mosul, to Damascus to deal with the situation. Mar Matthew, a 19th century Saul,[34] "breathing out threatenings and slaughter against the disciples of the Lord," was chosen for this purpose, as he had on many occasions shown his hatred of Catholicism. God, however, was waiting for him. The first seeds of doubt were sown in his mind when he applied the flame of a candle, lit from the "holy fire" at Jerusalem, to his deacon's beard, in the belief that the "miraculous" fire did not burn! Later, finding himself unexpectedly in the house of the Lazarists at Aleppo, he prayed, read and argued, until on November 27, 1832, he made a formal abjuration of his errors, and was reconciled to the Catholic Church. "Saul" the persecutor had become "Paul" the apostle.

Within two months he had won over fifty-four Jacobites in Mardin, as a result of which he was hailed before the Turkish governor, and imprisoned first in the common gaol and then in the monastery of Za'faran. In this latter place, Mar Matthew was beaten, struck on the mouth, and kicked from the top to the bottom of a flight of stairs. Nothing,

[34] *Act. Apost.*, IX, I.

however, could shake his constancy, and he was finally released by a Kurdish princess. Returning to his preaching, the confessor was appointed archbishop of Nabk and Keriatim, and died in 1868 in the college at Sharfeh, where he is buried. [35]

In all, five Jacobite bishops were converted, one of whom, Antony Samhiri of Diarbekir, eventually became Catholic patriarch.

The patriarch Mar Philip Arkus (1866-1874) assisted at the Vatican council; while the dissident hierarchy was approached by Mgr. Nicholas Castello, the apostolic delegate, in the hope that attendance at the council might lead eventually to reconciliation. The Jacobite bishops and many of the people seemed well disposed, but the patriarch, whom all feared, was hostile, and the project was abandoned. [36]

In the Catholic patriarchate of George Šelhot (1874-1892), eight thousand dissidents, including an archbishop and two bishops, were reconciled to the Church; while, to supplement the dearth of priests, the Congregation of the Brothers of St. Ephrem was reorganised, and a house built for them at Mardin.

Mar Benham Benni, his successor, visited Constantinople and Rome, and at the latter place attended a patriarchal reunion (1894).

The 20th century

He was succeeded by Mar Ignatius Ephrem Rahmani (1898-1929), a liturgical scholar of international repute, who received many Jacobite converts, and for administrative

---

[35] His own successor in the see of Mosul, the metropolitan of Mardin, a number of clergy and a thousand lay people received the gift of faith. Donald ATTWATER, *Golden Book of Eastern Saints,* p. 155.

[36] In 1913, a former patriarch and two bishops were reconciled, while in 1928 there were three priests and twelve hundred lay-folk.

reasons removed his place of residence from Mardin to Beirut. [37] Here, in 1931, Mar Gabriel Tappuni erected a church [38] under the title of St. Ignatius the God-bearer.

The war of 1914-18 brought devastation to Syria with the destruction of 5 dioceses and 15 missions, although there has been some attempt at reconstruction.

Mar Ephrem Rahmani was succeeded as patriarch in 1929 by Gabriel Tappuni, archbishop of Aleppo, who was raised in 1935 (December 16) to the sacred purple, [39] the first oriental member of the sacred college since 1895. The attendance of Cardinal Tappuni at the papal conclave in 1939 was the first time in history that a residential Eastern patriarch [40] has taken part. After the election, when the cardinal did homage to Pope Pius XII, the Holy Father embraced him and said: "In your person we embrace all the Christians of the East."

The Condition of the Jacobite Church

Since the 14th century, the importance and prestige of the Jacobite church have steadily declined. The dissident hierarchy [41] dwindled to about 20 bishops and 5 metropolitans, while the office of mafrian became little more than a patriarchal "vicar general."

[37] At the beginning of the movement towards Rome, the Catholic patriarchs fixed their residence temporarily at Aleppo.

[38] The building of the church was made possible by a generous gift from the pope.

[39] The Syrian cardinal received the title of the church of *Santi Apostoli*.

[40] Mgr. Hassun, the Armenian cardinal, had resigned the patriarchate before his elevation to the cardinalate.

[41] The *Notitia episcopatuum patriarchatus antiocheni* published by Mar Rahmani, says that the patriarchate of Antioch in the 6th century

Before the first world war (1914-1918)[42] the Jacobites had a patriarch, who resided at Deir el-Za'faran[43] near Mardin, 11 metropolitans, and 3 bishops, all of whom, with the exception of the *mafrian* of Jerusalem, lived in Mesopotamia at the north-east corner of Syria.

The number of adherents has been estimated at 100.000, but since 1915 statistics have not been very accurate.

The principal centres are Irak,[44] Turkey, Kurdistan, Syria, the Lebanon and Palestine, with colonies in Egypt and the two Americas. Their present numbers in Palestine are, in Jerusalem, 1,500 souls; in Bethlehem, 750; and 300 dispersed in other localities.

In 1937, a hundred families of Jerusalem and Bethlehem, comprising about 600 persons, returned to Catholic unity.

In Jerusalem, the Jacobites have the church and monastery of St. Mark, erected on the traditional site of the house of Mary, mother of John Mark; the chapel of Mar Behnam; and the dark chapel, called the "Tomb of Nicodemus" in the basilica of the Holy Sepulchre.

A new parish church has been recently consecrated in Bethlehem, and on the banks of the Jordan there is a chapel.

Since the 17th century, a Jacobite church has existed in

had a patriarch, 7 suburbicarian bishops, 2 bishops in attendance on the patriarch, 4 autocephalous sees, and 12 metropolitans with 128 suffragans: 154 in all.

Mgr. Hindo (*Disciplina Antiochena Antica* (Siri), IV, p. 53) gives a total of about 15 provinces and 220 bishoprics.

[42] It has been estimated that 96,000 Jacobites were put to death during the war of 1914-1918 in the district of Mardin. DE VRIES, *Cattolicismo e Problemi Religiosi nel Prossimo Oriente* (Rome, 1944), VI, p. 143.

[43] The patriarchal see was fixed at Deir el-Za'faran in 1080.

[44] In the region of Mosul, the Jacobites have about 10,000 souls, with 2 bishops, 14 churches, 16 priests and 12 monks. The community at Bagdad numbers about 400. The total number in Irak is about 12,000.

India, but it will be considered under the Malabarese [45] and Malankarese [46] rites.

The *Shamsiyeh* or "People of the Sun," a curious sect of about 100 families living at Mardin, are said to conform outwardly to the Jacobites, while practising pagan rites in secret. They are reputed to be the descendents of the heathen whom the Turks in 1762 threatened to kill unless they abandoned paganism. Their origins, however, are by no means certain, and a Catholic convert, who had been for twenty years a Jacobite priest, styled himself "Priest Catholic Shamsee."

The Jacobites are nominally in communion with the Copts, and the patriarch on his election sends an official intimation to his Monophysite brother of Alexandria.

Saints and Writers

The Syrian church is the heir to many saints and writers, whose holiness and learning have made the patriarchate of Antioch illustrious.

St. Ephrem (Afrem), who is honoured not only by the Syrians, but also by Latins, Byzantines, Armenians, Chaldeans and Copts, was raised in 1920 by Pope Benedict XV to the rank of Doctor of the Universal Church. In the encyclical *Principi Apostolorum* (October 5, 1920), the pope declared that the custom of St. Ephrem in introducing hymns to be sung in church has influenced the liturgy for all time. The antiphons of the liturgy together with its canticles, hymns and responses have the saint for their inspirer in that form. St. John Chrysostom introduced the custom in Constantinople; St. Ambrose in Milan; thence it

[45] Chap. IX.
[46] Chap. IV.

spread over Italy and Europe. St. Augustine, while still a catechumen, was touched by this singing, which he called an "oriental custom." This manner of singing was improved by St. Gregory the Great, and perfected still more after him.

St. Ephrem appears to have been born early in the 4th century at Nisibis, when the city was under the emperors, and at its capture by the Persians in 363 to have moved to Edessa, where he lived as a hermit. He visited St. Basil at Caesarea about the year 370, and received the diaconate at his hands. St. Ephrem died three years later, with a great reputation as theologian, orator and poet.

The hymns, [47] which are written in the dialect of Edessa, are the glory of the Syrian church, and provide a striking commentary on the faith and practice of the East in the 4th century.

Thus, the hymns, sung before the epistle in the liturgy, are redolent with Catholic eucharistic doctrine, and are known as "ephremetes." In another place, St. Ephrem writes: "Thou and thy Mother are the only ones who under every aspect are entirely beautiful, since in thee, O Lord, there is no stain, nor any blemish in thy Mother." A hymn on virginity affords the first known example of the use of oil at the consecration of an altar: "Oil is the staff of old age, the assistance of the sick, the rampart of health .... by it altars are anointed and become worthy of sacrifice."

It is probable, however, that some of the hymns bearing the name of St. Ephrem were not composed by him, and that he was claimed as the author, in place of one whose orthodoxy was not so well established.

The early translation [48] by St. Ephrem or other Syriac

---

[47] *Madrashê*, "*Instructions.*"
[48] Edmund BISHOP, *Liturgica Historica*, VIII, 4, p. 178, n. 3.

writers of pieces into Latin seems to have been largely responsible for the outburst of the cultus of the blessed Virgin in Spain in the 7th century. There is an almost identical devotional spirit [49] between many of the prayers and meditations of St. Ephrem on the one hand and of St. Ildephonsus's *De virginitate* on the other; while much of the Mozarabic missal and of the *Book of Cerne* show unmistakeable traces of Syrian influence, in respect to both devotion and piety. Canon 12 of the council of Seville in 618 gives an account of the conversion [50] to orthodoxy of a Syrian Jacobite bishop seemingly settled in Spain.

A considerable collection of metrical homilies (*mimrê*) has been ascribed to Isaac of Antioch (459-461), who is surnamed "the Great" and venerated as a saint.

Syriac literature, however, was enriched by the Jacobites no less than the Catholics, and from the middle of the 5th century till the end of the 7th we find many liturgists and spiritual writers.

James of Sarugh (451-521), bishop of Batnan, the "Flute of the Holy Spirit" and "Harp of the believing Church," is said to have written an anaphora [51] and about 760 homilies. His feast is observed by the Maronites and some Nestorians, although many allege that he corresponded with the Monophysite monks of Mar Bassus, accepted the *Henoticon*, and to the end of his life rejected the council of Chalcedon (451). At the present time there are those who maintain the orthodoxy of James of Sarugh, and the whole question is *sub iudice*.

Philoxenus, bishop of Mabug (485), was the author of

[49] *Ibid.*, p. 161.
[50] *"Ingressus est ad nos quidam ex heresi Acephalorum, natione Syrus (ut asserit ipse) episcopus."* Can. 12. S. Concil. Hisp., II.
[51] RENAUDOT, *op. cit.*, t. II, pp. 356-370.

two anaphoras [52] and a Syriac version of the New Testament.

James of Edessa (640-708) in a letter to Thomas the Presbyter concerning the *Mystical Ministry of the reasonable and unbloody sacrifice, that is to say touching the kurōbo or kurbōno*, professes to speak of the liturgy from the time of the apostles to that of his own day, and asserts: "This is the tradition that I have received from the fathers, and the same also I hand on." At a later period, Moses bar-Kepha, bishop of Mosul (813-903), who was known in the episcopate as Severus, wrote valuable treatises on the liturgy.

There was a renaissance of letters in the 12th century, and the Jacobite church produced several notable writers. James bar-Ṣalibi, bishop of Marash, who assumed the name of Denys (1154), was translated in 1166 to Amida, where he died five years later (1171). He wrote commentaries on the Old and New Testaments, an anaphora [53] and an explanation of the liturgy. Michael the Syrian ("the Great," 1166-1199), abbot of Barsauma and patriarch, was the author of several liturgical works and a chronicle. This last-named work formed the basis of the *Universal History*, which was compiled by Bar Hebraeus, a writer of Jewish descent, whose real name was John Abu'l Farag. He was raised to the episcopate, receiving the name of Gregory. In 1264, Bar Hebraeus became mafrian, and died in 1286. He was buried with his brother in the Jacobite monastery of Deir Mattai under a slab of grey Mosul alabaster. The epitaph, written in Karshuni, is said to have been composed by Bar Hebraeus himself: "O net of the world, in the year 1536 (1225) thou didst catch me; but my hope is that in

---

[52] RENAUDOT, *op. cit.*, pp. 300-320.
[53] *Ibid.*, pp. 448-454.

1597 (1286) I shall not be in thee"—an aspiration that was fulfilled!

Jacobite canon law is largely derived from the Nomocanon [54] of Bar Hebraeus. The same writer, also, was the author of the *Book of Thunderbolts* and the *Book of the Lamp of the Sanctuary*.

An exposition of the doctrine of the sacraments was given by James Bar' Sakkô († 1241).

Hierarchy

The Catholic and the Jacobite patriarchs both assume the name of Ignatius in memory of the 2nd century martyred bishop. The custom seems to have arisen in the 13th century, and since the days of Ignatius V (Bar Wahīb of Mardin, 1292) there has been no exception to the rule. The choice of the Jacobites is somewhat inconsistent, as St. Ignatius, [55] was the great opponent of Docetism, of which Monophysism is a revival.

The residence [56] of the Jacobite patriarch has changed many times in the course of history, and in 1924 he was compelled to leave Deir el-Za'faran [57] ("Monastery of the Yellow Rock") and take refuge in Mosul. The present patriarch resides at Homs (Emesa) in Syria.

The Catholic patriarch is elected by the synod of bishops,

[54] *Ktôbô d'huddôyo.*
[55] "I bear all things, sustained by him who became a perfect man." *Epist. ad Smyrn.*, IV, 2.
[56] The patriarchs have never resided at Antioch, although the patriarch Elias in the 9th century built a church in the city. Their residences have included Diarbekir, the convent of Barsauma (near Melitene), Mardin and Tur 'Abdin.
[57] The Jacobite patriarchs were formerly buried at Deir el-Za'faran.

and the appointment requires papal confirmation. The synod also elects the bishop from a number of candidates recommended by the clergy and people of the vacant diocese.

Statistics [58] published in 1932 give a patriarch; 8 dioceses, with 5 resident bishops and 3 titular bishops; 164 priests; 6 religious (men); and 71,354 faithful.

The Syrian dioceses are Mardin and Amida, the former patriarchal see, which is administered by a patriarchal vicar having the dignity of chorepiscopus; Bagdad; Mosul; Aleppo; and Damascus, which are archiepiscopal; Homs (Emesa) and Hama; Beirut; and Cairo [59] (patriarchal vicariate), which are episcopal.

Gazirah is ruled by an episcopal patriarchal vicar, while the see of Jerusalem is administered by a patriarchal vicar with the dignity of chorepiscopus. There is a patriarchal vicar with episcopal character in the Lebanon. All the bishops are directly subject to the patriarch.

The first great war (1914-1918) has greatly hampered the progress of the Catholic Syrians. Dioceses were wrecked, and Mar Flavian Michael Malkeh, bishop of Gazirah, in 1915 was murdered [60] in prison by the Turks, together with four of his clergy, while thousands of his people suffered a similar fate.

The second in command in the Jacobite hierarchy is known as the *mafrian*, [61] a title which has been in use since

[58] *Statistica della Gerarchia e dei Fedeli di Rito Orientale* (Tipografia Poliglotta Vaticana, 1932), pp. 68-75.

[59] The dioceses of Mosul and Bagdad have about 20,000 faithful with 35 priests. The number of Syrian Catholics in Egypt is estimated at 1,600.

[60] Eighteen clergy of the diocese of Gazirah are said to have been killed, and twenty-eight from the diocese of Mardin.

[61] *Mafryônô*, "fructifier;" *afri*, "to make fruitful," "beget."

the time of Marutha (✝ ab. 649), who made Tagrith on the Tigris a centre of Monophysite activity. Michael I (1166-1199) spoke of the mafrian under the Greek name *epītrō-nīsa,* [62] and he has also been known as *ǵathliq (katholikos)* and *wakīl.* [63] The mafrian became the head of the hierarchy in Persia, where he was permitted to ordain priests and consecrate the chrism. Since the 14th century, however, he has been forced to leave Persia, although the title is held by an assistant bishop and vicar general, who lives near the patriarch, and is known as "Metropolitan of Jerusalem, Mafrian and Katholikos of the East." The mafrian nominally has the right of succession to the patriarchate.

Chorepiscopi have retained their importance in the Syrian Catholic church, whereas the Maronite patriarch in April 1929 curtailed their prerogatives and privileges. Amongst the Chaldeans, the office of chorepiscopus is conferred without any ceremony, on the simple written nomination of the patriarch.

From at least the 3rd century, a chorepiscopus was the vicar of a bishop, functioning outside the episcopal town, with inherent power to confer minor orders and consecrate churches, and, by *express* delegation, to ordain priests.

The office seems to have disappeared from the Byzantine church in the 11th century, and to have been replaced by the titular archimandrite, although the auxiliary bishops in the church of Constantinople are in fact chorepiscopi.

In the West, the office was less well known, although we find traces of it in Gaul, perhaps on account of the intercourse between that country and the East.

The excessive number of bishops in ancient days in

---

[62] ἐπιθορῶ, ἐπιθρόνιζω " to make fruitful."
[63] Arabic, " vicar."

Ireland may probably be accounted for by confusing chorepiscopi with bishops. [64]

Charlemagne (742-814), since there was a tendency to encroach upon the rights of diocesan bishops, limited the functions of the chorepiscopi, while the council of Meaux (845) forbade the chorepiscopi to administer confirmation, consecrate churches and ordain priests. The title, however, persisted in the west until the 12th century, often in the sense of an auxiliary bishop, although the work was rather that of an archdeacon or vicar general.

Current discipline in the Syrian church admits of one chorepiscopus in each eparchy, but they are also appointed for the diaspora. [65]

The rite for the blessing [66] of a chorepiscopus has retained the simplicity of the early church. After the elevation in the liturgy, the bishop goes to the throne, while two choirs chant alternately and two lessons are read from holy Scripture. Then the candidate receives the imposition of hands at the corner of the altar, and the bishop covers him with his pontifical vestment. The new chorepiscopus, who is standing, is given the insignia of his office, a kind of hood (the colour of the vestment), which takes the form of a piece of material, shaped like the hood of a western cope, ornamented with rich embroidery, and falling on the shoulders. This is

[64] "It is supposed that they were introduced into Ireland by St. Patrick himself, which would render intelligible the statement of St. Aengus that the Apostle conferred their orders on 'seven times fifty holy bishops' The *Tripartite* puts the number up to 370." Ailbe J. LUDDY, *Life of St. Malachy* (M. H. Gill, Dublin, 1930), introduction, p. XVIII. St. Aengus mentions 141 places in Ireland each of which possessed at the same time *seven* bishops. *Ibid.,* p. XVII, n. I.

[65] e. g. the procurator of the Syrian patriarch in Rome.

[66] The synod of Sharfeh (1888) says: "De *benedictione* chorepiscopi."

the *masnaphtho,* [67] an ornament in appearance not unlike
the amice worn by a Latin monk.

The celebrant, after the blessing, receives holy communion himself, and gives it to the chorespiscopus. The
members of this order may not use either an omophorion or
a pastoral staff, but the patriarch as a mark of favour may
grant them the right to wear a pectoral cross and a ring, and
also to carry a hand-cross. The Catholic chorepiscopus, like
a bishop, wears a black cassock with violet buttons on ordinary days, and a violet cassock on feasts. The office in a real
sense is a stepping stone to the episcopate, and, if a bishop
elect is not already a chorepiscopus, he must be admitted to
that dignity eight days before he is to receive the plenitude
of the priesthood.

The Syrians, like the Maronites, have *periodeutes* or
"diocesan visitors," who are constituted by a rite similar to
that used for the chorepiscopi.

Priests [68] do not concelebrate at their ordination; while
deacons [69] receive a censer and make a signed profession of
faith.

There are three minor orders in this rite, singer, reader,
and subdeacon. [70] The first two are conferred at the elevation in the liturgy, when the singer receives the book of
psalms, and the reader the book of the prophecies and a
stole. In practice, the singer [71] makes the responses which
the rubrics ascribe to the people. The subdeacon, who
includes in his duties the offices of acolyte [72] and doorkeeper,

[67] The *masnaphtho* worn by the chorepiscopus in Rome, which was
blue in colour, had the appearance of an apparelled amice.
[68] *Kachicho, senex,* " elder."
[69] *Mchamchono, diacono.*
[70] *Houpodiacono.*
[71] *Mzamrono.*
[72] *Qoruyo, aghnusto.*

is given a taper, since he is required to light the lamps and candles. The exorcist[73] does not receive ordination, but only a special mandate from the bishop.

Among the Jacobites, the subdiaconate is conferred at the age of ten, if the boy can read.

Catholic priests, since the synod of Sharfeh (1888), have been bound to celibacy, but dispensations are sometimes given, especially in the case of convert Jacobite clergy.

In 1929, the patriarchal seminary at Sharfeh was entrusted to the Benedictines of the French province of the Cassinese Congregation of Primitive Observance, who since 1903 had directed the Syrian seminary at Jerusalem.[74] Sharfeh[75] in 1786 had become the residence of the Catholic patriarch, Michael Garweh, who founded there the monastery of St. Mary, which was confirmed by Pope Pius VI in the brief *Exposuit nobis*. The tombs of three patriarchs and twelve bishops lie in a small chapel, which is known as *beth qaddishe* or "house of the saints." A seminary was established here in 1801.

The church is now being furnished in accordance with strict liturgical principles. A Syro-Benedictine province has been formed at Sharfeh, and Pope Pius XI permitted ten religious to pass from the Latin to the Syrian rite. In November 1935 Fr. Stephen Rahhal made his profession as the first Syrian Benedictine of the Antiochene rite.

Cardinal Antonio Barberini, brother of Pope Urban VIII,

[73] *Maumyono.*
[74] The seminary, which is part of the monastery of St. Benedict and St. Ephrem, is maintained to-day as a junior seminary.
[75] Arabic, "an eminence." Sharfeh has a commanding view of the Mediterranean sea on the west; with Beirut on the south; and the mountains on the east.
[76] The offices are celebrated in the Syrian and Chaldean rites alternate weeks.

founded two burses for "Jacobites" in the Urban College of Propaganda, which in 1637 by the brief *Altitudo divinae* were approved by the pope.

In addition to Sharfeh and the College of Propaganda, aspirants to the priesthood go to the Syro-Chaldean college [76] of the Dominicans at Mosul, the monastery of Mar Behnam and to the university of the Jesuits at Beirut.

Monasticism

Pope Leo XIII is reported to have said: "I love the Syrians. They have only one shortcoming: they have no religious life." Attempts have been made from time to time to establish Catholic communities. Sharfeh in the time of the patriarch Michael Garweh († 1801) had served as a monastery (Our Lady of Deliverance) with a few religious.

The Catholic Syrians, however, possess several monasteries, some of which go back to a remote antiquity. The earliest is probably that of *Mar Behnam* near Mosul, containing the tomb of the royal boy-martyr, St. Behnam (4th century). The church has been described as a "monument [77] of Eastern Christian art, and certain parts go back to the 4th century." The monastery is now governed by a superior of the secular clergy. There are 10 students (religious) and 2 lay brothers. *Mar Musa* (Moses) *the Ethiopian*, 70 kilometres north of Damascus, on the road to Homs, is now empty and in a tottering condition, but the chapel, which may go back to the 7th century, has some frescoes of great beauty. *Mar Afrem* [78] (Ephrem) *of Raghem*, near Hammana in the Lebanon, was founded in the 15th century, and was

---

[77] Stephen RAHHAL, *Some Notes on the West Syrians. Eastern Churches Quarterly* (July-September, 1946), p. 379.
[78] The monastery of Mar Afrem gave several bishops to the Church.

governed by an abbot who was also a bishop, but the monks were massacred, and the building ransacked and burnt by the Druses in 1860.

The promising feature of Syrian religious life to-day is the Syro-Benedictine province, so long desired by Mar Ephrem Rahmani, the late patriarch, who often repeated these words: "The Rule which came from the East must go back there."

The missionaries of St. Ephrem form a congregation of "clerks regular," which in greatly depleted numbers survived the great war of 1914-1918. The congregation in its present form dates from 1882, although this was a revival of an order that existed from 1785 at Sharfeh. In 1932, the missionaries numbered only half a dozen priests, ministering to the faithful at Mardin, Golya and Kolosya.

An inter-ritual congregation for women, the native Sisters of the Sacred Hearts of Jesus and Mary, founded in 1857, works in Syria and the Lebanese republic. It has 39 houses and 266 religious.

Monastic life [79] among the Jacobites is to-day completely degenerate; there are 20 monks at the most, and of their numerous monasteries 12 remain. Of these, the most famous are Deir el-Za'faran, where a handful of monks are finishing their days; Deir Mattai ("the Old"), where a few monks live a kind of life which recalls that of the 4th century; and Mar Marcos in Jerusalem, where 5 monks reside with a bishop.

The Jacobite clergy receive their scanty training for the ministry in these monasteries, but "orders [80] are conferred on anyone of the faithful if he can read Syriac and Arabic,

---

[79] Stephen RAHHAL, Some Notes on the West Syrians. Eastern Churches Quarterly (July-September, 1946), p. 375.
[80] Ibid.

especially if he has a fine voice and an imposing presence."
The present Jacobite patriarch, Mar Ignatius Afrem Barsaum,
has had a better education than is customary. He was
educated at the Dominican Syro-Chaldean preparatory seminary at Mosul, and then reverted to schism.

Monastic regulations were revised and modifications were
introduced by the Jacobite council of 1930, when two canons
affecting the religious life were passed. The monks were
forbidden to serve parishes.

A strange legend is told of the Jacobite monastery of Deir
Mattai, on the heights of the Jebel Maqlub about 50 miles
south-east of Mosul. A Nestorian visitor in the 6th century
is said to have crept into the library, and with water miraculously produced from the floor to have washed all the parch-
ments free from writing. Jebel Maqlub at one time teemed
with monasteries, and it has been called the Monophysite
Mount Athos.

The monastic habit consists of a robe [81] of black wool,
leather girdle, [82] hood [83] and mantle. [84]

The tonsure is called *suphora*. [85]

Numbers and Dispersion

In 1931, the number of Catholics of the rite was given
by the Congregation for the Eastern Church as 71,354, of
whom 6,801 were in the United States.

The Jacobites, as we have seen, are said to number about
100,000.

[81] *Kuthino.*
[82] *Zunoro.*
[83] *Eskimo.*
[84] *Jubba.*
[85] *East Syrian, supára;* cf. Greek, στεφάνη, i. e. " anything that sur-
rounds or encircles the head," hence " tonsure."

The largest communities of Catholic Syrians [86] are in Mosul, Damascus, Aleppo and Cairo; while small colonies are found in South America (Argentina; Chile); Australia; [87] and the United States (New York; Boston; Cincinnati). In 1925, the former chapel of the Irish college in the Rue des Carmes, Paris, was given to the Syrians.

Ancient links had already existed between Paris and Syria, and Gregory of Tours [88] narrates how one Eusebius, a Syrian merchant, by means of his money was elected bishop of Paris (ab. 592). One of the first acts of the new bishop was—*abiciens omnem scholam decessoris sui*—to fill his household with people of his own nation. It may very well be therefore that this Syrian stranger expelled from the diocese the singers of that Paris song-school which Venantius Fortunatus [89] had so wholeheartedly extolled. Later, a church in Paris received the name of *St-Pierre-des-Arcis,* "St. Peter of the Assyrians." In the 6th century, Tours had many Syrian establishments.

Pope Benedict XV in 1915 conceded a church in Rome for the use of the Syrian rite, and St. Gregory, Via Leccosa, was chosen. The offer, however, never materialised, and it was only in 1920 that a former house and church of Benedictine nuns in Campo Marzio was granted to the Syrian patriarch.

The name of the church was changed from Santa Maria in Campo Marzio to that of the great Syrian doctor, St. Ephrem. The church in its arrangements is altogether Latin, and a small chapel is found in the house. In earlier

[86] The Catholic Syrians in Palestine number about 600.
[87] The archdiocese of Sydney has about 1,000 Syrians, and Brisbane about 700. A church of the rite was opened in 1929 at Brisbane.
[88] *Hist. Franc.,* Lib. X, chap. 26.
[89] *Carm.,* Lib. II, 9.

times, however, the Syrians in Rome had had a church of
their own.

The Catholic patriarch, Ignatius Peter Šahbadīn, in 1696
obtained permission from Propaganda to buy, with money
collected by the metropolitan of Mardin and Diarbekir
(Athanasius Safar), the house of the *Fatebenefratelli* and
the church of S. Maria della Sanità. [90] The name of the
church was changed to that of St. Ephrem, but in 1648 it
was sold, together with the house, to the Franciscan Con-
ventuals.

Architecture

"Syrian architecture," says Butler, [91] "in addition to
being one of the earliest expressions in stone of the faith,
and a lasting record, even in its ruins, of the zeal and beauty
of that faith, is also an important factor in the general growth
of Christian architecture."

The golden age was in the 5th and 6th centuries, but the
destruction caused by the Islamic barbarians has left little
beyond fragmentary ruins. [92]

Tur-Abdin, [93] a hilly plateau in a bend of the Tigris, has
many fortified monasteries, whose churches have walls of
stone, but vaults of brick. Mediaeval churches are found at
Qara Qosh. The deeply undercut lintels, peculiar to the
neighbourhood, with other distinctive features—seen at their
best in the monastery of Mar Behnam—have suggested to
an Arab geographer the intricacies of wood carving. The

[90] The church has since been destroyed. It was in the present Via
Agostino Depretis.

[91] *Early Churches in Syria, fourth to seventh centuries.* H. C. BUT-
LER, Princetown University, 1929, p. 264.

[92] A full description of the early churches of Syria is given by
Mgr. HINDO, *Disciplina Antiochena Antica (Siri)*, t. IV, pp. 13-58.

[93] "Mountain of the Servants of God."

facing of walls with sculptured panels of alabaster, as in the buildings of ancient Assyria, has created a type of decoration that is common to both churches and mosques. There is but little in the arches or the vaulting of the Jacobite church of Mar Tuma or the Catholic church of al-Tahira ("the Immaculate") to distinguish them from those in the mosque of Aun al-Din.

The church of St. Ignatius the God-bearer, attached to the new residence of the Catholic patriarch at Beirut, and blessed on June 28, 1931, is an example of modern architecture, fashioned according to the best traditional Syrian style, although some of the internal arrangements proper to the rite are wanting.

The description given by Bar Hebraeus [34] (1225-1286) of the consecration of a church agrees in many points with present day practice, e. g., the anointing of the altar and walls with chrism.

The Church and its Interior Arrangements

A Syrian church has three main divisions, the east end with the sanctuary, choir, and nave. In old churches there is also a narthex, and outside the main door there may be a portico (*atrium; impluvium*), where the divine office is sometimes recited in hot weather.

The east end traditionally terminates in one or more apses, in which there are altars. Catholics may offer the holy Sacrifice on any of the altars, but the Jacobites normally celebrate on the central one (*thronos*), using those on either side (*kenfo*, "wings") for concelebrants, or for the holding of accessories of worship.

---

[34] *Nomocanon.* Latin edition. Mai, *script. vet.*, t. X, p. 10.

The southern apse or its equivalent is called the *diacon-icon*, [95] where the sacred vessels are sometimes kept. The Jacobite custom, occasionally followed by Catholics, is to leave them on the altar, covered with veils, from one liturgy to the other.

The east end should be cut off from the rest of the church by a screen (without pictures), which may be a solid stone wall pierced with doorways or a wooden trellis. Curtains, [96] which are drawn at certain times during the liturgy, hang in each of the doors, although there is a tendency to dispense with screens and even curtains. Thus, the new Catholic cathedral at Beirut has neither screen nor curtain, and the same is the case at Cairo, Rome and Paris. The Jacobite church of Mar Marcos at Jerusalem, where legend says that our Lady received baptism, has an open trellis-work screen.

The sanctuary is variously known as the "holy place," [97] "holy of holies," [98] "house of the altar," [99] $\kappa\acute{o}\gamma\chi\eta$, [100] or *bema*. [101]

The altar [102] or throne, [103] which may be of wood or stone, normally stands under a ciborium supported by four pillars. A curtain hangs in front, which in some modern churches has been confused with the curtain of the main door of the screen.

---

[95] *Diyaqoniqon; beth diyaqon; beth rozê; secretarium.*

[96] Wilo (β ῆλο *velum*); sethro.

[97] *Qudsho; beth qudsho.*

[98] *Q'dhosh qudhshe.*

[99] *Beth madb'ho.*

[100] *Qankho.*

[101] *Bim.*

[102] *Pothur hayê*, "table of life;" *madb'ho*; θυσιαστήριον, "place of sacrifice."

[103] *Thronos.*

The gradines support a cross [104] and at least two candles; [105] while the book of the gospels and the holy vessels sometimes remain on the altar. Altar cards are not unknown, and the Jacobite church at Damascus has a single card containing the words of institution and the epiclesis.

The altar should stand away from the east wall to admit of the procession at the anthem or *qurobo*. The steps of the altar, of which the Syrians have three and the Malabar Jacobites one, are kissed liturgically. The *tablith* [106] or "altar stone" is oblong in shape, and a direction in the pontifical says: "the small tablets are made of precious wood, [107] chosen stone or other material." They are consecrated with chrism by the bishop on Holy Thursday or any Thursday from Easter to the Ascension. Each "stone" has the name of the bishop and the date, while the Syrians have the following inscription in two lines: "The Holy Ghost hath hallowed this *tablith* by the hands of mar N.," and across it "Year N."

The Jacobites speak of the Holy Trinity as having consecrated the "stone," which is covered by a cloth, folded into four and often embroidered. The Catholics have three cloths, and the synod of Sharfeh (1888) directed that Mass must not be said without a "corporal." [108]

Theodoret of Cyrus († ab. 393-457) said that in a case

---

[104] "It is not permitted to offer the Sacrifice without the gospel, the cross and the image of Christ." Yaḥya ibn-Garir (c. 1083); Al-Muršid, chap. LIV, *Of the Communion.* Modern practice favours a crucifix.

[105] The candles have replaced the standing or hanging lights.

[106] The *tablith* is about 18 × 12 inches.

[107] "Abdallah ibn-aṭ-Ṭayyib (1043) said that the use of wood was a concession introduced in the great persecution of Sapor II, which with short interruptions lasted for 39 years (340-379).

[108] *Kethons,* "linen;" Arabic, *Andimisi (antimension); mandil; mantile.*

of necessity a deacon might serve as the *"mensa;"* while we find the Jacobites permitting a priest to celebrate, while holding the vessels with his left hand in a scarf. The *Nomocanon* of Bar Hebraeus envisaged the possibility of a bishop sanctioning a leaf of the gospel-book to serve as an "altar stone." The use of a *"mensa"* in stuff or skin was prohibited by John, a Jacobite patriarch in the 7th century, thus apparently condemning the Byzantine and Nestorian customs of the *antimension* and the piece of ass's skin respectively.

The bishop of Sidon, who visited the Jacobites in the 16th century, said that the blessed sacrament was reserved in a wooden box without a light, although Bar-Hebraeus [109] († ab. 1286), citing the 23rd canon of the Nestorian katholikos, John bar-Abgar (10th cent.), had said: "One should not leave the holy sacrament on the altar without a lamp that burns throughout the night."

The same writer [110] forbids the reservation of the chalice, except in the case of the gravely sick and those who fast until late at night. James of Edessa († ab. 708) [111] condemns the practice [112] of reserving a part of the blessed sacrament, consecrated on Holy Thursday, until the following year. The eucharist [113] is kept in a paten or other vessel, and taken to

[109] *Nomocanon*, IV, 2.

[110] *Ibid.*, IV, 8, taken from James of Edessa (ob. 708).

[111] Can. 7.

[112] The Maronite *Kitab al Huda* (1059) orders the priest to reserve a portion of the *qurban* of Holy Thursday in a pyx (*qamtara*; cf. κάμπτρια or κάμπρα " box"), which is to be placed in the cupboard of the mysteries and given in holy communion the following Holy Thursday. The Greeks had a similar custom, which was condemned by Pope Benedict XIV (*Etsi pastoralis*). The practice was still mentioned in the last edition of the *Liturghier* of the Catholic Rumanians of Transylvania (edit. Blaj, 1931, pp. 225-227), although it is no longer in existence.

[113] John, bishop of Tel-Mauzalta (canon 8).

the sick in a linen bag or leaf of parchment, which is to be afterwards burned. In Lent enough of the sacred species was reserved each Sunday for the liturgy of the presanctified during the week; while churches [111] and religious houses were also to have the blessed sacrament for communion outside the liturgy and to take to the sick in their homes. James of Edessa, in answer to a question put to him by Addai, said that the reserved sacrament was placed in an open niche [115] in the sanctuary wall, but the modern practice among the Jacobites [116] is to reserve in a chalice with a cover on one of the gradines of the altar. The Catholic Syrians use a Latin tabernacle, [117] and the sacred host, which has been anointed with the precious blood, must be renewed every day.

There are two episcopal thrones on the north side of the sanctuary, one facing west for the office on solemn feasts, and the other facing south for the liturgy. As in Latin Christendom, the ancient position for the throne was against the east wall of the apse. The treasury (*beth gazo*) is a cupboard for valuables in the wall of the apse behind the altar. The Jacobites now keep the chrism, with the oil for baptism, in the north apse; the Catholics behind the altar or in the baptistery.

Lecterns sometimes support icons, especially that of our Lady on the north side of the church, but there has been a

[114] RAHMANI, *Les Liturgies Orientales et Occidentales*, p. 61.

[115] The Maronite nomocanon says to the right of the altar in the cupboard of the mysteries.

[116] The blessed sacrament is so reserved in the church of St. Mark, Jerusalem.

[117] The place of reservation is called the *paradiscus* ($\pi\alpha\rho\alpha\delta\acute{\iota}\sigma\kappa\sigma$) "cupboard;" Arabic, *beit qurban* (used by the Melkites for *artophorion*), "house of the oblation;" *tabut*, "ark."

protestantising movement among the Jacobites, which has discouraged the use of holy pictures. [118]

Dislike of images, however, is no new phenomenon, and in 488 we find Xenaias, a Monophysite bishop in Phrygia, forbidding their use in his diocese; while Syria in the 6th and 7th centuries was constantly being influenced by iconoclastic tendencies.

On the south side of the sanctuary there is often a memorial [119] to the patron saint, which frequently takes the form of a reliquary. [120]

The prohibition for the laity to enter the sanctuary is found in the writings of James of Edessa, but it is now very generally disregarded. A gospel book normally rests on a lectern [121] (*golgotha*) outside the central door of the screen, slightly to the north, and standard lights, on one of which hangs a censer, are placed on either side. The ambo [122] was originally used in the Syrian rite, and some remains are

---

[118] The use of statues, especially bas-reliefs, is not unknown to the Syrians. In the 4th century (restored in the 12th century) church of the monastery of Mar Behnam, to the right of the royal door, there are about 20 bas-reliefs, representing scenes from the life of the patron saint and of the founders of monasticism. To the left, also, is a large bas-relief of St. Behnam and his sister, St. Sara; while on the vaulting St. Peter and St. Paul are represented. The ancient church of Al-Tahira, Mosul, has a bust of our Lady that is said to date from the early middle ages. P. HINDO, *Disciplina Antiochena Antica (Siri)*, IV, p. 312, n. 1.

[119] *Beth kadiché*, "place of saints."

[120] Jacobites do not place relics in or under the altar, a practice forbidden by John Bar Cursos (519-538; canon 13), but they are normally kept in a *glusqomo* (γλωσσόκομον) or oblong stone box, in a cupboard. The blessed sacrament was formerly reserved in the same place. Special chapels (*martyria*) were sometimes built for relics.

[121] Janin (*Les Eglises orientales et les Rites orientaux*, chap. XIII, p. 442) says that the golgotha is on the south side of the sanctuary.

[122] The ambo took the form of a raised platform opposite the central door of the screen.

extant in the ancient churches of Mount Masius near Mardin (Zaz; Beth-Severina; Hebab). The section of the church between the sanctuary and nave, which is reserved for the singers, is known as the *catastroma*. [123] In Jacobite churches, this is now also the baptistery, [124] although some ancient churches in Mesopotamia use the *diaconicon* for the purpose, and Bar Hebraeus [125] says that it was usually on the south side of the altar.

The nave, [126] commonly in Jacobite churches and always in those of the Catholics, has an icon [127] of the blessed Virgin. The women worship in galleries, at the west end of the church or in the aisle behind a screen. The Syrians, to fulfil the requirements of their Turkish masters, used wooden boards struck by hammers instead of bells.

Many of the Catholic churches have introduced Latin ornaments, which present a hybrid appearance distasteful to both rites.

The altar vessels are similar to those in the Byzantine rite, but the lance is not used and the sponge, although retaining the name, has given place to the linen purificator. [128]

The paten is a round dish with the edges turned up; while the chalice [129] is of the Latin shape.

A star, [130] composed of two hoops of metal crossed and fastened together in the middle, is used to prevent the veil

---

[123] The *Catastroma* is also used for the choir.

[124] *Beth m'amuditho*, "house of baptism."

[125] *Nomocanon*, II, 3.

[126] *Haiklo*, "temple."

[127] *Yuqno*, εἰκων.

[128] Arabic, *siniyah;* Syriac, *pinco* (πίναξ), cf. "Nunc vos Pharisaei quod deforis est calicis, et *catini*, mundatis." Luc. XI, 39. *Piyalo; pilaso* (φιάλη); *kphophto.*

[129] Arabic, *kas;* Syriac, *koso.*

[130] *Kaukbo;* cf. asterisk.

touching the holy bread, although in some churches [131] the vessels are provided with covers bearing crosses.

The synod of Sharfeh (1888) enjoined that the paten and chalice should be consecrated with chrism by a bishop, but in earlier days it sufficed that a bishop or even a priest should bless them with the prayer: "O God of our fathers, who in ancient days...." etc.

A spoon [132] is used for holy communion by the celebrant and those who are in orders, but a hymn which is still sung at the funeral of a priest shows that this was not the primitive practice.

It is evident from its name that the sponge [133] was of levantine origin, but distance from the sea has caused the Jacobites to use a piece of silk. This sponge is required not only at the ablutions, but also at the frequent washing of the fingers, which the rubrics enjoin each time the Jacobite priest touches the host. Catholics keep the fingers joined from the consecration to the communion.

The metal vase of water which stands on the altar in Jacobite churches for the ablution of the fingers and the mixing of the wine and water at the offertory is termed the "deaconess." [134]

The small cushion [135] on which the spoon rests and with which the fingers and mouth are wiped and the paten purified is almost obsolete in Catholic churches.

---

[131] e. g. Sant'Andrea della Valle, Rome, and St. Ephrem, Paris. A Syrian priest informed the writer that "covers" are more liturgical than veils. Veils are used especially when the vessels are of the Latin shape.

[132] *Tarwodho; kalb'tho*, "tongs," cf. "et in manu ejus calculus, quem *forcipe* tulerat de altari." Isa. VI, 6.

[133] *Espugo;* Greek, σπόγγος.

[134] *M'shamshonito,* cf. *Rom.* XVI, 1.

[135] *Gomuro,* "perfecter."

Except in those churches where the holy vessels have metal covers or crowns, veils [136] of some pliant material are placed over the paten and chalice, [137] while a larger veil [138] envelops them both.

It seems that a veil originally covered the altar, and that it was lifted up by the priest and deacons at the beginning of the dialogue before the preface.

Cymbals (sesle) and the noqusho, a brazen cup fitted with a handle after the fashion of a tongueless bell and struck with a metal rod, are sometimes used at the more solemn parts of the liturgy—sanctus, words of institution, epiclesis, elevation, and the blessing before the communion of the people. In Malabar they are used also at the trisagion.

The liturgical fan, [139] which is used in processions, is a metal disc in the form of a seraph's face and wings with bells attached, fixed on a staff.

The censer (pirmo) is of the Latin shape, with shorter chains and bells, and swung at the whole length of the chain. It would seem that the censer was at one time placed on the altar. Thus, in canon four of the so-called Canons of the Apostles: "the offering of the incense that burns on the altar during the holy Sacrifice." Mgr. Rahmani [140] says that the use of a censer without chains still persists in the Syrian church, and that it is sometimes placed on the altar and sometimes, during funeral ceremonies, on graves.

St. Ephrem refers in a hymn to the use of incense in the

---

[136] Shushepo (singular).

[137] Huppoyo, the veil over the chalice.

[138] Annaphuro; Greek, ἀναφορά ; aimo, "cloud;" p'roso; keltho; shushepo; Arabic, nāfūr.

[139] Marwaḥ'tho; Arabic, mirwaḥah; flabella. The fans, when not in use, are placed against the sides of the altar.

[140] Liturgies Orientales et Occidentales, chap. II, p. 278.

liturgy: "I have built a church to Christ in myself and I have offered up the sufferings of my members as sweet smelling incense."

Eucharistic Bread and Wine

The eucharistic bread [141] is a round cake of leaven, about 3 inches in diameter, to which a little salt has been added. The Jacobites have also one or two drops of oil, but the Catholics [142] only anoint the mould at the moment of stamping the bread with the pattern. Oil, as an ingredient of the bread, is mentioned by John X Bar Susan, patriarch of Antioch ($\dagger$ 1072), in a letter to Christodulus, patriarch of Alexandria.

The moulds are now made of wood, but examples of stone may be seen in the museums at Cairo, Old Cairo and St. Stephen's Jerusalem. The whole surface of the cake is divided into four equal parts by two cross lines. The central part is demarcated by a circle, and the four segments thus formed are each marked with a cross.

Each of the four divisions on the remainder of the cake between the circle and the perimeter effected by the cross lines is further divided into two sections, each with a cross, thus making a total of twelve.

---

[141] *Būchro,* "first begotten," cf. Heb. I, 6: "Et cum iterum introducit *primogenitum* in orbem terrae." *Burshānah;* Syriac, *pūrshōno,* "portion set apart" (ἀγαίρεμα), cf. heave offering in *Leviticus; tabh'o,* "seal," as the cake is "sealed with crosses;" *p'rīsto,* "flat cake," "divided."

A particle broken from the consecrated host is called *g'murtho* "coal," cf. Isa., VI, 6-7, and used in this connection by St. Ephrem and James of Batnan; also *margonītho,* "pearl." *Qurbono* is the "oblation" as a whole.

[142] HANSSENS, *Instit. Lit. de Rit. Orient.,* t. II, pars I, chap. VII, sect. I, p. 122.

A rubric warns the celebrant not to mutilate one of the crosses in dividing the host for communion.

The synod of Sharfeh (1888) laid down requirements for the eucharistic bread, [143] and at the same time permitted in case of real necessity the use of ordinary bread. [144]

Catholics and Jacobites both leaven the sacred loaves with a portion of dough (h'miro) reserved from the last baking.

Many of the early fathers [145] have witnessed to the use of leavened bread in the liturgy, although St. Ephrem [146] for symbolical reasons has referred in hymns and homilies to both leaven and azymes.

A Syrian tradition, cited by St. Rabula, bishop of Edessa († 435); Lazarus Bar Sabta, bishop of Bagdad (9th century); the patriarch John III († 873); and the patriarch John X Bar Susan († 1072), maintains that our Lord after using azyme bread at the Last Supper abrogated the further use of it.

The synod of Sharfeh, also, enjoined that the eucharistic bread [147] on Maundy Thursday (*In feria autem 5. Paschatis*)

---

[143] The bread was to be divided into 12 parts, with a small cross on each part. It was to be moderately thick "according to custom." HANSSENS, *op. cit.*, pp. 175-176.

[144] *Ibid.*, p. 176.

[145] e. g. St. Epiphanius, bishop of Salamis (ab. 310-403), chap. XXX, *Book of Heresies;* St. John Chrysostom (ab. 344-407) *Homily XXIV on the Epistle to the Corinthians;* St. Rabula, bishop of Edessa († 435), *Letter to Gamalina*, bishop of Perin.

[146] "The bread of him who gives life to all, vivified his people, in place of the unleavened bread which gave death to those who have eaten it." ap. RAHMANI, *Les Lit. Orient. et Occiden.*, chap. II, 6, p. 63.

"He has immolated and eaten the passover, he has broken his body, has made the figure disappear and given the reality. In the day of unleavened bread he has eaten leaven, and by that his body has become for us the unleavened bread of reality." *Hymn on the Institution of the Eucharist*, ap. *ibid.*, p. 64.

[147] HANSSENS, op. cit., t. II, pars I, chap. VII, sect. IV, p. 176.

should, in accordance with an old custom, be stamped with a representation of a lamb.

Great care must be taken in the baking [148] of the bread, which, if possible, should be carried out in church or in the house of the bishop or parish priest, but not in the homes of the laity. It is fitting that psalms or other canticles should be recited during the work, which must on no account be undertaken by women. Priests may not consecrate with hosts which have been prepared by non-Catholics. The bread [149] should be baked fresh for each liturgy, but in the absence of a sacristan (*aedituus*) it is permitted for Catholics to use hosts which are two or three days old. It is forbidden, except in a case of necessity, to use bread which has not been baked specifically for the Syrian rite.

The baking of the bread on the day of the liturgy has been ascribed to the days of the apostles, [150] while John Bar Cursos, bishop of Telles (538), Denys Bar Salibi (1171), and Bar Hebraeus (1286) have all insisted on the practice, comparing the eucharistic bread with the manna. John of Telles, who referred to the custom of the faithful bringing the matter for the sacrifice, recommended the deacons to place the bread and the chalices at the four corners of the altar.

The Liturgy of St. James, in the diptychs of the living, has the prayer: "Be mindful, O Lord, of those who have *brought* these offerings to thy holy altar;" while a hymn [151] for the Ascension, ascribed to St. Ephrem, speaks of the "new bread" which mystically ascends to-day.

[148] *Ibid.*, sect. VIII, p. 207.
[149] Cf. BAR HEBRAEUS, *Nomocanon*, IV, 1.
[150] HANSSENS, *op. cit.*, p. 212.
[151] "*Panis novus* mystice ascendit hodie. Ita mysteria fuerunt explanata per corpus tuum, quod ascendit tamquam oblatio. Benedictus sit panis tuus."

A small furnace [152] for the baking is still to be found in the courtyards of some village churches.

Later usage prescribed the bringing of flour to the sacristan, a custom which is observed at Mosul, and families [153] in some parts of Syria continue to offer wheat for the liturgy.

A hymn for the fourth Sunday after the Holy Cross speaks of the eucharistic bread as "crowns," [154] an expression used by St. Gregory the Great (590-604). [155]

Salt as an ingredient of the bread is mentioned in the pseudo-Clementine homilies, while Isaac the Great of Antioch (459-461) alludes to oil in the *Song of the Holy Martyrs*.

Renaudot [156] thinks that a reference to oil in the bread of the liturgy is made in the prayer [157] after the epiclesis in the anaphora of John of Basora (8th century), but there is some doubt as to whether this is the correct interpretation.

The composition of the Jacobite eucharistic bread has occasioned much controversy with other dissident churches.

The proposed union of the Jacobite and Armenian churches in the 8th [158] and 11th[159] centuries was largely

[152] A small furnace for this purpose exists in a Coptic church in Old Cairo.

[153] Cf. Synod of Sharfeh (1888), canon 3.

[154] The fruits of the earth are called in Syriac the " crowns of the year."

[155] St. Gregory speaks of a priest bringing " *duas oblationum coronas.*" Lib. IV, *Dialog.*, c. 55.

[156] *Lit. Orien. Collect.*, t. II, p. 435, n. 7.

[157] " *Panem ex simila mistum cum oleo, et thure, in odorem suavitatis tibi offerimus.*" *Ibid.*, p. 426.

[158] Athanasius, Jacobite patriarch (724-740), and John III Oznezi, Armenian katholikos (717-728).

[159] John X Bar Šušan, Jacobite patriarch (1058), and Gregory Arsakuni, Armenian katholikos († ab. 1058).

wrecked through difference of opinion on this question.

The Jacobite patriarch, John VIII (1004-1033), who was exiled to Bulgaria, is said to have caused scandal to the Bulgars in respect to the bread of the eucharist and the way of making the sign of the cross.

Apologists, however, were not wanting, and the patriarch Isho Bar Shushan (1064-1073), who wrote under the name of John, produced a treatise in defence of the Jacobite practice, and Denys Bar Salibi [160] (1171) gave an elaborate mystical explanation for the various ingredients.

The Coptic church felt so strongly on the matter that in the patriarchate of Christodulus (1047) there was a schism between Alexandria and Antioch.

The Jacobites, unless there are no communicants when two hosts will suffice, insist upon an unequal number of breads, and some manuscripts have a rubric to that effect: "Besides two 'seals,' let no one place (on the paten) an equal number (of seals), but rather let him take care that they may be unequal."

This custom was supported by Denys Bar Salibi (1171) and Theodore Bar Wahbun (1192-3), although it was unknown for many centuries. John Bar Cursos, [161] bishop of Telles (538), plainly says: "The number of hosts is optional, either equal or unequal: for it is lawful to offer them equal and unequal, as is handed down from the holy apostles in the Book of Clement." Bar Hebraeus, the Jacobite canonist (1286), is forced to admit that there is no binding authority for the use of an unequal number.

---

[160] *Expositio Liturgiae,* chap. VI.
[161] Quoted by Daniel Bar Hattab, who flourished at the end of the 13th century, *Nomocanon,* chap. III, sect. BO II, 181.

The synod of Sharfeh (1888) forbade the use of unfermented wine in the liturgy, and expressed a preference for wine that was white in colour, as it does not stain the purificator at the ablutions.

Some Syrian anaphoras [162] specifically mention that our Lord mixed water with the wine at the Last Supper, and in that of Marutas [163] the Catholic the two elements are said to be in a *right proportion*.

The Jacobites have an equal quantity of wine and water, adding unconsecrated wine if the supply runs short. This practice was enjoined in the 5th canon of John Bar Cursos (538), and quoted by Bar Hebraeus: [164] "And there should be half wine and half water mixed in the chalice: and if the quantity of liquid (for the communion of the faithful) should fail, the priest himself can add to it from that which has not been consecrated."

The synod of Sharfeh (1888) [165] condemned the Jacobite custom, and said that according to the practice and tradition of the universal Church there was a definite quantity (*quantitatem determinatam*) of water put into the chalice.

The absence of water in the liturgy of the Gregorian Armenians was adversely commented on by George the Arabian (686-724); John X Bar Šušan (1058; 1064-1073); and Denys Bar Salibi (1171).

[162] St. James the Less; St. Xystus.
[163] "*Similiter prosequendo, accepit etiam vinum, et illud justa proportione, cum miscuisset aqua.*" RENAUDOT, *op. cit.*, t. II, p. 262.
[164] 1286, *Nomocanon*, c. IV, sect. I.
[165] HANSSENS, *op. cit.*, p. 244.

Vestments

A canon [166] warns the priest who dares to celebrate the liturgy without vestments of the fate that overtook the company of Core. [167]

Catholics of the rite are more faithful to Eastern tradition than the Maronites.

Special shoes (*m'sonê*) [168] are prescribed for the priest and the deacon.

The alb (Syriac, *kūthīno;* [169] Arabic, *l:amīs*) worn by the sacred ministers should be a long flowing tunic, which may be of cotton, linen or silk, of any colour and embroidered with crosses, but the seemingly inevitable laced alb is sometimes used by Catholics. [170] The cincture (*zūnnōro*) is not worn by the lower orders of the ministry. The priest has an embroidered belt, fastened by two clasps.

The stole (*urôrô; orarium; hamnikho*) is used by the celebrant and all the assistants, but each minister has his own way of wearing it. The priest, as in the Byzantine rite, has a broad strip of material with an aperture for the head, ornamented with crosses. The deacon carries the stole on the left shoulder, from whence it falls nearly to the ground before and behind, and originating in the long napkin still used in the East to wipe pots and pans. The archdeacon wears the stole in the Latin way, fastened on the right thigh. The subdeacon has the stole on the left shoulder, with the

---

[166] *Canones .... Syrorum,* can. 15. DENZINGER, *Ritus Orientalium,* I, 491.

[167] Num. XVI, 1-35.

[168] BAR HEBRAEUS († 1286), *Nomocanon,* IV, 2.

[169] Cf. Greek, χιτών.

[170] Anomalies of dress, however, are not confined to Catholics, and in 1931 a Jacobite priest was seen assisting in the church of the Holy Sepulchre, Jerusalem, dressed in cassock and biretta.

part pendant behind brought round under the right arm and thrown back over the left shoulder, after the manner of the Byzantine deacon. The stole of the reader [171] is worn round the waist as a girdle, with the two ends crossed behind, brought over the breast, and tucked into the part that forms the belt.

Long narrow cuffs (zendê; pedhitho) confine the sleeves of the kūthīno, a usage which may have suggested to the West the ornamentation of the sleeves of the alb.

The vestment (faino, phaino) is the ancient phelonion or paenula, but divided up the front, with a cross on the upper part of the back, and fastened by a loop and button—or clasp. The effect resembles a cope without a hood.

Some Syrian priests wear the Latin amice, but it is untraditional. Bishop and dignitaries, such as chorepiscopi, have also a masnaphtho or hood of the same material as the outer vestment, and received at their consecration. It covers [172] the head during the celebration of the holy Sacrifice: at the gospel, the consecration of the mysteries, and after the consecration it is placed on the neck. When a mitre is worn, the masnaphtho falls back on the shoulders. The "holy schema" (eskhimo; eskhim; qubh'uno) is used by bishops and monks, and it is never removed at Mass. It consists of a long strip of black material, with one end shaped like a hood, and the other hanging between the shoulders under the outer garment, so that the edge passes over the ears diagonally from the forehead to the back of the neck.

---

[171] The wearing of a stole by a reader was prohibited by the council of Laodicea (c. 370, can. 23): "Non licet lectoribus, ex fidelibus electis ad legendum, imponere orarium humeris suis, non enim habent perfectum ministerium sed imperfectum tantummodo. Legant ipsi libros Ecclesiae, ex psalmos canant."

[172] RAHMANI, op. cit., chap. II, 8, p. 79.

The schema of the Catholics, which is gold [173] for bishops and white for monks, has no ornamentation except a cross over the forehead. The Jacobites have a more elaborate head-gear, adorned with two white stripes, and the space in between covered with white crosses.

The lofty Latin mitre (*togho*), which has been adopted by Catholic bishops, [174] is worn over the schema. The omophorion (*hemnicho;* [175] *uoro rabbo;* [176] *homophoryon*) of white silk [177] has much the same shape as the priest's stole, but wider and double, hanging down in front and behind like a monastic scapular, with a number of crosses on it.

The pectoral cross is worn by Catholic bishops over the omophorion.

The Latin crozier also has been adopted by the united Syrians, and except at the entry, blessing, gospel and sermon, it is held by the archdeacon, raised slightly above the ground.

The eastern form of pastoral staff, [178] either taking the form of two serpents entwined, with between them a ball surmounted by a cross, or of a single serpent curved like the head of a Roman crozier, is occasionally used by Catholic bishops.

The Catholic patriarch carries a staff which terminates

---

[173] A plain red silk schema with a cross over the forehead was worn at a "low Mass" celebrated by Cardinal Tappuni (June 16, 1946).

[174] Latin mitres are also worn by the Jacobite bishops in Malabar.

[175] "Necklace;" cf. "Tulitque annulum de manu sua, et dedit eum in manu ejus: vestivitque eum stola byssina, et *collo torquem auream* circumposuit." Gen. XLI, 42.

[176] "Great orarion."

[177] At a "low Mass" celebrated in Rome (June 16, 1946) by Cardinal Tappuni the omophorion was of the same material as the vestments.

[178] *Muronitho; ḥutro; shabbuqto.*

in a ball surmounted by a cross, while the Jacobite patriarch has what appears to be an imperial sceptre, probably conceded by some emperor. The pallium is worn by the Catholic patriarch.

As we have seen, Mar Ignatius Gabriel Tappuni in 1939 was raised to the college of cardinals, but as the announcement of his elevation was only made a few days before the consistory there was no time for special robes, and no formal decision was taken as to how a cardinal of an eastern rite should dress. He has always dressed, at least in Rome, in the Latin manner.

The small hand-cross (*shushepo*) with pendant veil or "wrapper" is held in the right hand by all bishops, and is used for blessings. When not in use, it is carried in a left fold of their clothing, and Mar Ignatius Ephrem Rahmani [179] has suggested that this custom was the origin of the pectoral cross.

Catholic bishops have adopted the practice of wearing a ring, which the late patriarch [180] claims to have originated in the ring on which was engraved the name of the prelate, and which served as a seal for patents and letters.

Jacobite secular priests wear a black tarbush (*qaruqtho*), ornamented with seven white crosses, during the liturgy, which is removed at the gospel and from the preface until after the ablutions.

The outdoor dress of the clergy consists of a black or dark cassock (*abū; sultana*), with a wide-sleeved open gown and a peculiarly shaped black turban (*kawok; arf*). This turban is made by covering a stiff canvas frame with ingeniously plaited folds of black silk.

[179] *Lit. Orien. et Occiden.*, chap. II, 7, p. 75, n. 2.
[180] *Ibid.*, p. 76, n. 2.

Catholics have borrowed the Byzantine *kalemavkion* [181] (*kallosa*), and bishops wear a gold filigree button on the crown.

Calendar

On formal occasions, the Jacobites still reckon from the Seleucid era of Antioch (311 B. C.), fixed from the year that Seleucus Nikator entered Babylon as a conqueror, and reserving the Christian era for the affairs of every day life.

Some time before the synod of 1853, the Catholic Syrians adopted the Gregorian [182] calendar, and the Jacobite council of Mosul (1930) directed that except for Easter the new style should be adopted by the dissidents in the United States.

The liturgical year, which in its divisions bears a strong resemblance to that of the Chaldeans, begins in October with the Sundays of the Consecration [183] and Renewal (Dedication) of the Church. Then follow the Sundays of "Annunciation" (*Suboro*), namely the Annunciation of Zacharias, the Annunciation of the Mother of God, the Visitation, the Birth of St. John Baptist, the Revelation to St. Joseph, and the Sunday before the Nativity or the Genealogy of Christ. The *Suboro*, in the same order and under the same titles, is found in a Jacobite menology of the 12th-13th century and in the menology of Segestan (1210). At

[181] Syrians and Ethiopians are the only non-Byzantines to wear this kind of hat. Early in the present century, the Jacobite clergy of Jerusalem and Damascus adopted it.

[182] The Catholic patriarch Nehemetallah I (1557-1576), while an exile in Rome, took part in the commission of Pope Gregory XIII for the reform of the calendar.

[183] According to Baumstark, the consecration is possibly that of the cathedral of Edessa in 313. The eparchy of Mosul has *three* Sundays of "Dedication."

thee beginning of the 6th century, Advent at Antioch was observed by *two* Sundays, St. John Baptist and the Mother of God. [184] Christmas (*Beth yaldo*) was originally one feast with the Epiphany (*Beth denho*), [185] and a hymn for laudes on Feria III says: "In the month of April the angel Gabriel announced thy Incarnation and in the month of January we have seen thy birth." St. John Chrysostom speaks in a homily (386) of the separation of the two feasts in the church of Antioch about the year 375. On the vigils of Christmas and Easter, the liturgy is celebrated at about five in the afternoon, entirely in Syriac. [186] December 26, "Of the Praises of the Mother of God," is mentioned in an apocryphal document (*Transitus Mariae,* book IV) of the 5th or 6th century, and it was probably the first festival of the blessed Virgin to be celebrated in the Syrian church. The day following the Epiphany, which commemorates the Baptism of our Lord, is "Of the Praises of St. John Baptist." The Sundays after the Epiphany, of which eight is the maximum number, are known as the "Sundays of the Baptised." The three Fridays following the fast of Nineveh are "of departed priests," the "departed," and "deceased strangers" respectively. Each Sunday in Lent commemorates one of the great miracles of our Lord. The first [187] of the seven Sundays is the "Sunday of Cana" or "of the Entrance of the Fast," and the Saturday of that week is the feast [188] of St. Ephrem and St. Theodore Tyro.

The Wednesday after the fourth Sunday in Lent is

[184] St. Peter Chrysologus, archbishop of Ravenna (✝ ab. 450), speaks of the same two commemorations in his church.
[185] *Denho,* "rising;" cf. "in quibus visitavit nos, *oriens ex alto.*" S. Luc. I, 78.
[186] Also on the feast of St. Ephrem.
[187] Latin Quinquagesima.
[188] Since 1921, the feast is no longer a day of obligation for Catholics

observed as Mid-Lent,[189] with commemorations of the Exaltation of the Cross [190] and the Conversion of Abgar, king of Edessa. The sixth Friday in Lent is known as the "Friday of the Forty," as it is the fortieth day of the fast; while the following day is the Saturday of Lazarus. "Hosanna Sunday" begins the "Week of the Passion of the Redeemer," and the three days of the *Triduum Sacrum* [191] are called respectively "Pasch of the Mysteries;" "Great Friday of the Crucifixion," and "Saturday of the Annunciation" or "Saturday of Lights."

The gospel read on the Thursday (during the week of offices) in Assyria, but not in other districts of Mesopotamia and Syria, is borrowed, with some slight modifications, from the Harmony of the *Diatesseron* of Tatian (ab. 150-ab. 170).

Easter is the "Great Feast of the Resurrection," and the week-days in the octave are termed "of the white clothes;" while the Friday following, which is "of all Confessors", is a feast of All Saints.

Low Sunday is referred to as "New Sunday" or "of Renewal" (*In albis*).

Golden Friday, so called from the miraculous healing at the Gate Beautiful, [192] is the Friday after Pentecost.

The first Sunday after Pentecost is the first of the seven Sundays of the Apostles, and the eighth Sunday, the first of the Sundays of Summer, which end before Holy Cross day.

[189] "Oil of anointing" or "of gladness," as the oil of catechumens is blessed on this day, if the chrism was not consecrated on Maundy Thursday.
[190] The cross is placed on an altar in the middle of the church, where it is censed, venerated, and adorned with flowers. It remains exposed on a secondary altar until Good Friday. *Liturgia*, XIX, p. 625.
[191] Wednesday in Holy Week is called the "Wednesday of anguish" or "of plots."
[192] *Argentum et aurum non est mihi.* Act. III, 6.

The two series together make up the Sundays after Pentecost, which vary in number from thirteen to seventeen.

There is another arrangement with twelve Sundays after Pentecost, followed by the Sunday after the Transfiguration, and four Sundays after the Assumption.

The year is concluded with six or seven Sundays of the Holy Cross.

Ancient manuscripts have other systems, one of which is based on the commemoration of the Three Children, whose feast in the 9th century was assigned to August 22.

The Catholics also observe Trinity Sunday; Corpus Christi, with an octave, procession of the blessed sacrament and benediction; and the feast of the Sacred Heart.

There are three classes of feasts, but the third category is a mere commemoration. [193]

The church of Antioch has comparatively few saints.

Some festivals are kept on different days from the Latin church, but Catholics observe St. Joseph (March 19); All Saints (November 1); and the Immaculate Conception [194] (December 8).

The synod of Sharfeh (1888), reducing the number of feasts by thirty, enjoined twenty-four holidays of obligation—Circumcision with St. Basil and St. Gregory (January 1); Epiphany (January 6); Praises of St. John Baptist (January 7); Presentation of our Lord in the Temple (February 2); Forty Martyrs of Sebaste (March 9); St. Joseph (March 19); Annunciation of our Lady (March 25); St. Geor-

[193] The *shehimo* or West Syrian ferial office, published at Sharfeh in 1944 for the Catholics, has inserted the feast of St. Benedict (March 21) in the calendar as a memorial of the third degree.

[194] The Jacobites keep the feast on December 9 under the title of the Conception of St. Anne. A recent work on the Oriental churches (*Incontro ai fratelli separati di Oriente*, p. 370) says that the dissidents do not keep this feast.

ge (April 23); St. Peter and St. Paul (June 29); Transfiguration (August 6); Assumption of our Lady [195] (August 15);
Nativity of our Lady (September 8); Exaltation of the Holy
Cross [196] (September 14); All Saints (November 1); Immaculate Conception (December 8); Christmas (December 25); Praises of our Lady (December 26); and Holy
Innocents (December 27).   St. Ephrem (first Saturday in
Lent); Easter Monday; Easter Tuesday; Ascension (Sulôqo);
and Corpus Christi are moveable feasts. Some dioceses also
have additional holy days of obligation, but, since 1921,
St. Stephen; Forty Martyrs; and Easter Tuesday are no
longer holidays; while the feast of St. Ephrem is kept on the
Latin date (June 18).

The Syrians of the Aleppo district have a curious custom
on the Assumption of gathering in cemeteries, where, sitting
on the graves of the dead, they eat blessed grapes, and give
what is left over to the poor. The Syrian ritual has a formula
of blessing, and the Byzantine euchologion has a prayer for
the blessing of grapes on this day, although there is no
mention of the dead. The feast of the Assumption was
referred to in three mediaeval Syrian calendars as a vintage
festival, [197] but the connection seems to have been quite
arbitrary, though doubtless made with the object of giving
a Christian character to this ancient popular celebration. The

[195]   *Shunoyo, Transitus.*

[196]   In two old Syrian calendars (7th and 9th centuries), the Finding
of the Cross is coupled with the memorial of the emperor Constantine
on May 22, a feast which corresponds with the Byzantine one of St. Constantine and St. Helena on the previous day. H. W. CODRINGTON, *Eastern
Churches Quarterly* (April-June 1944). *Egypt and the West*, p. 287.

[197]   "Decease of the Mother of God over the grapes." Brit. Mus.
Add. 17232 (1210), from Sijistan; "Translation of the Mother of God
over the vines." Brit. Mus. Add. 17261 (13th-14th century); "Decease of
the Mother of God over the vines." Vatican Syr. LXVIII (1465).

feast is not mentioned in the Syrian Jacobite "Codex of Commemorations" [198] of A. D. 675, and its institution perhaps
may be assigned to the patriarchate of Constantinople. Progressive Byzantine infiltration in the course of ages is very
marked in Jacobite calendars.

This vintage festival was not peculiar to Syria and Palestine, and on August 15 the ecumenical patriarch [199] was
accustomed to bless the imperial vintage in the palace of
Blachernae, while the Armenians still bless grapes on this
day. The Greeks [200] also bless figs, and the Melkites fruits.
The blessing of grapes [201] is carried out on August 6, as was
at one time the custom at Rome.

Holy Cross Day is observed throughout Syria with
especial solemnity, and on the night of the feast, on every
hill top and even on the flat roofs of the houses, beacon fires
are lighted as dusk falls. Cries of joy are heard everywhere,
as the fires kindled and the signals flashed from Jerusalem to
Constantinople long years ago are commemorated.

The Syrian church keeps also the feasts of St. James,
brother of our Lord (October 20); St. Ignatius (December 20); Our Lady of the Seed Sowing [202] (January 15);

[198] Brit. Mus. Add. 17134.

[199] GOAR, Euchologion, p. 694. Paris, 1647.

[200] NEALE, Holy Eastern Church, chap. I, I, p. 1042; Euchologion,
Jerusalem, 1865.

[201] PARISOT, La Bénédiction liturgique des raisins. Revue de l'Orient
chrétien, 1899, p. 354.

[202] The feast has been thought to be Edessene rather than Antio-
chene, as it does not appear in the calendar of the British Museum.
Add. 17134 (7th century) and Add. 14504 (9th century). H. W. CODRING-
TON, Eastern Churches Quarterly (April-June 1944). Egypt and the
West, p. 286.
There are thus three cultivation festivals in the Syrian calendar:
January 15, May 15, and August 15—all connected with our Lady. The
first two of these festivals were probably pre-Christian; the third was
certainly so.

Translation of St. Ignatius (January 28); Our Lady of the
Corn Ears (May 15); the Four Evangelists (May 20); De-
dication [203] of the first church in honour of the Mother of
God (June 15); All Apostles (June 30); and St. Simon
Stylites (September 2).

The Catholics have adopted many Latin practices, such
as Benediction with the blessed sacrament, rosary, stations
of the cross, the Carmelite scapular, etc.

Until recently, the versicle and collect of the Roman rite
were sung at Benediction, translated into Arabic, but some
years ago, at least in the seminaries of Sharfeh and Jerusalem, a *teshmeshto* ("service") in honour of the holy eucharist, composed in Syriac and in accordance with the Antiochene rite, has been substituted.

Gregory Bar Hebraeus, [204] the Jacobite canonist of the
13th century, enjoined the sign of the cross to be made
"from the forehead to the breast, and from the left to the
right."

The Catholics, however, in view of the Jacobite practice
of using one finger (middle finger) [205] in token of their
heresy, bless themselves *more Romano* with the open hand.

In the blessing of objects, four movements [206] are made,
as it were punctuating the extremities of the cross with dots.

For many centuries, the Syrians observed the Mosaic
prohibitions of blood, things strangled, and unclean animals.

Wednesday and Friday, except in Christmastide and the
Paschal season, are days of abstinence. The Nineveh fast [207]

[203] The feast has been borrowed from the Copts, the Dedication of
the Sovereign Lady at Atrib.
[204] *Nomocanon*, V, 5.
[205] In Jerusalem, at least, the first two fingers and thumb are joined.
[206] The two fingers and thumb are joined.
[207] The fast dates from the 6th century, when it was observed in
consequence of an outbreak of plague.

is kept on the first three days in the third week before Lent, and the fast of great Lent for forty days, excluding Saturdays and Sundays, from the Monday after "Quinquagesima." The fast of the apostles (June 16-June 28) is said to be seldom observed among the Jacobites, but it is kept by the Catholics from June 25-June 28. The Assumption fast is held from August 8-August 14, and the Christmas fast from December 16-December 24 (originally lasting for 25 days).

Music

The ecclesiastical chant, which, as Mgr. Paul Hindo [208] says, "gives out the primitive soul," is very complicated, and for many generations the "notation" was not committed to writing. Singers therefore were compelled to learn the airs by heart, and there was a great variety in transmitting them. Strangers are apt to find the grave music somewhat melancholy and monotonous, but the rhythm is very rigorous and most of the liturgical compositions are metrical. Syrian music is richer than that of the Maronites and the East Syrians, and the former have a large number of Arabized chants. The chant is essentially popular both in origin and use, and it is not uncommon to see three generations assisting at the liturgy—the father vested as subdeacon, the son as lector, and the grandson as cantor.

The normal accompaniment to the singing consists of cymbals, bells and *bubboli* or *sonagli* with which the *flabella* are adorned. Of recent years the chant has been the subject of considerable study. Thus on the Catholic side there have

---

[208] *Cantus sacer Syrorum. Conferenza al Pontificio Istituto di Musica Sacra.* 5 Marzo 1942.

been Mar Ephrem Rahmani, Dom Jules Jeannin, [209] a monk of the abbey of Hautecombe and the Benedictines [210] on the Mount of Olives; while the Jacobite council, [211] held in 1930 at Mosul, have at last realised the importance of clarity and order in liturgical matters.

There are 15 kinds of Syrian melodies, [212] and, as in the Byzantine rite, there are 8 tones, the characters of which are almost identical. "Syrian poetry," says Grimme, [213] "has really been the school-mistress (*lehrmeisterin*) of the Western

---

[209] Dom Jules is said to have collected about 900 melodies out of a total of about 2,460.

[210] The Benedictines have recently transcribed these Syrian melodies in modern musical notation, but written from right to left, on account of the Syriac text. Two volumes, published by the Jesuit press in Beirut, have already appeared, but the volume containing the Chaldean melodies has not yet been produced. The first volume of *Mélodies Liturgiques Syriennes et Chaldéennes* contains a musical introduction by the late Dom Jules Jeannin, the second a liturgical introduction by Dom Anselm Chibas-Lassalle, titular abbot of our Lady of the Valley of Josaphat and prior of the monastery of the Mount of Olives.

[211] The council passed the following canons: 1. That a seminary be established, and that uniformity be introduced into the chant and the liturgy. 2. That schools be established, in which religion, Syriac and the liturgical chants shall be taught in a uniform manner. 4. That certain persons be entrusted with the revision of the liturgical books, which revision is to be subsequently referred to the patriarch and three bishops. 5. That the chant be transcribed in musical notation. 7. Permission is given to use an organ during the holy liturgy, especially on Sundays and feasts. 8. Henceforth women may take part in the chant, but outside the sanctuary, and schools for girls are to be established.

The apparent innovation of permitting an organ finds a precedent in the 13th century, for Bar Hebraeus (1226-1286) wrote: "the use of the organ in the churches, of the East as well as of the West, is admitted and received." Thus, he accepted "the use of the organ with *tubi* as that which is adopted in the churches of the Romans" (Latins).

[212] Antiphonal singing was referred to by James Bar Šakkô (✝ 1241) and Bar Hebraeus (✝ 1286).

[213] Article in *Zeitschrift der deutschen Morgenlandischen Gessellschaft*, t. LIII, p. 112.

peoples, and especially of the Byzantines," although it is from these last-named that the Syrians have derived the Greek canons (*qonune yawnoye*).

The *bo'wotho* ("supplication," "petition") is a hymn, generally divided into four strophes, the last of which has the doxology. They have eight modes. James of Sarugh (451-521) is said to be the author of more than half of them, but some have been ascribed to St. Balay, chorepiscopus of Aleppo (end of the 4th century), and to St. Ephrem (306?-373).

The *qolo* [214] ("voice," "tune"), of which there are three kinds, normally follows a passage from Scripture. It is an essentially popular chant, which, according to Bar Hebraeus, [215] was composed by a potter of the village of Gesir, from whom James of Sarugh made a collection and then called it by his name (*Quqoyoto* or *Qolo Quqoyo*).

The *madrosĕ* ("instruction," "meditation," "debate") is a hymn of strophes with chorus, dating from the golden age of Syrian hymnology. Its creator was Bar-Daysan (154-222), a Gnostic, who to further his heresy composed 150 canticles.

Later, to counteract this bad influence, St. Ephrem organised choirs of virgins to sing orthodox *madrosĕ*.

The *sughito* is a kind of metrical treatment of various strophes with acrostic or alphabet, [216] and modelled on the *madrosĕ*, as much by metre as by melody. The Ephremite[217] *madrosĕ* formed the model for the Byzantine *kontakia*, and especially those of the great melodist Romanus (✝ ab. 555).

---

[214] The Maronites call it *qolo fŝito* or " simple."

[215] *Chron. Eccl.*, I, 191.

[216] Cf. Lamentations at Tenebrae in the Roman rite.

[217] " *Dicitur (Ephrem) circiter tricies centena versuum millia in universum scripsisse.*" SOZOMEN, *Hist. Eccl.*, III, 16.

Sebeltho [218] ("ladder") is a kind of mosaic composed of pieces, taken from here and there, and adapted for the use of a choir. They are similar to the *madrosĕ*, and St. Ephrem is claimed as their author.

The four *'enione* ("response," "responsary") form the psalmody *par excellence*. A rhythmic antiphon is interpolated between the psalm verses.

About the 4th century we find the Edessene hymnology in use at Antioch, Jerusalem and Caesarea. This Syrian system of responsorial psalmody passed to churches of Greek speech through the works of Flavian, patriarch of Antioch (381-404), and Diodore of Tarsus († before 394), as Theodore of Mopsuestia [219] († 428) says: *Illam psalmodiae speciem, quas antiphonas dicimus, illi ex Syrorum lingua in graecam transtulerunt.*

It is characteristic to end in a short acclamation, which is always identical with one or more words of the psalm.

The *'enione* is sung on eight modes, but every mode has thirteen to twenty-two melodies. [220] There are various types of *'enione*, such as the *quqelion*, [221] *zumoro*, [222] *hulolo*, [223] *ma'nitho*, [224] and *mawerbe*. [225]

[218] The name for these hymns is not ancient, and in the 6th century the word signified a book for the choir.

[219] MIGNE, *Pat. Graec.*, t. CXXXIX, col. 1930.

[220] The total number of these melodies equals that of the psalms, 150.

[221] A psalm chant with one or two alleluias interpolated. The name is derived from the Greek κύκλιον or κουκούλιον. It has been attributed by Bar Hebraeus to Abba Quqma (Cosmas of Maiuma, † 750).

[222] An antiphon before the lessons. Maronite, *mazmuro d'tešbuhto;* Chaldean, *šuraya;* cf. Byzantine, *prokeimenon* and Gallican, *psalmellus.*

[223] The *zumoro* preceding the gospel; cf. Roman *gradual.*

[224] A kind of responsary for great feasts. First introduced by St. Simon bar-Sabba'e, bishop of Seleucia († 341). Others were composed by Severus of Antioch, etc., and a revision was made in 675 by James of Edessa.

[225] Antiphons to the *Magnificat*.

The *qatismata* (καθίσματα) are chants sung during the censing and the fraction.

The *Greek canons* were introduced into Syria in the 8th century, the "golden century of Greek melodies," as Bar Hebraeus called it. [226] *Takhšfotho* ("supplication") is a hymn, which is sung during the communion, at funerals or at the end of nocturns (*lilyo*). [227]

They are mainly addressed to our Lady, and, according to tradition, their chief author was St. Rabula, bishop of Edessa († 435).

Chants and hymns of the liturgy. There are various kinds of hymns, as for example *mimro*. [228] The homilies of the Syrian fathers are measured with five, seven or twelve syllables.

The ancient collection of hymns for the liturgy has very many responsaries and canticles under different rubrics. Thus, there are *suboho* (praises), *Qole d'Ma'elto* (canticles for the offertory), *Ma'nitho d'roze* (hymn of the holy mysteries), *Ma'nitho d'qurobo* (hymn of sacrifice) and *Qatismatas* (non-measured hymns sung seated). There were originally more than 800 melodies, but the greater part of them has been lost. Mar Ephrem Rahmani in 1905 made a collection of chants, but without the original melodies.

The *trisagion* (*Qadišat Aloho*) is sung on eight tones, with special melodies for certain feasts. It was attributed by Moses bar Kepha (903) to St. Ignatius of Antioch.

The most customary mode for στῶμεν καλῶς after the gospel is called *hiǧaz*, and may be compared with the mode used by the muezzin of a mosque on Fridays.

---

[226] *Ethicon* I, 5, 4; ed. Bedjan, pp. 65-66.
[227] Cf. Ἀπολυτίκιον of the Byzantine rite.
[228] From the verb *emâr*, "to say" and thence λόγος., "prayer."

The *tešebhotho* is a special kind of very ancient acclamation of praise, inspired by *Exodus* (XV, 20) and sung on some solemnities before the gospel at the liturgy and vespers, in honour of Christ the King.

Liturgical Language

Syriac, the hieratic language [229] of the rite, is also used by the Maronites, Chaldeans and Nestorians, although there are differences in pronunciation, forms of the consonants, and the system of representing the vowels. Thus, in the Syrian liturgy the usual vowel points are Greek letters, and the vowel *zekopho* is sounded O. This Western or Palestinian dialect (Aramaic) was spoken by our Lord, and it is represented by several passages in the Old [230] and New [231] Testaments, the Targums, and, to a considerable extent, in Hebrew literature. Aramaic is a sister language to Hebrew, in much the same way as Spanish is to Italian. Estrangelo (Greek, στρογγύλος "round"), the earliest form of Syriac alphabet, consisting of uncial characters, was in constant use, by West and East Syrians alike, until about the 12th or 13th century. Tradition asserts that Bar Hebraeus invented the present characters, as well as the system of vowel and diacritical points. Jacobites and Nestorians, for ornamental

---

[229] "Syriac belongs to the Eastern group of Aramaic dialects, became a literary language at Edessa (whose evangelization began during the second half of the 2nd century), and eventually supplanted all other dialects as a liturgical and literary language among all (or nearly all) Aramaics-speaking Christians. Some of these Aramaic dialects are still spoken in some places." Dom Benedict MORRISON, *Some Notes on the West Syrian.— Eastern Churches Quarterly* (July-September, 1946), p. 372, n. 4.

[230] e. g. "Responderuntque Chaldaei regi *Syriace.*" Daniel. II, 4.

[231] *Vide* Chapter III.

purposes, occasionally use this ancient script, but the normal writing of the West Syrians is known as *Serto*.

The original language of the liturgy (St. James) was Greek, as words and expressions still in use show:—*Stumen* kālus [232] (στῶμεν καλῶς) *Kurye elaisun* (κυριε ελέησον); *Sufiyâ* (σωφία); *Prushumen* (πρόσχωμεν);—although they are not as numerous as in the Coptic rite. Greek was the tongue of the upper classes and the intelligentsia, but by at least the 5th century the liturgy was commonly celebrated in Syriac. In the 4th century, the *Peregrinatio Etheriæ* (*Egeriæ*) mentions Greek as the language at Jerusalem, although the lessons, *propter populum*, were read in Syriac. With the coming of the Arabs in the 7th century, Arabic gradually became the vernacular language, and to-day Syriac is only spoken in three villages near Damascus; Tur Abdin (Mesopotamia, between Nisibis and the Tigris); Kurdistan near Urmia; and the north of Irak. Since the 15th century, a number of the pro-anaphoral prayers have been recited in Arabic, [233] and in some places the Jacobites use Kurdish or Turkish.

The chief prayers in Arabic are the prayers of the beginning and of incense; *hussoyo;* Lord's prayer; and creed.

The rubrics are written in Karshuni, that is Arabic in Syriac script.

Bible

The *Peshitto* ("simple") version of the Bible, which was the first translation of the Hebrew Scriptures in the Edessene dialect made for and by Christians, has been in circulation

---

[232] Bar Salibi always quoted this expression in Syriac, *'nkum shafir.*

[233] Yaḥya ibn-Garîr, a Syrian Jacobite writer of the 11th century, said that it was permissable for Arabs of the patriarchate of Antioch to celebrate the liturgy in Arabic. He mentions that the met-

since the 4th century. The name has been variously derived,—"literal fidelity;" as giving an implication of "vulgate"
or *"communis;"* or as expressing a distinction from the
version of Paul of Tella, its source, which contains the crit-
ical additions of the Haxapla text.

The Dominican press at Mosul (1887-1891) published
the *Peshitto* version for the use of the Catholics of the rite.

The Lord's prayer, however, in the time of James of
Edessa († 708), as we have shown elsewhere, [234] was not in
agreement with the Peshitto.

Liturgical Books

The Book of the Sacrifice (*Kthobo Dkhourobo*) or missal
is also called the *Annafura.* The version used by the Catholics has seven anaphoras. The missal printed in 1594 at
Rome was the exemplar quoted by Le Brun in his work on
the Mass. [235] An edition was published in 1843 (Rome), [236]
in which the audible prayers were written in Syriac and
Karshuni, with the rubrics in Karshuni only.

The missal produced in 1881 at Mosul attached the
anaphora of St. Xystus to the *Ordo communis,* [237] but in
1922 this anaphora was suppressed; [238] while the preparatory

ropolitan of Tagrit, Mafrian Thomas III (912-934?), consecrated an
Arab as bishop, who was accustomed to celebrate in Arabic and " on the
book of the gospels." The bishop was probably a member of a nomadic
tribe in the Yemen. P. HINDO, *Disciplina Antiochena Antica (Siri).*
t. III. *Introd.,* pp. 3-4.

[231] Chapter III. Maronite rite.
[235] *Explication de la Messe,* t. II, p. 585.
[236] *Missale Syriacum iuxta ritum ecclesiae antiochenae syrorum.*
[237] Syriac, ṭīchso dᵉ ḳūrbōno; Arabic, rutbat alḳuddās.
[238] *Missale iuxta ritum ecclesiae apostolicae Antiochenae Syrorum
auctoritate recognitum. In Seminario Sciarfensi de Monte Libano.*

prayers, that were translations from the Latin and had been inserted in 1843, were abolished.

The patriarch, in an assembly at Beirut in June and July 1931, discussed the publication of a new edition of the liturgical books, and also the question of the codification of Eastern canon law.

The Jacobite council at Mosul (November 1930), not only attempted to obtain liturgical uniformity, but also agreed that the service books, for the first time, should be printed, and for the vernacular parts of the liturgy a Karshuni text [239] should be published side by side with the Syriac. Some of the manuscripts that had been in use dated from the 9th and 10th centuries.

The Catholic *Diaconale* [240] (*K'tobo d'teshmeshto*) or "Book of the clerks used in the ecclesiastical ministries" was published in 1888; while the ritual and lectionary were printed at Mosul in 1872 and 1879 respectively.

The *Penqitho*, which was published by the Dominicans (Mosul) in 1860, contains vespers, nocturns, matins and terce for Sundays, greater feasts and Lent. *The Shehimo* or West Syrian ferial office has three Jacobite [241] and six Catholic editions. [242]

The divine office is only of obligation for the Jacobites in choir, and, outside, a station consisting of the trisagion and the Lord's prayer takes the place of each office. Catholics, however, have been bound to the office since the synod of Sharfeh (1888).

A new edition of the anaphora-book is being prepared. The manual for the server is called the *Kthobo*

---

[239] Syriac only in Malabar.
[240] A *Book of the Minister* was published in 1596 at Rome.
[241] 1890; 1913; 1936.
[242] 1696; 1787; 1853—all in Rome. 1902; 1937; 1944—all in Sharfeh.

("Book"), and the book of the gospels the *Ewanghelion*. The other lessons are contained in the *Egroto Dashlihe* ("Epistles of the Apostles").

In 1939 a commission within the Congregation for the Eastern Church undertook to make a revision of the Syrian Pontifical, which is now (1945) virtually completed. A revision and rearrangement had been carried out in the 13th century by the patriarch Michael the Great, but many very old prayers and rites had been left unaltered.

Concelebration

Concelebration with several celebrants together at the same altar, as in the Byzantine rite, is unknown, but on Holy Thursday the following form of service takes place: The chief officiant stands facing west at a table set up in the sanctuary, while other priests, each with altar vessels and a *tablītho*, stand facing each other on either side. The senior priest [243] alone is permitted to raise his voice, unless one of the concelebrants has been authorised to chant some of the prayers, but, even so, he may not recite aloud the central portion of the liturgy, from the preface to the epiclesis, nor may he give a blessing. Each priest receives in holy communion that which he has consecrated himself; while the people are communicated at the end of the liturgy. In the dissident church, the chief celebrant is at the high altar, and the concelebrants use separate or secondary altars, [244] a custom followed by the Catholics on the first Monday of Lent ("Monday of Forgiveness").

[243] Synod of Sharfeh (1888). Chap. V, art. 5, no. 7.
[244] *Madhb'he gh'nize*, "hidden altars."

History of the Rite

The Syrian rite or *Ritus Antiochenus Syrorum purus* [245] (*Ritus Syro-Antiochenus*), in order to distinguish it from that used by the Chaldeans (East Syrian), is often known as the "West Syrian." Catholics, in speaking of the dissidents, sometimes use the courtesy expression our "Oriental brethren;" while the Monophysites return the compliment by calling the united Syrians our "Western brethren."

The usual Syrian term for the liturgy is *qurobho*, "approach" [246] from the same root as *qurbono*, "oblation," which in practice connotes "offering." Mass is also known as *quddosh roze; quddosho*, "hallowing of the mysteries" or "hallowing." The verb *qaddesh* is used absolutely for saying Mass; while *quddas* is the word for "Mass" with all Arab-speakers.

The Liturgy of St. James, "which he heard and learnt from the mouth of the Lord," is the norm, and will be described in detail. The pro-anaphoral part of the liturgy, although differing in many particulars from the original Greek form, is invariable. While it is improbable, to use no stronger word, that St. James was the author of the liturgy, the anaphora was certainly in use before the 5th century, as it is found in churches which then ceased to be in communion with each other. It seems clear, also, that its first provenance was Jerusalem rather than Antioch, as the intercession has a prayer "for the holy Sion, the mother of all churches," and St. Cyril of Jerusalem (348) was cognizant of it. The liturgy has remarkable similarities with the eighth

---

[245] The rite of the West Syrians is sometimes known as the " pure Syrian" rite, but the term is unfortunate, as it would seem to presuppose the existence of " impure" rites.

[246] Cf. προσαγωγή

book of the *Apostolic Constitutions* and the rite of Alexandria.

Ancient manuscripts speak of the "Anaphora of James, the brother of the Lord, according to the careful recension of James of Edessa," but no manuscript exists prior to the 8th century, although fragments of that and the two succeeding centuries have been preserved.

Among the commentators of this rite, the most noteworthy are James of Edessa (708), writing to a priest named Thomas; Moses bar Kepha (903); [247] and Denys bar Salibi (1171). [248]

The liturgy, in accordance with oriental custom, should have the assistance of a deacon, and, if several are present, they should alternate in the recitation of the litanies and diptychs.

Moses bar Kepha pointed out that, whereas in the Byzantine and Nestorian churches the deacon sometimes addressed the priest, the Syrian minister always spoke to the people.

The Catholics have adopted the practice of "low Mass," although bar Salibi [249] quotes James of Edessa [250] as making provision for a liturgy without a deacon. Thus, the celebrant is not compelled to say the diaconal proclamations, especially in the great intercession (diptychs), but he answers the responses in which the people join: "They are with the Lord our God;" "It is meet and right;" "One holy Father" etc.

The celebrant, also, is required to sign himself with the cross, when the assistant ministers are normally blessed to the right and the left.

Bar Salibi, however, unlike James of Edessa, considers

---

[247] *Exposition of the Mysteries of the Oblation.*
[248] *Exposition of the Liturgy.*

that the absence of all help in the sanctuary necessitates the postponement of the liturgy, and Moses, bishop of Charka (ab. 540),[251] holds the same view. The Catholic synod of Sharfeh (1888)[252] enacted that, in the absence of a deacon or a priest to act as deacon, a cleric might assume the office, so long as he neither wears diaconal vestments nor offers incense. A layman, with the permission of the bishop, so long as he is of good character, not married more than once, and then not to a widow, may perform the duties of a subdeacon or lector, and he may sing in the choir, provided that he does not enter the sanctuary or put on clerical dress.

The liturgy follows vespers on all the days of Lent except Saturdays, Sundays, and Holy Saturday, and also on the vigil of Christmas. At Easter it follows matins.

Liturgy of St. James

The sacred vessels,[253] before the beginning of the liturgy, are placed uncovered on the altar, with the veil towards the gospel side, hanging over the edge. The missal remains on the epistle side of the centre of the altar.

[249] *Exposition of the Liturgy*, chap. III.

[250] *Scholion to George, Stylite of Sarug.* James of Edessa (*Scholion of the Sacrifice*) also permits, in a case of necessity, a solitary Mass "with no one behind the priest."

[251] Moses warns the people not to receive communion from the hands of a priest who celebrates without an assistant, as the oblation is neither perfect, nor holy, nor does the Holy Spirit descend upon it. *Liber bonorum morum*, quoted by Elias of Damascus (after 900) in the *Nomocanon*.

[252] HANSSENS, *Instit. Lit. de Rit. Orient.*, t. II, pars I, sect. 544, pp. 306-307.

[253] Ceremonial details are not identical in every Syrian church, and the writer has only personal knowledge of the rite from Catholic liturgies celebrated in Cairo, Rome and Paris; and from the liturgy of the Jacobites in Jerusalem.

At a pontifical liturgy, the bishop enters the church in a black cloak over a western cassock, and a *zucchetto*, while the priest assistant is vested in "alb," cuffs and stole, and the two taperers in "albs" and stoles. A bishop, even at the recital of the words of institution, blesses persons and things with a hand-cross. A *lavabo* is taken before the preparatory prayers.

The priest, in outdoor dress, comes to the foot of the altar (within the veil, if it used), where with his arms crossed on his breast he recites the preparatory prayers.

This part of the rite, originating in the private prayers of the celebrant, [254] has been subject to a certain amount of modification, and the prayers of the Greek St. James have been considerably expanded.

A bishop, standing at the throne, begins the preparatory prayer, and then sits down, while a priest, acting as archdeacon, goes up to the altar and prepares the matter of the sacrifice, saying the prayers as if he was himself the celebrant. He returns to the throne in time to assist at the vesting of the bishop.

The liturgy, in the first *teshmeshto*, [255] which is recited standing [256] before the gate of the altar, opens with an outburst of praise: "Glory be to the Father and to the Son and to the Holy Ghost: and upon us weak and sinful be

---

[254] Cf. Roman rite.

[255] "Service of psalms," which originally corresponded with the Byzantine ἀντίφωνα. A similar beginning is found in the East Syrian liturgy. By the 16th century it had been duplicated, the preparation of the oblata, offertory and vesting being intercalated in the 1st and 2nd *teshmeshtos* so formed. The two *teshmeshtos*, unless the liturgy has great solemnity, are said while the office is being recited by the choir.

[256] The Jacobite priest, during this prayer and the psalm which follows, squats on his haunches.

mercy and grace in both worlds, now, always and for ever and ever, Amen."

This is followed by the "prayer of the beginning" (*slouto dshouroyo*): "Vouchsafe unto us, O Lord God, commiserator and lover of men, with knowledge and fear and beauty of the spiritual order to stand before thee in purity and holiness and to serve thee as the Lord and Creator of all, to whom worship is due from all, Father, Son and Holy Ghost now, always and for ever."

Psalm L (*Miserere*) is then said, and at its conclusion: "And thee glory befitteth, O God, now and at all times for ever."

The celebrant, asking forgiveness from the clergy and people, says to the assembled priests: "Bless, O Lord, for pardon," and they answer: "Remember me in thy sacrifice."

To the people, he continues: "Brethren and beloved, pray for me from the love of the Lord."

Then, ascending to the altar, he says: "I will go unto the altar of God, to God who giveth joy to my youth," and, bowing before the holy table: "Into thine house, O Lord, have I entered and before thy sanctuary have I worshipped, O heavenly King: pardon me all wherein I have sinned against thee."

The celebrant kisses the altar three times, and, saluting the side, he says: "Bind our solemnities in chains, O Lord, even unto the horns of the altar. My God, I will confess thee. My God I will glorify thee."

The rubrics direct that the following prayers are to be said at the lighting of the altar candles: *a*) (right): In thy light we shall see light, O Jesus, full of splendour, because thou art the true light, that illuminates every creature, O splendour of the heavenly Father," *b*) (left): "O pious and holy one, who dwellest in the habitations of light, take away from us evil passions and harmful thoughts, and grant that we may carry out the works of justice in purity of heart."

The priest then spreads the "corporal," [257] and uncovers and arranges the sacred vessels, with the sponge, spoon and paten on the left, and the chalice on the right.

The celebrant [258] takes the bread in both hands, as he says: "As a lamb he was led to the slaughter, and he was silent as a sheep before his shearer, and he opened not his mouth in his humiliation."

The "seals" [259] are arranged on the paten; if they are many, they are placed on the four sides of the paten cross-wise, if few one above the other.

Covering the paten with both hands, the priest continues: "First begotten of the heavenly Father receive this first begotten from my hands, your worthless servant. The place, O Lord, which thou hast made for thee to dwell in: thy sanctuary, O Lord, which thy hands have established. The Lord shall reign for ever and ever."

The wine and water are sometimes mixed in a special

[257] The Jacobite priest spreads a square of coloured material.

[258] The Jacobite priest here receives his vestments. In the Catholic rite, the position of the prothesis and vesting does not appear to be always the same. The prothesis may follow the vesting during the second *teshmeshto*, or the vesting may precede the prothesis in the first *teshmesto*. H. W. CODRINGTON, *Syrian Rite*, p. 49. *Eastern Churches Quarterly*. April 1936. In a "low Mass" celebrated by Cardinal Tappuni (Rome, June 16, 1946) the vesting followed the prothesis. It may be noted that, unlike the Byzantine arrangement, the preparation at the prothesis has retained its original simplicity.

[259] This is a rubric in the 1922 missal, and the wording is found in a canonical decision attributed to John of Tella († 538) in *Nomocanon* IV, 4. It is repeated by John of Harran (can. 1). The Jacobites normally use only one "cake," as the communion of the people is infrequent.

At a "low Mass" celebrated in Rome (June 16, 1946) by Cardinal Tappuni a Latin wafer was used.

vessel, [260] with the accompanying prayer: "As thy divinity was united to thy humanity, may this water, O Lord, be as one with this wine."

The mixture is then poured into the chalice, as the priest says: "Our Lord Jesus Christ was crucified between two thieves, on the tree in Jerusalem: and was pierced in his side with the lance, and there flowed from it blood and water, for the propitiation of the whole world, and he who saw it bare record, and we know that his record is true."

Slightly raising the chalice, the celebrant continues: "What reward shall I give unto the Lord for all that he has done unto me? I will receive the cup of salvation and call upon the name of the Lord: and I will pay my vows unto the Lord before all his people."

The prothesis ends with the covering of the paten and chalice, as the priest says: (for the paten) "The Lord reigned and put on beauty." (for the chalice) "The Lord put on and girded himself with strength: and made fast the whole earth, that it should not be moved."

Deacon: "Stand we well. Have mercy on us, O Lord."

The priest then descends from the altar, and recites the *proem* [261] and *sedro* [262] "of penitence," together with a *qolo,* [263] in which forgiveness of sins is asked.

---

[260] The Jacobites pour wine and water in equal quantities into a vessel called the "deaconess."

[261] *The proem (p'rumiyon, p'romiyon, προώίμιον)* or the introduction" of praise is usually preceded by a diaconal exclamation and the *Kyrie.* It always has a proclamation (*koruzutho*) or "beginning" (*shuroyo*) of the "propitiation" (*hussoyo*) — "Praise and confession," etc. The *hussoyo* was originally recited below the altar during the offering of incense. It consists of three main divisions.

[262] *Sedro* or "order" (of incense) is a long prayer in prose or verse, generally in the form of a litany, which may end with a *huttomo* or "seal."

[263] *Qolo,* "voice" or "tune," normally consists of four short anthems

Proem: "Praise and confession, glory, laudation and holy exaltation without ceasing, continuously, at all times and at every hour may we be accounted worthy to offer to the one merciful Father, who hears sinners calling upon him: to the clement only Son, who receives penitents knocking at his door: to the one Holy Spirit, who pardons the guilty that beseech him; since glory and praise befits him at this moment and at all feasts and times and hours and moments, all the days of our life for ever. Amen."

Thus, the *proem* is a doxological introduction addressed in turn to each of the divine persons; while the *sedro* is a plea that the sacrifice about to be offered may be acceptable to God.

Sedro. "O God who art gentle and kind, humble and a lover of man, who delightest in mercy and not in sacrifices and who lovest a contrite heart rather than burnt offerings and receivest a humble spirit rather than the blood and the smell (of the fat) of bulls and fat lambs, receive our spiritual sacrifice at this moment on thy reasonable altar and account us worthy to present unto thee our souls, a living and acceptable sacrifice, pleasing to thy will in reasonable service, and to sacrifice unto thee spiritual sacrifices in a contrite heart and a humble spirit on the altar on high; and may we be unto thee a flock resplendent and stainless, that being changed with a new change and strengthened as neophytes for the new world, with souls reasonable and wise with the fair lamps of faith we may all be accounted worthy to say; Glory be to the Father, and to the Son, and to the Holy Ghost, now and for ever and ever. Amen."

(*baito,* "house," cf. stanza) on a framework of hemistichs (*pethghome*), which are usually taken from the psalms. The third anthem is preceded by "Glory be to the Father" etc., and the fourth by "Now always and for ever and ever."

A prayer, known as the *m'hass'yono hokhil* ("propitious therefore,"), is recited on certain occasions between the *proem* and the *sedro*.

Qolo: a) "At thy door, O our Lord, do I knock and from thy treasure-house do I ask mercies. I, a sinner of years, have turned aside from thy path. Grant me to confess my sins and to turn from them and to live in thy grace." *b*) "At what door shall we go and knock save at thy door, O gracious one our Lord, and whom have we to plead with thee for our error, if thy mercies plead not with thee, O King whose honour kings worship? Glory be to the Father, and to the Son, and to the Holy Ghost." *c*) "O Father, Son and Holy Ghost, be thou to us a high wall and a house of refuge from the evil one, who with his armies fights against us: under the shadow of thy mercy protect us when the good are separated from the wicked. Now, always and for ever, Amen." *d*) "May the voice of our prayer be a key that opens the gates of heaven: and may the archangels say from out their ranks," "How sweet is the voice of the children of dust and may the Lord swiftly answer their petitions." (Deacon) Then have mercy on us, O Lord, and help us."

The *'etro* [261] ("smoke") or prayer of incense follows, although the thurible is not used until after the vesting of the priest: "May the savour of our prayers be pleasing unto thee, O my Lord, at all times, and may the smoke of our incense be for thy satisfaction and be thou reconciled unto thy creation thereby for thy mercies sake, now and at all times and world without end. Amen."

The first part of the Liturgy, which is called the "Sacrifice

---

[261] *Etro*, "smoke," "prayer of the smoke;" prayer of the *qubbol pirmo*, "acceptance of incense;" prayer of the *pirmo*, "censer," "incense." The prayer is always short, and, if a bishop is present, he says it.

of Melchisedech," is concluded by the *'eqbo*, [265] a short
anthem of a single verse: "O Christ, who didst receive the
offering of Melchisedech, the great pontiff, receive, O my
Lord, the prayer of thy servant and pardon the offences of
thy flock."

The *Kyrie eleison* is recited three times, together with
the following petition: "O our Lord, have mercy on us. O
our Lord, be propitious and have mercy on us. O our Lord,
hear us and have mercy on us. Glory to thee, O our Lord
(twice). Glory to thee, O our hope, for ever. Our
Father" etc.

This is followed by a *huttomo* or "seal": "O Lamb
pure and spotless, who didst offer thyself to the Father
an acceptable oblation for the pardon and salvation of the
whole world, account us worthy to offer unto thee ourselves
a living sacrifice pleasing to thee and imitating thine immolation for us, O Christ our God, for ever and ever. Amen."

At a pontifical liturgy, the "Sacrifice of Melchisedech"
is performed by the deacon, and the bishop, having chanted
the preparatory prayer, remains seated on the throne.

The second office of oblation or "Sacrifice of Aaron"
begins, as the first office, with a paean of praise: "Glory be
to the Father, [265] and to the Son, and to the Holy Ghost:
and may the divine mercies and kindnesses be poured in
both worlds upon us weak sinners, now and always and for
ever and ever."

A prayer follows: "Grant us, O Lord God, having our
hearts sprinkled and clean from all evil conscience, to be
accounted worthy to enter into thine holy of holies, high
and exalted, and in purity and holiness to stand before thy
holy altar and present unto thee reasonable and spiritual

---

[265] *'Eqbo,* "heel," "end."

sacrifices with true faith, Father, Son, and Holy Ghost, now, always and for ever. Amen."

A bishop is vested at the throne, assisted by the deacon.

The rubrics direct a priest to put on his vestments in the church, although in practice this is frequently done in the sacristy. First, the *jubba* is laid aside with a suitable prayer. Then the celebrant, making the sign of the cross, [266] receives the vestments, as he recites prayers chiefly taken from the psalms.

He returns fully vested before the "table of life" and within the veil, where he says secretly: "O Lord God Almighty, who takest away the sins of men, who desirest not the death of a sinner: to thee do I extend the hands of my heart, and from thee I beg, albeit unworthy, the remission of all my faults, but I beseech thee, that thou wouldest keep my mind from all the works of the enemy, mine eyes that they look not incontinently, mine ears that they listen not to vanities, my hands from the perpetration of hateful things, and my reins that they be moved in thee, so that I be entirely thine. And from thee be there granted unto me the gift of thy divine mysteries, now, always and for ever and ever. Amen."

Then, kissing the step, [267] the priest ascends to the altar, where he uncovers the sacred gifts, placing the veil of the paten towards the south and the veil of the chalice towards the north.

Crossing his right hand over the left, the celebrant takes the paten in the right and the chalice in the left, while he recites a long offertory prayer, which has been borrowed from the Byzantine rite:

[266] Once, twice or even three times.
[267] "*medium altaris,*" P. M. S. (i. e. Latin translation of Prince Maximilian of Saxony).

"We make the memorial of our Lord, God and Saviour
Jesus Christ and of all his saving dispensation [268] on our
behalf: especially of his annunciation by an archangel, his
nativity in the flesh, his baptism in the Jordan, his saving
passion, his elevation on the cross, his vivifying death, his
honourable burial, his glorious resurrection, his ascension
into heaven, his installation at the right hand of God the
Father: we make the commemoration at this eucharist
placed before us. And in the first place we commemorate our
father Adam and our mother Eve, Mary, the holy Mother of
God, the prophets, apostles, preachers, evangelists, martyrs,
confessors, just men, priests, holy fathers, true pastors, orthodox doctors, hermits, monks, those who pray with us together with all those who in time have pleased thee, from
Adam and Eve down to this day. We also commemorate
our fathers and brothers, our superiors who have taught us
the word of truth rightly, our dead and all the faithful departed, especially and notably our relations and those who
have had or have a share in the upkeep of this holy place,
and whomsoever is in communion with us, whether by word
or action, in great things or small and particularly him (N)
for whom this sacrifice is offered to-day."

If the liturgy is being offered for a sick person, the
following prayer is repeated three times: "O merciful God
have mercy on N. N. and grant to him health of soul and
body through the prayer of thy Mother and of all thy
saints."

An alternative prayer is said, if the intention is for the
departed.

---

[268] *m'dhabb'ronutho*, "economy;" *methdakhronutho, meth'ah'dho-
nutho*, "commemoration."

Two further prayers are then said, each three times: [269]
a) "God, thou hast become a sacrifice and to thee sacrifice is offered, receive this sacrifice at my sinful hands, for the soul (or for the intention) of N. ....;" b) O God, in thy clemency, grant rest and a good memorial to my father and my mother and my departed brothers and sisters and relatives."

The priest, placing the holy vessels on the altar, with the chalice towards the east and the paten towards the west, covers the sacred gifts with the great veil, as he says: "The heavens have been covered with his glorious splendour and the earth has been filled with his praise."

Liturgy of the Catechumens

The remainder of the liturgy is called the "Sacrifice of Jesus Christ."

The liturgy of the catechumens begins with the "*Stomen kalos*" ("Stand we well") of the deacon and the "*Kyrie eleison*" of the people.

The priest now descends from the altar, where he blesses the incense [270] and begins the general *sedro:* "To the praise and honour of the holy and glorious Trinity, sweet smelling gums are offered by my weak and sinful hands. Let us all pray and beg for mercy and grace from the Lord. O Lord God, have mercy on us and help us."

This combination of *sedro* and incense was commented on by Denis bar Salibi (1171), but it appears to have been unknown to Moses bar Kepha (903).

---

[269] The Italian translation (*La Santa Messa in rito Siro-Antiocheno* (Rome, 1942, p. 8) enjoins the threefold repetition only for the first of these prayers.

[270] The incense is blessed both before and after it is put into the thurible.

Proem: "Praise and confession, glory, laudation, holy exaltation ceaselessly, continuously, at all times and at every moment may we be worthy of offering to this desirable fruit which hath budded in the virginal womb, has magnified the memory of his Mother in heaven and on the earth and has rendered her eternal; to this adorable Lord, of whom the choirs of his saints celebrate glory, to this God, living and life-giving, who, by his imperious voice, raises the dead and with him gives to them joy in his glory, to him to whom belongeth praise and honour in this time of this offering of this eucharist, and at all feasts and times and hours and moments and all the days of our life for ever. Amen."

The priest then takes the thurible and censes the altar (three times), as he says the *sedro: a)* "We adore thee, we confess thee, we praise thee, Creator of the worlds, and architect of the universe, blessed stem that has budded and been brought forth from a thirsty earth. Mary has filled every creature with the perfume of his wonderful sweetness, has chased away the pernicious infection of impiety, on every side, by his glorious doctrine;" *b)* "We offer this incense before thee after the example of the priest Aaron, who offered thee pure incense and stayed the plague from the people of Israel;" *c)* "We beseech thee, O Lord God, receive this sweet-smelling incense which our lowliness offers unto thee, by reason of our sins and shortcomings, for rich and poor, widows and orphans, those in anguish or affliction, the sick and ill, all those who have asked or ordered us to remember them in the prayers which we address to thee, O Christ our God, for the living and the dead, the repose of the souls of those who are in the heavenly Jerusalem: by the supplications of our father Adam and our mother Eve, by the supplications of Mary, thy mother, by the prayers of the prophets, apostles, martyrs, confessors, fathers, orthodox doctors, by the invocations of the virgins of both sexes, and of all the saints and the just, and we offer thee, O Lord, glory, praise and adoration, and to thy Father, and to thy Holy Spirit, now, always and for ever. Amen."

The priest now ascends to the altar, where he raises the censer over the mysteries towards the east, as he says: "Over [271] the sweet-smelling incense, may there be a memorial of the virgin Mary, Mother of God." Towards the west: "Over the sweet-smelling incense, may there be a memorial of the prophets, apostles and holy martyrs." Towards the north: "Over this sweet-smelling incense, may there be a memorial of the doctors, priests, the just and the righteous." Towards the south: "Over this sweet-smelling incense, may there be a memorial of the holy Church and of all her children." [272]

The priest, making three circles with the censer over the mysteries, says: a) "Receive, O Lord, through thy love the incense of thy servants;" b) "Be appeased through the incense (perfuming) of thy priests;" c) "Deign to accept the ministry of those who adore thee, and magnify through it the remembrance of thy Mother and of thy saints, and give rest to the faithful departed who have put their hope in thee, O Christ the Son, adored and glorified with thy Father and thy Holy Spirit, now, always and for ever. Amen."

Then, three times censing the middle of the "table of life, which is the type of the Father," he says: "Adoration

---

[271] Some editions of the missal have "with" instead of "over." The people repeat the words immediately after the priest. *La Santa Messa in rito Siro-Antiocheno* (Rome, 1942), p. 10.

[272] The Byzantine deacon, after the epiclesis and at the commemoration, of the living and dead, censes round the altar; cf. *Ecclesiast.* XLIX, I : "*Memoria Josiae in compositionem odoris facta opus pigmentarii*"

to the merciful Father;" censing a like number of times the
"north side of the same table, which is the type of the Son":
"Adoration to the compassionate Son;" and censing "three
times also the south side, which is the type of the Holy
Spirit:" "Adoration to the Holy Spirit, the giver of life."

The priest continues: "May Mary who bore thee, and
John who baptized thee, pray to thee for us. Have mercy
on us. May we be worthy, O Lord, to offer thee, in the
odour of sweetness, the sacrifices of praise in the priestly
ministry. May our thoughts, words and deeds be holocausts
without spot and pleasing to thy divinity, and may we appear
before thee, in all the days of our life, O Christ, Lord God.
Amen."

Then, once again, the priest descends the steps of the
altar, as he says: "*Kyrie eleison*" (three times).[273] "Have
mercy on us, O Lord. Vivify us, O Lord, and have mercy
on us. O Lord, hear us and have mercy on us. Glory to
thee, O Lord. Glory to thee, O Lord, our hope, for ever.
Our Father...."

In solemn masses, when the three adorations are sung,
the deacon chants the *kyries*, while the priest says the "our
Father."

The people are censed by the celebrant, as he asks for
the intercession of the saints:[274] "Through the prayer of
the Mother who bore thee, and of all thy saints."

The veil is drawn during the second *teshmeshto*.

The anthem of the *quorobho*[275] is preceded by a hemis-

---

[273] The prayers are almost identical with those at the end of the
first service (Sacrifice of Melchisedech).

[274] *P. M. S.*, p. 15. The Italian translation (Rome, 1942, p. 10)
says that when the priest censes the people, *they say together*: "The
only Son and Word of the Father..."

[275] *M'anitho dh'qurobho.*

Mar Gabriel Tappuni

Syrian Patriarch of Antioch and Cardinal of the Holy Roman Church

(*Left to right*) Chorepiscopus - Patriarchal Vicar in Egypt - Mar Gabriel Tappuni, Patriarch of Antioch - Archbishop of Bagdad - Newly ordained Chorepiscopus

(*Left to right in vestment*) Syrian priest - Chorepiscopus - Patriarchal Vicar in Egypt - Mar Gabriel Tappuni, Patriarch of Antioch - Archbishop of Bagdad - Newly ordained Chorepiscopus

Ordination of a Chorepiscopus in the Syrian rite
S. Maria in Campo Marzio (S. Ephrem), Rome

tich, [276] sung by the people, which begins with the opening words of psalm CXLIV: "I will exalt thee, O Lord, only begotten King, Son and Word of the heavenly Father, who in thy substance art immortal."

The anthem [277] itself, which is a free rendering of the Byzantine *Monogones*, is attributed by the Jacobites to Severus of Antioch: (Choir) "He accepted and came through his grace, for the living and for the salvation of the human race, (Priest) and was incarnate by the holy, praiseworthy and pure virgin Mary, Mother of God. (Choir) He became man without change, and was crucified for us, Christ our Lord, (Priest) who by his death trod under foot and slew our death, being himself one of the Trinity, (Choir) to be equally adored and glorified with his Father and his Holy Spirit. Spare us."

This hymn, in solemn and conventual Masses, is sung as the priest and his assistants are making a procession [278] round the altar. The celebrant, who is accompanied by crucifer and taperers, carries the book of the gospels, and is himself censed continuously by the deacon. At the close of the procession, when the altar steps are reached, the deacon incenses the priest, ministers and people. The gospel book is placed on a lectern [279] in the sanctuary.

---

[276] *pethghomo*, which is the theme of the single stanza or anthem which follows.

[277] The Mass of the catechumens, as we have seen, rightly begins before the incensing, but in practice it is at the end of the 2nd *teshmeshto*, when, the office, usually sext, being over, Mass proper starts with the anthem of the *qurobho*.

When lessons from the Old Testament are read (without introductory chants or prayers), they come before the anthem.

[278] *K'rokhyo*, "circuit," which serves as the "little entrance." Jacobite priests, who are present at the liturgy, put on stoles for the procession, and retain them until the dismissal.

[279] Alternatively, it may be placed on the north corner of the altar.

The celebrant then ascends to the altar, and, thrice signing the mysteries and himself, three times recites the trisagion: "Thou art holy, God" (*Qadîshat Alohô*); "Thou art holy, O strong" (*Qadîshat Haïltono*); "Thou art holy, O immortal" (*Qadîshat lô Moïoutô*).

To each clause the deacon responds: "Have mercy on us," and after the last: "*Kyrie eleison*" (three times).

The *Kyrie* may well be a survival of a litany which was recited here.

This is the form of the trisagion used by the Catholics, but there has been nearly as much controversy in the Syrian church in regard to the manner of its recitation as in the Byzantine church concerning the *filioque* clause in the creed.

The chant was probably first used in the middle of the 4th century, and it is found in the *acta* of the council of Chalcedon (451), but there is little foundation for the legend connecting the trisagion with the earthquake, which occurred at Constantinople in the reign of the younger Theodosius (408-450).

Peter the Dyer (Fuller), patriarch of Antioch (470-488), in support, it is said, of the Theopaschite heresy, [280] inserted the fateful words "who wast crucified for us." [281] This interpolation introduced the possibilty of serious theological error, as the hymn was traditionally addressed to the Holy Trinity. [282]

Riots followed the insertion of the clause. The orthodox patriarch Calandion, [283] the second successor of Peter the Dyer at Antioch, suggested the adoption of the phrase "Christ the King, who was crucified for us." The compro-

---

[280] The heresy asserted that the divine nature suffered on the cross.
[281] Greek, ὁ σταυρωθεὶς δι' ἡμᾶς ; Syriac, *how deṣṭlebth hlôfain*.
[282] Cf. Isaias, VI, 3.
[283] *Dictionnaire de Théologie Catholique*, t. X, coll. 2240-2241.

mise, however, was unsatisfactory, as it made the chant refer
directly and unequivocally to the Incarnate Word. Then
some Scythian monks at Constantinople, led by John
Maxentius, proposed a formula, which obtained, though not
without difficulty, the approval of the emperor Justinian
(March 15, 553): "One of the Trinity was crucified." In
521, Pope Hormisdas (514-523) considered the compromise
to be of but little importance, but it was commended by
Pope John II (532-535) in 534, and imposed under anathema
as orthodox by the second council of Constantinople (553).
The clause "who was crucified for us" was condemned by
the second council in Trullo (692). [284]

Monophysite writers, [285] however, have been at pains to
defend the interpolation, and Denys bar Salibi (1171) in the
Explanation of the Liturgy suggests that three choirs of
angels carried the body of our Lord to the grave, and the
first choir sang "Holy God," the second "Holy and strong,"
and the third "Holy and immortal;" while Joseph of
Arimathea and Nicomedus added "who was crucified for us."
The anonymous author of the *Explanation of the Mass*
asserts that the expression "Holy God" implies an address
to the Holy Trinity, whereas "Thou art holy God" refers
exclusively to the second person.

The Jacobites have six lessons [286] in the liturgy, three
from the Old and three from the New Testament, but except
on solemn occasions the Catholics have reduced the number
to two, the apostle and the gospel. [287]

When the trisagion is concluded, the deacon says three

[284] Canon 81.
[285] e. g. John bar Cursos, bishop of Tella (÷ 538); David bar Paulos
(8th century).
[286] Prophets; Acts; "Book of Paul;" Gospel.
[287] *Sh'liho.*

times "Have mercy on us" and three times "*Kyrie eleison.*"

This is followed by the *zumoro*.

In a solemn liturgy, when there are extra lessons, those from the Old Testament are read by subdeacons, who carry lights.

Another *zumoro* and prayer precede the lesson from the Acts (*Praxis*) or the catholic epistle, which is also read by a subdeacon.

It would appear that in some places the Old Testament lesson and the *praxis* are read at the north door of the screen, but, contrary to all old custom as described by commentators, the missal of 1843 directed that the Old Testament lesson should be read immediately before the trisagion, and the Praxis after it.

The deacon, before the apostle, recites this antiphon: "I have heard the blessed Apostle Paul say: [288] 'If anyone, even though it be an angel from heaven, should come and preach to you a gospel other than what we have preached to you, let him be anathema from the Church.' Lo, different teachings arise on all sides, blessed is he who has begun and ended in the doctrine of God."

The priest in the meanwhile says a secret prayer: "Accept, O Lord God, our prayers and our supplications which are at this time before thee, and account us worthy with purity and holiness to keep thy commandments and those of thy divine apostles, and of Paul, the architect and builder of thy holy church, O our Lord and our God for ever." The apostle (epistle) is read [289] in Arabic by the deacon, who asks a blessing: "Bless, Lord. From Paul the Apostle."

[288] Galat. I, 8.
[289] The deacon stands at the door of the screen, facing west.

The *hulolo*, [290] which, like the Roman gradual, is the alleluia with a verse, is sung before the gospel by the deacon, and there is a proper for each of the holidays of obligation and for the common of martyrs, confessors, virgins etc.

On ordinary days the deacon sings: "Alleluia, alleluia, alleluia. Offer sacrifices to him, bring oblations, and ascend into the courts of the Lord; worship him before the temple of his holiness. Alleluia."

The priest, as before the apostle, recites a secret prayer, the prayer of preparation for the gospel: "Grant us, O Lord God, the knowledge of thy divine words and fill us with the understanding of thy holy gospel and the riches of thy divine gifts and the indwelling of thy Holy Spirit and give us with joy to keep thy commandments and accomplish them and fulfil thy will and to be accounted worthy of the blessings and the mercies that are from thee, now and at all times and for ever. Amen."

The diaconal injunctions: [291] "Be attentive;" "Keep silence" have long since disappeared from the rite, and the priest, taking the gospel-book from the altar, goes to the main door [292] of the screen, where he blesses the people: "Peace be with you all." [293]

The response is made: "And with thy spirit."

Then the gospel is announced: "The holy gospel of our

---

[290] Arabic, *mazmur*, " psalm."

[291] Cf. Mozarabic rite.

[292] Where there is no screen the gospel is read by the priest from a portable lectern, standing *in plano* and facing west, or the book may be held by assistants. At a " low Mass" celebrated in Cairo (May 22, 1924) the gospel was read from a lectern on the footpace of the altar, while the single assistant, a small boy in ordinary clothes, held a candle.

[293] This is the common social greeting as well. When the priest uses it liturgically, he extends his right arm in the manner of the old Roman —and recent fascist—salute.

Lord Jesus Christ, message of life, according to *N.*, Apostle (Announcer), who announces life and salvation to the world."

The people answer: [294] "Save us and protect us, O Lord."

The deacon continues: [295] "Blessed is he who cometh and who is to come, praise to him who sent him, and may his mercy be always upon us."

The rite has a somewhat elaborate equivalent of *In illo tempore:* "At the time of the dispensation of our Lord, and our God, and our Saviour Jesus Christ, vivifying Word, God incarnate from the holy Virgin Mary, these things were done."

The deacon (people) answers: "We believe and confess."

On feasts, the expression "dispensation" is replaced by the specific commemoration. Thus on festivals of our Lady: "at the time of the feast of the Assumption (Annunciation, Immaculate Conception, etc.) of Mary, Mother of our Lord and our God," etc.

At a pontifical liturgy, the bishop lays aside the mitre, and places it on the altar.

The gospel [296] is read by the celebrant in Arabic, attended by lights, *flabella* (sometimes) and incense; while at the end of each sentence the deacon makes an impulsion with the thurible. [297]

After the gospel, the priest blesses the people with the book, [298] and says: "And peace be with all."

On some feasts, [299] the celebrant pauses in the singing of

---

[294] Italian translation, p. 11; not in *P. M. S.*

[295] *P. M. S.*, p. 17.

[296] "*Sacerdotes legant Evangelium ubi reperientur, nullique erunt diaconi.*" Constitution of Rabula, bishop of Edessa (411-2/435), art. 70.

[297] Cf. Rite of Lyons.

[298] The bishop blesses with the hand-cross.

[299] e. g. Christmas, Presentation in the Temple, Palm Sunday.

the gospel, in order that he may with especial solemnity chant the verse which directly recalls the incident of the day, and the choir, before the gospel is concluded, sings some verses of a hymn.

This practice is intended to sustain the fervour and interest of the faithful.

A homily [300] on the gospel taken from one of the fathers was formerly read on feasts, but the custom has fallen into desuetude. Catholics, however, have a sermon after the gospel, whereas the dissidents normally preach either after the blessing before the fraction or after the elevation and before the communion of the priest.

Bowing down, the priest says the "prayer after the gospel": "To our Lord Jesus Christ be our hymns, praises and blessings for his lifegiving words to us, to his Father who has sent him for our salvation, and to his living and Holy Spirit who giveth us life, now and at all times and for ever and ever. Amen."

In the meanwhile, the choir [301] sometimes sings the following memorial (variable): "Let us remember the prophets and apostles, who preached thy annunciation among the nations; let us remember the upright and the just, who were famous and were crowned; let us remember the martyrs and confessors, who suffered torments and pains. Let us remember the Mother of God and the faithful dead."

Deacon: "Stand we rightly." People: "O Lord, have mercy on us."

The liturgy no longer calls upon the catechumens, energumens and penitents to leave the church, although the

---

[300] e. g. "*Christus nascitur, laudate,*" the Christmas *commentary of St. Gregory Nazianzen.*

[301] The whole is recited by the deacon. *P. M. S.,* p. 17.

dismissal [302] is mentioned by Denys bar Salibi (1171). Reference to them, however, is still found in the consecration of the chrism and the blessing of the water on the feast of the Epiphany: "Let none of the catechumens, let none of the energumens, let none of those with whom it is forbidden for us to pray (remain)." Allusion, also, is made in a hymn sung on the Sundays after the Epiphany: "He who has not received the seal (of baptism), let him go out: thus proclaims the church. You children of baptism, penetrate up to the altar. Woe to the man whose spirit goes wandering in the bazaars during the celebration of the holy mysteries. Here is the table of life prepared on which will be placed the bread of life and the chalice containing the blood which flowed from the breast of the Lord, for the remission of sins. Alleluia."

In the primitive church, when the catechumens had gone out and the faithful had been bidden to "recognise one another" (Ἀλλήλους ἐπίγνωτε), a cry of "the doors" (τὰς θύρας) was raised as a warning to the *ostiarius* to guard the entrance, lest unbelievers should enter the church during the liturgy of the faithful. The monition has long since vanished, although in the time of James of Edessa (708), when the primitive discipline was already a thing of the past, there seems to have been a ceremonial shutting of doors, expressly designed to keep out the "Hagereans." [303]

---

[302] The canonical replies, which the Jacobite bishops, about the year 538, gave to superiors of monasteries, expressly mention the prayers for these several classes.

Liturgy of the Faithful

The liturgy of the faithful begins with a *proem* and *sedro,* said at the foot of the altar and known as the "prayer of the entrance." [304]

The name would seem to have reference to a procession of the *oblata,* such as we find in the Byzantine rite, but the word "entrance" rather implies the "beginning" [305] of the Mass of the faithful or the entrance [306] of the priest and his ministers from the *catastroma* into the sanctuary. The Jacobites, however, once had a procession of the mysteries, and Denys bar Salibi (1171) describes such a one, which must have been rather a meaningless imitation of Byzantine custom, [307] as the holy offerings had rested on the altar from the beginning of the liturgy.

There are a *proem* and *sedro* proper to Sundays and feasts.

The *proem* said on ordinary days is as follows:

"Praise and confession, glory, homage, holy exaltation without interruption and continuously may we be worthy to offer to Jesus Christ, the high priest of our faith, pure and holy victim, who of himself has blotted out our sins, and who, offering himself as a holocaust, has brought innocence to a guilty world: to whom belongeth praises, honour and power, and to his Father and the Holy Spirit, now in this

---

[303] The followers of the Hegira, *i. e.* Mohammedans.

[304] *Sedro d⁰ Ma'altho.*

[305] Cf. "Entrance of the fast."

[306] East Syrian or Nestorian rite.

[307] Cf. Greek St. James, which has a genuine great entrance and chant — Σιγησάτω ("Let all mortal flesh keep silence"), which is sung in the Byzantine rite on Holy Saturday.

eucharist and in all feasts and times and hours and moments all the days of our life and for ever and ever."

The priest then puts on incense, and the deacon says:

"Before the merciful God, before his altar of pardon, before those sublime, holy and celestial mysteries, and before this terrible and holy sacrifice, incense is poured from the hands of the priest, let us all pray and beseech mercy and love from the Lord.   O merciful Lord, have mercy on us and help us."

The priest continues: "My Lord, pardon, purify, forget and blot out our faults and be not mindful of them; by thine infinite mercy put away our terrible sins which are innumerable, and the sins of thy faithful people. Look kindly upon us.   Have mercy upon us, our fathers, brothers, masters, superiors, our dead and all the faithful departed, sons of the holy and glorious Church.   Give rest, O Lord God, to their souls and bodies, that the dew of thy mercies may refresh their members. Pardon us, O Christ, our King and our God, Lord full of glory, hear us and hasten to succour and deliver us. Accept our prayers, keep from us, O God, cruel punishments, do not retaliate upon us, make us worthy of eternal happiness, O Lord of peace and safety. Finally, grant us a most christian end, such as thy holy will would desire, and we offer thee glory and thanksgiving, now and always and for ever and ever. (Deacon or people) Amen."

The priest then says the *sedro:* "O God, Lord of all things, who didst receive the sacrifice of thanksgiving from all those who call upon thee with all their hearts, accept this incense which is offered to thee by the hands of thy miserable servants, make us worthy to approach thy holy altar, grant that we may offer sacrifices and spiritual holocausts for our sins and the crimes of thy people, grant that our oblation may be agreable to thee, and that thy Holy Spirit may descend on us, these offerings, and on all thy people who believe in Jesus Christ our Lord. [308] (Deacon or people) (Amen."

The Syrians call this *sedro* the "prayer" or "supplication of the entrance," and several forms exist, some of which are attributed to the Monophysite patriarch John (648). It is known to the Byzantines as the "prayer of the offertory," and examples are found in the liturgies of St. Basil and St. John Chrysostom, both of which are in the Syrian rite. [309]

The deacon in the meanwhile censes the altar, celebrant, choir, people, and altar again.

Then, half turning to the people, the priest gives his blessing: "Peace be with you all," and the deacon answers: "And with thy spirit. May the Lord receive thy ministry and may he aid us by thy prayers."

The priest continues: "May we receive from God the remission of our faults, the pardon of our sins and a holy remembrance for the faithful departed, in both worlds, and for ever and ever. (Deacon or people) Amen."

He blesses the censer and signs himself, holding one of the chains in his left hand, as he chants: "Holy is the holy Father. (Deacon or people) Amen." Again blessing and holding another of the chains, he continues: "Holy is the holy Son. (Deacon or people) Amen." Finally, grasping all the chains of the thurible, the priest chants: "Holy is the living and Holy Spirit, who sanctifies the incense of the sinner his servant, who is propitious and has pity on our souls, the souls of our fathers, brothers, superiors, our dead and of all the faithful departed, faithful to the Holy Church in both worlds, for ever and ever."

[308] *P. M. S.* has a doxological termination.
[309] The first begins: "O Lord God all powerful;" the second: "O Lord God, who hast created us." Cf. Greek St. James.

The deacon, having responded "Amen," prepares the faithful for the creed: "*Sufiyâ. Prushumen.*"[310] "Stand we well in the prayer of our honoured father,[311] and let us cry out, saying."

Then the priest, at the foot of the altar and holding the censer, chants: "We believe in one God," continuing the creed,[312] with the *filioque*, in a low voice and inclined before the altar.

The deacon or other minister[313] proceeds with the singing of the Nicene symbol, while the priest censes the altar (*oblata*) three times, the clergy and the people.

The Jacobites recite the creed without the Constantinopolitan additions ordered at Chalcedon, and of course the *filioque* is omitted. It would seem also that the dissidents cense only the mysteries.

The creed was apparently first said in the liturgy as a protest against the council of Chalcedon (451), and introduced at the end of the 5th century by Peter the Fuller (Dyer), Monophysite patriarch of Antioch, and Timothy of Constantinople. The custom was commented on by John bar Cursos (519-538) in canon 17.

The priest, when he has given up the censer, washes[314] his hands, as he says: "Wash away, O Lord, the foul pollution of my soul and cleanse me with thy sprinkling of life that in purity and holiness I may be accounted worthy to go into the holy of holies, thine holy and hallowing house, and

---

[310] "Wisdom. Let us attend."

[311] This is the formula if the celebrant is a priest; "venerable father," if he is a bishop; and "blessed father," if he is the patriarch.

[312] Syriac, *haiyimōnūtho, kanūno dhaiy* ("Catholic;") Arabic, *amānah.*

[313] The creed is occasionally sung by the people.

[314] The *lavabo* is mentioned in this position by Denys bar Salibi (1171).

without defilement to handle thine adorable and divine
mysteries, that with a pure conscience I may offer unto thee
a living sacrifice that may be well-pleasing to thy Godhead
and like unto thy glorious sacrifice, our Lord and our God,
for ever and ever. Amen."

At a pontifical liturgy, the bishop censes the altar, while
a priest or deacon censes the clergy, choir and people. The
ancient diaconal proclamation, [315] beginning with the words:
"Here is the time of prayer," is recited after the *lavabo* in a
pontifical Mass.

It has been referred to by several commentators, including Moses bar Kepha (903), and it was formerly recited
by the deacon on the steps of the ambo. The faithful
are exhorted to purify their intentions and to pray with
fervour.

The celebrant, turning towards the people, now seeks
their intercession: "Pray for me, my brethren and friends."

Then, bowing down or kneeling before the "table of life,"
he says a short prayer of preparation, and remembers the
living and dead: "O holy and glorious Trinity, have mercy
upon me: O holy and glorious Trinity forgive me my sin:
O holy and glorious Trinity, receive this offering from my
weak and sinful hands. O God, in thy mercy make rest and
good remembrance on thy holy and heavenly altar for thy
Mother and for thy saints and for all the faithful departed.
O God, pardon and remit in this hour the sins of thy sinful
servant, and help my weakness which crieth unto thee at
all times, and by the prayers of thy Mother and all the saints,
O God, in thy loving-kindness pardon and remit the sins
of these of our blood, our fathers, our brethren, our masters,

---

[315] The name kathisma has been applied to the proclamation. COD-
RINGTON, *Eastern Churches Quarterly.* No. 2, vol. I (April 1936), p. 44.

and of him for whom and on behalf of whom this sacrifice is offered (here he mentions whomsoever he will)."

The priest, who since the gospel has been *in plano*, now ascends to the altar and, having kissed it, [316] begins the anaphora, which is commonly called by the dissidents the "approach." [317]

Anaphora of St. James

"The Annaphura of Mar James, the brother of our Lord" is given in some detail, but the general arrangement and subject matter of the other anaphoras are substantially the same.

The council of Laodicea (ab. 370) [318] enjoined three prayers to be said after the dismissal of the catechumens. These prayers now include those "before the peace," "of the imposition of hands," and "of the veil." They are referred to by James of Edessa (708) in his *Epistle to Thomas the Presbyter,* and the "prayer of the veil" is described as "that wherewith they uncover the table and signify thereby that the doors of heaven are then opened."

The priest, with hands folded on the breast, says aloud the "prayer of the peace:" O God and Lord of all, make these our unworthy selves worthy of this salvation, O thou lover of men, that cleansed from all guile and all hypocrisy we may salute one another with a holy and divine kiss, united with the bond of love and peace: through our Lord and

[316] The rubric speaks of "kissing the step."

[317] Syriac, *kurobho;* Greek, προσαγωγή cf. "quoniam per ipsum habemus *accessum* ambo in uno Spiritu ad Patrem." Ephes. II, 18. *Kurobho,* however, means also "sacrifice" or "offering," from the Syriac verb *kareb,* "to offer."

[318] Canon 16.

Saviour Jesus Christ, thine only Son our Lord, through whom and with whom to thee belongeth glory, honour and dominion, with thy Spirit, all holy, good, adorable, life-giving and consubstantial with thee now, ever and world without end. (Deacon or people) Amen."

A blessing follows: "Peace be with you all," and the response: "And with thy spirit."

There appear to be several methods of transmitting the kiss [319] of peace. If the minister is below the order of deacon, he kisses the altar after the priest, then the hand of the priest, and finally the other side of the altar; while, if he is a deacon or a priest, the minister kisses the altar, receives the *accolade,* and then kisses the celebrant's hand. This is the normal method of conveying the peace, but the deacon may take the priest's hands between his own and then pass his own down his face; or the deacon may cense the priest, who makes a gesture of catching the smoke and putting it to his face. The assistants and people receive the "peace" in one of these two last ways.

The giver of the *pax* says: "Let us give the peace mutually, each to his neighbour, in a holy embrace, with the love of our God, and having received this holy peace let us prostrate ourselves before the God of mercy."

The anonymous author of the *Explanation of the Mass* speaks of the custom of "kissing each other's shoulders." [320]

The prayers, referred to by Moses bar Kepha (903) and Denys bar Salibi (1171), which were said at the will of the celebrant either before or after the "prayer of the peace," were retained in Mesopotamia until the 13th century.

---

[319] The Jacobites use the word *sh'lomo* (Syriac); Syrian Catholics and Maronites the Arabic *salām.*

[320] Cf. Roman rite.

Moses bar Kepha speaks also of the "Book of Life," [321] which was read by the deacon from the sanctuary after the *pax* on feasts of our Lord. This *Liber Vitae* contained the names of those who had died in the fear of the Lord, and, when they were read for the encouragement and imitation of the faithful, the deacon omitted the three last diptychs (saints; fathers and doctors; dead) in the great intercession. Thus, the same commentator says: "The diptychs that the deacon proclaims are six: three of the living and three of the dead. And whenever the book of the living is not read at the altar, it is not necessary to abbreviate them." It would seem that the reading of the *Book of Life* by the Jacobites was borrowed from the East Syrian church.

The diptychs, as a formalized and ritualised recital of names, were said in the early years of the 5th century. In the first three centuries the commemoration of the dead was confined to private celebrations or to groups or categories, although the recital of particular names at the public liturgy was, by the middle of the 4th century, the custom in the Delta of Egypt. [322]

The Syrian church [323] about the 11th century abandoned the reading of the *Book of Life*, but several manuscripts have preserved the text.

The "prayer of the imposition of hands" or of "inclination" [324] is prefaced by a diaconal bidding: "Let us bow

---

[321] *Se pharhaiye; cf.* " Evodiam rogo, et Syntychen deprecor idipsum sapere in Domino. Etiam rogo, et te germane compar, adiuva illas, quae mecum laboraverunt in evangelio cum Clemente, et ceteris adiutoribus meis, *quorum nomina sunt in libro vitae.*" *Philip.* IV, 2, 3.

[322] Cf. *Euchologion* of Sarapion.

[323] RAHMANI, *Les Liturgies Orientales et Occidentales.* Chap. IV, 4, pp. 171-172. Cf. Chaldean rite; Syrian anaphora of St. Peter; Maronite rite.

[324] Syriac Jacobite, *syomidiho;* Arabic, *wad'yad.*

down our head before the Lord," and the response of the
people: "Before thee, O Lord."

The priest, with hands [325] folded on the breast, says:
"Thou who alone art a merciful Lord, send thy blessings on
them that bend their necks before thine holy altar, O thou
that dwellest on high and yet has regard to the lowly, bless
them through the grace and mercies and love towards mankind of Christ, thine only Son, through whom and with
whom to thee belongeth glory, honour and dominion with
thy Spirit, all holy, good, adorable, life-giving and consubstantial, with thee now and ever and world without end.
(People) Amen."

The prayer of the veil [326] follows (aloud): "O God the
Father who for thy great and unspeakable love towards
mankind didst send thy Son into the world to bring back the
sheep that had gone astray, turn not away thy face from us
in the moment we offer this fearful [327] and unbloody sacrifice: for we trust not in our own righteousness but in thy
mercies. We entreat therefore and beseech thy goodness
that this mystery which is administered for our redemption
be not for judgment unto thy people, but for the wiping out
of sins, for forgiveness of trespasses and for thanksgiving
unto thee; through thy grace, mercies and love towards
mankind of thine only Son, through whom and with whom
to thee belongeth glory, honour and dominion, with thy
Spirit, all holy, good, adorable, life-giving and consubstan-

---

[325] H. W. CODRINGTON, *The Eastern Churches Quarterly* (July,
1936), vol. I, no. 3, p. 89. Rahmani (*op. cit.*, p. 180) says that the priest
stretches his right hand over the faithful, whilst he demands for them
help and grace from on high. The faithful in the meanwhile stand
before the altar with heads inclined.

[326] Cf. Coptic St. Basil.

[327] Another codex has " spiritual."

tial, with thee now, ever and world without end. (People) Amen."

The veil [328] to which reference is made would seem to be that which covered the offerings rather than the veil [329] which screened the altar from the sight of the people.

The late Syrian patriarch, [330] however, connected the prayer of the veil with the veil hanging before the altar, and by way of example quoted the *Testamentum* [331] *Domini:* "*Dum offert episcopus oblationem, velum sit expansum .... et offerat intra velum."*

The celebrant now removes the veil [332] that covers the oblations, and raises and lowers it three times over the mysteries, as he says in a low voice:

---

[328] Cf. *Oratio super sindonem* in the Ambrosian rite. The same title is also found in Syriac, and the Antiochene liturgy of St. James has a corresponding prayer. RAHMANI, *op. cit.,* 673.

The *Expositio Missae,* a commentary on the liturgy composed by Denys Bar Salibi († 1171) and later adapted by an anonymous Maronite, definitely states that the prayer derives its name from the removal by the priest of the veil.

[329] The anonymous writer of the 5th century, Denys the pseudo-Areopagite, appears to suggest that such a veil was unknown to him, for he contrasts the catechumens etc. with the faithful, in that the former are not called to the *sights* and services that follow their dismissal, which are reserved for the perfect *eyes* of the initiated. *De eccles. hierarch.,* cap. III, 6; ap. MIGNE, *P. G.,* III, col. 432 C.

[330] RAHMANI, *Les Liturgies Orientales et Occidentales,* p. 180.

[331] ab. 350 or earlier.

[332] "Pseudo-Germanus," describing the Gallican liturgy, alludes to the ceremony of removing the great veil which covers the mysteries: "*Nomina defunctorum ideo hora illa recitantur qua pallium tollitur."* L. Duchesne. *Christian Worship,* chap. VII, p. 208. London: S. P. C. K. In the time of Duchesne it was generally thought that the author of the description of the Gallican liturgy was St. Germanus (576), but it is now agreed that the two letters were written by an anonymous writer at the end of the 7th century or even a little later. *Dict. d'Archéol. Chrét. et de Lit.* D. WILMART, Art. *Germain de Paris,* t. VI, col. 110?

"Thou art the corner stone which gave out twelve rivers of water and gave to drink to the twelve tribes of Israel. Thou art the corner stone which was placed on the sepulchre of our Saviour."

The deacon in the meanwhile exhorts the people to have the right dispositions: "Let us hold ourselves worthily, with fear, purity, holiness, charity and true faith and above all with the fear of God, looking upon this holy oblation which is set out before us and which offers itself for us, a living victim to God the Father, by the hands of his priest."

The celebrant now blesses himself, the assistants and the people as he says: "The love of God the Father and the grace of the only-begotten Son and the fellowship and descent of the Holy Spirit be with you all, my brethren for evermore. (People) And with thy spirit."

The formula of blessing must have been changed to the Pauline [333] exemplar some time subsequent to the beginning of the 8th century, as James of Edessa (708) gives "Peace be with you all."

The dialogue, common in some form to all liturgies, follows:

Priest: "On high where Christ sitteth at the right hand of God the Father be the minds and intellects and hearts of us all at this hour."

Deacon or people: "They are with the Lord our God."

Priest: "Let us give thanks unto the Lord in fear."

Deacon or people: "It is meet and right."

The priest now begins the "prayer of the thanksgiving" (*eucharistia*), which is the preface of the Roman rite, but comprising the anaphora to the end of the epiclesis.

The "preface" has two parts, the first said in secret,

---

[333] Cf. 2 *Cor.* XIII, 4.

while the priest bows down [334] fluttering his right hand over
the paten and his left over the chalice; the second said aloud,
as he stands up [335] and stretches out his hands:

"It is very meet, right, fitting and our bounden duty to
praise thee, to bless thee, to celebrate thee, to worship thee,
to give thanks to thee, the Creator of every creature visible
and invisible."

Then, aloud and standing erect: "To whom the heavens
and the heaven of heavens praise and all the hosts of them,
the sun and the moon and all the choirs of the stars, the
earth and the sea and all that in them is, the heavenly
Jerusalem, the church of the first born that are written in
heaven, angels, archangels, principalities, powers, thrones,
dominations, virtues high above the world, heavenly servants, the many-eyed cherubim, and the six-winged seraphim, who with two of their wings veil their faces, and
with twain their feet, and with twain they do fly one to
another, with unceasing voices and unhushed theologies, a
hymn of victory, majesty and excellent glory with clear voice,
hymning, crying, shouting and saying."

The celebrant silently continues the *sanctus* and *post-
sanctus*, while the people sing: "Holy, [337] holy, holy,
Lord God of Sabaoth, of the glory and honour of whose
majesty heaven and earth are full. Hosanna in the highest.
Blessed is he that came and *will come* in the name of the
Lord. Hosanna in the highest."

---

[334] Syriac, *ghōntho, ghântâ,* "inclination," so the rubrics describe a
secret prayer said by the celebrant as he bows down; cf. Arabic, *khuḍū;*
Greek, μυστικῶς

[335] Syriac, *tlīthâ, tᵉlītho,* "erect," as the celebrant is standing
erect; cf. Greek, ἐκφώνησις

[336] Cf. Liturgy of Alexandria.

[337] The beginning of the sanctus (*quadish*) has more similarity to
the Roman than the Byzantine rite.

At the *sanctus,* the bell is rung in the Catholic rite, and fans are sometimes shaken; while the bishop in a pontifical liturgy removes his mitre.

The *post-sanctus,* during which the priest flutters his hand three times over the mysteries, leads directly to the consecration: [338] "Thou art truly holy, King of the worlds and giver of all holiness, and holy also is thine only-begotten Son, our Lord and our Saviour Jesus Christ, and holy also is thine Holy Spirit who searcheth all things, even the deep things of thee, God and Father. For holy art thou, omnipotent, terrible, good, of fellow-feeling and especially as touching thy creature: who madest man out of earth [339] and gavest him delight in paradise. But when he transgressed thy commandment and fell, thou didst not pass him by nor forsake him, O good, but didst chasten him as an exceeding merciful Father. Thou hast called him by the law, thou hast led him by the prophets, and last of all hast sent thine only-begotten Son into the world that he [340] might renew thine image: who, when he had come down and become incarnate of the Holy Ghost and of Mary, the holy Mother of God and ever Virgin, and conversed with men and done all things for the redemption of our race (aloud) and when he was about to accept a voluntary death for us sinners, himself without sin,

in the same night in which he was delivered up for the

[338] The following Syrian writers unequivocally speak of the words of our Lord as effecting the consecration — Severus of Antioch (✝ 538), John, bishop of Dara (8th-9th century), Denys bar Salibi (✝ 1171), and Bar Hebraeus (1286).

A text of St. Ephrem (373) seems to infer that in the 4th century the epiclesis was recited *before* the consecration. P. HINDO, *Disciplina Antiochena Antica* (Siri). T. III, pp. 47-49.

[339] Greek St. James has "in thine own image and likeness."

[340] The missal of 1922 has "that *thou* might."

life and salvation of the world took bread (takes bread and
places it on the palm of his left hand) in his holy, spotless
and unpolluted hands, and showed it to thee, God and
Father, and when he had given thanks † he blessed †,
hallowed †, brake (breaks it slightly at one of the middle
crosses, taking care not to separate the halves) and gave to
his disciples and holy apostles, saying: Take, eat of it, this
is my body, which for you and for many is broken (turns
the host half a circle on the left and breaks it slightly at the
bottom, again without dividing it) and given, for the remission of sins and for eternal life" (lays the host on the
paten).

The people respond: "Amen."

A Catholic priest at each consecration steps back a pace
and makes a profound bow. [341]

The celebrant continues: "And likewise also the cup
(takes the chalice by the middle in his right hand and lifts
it up over the *tablītho*) after he had supped, when he had
mixed with wine and water, he gave thanks (takes the chalice
in his left hand) †, blessed †, hallowed †, and gave to his dis-
cliples and holy apostles, saying: Take, drink ye all of it
(places his right hand on the lip of the chalice), this is my
blood of the New Testament, which for you and for many is
shed (takes the chalice in the same hand, and lifts or tilts it
slightly over the *tablītho*, moves it crosswise, and puts it
down in its place) and given, for the remission of sins and for
eternal life. (People) Amen."

The bell is rung at each consecration; lights are carried;

---

[341] The genuflection or shortened form of prostration, known as
matouniat, is in the East an expression of penitence, which is performed
in Lent and the fast of Nineveh; cf. Greek, μετάνοια.

fans shaken; and the blessed sacrament is censed by the deacon.

The seven anaphoras in the Propaganda missal (1843) all have the same formula of consecration, but in 1922 a return was made to the ancient practice, [342] by which each anaphora had its own distinctive words of institution.

The priest then says: "Do this in remembrance of me: for as often as ye eat this bread and drink this cup ye do proclaim my death and confess my resurrection until I come." [343]

The people respond: "Thy death, O Lord, we commemorate, and thy resurrection we confess, and thy second coming we look for, and we ask of thee mercy and compassion, and we implore the forgiveness of sins. Thy mercies be upon us all." [344]

The anamnesis, which is said aloud, has the unique peculiarity of being addressed to God the Son [345]: "Commemorating therefore, O Lord, *thy* death, and *thy* resurrection on the third day from the tomb, and *thine* ascension into heaven, and *thy* session at the right hand of God the Father, as well as *thy* second coming fearful and glorious, wherein *thou* shalt judge the world in righteousness, when *thou* shalt render to every one according to his deeds. We offer thee this fearful and unbloody sacrifice, that thou deal not with us after our sins, O Lord, neither reward us after our iniquities; but after thy leniency and thy great and unspeakeable love towards mankind, blot out the sins of us thy servants who entreat thee. For thy people and thine

---

[342] The words of institution in the several anaphoras are the same as those found in the liturgy of the dissidents.

[343] Cf. Alexandrine rite.

[344] Cf. Alexandrine rite.

[345] Greek St. James is addressed, as is usual, to God the Father.

inheritance beg thee and through thee and with thee the Father, saying."

The people [346] respond: "Have mercy on us, O God the Father almighty, have mercy on us."

Then the priest continues: "We also give thee thanks while receiving thy gifts, O Lord, we praise thee for all and because of all."

The deacon, while the priest silently invokes the Holy Spirit, now recites a formula peculiar to the Syrian rite:

"How terrible is this hour; how fearful this time, in which the life-giving and Holy Spirit comes down from the topmost heights of heaven, descends and glides down upon this eucharist [347] laid in the sanctuary and sanctifies it; be in fear and trembling, standing and praying. Peace be with us, and the security of God the Father of us all. Let us cry out and thrice say, *Kyrie eleison.*"

The people respond: "Lord, have mercy on us. Lord, have mercy on us. Lord, have mercy on us."

In the meanwhile, the priest, bowing and three times fluttering with his hands over the *oblata,* begins the invocation (*q'roito*) of the Holy Spirit:

"Have mercy on us, O God the Father almighty, and send thy Holy Spirit, the Lord and giver of life, who is equal to thee on the throne, and equal to the Son in his kingdom, consubstantial and coeternal; who spake in the law, the prophets and the New Testament; who came down in the likeness of a dove on our Lord Jesus Christ in the

---

[346] "Deacon." *P. M. S.,* p. 29.

[347] The use of the word "eucharist" shows that it was the belief of the compiler of this prayer that the consecration had already taken place. Before the consecration, the offerings are otherwise designated. *Disciplina Antiochena Antica (Siri),* t. III, p. 45.

river Jordan; who descended upon the holy apostles in the likeness of tongues of fire." [348]

Deacon: *"Kyrie eleison"* (three times).

The epiclesis [349] itself, which is said aloud, is unmutilated:

"That coming down he may make of this bread the body † of Christ, amen, the life-giving body, the redeeming body † of our souls and bodies, the very body † of our great Lord God and Saviour Jesus Christ, for the remission of sins and eternal life to them that receive. (People) Amen."

"And the mixture that is in this cup, the blood of Christ, amen †, the blood † purifying our souls and bodies, the very blood † of our Lord God and Saviour Jesus Christ, for the remission of sins and eternal life to those who receive it. (People) Amen."

During the recitation of the epiclesis, the priest flutters [350] three times with his right hand over the host, and again three times over the chalice; while after each part of the invocation he makes an inclination. [351]

At a solemn liturgy, the deacon, who from the beginning of the anaphora to the end of the epiclesis is standing below

[348] Before the missal of 1922, the celebrant was now directed to smite his breast and say: "Hear me, O Lord, hear me, O Lord, hear me, O Lord; be merciful and have pity on us."

[349] Catholics use the Arabic Word *da'wah;* Jacobites the Syriac *kerytho.*

[350] A gesture referred to by St. Ephrem. RAHMANI, *op. cit.*, IV, pp. 216-217.

[351] St. Ephrem says that the celebrant bends both knees. RAHMANI, *op. cit.*, pp. 143, 217 (*vide* Maronite rite). Narsai of Nisibis (end of the 5th century) forbids the assistants to bend the knee during the liturgy, and also the celebrant after the epiclesis, as genuflection symbolises the silence and death of the Saviour lying in the tomb—and the priest by the epiclesis renews the mystery of the resurrection. *Liturgia* XII, p. 383. Paris, 1930.

the altar on the right, continues to cense the holy mysteries. A bell is rung and the fans are shaken.

The third division of the epiclesis (first diptych), [352] which is for the communicants, is said by the priest, who stands upright with arms outstretched:

"That they may be the body and blood of Jesus Christ to all who receive them and who partake of them, the hallowing of souls and bodies, fruitfulness in good works, the confirmation of thy holy Church, which thou hast founded upon the rock of faith, and the gates of hell shall not prevail against it, delivering it from all heresy and from every stumbling block of them that do iniquity, even unto the end of the world. [353] (People) Amen."

A Jacobite assertion to the effect that the consecration by the Byzantines is null and void is expressed in a letter, said to have been written by Philoxenus, bishop of Mabug (532) to Abi'Afr, the military governor of Hirta of Numan, although it was more probably composed by a Monophysite writer, who lived after the Islamic conquest (ab. 760-790) in or near Bagdad:

"When the priest prays on the altar, the Holy Spirit comes down and sanctifies the mysteries, and changes them into the body and blood of God; the contrary would be the case if the name of one of those blasphemers of the unholy, wicked and pervert council of Chalcedon was invoked."

James of Edessa (708) in his commentary on the liturgy

---

[352] The general intercession *after* the epiclesis is a characteristic of the West Syrian type of liturgy.

[353] In the Catholic missal of 1922, the diptych ends here, but the missal edited at Rome had as a conclusion: " by the grace and mercies and love towards mankind of thine only Son through whom and with whom to thee belongeth glory, honour and dominion, with thy spirit, all holy, good, adorable, life-giving and consubstantial, with thee now, ever and world without end."

compares the respective positions of the intercession in the Antiochene and Alexandrine rites: "In the imperial city (Constantinople) and in the province of Greece the liturgy is celebrated as with us, first the rite of sacrifice which consecrates and then the commemorations. However, the fathers of Alexandria celebrate the liturgy differently: first the commemoration and then the consecration and oblation."

"That the two liturgies,[354] Sarapion and St. James (as represented in St. Cyril of Jerusalem), were in use at one and the same time in churches not far apart is a fact full of instruction for the enquirer into the history of liturgical development."

In the Syrian rite, the great intercession comprises six prayers, three for the living (fathers or pastors; faithful brethren; faithful kings) and three for the dead (Mother of God and the saints; fathers and doctors; departed in general). Each prayer consists of two parts. The first is said secretly by the priest, bowing [355] down with hands folded, while the deacon recites aloud the diptych [356] or canon, at the end of which the people answer: "*Kyrie eleison*" or "Amen." The second part is said aloud [357] by the priest, who stands with forearms outstretched, and at its conclusion lowers his arms by the mysteries "and in his hands takes a blessing from them." The people respond: "Amen."

Lazarus bar Sabta, Jacobite bishop of Bagdad, who was deposed in 829 by Denys of Tell Mahré, objected in a liturgical commentary to the practice of saying a secret and

[354] Edmund BISHOP, *The Journal of Theological Studies,* vol. XIV (Oxford Clarendon Press, 1913). Notes and Studies. Liturgical Comments and Memoranda. VIII, p. 49.

[355] *G'honto,* "inclination."

[356] *Diphtucho; kanuno; qanuno.*

[357] *T⁾litho,* "elevation," namely of the voice (cf. ekphonesis); *p'shto,* "extension," namely of the hands.

an audible prayer after each diaconal interpolation, on the ground that the practice was a late addition. The sense, also, was spoilt and the commemorations disjointed, so that only two prayers should be said, one secret and one aloud. The Anaphora of the Twelve Apostles retains the original arrangement.

The priest, inclining, begins the intercession in a low voice: "Wherefore we offer unto thee, O Lord, this fearful and unbloody sacrifice for these thine holy places, which thou hast glorified by the manifestation of Christ, thy Son, and especially for the holy Sion, the mother of all orthodox churches, and for thy holy Church throughout the world, grant her, O Lord, the rich gifts of thine Holy Spirit."

The reference to Jerusalem shows that the Antiochene liturgy originated in the holy City, and St. Ephrem (373) in his hymns apostrophises the scene of the institution of the blessed sacrament: "O happy place, which has seen what none other has ever seen nor ever will see," and again: "O blessed Cenacle in which was broken the bread made from the blessed sheaf and was expressive of the cluster of grapes gathered in the womb of Mary."

The priest then remembers before God the sacred hierarchy, and the deacon recites the corresponding diptych: "Bless, O my lord. Pray we and beseech our Lord and our God at this great and terrible and holy moment for all our fathers and rulers who stand at our head this day and in this present life and tend and rule the holy churches of God in the four quarters of the world, our holy venerable and blessed fathers, [358] the great pontiff mar N. pope of Rome, and mar Ignatius N. our patriarch, and our father mar N.

[358] The Jacobites commemorate "our patriarchs Mar Ignatius and Mar Basil," that is the patriarch and the mafrian.

our sacred metropolitan (bishop); may they be stablished in God, with the residue of all the orthodox bishops: their prayer be a wall to us. Let us beseech the Lord."

The priest continues: "For those among our brethren who are cast into bondage, and are in prison and exile, them that are sick and ill, and them that are oppressed and vexed of evil spirits. Remember also, O Lord, the air, the rains and the dews and the fruits of the earth."

Then, aloud, he says: "And deliver us, O Lord, from all oppression and wrath, and straits, and all hurt and opposition of wicked men, and from all force and violence of devils, and from every scourge sent from thee, O God, which is brought upon us by reason of our sins, and preserve us in the orthodox faith and the keeping of thine holy life-giving commandments, us indeed and all that are accounted worthy to stand before thee, and to wait for the rich mercies which come from thee: for thou art a God that taketh pleasure in mercy, and to thee we offer up glory and to thine only Son, and to thy Spirit, all holy, good, adorable, life-giving and consubstantial with thee, now, ever and world without end. (People) Amen."

The deacon then recites the diptychs of "all our faithful brethren, true Christians;" for those who are in temptation; and for "this city;" while the priest remembers before God those for whom the holy Sacrifice is being offered.

The celebrant continues aloud: "Remember, O Lord, all those whom we have mentioned and those whom we have not mentioned: according to the greatness of thy reconciliation (loving-kindness) afford them the joy of thy salvation, receiving their sacrifices on the expanses of thine heaven, granting unto them visitation and succour from thee: strengthen them with thy power and arm them with thy might, for thou art merciful and hast pleasure in mercy.

To thee belongeth honour, glory and power, to thine only Son and to thy Spirit."

Prayer is made in the memorial for "all faithful kings;" for those "who in the four quarters of this world have founded and established churches and monasteries of God: and for every Christian polity, the clergy and the faithful people, that they be exercised in virtue."

The priest says aloud: "For thou art a house of refuge and salvation, a helping power and a victorious leader of all them that call unto thee and hope in thee, O Lord, and to thee belongeth" etc.

It would seem to have been the custom at one time for the Jacobites to have omitted this diptych, as there were no orthodox (Monophysite) kings, but Lazarus bar Sabta, a 9th century commentator, forbade the practice, and, in point of fact, there were Christian rulers amongst the Cusites, Ethiopians and Iberians.

The diptychs of the saints, as Philoxenus, [359] bishop of Mabug (523) pointed out, begin with "her who is to be called blessed and glorified of all generations of the earth, the holy and blessed and ever-virgin Mother of God, Mary." Mention is made also of St. John Baptist "messenger and forerunner" and of St. Stephen "chief of deacons and first of martyrs."

The precedence of our Lady, however, exists only in the diptychs recited by the deacon, and in the *gehonto* [360] said

---

[359] In his writings against Julian the Phantasiast.

[360] "Forasmuch then, O Lord, as thou hast the power of life and of death and art a God of mercies and of love towards mankind, vouchsafe to remember all those who have been well-pleasing unto thee since the world began, holy fathers and forefathers, prophets and apostles and John the forerunner and baptist and St. Stephen chief of deacons and first of martyrs, and the holy and glorious Mother of God and ever-virgin Mary and all saints." BRIGHTMAN, *op. cit.*, pp. 92-93.

by the priest the ever-virgin Mary is given a place *after* "John the forerunner and baptist and St. Stephen chief of deacons and first of martyrs." Edmund Bishop [361] has shown that a similar position is held by our Lady in the diptychs of the Stowe missal, which describes a liturgy older than the 9th century, and he speaks of "the indubitable influence of the Syrian (in the sense of Syriac) devotion and piety on Ireland, remote from each other geographically and historically as the churches of these two regions are."

"This Syrian religious influence," the same liturgist [362] goes on to say, "with its thoughts, forms of expression, even formulae, made itself felt in Spain and it was the Spanish church that inoculated the Irish, although it is possible that the order 'John, Mary' in the Stowe diptychs was derived by some Irishman—and the Irish were in those days a people enamoured of the strange, the odd, the rare—directly from some Syrian, and taken directly to Ireland."

The priest then prays aloud: "Unite us to the blessed church, number us with that church, give us a place through thy grace among the first born which are written in heaven, For, for this cause we remember them that they too while they stand before thy lofty tribunal may remember our misery and poverty, and may offer unto thee with us this fearful and unbloody sacrifice, for the care of them that live, for the assurance of us who are miserable and unworthy, and for the repose of all them that have fallen asleep aforetime in the belief of the truth, our fathers and brethren."

The memorial of the "doctors" or "fathers" recalls those who have preserved the orthodox faith, especially in the holy ecumenical councils, [363] speaking of Cyril as "a lofty

---

[361] *Liturgica Historica*, VII, n. 8, pp. 161-163. Oxford, At the Clarendon Press, 1918.
[362] *Ibid.*, pp. 162-163

tower and interpreter who expounded and explained the Incarnation of the Word of God made flesh."

The dissidents have inserted the names of Monophysites, and the Jacobite diptych includes Dioscorus, "our patriarch mar Severus the eloquent mouth and pillar and doctor of all the holy Church of God, and our sacred holy father mar James Baradaeus, establisher of the orthodox faith."

The priest continues aloud: "the luminaries and teachers of thy holy church, even them that have fought a good fight of faith, who have carried thy holy name before the Gentiles, kings and the children of Israel: by whose prayers and supplications grant thy peace to thy church. Their doctrines and their confessions confirm in our souls, speedily destroy heresies which trouble us, and grant us to stand before thy dread judgment seat without shame. For thou, O Lord, art holy and dwellest in the holy place, who art the perfecter of the saints and to thee we offer up glory..."

In the memorials of the dead, the celebrant places his thumb [364] on the host, and then makes the sign of the cross three times over a small tablet, [365] on which are inscribed the names of those for whom prayers had been asked and alms received at the commemoration before Lent.

An interesting parallel once existed in the Roman rite, and some ancient manuscripts of the Canon, after the words "*et omnium circumstantium,*" added "*et eorum quorum nomina ad commemorationem transcripsimus ac super altare*

---

[363] The deacon in the diptych of the doctors makes express mention of the first four general councils, as the emperor Justinian ordered (Anon. writer, 6th cent., *Chronicon Edessenum*, LXXXVIII).

[364] "Palm of the hand." *Liturgia*, XXIII, 2, p. 916, n. Paris, 1930.

[365] Cf. *Liber Vitae*. The reading of the *Liber Vitae* was referred to in the 10th century by Moses bar Kepha.

tuum scripta videntur," in allusion to a parchment [366] lying on the altar containing the names of benefactors and
others.

The deacon prays for the faithful departed "from this
holy altar, this town, this place and from all places and
quarters," that God may "vouchsafe them in his great
mercies, pardon of offences and remission of sins."

The diptych concludes: "Together let us cry and say
thrice *Kyrie eleison, Kyrie eleison, Kyrie eleison.*"

The priest in the meanwhile says silently: "Remember,
O Lord, the orthodox presbyters who have gone to their rest
aforetime, deacons, subdeacons, singers, readers, interpreters,
exorcists, monks, solitaries, hearers, perpetual virgins and
seculars who have departed in the true faith, and those for
whom each has offered the Sacrifice, or that he has·in his
intention."

Then aloud: "O Lord, Lord God of spirits and of all
flesh, remember, O Lord, those whom we have mentioned
and those whom we have not mentioned, who have passed
from this life in the orthodox faith. Give rest to their souls,
bodies and spirits, deliver them from eternal punishment to
come and grant them delight in the bosom of Abraham,
Isaac and Jacob, where the light of thy countenance visiteth,
whence pains, tribulations and sighings are fled away.
Impute to them none of their offences and enter not into
judgment with thy servants, for in thy sight shall no man
living be justified: for there is no man that is not guilty of
sin and that is pure from defilement of them that are among
the sons of men upon the earth, save only our Lord and
God and Saviour Jesus Christ, thine only begotten Son,

[366] MARTÈNE, *De Antiquis Ecclesiae Ritibus,* lib. I, chap. IV,
art. VIII.

through whom we too hope to obtain mercies and forgiveness of sins for his sake, both for ourselves and for them."

The people respond: "Grant them rest, remit and purify, O God, the offences and the shortcomings of us all, which we have done knowingly or unknowingly, willingly or unwillingly;" while the priest continues silently to pray for the holy dead and to seek pardon for the faults and failings of those present.

Then aloud he says: "Preserve our end Christian and sinless, gathering us beneath the feet of thine elect, when thou wilt, only without shame by reason of our faults, that in this, as in all things, thine all-honoured and blessed name may be glorified and extolled, with the name of our Lord Jesus Christ and thy Holy Spirit, now and always. [367] Amen."

The great intercession is concluded with the chant of the people: "As it is, and was, from generation to generation, and to the future centuries for ever. Amen."

Priest: "Peace be to you all." People: "And with thy spirit."

Then the celebrant passes his right hand over the chalice, as if to take a blessing from it. He signs himself, and also the right and left corners of the altar.

Finally, he turns to the people and blesses them three times, as he says: "May the mercies of the great God and of our Saviour Jesus Christ be upon you all, my brethren, for ever."

The veil is now drawn, and the priest, uncovering the chalice, begins the "order of breaking and signing." [368]

During the fraction, [369] consignation [370] and commixture,

[367] Cf. Coptic St. Cyril.
[368] *Tukkoso dh'-q'soyo w'rushmo.*
[369] Syriac (Jacobite), *kasyo;* Arabic, *kismah.*
[370] Syriac (Jacobite), *rūshmo,* "signing."

the deacon chants hymns which vary according to the season
or feast, but the Jacobites have retained the *kathuliki*, [371] a
general intercession for all sorts and conditions of men,
which gives the people a subject for prayer. The "catholic,"
which some codices refer to as the *brodiki*, [372] dates back to

[371] "Catholic:" "Bless, O Lord, again and again by this pure holy
oblation and propitiatory sacrifice which has been offered to God the
Father and consecrated and accomplished and consummated by the
descent of the living Holy Ghost; for our father the illustrious priest who
offered and consecrated it, for the altar of God whereon it is celebrated,
for the blessed folk who draw nigh and receive it in the belief of the
truth and those for whom it is offered and consecrated again more
especially we are praying. Behold a time of fear and behold an hour
full of trembling. Those on high stand in fear and minister with trembling: trembling is cast away among the children of light and earthborn
men feel it not, and from the hour wherein pardon is brought nigh
sinners flee away. Tremble ye ministers of the church for that ye
administer a living fire, and the power which ye wield surpasseth the
seraphim's. Blessed is the soul which is present in the church in purity
at this time, because the Holy Ghost writes down its name and uplifts
it to heaven. My blessed lady Mary, beseech with us thine only begotten
that he be appeased through thy prayers and perform mercy on all. Look,
O Lord, with a merciful eye on our father who stands before thine altar:
receive, O Lord, his oblation, like those of the prophets and apostles.
Remember, O Lord, by thy grace and by thy divine compassion the
fathers and pontiffs; may their prayers be a wall to us. Remember, O
Lord, our fathers and brethren again and our teachers and us and account
them worthy by thy mercy of the heavenly kingdom. Remember, O Lord,
them that are absent, have mercy on them that are here: give rest also to
the spirits of the departed and have mercy upon sinners in the day of
judgment. The departed who are severed from us and have passed from
this world, grant rest, O Christ, to their spirits with the righteous and
the just; be thy cross a bridge to them and thy baptism a covering: thy
body and holy blood a way to lead them to the kingdom. May we be
accounted worthy to lift up everlasting praise and acceptable worship
from the midst of the sanctuary to the Father and the Son and the living
Spirit of holiness, that the true God may accomplish towards us his grace
and blessing, compassion and loving-kindness, now, henceforth and for
ever. And let us all with prayer beseech the Lord. (People) Amen."
[372] *B⁽ᵉ⁾rūdīki*, "proclamation." The Jacobite *diakonale* calls it
kathisma.

early times, [373] although Lazarus bar Sabta (after 829) says that psalm CXVIII is sung during the fraction in some towns of Syria.

After the "catholic," Codrington [374] inserts a litany, which begins with the petition: "An angel of tranquillity and of peace and of mercies and of grace, my brethren, at all times let us implore of the Lord."

Each petition (takhshephtho) has the response "Kyrie eleison," except the last: "Our lives let us commit into thy hands, O Lord merciful God, and ask for mercies; be propitious, O good one, and have mercy on us."

The fraction and consignation were originally made immediately before holy communion, [375] to prepare the host for its reception by the faithful, but its present position is commented on by James of Edessa (708) in a letter to Thomas the Presbyter.

In the 8th and 9th centuries a controversy arose regarding the prayer to be said at the fraction. The formula "We are breaking the heavenly bread...." seems to have been in use until the time of the patriarch George (758-790). About that time, this prayer was omitted, and there is a manuscript [376] in the British Museum in which it has been erased, with a note to the effect that "the priest breaks the host in silence."

The controversy was examined at a synod [377] held under the patriarch Cyriacus in 795 at Beith Botin in the diocese of Harran, but without a condemnation of either side. The

---

[373] Cf. St. John Chrysostom, In Math. Hom. XXV.

[374] Eastern Churches Quarterly, no. 3, vol. I, p. 92. July, 1936. Renaudot (op. cit.) and Brightman (op. cit.) make no mention of the litany.

[375] Cf. St. Ephrem (÷ 373).

[376] Addit. 17178 f. 38.

[377] P. Hindo, Disciplina Antiochena Antica (Siri), pp. 257-258.

synod of Callinicum (818) came to a similarly inconclusive decision. The whole question is fully discussed in the *Chronicle of Michael the Syrian* (1166-1199), where valuable contemporary documents are given.

The prayer finally adopted has been ascribed by the Jacobites to Denys bar Salibi (1171), although in reality it is an adaptation from his work on the liturgy, in which this passage has been copied from the 9th century commentator, Moses bar Kepha:

"Thus truly did the Word of God suffer in the flesh (priest breaks the host in the midst, saying) and was sacrificed and broken on the cross (he divides and separates the halves slightly) and his soul was separated from his body (he unites them) though his Godhead was in no wise separated either from his soul or from his body (he dips the top of the half in his right hand, making a cross in the chalice, and with the moistened top signs the broken edge of the left hand half) and he was pierced † in his side † with the lance (he dips it again) and therefrom flowed forth blood and water, the propitiation for the whole world, (and signs the left half again) and his body was stained therewith (he joins the halves and turns them half a circle, from right to left). And for the sin of the circle of the whole world (he dips the original left hand top, now at the right bottom, and signs the blood inversely, *viz.* from west to east, etc.) the Son † died (and signs the half now in his left hand as before) upon the † cross (he joins the halves). And his soul came back and was united with his body (he elevates them so joined and bows); and on the third day he rose from the tomb (he lowers them and turns them round half a circle from left to right) and he turned us from a left-hand (evil) conversation to that of the right hand (good) (he proceeds holding the whole host with the two moistened tops uppermost) and by the blood of his cross reconciled and united and joined heavenly beings with those of earth and the people with the nations [378] and the soul with the body. And he is one Emmanuel and not divided after the indivisible union into two natures. [379] Thus we believe and thus we confess and thus we declare (he places the right half over the left half crosswise and holding them in the fingers of his left hand breaks a 'coal,' that is the top from one half, and places it in the chalice) that this body belongeth to this blood (he breaks a 'coal,' that is the top of the other half, brings it near to the mouth of the chalice, and then to the half from which it was broken) and this blood to this body."

Thus, there are six crosses, three on the body and three on the blood.

At the end of the prayer, the priest places the two halves in his left hand on the paten. He now holds the paten in his left hand with the 'coal' between his fingers and dips this particle in the chalice and signs on the left half of the host; dips it again and signs on the right half; and, finally, dips it once more and signs both halves together. He then places the 'coal' upon the two halves and replaces the paten on the altar.

A rubric orders the celebrant to take the greatest care lest he should break one of the crosses on the sacramental bread.

The prayer of the fraction, which the patriarch George had given up, was restored to the Catholic missal of 1922: "We are breaking the heavenly bread in the name of the Father, Amen, and of the Son, Amen, and of the living

[378] i. e. the Jews with the Gentiles.
[379] Catholics, until 1922, used this prayer purged of Monophysism. Thus, in place of the above, they said: " One Emmanuel who is one person in two natures."

and Holy Spirit, Amen. O Father of justice, [380] here is thy Son who sacrifices himself to appease thy anger. Accept him, he died for me, so that I might obtain pardon. Through him accept this sacrifice, presented by my hands, and forgive me. No longer remember the faults that I have committed before thy majesty. Behold his blood, shed † on Calvary by malefactors. [381] He prays for me, hear my prayer because of his merits. As great as are my offences, so great are thy mercies, if thou shouldest weigh them. But thy mercy weighs infinitely heavier than the heaviest mountains. [382] Look upon the sins, but look also upon the sacrifice † offered for them. The sacrifice and the victim are infinitely superior to the sins. It is because I have sinned that thy well-beloved has suffered the piercing of the nails † and the wound of the lance.

His sufferings are sufficient to appease thee, and it is by them that I obtain life. Glory be to the Father, who has given his Son for our salvation. Adoration to the Son, who has died on the cross and has given us life. Honour to the Holy Spirit, who has begun and achieved the mystery of our redemption. O august Trinity, have mercy on us all. [383]

By the same mercy, with which thou hast pardoned the thief that was placed on thy right hand, pardon us, O Lord, and have mercy on us.

Thou art Christ, our God, who was cleft in his side on

---

[380] Cf. James of Sarugh, *Sermon* XCV.

[381] "*Peccatori.*" Italian translation, p. 25.

[382] "*Ma la Tua misericordia supera infinitamente il peso dei miei peccati.*" *Ibid.*, p. 25.

[383] This prayer is substantially the same as the second of the three prayers given by Brightman (*op. cit.*, pp. 98-99), where it bears the name "of mar Jacob the doctor."

the height of Golgotha in Jerusalem for us. [384] Thou art the lamb of God that taketh away the sins of the world. Do thou pardon our offences and forgive our sins; grant that we may be able to sit at thy right hand, O Lord, our God, for ever. [385] Amen."

The following description of the fraction was sent to the writer by Dom Maurus Massé, O. S. B., a monk at the junior seminary of St. Benedict and St. Ephrem, Jerusalem.

The ceremony is symbolical of the passion and resurrection of our Lord.

The priest breaks the host into two equal parts, and each half is partially dipped into the chalice. Then the one particle is anointed, [386] not sprinkled, with the other; while a small fragment for the communion of the priest is placed in the chalice. Another piece is several times dipped into the chalice, and with this the priest anoints three times the remaining portions of the host, which will be used for the communion of the lower clergy and the people.

We have already had occasion to comment on a similarity in the diptychs between the Syrian rite and the missal of Stowe, and in the ceremony of intinction [387] there is a further connection. Thus, following the *per quem haec omnia* in the Irish book, a rubric adds *ter canitur* and then in Irish: "Here the oblations are raised above the chalice, and half the bread is plunged into the chalice."

---

[384] The words "in Jerusalem" are not found in the Italian translation of this prayer (*La Santa Messa in rito Siro-Antiocheno*, p. 26).

[385] The third of the three prayers given by Brightman (*op. cit.,* p. 99).

[386] The "painting" of the host is referred to by St. Ephrem in several hymns. *Vide* Maronite rite.

[387] *The Mass of the Western Rites.* Dom Fernand CABROL, chap. VIII, p. 165. London, Sands & Co., 1934.

The veil is now drawn back, and the priest, with out-stretched hands, says aloud the prayer of the our Father:

"O God the Father of our Lord Jesus Christ, the Father of mercies and God of all comfort, who sittest above the cherubim and art glorified of the seraphim, before whom stand a thousand-thousand archangels, ten-thousand-times-ten-thousand angels, hosts rational and heavenly, who hast vouchsafed to sanctify and perfect the offerings and gifts and perfection of fruits which are offered to thee for a sweet smelling savour by the grace of thine only-begotten Son and by the descent of thine Holy Spirit: sanctify, O Lord, our souls and our bodies, that with a pure heart and with soul enlightened and with face unashamed we may make bold [388] to call upon thee, O God, heavenly Father, almighty, holy, and to pray and to say, Our Father, who art in heaven."

The people continue the Lord's prayer in Arabic, and in some districts pray with arms [389] outstretched, after the manner of the primitive *orantes*.

James of Edessa says that the Lord's prayer was introduced by the ancient fathers. [390]

The final ascription [391] is found in the Peschitto version of *St. Matthew* and in the *Didache*.

The celebrant continues with the embolism, also aloud and with arms outstretched: "Yea, O Lord our God, lead us not into temptation which we are not able to bear, but make with the temptation also a way of escape, that we may be able to bear it and deliver us from evil: by Christ Jesus our Lord, through whom and with whom to thee is fitting

[388] Cf. *Praeceptis salutaribus moniti* of the Roman rite.
[389] RAHMANI, *op. cit.*, part I, chap. IV, p. 241.
[390] *Ibid.*, p. 240.
[391] Cf. Coptic rite.

glory and honour and dominion, with thy Spirit, all holy, good, adorable, life-giving and consubstantial, with thee now, you all for ever. (People) Amen."

The Inclination

The priest says: "Peace be to you all," and the people respond: "And with thy spirit."

Then, as in the Byzantine rite, the deacon announces: "Let us bow down our heads unto the Lord," to which the people answer: "Before thee, O Lord our God."

This is the version given by Brightman, [392] but in the recent Italian translation [393] of the Catholic rite the minister says: "Bow down before the God of mercy, before the propitiatory altar, before the body and blood of our Saviour: in him they have the life which they receive. Receive a blessing from the Lord."

There is no response on the part of the people.

The celebrant continues with the prayer of inclination or "prayer of the laying on of the hand," which seems to have developed from the people bowing their heads in response to the blessing of the priest. Theodore of Mopsuestia says: "When .... he blesses the people with the peace, (the people) also themselves return the accustomed reply, which is prayed by all who are present whilst bowing their heads fitly."

The priest says: "To thee thy servants bow down their heads, awaiting the rich mercies which come from thee. Send, O Lord, the rich blessings which come from thee and

[392] Op. cit., p. 100.
[393] La Santa Messa in rito Siro-Antiocheno (Rome, 1942), p. 27. In reply to the blessing of the priest, P. M. S. gives: "Deacon: And with thy spirit. Before we receive this divine mystery, which has been offered, let us bow our heads before the merciful God" (p. 40).

sanctify our souls and bodies and spirits, that we may be worthy to partake of the body and blood of Christ our Saviour: by the grace and mercies and love towards mankind of Christ Jesus our Lord, with whom thou art blessed and glorified in heaven and on earth, with thy Spirit all-holy, good, adorable, life-giving and consubstantial, with thee now and ever and world without end. (People) Amen."

Again, the priest says: "Peace be to you all," and the people respond: "And with thy spirit."

The six signs of the cross which follow are similar to those made by the celebrant after the intercession, but the wording of the blessing is different: "May the grace and the mercies of the Trinity, holy and glorious and uncreated, essential and eternal, adorable and consubstantial, be with you all for ever. (People) Amen."

The elevation [394] is preceded by a diaconal monition: "Bless, O my Lord. In fear and trembling let us give heed," to which the people respond: "Be propitious, O Lord, and have mercy upon us."

Then the priest takes the paten in both hands and raises it to the level of his eyes, moving it crosswise from east to west and from north to south, as he says: "The holy things are given to those who are holy and pure."[395]

The assistant replies: "The one Father is holy, the one Son is holy, the one living Spirit is holy." [396]

The priest touches his eyes with the paten, kisses it, replaces it on the altar, and worships.

---

[394] Syriac, zūyoḥo, "shewing;" Arabic, raf'ah.

[395] Kudshe lḳaddīshe.

[396] The Italian translation (p. 28) adds the following: "Blessed be the name of the only Lord in heaven and on earth. To him be glory for ever. Glory be to the Father and to the Son and to the Holy Ghost, who sanctifies all and grants every remission."

The chalice is then uncovered and elevated with the same ceremony, while the people respond: "Glory be to the Father and to the Son and to the Holy Ghost, only one for ever and ever. Amen."

During the elevation, the deacon censes the blessed sacrament, two lights are carried, fans are shaken, and the bell is rung.

The touching of the eyes with the holy mysteries was referred to by St. Ephrem in the hymn which the priest recited after the liturgy: "That my eyes to which I have applied thy body may see thy mercy." The kissing of the host was once common to both the Syrian [397] and Roman [398] rites.

The double elevation, which is peculiar to this liturgy, is said to have originated in the oriental custom of carrying in triumph the person whom one wished to honour.

Originally, the priest chanted in the singular: "the holy to the holy," a practice mentioned by James of Sarugh (451-521): "That is why the priest cried in a loud voice: the holy who comes down and dwells in the holy.'"

The priest next takes the paten in his right hand and the chalice in his left, and, holding the right over the left crosswise, he says: "The one holy Father is with us, who created the world by his grace. (People) Amen." "The one holy Son is with us, who has saved us by his own precious sufferings. (People) Amen." "The one living and Holy Spirit is with us, the author and consummator of all

---

[397] "The angels in heaven are astounded at the dignity to which those on earth have attained. The angels proclaim him holy in silence, without troubling where he dwells, whilst men embrace and kiss him." St. Ephrem, *Hymn on the Priesthood*.

[398] Cf. MARTÈNE, *De Antiquis Ecclesiae Ritibus*, lib. I, chap. IV, art. 9.

things that are or have been. Blessed be the name of the Lord, from everlasting and to world without end. (People) Amen."

The priest places the paten and chalice on the altar, covers the paten with the star, and the holy vessels with their veils.

Then, [399] coming down from the altar, the celebrant, bowing down or kneeling with hands folded on his breast, says a short prayer preparatory to communion.

Three prayers are given in the missal, from which he may take his choice. *a*) "Grant me, O Lord, to eat thee in holiness, and by the eating of thy body may my evil desires be driven away, and by the drinking of thy cup of life may my passions be quenched, and by thee may I be deemed worthy of the remission of my faults and pardon of my sins, O our Lord and our God, for ever. Amen."

b) "Grant, O Lord God, that our bodies be made holy by thy holy body, and our souls be illuminated by thy propitiatory blood, and may it be for the remission of our faults and the pardon of our sins, O our Lord and our God, for ever. Amen."

c) "Grant us, O Lord, to eat thy holy body and to drink thy propitiatory blood, and may we be heirs in thy heavenly kingdom with all who have been well pleasing to thy goodwill, O our Lord and our God, for ever. Amen."

The cantors in the meanwhile sing the "Verse. In oblations and prayers. Let us remember our fathers who taught us whilst alive to be children unto God in this world that passeth away, O Son of God, rest them in the kingdom of heaven with the just and with the righteous in the world that passeth not away."

---

[399] Some Jacobite books here insert a *teshmeshto* of our Lady or a *kyklion* of the departed.

This is followed by an appropriate anthem called the *shubboho*.

The priest returns to the altar, uncovers the mysteries, and with a spoon takes the "coal" from the chalice, as he says: "I hold thee who holdest the bounds of the world, thee I am grasping who orderest the universe here below, and I place thee, O God, in my mouth. By thee may I escape fire unquenchable and merit the pardon of my sins like the sinful woman and the robber. Thou art our Saviour and our God for ever and ever."

Then, lifting the "coal" with the spoon to receive the particle in holy communion, [100] he continues: "A propitiatory particle ('coal') of the body and blood of Christ our God is given to me his feeble servant and sinner, for the pardon of faults and the remission of sins, in both worlds for ever and ever. Amen."

The priest puts the other "coal" which was placed on the paten into the spoon, and so into the chalice, which he then consumes, saying: "By thy living and lifegiving blood, shed on the cross, may my faults be remitted and my sins pardoned, O Jesus, Word of God, who didst come to save us. May it be for our resurrection in eternity, our Saviour and our God, for ever. Amen."

The number of "pearls" necessary for communion are now broken off from the host and put into the chalice, and the clergy are communicated in a spoon with these particles.

The celebrant says: "The propitiatory coal of the holy body and the propitiatory blood of Christ our God is given to the pious priest (modest deacon; truly faithful subdeacon; Antonian monk) and steward of the house of God for pardon

---

[100] Syriac, *shauthōphūtho;* Arabic, *tanāwul.*

of offences and forgiveness of sins; his prayer be with us. Amen." [401]

The veil, which has been drawn during the communion of the clergy, is now opened.

The priest, taking the paten in his right hand and the chalice in his left, then goes to give holy communion to the people, accompanied by two torch bearers and assistants with fans, while on more solemn occasions the deacon walks backwards censing the holy mysteries.

Moses bar Kepha (903) speaks of the deacon carrying the chalice, to the accompaniment of lights, fans and incense.

The following prayer is said by the priest as he leaves the altar: "From thy altar of pardon let there come down pardon on thy servants, O Son of God, who came for our salvation and shall come for our resurrection and the renewal of the human race, for ever. (People) Amen."

The people are blessed with the paten, as the celebrant makes the sign of the cross from west to east and from right to left, as he says: "Stretch forth, O Lord, thine invisible right hand and bless the multitude of thy worshippers, which receive thy body and precious blood for the pardon of faults, remission of sins and the recovery of innocence before thee, O our Lord and our God for ever. (People) Amen."

Then the priest, crossing his right hand over his left, descends from the step to the place of communion, as he

---

[401] At Sharfeh, the deacon brought a chalice, purificator and spoon for his own communion. The priest took the spoon and communicated the deacon, while the latter held his chalice under his chin. He then went to the *diaconicon* and took his own ablution. CODRINGTON, *Eastern Churches Quarterly*, No. 3, vol. I, p. 95. July, 1936.

If a bishop is assisting at the liturgy, he communicates himself from a spoon.

recites aloud: "May the mercies of Almighty God and our Saviour Jesus Christ descend upon those who carry these holy things, and upon those who distribute them, and upon those who receive them, and on whomsoever officiates and communicates. May the mercy of the Holy Trinity be with us, in this world and the next, for ever. (People) Amen."

The deacon responds: "Glory to God in heaven, exaltation to his holy Mother, a crown of praise to the martyrs, and pity and mercy for the dead."

The people, who stand with hands joined on their breasts, receive the blessed sacrament under the species of bread,[402] which at the time of the fraction was anointed with the precious blood.

The Jacobites receive particles, which the priest takes with his hand from the chalice.

The writer has himself received holy communion[403] in

---

[402] The earliest method of receiving holy communion was that described by St. Cyril of Jerusalem. The priest placed the host in the palm of the right hand, which was supported by the left, and the people communicated themselves. Then they drank of the chalice. This practice is recalled by a prayer recited by the priest after communion: " May the hands which have extended their palms and have received thee, O Son of God, the gage (of eternal life), not contract in the day of judgment .... by the heat of the flame." *Missale juxta ritum Ecclesiae Apostolicae Antiochenae Syrorum* (Sharfeh, 1922), p. 98.

This was the method of receiving communion in the time of the mafrian Marutha (629-648), but in the 9th century we have the testimony of Yaḥya ibn Garir (*Al-Muršid*, chap. LIV, *Of Communion*) for the use of the spoon, and the custom is confirmed by Bar Hebraeus (*Book of the Rays*, VII, 3, 2).

The Jacobite canonist (*Nomocanon*, IV, 5) said also: "in the 13th century, in the western part of the patriarchate, the priest dipped particles in the chalice held by the deacon and so gave to the people; whereas, in the 'east,' each particle was dipped at the fraction,"

[403] The use of the spoon is liturgically permissable in the Syrian Catholic church, although it is now normally reserved for the deacon and, sometimes, the lector.

the Catholic Syrian rite both with the use of the spoon and also the intincted species from the hand of the celebrant.

The formula of communion for the people is similar to that for the clergy, but "true believer" is substituted for "pious priest." The communicant answers "Amen," bowing and taking a few steps backward before returning to his place.

An anthem or hymn is sung during the administration of communion.

One of these is called "the one whom the illuminated": [404] "Come in peace, O pontiff, who bearest the sacraments of thy Lord and who distributest life to men with thy hand."

Another, ascribed to James of Sarugh, makes the strange assertion that Judas, at the last supper, received unconsecrated bread: [405] "to whom the Lord by no means gave his body."

Psalm CVIII (*Beati immaculati*), whose strophes are alphabetical, was at one time sung during the communion of the people, a practice alluded to by St. Cyril of Jerusalem (4th century) and Lazarus bar Sabta, bishop of Bagdad (9th century).

On the Epiphany, the choir chants: "John Baptist saw the Son of God, but he did not eat him. We, however, who were baptized in his name, approach to eat him. John Baptist placed his hand on the head of his Creator, but we apply our lips to the source of grace."

It would seem that a table outside the sanctuary is required, as the paten and chalice are covered when they are brought down from the altar. It is in fact mentioned in

---

[404] *Haou dnourone*, a hymn to the blessed sacrament.

[405] Innocent III and Stephen Euodius Assemani († 1782) maintained that this referred only to the *effect* of the sacrament.

Greek St. James, [406] and it is used to-day in the Jacobite church of Malabar.

This is certainly the correct place for communion, but an abuse has crept in of deferring holy communion until immediately before the ablutions. This practice was condemned by the Catholic synod of Sharfeh (1888).

In the *Hymn on the Priesthood, St. Ephrem* [407] († 373) speaks of the priest carrying the blessed sacrament and elevating it with veneration prior to giving communion to the faithful.

The laity in the time of the Syrian doctor appear to have washed their hands and mouths before reception, and to have used a reed [408] for the precious blood.

The Catholic Syrians also give holy communion from the reserved sacrament, especially in the case of women, who in some dioceses are separated from the men.

Communion immediately after baptism and confirmation, except in the case of adults, has been abolished by the Catholics.

When the celebrant has finished giving communion, he blesses [409] the people first with the paten and then with the chalice, as he says:

"Glory to thee, glory to thee, glory to thee, our Lord and our God, for ever. O our Lord Jesus Christ, let not thy

---

[406] παρατράπεζον

[407] RAHMANI, *op. cit.*, chap. IV, p. 244.

[408] Cf. "*Suck* his blood and rejoice, kiss his body and exult." Hymn at nocturns on the fifth Sunday after Pentecost. On the other hand, another hymn says: "Receive the holy in your palms and the life (blood) on your lips."

In regard to the reception of the precious blood by means of a fistula cf. the pope and the deacon at a solemn papal Mass.

[409] The Italian translation (p. 31) only says: "the priest, holding the paten and chalice in his hand turned towards the people, says ...."

body with which we have been nourished and thy propitiatory blood which we have drunk be to us for our judgment
and condemnation, but for the eternal life of all of us and
our salvation, and do thou have mercy on us."

Then, returning to the altar, the priest replaces the
mysteries on it.

The deacon [410] says: "The world bends and adores
thee, every tongue proclaims thy name, for thou art the
resurrection of the dead and the sweet hope of the departed.
We praise thee, O God, and we offer thee our thanks."

The priest, with hands folded on the breast, now says
aloud the prayer of thanksgiving: "We give thee thanks,
O Lord God, and in particular we praise thee on account of
thy immense and ineffable love towards mankind, O Lord,
who hast accounted us worthy to partake of thy heavenly
banquet. Do not condemn us by reason of the reception of
thy holy and unspotted mysteries, but preserve us in justice
and holiness, that being worthy to partake of thy Holy Spirit
we may find a portion and a lot and an inheritance with all
the saints who have pleased thee in the world. By the grace,
mercies and love towards mankind of thine only Son,
through whom and with whom belongeth glory and honour
and power with the Holy Spirit, now, always and for ever.
(People) Amen."

This prayer [411] has every appearance of being in historical and literary relation with the prayer immediately

[410] The Italian translation (p. 31) says the "people." Brightman
(op. cit., p. 104) and Codrington (op. cit., p. 97) in place of the above
have the following:—Deacon: "Stand we fairly all of us after that we
have eaten." People: "We give thanks to thee especially on account of
thy benefit towards us."
[411] Edmund BISHOP, The Journal of Theological Studies, vol. XIV
(Oxford, Clarendon Press, 1913). Notes and Studies. Liturgical Comments and Memoranda, VIII, p. 61.

following the epiclesis in Greek St. Basil. It would seem therefore that the prayer in St. James has been removed from its original position and worked up into the form of a thanksgiving after communion by the simple expedient of changing the reference of the verbs from the future to the past tense; while in St. James the prayer for the communicants immediately following the epiclesis seems in some way to have been tampered with.

The prayer is followed by "Peace be to you all," and the response of the people: "And with thy spirit."

Then the deacon gives the monition: "Let us bow down our heads unto the Lord," and the people answer "Before thee, O Lord our God."

The priest continues with the "prayer of inclination": "O God, who art great and marvellous, who didst bow the heavens and come down for the salvation of our humanity, look upon us according to thy mercies and grace; bless thy people and preserve thine heritage, so that for all time we may praise thee, because thou art our true God, [412] with God the Father, who hast begotten thee, and thy Holy Spirit, now, always and for ever. (People) Amen."

In the dismissal, the words "Bless, O Lord" are said by the people, [413] although the deacon proclaims: "Go in peace ye who in the name of Christ our God are dismissed."

The people reply: "In the name of the Lord our God," and the priest says a variable "seal" (huttomo) or final prayer.

The people or deacon then recite an 'eqbo, such as the following: "By the prayer of thy Mother and of all thy

---

[412] Note the very clear expression of the divinity of our Lord.

[413] "In dimissione verba .... 'Benedic Domine' a populo proferuntur. Diaconus autem proclamat .... 'Ite in pace.' HANSSENS, Instit. Lit. de Rit. Orien., t. II, part I, chap. X, II, p. 388.

saints, pardon us, O our Lord, and grant rest to our departed. Bless, O my Lord."

The prayer: "Bless us all, preserve us all ....," which Brightman [414] gives as the last prayer of the Anaphora of St. James, is "not found" [415] in the Catholic liturgy.

The dismissal prayer or commendation [416] since 1922 has been said aloud in Arabic, whereas prior to the new edition of the missal it was said in Syriac and in a low voice, with the exception of the final words: "Go in peace while rejoicing and contented, and pray for me," which were said aloud in Arabic.

The celebrant, half turning towards the people, blesses them and says: "† Go in peace, O our brethren and beloved, we commit you to the grace and the mercy of the Holy Trinity, with the viaticum and the blessings which you have taken from the purifying altar of the Lord, the far off and the near, the living and the dead, the saved † by the victorious cross of the Lord and the signed by the mark of holy baptism. May the Holy Trinity pardon your sins and forgive your faults, may he give rest to the souls of your dead, and have mercy on me miserable sinner, and may your prayers help me. † Go in peace while rejoicing and contented, and pray for me."

During the blessing, the priest keeps his arm raised, and bows to the altar at the words: "may he have mercy on me."

The people are blessed with a single sign of the cross, whereas the normal practice in the liturgy is to give a threefold cross. Lights are carried in a solemn liturgy.

The traditional place for the ablutions is after the dismis-

---

[414] *Op. cit.*, pp. 105-106.
[415] Information given by Fr. Zacharia Malké.
[416] *Magh'lonutho.*

sal, although they are sometimes taken, *more Romano*, [417] when the communion is finished.

The celebrant makes his communion for the second time, as he had previously received only one particle of the host and two spoonfuls of the precious blood.

The details of the ablutions are not identical in all the the missals, and although the prayers are the same, we find many small differences [418] of ceremonial.

The following description is taken from the Syro-Malankara missal of 1934, and agrees substantially with the Latin translation [419] of the Syrian liturgy made by Prince Maximilian of Saxony.

The veil is drawn, and the priest, descending from the altar and bowing down or kneeling, says two prayers in secret: *a*) "By the sacrifice which we have offered this day may the Lord God be appeased and his elect and holy angels, and may he make rest and good remembrance for his Mother and for his saints and for all the faithful departed and especially for him for whom and on behalf of whom this sacrifice has been made this day;" *b*) "Thy sacred and holy mouth, O my Lord, hath promised and said on this wise: 'Whoso eateth my body and drinketh my blood and believeth in me dwelleth in me and I in him and I will raise him up at the last day.' And to us, O Lord, who have eaten thy holy body and drunk thy propitiatory blood, let it not be for judgment, for vengeance nor for condemnation nor accusation to me and to thy faithful people, but for the pardon of

[417] The ablutions were taken *more Romano* in a pontifical liturgy sung in Sant'Andrea della Valle, Rome, in 1928, and also at a solemn liturgy in Paris in 1931.

[418] The liturgies in Rome and Paris followed the Roman method, but with water on the spoon; whereas the Syrian church in Cairo had water only for the second ablution and water on the paten.

[419] *Missa Syriaca-Antiochena.* Pustet, 1908.

offences and for the remission of sins and for a blessed resurrection from the house of the dead and for boldness before thy fearful judgment-seat, O our Lord and our God, for ever."

Then the priest goes up to the altar, uncovers the paten and chalice, places the spoon in the chalice, and receives [420] any "coal" that remains, as he says psalm (XXIII), "*Dominus regit me.*"

The smaller fragments are swept into the chalice with two fingers, [421] as he says: "If there be any member (particle) remaining it remaineth to thy knowledge which created the world; if there be any member remaining, may the Lord be its keeper and be propitious to us and to you."

The paten is replaced on the altar, and the priest "ministers the chalice," consuming what is left of the precious blood, as he says: "What reward shall I give unto the Lord .... I will pay my vows also unto the Lord."

A second prayer is called in Brightman [422] "With the sign of mar James": "O son of God, who by his immolation saved the guilty, by thy living sacrifice dispel my passions and heal mine infirmities. Good is he that came and they pierced his side on Golgotha. By the blood and water that flowed therefrom quench thou my thirst."

The paten is washed with wine, which is poured into the chalice [423] and consumed by the priest, who says:

[420] Communion is sometimes given here, but, as we have seen, this practice was forbidden to Catholics by the synod of Sharfeh (1888). The Italian translation of the liturgy (p. 32) says that communion is given here to the faithful who were unable to be present at the time of communion.

[421] The Jacobites use a *gomuro*, the small cushion on which the spoon rests.

[422] *Op. cit.*, p. 107

[423] The dissidents use a finger bowl for the ablutions called the "deaconess."

"They shall be satisfied with the plenteousness of thy house," and the rest of psalm XXXV (XXXVI).

Water is then put into the paten, and the spoon and star are washed, while the water is poured into the chalice, which the celebrant drinks.

The priest washes his fingers in the paten, first those of the right hand and then those of the left.

Water is again poured into the chalice, and the priest takes a third ablution, although this is sometimes consumed by the deacon. [424]

"And when he ministers his hands," [425] the priest says: "The living fire of the glorious body and blood of Christ our God quench the flame of the fire and the dread and vehement torments from my members and from the souls and bodies of the faithful departed, who have put thee on by water and the Spirit, and do thou call and set them on thy right side at the last day as thou hast promised, O our Lord and our God."

"And when he ministers his fingers, first of his right hand three times, he says: Let my fingers rehearse thy praises and my mouth thy thanksgiving. By the nails in thy hands

[424] Mar Ephrem Rahmani (op. cit., p. 250) says that the deacon cleanses the sacred vessels, wipes them, and takes them to the sacristy. In a pontifical liturgy celebrated in the church of Sant'Andrea della Valle, Rome (1928), the vessels were left uncovered on the altar, and a server, after the Mass, carried them to the sacristy.

John, bishop of Manzalta († 1165) recommended (canon 6) the deacon, when he had consumed the sacrament, to pay attention to all the small particles which could adhere to the linen, etc.; to pour wine and water into the chalice, which he was to drink; and to wipe the vessels with the sponge.

[425] BRIGHTMAN, Ibid., p. 107. Prince Maximilian in his translation of the liturgy gives the prayer "The living fire" as said when the celebrant washes the spoon (p. 49).

and thy feet, by the spear which pierced thy side pardon me mine offences and my sins."

"And when of the left hand, he says: Keep me, O Lord, from all deceitful men and let thy right hand help me and from wicked works preserve me for ever. Amen."

"They shall be satisfied with the plenteousness of thy house" etc. is said for the second time, when the priest again drinks from the chalice. [426]

The paten and chalice are wiped with a "sponge," and the celebrant says: "(In mar Ephraim) Wipe away, O Lord, with the sponge of thy mercy all mine offences, and the sins which I have committed before thee pardon in thy loving-kindness, O Christ the King, who givest us life, whose holy mysteries I have ministered. Vouchsafe me with the just who have loved thee and with the righteous who have desired to serve thee, O my Lord, in thine heavenly kingdom which is everlasting, continually, O my Lord, and amen, now, always and for ever."

Then the priest [427] arranges the sacred vessels, and goes to the diaconicon, where he washes his hands, reciting psalm XXV (XXVI), "*Judica me.*"

He says, as he dries them, psalm XXVIII (XXIX), *Afferte Domino.*

A *teshmeshto* [428] of the departed is said by the priest as he unvests, at the *'eqbo* of which he puts on his usual outer garment.

Finally, [429] having kissed the altar in the middle and on

[426] "Deaconess" in the Jacobite liturgy.

[427] CODRINGTON, *Eastern Churches Quarterly, op. cit.,* p. 98.

[428] *Proem.; sedro;* Kyrie eleison (three times); prayer; Lord's prayer.

[429] Mgr. Paul Hindo (*Disciplina Antiochena Antica (Siri)*, IV, p. 253, n. 2) has suggested that this conclusion of the Syrian liturgy might have been borrowed by the Mohammedans for the final ceremony

either side, he takes his leave of the altar in the following
prayer: "Remain in peace, O holy and divine altar of the
Lord. Henceforth I know not whether I shall return to thee
or not. May the Lord vouchsafe me to see thee in the church
of the firstborn which is in heaven, and in this covenant do
I trust.

Remain in peace, O holy propitiatory altar of the holy
body and propitiatory blood which I have received from
thee. May it be to me for the pardon of offences and for the
remission of sins and for boldness before thy fearful judgment-seat, O our Lord and our God, for ever.

Remain in peace, O holy altar, table of life, and entreat
our Lord Jesus Christ for me that my remembrance may not
cease from thee, henceforth and for ever. Amen."

"The order of the *Kurbono* is complete without defect." [430]

Bread [431] is blessed and distributed on the days of the
holy fast of the forty days and "on vigils after the *kuddūs,*
which is celebrated at midday during the fast and in the
evening on vigils."

There are alternative prayers for the blessing.

The shorter form is as follows: "May the grace of the
Holy Trinity come from heaven and abide upon this †††
būrc°tho: and upon them that give it and them that receive
it and them that minister it and all that have partaken and
are partaking in it be the mercies of God in both worlds for
ever and ever. (People) Amen."

---

of all their prayers, which is called *taslimah* (of *salam,* "peace"), and
consists in turning the head to the right and to the left, and in saying
the word *salam.*

[430] BRIGHTMAN, *op. cit.,* p. 109.

[431] Syriac (Jacobite), *būrc°tho,* "blessing;" Arabic (Catholic), *khubz
moubārak,* "blessed bread;" *baracah,* "blessing."

"Then the bishop shall take a piece and eat it and distribute portions to each of the clergy: but if the bishop be not present then each of the priests shall take a piece in his hand, saying: "Grant us, O Lord God, by this būrcᶜtho pardon of offences and remission of sins." And the priest who takes last shall distribute to the rest of the clergy and then one of the deacons shall distribute the *eulogia* to the people."

Liturgy of the Presanctified

The Liturgy of the Presanctified [432] was restored to the Syrian rite by the late Catholic patriarch Ephrem Rahmani in the missal of 1922, and it has passed to the Syro-Malankara book of 1934. It is celebrated by the Catholics on the ferias of Lent after vespers [433] and on Good Friday morning.

The liturgy, which is found in ancient manuscripts, has been chiefly taken from St. Basil, and consists of Mass of the catechumens, with little entrance and lessons, and Mass of the faithful, with great entrance, litanies, Lord's prayer, fraction, communion, thanksgiving and dismissal.

The presanctified is now obsolete among the Jacobites, [434] although a form of the "Signing [435] of the Chalice" was mentioned by John bar Cursos, [436] bishop of Telles (503-

[432] Syriac, *r'shom koso*, "signing of the chalice;" Arabic, *bruyigyasmana, alsabik takdisuha.*

[433] CODRINGTON, *Eastern Churches Quarterly*, No. 3, vol. I (July, 1936), p. 98.

[434] A Liturgy of the Presanctified for the Jacobites was edited in 1902 by H. W. Codrington. It is remarkable for a formula of epiclesis addressed to our Lord.

[435] Liturgical books speak of the Presanctified as the "Signing of the Chalice," since the intincted host is signed over a chalice of wine and water.

[436] *Resolutiones canonicae*, n. 10; canon 8.

519); James, bishop of Edessa (633-708); [437] and Theodosius, patriarch of Antioch (887-896). [438]

Assemani thinks that the church of Syria adopted the rite as early as the 5th century, and Bar Hebraeus († 1286), describing the presanctified according to the use of his church, speaks of Severus of Antioch († 538) as the author. No manuscript, however, subsequent to the 13th century makes any mention of it, and it is thought that it was abandoned about that time.

Other Anaphoras

Anaphoras [439] are plentiful, and no less than sixty-four are known to have existed. The Catholic Syrians have reduced the number to seven, but the Jacobites have still the choice of more than thirty.

Many of the alleged authors have little or nothing to do with the liturgies that bear their names, but the earliest anaphoras [440] show traces of very ancient Antiochene forms.

Some of the liturgies are without the words of institution [441] or are unduly composite and deficient; [442] while those of later authorship are lenghty, inflated and full of bad rhetoric.

It would seem that the last Syrian anaphora to be written

[437] *Apud* Bar Hebraeus. *Nomocanon,* chap. IV, sect. VIII.

[438] *Ap.* Bar Hebraeus. *Nomocanon,* cap. IV, sect. I.

[439] Renaudot (*op. cit.,* t. II, pp. 45-560) cites 39 anaphoras. Mgr. Paul Hindo (*Disciplina Antiochena Antica (Siri),* t. III, p. 181) gives a total of 72 anaphoras, "like the 72 disciples of our Lord."

[440] e. g. St. Ignatius; St. Athanasius, which was probably for the use of Syrians in Egypt.

[441] Denys Bar Salibi, bishop of Amida.   In the Roman edition ascribed to Dionysius the Athenian.

[442] Thomas of Heraclea, a Jacobite bishop of about the end of the 7th century.

was that of Ignatius (Joseph Ibn Wahib), patriarch of Antioch
(1293-1308).

Stephen Evodius Assemani (1707-1892), the Maronite
writer, says that in his day the Catholic Syrians had
twenty-five anaphoras, but in 1843 their number had been
reduced to seven,—St. Xystus; St. James; St. Peter; St. John
Chrysostom; Matthew the Shepherd (one of the seventy
disciples); St. Basil of Caesarea; and St. John the Evangelist.

The normal anaphora for use on Sundays was St. James;
on week days in Summer (Easter to Dedication), St. Xystus;
and on week days in Winter (Dedication to Easter), St. John
Chrysostom.

The missal published in 1922 has retained the same
number of anaphoras, but some of them are different from
those formerly used. Thus, St. James; St. John; Twelve
Apostles; St. Mark; St. Eustathius, Patriarch of Antioch;
St. Basil of Caesarea; St. Cyril of Alexandria; with the
Liturgy of the Presanctified for Good Friday.

The rubrics of the anaphora [443] indicate the days on
which the Liturgy of St. James and others are to be said.

Thus, St. James is used on all feasts [444] of our Lord,
Sundays in Lent, at the enthronement of the patriarch, consecration of a bishop, ordination of a priest, consecration of
a church or altar-stone, and at the first liturgy of a priest or
bishop.

The anaphora of St. John in used on feasts of our Lady.

The other anaphoras are left to the choice of the celebrant, but the normal liturgy on ordinary days is that of the
Twelve Apostles.

The evening liturgy on Holy Saturday and Christmas

[443] p. 57.
[444] e. g. Easter, Christmas, Ascension.

Eve, as well as that on the feast of St. Ephrem, is celebrated entirely in Syriac, while on Holy Thursday the liturgy is concelebrated.

As we have seen, the anaphora *par excellence* of the Syrian rite is *St. James.* There is, however, no historical foundation for the tradition that it was composed by St. James the brother of the Lord at divine dictation, although it is used on the Wednesday after Pentecost in commemoration of the legend that the apostle celebrated the liturgy on that day.

The story is referred to in the *Commentary* of Denys bar Salibi (1171), which said that when St. James was asked whence he had taken the liturgy he replied: "As the Lord lives I have neither added nor taken away anything from what I heard from our Lord."

St. John, the anaphora reserved for feasts of our Lady, was formerly used on other great solemnities: [145]

"O Lord, mighty God, who art true charity, imperturbable peace and a hope that does not confound."

The *Twelve Apostles* [146] and *St. Mark* are also used by the Maronites, and short references to them will be found in the following chapter.

St. Eustathius, patriarch of Antioch, is claimed as the author of the anaphora which begins with the words: "O Lord God, clement and of great pity, who truly hearest those who without doubting call upon thee."

The anaphora of Basil Lazarus bar Sabta, bishop of Bagdad ("O God, ocean of peace, stream of love, and source of purity"), has been falsely ascribed to *St. Basil of Caesarea,* whose genuine liturgy is used to-day by the Catholic Syrians:

---

[145] *"Imprimis in magnis solemnitatibus adhiberi solet."* Maximilianus, *Missa Syriaca-Antiochena. Introd.,* p. VI, Pustet, 1908.

[146] The writer assisted at the Liturgy of the Twelve Apostles on May 22, 1924, in the Syrian (Catholic) church, Cairo.

"O everlasting God, who from the beginning didst create men for immortality."

The eucharistic prayer in St. Basil is almost identical with the prayer assigned to the same author in the Byzantine liturgy that bears his name.

Its style shows, not only by the exact choice of words, but also by a facility of expression, that the translator lived not later than the 7th or 8th century, at a time when Syriac literature was flourishing, although the extant manuscripts may be of more recent date.

A difference from the Greek St. Basil exists in the allusion [447] to the two "honourable animals," signifying the cherubim and seraphim, which has been borrowed from the prophet Ezechiel. [448] The same prayer also says that the seraphim and cherubim veil their faces with their two wings, as they do not fathom the mystery of the divinity.

The late Syrian patriarch [449] has shown that the Syriac translation of St. Basil has preserved expressions [450] which have disappeared from the extant Greek version. The Coptic St. Basil has borrowed the prayer [451] of the peace with which this anaphora begins.

---

[447] The *Euchologion* of Sarapion has a similar reference.

[448] "*Et elevata sunt cherubim: ipsum est animal, quod videram juxta fluvium Chobar.*" Ezech. X, 15. "*Ipsum est animal quod vidi subter Deum Israel juxta fluvium Chobar: et intellexi quia cherubim essent.*" Ezech. X, 20. Cf. Coptic Liturgy of St. Mark, known as St. Cyril.

[449] Ephrem RAHMANI, *op. cit.*, part. II, chap. III, p. 405.

[450] *Syrian liturgy:* "Thou hast sent the prophets who had already announced the salvation that was to come. Thou hast worked miracles and marvels by thy saints, and thou hast testified that they are the ministers of thy power."

Greek Liturgy: "Thou hast sent prophets and worked miracles by thy saints, who have flourished at all times."

[451] Cf. James of Sarugh.

Finally, it may be noted that the phrase in the epiclesis: "the *type* [452] of the body and blood of thy Christ" can be understood in an orthodox sense, as the body and blood are the types or symbols of that body which suffered upon the cross, notwithstanding that the body on the altar is one and the same body as suffered on Calvary.

The anaphora of *St. Cyril,* which begins with the words: "O Lord, merciful, holy and omnipotent," [453] is a translation from the Greek.

---

[452] Narsai in *Homily XXXII, "On the Church and Priesthood"* (Connolly, p. 67), says: "And he (priest) stretches out his hands and breaks the spiritual bread; and he signs the *type* of the body and blood that died and was raised up." Whereas in *Homily XVII, " An Exposition of the Mysteries" (Ibid.,* p. 17), he writes: " He (Christ) did not style them a type or a similitude, but body in reality (literally "in exactness") and blood in verity."

[453] Cf. preface to the Lord's prayer in the *Apostolic Constitutions.*

Syrian Catholic Patriarchate, Beirut

Syrian Catholic Church of Santa
Maria in Campo Marzio
(S. Ephrem), Rome

Invitation to Holy Communion in
the Syrian rite
Celebrated by a Chorepiscopus

(*Left to right*) Procurator to the Holy See · Bishop of Damascus · Mar Antony Peter Arida, Patriarch of Antioch of the Maronites · Bishop of Tripoli

Visit of the Maronite Patriarch to the Ruthenian College, Rome

BIBLIOGRAPHY

1. *Annuaire Pontificale Catholique.* 1930. E. Chardavoine. Paris: 5 Rue Bayard.

2. *Antioche, patriarcat syrien-catholique. Dictionnaire de Théologie Catholique. S. Vailhé.* T. I, col. 1430-1433.

3. *Cantus sacer Syrorum.* Conferenza al Pontificio Istituto di Musica Sacra. P. HINDO. 5 Marzo 1942.

4. *Disciplina Antiochena Antica, Siri,* III. Paolo HINDO. Fonti. Serie II, fascicolo XXVII. Tipografia Poliglotta Vaticana. 1942.

5. *Disciplina Antiochena Antica, Siri.* IV. Paolo HINDO. Fonti. Serie II, fascicolo XXVIII. Tipografia Poliglotta Vaticana. 1943.

6. *The Golden Book of Eastern Saints.* Donald ATTWATER. The Bruce Publishing Company, Milwaukee. 1938.

7. *Liturgica Historica.* Edmund BISHOP. Oxford: At the Clarendon Press. 1918.

8. *Manuel de Prières* à l'usage des Fidèles qui assistent à la Sainte Messe *selon le Rite Syrien. Mission Syrienne.* 15 Rue des Carmes, Paris. 1926.

9. *Missa Syriaca-Antiochena* quam ex lingua Syriaca in idioma Latinum traduxit cum commentario praevio *Maximilianus Princeps Saxoniae.* Sumptibus et typis Friderici Pustet. 1908.

10. *Petit Manuel de la Messe Syrienne.* Publié par ordre de S. B. Mgr. Ignace Rahmani. 2me édition. Paris: Maison de la Bonne Presse. 1923.

11. *La Santa Messa in rito Siro-Antiocheno.* Chiesa di S. Maria in Campo Marzio, Roma. 1942.

12. *The Syrian Liturgy.* H. W. CODRINGTON. *Eastern Churches Quarterly.* Vol. I, Nos. 1-4 (January-October), 1936.

13. *The Syrian Liturgy.* Donald ATTWATER. *Orate Fratres* (January-February), 1942.

ACKNOWLEDGEMENTS

1. His Eminence Cardinal Tappuni, Patriarch of Antioch of the Syrians.

2. Mgr. Paul Hindo, Chorepiscopus, Procurator of the Syrian Patriarch of Antioch to the Holy See.

3. Fr. Gabriel Khouri, Rector of the Syrian Church, Paris.

4. Fr. Isaac Armaleh, Syrian Catholic Patriarchate, Beirut.

5. Fr. Zacharia Malke, Rector of the Seminary of Sharfeh, Lebanon.

6. Dom Maurus Massé, O. S. B., Monastery of St. Benedict and St. Ephrem, Jerusalem.

Chapter III

MARONITE RITE

The Maronite rite is a variant of the West Syrian liturgy, which in the course of centuries has been considerably Romanised. It has the distinction of being the only Oriental rite which is not used by any body of dissidents.

Since at least the 16th century the whole "race" has acknowledged the supremacy of the Apostolic See, but the claim to *continuous* orthodoxy, asserted by Maronite writers, is without foundation.

History

The Syrian *Marunôyê*,[1] from which the rite takes its name, is derived from Maro, a 5th century solitary who lived near Cyr, between Emesa and Apamea on the banks of the Orontes. The details of his life[2] have been preserved by a near neighbour, Theodoret, bishop of Cyr.

It was probably to this recluse that St. John Chrysostom wrote from his exile in Cucusus (405), having made his acquaintance while Maro was studying under Libanius at Antioch. St. Maro is thought to have died[3] about the year

---

[1] Arabic, *Mawarinah.*
[2] *Dict. d'Arch. Chrét. et de Lit.* H. Leclercq. Art. *Maron.*, t. X. col. 2188.
[3] *Ibid.*

410, and his disciples [4] erected the monastery [5] of Beit-Marun to his memory.

Beit-Marun for more than five hundred years was a source of great influence in Syria, and may be described as the cradle of the Maronite people. When attacked by Monophysites, the monks, not only remained loyal to Chalcedon themselves, but also kept a part of the neighbouring population faithful to orthodoxy.

Procopius [6] speaks of Beit Marun as a bulwark of Byzantine language, culture and faith, set in the midst of a heretical and hostile population. The early history of the Maronites is impossible to unravel, and it does not seem at all clear when a nation or church was evolved. The text [7] of Denys of Tell Mahré († 845) shows that in the 7th century the term "Maronites" still implied the monks of Beit Marun.

In 517, the monks of *Syria Secunda* sent a report to Pope Hormisdas and to the metropolitan of Apamea on the persecutions inflicted by the emperor Anastasius I and the Monophysite patriarch of Antioch, Severus, in which the first signature was that of Alexander, archimandrite of St. Maro. The *mémoire* to the pope, which is preserved in the *acta* of the fifth general council, refers to him as the "common father of the whole Church" and the "infallible father." The apocrisarius Paul, in the name of the monks

---

[4] THEODORET, *Religionis Historia*, XVI; ap. MIGNE, *P. G.*, LXXXII.

[5] The Arab historian Abulfida († 1331) says that Marcian in the second year of his reign (452) enlarged the monastery: *Historia praeislamica*, ed. H. Fleisher, 1831, p. 113. Abulfida entitles it: *Ancient History*. The monastery of St. Maro is thought to have been situated near Afamyah (Famyah) in the valley of the Orontes, which is known to-day as Qalhat al-Madiq.

[6] *De Aedificio*, V, 9.

[7] *Dict. d'Arch. Chrét. et de Lit.*, t. X, col. 2192.

of St. Maro, subscribed in 536 at Constantinople to the decrees of Chalcedon; while the same monastery at the second council of Constantinople (553) was represented by the priest John and the deacon Paul. The letter [8] of the monks of Beit Marun to the Jacobites, written a little after 591, puts into relief the orthodoxy of the community in the 6th century, and at the same time witnesses to the pre-eminence of their monastery in Syria. The letter was addressed to "the particular sect of monks, who shave their heads: to the partisans of Peter, who form one of the many sects of Eutychius and Severus .... from the orthodox Maronite monks, sons of the holy Catholic Church."

Theodore, a Jacobite monk of the monastery of Beit Mar Arbaz, answered in a "reply and refutation of the five chapters that the monks of the monastery of Maro, after having left Antioch, sent from the village of Armenaze to the orthodox monks of the holy monasteries of Gzara, to the branches of the root of Leo, the Maronite monks, Philip and Thomas."

The monks of Beit Marun represented the Greek or imperialist element, which, apart from theological differences, the Jacobites cordially hated, and throughout the 6th century the official language of the monks was Greek.

The emperor Heraclius [9] (575-641) in 628 visited Beit Marun and enriched it with many gifts, and the monks for their part were staunch supporters of the religious policy of the emperor.

---

[8] The manuscript (8th century), which is in the British Museum, takes the form of a treatise in five chapters, with the Jacobite reply.

[9] Dict. d'Arch. Chrét. et de Lit., t. X, col. 2191. The visit is recorded by Eutyches, patriarch of Alexandria. MIGNE, P. G., CXI, col. 1089.

Monothelitism

The propositions made by Heraclius to the Jacobite patriarch, Athanasius, already contain ideas essential to Monothelitism. In 638, the emperor, believing that the only certain bulwark against the dismemberment of the Empire by the Arabs lay in a common uniform faith, in an attempt to win the support of all parties, issued the *Ekthesis*. This well-intentioned document, however, had the effect of producing yet another heresy, Monothelitism. It forbade as blameworthy the use of such expressions as "one" or "two energies," and affirmed in Christ one single will, without any confusion of the two natures, which each preserve with their own attributes in a single person, the Word made flesh, who has worked miracles and endured sufferings.

The compromise reduced the human nature of our Lord to the "irrational irresponsible instrument of his divinity," thereby denying the real and perfect humanity.

At first, the longed-for healing of the schism appeared as practical politics, and the prospect of one great Church overjoyed Sergius I, patriarch of Constantinople (610-638), the author of the compromise, and the emperor. Sergius wrote that controversy was at an end by the adoption of the simple phrase, "one will, one energy;" while all those who were again united named Leo and Chalcedon in their diptychs.

Even the pope [19] (Honorius I, 625-638) seemed to acquiesce in the new teaching, although, injudicious and

---

[19] Pope Honorius neither defined nor condemned; he praised Sergius for dropping the expression "one operation" (or "energy"), but agreed with him that no reference should be made to "two operations" either; and admitted that "there being only one principle of action or one direction of the will in Christ, therefore there must be one will also." Unless

indiscreet as he was, he was preserved from formal heresy. Many, however, were undeceived by the real implications of the *Ekthesis*. The Monophysites saw in it a betrayal of Chalcedon,—"We have not gone to Chalcedon: Chalcedon has come to us;" while Sophronius, patriarch of Jerusalem (634-638), the unflinching orthodox opponent, realised that the formula was contrary to Catholic doctrine.

The bishops of Cyprus in 643 sent a letter to Pope Theodore (642-649), in which they said: "disperse the rule of the foolish with the light of thy divine knowledge, O most holy. Destroy the blasphemies and insolence of the new heretics with their novel expressions."

The Lateran council (649), held under Pope St. Martin I (649-655), formally condemned the *Ekthesis* (638) and the *Typos* [11] (648), as well as the altogether insufficient expression formulated by Severus of Antioch, *Una deivirilis operatio,* [12] by which all the actions, divine as well as human, are performed.

An encyclical letter was sent to the "entire sacred plenitude of the Catholic Church," ordering the deposition of those bishops who refused to accept the findings of the council. The emperor, [13] Constans II (641-668), sent his exarch to kidnap the pope, with instructions to bring him

he meant by "one will" simply a perfect concord of the divine and human wills, this is Monothelite heresy. In any case, this was not an *ex cathedra* decision; its whole tenor disclaimed any intention of settling the disputed matters; he wrote: "we must not wrest what they say into church dogmas." Donald ATTWATER, *A Dictionary of the Popes* (London, 1939), p. 65.

[11] The *Typos*, which was published on the initiative of the patriarch of Constantinople (Paul) to put an end to the discussions on Monothelitism, forbade speaking of either one or two energies or wills.

[12] μία θεανδρικὴ ἐνέργεια

[13] The Byzantine church was in schism, with 7 Monothelite patriarchs, from 640-681.

to Constantinople. St. Martin I was banished to the Crimea, where he died [14] as a result of his ill treatment (September 16, 655). The West remained firm in its opposition to Monothelitism, but, although the Eastern church was officially compromised, there were not wanting martyrs to orthodoxy. Thus, St. Maximus, abbot of Chrysopolis (Skutari), was so maltreated that he died in great suffering (662). In the same year, also, his disciple Anastasius fell a victim to the hatred of the heretics; while four years later that other Anastasius, the apocrisarius, suffered a like fate.

Constantine IV Pogonatos (668-685) in 680 [15] presided at the sixth ecumenical council, the third of Constantinople, in which the Eastern church returned to Catholic unity, although the Maronites refused to accept the council. The decisions of the Lateran Council (680) against Monothelitism were accepted and, although Honorius was condemned for his pusillanimity, the inerrancy of the Apostolic See was affirmed.

The short reign of Philippicus (712-713) saw a recrudescence of the heresy in the Byzantine empire. In an edict addressed to Pope Constantine (708-715), the emperor ordered his subjects to acknowledge one single will in our Lord; while the memory of Patriarch Sergius, Pope Honorius and all those who had been condemned by the sixth council were rehabilitated, with their names restored to the diptychs. On the accession of Anastasius II (713-715), orthodoxy was reestablished, and Monothelitism was never again promulgated as the religion of the empire.

The monks of Beit Marun, as we have seen, supported the religious policy of the emperor Heraclius, and there is

---

[14] St. Martin I was the last martyr pope. He is honoured by Rome on November 12, and by Constantinople on April 13 and September 20.

[15] *Incontro ai fratelli separati di Oriente* (Rome, 1945), p. 19.

little doubt that they continued to give the same assistance to his successors. The Chronicle of Michael [16] the Syrian, which was taken in great part from that of Denys of Tell Mahré († 845), speaks of the Maronite community affording active help to the emperor in trying to coerce the Jacobite monks into accepting the new formula. In 659, a public dispute took place at Antioch between the Maronites and Jacobites, in which the latter were worsted and compelled by the Arab authorities to pay a fine.

When the emperor returned to orthodoxy (680), the monks of Beit Marun seem to have retained the Monothelite [17] creed, and to have similarly influenced the neighbouring population.

The Chronicle of Michael says: "The Maronites remained as they are now. They ordain a patriarch and bishop from their convent. They are separated from Maximus in that they confess only one will in Christ, and say, 'who was crucified for us.' But they accept the synod of Chalcedon." The orthodox thus came to be called "Maximists," in memory of the martyr.

In 727 a dispute was said to have taken place between the Maximists and the party of Beit Marun, when it was alleged that the bishop and his monks had perverted the neighbouring Melkites and had contended with the orthodox for possession of a church at Aleppo.

St. Germanus [18] of Constantinople (ab. 735) spoke of "some heretics who, rejecting the 5th and 6th councils, nevertheless contend against the Jacobites. The latter treat them as men without sense, because, while accepting the

---

[16] Jacobite patriarch of Antioch, 1166-1199.
[17] The Monothelitism may have been verbal rather than real.
[18] *De Haeresibus et Synodis.*

4th council, they try to reject the next two. Such are the Maronites, whose monastery is situated in the mountains of Syria."

St. John Damascene [19] (749) regarded the Maronites as heretical, as they continued to add the words σταυρωθεὶς δι' ἡμας to the trisagion.

The continual persecution by the Jacobites, who had made common cause with the Arabs, compelled the Maronites to invoke the aid of the Nestorians, who had found favour at the court of Bagdad. Such an alliance, however, could not have any lasting effect, and the Nestorian patriarch, Timothy I (780-823), required the acceptance of the formula, "Two natural hypostases in one *prosopon* of the Son," in addition to the approval of Nestorius, Theodore and Diodore, and a denunciation of "that heretic Cyril." Further evidence as to the Monothelitism of the Maronites is forthcoming from the Melkite controversialist, Abukara [20] († ab. 820); the Jacobite theologian, Habib Abu-Raita; and the treatise *On the Reception of Heretics,* attributed to the priest Timothy.

In spite of the evidence, however, Maronite historians, since the 16th century, have maintained the continuous orthodoxy of their church, although it is difficult to see how there could have been two Syrian churches both in communion with Rome, and yet treating each other as mutually heretical. Boulos al-Raheb, bishop of Sidon (end of the 13th century), certainly thought that the Maronites were heretical, and said that they admit only one divine will and one single

[19] μαρωνίσομεν προσθέμενοι τῷ τρισαγίῳ τὴν σταύρωριν:"We shall be following Maro, if we join the crucifixion to our trisagion."*De Hymno Trisagio.* Chap. V; cf. περὶ ὀρθοῦ φρονήματος.
[20] Metropolitan of Harran, who reproached the Maronites for not accepting the 5th and 6th general councils.

divine energy in our Lord; while no papal letter was received by them prior to the bull [21] of Innocent III in 1215.

The upholders [22] of continuous orthodoxy maintain that the controversy concerning the two wills did not reach Syria before the year 727, when it was introduced by some prisoners of the Arabs. The Maronites [23] even then, the apologia continues, were not Monothelites in the sense in which the heresy had been condemned, for, until they were enlightened by the Crusaders, they had never heard of the council! The narrative of Denys of Tell Mahré, which was reproduced in the Chronicle of Michael the Syrian, is described as "interpolated, badly interpreted or falsely attributed to ancient authors;" while the accusation of heresy is largely attributed to the evil testimony of William of Tyre († 1190), who copied the mendacious history of Eutychius, patriarch of Alexandria (10th century). Those Maronite manuscripts which appear to contain heresy have had the misfortune to fall into the hands of careless or unscrupulous copyists.

In their beginnings, the Maronites lived in and around the monastery, from whence they spread in the valley of the Orontes, and to Mabug (Hierapolis), Qennesrin, Aleppo and, finally, Antioch. Several bishops by the beginning of the 9th century would seem to have formed the nucleus of a hierarchy, but long before this the Maronites themselves affirm that they had a succession of patriarchs [24] of Antioch, who were in communion with Rome. If however such had existed, they would have sent representatives to the general

[21] *Quia divinae sapientiae.*

[22] *Dictionnaire de Théologie Catholique.* P. DIB, Art. *Maronite* (*Eglise*), vol. X, col. 12.

[23] *Ibid.,* col. 16.

[24] Mons. Peter Sfair (*La Messa Siro-Maronita,* Rome, 1946, p. 120) maintains that the Maronite patriarchate was instituted in 685, after the death of Theophanes, catholic patriarch of Antioch.

councils of 787 and 869, after the example of their Greek colleagues of Antioch, Jerusalem and Alexandria.   Their abstention would be inexplicable for patriarchs who place the recognition of papal supremacy at the basis of their religious connections, and who yet abstain from appearing at the councils which the popes of Rome summon.   On the other hand, Denys [25] of Tel-Mahré († 845) speaks of the Maronites "ordaining a patriarch and bishops from their monastery." A list of patriarchs from John Maro († 707) to the beginning of the 12th century is given by Le Quien in *Oriens Christianus*, but it is entirely worthless and largely mythical.

John Maro, not to be confused with the earlier hermit of the same name, is said by the Maronites themselves to have preserved the autonomy of his people by defeating the Greeks near Amium (649), after the monastery had been destroyed by the forces of Justin II, since the monks had refused to follow the emperor in his heresy.   He is alleged also to have been patriarch of Antioch (685-707), although the evidence for his existence [26] is very slender.   It has no other guarantee than an anonymous chronicle written in Syriac and Arabic in 1305, and no other ancient author, whether Christian or Mussulman, makes the least allusion to him, beyond a reference by Eutychius, [27] the 10th century Melkite patriarch of Alexandria, to a monk named Maro who lived in Syria in the time of the emperor Maurice (582-602), and affirmed in Christ two natures, one will, one operation, and one person.

The alleged life of John Maro was first published in 1495 by Gabriel Barclai, Maronite bishop of Nikosia, and

---

[25] In the Chronicle of Michael the Syrian, ed. Chabot, II, 511.

[26] *Qui nunquam fuit.*"   RENAUDOT, *Lit. Orient. Collect.*, t. II, p. 343.

[27] *Dict. d'Arch. Chrét.*, t. X, col. 2197-2198.

translated into Latin by the Franciscan Quaresmius in 1639. No reliability therefore can be placed in the supposed works of John Maro. The *Exposition of the Liturgy of St. James* is probably a commentary made by the 12th century Monophysite, Denys bar Salibi, and altered later to suit the liturgical changes of the Maronites; while the *Treatise on the Faith* is very similar to the theological treatise of Leontius of Constantinople. This latter book is presumably from the second half of the 6th century and the first half of the 7th, so that it is earlier than the alleged date of John Maro, and contains no reference to a heresy unknown at the time.

The Maronites are permitted to keep the feast of this John Maro on March 2, although the Congregation of Sacred Rites (1715) and the bull *Inter Caetera* (September 28, 1753) have both made a careful distinction between the solitary of the 5th century and the 7th century "patriarch."

The Coming of the Arabs

The invasion of the Arabs caused the Maronites to abandon the rich plains of Syria and to take refuge in the mountains of Lebanon. This emigration did not take place all at once, but it began at the end of the 7th century and continued progressively. Thus it came about that the Maronites had henceforward a definite country, and by the middle of the 8th century they had begun to build churches. [28]

The original monastery of Beit Marun for a long time continued to be a centre of prosperity, although the Maronite

---

[28] e. g. Mar Mâmâ at Ehden, built in 749. *Dict. d'Arch. Chrét. et de Lit.*, t. X, col. 2202.

migrations necessarily affected vocations. The exact date of the ruin and destruction of the monastery is unknown. The reply of the Nestorian patriarch to the Maronite request for protection suggests that it was in full activity in 791, and one learns from Denys of Tell Mahré († 845) that the community was flourishing in the first half of the 9th century, since bishops [29] were chosen from among the members of the community. It would appear likely that the disaster took place in the 10th century, before 939, when the seat of the patriarchate was moved from Beit Marun to the Lebanon. The Arab historian Macudi († 956) tells us that the monastery "was devastated, as well as the cells which surrounded it, as a result of the repeated invasions of the Arabs and the violence of the sultan," but he does not give any clue as to the name of the sultan.

Catholic Unity

The Crusades brought the Maronites into personal contact with the Latin west, and William of Tyre,[30] after a long residence in Syria, has told the story of the conversion in 1182 of 40,000 souls. Mgr. Dib,[31] determined at all costs to maintain the theory of continuous orthodoxy, has suggested that this "conversion" was nothing more than a public act of recognition on the part of the Maronites of the true pope as against his rival! The narrative, however, is incompatible with such an explanation: "After they (the nation which had

[29] The monastery of St. Antony the Great at Kosaya ("Weariness [or "Treasure"] of Life"), which is first mentioned in a document of the year 1104, claims in another, dated 1215, to be the seat of the first Maronite bishops. Donald ATTWATER, *Golden Book of Eastern Saints*, p. 158.
[30] *Historia rerum transmarinarum*, lib. XXII, chap. VIII.
[31] *Dict. de Théol. Cath.*, t. X, col. 23-24.

been converted near Bylos) had for five hundred years adhered to the false teaching of a heresiarch named Maro, so that they took from him the name of Maronites, and, being separated from the true Church had been following their own peculiar liturgy (*ab ecclesia sequestrati seorsim sacramenta conficerent sua*), they came to the patriarch of Antioch, Amaury, the third of the Latin patriarchs, and having abjured their error, were, with their patriarch and some bishops, reunited to the true Church. They declared themselves ready to accept and observe the prescriptions of the Roman Church. There were more than forty thousand of them, occupying the whole region of the Lebanon, and they were of great use to the Latins in the war against the Saracens. The error of Maro and his adherents is and was, as may be read in the sixth council, that in Jesus Christ there was, and had been since the beginning, only one will and one energy. And after their separation they had embraced still other pernicious doctrines." This "inspiration of heaven," as William of Tyre called the conversion, is said by some Maronite apologists to have affected only a small part of the nation, which through ignorance had been led into heresy by Bishop Thomas of Kfar-tas, whereas the majority of the people had remained faithful to Catholicism.

Jacques de Vitry,[32] bishop of Tyre (ab. 1160-1240), gives an account of the conversion similar to William of Tyre: "A people called Maronites from the name of a certain man, their master, Maro, a heretic, who affirmed that there was in Jesus but one will or operation. They remained separated from the Church nearly five hundred years. At last, their hearts being turned, they made profession of the Catholic faith in the presence of the venerable father Amau-

---

[32] *Historia Hierosolymitana.*

ry,[33] patriarch of Antioch, and adopted the traditions of the Roman Church."

The era of the Crusades was productive of a renaissance[34] in the Maronite church, and the period was one of great building activity. Examples of the period, showing a Syrian style influenced by the Byzantine, may be found in the churches of Hattun, Meïphuq, Helta, Scheptïn, Tula, Bhadidat, Ma'ad, Khura and Semar-Jebaïl.

Early in the 13th century, Pope Innocent III excommunicated the patriarch Luke († 1209), a prelate whose existence has been attested by Faustus Nairon and Le Quien, although Mgr. Dib has maintained that so early as 1183 the Maronite church had been governed by Jeremias II, a staunch Catholic. Jeremias was certainly present at the Lateran council of 1215, and he returned to Syria accompanied by a cardinal legate, who summoned a synod at Tyre. The pope, also, wrote to the patriarch to obtain an express acknowledgement of the two wills in our Lord.

The Jacobite Gregory Bar Hebraeus, who died in 1286, declared that the Maronites were infected with the heresy of Monothelitism.

In 1342, the Maronites of Jerusalem were certainly in communion with the Catholic Church, for in that year Pope Clement VI, in the bull *Gratias agimus,* confirmed the donation of the Upper Room of the Last Supper to the Franciscans, which had been made about nine years earlier by Robert of Anjou, king of Naples, and Sanchia, his wife. It had been the liberality of this queen that gave the Maronites the chapel of the Holy Cross in the church of the

---

[33] The third of the Latin patriarchs whom the Crusaders had set up at Antioch.

[34] *Dict. de Théol. Cath.,* t. X, col. 38-39.

Holy Sepulchre, and the right to use altars in four other churches, one of which was the Upper Room.

The succession of patriarchs before the 15th century seems very uncertain, and the difficulty as to names is seen by comparing the list given by Mgr. Dib [35] with that supplied by Le Quien. [36]

The council of Florence (1438-1445) promulgated a decree (August 7, 1445, *Benedictus sit Deus*) affecting the Maronites, but it contained nothing beyond the requirements for the oriental churches in general. Isaac, a delegate of Elias, archbishop of Cyprus, was present at the council and made a profession of Catholic faith.

Since the patriarchate of James of Hamet (1439-1458), all the Maronite patriarchs have been strictly orthodox.

In 1445, many of the Maronites of Cyprus, [37] under Archbishop Elias, returned to Catholic unity, although a letter of Pope Pius II (1458-1464) to Mahomet II speaks of the nation as still heretical. An apostolate in Cyprus was carried out in the latter part of the 15th century by Gryphon, a Flemish Franciscan, and several of his converts became members of the order. One of these, Gabriel Glai, [38] suc-

---

[35] The list is based on that of Duaihi, a 17th century patriarch.

[36] This list has been taken from Gabriel Glai, Faustus Nairon and even from Duaihi himself.

[37] The first settlement of Maronites in Cyprus probably dates from the 9th century, at the time of the persecution in Syria and Palestine under Al-Mamun (813-833). A second immigration followed the failure of the Crusades.

At one time there were 72 Maronite villages in Cyprus, but Turkish rule has had the effect of reducing their number to 5, with a population of about 1,000. The villages lie across the northern part of the island following the Kyrenia range of mountains, with Kormakiti as the chief place.

The Maronite bishop of Cyprus lives in the Lebanon.

[38] Barclaïus, Benclaïus.

ceeded to the bishopric of Lefkosia (Cyprus). He has been claimed by Mgr. Dib [39] as one of the principal precursors of the latinisation of the Maronite liturgy and discipline, and he was perhaps the first scholar to advance the theory of the continuous orthodoxy of his church. In 1495, Gabriel Glai published a letter, taken from a document written in 1315, in which he gave a list of the eighteen Maronite patriarchs who were alleged to have ruled at Antioch.

Pope Paul II in a reply (1468) to Peter, the Maronite patriarch, referred to the former heresy of his church; while Fr. Suriano, a Franciscan who was sent to Syria in 1515 by Pope Leo X to correct abuses, definitely maintained that the patriarch John Maro was a heretic.

In respect to the conversion of the Cypriot Maronites, Mgr. Dib again sees nothing but misrepresentation on the part of the apostolic visitors to the island, with William of Tyre still the *fons et origo* of all the mischief. Thus, Andrew of Colossus, who had been charged by Pope Eugenius IV (1431-1447) to visit the Maronites, is said to have contented himself with studying the crusading author, a vade-mecum of all pontifical delegations, and in this way to have convinced himself of the Monothelitism of the Maronites! It seems strange, however, if Mgr. Dib is correct in his theory, that there was no protest on the part of the misrepresented and maligned Maronites; while the apostolic visitor showed singularly little loyalty to his mission in confining his activities to a study of William of Tyre, and neglecting all other sources of information.

The presence of Maronites at the council of Nikosia (1340) goes for nothing, as Byzantines and Jacobites were also present, and it appears to have been the custom in

[39] *Dict. de Théol. Cath.*, t. X, col. 48.

Cyprus to class all orientals as subject to the Latin hierarchy.

Unfortunately, more direct intercourse with Rome tended to latinise the Maronite church, and we find the patriarch Simon Peter writing to the Lateran council of 1516, in which he expressed the view that Rome should be the norm in regard to the offices.

The first known Maronite council was held on Maundy Thursday 1557 under the patriarch, Moses of Akkar, when, in the presence of 8 archbishops and about 400 priests, the chrism was consecrated. In 1562, Pope Pius IV granted the patriarch authority to absolve certain heretics, at the same time commending his loyalty to the Apostolic See. Patriarch Michael in 1577 received the pallium from Gregory XIII, together with an Arabic translation of the decrees and canons of the council of Trent and a catechism suitable for parish priests. The synod of Kannobin, held by the patriarch Sergius on March 19, 1596, specifically anathematised the errors of which the Maronites had been accused: Monothelitism; denial of the double procession of the Holy Spirit, purgatory, and of original sin. The following propositions were also condemned: that one can lawfully deny the faith with the lips, at the same time retaining it in the heart; confirmation is not a sacrament distinct from baptism; and divorce is permissable for adultery and incurable disease.

In 1581, Pope Gregory XIII, in the bull *Exigit incumbentis*, permitted a hospice for Maronites in Rome, which was established by the bull *Salvatoris nostri* near the church of San Giovanni della Ficoccia in the rione of *Trevi*. The hospice in 1584 was transformed by the bull *Humana sic ferunt* into a college, which lasted until the French Revolution. The site was later occupied by the Polish college, but the retention of the name Via dei Maroniti recalls the original foundation.

A seminary (St. Ephrem) for the rite was founded by Pope Innocent X (1644-1655) at Ravenna, but it was unsuccessful, and in 1665 it was united with the Roman college.

At the beginning of the 17th century, a Maronite monk named Victor Scialak taught oriental languages at Rome. He translated into Latin the several liturgies ascribed to St. Basil, St. Gregory of Nyssa and St. Cyril of Alexandria. The collection was printed at Augsburg in 1604.

Many well known *savants* have been connected with the Roman College. George Amira, [40] the "Grammarian," who later became patriarch (1633-1644), was distinguished for his great devotion to the Holy See, and had the singular privilege [41] of celebrating Mass in the "Latin language and ceremonies and in Syriac with the ceremonies of the Maronites, according to the time and his devotion he officiated in either language."

Other famous *alumni* include Isaac of Schadre; Gabriel Siuni († 1648), who was a professor at the *Sapienza*, interpreter to King Louis XIII of France, and collaborator in the Polyglot Bible; Abraham of Hakel (*Ecchelensis*); and the Assemani.

Four members of the family of Assemani have distinguished themselves in the realm of letters—Joseph Simon (1687-1768); Stephen Evodius (1707-1782); Joseph Aloysius (1710-1782); and Simon (1752-1821). Joseph Simon, Maronite archbishop of Tyre, was the author of the *Bibliotheca Orientalis*, a work which appeared in Rome between the years 1719 and 1728. Joseph Aloysius, his nephew, wrote

---

[40] Pope Urban VIII spoke of him as the "Light of the Eastern Church." *Dict. de Théol. Cath.*, t. X, col. 66.

[41] Quoted by Fr. Eugène Roger, a contemporary of the patriarch, ap. *Ibid.*

the *Codex Liturgicus Ecclesiae,* but only nine volumes out of the proposed sixteen were published.

It is largely through the work of these Maronite scholars that European *savants* have been made aware of the literary riches to be found in the Syrian manuscripts.

A further stage in latinisation was reached in the patriarchate of Joseph Risi, who held a council in 1598 at Moise. Eight years later (1606), the Maronites adopted the Gregorian calendar, the second [12] oriental church to abandon the Julian mode of reckoning. The liturgical changes appear to have been moderate in character, but Pope Paul V (1605-1621) by the brief *Fraternitatis suae litteras* in 1610 directed the patriarch, John Makhluf, to restore the "ancient (Maronite) customs not contrary to the Catholic faith."

In the 17th century, [13] two Maronite patriarchs [44] earned a reputation for success in the conversion of Jacobites; while a third, Stephen Duaihi of Ehden (1670-1704), an *alumnus* of Rome and an international scholar of repute, founded a seminary at Kannobin, and reformed the monastic life in the country.

Peter James II Aued was deposed and degraded from the office of patriarch for alleged misdemeanours, but, although a successor (Joseph Mobarak) was nominated, Rome refused to accept the new appointment, and in 1713 James was reinstated, and governed the patriarchate until his death (1733).

[12] The Italo-Greeks had received the Gregorian calendar in 1582. It was not before 1836 that the Syrian and Chaldean churches accepted the new method of reckoning.

[43] The Maronites in this century underwent a severe persecution, and among those who suffered martyrdom one of the most noteworthy was Yunes Abu Risq, a rich and influential layman of the Lebanon (1697).

[44] Joseph III 'Akur (1644-1647); John XI Soffra (1648-1656).

The council of the Lebanon (*al-magmah allubnāni*) was held in the time of Joseph Dergham Al-Khazan, but the Maronite hierarchy had opposed the summoning of the assembly, as they feared lest their privileges might be curtailed, and resented the abolition of abuses which long custom had made dear to them.   Joseph Simon Assemani and Stephen Evodius Assemani were present as the delegates of Pope Clement XII (1730-1740), with an express mandate for the publication of the decrees of the council of Trent. The council met in 1736 in the monastery of St. Mary of Luweiza, [15] and it may be said to have given the Maronite church its constitutional charter.   Sixteen eastern bishops assisted at the sessions, fourteen Maronites, one Syrian, and one Armenian. The chief abuses which the council corrected were summarised in a letter, written shortly before the opening of the assembly:

a) Maronite bishops by ancient custom had a number of religious women in their households, whose lodgings were often separated from the prelates, by a communicating door.

b) The patriarch, who in accordance with eastern usage reserved to himself the sole right of consecrating the holy oils, was accustomed to demand a fee when distributing them to his bishops and clergy.

c) The blessed sacrament, except in monasteries of men and women, was rarely reserved, although the *Nomocanon* known as the *Directorium* had enjoined that "the priest should take one of the hosts that the bishop consecrated on Maundy Thursday, to keep it in the tabernacle of the mysteries, which is in the sanctuary, until the Maundy Thursday of the following year. He will then distribute it to the faithful and replace it by a newly consecrated host." The same

[15] *Deir Saidat al-Luaizeh*, "our Lady of the almond trees."

canon, also, directed that the chrism should be kept in the same receptacle as the sacrament.

James of Edessa († 708) in the seventh answer to his disciple Addai severely censured the practice of keeping the host for a whole year.

d) Marriage dispensations were granted for money payment.

e) Churches lacked becoming ornaments and "the members of Jesus Christ, necessary succour."

f) Bishops, [46] who were altogether too numerous, had neither fixed boundaries to their sees nor residences.

g) The Maronites of Aleppo, for the last 10 or 12 years, had made a practice of celebrating the liturgy in Arabic.

h) Priests [47] were forbidden to translate the Syriac text into Arabic during the liturgy.

In addition to reforming abuses, the council ordered the insertion of the *filioque* into the creed; the restoration of the name of the pope to the diptychs; the restriction of administering confirmation to bishops; and the blessing of the chrism and holy oils on Maundy Thursday. Other enactments prescribed azyme bread, which was to be made with flour and water, and without the Syrian addition [48] of oil and salt;

[46] There were 15 bishops to 150 parishes.
A somewhat similar multiplicity of bishops without fixed sees existed at one time in Ireland, a state of affairs partially rectified by the national synod of Rathbreasil (Westmeath) in 1110. Ailbe J. LUDDY, *Life of St. Malachy* (M. H. Gill, Dublin, 1930), chap. II, pp. 9, 12, 13.

[47] There was no objection to Arabic translations of the liturgy, but it was thought that if translations were made at sight for the people it might be possible for a hasty rendering to give rise to unorthodox expressions.

[48] "*Sedulo curent ii quorum munus est eucharisticum panem preparandi et ferro ad id preparato coquendi, ne praeter farinam et aquam naturalem quidquam aliud admisceant. Oleum enim et sal quae Jacobiti,*

while the reception of the chalice was restricted to priests and deacons. The hierarchy was definitely organised, with the number of bishops reduced to 8, who could not be deposed without the sanction of the Holy See; while the ceremonial of ordination was revised and supplemented. The number of councils recorded in the synaxary was increased from 6 to 10, by the addition of II Nicaea (787); IV Constantinople (869); Florence (1438-1445); and Trent (1545-1563). The council of the Lebanon admitted the continuous orthodoxy of the Maronites; while it confirmed the privileges of the patriarch in the following particulars: the consecration of all bishops; consecration of the chrism (*meirûn*); nomination of all *periodeutes* ("vicars forane"), archpriests and chorepiscopi; reservation of certain sins; [49] and the right of *ius liturgicum*, which included not only the approval of all service books and catechisms, but also the prohibition, without express permission, of any translation from Syriac into Arabic.

More than a century elapsed before the decrees of the council were all fully put into practice. The canons were promulgated (1788) in the Lebanon in Arabic, whereas the Latin text, which alone had received approval *in forma specifica,* [50] contained many notable differences.

An example of the fondness of the oriental for hyperbole may be seen in a letter sent by the Maronite patriarch to the pope after the conclusion of the council: "God so loved the world that he sent his only-begotten Son; so most

ac Nestoriani in suis hostiis fermentatis addunt, nec in sacra historia in pane illo a Christo consecrato fuisse leguntur, nec ab iis ecclesiis, in quibus azymorum aut fermenti usus vigent, admittuntur."

[49] Apostasy; use of holy things for sorcery; attack on the person of a bishop; expulsion of a parish priest by his parishoners.

[50] Constitution *Singularis Romanorum,* 1741.

blessed father thou hast loved us as to send a man most acceptable to thee and us."

In 1743, Pope Benedict XIV (1740-1758) dismissed the claims of two rival patriarchs, and appointed *motu proprio* Simon 'Auad, archbishop of Damascus. A dispute was settled between Maronites and Melkites, and the pope forbade the former either to mix in Melkite affairs or to proselytize, [51] as, on the strength of an ancient Roman constitution authorising the Maronite patriarch to receive heretics and schismatics, efforts were being made to change Melkites into Maronites. By way of retaliation, Cyril VI, the Melkite patriarch, had destroyed pictures of St. John Maro, asserting that he and his followers had been Monothelites. The pope, in the bull *Inter Caetera* (1753), gave a stern rebuke to Cyril, and restored peace.

A profession of faith, based on the constitution *Nuper ad nos* (March 16, 1743), was demanded of the Maronites, who were required to give a formal adhesion to the first eight general councils, as well as to those of Florence and Trent. Acceptance of Chalcedon [52] included a condemnation of the Monophysite addition ("who was crucified for us") to the trisagion; while that of the third council of Constantinople [53] entailed a refutation of Monothelitism.

[51] *Demandatum Caelitus*, clause XII.

[52] "*Per quam definitionem damnatur impia haeresis illorum, qui Trisagio ab angelis tradito et in praefata Chalcedonensi Synodo decantato.*" "*Sanctus Deus, sanctus fortis, sanctus immortalis, miserere nobis,*" addebant: "*qui crucifixus est pro nobis*" atque ideo divinam naturam trium personarum passibilem asserebant et mortalem."

[53] "*Profiteor, quod in illa contra Monothelitas definitum est, in uno eodemque Domino nostro Jesu Christo duas esse naturales operationes indivise inconvertibiliter, inseparabiliter, inconfuse, et humanam ejus voluntatem non contrariam sed subjectam divinae ejus atque omnipotenti voluntati.*"

The profession of faith also demanded explicit belief in the seven sacraments, apostolic and ecclesiastical tradition, indulgences, and the supremacy of the pope.

Modern History

In the latter half of the 18th century, the Maronite church was disturbed by the eccentricities and obstinacy of Anna Aggemi, a nun of Aleppo, who from her alleged nocturnal visits to India in the grasp of spirits was known as Idjaïme Hindîyé. She founded a congregation of the Sacred Heart at Bekorki in 1750, but spread many errors, even claiming to be hypostatically united to Christ.

The patriarch, Joseph Estephan, was deceived, and so warmly espoused her cause that he was delated to Rome. The pope by the brief *Ad Supremum* (1752) had in the time of his predecessor already suppressed the congregation, but little attention had been paid to the condemnation. The case of Hindîyé dragged on for some years, and was the cause of much controversy and disorder. In 1779, the patriarch was suspended from the exercise of his functions, and the suppression of the congregation was finally achieved; while the nun who had been responsible for so much trouble was sent to the convent of Saidat Al-Haqlah (Our Lady of the Fields), where in 1798 she died. Joseph Estephan submitted to the Holy See, and by the brief *Maximum nobis* (1784) was reinstated in the patriarchate. A synod was held at Bekorki in 1790, with the object of obtaining compliance with the statutes of the council of Lebanon, and in 1818 a synod [54] met at Loaïsah (Luweiza) for the same purpose, but it was not before the patriarchate of Joseph

[54] In the patriarchate of John Al-Helu.

Hobaich (1823-1845) that complete obedience was achieved. Joseph Estephan († 1793), perhaps on account of the congregation of nuns under that title, had been a warm supporter of devotion to the Sacred Heart, [55] establishing the feast with a solemnity similar to Easter and the Ascension.

Joseph Hobaich showed a zeal for discipline and ecclesiastical education, but his rule was not so happy in respect to liturgical matters, and he displayed a marked approval of latinisation: [56] *Aux yeux des liturgistes au moins, cette malencontreuse réforme du rit traditionnel projette une ombre sur ce pontificat, par ailleurs si bienfaisant.*

In 1867, the patriarch (Paul Mas'ad), for the second time in history, visited Rome in person, on the occasion of the 18th centenary of St. Peter and St. Paul. [57] He was not present, however, at the Vatican council (1870), for it is said that he was fearful of losing his privileges should the bull *Reversurus* be applied to the Maronites. Four bishops of the rite attended the sessions in St. Peter's, and voted with the minority until the day of the definition of papal infallibility.

Under Turkish rule, the Maronites in the mountains [58] of the Lebanon were granted semi-independence, with feudal power centralised in an emir, but until the second half of the 19th century there was always the possibility of an outbreak of persecution. The letters of the patriarchs to Rome continually refer to the hardships which the Maronites had to suffer for the Catholic faith, and Pope Alexan-

---

[55] *Dict. de Théol. Cath.*, t. X, col. 93. The Maronite people on May 29, 1921, were consecrated by the patriarch, Elias Hoyek, to the Sacred Heart.

[56] *Dict. de Théol. Cath.*, t. X, col. 104.

[57] The first patriarch to visit Rome was Jeremias Al'Amchiti, who died in 1230.

[58] *Jebal Libnân*, "White Mountain."

der VII [59] referred to them as roses set among thorns: *Veluti rosas esse inter orientalium infidelium, haereticorum et schismaticorum spinas, gratia Dei florentes.*

With the fall of the emir Bashir, at the beginning of the 19th century, their position became more precarious and the power of the Druses, the hereditary enemies of the Maronites, increased.

Two emirs were appointed with the title of *kaimakam,* one from each nation, but war broke out between them in 1845. Fifteen years later, a frightful massacre of the Maronites took place, when the Turks, faithful to the motto *Divide et impera,* stood aside and permitted the atrocities. The abbot of Deir al-Kamar was flayed alive, and his twenty monks pole-axed; while it has been reckoned [60] that in the space of twenty-two days 7771 persons were murdered, 360 villages were destroyed, 560 churches overthrown, 42 monasteries burnt, and 28 schools destroyed. "The blood of the martyrs is the seed of the Church," and, beyond that white robed company which is known only to God, Damascus has given eleven *beati.* Eight friars minor and three Maronite laymen—Francis Masabki, Abdulmuti Masabki, and Raphael Masabki—suffered for the faith on July 10, 1860, and were beatified by Pope Pius XI on October 10, 1926. Finally, the intervention of France under General de Beaufort d'Hautpoult and the strong character of the patriarch brought peace and a new form of government to the Maronites.

In the first great war (1914-1918), there were many victims of Turkish frightfulness among the Maronites, although the fastnesses of the Lebanon, as in times past, provided an asylum for the persecuted Christians.

[59] ASSEMANI, *Bibl. juris.,* t. I, pp. XVII-XVIII; ap. *Dict. de Théol. Cath.,* t. X, col. 114.
[60] *Dict. de Théol. Cath.,* t. X, col. 56.

The constitution of "Great Lebanon" was organised in 1920 by General Gouraud, and under the form of a Lebanese republic was revised six years later (May 1926).

Recently, in response to national aspirations, the French mandate has been withdrawn, and the country has attained the status of a sovereign independent state. There is, however, a very grave danger [61] that the rising tide of pan-Arab nationalism, with its baggage of Mohammedan fanaticism, will exert itself to sweep the Lebanon out of existence in the interests of Syrian unity. The influence of England and the United States could save it, but "Arab appeasement" will probably interest those countries more than Christian justice, particularly as they have nothing to gain materially from the Lebanon.

Present Conditions

From the statistics [62] compiled in 1932 for the Sacred Congregation for the Eastern Church, the Maronites of the patriarchate number 366,015; while of the diaspora, 38,000 live in the United States, 16,000 in Uruguay and about 5,000 elsewhere.

Two chorepiscopi with quasi episcopal powers and thirty-nine priests minister to the Maronites in the United States, where in 1941 there were 44 churches of the rite. Canada

[61] In November 1945, Elias Karain, Orthodox archbishop of the Lebanon, appealed to the pope in respect to this "danger which threatens all the Christians of the Near East." "The Christians of the whole world," says this Orthodox prelate, "have been accustomed, in every age, in every place, to look towards Rome in their times of trouble."

[62] *Statistica della Gerarchia e dei fedeli di Rito Orientale* (Tip. Pol. Vat., 1932), pp. 56-63, 545.

The *Manuel du Catéchiste en Orient* (p. 62, Cairo, 1939) gives the total number of Maronites as 420,000-300,000 in the patriarchate of Antioch and 120,000 in the New World.

had 3 churches, Mexico 3, Cuba 2, Argentine Republic 3, Brazil [63] 1 and Uraguay 1.

Maronite churches are found also in Leghorn [64] (S. Maria del Rosario), Paris [65] (N.-D. du Liban, 1915), Sydney and Johannesburg (1937).

The last named is the only Catholic church in South Africa where an eastern liturgy is celebrated.

The Maronites [66] form the largest body of oriental Catholics outside Europe, and in the absence of their own churches and schools they willingly attend those of the Latins.

The Lebanon, which has been called the "boulevard of Catholicism in the Christian East," follows the sea-coast in a general northerly direction from a point midway between Tyre and Sidon to a point somewhat north of Tripoli (ab. 120 miles), with 25 to 30 miles its greatest breadth. In the Kesrawan, north of the Dog river and Belad Bsherreh, below the cedars, the population is exclusively Maronite.

Many of the returning emigrants are said to be anti-clerical, which is accentuated by the amount of property (over one-third in the Lebanon) owned by the religious orders, and by the sight of so many monasteries perched on hills dominating the landscape.

[63] The chief centres in Brazil are in Rio de Janeiro, San Paolo, Porto Alegre and Marianna. By a decree of May 3, 1946, a new parish was created in Rio de Janeiro, dedicated to our Lady of Lebanon, and under the care of the Missionaries of Kraïm.

[64] In 1929, the church was enlarged and blessed, but there are now no Maronites in Leghorn.

[65] A former Jesuit chapel in the Rue d'Ulm, near the Pantheon. The Maronite population is about 250.

[66] There are 3,431 Maronites in Palestine, and 7,000 in Egypt.

Religious Orders

At the coming of the Arabs, the monks had fled to the rocky gorges of the Kadicha, which until the 17th century had remained their chief home.

In 1695, Germanos Farhat, archbishop of Aleppo, gave the first written rule to Maronite monks. A house was founded at Ehden, which in 1700 received canonical recognition, and in 1725 statutory approval from the patriarch (James 'Auad). The order was confirmed by Rome in the brief *Apostolatus officium* (1732). The monks were first known as Aleppines (*Halabiyeh*) and later as the Lebanese monks of St. Antony. Pope Clement XI in 1707 gave the old church of St. Peter and St. Marcellinus, Rome, and its adjoining house to be a house of study for the order and a hospice for pilgrims.

In 1753, by the brief *Alias porrectus,* Pope Benedict XIV authorised the removal of the monks to a house adjoining the little church [67] of St. Antony the Hermit near the Eudoxian basilica of St. Peter in Chains, which in 1770 became the exclusive property of the Aleppine congregation. The house was enlarged and restored in 1908.

The abbot-general of the order lives in the monastery of the Assumption, Luweiza, near Zuk-Mihail. There are 2 provinces with 12 houses and 132 religious.

In the pontificates of Benedict XIV and Clement XIII, discord between the Aleppines properly so called and the monks of the mountains of Lebanon produced a second order, which became known as that of the Baladites [68] or

---

[67] The small church is quite featureless and altogether Latin, even to an oleograph of St. Aloysius Gonzaga (1944). This picture has now (1947) been replaced by one of St. Teresa of Lisieux.

[68] *Lebnaniyeh; Beladiyeh,* "natives" or "country monks."

"country monks." The separation was effected in 1757, and by the brief *Ex Injuncto* (1770) received papal sanction. The abbot-general lives at Sa'dat al-Ma'ūnāt (Our Lady of Succour) near Gebail. There are 5 provinces with 33 houses and 645 religious. In 1931, 19 monks of the Baladite congregation were extern students at the oriental seminary, Beirut.

The congregation [69] of St. Isaac dates from 1700, when Gabriel of Blauza (later patriarch) sent a number of priests from the monastery of the Virgin at Tamish to the monastery of Mar Ishaya. Official recognition was accorded in 1740 by the brief of Clement XII, *Misericordiarum Pater*. The abbot-general lives at St. Roch, Dekwāneh near Beirut. There are 4 provinces with 25 monasteries and 130 religious.

The three congregations are all subject to the same rule, but under their own abbots-general and councils of four assistants. The monastic vows are renewed annually on the feast of St. Antony (January 17).

In 1931, Maronite Antonians were computed to number 520 hieromonks and 221 lay monks, with 70 monasteries.

Hermits, also, living after the primitive manner, are still to be found in the fastnesses of the Lebanon.

The causes of beatification of two Maronite monks [70] and a nun were begun at Rome in 1928—Nematalla al-Hardini (1808-1858), Sharbel of Beka Kafra (1837-1898), Rifka al-Rayes (1833-1914). Fr. Nematalla was a monk of the monastery of Kosaya, who became one of the four assistants of the abbot general. He is buried in the church at Kfifan, where for six years he was in charge of the young students.

[69] The procurator of the congregation lives in the Via Angelo Masina, Rome.
[70] The account of these three Maronite religious is taken from Donald ATTWATER'S, *Golden Book of Eastern Saints*, pp. 157-166.

Fr. Sharbel lived fifteen years in the community at Annaya and twenty-five years as a hermit. In December 1898, he was taken ill without warning while celebrating the liturgy. He found himself unable to replace the chalice on the altar without assistance, as he was reciting the prayer beginning, "O Father of Justice, behold thy Son who as a victim offers satisfaction to thee." He was taken to his cell, and never got up from his bed again.

Sister Rifka joined the teaching nuns at Bikfaya, and for ten years taught in various village schools of the Lebanon. Then in 1872 she was admitted among the contemplative nuns at the Maronite convent of St. Simon al-Karen, where she suffered from continual ill health.

In 1840, a congregation of missionaries was founded by the patriarch, but difficult times forced it to be dissolved. A second attempt in 1865 by John Habib, archbishop of Nazareth, was more successful, and the Lebanese Maronite Missionaries [71] of Kraīm, founded on the model of the Redemptorists, came into existence.

The priests wear a black tunic, leather girdle, hood, mantle and sandals. The congregation has three houses— Kraīm, Junich (Lebanon), Buenos Aires.

In 1931, the total number of Maronite male religious was 1,016.

Maronite nuns of the ancient observance are also divided into three groups: a) Antonians of the Lebanese congregation, affiliated to the Baladites, with 5 houses and about 100 religious; b) Antonians of the Congregation of St. Isaias, with 3 houses and 32 religious; and c) Five houses following

---

[71] The Missionaries of Kraīm publish two reviews (*Al-Manaret; Sayedat-Lobnan*) and a paper (*Al-Moursal*).

the rule given by 'Abdallah Qara 'Ali, bishop of Beirut († 1742), for the convent of St. John Baptist, Heras.

The Maronite Visitandines have 2 houses, and the Congregation of the Holy Family, the first active order of the Eastern rite in Syria, have 19. The last named was founded in 1895 at 'Ebrîn, near Batrun. The Mariamettes or Sisters of the Sacred Hearts of Jesus and Mary (1853) are an inter-ritual congregation, with a large proportion of Maronite members.

In 1931, the total number of female religious was said to be 420.

Hierarchy

The "Patriarch of Antioch and of all the East," after his election has been notified to the Sacred Congregation for the Eastern Church and ratified by the pope, is vested with the pallium.

Each patriarch, in memory of the apostolic founder of the see of Antioch, receives the name of Peter.

The title *Patriarcha Antiochenus Maronitarum* was conceded in the year 1254 by Pope Alexander IV, although it seems to have been granted by Calixtus II in the 12th century. A synod of the bishops is summoned every three years, while an *ad limina* visit to the pope is paid every ten years.

The patriarchal residence has varied through the centuries, but in the time of Joseph Hobaïch (1823-1845) it was moved from Qannubin (1440) and fixed at Bekorki [72] (Bkerke) in winter and at Dîmâm in summer.

---

[72] *Bkerke rappresenta per loro* (Maronites) *il Vaticano del Libano.* DE VRIES, *Cattolicismo e problemi religiosi nel prossimo Oriente* (Rome, 1944), II, p. 43.

As is often the case in the East, the title metropolitan [73] is only honorific.

There are seven archbishops—Aleppo, Beirut, Cyprus, Damascus, Sidon, Tripoli, and Tyre—and three bishops [74]— Batrûn and Gibail, Baalbek, and Cairo of the Maronites (1946).

The patriarch, who is *ex officio* archbishop of Aleppo, is assisted by patriarchal vicars, normally in episcopal orders, who act as secretaries and delegates.

Jerusalem has a patriarchal vicar, and a procurator of the patriarch lives in Rome.

A bishop must be celibate, although he is not necessarily a monk. The chorepiscopi, [75] who may be compared to deans in the Latin church, have the right to use a mitre and crozier, and, with the permission of the patriarch, they may administer confirmation and confer minor orders. They perform also many of the duties undertaken in the towns by archpresbyters, and they are permitted to consecrate [76] altars. The bishop at their ordination prays that they may be worthy "to place in the churches under their charge, baptismal fonts and altars, that they will anoint with sweet-smelling oil." In April 1929, some of the privileges of the chorepiscopi were curtailed by the patriarch.

The *economi*, who carry out many of the duties of archdeacons, [77] supervise church property and attend to the

---

[73] *Maphryono; maphrian,* commonly referred to the root *ph'ro, fecundus fuit, genuit,* as an essential function was the continuance of the hierarchy by the consecration of bishops.

[74] *Episqupo; rabkohno, khasvo,* "holy" or "venerable."

[75] *Kurepisqupo;* ἐπίσκοποι τῆς χώρας, χωρεπίσκοποι, "country bishops."

[76] Cf. *periodeutes.*

[77] *Rish-m'shamshono.* The rites of ordination for an archdeacon and archpriest (MARTÈNE, *De Antiquis Ecclesiae Ritibus,* t. II (1736 edition),

episcopal *mensa;* while the *periodeutes*[78] or "vicars forane" visit country parishes, consecrate baptisteries and churches, and, with the express permission of the patriarch, they may carry a crozier and administer confirmation. A priest[79] must be at least thirty years old (twenty-five by dispensation), and a deacon[80] twenty-one. The majority of the married clergy live in country districts, where they eke out a scanty living from *honoraria* and gifts of farm produce, supplemented by personal tillage of the soil.

Minor orders are given early, and a singer,[81] if he can read, may be seven years old, while lectors[82] and subdeacons[83] are sometimes not more than twelve. A subdeacon combines the duties of doorkeeper and acolyte.

There are said to be about 850 Maronite parishes with 1,200 secular clergy, but although 7 patriarchal and diocesan seminaries exist, as well as colleges in Beirut and Rome, the general standard of ecclesiastical education is not high.

In 1931, there were 50 Maronite students in the seminary at Beirut, and three years later a general seminary for the whole patriarchate was established at Ghazir.

The college in Rome, which came to an end at the time of the French Revolution, was reestablished in the Via Porta Pinciana in 1891 by the brief *Sapienter olim.* The spiritual direction of the house was given to the Jesuits, and Maronite

pp. 286 and 290) have an interesting analogy in the Mozarabic *Liber Ordinum* (Férotin, Paris, 1904, pp. 50-51, n. 2).

[78] Greek, περιωδεύτης, "visitor;" *barduts.*

[79] *Qashisho,* "presbyter;" *kohno,* "priest;" *kumro,* "sad one," and seemingly derived from sad coloured garments or solemn demeanour.

[80] *M'sham-shono.*

[81] *Mazmorono,* "psalter."

[82] *Quoroyo.*

[83] *Phelguth-M'shamshono,* "half deacon."

priests served the neighbouring church of St. Maro in the Via Aurora.

The college was reorganised in 1920, and in 1935 there were 12 students. At the outbreak of the second world war the house was closed, but the church was served by the Maronite procurator to the Holy See. By a strange coincidence [84] the college buildings were later temporarily acquired by the Polish army as an officers' club. The Maronites had no regular ordaining prelate at Rome, but Mar N'amatallah Karam, the rector of the college from 1913-1931, held this position.

Latinisation is forbidden. Students must receive both confirmation and ordination in their own rite, while those who show signs of undue Western influence are sent back to the Lebanon.

Since at least the council of the Lebanon (1736), the recitation of the divine office has been obligatory for priests and deacons.

Liturgical Language

The hieratic language of the rite is Syriac, which to-day is spoken only in a few villages about the Upper Tigris and Damascus. Arabic is now used in the occasional offices and in certain parts of the liturgy. The Bible (*Peschitto*) is also written in Arabic, but the rubrics of the liturgy are in Karshuni, which is Arabic in Syriac characters.

The original language was Greek, and it would seem that Syriac took its place when Maronite influence ceased in the hellenized lowlands. Theophilus of Edessa at the end of the 8th century was able to translate the Homeric poems,

---

[84] The site of the first Maronite college in Rome was later occupied by the Polish college.

and it is probable that Greek was spoken in Maronite monasteries until their destruction by the Arabs in the late 9th or early 10th century. Mar Ephrem Rahmani [85] has ascribed the frequency with which Greek expressions are found in the liturgy to the fact that several Syrian towns, especially on the coast, were the residence of the upper classes who were Greek-speaking. Consequently, the deacon used that tongue, as was the custom in addressing the governors and imperial functionaries.

A title of glory and justifiable pride to the Syrian and Maronite churches is the belief that their hieratic language is the nearest approach to the Aramaic [86] of the Babylonish Captivity, which was spoken by our Lord at the Last Supper.

It is found to-day in the vernacular Scriptures in such expressions as *Bar Jona* (S. Matt., XVI, 17), *Golgotha* (S. Matt., XXVII, 33), *Eloi, Eloi, lama sabacthani* (S. Matt., XXVII, 46), *Talitha cumi* (S. Mark, V, 41), *Ephpheta* (S. Mark, VII, 34), *Haceldama* (Acts, I, 19), *Maran-atha* (I Cor., XVI, 22).

Liturgical Books

The missal was in manuscript until the end of the 16th century, and three exemplars are now in the Vatican library.

The number of anaphoras has varied, and the 1536 manuscript has 22; 1564 and 1579 have 10; while one which has been copied on a codex of 1527 has only 7. The first printed missal, which was published at Rome in 1592—*Missale Chaldaicum juxta ritum Ecclesiae nationis Maronitarum,*—was enjoined by the synod of 1596. The book included 14 anaphoras and a series of gospels for the days of the

---

[85] *Les Liturgies Orientales et Occidentales*, chap. III, p. 111.
[86] *Aram*, North Syria.

week and some Sundays and feasts. Two important alterations had been made in the liturgy in regard to the words of
institution and the epiclesis. Prior to 1592, the formula [87]
of consecration had varied with the anaphora, but in that year
a translation of the Roman form was made obligatory; while
the epiclesis was changed from an invocation on the *oblata*
to one for the benefit of the faithful. This missal, which
the synod [88] of 1596 had ordered to be used, was superseded
in 1716 by another edition published in Rome.

The alterations made in the previous book were retained;
while certain anaphoras were suppressed and replaced by
others, although the number remained at 14. The most
notable change was the insertion of the anaphora of the
Roman Church, which was inspired by the Latin canon and
contains prayers of Latin origin. The liturgy of the Presanctified was also added to the missal, as well as an Arabic
translation of several western prayers. The publication was
mainly the work of Andrew Alexander of Cyprus, who at the
request of Joseph Assemani had been commissioned by Pope
Clement XI (1700-1721).

The synod [89] of 1736 apparently desired to restore some
of the ancient formularies to the liturgy, but nothing was
accomplished, and the books of the rite were described in
Latin terminology.

[87] Cf. Ethiopic rite.
[88] "*Missali Romae sanctissimi domini nostri Papae approbatione
nuper impresso, atque ad nos transmisso utantur omnes, nec alio nisi ad
Patriarcham delato, at ad Romanum emendato, ejusque manu subscripto,
ac solito sigillo confirmato uti liceat.*" Canon 8.
[89] *Eundem sensum (atque forma romana consecrationis) reddunt
verba, quae in diversis syrorum liturgiis diversi modo pronuntiantur. Sunt
autem accuratissime recognoscenda, quando missale auctoritate reveren-
dissimi domini patriarchae imprimetur ne quid substantiale in iis deside-
retur, quemadmodum in nonnullis manuscriptis codicibus additum vel
detractum ab haereticis reperitur.*

In 1762-3, a third edition of the missal was printed in Rome, and the number of anaphoras was reduced to eight, with a liturgy of the presanctified.

The liturgical books in more recent years have been published in the monastery of St. Antony, Kosaya, and at Beirut (1888).

In the seventh edition of the missal, the anaphora of the Roman Church, through the influence of Joseph Debs, archbishop of Beirut, was given the first place.

The first edition of the missal, that was printed in 1592, was supplied with rubrics, but they were too few, and were therefore insufficient. In the missal of 1716, however, they were more detailed, while in 1907 a book was published entitled *Manà'ir at-taqsiyyàt*, in which the ceremonies were described in extenso, and the liturgy was divided into six parts.

The Roman practice of the "three voices" for the celebrant is prescribed for the Maronite priest.

There are fourteen liturgical books of the rite.

The missal is called the "Book of the Oblation." Deacons and clerks use the "Book [90] of the Ministery" (*Diaconicon*), in which there are rubrics for the deacon, server, choir and people.

A new Maronite ritual was published in 1942 at the printing press of the Jesuits in Beirut. The former edition had been so latinised that to all intents and purposes it had become a Western book. The new edition shows signs of a revival of traditional usages, representing a more specifically Maronite recension, purified of hybridism and judiciously abridged. It was been largely based on ancient manuscripts in Europe and the Lebanon.

[90] *C⁪ thobko Teshmeshto.*

The pontifical has remained in manuscript, and it has retained as a whole the traditional framework of the usages of the Antiochene patriarchate. At the time of the recent revision of the Syrian pontifical (1939-1945) it was thought better not to attempt a unification of the Syrian and Maronite forms. The Maronites therefore must continue to use their manuscripts or adopt the Syrian book, which could be done with nothing more than the abandonment of a certain number of textual or ceremonial variants.

Church Architecture and Furniture

The Maronites, having lived for centuries with arms in their hands, have no splendid churches, but some dating from the time of the Crusades are in existence.

A typical specimen of a church shows two domes linked together, with the men gathered for worship under the dome nearest the altar. The sexes are sometimes separated by a latticed screen or gallery. The iconostasis is unknown; while the three altars, and Latin furniture and ornaments often make the Maronite churches indistinguishable from those of the Roman rite.

The altar or "table of life" (*madhbah*), at which more than one Mass may be said daily, is Western in shape, but a small oblong piece of consecrated wood or stone (*tablīth*), which may be compared to the Byzantine *antimension*, is placed on the *mensa*. The term "throne" is sometimes applied to the altar, but the word more accurately describes the central portion on which the holy vessels rest.

The asterisk,[91] once used in this rite, has been replaced by the Latin pall.

---

[91] *ita* Dandinus.

Three silk veils (*gitā*) cover the oblations, i. e. for the paten (*gitā absainiyah*), for the chalice (*gitā alcās*) and for both vessels together (nāfūr).

The vessel into which the celebrant "ministers" (*mᶜshamesh*) or washes his fingers is sometimes called the "deaconess" [92] (*mᶜshamshōnōitho*); the term "minister" (*shᶜmash*) is also used for cleansing the vessels after holy communion.

Eucharistic Bread

Azyme bread [93] was enjoined so long ago as 1215, in the bull of Pope Innocent III to the patriarch Jeremias Al-Amchiti: "You have received these things with piety and humility. We encourage you, dear brothers and sons, with love in the Lord. Enjoy St. Peter's protection and ours."

It seems probable that the Maronites from at least the 5th to the 12th century used leavened bread, and the tract *De Liturgia secundum ritum Syriacum*, which, bearing the name of John Maro, would suggest the use of azymes in the 7th century, cannot be traced back earlier than the 13th century. The *Nomocanon* [94] of the Maronites, known as the *Liber Directionis* or *Directorium*, which was translated from Syriac into Arabic in 1069 by the metropolitan David, speaks of the leavened bread which is to be made on the day of the celebration of the liturgy. ·

---

[92] It has the same name in the Syrian rite; cf. "Commendo autem vobis Phoeben sororem nostram, quae est *in ministerio* Ecclesiae, quae est in Cenchris." *Epist. Rom.*, XVI, 1.

[93] Arabic, *burshānah*, possibly derived from ἀπαρχή, a word often found in the Coptic books, and signifying "firstfruits" or "oblations;" Syriac, *kurbān; qūrbōro*, "offering;" *paristo, katzto*, "sacramental bread."

[94] Chap. XVII; ap. RAHMANI, *Les Liturgies Orientales et Occidentales,* chap. II, 6, p. 66.

The council of the Lebanon (1736) discussed the question of altar bread, but it is clear that azymes had been in use for many centuries. [95] It was enjoined that the eucharistic bread should be thin and always ornamented with some figure. [96] The greatest care was to be taken in regard to the baking, which, if possible, was to be undertaken by clerics or monks, [97] who were to sing psalms as they worked. The irreligious and the heterodox were forbidden to take part.

The custom of insisting upon an unequal number of breads in the liturgy was condemned as "useless and absurd" by Joseph Assemani [98] (1710-1782) in the *Liturgical Codex of the Universal Church.*

Vestments

Vestments [99] may be either of the Syrian or Roman pattern, but unfortunately there has been a growing tendency to latinise, although of recent years there are signs of a healthy reaction among some of the faithful of the rite.

Pope Innocent III (*Quia divinae*, January 3, 1215) authorised the use of Latin vestments, and other popes have enjoined the same, while the synod of the Lebanon (1736) definitely sanctioned the custom.

Clement XI (1700-1721) ordered the Maronites in Rome to wear Latin vestments, but the eastern form is used to-day in Paris.

---

[95] *Ab immemorabili tempore obtinuit.* Ap. HANSSENS, *Instit. Lit. de Rit. Orien.,* t. II, part I, p. 127.

[96] HANSSENS, *op. cit.,* p. 176.

[97] *Ibid.,* p. 207.

[98] *Codex liturgicus ecclesiae universae in quindecim libros distributus,* t. IV, 2, p. 272.

[99] *Thiyab altakdis.*

Bishops are more commonly faithful to their traditional vesture.

Singers and lectors [100] have long albs with bands of ornamentation, and sometimes, by abuse, stoles worn over the right shoulder; while a subdeacon, equally improperly, has a stole on the neck.

The deacon, [101] as in the Syrian rite, lets the stole fall from the left shoulder.

The ornaments of the priest consist of an amice [102] worn over the alb, alb, [103] girdle, [104] stole, [105] cuffs [106] and chasuble. [107]

A bishop [108] has also a Latin mitre and crozier, [109] ring, pectoral cross, and masnaphtho; [110] while the patriarch wears the pallium.

The liturgical shoes, referred to by Severus († 538) in his work on the *Paschal Lamb,* if they ever had more than a mystical significance, have long since disappeared.

The inconsistency of priests in regard to the vestments

[100] The Maronite lector at ordination has a folded orarion laid across his extended hands. DENZINGER, *Rit. Orien.,* pp. 229, 233.

[101] The deacon and subdeacon at a solemn Maronite liturgy celebrated in S. Andrea della Valle, Rome, on the feast of the Epiphany, 1947, wore the Latin vestments of their respective orders.

[102] *Masnaphtho,* a Syriac term, is used also for the hood worn by the patriarch and others.

The amice is taken after the girdle, and it should be worn so as to form a collar to the vestment. It has in the centre a cross in relief.

[103] *Citūnah* (Greek, χιτώνιον), *kuthino.*

[104] *Zunnār, zunoro.*

[105] *Bitrashīl* (Greek, ἐπιτραχήλιον), *uroro* (Greek, ὡράριον).

The stole is not crossed on the breast.

[106] *Cummin, zende.*

[107] *Phaino* (Greek, φαινόλιον), *rida.*

[108] A chorepiscopus at a solemn liturgy also has the right to *pontificalia.*

[109] A staff surmounted by a triple cross is sometimes used.

[110] Cf. Nestorian *birun.*

is seen in the following particulars: the maniple or eastern cuffs are worn indifferently; the traditional cincture ornamented with embroidery has given place, except in some monasteries, to the Latin girdle; the ample *ridā* at a solemn liturgy is exchanged before the consecration for a Roman chasuble, [111] generally of bad design.

The outdoor dress of the clergy consists of a black cassock, [112] girdle, black cloak and round stiff quilted turban, [113] wound about with a dark blue cloth. The old Syrian headgear is now very commonly replaced by a round black cap, but bishops have retained the turban, which they wear over the *masnaphtho*.

The students in Rome have Latin cassocks and birettas.

At solemn liturgies, the priest blesses the people with a hand-cross, which dignitaries also use for "low Mass." A silk streamer is attached to the cross.

Calendar

According to the *Sinksar,* the Maronite year begins in October (*Teshrin*), with feasts kept on the first day of the month, a little in advance of the dominical computation, but the rite has nothing corresponding to the Chaldean division of the year into *shawu'a* or seven week periods.

The six Sundays before Christmas have a festal character, recording events that took place before the birth of our Lord.

As in the Syrian rite, they are known as *Suboro* or "Annunciation," and are in fact identical.

On December 15, some churches begin a devotion to the

[111] *Nella Messa solenne il sacerdote indossa un piviale che cambia colla pianeta al Sanctus. Messa Siro-Maronita* (Rome, 1943), p. 6.

[112] Bishops wear a violet cassock, the patriarch a red one.

[113] *Tabieh.*

nine months' conception of our Lady, consecrating on that
day two hosts, one of which is placed in the "house of the
body" on the altar. Every evening until December 24 the
host is taken from the tabernacle and elevated, and on the
last day of the novena it is consumed. Other churches keep
the devotion on the nine days preceding Christmas by carrying in procession a picture of the Christ-child. Cribs have
been introduced into Maronite churches, but they are still
uncommon in the Lebanon.

December 26 is the solemnity "of the praises of the
Mother of God," and the Sunday after Christmas commemorates the Finding of the Child Jesus in the Temple; while
January 1 combines St. Basil and St. Gregory Nazianzen
with the feast of the Circumcision. Water is blessed before
the midnight Mass of the Epiphany [114] and on the feast of
St. Peter and St. Paul.

Sundays are named after the Epiphany, while the three
weeks immediately preceding Lent are "of deceased priests,"
"of the just and holy," and "of all the departed" respectively.

The day answering to the Latin Quinquagesima is called
the "first Sunday of the Great Fast" (*Saumo Rabbo*) or "of
the Wedding Feast at Cana."

Ashes are imposed on the first Monday in Lent; while in
Passiontide the pictures are covered, and a black curtain, [115]
bearing the symbols of the Passion, hides the altar. The first
lenten Sundays commemorate the fasting and miracles of
our Lord.

On Maundy Thursday, every church has the *mandatum*,
and on Good Friday adoration of the cross ("burial") with-

---

[114] The liturgy is celebrated at midnight at Christmas, Epiphany and
Easter.

[115] Cf. Lenten veil in the churches of Western Sicily and in those
of the Cistercians of Strict Observance.

out the Mass of the Presanctified sometimes takes place in the afternoon.

It is permissable for all priests to say Mass on Holy Saturday. Easter Week is known as the "Week [116] of Rest," and Low Sunday the "Sunday [117] of Renewal."

Trinity, Corpus Christi and the Sacred Heart now find a place in the calendar.

Weeks are reckoned "after Pentecost" until September 14, when they are called "after the Exaltation of the Cross."

Before the Sundays of the "Annunciation" are the Sundays "of the Sanctification [118] of the Church" and "of the Dedication [119] of the Church," but there is no indication as to what church is commemorated.

Twenty-three days are observed as days of obligation, which include St. Antony, Patriarch of monks (January 17). The national feasts of Mar Marun [120] (February 9); Patriarch John Marun (March 2) and the 350 Martyred Monks [121] of Mar Marun (on Mount Lebanon, July 31) are kept with especial solemnity.

Old Testament saints figure largely in the calendar: Mar Elias (H. O., July 20); Malachias (January 3); Agabus the Prophet (N. T., April 10); Jeremias (May 1); Isaias (May 9);

---

[116] *Shabto damyokhto; shabto d'Khewose;* cf. *Dominica in Albis.*

[117] *Khato;* cf. κυριακὴ τῆς διακαινησίμου.

[118] *Qudoshidto.*

[119] *Khudoto;* ἐνκαίνια.

[120] A memorial of Mar Marun is observed on the second Sunday in each month. The head of St. Maro is said to be preserved in the cathedral of Foligno.

[121] The 350 martyrs are all venerated as Maronites, although in reality they belonged to all the monasteries of *Syria Secunda,* which were attacked by the emperor Anastasius I and the Monophysite patriarch, Severus of Antioch, in the early years of the 6th century.

Eliseus (June 14); Aaron (July 1); Machabees [122] (H. O., August 1); Daniel (August 3); Samuel (August 21); Zacharias (September 5); Jonas (September 23); Baruch (October 30); Nahum (December 1); Habacuc (December 2); Sophonias (December 3); Aggeus (December 16); Daniel (second feast, December 18).

There is no proper of saints, as in the Roman rite, but the lessons, and sometimes also the *proemia* and *sedra,* are variable.

The Maronites [123] seem to honour a foe of Chalcedon by observing the feast of James [124] of Sarugh, bishop of Batnan (451-521), who was a supporter of the *Henotikon.*

Many Western devotions have been introduced, such as benediction with the blessed sacrament and stations of the cross, together with the observance of such feasts as the Holy Name of Mary (Sunday after September 8); Rosary Sunday (first Sunday in October); St. Joseph; and Corpus Christi ("Thursday of the Body"). The last named feast follows the regulations of Pope Urban IV (1261-1265). It has a liturgy composed in the 18th century, and a solemnity prolonged for an octave, when benediction is given every day, with a procession of the blessed sacrament on the first and last days. [125] At the moment of benediction, the deacons say: "We come to see, under the species of bread and wine, him

---

[122] The feast of the Machabeean martyrs is very ancient, and almost universal. It is appointed for this day in the primitive Syriac Martyrology of the 4th century, in the Calendar of Carthage, and in the Martyrology of St. Jerome. Ildefonso SCHUSTER, *The Sacramentary,* vol. IV, p. 399.

[123] The feast is also observed by the Nestorians.

[124] The author of a Syrian anaphora and 231 hymns. He was known by the Monophysites as the "Flute of the Holy Spirit" and the "Harp of the believing Church."

[125] Cf. Carthusian rite.

whom the cherubim fear." At Christmas, on a similar occasion, the people chant: "Holy, holy, holy is the august Lord, who is alone in his divinity."

Regulations relating to fasting and abstinence were fixed by the council of the Lebanon (1736).

There are four "Lents," as in the Byzantine rite. a) Great Lent, from "Quinquagesima" until Easter. b) Lent of the Apostles, which now lasts only four days—June 25-28. c) Lent of the Assumption, August 7-14. d) Lent of Christmas, December 13-24. The Rogation of the Ninevites is observed in the week before the Latin Septuagesima.

There are no ember days or vigils, but all Wednesdays and Fridays, unless they fall in Christmastide, the Paschal season or on certain feasts, are days of abstinence from meat and milk foods.

Music

Bells are said to have been introduced at the time of the Crusades.

The only form of accompaniment to the liturgy, at least in the Lebanon, are cymbals and noisy bells.

Harsh sounds and quick changes are marked features of the chant. The liturgy is remarkable for the number of hymns, although many of them owe little to St. Ephrem, [126] despite his alleged authorship and genuine reputation as a hymnologist. Some of them seem to have been Nestorian in origin, with heterodox expressions deleted, and the names of the authors either suppressed or changed to St. Ephrem. In others, the general arrangement has been altered and refrains added.

---

[126] St. Ephrem wrote 21 hymns on the holy Eucharist.

History of the Rite

The liturgy is a Syriac version of St. James, [127] revised by James of Edessa (ab. 633-708), and known as the "Anaphora of St. James, brother of the Lord, according to a careful recension of James of Edessa."

Thus the rite, although latinised, is substantially the same as that of the Syrians. Innocent III (1198-1216), as extant bulls show, encouraged the general policy of latinisation, but systematic hybridism does not seem to have become a feature before the end of the 16th century, at a time when the liturgical revision of St. Pius V (1566-1572) was thought by many to be the eventual norm for the Church throughout the world.

In 1610, Pope Paul V (1605-1621) ordered a return to the *status quo,* annulling the innovations introduced by the Maronite patriarch, but the revival of traditional usages was not of long duration. The congregations in 1631 encouraged the importation of the Roman episcopal insignia, the Latin sign of the cross, and the Western baptismal customs while in the 18th century the liturgical school at Aleppo proved a further hindrance to the maintenance of the purity of the rite.

To-day, however, signs are not wanting of a movement towards a fuller restoration of oriental usages, and when in 1881 a Maronite priest desired to join the Congregation of the Mission and sought permission to use the Latin rite, the concession was only granted for the time of his novitiate.

The foes of the Syrian rite have been the Maronites themselves, for surrounded by enemies they have turned instinctively to Rome for imitation as well as for sympathy and help.

---

[127] A 4th century Antiochene liturgy, received from Jerusalem.

The council of the Lebanon (1736) spoke of the liturgy as a "veritable dialogue between priest and people," by reason of the large share which the faithful take in it, although this assistance is now generally given by the deacon or server.

The devotions and hymns which are recited during the secret prayers of the priest probably date from before the schism in the 5th century. They were referred to by the commentator who bears the name of "John Maro," as well as by the schismatic John of Dara.

Under Latin influence, a fully developed "low Mass (*Missa Romana*) has been evolved, which, at least in churches [128] in the West, is sometimes celebrated without the normal accompaniment of incense. [129]

Concelebration was restricted by the council [130] of the Lebanon (1736) to solemn feasts, a requiem with the body present, and anniversaries of the dead.

The Liturgy with the Anaphora of the Roman Church

The liturgy [131] begins with the celebrant washing his hands and vesting at the foot of the altar, as he recites appropriate prayers, although in practice this is often done in the sacristy.

[128] e. g. N. D. du Liban, Paris; St. John Maro, Rome.
[129] The frequency with which the Maronites use incense was commented on by two French travellers: "*Jamais je n'ai vu de Messe où l'on encense davantage: leur office n'est qu'un parfum.*" Jerôme et Jean THARAUD, *Le Chemin de Damas*, p. 75. Plon (1913), Paris.
[130] Part II, chap. XIII, No. 18.
[131] *Qurobo, qurboro,* " the offering;" *qudosho,* " the hallowing."
Throughout the liturgy, the missal remains on the gospel side of the altar.

Before ascending to the altar, the priest [132] says: "O praise the Lord, all ye nations, Alleluja," and at the footpace the versicles taken from the Roman rite: "I will go to the altar of God, to God who giveth joy to my youth."

Then, moving his head in the form of a cross and making a genuflexion, the priest continues: "O God, I have entered into thy house, and kneel before thy throne: O heavenly king, forgive me all the sins which I have committed against thee. Vouchsafe, O Lord, on these days of solemnity, to lead our victims, bound with chains, to the horns of the altar, where they shall be immolated."

At a pontifical liturgy, [133] the bishop, before proceeding to the throne for the vesting, gives a blessing with the hand-cross from the footpace of the altar.

The *Treatise* [134] *on the Liturgy of St. James* and, according to some authorities, Denys bar-Salibi [135] maintained that the bread and the wine were placed on the altar after the expulsion of the catechumens and following a procession of the Byzantine type, but in the narrative [136] of the papal envoy the Maronites are definitely said to offer the elements before taking the sacred vestments. This latter practice is followed to-day, and the word "offer" implies that they are actually set on the altar at this time, although there is no specific mention of the sacrificial matter. The Maronite rite now requires the priest to vest *before* proceeding to the offertory,

---

[132] At a solemn liturgy, the deacon.

[133] At a pontifical liturgy celebrated by a chorepiscopus (S. Andrea della Valle, Rome, January 6, 1947), the celebrant, apart from a cope-like vestment, worn until the *Sanctus*, was vested *more romano*, while the the deacon and subdeacon had a Latin dalmatic and tunicle respectively. The servers had laced cottas.

[134] 7th century, once ascribed to the patriarch, "John Maro."

[135] Metropolitan of Amida, † 1171.

[136] Jerome DANDINI, *Voyage of Mount Lebanon*, 1675.

and the patriarch, Joseph Risi (1596-1608), added a canon [137] to the decrees of the synod of 1596 enjoining this.

Incense, as we have seen, is normally used in the liturgy, and at the offertory the boat is placed on the altar, while its contents are blessed before putting a spoonful into the thurible, with the following prayer: "To the glory and honour of the holy and glorious Trinity, my sinful hand strew this incense. Let us pray together, and beg of the Lord his grace and his mercy."

The priest then takes the chalice [138] in his left hand and the paten in his right, and, signing himself with the paten, holds each of the inverted vessels [139] over the smoking censer, as he says: "In the name of the Father and of the Son and of the Holy Ghost."

The choir in the meanwhile sings *Maestaeddon:* "My heart is ready, O Lord, my heart is ready. I will sing, I will give praise with my glory;" and *Barekmore:* "O living Son of God, who hast died, hast risen and given life, hope and courage to the dead, grant to those who believe in the mystery of thy Holy Trinity, to rise to the glorious and eternal life. Alleluia." The vessels are replaced on the corporal, and the chalice is covered with the paten.

The priest takes the altar bread in both hands, as he recites in a low voice a prayer that asks for grace to be given

[137] *In sancto missae sacrificio peragendo quosdam accepimus, antequam sacras vestes induant, panem et vinum offerre; alios primum vestes assumere, tum offerre. Unius gentis ac populi unum oportet esse ritum, unam divini cultus formam. Est autem rationi atque ecclesiasticae consuetudini magis consentaneum, ut sacris indutis vestibus ad altare sacerdos accedat.*

[138] The vessels are normally placed on the altar before the liturgy, with the chalice veil on the south side, hanging over the edge of the altar.

[139] "He turns the chalice and paten, the altar bread, the pall and the veil to be incensed by the server." SFEIR, *The Syrian Maronite Mass in English*, pp. 20-21.

to those who have presented the offerings: "O God who art always great and honourable, who hast accepted the offerings, the vows, the first-fruits and the tithes of thy faithful servants, accept also these offerings which thy servants [140] have set apart for thee, and which they offer for thy love, and for the sake of thy holy name. Protect them, and bless them with all spiritual blessings. Rejoice them with the happiness that will never end, and with the hopes which are the inheritance of thy saints. Make, O Lord, thy blessings to descend on all that belongs to them; grant to their bodies health and purity, and to their souls innocence and holiness; give also, unto the souls of their dead, the repose of thy happy and external mansions, and in place of these earthly things give them life and the kingdom of heaven. Amen."

The bread is turned to the gospel side of the altar to be censed by the server (deacon), as the celebrant continues: "He was led as a sheep to the slaughter, and in his humility he was silent and opened not his mouth, and was dumb as a lamb before his shearer."

Then, turning back to the middle of the altar, the priest [141] says: "O God, who didst accept the sacrifice of Abel on the plain, of Noe in the ark, of Abraham on the top of the mountain, of David on the threshing-floor of Areuna the Jebusite, of Elias on Mount Carmel, and the mite which the poor widow cast into the treasury; accept also, O Lord God, these offerings which are presented to thee, through the mediation of my weakness and of my misery. O Lord God, for the sake of these gifts, remember the living and the dead, for whom we offer them to thee, and bless the house of those who offer them. Amen."

---

[140] An allusion to the time when the faithful brought the matter for the eucharist.

[141] Cf. A similar prayer in the Chaldean and Ethiopic rites.

The host is replaced on the paten with the accompanying prayer, which is taken from the Syrian liturgy: "Thou hast made to thyself, O Lord, a sanctuary in which to dwell: O Lord, strengthen thy holy place; through thee, O Lord, we shall reign for ever and ever."

Then, taking up the paten before it is censed (by the deacon) and covered with the small veil, the priest says: "The Lord hath reigned. He is clothed with beauty, Father, Son and Holy Ghost. Amen."

Receiving the chalice in like manner and turning to the north side of the altar, he continues: "I will take the chalice of salvation and I will call upon the name of the Lord, and I will pay my vows to him."

Then, pouring the wine into the chalice, he says: "This wine, which is a figure of the blood which came forth for us from the side of thy beloved Son, our Lord Jesus Christ, I pour forth into the chalice, which is the chalice of salvation. In the name of the Father and of the Son and of the Holy Ghost. Amen."

Water is blessed and added to the wine with the following prayer: "This water, which is a figure of the water which came forth for us from the side of thy beloved Son, our Lord Jesus Christ, I mingle in this chalice, which is the chalice of salvation. In the name of the Father and of the Son and of the Holy Ghost. Amen."

Placing the chalice on the altar, the priest says: "I place the chalice of salvation upon this holy stone."

Covering it with a small veil (pall), which has been censed and placed against the chalice: "The Lord is clothed with strength, and hath girded himself, for he hath established the world, which shall not be moved, Father, Son and Holy Ghost. Amen."

Covering both paten and chalice with the large veil,

which has been censed and placed against the sacred vessels:
"Before the splendour and glory of the Lord, the heavens are
hid, and his glory hath filled the entire earth. To him be
glory for ever and ever. Amen."

The Maronite rite has no prayer (*sedro*) of penitence,
which is said in the Syrian liturgy after the preparation of the
oblations, but, withdrawing to the foot of the altar, the priest,
in imitation of the Roman rite, recites a form of *Confiteor*
in Arabic, which may be compared with the prayer said by
the Latin celebrant as he ascends to the altar. It is an
amplification of a little prayer which is said at the beginning
of the Maronite offertory. There is no evidence of its use
before the 16th century, and it was placed in its present
position in the missal of 1716.

The priest genuflects and signs himself (a bell is sometimes rung), as he says: "In the name of the Father and of
the Son and of the Holy Ghost. Amen. O God, I beseech
thee, render me worthy to approach thy pure altar without
stain or defilement, for I am a sinful servant. I have committed sins and offences before thee, and I am unworthy to
approach thy pure altar and thy holy mysteries. But I entreat
thee, and address myself to thy liberality and to thy mercy.
O clement! O merciful! O thou who lovest men, cast upon
me a glance of mercy and of kindliness; grant that I may
become worthy to keep myself in thy presence, now and at
all times; grant that the grace of thy Holy Spirit may descend
upon me; purify me from my sins; sanctify this oblation,
vouchsafe through it to grant pardon of offences and remission of sins to those for whom I offer it to thee: to my father
and mother, and to all the faithful, living and dead, who
have shared my tribulations and have been associated with
me. Remember them, O Lord, in thy heavenly kingdom,
and place them with the just, and with the saints who have

accomplished thy will by their works of piety; through the intercession of our Lady, mother of light, of St. John Baptist, and of all the saints. Amen."

The priest, moving his head in the form of a cross, now recites, alternately with the choir or server, the entrance chant (*lbaitokh*), or introit: "O God, I have entered into thy house, and have knelt before thy throne: O heavenly King, forgive us all the sins which we have committed against thee."

Then, turning to either side and with hands crossed on his breast, the priest asks for the prayers [142] of the people: "Pray to our Lord for me."

The choir (server) responds: "May God accept thy oblation, and show us mercy through thy prayers."

Incense is now blessed for the second time, and the priest censes the oblations, cross, altar, people, [143] and the space between himself and the altar, as he says: [144] "O thou, who lovest sinners, accept in the sweetness of thy clemency and as a satisfaction to thy divinity the sweet-smelling incense, which the faithful children of the Church offer to thee by the hands of the priest, the head of all the faithful; as thou didst accept the sacrifice of Abraham upon the top of the mountain, and wast pleased with the odour of incense which the priest Aaron offered to thee, deign to accept as pleasing to thee the perfume of our incense, as a satisfaction for our offences, O most merciful God."

The deacon then censes the priest.

---

[142] Cf. *Orate fratres* in the Roman rite.

[143] The priest makes a complete circle. The people say together: "O Christ, guard thy Church."

[144] "Singing with the choir." SFEIR, *op. cit.*, p. 23.

Liturgy of the Catechumens

The priest and the assistant now say *Kyrie eleison* (three times) and the trisagion: "Holy God, holy and mighty, holy and immortal, have mercy on us. O Lord, have mercy on us; O Lord, pardon us and have mercy on us; O Lord, help us and have mercy on us; O Lord, accept our service and our prayers; come to our aid and have mercy on us."

The Lord's prayer is said with the doxology: "for thine is the kingdom" etc.

The priest, making the sign of the cross, continues: "Glory be to the Father and to the Son and to the Holy Ghost in our beginning and in our end; may his graces descend upon us, weak and sinful as we are, in both worlds, now and always and for ever and ever. Amen."

The minister (choir) recites a prayer, [145] similar in character to the great *synapte* of the Byzantine rite: "For the peace and salvation of the whole world, for the faithful of Christ from one end of the world to the other, for those in weakness and in tribulation, and for the souls which lie in affliction, and for our fathers and brethren and teachers; and also because of our sins and our failings, and the vices of all; and for the faithful departed who have gone before us, we entreat the Lord."

In the meanwhile, the priest, extending his hands, says the prayer of the introit: [146] "O Lord God, render us worthy to enter with courage into thy dwelling, to knock with confidence at thy gate, and to adore thee with purity in thy temple. Hear our supplications with favour, and in thy mercy grant our desires, and we will joyously glorify

[145] *Karozutho;* Greek, κηρύξις.
[146] Each part of the divine office and every rite of blessing, consecration etc., begins with a prayer known as *shuroyo* ("of the beginning").

thee, O triune God, Father, Son and Holy Ghost, now and
always, for ever and ever."

Then he turns to the right [147] and blesses the people, as
he says: "Peace be to the Church and to her children."

This is followed by a form of the *Gloria in excelsis,*
said with the deacon: "Glory to God in the highest, and on
earth peace to men of good will. Glory be to the Father and
to the Son and to the Holy Ghost, now and for ever and
ever. O Lord, thou wilt open my lips, and my tongue will
announce thy praise: O Lord, open my lips, and they will
sing thy praises. Set a watch, O God, before my mouth,
and a door round about my lips. Incline not my heart to
evil words, to make excuses in sins. O Lord, remember thy
goodness and thy mercy, which thou hast made to appear in
all times; remember not the sins which I have committed,
but in the abundance of thy mercies remember me. I have
loved, O Lord, the beauty of thy house and the place where
thy glory dwelleth. Holiness becometh thy house, O Lord,
for ever. O praise the Lord, all ye nations; praise him all
ye people; for his mercy is confirmed upon us; and the
truth of the Lord remaineth for ever. Glory be to the Father
and to the Son and to the Holy Ghost, always and for ever
and ever. Peace on earth to men of good will."

The solemn prayers, said to have been composed by
fathers of the Church, are known as *sedra* ("order"); while
their doxological introductions are called *proemia.* [148]

The *sedro,* which is a prayer of praise said aloud by the
priest as the censer is swung, is built up by the insertion of
verses into a more or less constant framework, commemor-

[147] The blessing is given facing the people at three solemn moments
in the liturgy,—before the gospel; before the greater elevation; and at
the end of the liturgy.
[148] Greek, προοίμιον.

ative of season or feast. It would seem to be a survival of the old psalm verses with the *Gloria.*

Extending his arms, the priest first says a *proem* in honour of our Lady: "May we be working to give praise and glory, thanksgiving and honour to the most High, who, having humbled himself, magnified the humble Virgin; to God, who became man, and who hath saved men, to the lofty one who hath humbled himself and raised on high the lowly; to God, who is above all others and to whom belongs glory and honour at this moment, in all festivals and at every instant of our life, now and always, for ever and ever. Amen."

A *sedro* [149] follows: "While we sing the praises, the glories and the melodies of the Holy Spirit, in honour of the blessed Mary, Mother of God and ever virgin, and while we present the supplications and the prayers which she makes for us before her Son, who was born of her womb, we say: O Lord, we beseech thee, through the supplications of thy Mother, put far from the land and from all its inhabitants all the evils and the scourges of thy anger; let adversities and uprisings disappear; let war, exile, famine and epidemics cease; have compassion on our weakness; heal our maladies; succour us in our misery; save us from injustice; give eternal rest to the faithful departed, and grant that we too may leave this world in peace, in order to render glory to thee, for ever and ever. Amen."

The deacon [150] or server responds with the *Innana*

---

[149] An alternative *proem* and *sedro* are given in the Latin translation of Prince Maximilian of Saxony. Further references to this translation will be noted as *P. M. S.* In Arabic, this prayer takes the name of the "prayer of pardon"—*hussayah or hussay,* from the Syriac *hussoyo* "pardon." Pietro SFAIR, *La Messa Siro-Maronita* (Rome, 1946), p. 27, n. 11.

[150] "Choir sings." SFAIR, *op. cit.,* p. 25.

nazkor: "Be there remembrance of Mary, the Mother of God, of the prophets, the apostles, the martyrs and the just, of the priests and all the children of the Church, from generation to generation, and for ever and ever. Amen."

The commemorations which follow are variable.

The commemoration in honour of the blessed Virgin is said secretly, with bowed head and joined hands: "O Jesus, only begotten and eternal Son, we offer thee this incense of sweet perfume, in memory of thy Mother and of all the saints. May it be pleasing to thee, according to thy will, and that of the Father and of the Holy Ghost, now and for ever. Amen."

The deacon [151] (server) answers *Salatooke maana:* "Let thy intercession be with us, Mother most pure, and assist our poverty, as is thy wont. Behold us, exiles on the earth, seeing our end approaching—and now we are perishing—succour us by thy prayers, O Virgin most pure and holy, and be thou always our advocate, lest we perish through our own malice. O blessed one, supplicate and plead for us before God, who was born of thy womb, that he may show us mercy through thy prayers, O most holy one."

Other memorials include those of the prophets, apostles, martyrs, saints and the holy dead. The last-named describes the effects of receiving the blessed sacrament: "Be not sorrowful, all you who sleep in the dust, for the corruption of your bodies. The living body which you have eaten and the blood of propitiation which you have drunk, can vivify you all and clothe your bodies with glory. This is the way, and the bridge through which you shall be led to the place of life. O Christ, who didst come and reconcile through thy blood all height, all depth and all regions, grant, O Lord, that

---

[151] " Choir sings." *Ibid.*

the souls of thy servants may rest externally in the promised life."

Kyrie eleison (thrice) is followed a secret prayer, answering to the *super oblata* of the Roman rite.

The priest places his hands [152] in the form of a cross over the oblations, as he says: "We now make the commemoration of our Lord Jesus Christ, our God and our Saviour, and of the whole of that life which he led amongst us for our redemption, upon this host which is placed before us; and of Adam our father and Eve our mother, and of all the children of men who have pleased God, from the time of Adam to this day; above all and especially of the holy, glorious and ever virgin, blessed Mary, Mother of God. We offer it also in honour of the prophets, apostles, martyrs, confessors, the just, priests, holy patriarchs, doctors of the true faith, hermits eminent for the fear of God, virgins and the saint (*N.*) upon whose altar we make our oblation, and we recommend to you our fathers and brothers, our masters spiritual and temporal, and all the faithful departed, children of the holy Church (*N. N.*). Especially by name thy servants (*N. N.*) for whom this oblation is made. O Lord God, pardon their offences and blot out their sins. Grant eternal rest to the souls of their dead and preserve them from all evils and chastisement. Amen."

Commemorations are now made for the sick, the dead, parents, the saint of the day and our Lady.

The priest then strikes his breast three times, as he says: "O Holy Trinity, have mercy on me; O Holy Trinity,

---

[152] Cf. the Jewish priest placing his hands on the head of the holocaust (Levit., I, 4; Exodus, XXIX, *passim*), and also on the head of the scapegoat (Levit., XVI, 21) which St. Paul (Heb., XIII, 11-12) says is symbolised by Christ.

forgive me my sins; O holy and glorious Trinity, accept this oblation from my sinful hands."

Joining his hands over the oblations, he continues: "O God, for the sake of this oblation which we present to thee upon this holy altar (N.), remember our fathers, brothers, masters who have died and all the faithful departed. O God, pardon, blot out and forgive in this moment my sins, my offences and the sins of those who invoke thee through my mediation, with true faith. Remember especially, O Lord, those for whom this sacrifice is offered and those who have asked us to remember them before thee. Be mindful of them, O Lord; blot out their faults and their sins, through thy infinite mercies. Amen."

Then, extending his hands, the priest says: "O Lord, God Almighty, who dost blot out the sins of men, and who desirest not the death of a sinner, I stretch forth my hands to thee, and beg of thee the pardon of all my disobedience to thy laws. And, although I am not worthy, I beseech thee to protect my understanding against all the deceits of the enemy, my eyes against all sinful sights, my ears against all useless and idle words, my hands against all dishonourable deeds, and my whole being which moves in thee. Grant me the grace to receive thy divine mysteries. O Lord God, glory be to thee for ever and ever. Amen."

The entrance chant (*Lbaitokh*) is repeated as before, with the priest moving his head in the form of a cross: "O God, I have entered into thy house, and have knelt before thy throne: O heavenly King, forgive us all the sins which we have committed against thee."

Then the prayers of the people are asked: "Pray to our Lord for me," and the choir or server responds: "May God accept thy oblation, and show us mercy through thy prayers."

The priest, making the sign of the cross, recites "Glory be to the Father etc." and the people answer "Amen."

Once again the deacon (server), as in the Byzantine rite at the *synapte*, says: "For the peace and salvation of the whole world, for the faithful of Christ from one end of the world to the other, for those in weakness and in tribulation, for the souls which lie in affliction, for our fathers, brethren and teachers, and also because of our sins and failings and vices of all, and for the faithful departed who have gone before us, we entreat the Lord."

The prayer of humble access, which follows, is sometimes called the prayer for the catechumens, as it was originally said on their behalf, and also for the penitents: "O Lord, God of mercy, who lovest all men, make us worthy to stand with purity in thy presence and with attention, fear and respect; that we may serve thee holily, and glorify thee as the Lord and Creator of all things, to whom is due the adoration and reverence of all creatures, our Lord and our God. Glory be to thee for ever and ever."

Still concerned with the unworthiness of those who stand before the altar, the liturgy directs the priest and deacon to recite in Arabic the *Miserere* (*psl.* L), while the former [153] censes the oblations (three times in the form of a cross), and altar, and the latter the people.

Then, with outstretched hands, the priest says: "Have mercy on us, O Lord, according to thy mercy; blot out our sins in thy clemency and cleanse our iniquities in the abundance of thy goodness; create a clean heart in us and a spirit of uprightness and humility; sanctify our thoughts; purify us anew from the sins which require whole burnt-offerings and

[153] At a pontifical liturgy, the priest assistant censes the oblations and altar, while the bishop remains at the throne.

Maronite Chorepiscopus

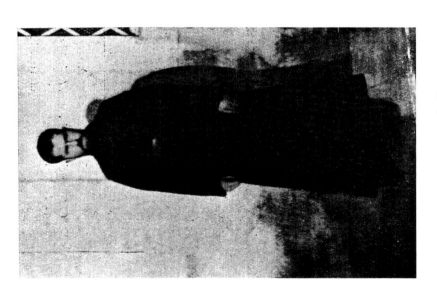

Aleppine Maronite monk, Rome

(*Left to right*) Mar Ivanios, Archbishop of Trivandrum (Syro-Malankara rite) · Mar Augustine, Archbishop of Ernakulam (Syro-Malabarese rite) · Mar Theophilos, Bishop of Tiruvella (Syro-Malankara rite)

legal victims. Teach the unjust thy ways; convert the wanderer to thee, in order that every tongue may proclaim thy justice and praise thy eternal mercies, Father, Son and Holy Ghost, now and for ever and ever. Amen."

The deacon responds: "Stand we well in prayers and supplications before the God of gods, the Lord of lords, the King of kings, the altar of propitiation and before the glorious and divine mysteries of our Redeemer. Let us plead for thy mercies, O Lord, with sweet-smelling gums which are offered before thee."

This is followed by a *proem* and *sedro:* (on ordinary days).

Proem. "May we be worthy to offer him praise, glory, thanksgiving and honour."

Sedro. "It is the most high God who hath given all things being."

(Wednesdays, Saturdays and feasts of our Lady).

Proem. "May we be worthy to offer her praise, thanksgiving and honour."

Sedro. " I salute thee, Mary, who hast preserved thy virginity. Praise to thee, O Lord, born of a virgin, who hast become man, and hast united two natures and two wills in one person."

A variable hymn, [154] composed by St. Ephrem or at least built up after his style, is recited here, and at a solemn liturgy it is chanted alternately by the priest and choir.

When the *sedro* is finished, the deacon gives the monition: "Stand we well in prayers and supplications."

The oblations are now censed with three swings in the form of a circle, as the priest says (three times) the trisagion

---

[154] The missal gives seven hymns; *P. M. S.* 5; cf. sequences of the Roman rite. The hymns are called " Ephremites" or, if they are according to the mode of St. James, " Jacobites."

(*kadishat Aloho*): "Thou art holy God; thou art holy mighty; thou art holy immortal."

The choir responds: "Have mercy on us."

On Good Friday, the choir answers: "O Christ, who hast been crucified for us, have mercy on us;" and at Easter: "O Christ, risen from the dead, have mercy on us."

It seems likely that the words "thou art" were inserted in the trisagion at a time subsequent to the Crusades, when a number of Jacobites were reconciled to the Church, although the interpolation appears out of place in a liturgy of "Dyophysites."

The Maronites, in common with other Syrians, at one time had two methods of reciting the trisagion, *a*) a hymn to the Holy Trinity and *b*) a hymn to our Lord. This twofold use existed in the patriarchate of Antioch in the time of the patriarch Ephrem of Amida [155] (529-545). It was referred to in the Maronite synod of 1596, [156] at which Jerome Dandinus, the Roman legate, presided.

Commemorations of the birth, crucifixion and death of our Lord were added to the second form.

In 1578, Pope Gregory XIII sent two legates [157] to the Maronite patriarch, Michael El-Ruzzi, who among other reforms ordered the insertions in the trisagion to be removed from the liturgy.

The wishes of the pope were acceded to by the synods of 1580 [158] (Kannobin) and 1596 (Kannobin), and the missal of 1592 was produced without the insertion "who was crucified for us."

---

[155] *Dict. de Théol. Cath.*, t. X, col. 20.
[156] HANSSENS, *Instit. Lit. de Rit. Orien.*, t. III, *pars altera*, p. 148.
[157] *Ibid.*, pp. 146-147.
[158] "*Nihilominus, petente Sancta Sede, omnis insertio in trisagio apud Maronitas eodem saeculo XVI prohibita est.*"

After the trisagion, the oblations, cross and altar are again censed, as the priest says: "O holy Lord, glorified, strong and immortal, who dwellest with thy saints and whose holy will is not pleased except with thy saints, sanctify our thoughts and purify our intentions from all foulness of sin, in order that from the bosom of thy Church we may make continual praises to ascend to thee, now and always, for ever and ever."

The *monogones*, [159] once sung at the gospel procession, has long since disappeared from the Maronite rite.

From at least the 17th century, [160] the liturgy has had only two lessons, [161] and the subdeacon, as in the Roman rite, is associated with the singing of the epistle. On less solemn occasions this is recited by the server.

The missal, printed at Rome in 1592, had seven Pauline lessons, one assigned to each day of the week.

The subdeacon (deacon) raises his voice and says: "The psalm of praise is said before our father (celebrant). Bless, Lord," and the priest responds: "Sing and glorify thy Creator."

A variable psalm follows, with the deacon reciting the first verse and the celebrant the second.

Then the deacon continues: "He whom Moses saw in the bush and Ezechiel on the chariot is offered on the altar, and the people receive him and live through him, whom the cherubim and seraphim serve with great fear. And lo he is offered on the altar and the people receive him and live through him. O God, who hast received through thy

[159] Cf. Byzantine, Armenian and Syrian rites.
[160] DANDINI, *Missione apostolica al Patriarca e ai Maroniti del Monte Libano,* p. 80. Cesena, 1656.
[161] In a solemn liturgy, one candle is held for the epistle, two for the gospel. S. Andrea della Valle, Rome, Epiphany, 1947.

mercies the sacrifices of the first just man, receive through thy mercies our sacrifice and be reconciled by our prayers."

The lesson has by way of preface: "I read, over these pure and holy mysteries before our father, from Paul, the apostle of our Lord Jesus Christ according to the will of God. Bless lord."

The priest blesses the reader: "Glory be to the Lord of Paul, of the prophets, and of the apostles; may the grace of God be upon them that read and them that hear, upon this city and its inhabitants for ever."

The epistle is recited in Arabic (sometimes Syriac and Arabic) facing north, and the reader holds a censer.

In a pontifical liturgy, the subdeacon faces west, with a portable light by his side.

At the conclusion of the lesson, the subdeacon says: "And we lift up to the Lord our praises, thanksgivings and adorations in the church before this altar and before our father. Bless, lord." Then, preparatory to the alleluiatic chant, he continues: "The psalm of David is sung before our father. Bless, Lord."

The subdeacon, in a pontifical liturgy, is now blessed by the bishop, but there is often a lack of uniformity in the ceremonial of different churches.

The oriental rites present a strange mixture of extreme conservatism and "all-anyhow-ness." [162]

The celebrant then says: "May God accept thy praises (hulolokh) and rejoice the hearts of thy hearers in the kingdom of heaven for ever and ever."

After a twofold "alleluia," the deacon recites psalm

---

[162] Improvisation in the East, however, never causes any loss of the liturgical sense.

verses [163] of thanksgiving: "Offer to him the sacrifice of praise; *take the offering* and go up to the house of the Lord, adore him in his holy temple, glorify and bless his name, for he hath given life to us. Alleluia."

Dom Edmund Martène [164] thinks that the words "take the offering" (*ferte oblationes*), which are said here, allude to a procession of the sacred gifts that formerly took place after the epistle. A recent writer, [165] quoting the learned Maurist, has said: "one knows that the Maronite rite has undergone some western influences, and French in particular." There does not seem to be, however, any evidence for such a procession at this point of the liturgy, and the words quoted above are probably no more than a rendering of the 8th and 9th verses of psalm XCV. [166]

Then the deacon presents incense to the priest, as he says: "We implore thy mercies, O Lord, in the presence of the announcement of thy Saviour which foretells life to our souls, through sweet-smelling gums which are placed before thee."

Kyrie eleison is chanted three times, and the priest blesses from the left side: "Peace be with you all" (*Shlomo lkoolkhoon*), while the people respond: "And with thy spirit."

---

[163] Cf. Gradual of the Roman rite.

[164] *De Antiquis Ecclesiae Ritibus*, t. I, lib. I, chap. IV, art. V, col. 136. Antwerp, 1763. Dom Martène writes of a solemn procession of bread and wine to the altar which existed in his day in the church of Tours, and then goes on to say that *ferte oblationes* in the Maronite liturgy "seems to allude to this rite" (*ad hunc ritum alludere videtur*).

[165] Dom Denys BUENNER, *L'Ancienne Liturgie Romaine. Le Rite Lyonnais*, chap. VI, p. 276, n. 1, Lyon, 1934.

[166] "*Afferte Domino gloriam nomini ejus. Tollite hostias, et introite in atria ejus; adorate Dominum in atrio sancto ejus. Commoveatur a facie ejus universa terra.*"

The deacon [167] gives the monition: "Draw near, brethren, be still and hear the announcement of our Redeemer
from the holy gospel, which is read to you."

This is followed in a solemn liturgy by the procession of
the gospel. The deacon carries the book on his breast, and
the subdeacon censes during the procession.

The gospel is then announced: "Let us hear for the good
of our souls the glad tidings of life and salvation, the holy
gospel of our Lord Jesus Christ: Preaching of St. (N.),
Apostle (Disciple), who hath preached life to the world."

The deacon again enjoins silence and attention: "Be
hearers in silence, for lo the holy gospel is read. Brethren
attend, hear and glorify the word of the living God and give
thanks for it."

The priest continues: "In the time therefore of the
dispensation of the salvation of our Lord and God and
Saviour Jesus Christ, he said to his disciples and to the
multitudes."

In response to the request of the people: "Father, bless
us," the celebrant turns to the faithful and gives a blessing
three times with the hand-cross, as he says: "May the right
hand of our Lord Jesus Christ, the strong arm of his om-
nipotence, the hidden power of his grandeur, which brings
with it all blessings and all the gifts of life, which rested
upon the apostles in the cenacle of Sion, sanctified and blessed them on the Mount of Olives, descend, rest upon and
dwell among my brethren, who read and hear, and be their
protection. May it protect also this place and the faithful
who are present, this city and its faithful inhabitants; may
it grant eternal rest to the departed souls who have died here,

[167] The translation of *P. M. S.*, before the monition, has further
prayers by the priest and deacon.

may it preserve the faithful who are living and dwell here, always and for ever and ever."

Then the priest says: "Behold that which happened in the life of Jesus Christ, our Lord, our God and our Saviour, the Word of God which was made man for us (People: "Lord have mercy on us"), may our Lord have mercy on us, on you and on all the children of the holy Church by the baptism which cleanseth."

On Christmas Day, the gospel is read in both Syriac and Arabic. At a "low Mass," the priest sometimes reads the gospel from a lectern facing the people.

A bishop, holding his crozier and accompanied by portable lights, recites the gospel from the throne, and, at its conclusion, blesses the faithful with the hand-cross, which he kisses after touching the book.

The celebrant and deacon at a solemn liturgy both kiss the book of the gospels.

As he signs his breast, the priest says: "In the name of the Father and of the Son and of the Holy Ghost," and, blessing the people at the conclusion of the gospel: "Peace be with you all."

The following prayer to the Holy Trinity is said at the salutation of the book: "To Jesus be glory, praise and benediction, for the vivifying word which he hath addressed to us; to the Father, who sent him for our salvation, and to the Holy Ghost, now and always, for ever and ever."

The deacon gives a further monition: "Let us all stand in prayer before the God of mercy and with such words as may appease him, let us cry to God in peace. Let us ask the hidden Father, his glorious and holy Son and the Holy Spirit the Comforter, that in pity he may receive our sacrifice. May thy announcing, O Lord, which has been foretold in thy Church over thy flock be as leaven to our souls and through it grant us pleasant food. May the priests who have read it be reconciled, the deacons justified and the subdeacons and lectors receive pardon from thee. Be favourable upon thy people, O God, and have mercy upon thy flock and may we lift up a threefold voice of praise to the Trinity."

The dismissal of the catechumens which took place at this point of the liturgy no longer exists, although some manuscripts have retained the formula for sending away hearers and penitents before the prayer preceding the "peace."

Liturgy of the Faithful

A prayer [168] or hymn [169] in honour of our Lady is now immediately followed by the liturgy of the faithful.

The priest and deacon say or chant together a prayer, which may be compared with the Roman offertory: "The Lord reigneth, he is clothed with beauty, Alleluia. Our Lord said: I am the living bread, which came down from heaven upon the earth, in order that the world may find life in me. The Father sent me, his Word, without flesh, and the womb of Mary received me, as a rich grain of wheat in a fertile soil. [170] And behold the priests carry [171] me in their hands on the altars. Alleluia. Accept our oblation."

---

[168] At a " low Mass."

[169] In a solemn liturgy and on feasts.

[170] The ancient manuscripts, in place of "as a rich grain .... soil," had the words: "as a tiller of the soil Gabriel has sown me." The change was effected in the first edition of the missal and in all successive books, lest the simple might be led to suppose that the seals of the virginity of Mary had been violated. *La Messa Siro-Maronita*. Pietro SFAIR (Rome, 1946), p. 47, n. 19.

[171] The prayer refers to a procession of the elements from the prothesis, which formerly took place during its recitation. Sometimes the choir also joins in this eucharistic hymn. SFAIR, *op. cit.*, pp. 47-48, n. 20.

(Deacon) "The Lord hath put on strength and clothed himself."

(Priest) "Glory be to the Father and to the Son and to the Holy Ghost. Alleluia. Be mindful, O Lord, of the departed and grant rest to those who have been clothed in thee in baptism, and have received thee."

(Deacon) "May those who have received thy holy body and drunk thy blood, the chalice of redemption, rejoice with Abraham in thy kingdom and on thy right hand may they cry out: "Glory be to thee, O Lord." Alleluia. Grant them rest, O Lord."

The creed, with the conciliar "*we* believe" and the *filioque,* is recited in Arabic by the deacon or choir, and said silently by the priest.

Renaudot [172] quotes the rubric: "Then they recite the symbol of the three hundred and eighteen Fathers at Nicaea."

In the meanwhile, the priest, [173] in the third and last censing, [174] censes the cross and the altar, while the deacon censes the people.

The *lavabo,* at which the priest recites a few verses of psalm XXV, follows, and the choir sings either *Falnahef* or a hymn.

The former is a chant of praise: "Let us all stand, with reverence, praising and thanking our Saviour, the lamb of God who is being offered upon our altar. *Kyrie eleison.*"

The priest now returns to the altar for the anaphora, first moving his head crosswise and repeating the entrance

[172] *Op. cit.,* t. II, p. 10.
[173] At a pontifical liturgy, the censing is carried out by the assistant priest.
[174] The Maronite rite has three censings,—at the *Miserere,* at the trisagion, and during the creed,—although a Syriac manuscript, dating from 1536 and preserved in the Vatican library, has but one, at the chant (*sedro*) after the *Miserere.*

chant [175] (*Lbaitokh*) for the third time: "I have entered into thy house, O God, and have knelt before thy throne: O heavenly King, forgive us all the sins which we have committed against thee."

Then, turning to either side and with hands crossed on his breast, the priest asks for the prayers of the people: "Pray to our Lord for me."

The response is made: "May God accept thy oblation, and show us mercy through thy prayers."

Anaphora

The choice of anaphora rests in theory with the individual celebrant, but in practice it would be unusual if the priest, except on certain days, deviated from "The Canon of the Mass, taken from the Canon of the Holy Roman Catholic Church, mother of all the Churches."

This anaphora, which is peculiar to the Maronite rite, is not a translation of the Latin canon, although it has been influenced by it. It was drawn up for the missal of 1716 by Andrew Alexander, a Maronite of Cyprus, at the instance of the Sacred Congregation of *Propaganda Fide*. The type or model for the anaphora was the Anaphora of the Twelve Apostles, in which the diptychs and some other parts have a more concise and freer form than the others.

The priest signs himself with the cross, saying: "Glory be to the Father and to the Son and to the Holy Ghost, now and always, for ever and ever."

Then, extending his hands, he continues aloud: "O Lord, [176] Jesus Christ, who saidst to thy apostles: peace I

---

[175] A defect of this liturgy is the frequent repetition.

[176] Cf. the first prayer before the communion of the priest in the Roman rite. In the printed Syriac missal, this prayer, with others, is written in Arabic.

leave with you, my peace I give unto you; let thy holy will be accomplished, and grant us protection and peace, that we may make praise to rise to thee, now and always, for ever and ever. (People) Amen."

Then the deacon gives a monition: "In the midst stand we well." This is followed by a *koruzuto* (homily): "And let us pray, confess, adore and glorify the living lamb of God, who is offered upon the altar. O God, who didst incline and come down to sinners, sons of Adam, and didst redeem them from the error and slavery of sin, we are mindful in this sacrifice of the pure Virgin Mary, the prophets, apostles and martyrs, as well as of the innocent and the just. The sacrificial vessels are given to our father that he may kiss them. May our father remember in the sacrifice all the faithful in Christ. Lord have mercy on us."

The priest, bowing and joining his hands, says secretly: [177] "O Lord God Almighty, who in the abundance of thy mercies hast created us and hast appointed us, miserable sinners, to stand before thy majesty as ministers at thy holy altar, pour upon us now, O Lord, thy countless blessings; fortify us by the power of the Holy Spirit, and grant that we may open our lips to invoke thy Holy Spirit in all things upon this oblation, which is placed here for the pardon of our sins and the salvation of our souls, and that we may give the kiss of peace one to another. We shall then be rich in thy love and in thy mercies, and will make praise and glory to ascend even unto thee, to thine only Son and to thy Holy Spirit, now and always, for ever and ever."[178]

---

[177] *G'honto,* "inclination;" cf. μυστικῶς.

[178] This secret prayer is found in the Anaphora of St. Peter that begins with the word *Sharar* as the second of the three prayers that precede the *pax.* It was included in the first printed missal (1592), but the following editions suppressed it. Andrew Alexander inserted the

Then the deacon (server), moving to the left side and kissing the altar, on his knees gives to the celebrant the end of the large veil, which is kissed, folded and placed over the chalice.

The priest, extending his hands, says aloud the "Prayer of the imposition of hands": "We adore thee, O Lord, and we supplicate thee, O merciful one, to grant us thy protection, so as to be protected from evils (he joins his hands) and we will make praise to ascend to thee, now and always, for ever and ever. (People) Amen."

The celebrant continues with the "Prayer of the Veil:"[179] "Receive, O Lord, our oblation, establish our days in peace, save us from eternal damnation, place us in the number of the sheep, thy elect, and we will make praise to ascend to thee, now and always, for ever and ever. (People) Amen."

Then he touches the altar, paten and chalice with his right hand, each time kissing the index finger, as he says: "Peace be to thee, altar of God; peace be to the holy mysteries which are upon thee." The priest now touches the hand of the deacon (server), and says: "Peace to thee, minister of the Holy Spirit; peace to the Church and to all her children."

The response is made: "I come in peace, venerable father and priest."

The assistant kneels down and, extending his right hand on the edge of the altar, kisses the hand of the priest and blesses himself.

---

prayer as the second in the Anaphora of the Holy Roman Church, while the Anaphora of St. Peter, that begins with the words *Aloho dashlomo*, has the prayer as the second of the *four* prayers before the *pax*.

[179] James of Edessa (*Bib. Orien.*, I, 481) says that the removal of the veil symbolises the opening of the gate of heaven.

The "peace" (*salâm*) is given to all those in the sanctuary by placing joined hands [180] between the hands of each in turn, while the deacon (server) chants: "Let us all give peace one to another with love and loyalty well pleasing to God; please grant peace, most reverend father."

The priest, uncovering the oblations, says: "Thou art the stone from which burst the twelve fountains of water for the twelve tribes of Israel."

Then he waves the veil over the mysteries and over the congregation from the left and the right side of the altar, symbolising the descent of the Holy Spirit, as he asks for the blessing of the Holy Trinity: "May the charity of God the Father, the grace of the only-begotten Son, the communication and the indwelling of the Holy Spirit be with you all, my brethren, for ever. (Choir) Amen."

This solemn formula of benediction was a later addition to the liturgy than "Peace be with you all," but it was referred to in a letter of Theodoret of Cyrus († ab. 457) to John the Cellerar (*Oeconomus*) — *illam esse Liturgiae Proemium*. [181]

After the response: "And with thy spirit," the priest removes the veil from the oblations and, signing himself three times, he says thrice: "Glory be to the Father and to the Son and to the Holy Ghost, the adorable and glorious mystery, in whom there is no division, now and always, for ever and ever. (People) Amen."

In a commentary on the liturgy, James of Edessa (ab. 633-708) says: "Three prayers are made after the recitation of the creed,—those of the *pax*, the imposition of hands (recited over the people) and the uncovering of the anaphora or veil."

---

[180] The joined hands signify that they are powerless to do harm.
[181] Cf. Office of baptism in the Maronite rite.

This is followed by the *Sursum corda* and its dialogue:

Priest (raising his hands): "Let us lift up our thoughts, our minds and our hearts."

People: "They are raised to thee, O Lord."

Priest (extending his hands and bowing): "Let us glorify God with fear, and adore him with trembling."

People: "It is meet and just."

Deacon: "To thee, O God of Abraham and Isaac and Jacob, O glorious and holy king of Israel for ever."

Priest: "Glory be to the Father and to the Son and to the Holy Ghost, now and for ever world without end."

Deacon: "Before the glorious and divine mysteries of our Redeemer, with the pleasant things which are imposed, let us implore the mercy of the Lord."

People: "It is meet and just."

The preface or "Prayer of Triumph" is begun in a low voice, the hands of the priest resting on the altar: "It is truly meet and just that we glorify thee faithfully, O God almighty. (aloud) The angels glorify thee, the dominations adore thee and the powers tremble with fear. The heavens with the virtues and the blessed seraphim celebrate together thy greatness. Render us worthy to lift up our humble voice and to say with them."

As the priest recites the *sanctus*, he three times waves with his hand over the oblations to symbolise the flying of the angels, whom the prophet Isaias saw flying before the throne of God, singing "Holy, holy, holy."

In the meanwhile, the people sing (bell is rung): "Holy, holy, holy Lord God of hosts. Heaven and earth are full of thy glory and thy honour and thy greatness, hosanna in the highest. Blessed is he who cometh and who art to come in the name of the Lord. Hosanna in the highest of heaven."

In some churches, [182] the cope-like Syrian vestment is exchanged at the *sanctus* for a Roman chasuble.

A short *post-sanctus* is said secretly, during which the priest three times signs the oblations: "Holy art thou, O God the Father, who for our salvation hast sent thy only Son, our Lord Jesus Christ."

The words of consecration are similar to those in the Roman rite, but they are chanted with a poignant sorrowful rhythm, in keeping with the anguish of our Lord on the eve of his death:

"Who, the day before he suffered took bread into his holy and venerable [183] hands, and with eyes lifted towards heaven, unto thee, O God, his almighty Father, giving thanks to thee †, did bless †, break †, and give to his disciples, saying: Take, and eat ye all of this: For this is my body. (Minister) Amen."

"In like manner, after supper, taking also this excellent chalice into his holy and venerable hands, and giving thanks to thee †, he blessed †, and sanctified [184] †, and gave to his disciples, saying: Take, and drink ye all of this: For this is the chalice of my blood of the new and eternal testament: the mystery of faith; which shall be shed for you, and for many, for the remission of sins. (Minister) Amen." [185]

Prince Maximilian in the Latin translation has added the word "sanctify" before "break" in the consecration of the host.

---

[182] e. g. At a pontifical liturgy at St. Andrea della Valle, Rome, on the feast of the Epiphany, 1928. *La Messa Siro-Maronita,* p. 6, Roma, 1943.

[183] Omitted by *P. M. S.* and Sfeir.

[184] The word " sanctified" is found in all the Syrian anaphoras, but it was omitted in the Missal of 1592 that adopted the Latin formula of consecration. Recent editions have inserted it.

[185] Sfeir adds " *Kyrie eleison,*" *op. cit.,* p. 34.

The priest, as he says "break," is directed to touch the host four times, as if he would make a fraction.

The bell is rung after each consecration, and a single genuflection is made without an elevation, but the host is placed over the chalice. The synod [186] of 1596 directed the celebrant to keep his fingers joined from the consecration until after the ablutions.

The anamnesis is said aloud: "As often as ye do these things ye shall do them for a commemoration of me."

The minister (people) responds: "O Lord, we make the commemoration of thy death; we believe in thy resurrection; we await thy second coming; we pray thee to grant us thy grace and thy mercy; we beg of thee the pardon of our sins. May all the graces be poured upon us."

The priest, crossing his hands on his breast and bowing, says in a loud voice the "Prayer of the dispensation" [187] and the "Prayer of thanksgiving:" "O Lord God, we make the commemoration of thy sufferings which have redeemed us, of thy resurrection from the dead, and of thy glorious ascension into heaven; for which reason thy Church presents to thee this holy and immaculate victim, praying."

It may be noted that there is no reference in the anaphora either to the session at the right hand of the Father or to the second coming at the end of the world.

The minister (people) responds: "Have mercy on us, [188] O God, Father almighty, have mercy on us," and the priest continues: "We also, O Lord, thy weak and sinful servants, while we receive thy graces, we render thee in return the glory of all these blessings and for all these blessings."

---

[186] Canon 10.
[187] "Economy" or "dispensation" is called in Syriac *mdabronuts*. In other rites, the prayer is called the Anamnesis.
[188] *P. M. S.* adds "We glorify thee."

The minister answers: "We glorify thee, we adore thee, we believe in thee, and we address our supplications to thee; pardon us, O Lord God; have mercy on us and hear us."

This is followed by a memorial of our Lady said by the priest:

"Again, and above all, we make the commemoration of the holy, glorious and ever virgin, the blessed Mary, Mother of God. (said secretly) O Mother of our Lord Jesus Christ, ask thy only Son, who was born of thee, to pardon my faults and my sins, and to accept from my weak, sinful hands this victim, whom in my lowliness I offer upon this altar; O holy Mother, obtain for me these favours through thy prayer."

The deacon in the meanwhile continues the memorial: "Be mindful of her, O Lord, and through her pure and holy prayers be clement, have mercy on us and hear us."

Before the epiclesis, the priest moves his hands three times over the oblations in the form of "waves," as he says: "Have mercy on us, O Lord, and send on us thy Holy Spirit, the Creator of life."

Then the deacon gives a monition: "Bless, lord. How awe-inspiring is this hour and how terrible is this time, my beloved, in which the life-giving and Holy Spirit flies from the highest heaven and comes down and moves over this eucharist, which has been placed in the house o four sanctuary for our reconciliation. Stand and pray with silence and fear. May salvation and the peace of God our Father be with us all. Let us cry aloud and say thrice."

The phraseology of the monition seems to indicate that at the time of its composition it was generally believed that the consecration had already taken place, and consequently was not dependent on the epiclesis.

The priest, in response to the diaconal invitation,

kneels [189] on both knees, touches the altar three times with his hand, kisses it, and recites the prayer to the Holy Spirit: "Aid me, O Lord; aid me, O Lord; aid me, O Lord; and may thy living and Holy Spirit come and dwell in me and in this oblation."

The minister (people) answers: *Kyrie eleison* (three times). Then (bell rings), rising to his feet, the priest continues: "May he also make this † mystery, † the body † of Christ, our God, to be for our salvation. (Minister or people) Amen."

"May he also make this † chalice, † the blood † of Christ, our God, to be for our salvation. (Minister or people) Amen."

St. Ephrem († 373) in the hymn on the priesthood refers to the prayer before the epiclesis, and speaks of the priest as kneeling, while he prays to the Father that he may send his Holy Spirit upon the sacrifice.

It will be observed that the epiclesis has been altered and mutilated, and only that part has been retained in which it is asked that the fruits of the sacrifice may be applied to souls in holy communion.

So early as the 15th century, we find examples of tampering with the text of the invocation, although traces of the original wording were found in the missal of 1592, in the anaphoras of Matthew the Shepherd, Eustathius and the Twelve Apostles. Other forms of epiclesis also exist in four anaphoras of the liturgy of 1716, and in two anaphoras of the missals published in Beirut (1888; 1908). The council [190]

---

[189] This unusual posture for the celebrant in the offering of the holy Sacrifice may be noted.

[190] "*Maxime autem probamus aliam ejusdem invocationis formulam, quae in plerisque liturgiis legitur, et apud nos jam obtinuit, ut non per illam petatur panis in corpus et vini in sanguinem Domini conversio, sed*

of the Lebanon (1736) specifically approved the altered phraseology in the invocation of the Holy Spirit.

The intercession, which resembles a rather rambling paraphrase of the Roman canon, although it is not divided by the consecration, begins with the priest saying aloud: "We pray thee, O Lord God, to grant us thy grace in this world and thy kingdom in the next, through the meditation of these mysteries, and we glorify thee now and always, for ever and ever."

At a solemn liturgy, the deacon then gives a bidding: "Bless, lord. Let us pray and beseech our Lord God at this great, terrible and holy moment for our fathers and leaders, who rule over us to-day in this life and who feed and guide the holy churches of God. Let us beseech the Lord for our honourable and holy Lord (*N*.), Pope of Rome, our Lord (*N*.) Peter, our Patriarch, and our Lord (*N*.), Metropolitan, together with all other honourable and orthodox metropolitans and bishops."

The people respond: *Kyrie eleison,* and the priest silently continues the prayer for the hierarchy: "We supplicate thee, O God, Father of mercies, etc."

Then he says: "*Remember* the immaculate and glorious, the blessed and ever virgin Mary, Mother of God: remember the Saints Peter and Paul: .... Remember, O Lord, thy servants, who have slept in the true faith, and who repose in the sleep of peace."

The deacon in the meanwhile recites a long intercession for all sorts and conditions of men; for peace and tranquillity; Christian rulers; founders of churches and monasteries; and for the whole state of Christ's Church.

---

hoc tantum postulet sacerdos, ut corpus et sanguis Domini fiant sumentibus ea in remissionem peccatorum." Part II, chap. XII, n. 8-9.

This is followed by a commemoration [191] of saints,—our Lady; John Baptist; Stephen; the fathers of the first four general councils; James, "who was apostle, martyr and leader of bishops;" Ignatius; Dionysius; Athanasius; Basil; Gregory; Cyril, "who is the true tower and demonstrator of the Incarnate Word;" Maro, "who was a blessed and holy father, whom the holy Roman Catholic Church received;" James; Ephrem,—and a further memorial of the dead.

The prayer concludes: "At the same time let us thrice cry out and say, *Kyrie eleison,*" and the priest in an audible voice thus ends the intercession: "Give to them, O Lord, and to those who are asleep in Christ, the repose of the habitations of light and of rest, and grant to them and to us thy mercy."

The minister (people) responds: "Grant them eternal rest, O Lord, and blot out and pardon the sins which they have committed whether deliberately or through ignorance."

The eucharistic intercession ends with those eighteen benedictions, which Janin [192] calls a seeming echo of the prayer of the eighteen benedictions in the worship of the synagogue.

The next prayer [193] is said in Arabic: "Our hope is strong in thy abundant mercies, O Lord, our God. It is for this we implore thee to make us worthy of the happiness of thy saints, through the intercession of thy only Son, our Lord Jesus Christ, with whom thou art blessed and glorified, with the Holy Spirit, now and for ever."

[191] When the anaphoras of the Roman Church and the Twelve Apostles are used only the first commemoration is said, but on other occasions the assistant recites all the six.

[192] *Les Eglises orientales et les Rites orientaux,* chap. XVI, p. 547.

[193] According to Bar Salibi (*Expos. Lit.,* pp. 84-85) the second prayer after the diptychs also makes mention of the dead. This is done in the other anaphoras, but it is omitted in the Anaphora of the Roman Church.

The people respond "Amen," and the deacon answers:
"As it was and is and will be for all generations and to the
generations of future aeons for ever. Amen."

The celebrant [194] then gives a blessing: "Peace be with
you all," to which the reply is made: "And with thy spirit."
This is followed by a prayer, said with hands joined: "May
the blessing of God the Father and of our Lord Jesus Christ
and the gifts [195] of the Holy Ghost be with us and with
you all, my brethren, for ever and ever. O Lord God, grant
a participation in this sacrifice, to our fathers, our brethren,
our masters, our instructors, those who have died amongst
us, all those who have been and are in communion with us
in these mysteries, and who have helped to build up the edi-
fice of the holy Church from the beginning until our days."

The deacon now makes intercession for the living and
dead in the "catholic" [196] or *bodiki*, [197] a prayer referred to
by Denys bar-Salibi: [198] "Bless, Lord, again and again by
this pure and holy sacrifice."

In the meanwhile, the priest, having made a genuflection and taken the host in his hand, continues: "We have
believed and we have offered: we now consummate [199]
and break this host (he takes the host), the bread of heaven,
the body of the Word of the living God and we † sign
the chalice of salvation and of grace [200] with the fiery

[194] A bishop uses the hand-cross, and the priest in solemn liturgies.
[195] P. M. S., *obumbratio*, "overshadowing." In this prayer, the
priest formerly made three signs of the cross.
[196] Greek, καθολική, "general."
[197] *Prodiki*, proclamation and prayer said in a low voice.
[198] "*Incipit diaconus Catholicam: et illa generalis oratio est, quia de
omnibus memoriam revocat. Quidem dicunt, Apostolorum temporibus
non exstitisse Catholicam illam, quae ab illis verbis incipit: Iterum atque
iterum.*"
[199] P. M. S., *signamus*, "designate."
[200] P. M. S., *confessionis*, "confession."

coal. [201] In the name of the living † and vivifying † Father †
and through the life † of the Holy † Ghost †, the beginning,
perfection and consummation of all that has been and that is
in heaven and upon earth †, the † same † strength †, the †
same power †, the † same † will †, one only true, blessed and
exalted God, in whom there is no division, and of whom life
is derived, for ever and ever. (Minister or people) Amen."

In the Latin translation [202] of Prince Maximilian, the
name of the Son has been interpolated: "through the life
and of the only-begotten and holy Son †, living † and vivifying † in like manner, who is born from him."

In all, the priest is directed to make the sign of the cross
no less than eighteen times.

It would seem that the fraction was once made here,
although its postponement until after the elevation dates
from at least the 16th century.

Then, raising both host and chalice over the altar (bell
is rung), in a rite peculiar to the Maronites, the priest continues: O desirable victim, who dost offer thyself for us; O
purifying victim, who dost present thyself to the Father;
O lamb, who art at the same time the priest who maketh the
offering; grant that through thy grace our prayer may be
accepted, as of incense, for it is by thee that we offer it to
thy Father."

The priest, holding the host in his right hand and the
chalice in his left, now recites the following prayer of Mar
James of Sarug: "O Father of justice, [203] behold thy Son

[201] "Coal," a common oriental name for the blessed sacrament.
St. Ephrem and James, bishop of Batna, both apply the vision of Isaias
and the coal to the eucharist; cf. gamourto, "body;" margarita, "pearl,"
which purifies and is full of mysteries.
[202] This appears to be the current usage, as it is also found in La
Messa Siro-Maronita (Sfair, Rome, 1946), p. 71.
[203] P. M. S., veritatis, "truth."

as a victim, who offers satisfaction to thee. Accept it (the sacrifice) because he died for me, and by him I shall be cleansed. Behold the offering: accept it from my hands as a satisfaction for me, remember not the sins which I have committed before thy majesty (he puts down the chalice). Behold his blood, which flowed † on Golgotha for my salvation, and which prays for me; accept my offering [204] for its sake. How numberless are my sins, yet how much more abundant are thy graces. If thou weighest them in the balance, thy mercy is greater, for it outweighs by far the weight of the mountains, which thou knowest [205] (he places [206] the host on the paten). Look upon my sins, and look upon the sacrifice † offered for them: the sacrifice and the victim are greater than my sins; I have sinned indeed, but thy well-beloved hath suffered the nails † and spear, and his sufferings are sufficient to appease thee, and by them I will obtain life. Glory be to the Father, who hath sent his Son for us; adoration to the Son (he genuflects), who hath delivered all men by his cross; praise to the Holy Spirit, by whom the mystery of our redemption has been accomplished; blessed be he who has vivified all of us by his love; praise be to him."

The translation of Prince Maximilian adds also: "By the mercies that spared the robber, who wast on the right hand, spare us, O Lord, and have mercy on us," and before the blessing: "May thy cross, O my Lord Jesus Christ, be our perpetual protector against the evil spirit and his powers."

[204] *Ibid., orationem,* " prayer."
[205] Cf. " *Quis appendit tribus digitis molem terrae, et libravit in pondere montes, et colles in statera?*" Isaias, XII, 40.
[206] According to the ancient rubrics, the priest lays down the host and chalice before beginning the metrical prayer of Mar James, and then says the prayer with hands crossed on the breast and head slightly inclined.

In the meanwhile, the choir sings *Sabehoo* or *A ya rabe*.

Sabehoo: "Praise the Lord from the heavens; praise ye him in the high places. Praise ye him all his angels; praise ye him all his hosts. Praise ye him, O sun and moon; praise ye him all ye stars."

A ya rabe: "O Lord, have mercy, and deign to accept our offering. This is the victim offered for sin, as you have instituted in thy infinite generosity."

The introduction to the Lord's prayer is similar to that found in the Roman rite: "Directed by thy saving precepts and following thy divine instruction, we make bold to say: Our Father."

The priest, as the "tongue [207] of the body of the Church," says the first words of the prayer aloud, and the choir or people take it up. This custom was referred to by James of Edessa (ab. 633-708), who said: "then he begins the Lord's prayer, which is thereupon recited by all the people."

It is now said in Arabic, but Renaudot [208] (1648-1720) specifically states that in his day it was in Syriac, even though the people did not understand the language, although Arabic might be used in private prayer.

A 13th century manuscript (1224) of the *Commentary on the Liturgy* by James of Edessa, which has been preserved in the Syrian seminary at Sharfeh, has the text of the Lord's prayer in the Prepeshilla version, before it had been corrected by the Peshitto. Thus, it has: *fiat voluntas tua in terra sicut in coelo* and *panem diei da nobis*.

The embolism is considerably shorter than the Roman: "Deliver us, we beseech thee, O Lord, from all evils, past, present and to come, by the intercession of thy Mother and

---

[207] Denys bar-Salibi, ap. RENAUDOT, *Lit. Orient. Collect.*, t. II, p. 113.

[208] *Ibid.*

thy saints, and we will cause glory to ascend to thee, now and for ever and ever. (Choir) Amen."

At the conclusion of the embolism, the deacon directs the people to bow down their heads, not indeed for the solemn blessing before holy communion, but in preparation for the confession of faith expressed in the formula: "One only Father."

Thus, the deacon enjoins: "Bow your heads before the merciful God, and before the propitiatory altar, and before the body and blood of our Redeemer, which have been placed on it as life to those who partake, and receive a blessing from the Lord."

Then the priest says: "Peace be with you all;" a short Arabic prayer; and again "Peace be with you all," while the people respond: "And with thy spirit."

In the meanwhile, the priest places the host over the chalice, and elevates the two species together.

The prayer "of the Imposition of Hands" asks that the faithful may be strengthened in goodness: "Strengthen, O Lord God, the hearts of thy servants by the power of thy heavenly benediction, for the sake of these divine mysteries, lest we deviate from the observance of thy commandments; and we will make glory to ascend to thee, now and for ever."

The priest, turning to the people, now gives the blessing, which on very solemn occasions is repeated three times: "May the grace of the Holy Trinity, which has neither beginning nor end, uncreated and consubstantial, be ever with you all, my brethren."

As the priest genuflects and takes the host into his hand, the deacon says: "Let everyone look to God with fear and trembling, and seek mercies and love from the Lord."

The priest in the meanwhile recites secretly the following prayer: "Holy, holy, holy art thou, O Lord, the strong God of hosts; heaven and earth are full of thy glory. Thy glory, O God, is exalted above the heavens, and over all the earth. I have lifted up my eyes to thee, O God, who dwelleth in the heavens. As the eyes of the servants are on the hands of their masters; and as the eyes of the handmaid are on the hands of her mistress. so are our eyes unto thee, O Lord our God, till thou have mercy on us. Have mercy on us. Have mercy on me, O God, according to thy mercy, and blot out my sins, according to the abundance of thy graces. Have mercy on me, O God, for my soul trusteth in thee, and in the shadow of thy wings will I seek shelter; have mercy on me, O God, for man hath trodden me under foot. Save me, O God, from the hands of my adversaries, and deliver me from those who rise up against me. Save me, O Lord, from the evil man, and defend me against men of iniquity. Remember me, [209] O Lord, when thou shalt enter into thy kingdom."

Then, genuflecting and elevating the host (bell is rung), the priest makes the sign of the cross and says aloud: "The holy things are given to the holy, with peace, purity and sanctity."

The choir (people) responds in a magnificent confession of faith: " One only Father, the holy; one only Son, the holy; one only Spirit, the holy. Blessed be the name of the Lord, who is one in heaven and on earth. Glory be to him, for ever and ever."

In the Greek St. James, the affirmation is addressed throughout to the second person of the Trinity: "One holy, one Lord Jesus Christ, in the glory of God the Father, to whom be glory for ever and ever."

The chalice also is elevated (bell is rung), and the priest says: "In truth we have believed, and we do believe firmly

[209] Cf. Byzantine rite.

in thee, O Lord, as the holy Catholic Church hath believed
in thee: that thou art one Father, the holy, praise be to him,
amen; one Son, the holy, glory be to him, amen; one Spirit,
the holy, praise and veneration [210] be to him for ever and
ever, amen."

The choir (people) responds: "Glory be to the Father
and to the Son and to the Holy Ghost, who sanctifieth all
and pardoneth all."

At a solemn liturgy, psalm CXLVII [211] or a hymn is sung,
and the deacon says: "In the resurrection of Christ the
King let us receive in faith pardon for our souls, and let us
all in like manner say to the Son, who saved us by his cross:
Blessed be our Saviour. Holy, holy, holy art thou in every
place, exalting the memory of thy Mother, the saints, and
the faithful departed. Alleluia. The heavenly powers stand
with us in the midst of the sanctuary and present service to
the body of the Son of God, who was immolated for us.
Draw near, receive from him pardon of sins and offences.
Alleluia. On thy holy altar, O Lord, let there be the memory
of our fathers, brethren and doctors, and may they rise upon
thy right hand in the day of the appearing of thy majesty,
O Christ the King. Alleluia. Blessed be Christ, who gave
us his living body and blood, that through them we may obtain pardon. Alleluia. Adored and praised be the Father, the
Son and the Holy Spirit, for ever and ever to him be glory."

The priest genuflects and says with hands extended: [212]
"Praise to the Father who hath sanctified; praise to the Son
who hath pardoned; praise to the Holy Ghost who hath

[210] *P. M. S.*, "thanksgiving."
[211] *Lauda Jerusalem Dominum.*
[212] The present rubric says "in a loud voice," but formerly the
prayer was said in a low voice, which is often the case to-day as the
assistant is singing a hymn.

filled; the beginning, perfection and end of all that hath been and now is, in heaven and on earth. He hath come down in his mercy; he hath abased himself in his goodness; he hath come and sanctified this oblation, and hath signed the Church and her children by the great power of the cross. May he make the right arm of his mercy to descend on this place, and over its faithful inhabitants, over this city, and over all the faithful departed, who have left it, and be the hope and protection of those who dwell in it, and all classes of its inhabitants. May God keep them under the protection of his mercy. Glory be to thee always, O Lord our God. Amen."

Deacon: "When you priests stand in the sanctuary, open the doors of your hearts, say the psalm and bless on this eucharist what has been placed in the sanctuary."

According to the translation of Prince Maximilian, the people (choir) now say psalm CL and also "And to thee, O God, it becometh glory," whereas in some other versions of the liturgy these find a place immediately before the communion of the priest.

Then the priest, signing the mysteries, says silently: "Bless, O God, this bread which is found in thy sanctuary, bless the seed, and the earth from which it hath sprung, and grant repose and pardon to those for whose sake we have offered and sanctified it."

The mingling of the body and blood on the altar symbolises the union of the body and blood of our Lord in the resurrection.

The choir sings *Biserre Kiamat*: "Through the mystery of the resurrection of the Lord let us ask for his forgiveness, saying: Blessed is he who delivered us from damnation by his cross."

The priest, having genuflected, divides the host into

three parts and, intincting one of them, says: "Render
worthy, O Lord, my weak and sinful hands, that they may
offer and break the sacred body, and distribute it with true
faith to the children of the holy Church for ever and ever.
Blessed be thou, O Lord Jesus Christ, the living bread, which
came down from heaven, and hast become life to those who
receive thee, for ever and ever. Every one of the faithful,
who associates himself with us in this eucharist, do thou
associate him, O Lord God, in thy heavenly kingdom, for
ever and ever. May thy body and thy blood be not on the
day of judgment for our condemnation and our confusion,
for ever and ever. O Lord Jesus Christ, grant that we may
be acceptable before thee, when thou shalt appear with thy
angels in thy great glory, for ever and ever. May the living
and the dead find in thee graces and mercies unto the day
of judgment, for ever and ever."

At a solemn liturgy, the deacon now says: "We implore
thee, O Lord God, on behalf of the sick and sorrowful, for
those troubled with evil spirits, for both living and dead, for
those who are near as well as for those who are far off, for
those for whom this sacrifice is being offered, and for our
brethren who take care of this city. Help and preserve them,
O Lord, and may thy peace and salvation dwell in thy
churches amongst thy people and in the four quarters of the
globe. Drive from them and from all the faithful in Christ
the rod of thy anger. May we all thrice pray and repeat."

The choir (people) responds: "*Kyrie eleison, Kyrie eleison, Kyrie eleison.*"

The priest takes the intincted particle and makes three
crosses [213] with it on the other particles, as he says: "May

---

[213] The intinction of the host with the chalice symbolises the
resurrection, so the ceremony is not permitted at Mass of the Presanctified, which commemorates the burial of our Lord.

the blood of our Lord sprinkle his holy body. In the name
of the † Father and of the † Son and of the † Holy Ghost.
Glory be to thee, for ever and ever."

St. Ephrem [214] in his hymns makes allusion both to the
fraction and to the anointing of the sacred particles with the
precious blood. Thus, he says: "The priest .... breaks the
host and divides it ...., he immolates on the altar the second
of the divine persons and distributes to men the giant who
carries the universe ...., he breaks it with his right hand and
divides it into parts ...., he symbolically immolates the first-
born Son before his Father, he separates the particles and
lays them aside, then he communicates in eating the first
particle."

In another hymn, [215] he describes the rite of " signing" :
"Your image is here painted on the (sacred) bread by the
blood of the grape. It is also painted on our hearts by the
finger of the Holy Spirit with the colours of faith. Blessed
be he who has effaced the image of paganism by that of
truth."

Then the priest makes the commixture, as he says:
" Thou hast united, [216] O Lord, thy divinity to our humanity,
and our humanity to thy divinity, thy life to our death, and
our death to thy life. Thou hast taken that which was ours,
and hast given us that which is thine, for the life and
salvation of our souls. Glory be to thee, for ever and ever."

Then, withdrawing a little from the altar, and making

[214] Ap. RAHMANI, op. cit., pp. 234-235.
[215] The eleventh hymn, " on the birth of our Lord."
[216] In conformity with the ancient manuscripts, the missal of 1592
had " hast mingled" in place of " hast united." The present expression
was first inserted in the Roman edition of the missal published in 1716.
Joseph Aloysius Assemani (*Codex liturgicus*, lib. IV, part II, p. 208)
writes " hast mingled."

three genuflections, three signs of the cross and three inclinations, the priest, thrice striking his breast, recites a prayer [217] of humble access (the bell is rung):

"Render us worthy, O Lord God, to sanctify our bodies with thy holy body, and to adorn our souls with thy blood which purifies, and may this be for the pardon of our sins and the remission of our offences, O our Lord and our God. Glory be to thee, for ever and ever."

During the communion of the celebrant, it is customary for the assistant to sing the hymn "For the resurrection of Christ the King," followed immediately by the chant or recitation of the exhortation that begins "O priests," psalm 150 and a prayer. All these follow uninterruptedly, but when the priest has made his communion the assistant concludes at once with the last four words of the prayer.

Before holy communion, the priest, turning to either side, asks for the prayers of the faithful: "Pray for me."

Then he receives the host (the bell is rung), as he says: "May the body of our Lord Jesus Christ be given to me for the pardon of my sins and the remission of my offences, and for life everlasting."

A portion only of the host is consumed here, a practice recalling the primitive custom of giving particles of the *same* host to the people in holy communion.

Receiving the chalice, the priest says: "By thy living and purifying blood, may my sins be remitted to me, and my offences blotted out, O Jesus, the Word of God, who didst come for our salvation."

The faithful are directed to say at the moment of communion: "Lord Jesus Christ, I am not worthy and I do not deserve that thou shouldst enter under my roof, but speak

---

[217] Cf. *Domine non sum dignus* in the Roman rite.

only one word and my soul shall live. O lamb of God, who takest away the sins of the world, have pity on me."

The original custom, when the commixture immediately preceded communion, was for the people to receive intincted particles, and the synod of Kannobin (1596)[218] enjoined: "The celebrant should not give holy communion to the people (under the species of bread) before he has received the chalice himself. Let him distribute to the people particles of sacred bread, either intincted with blood from the chalice or with some part of the blood."

Until at least the 17th century,[219] the laity were permitted to receive under both kinds, but the council of the Lebanon (p. II, lib. XII, n. 25; 1736) restricted the privilege to deacons and archdeacons, "particularly in a solemn Mass."

Thus to-day, the deacon of the liturgy receives the host intincted in the chalice.

So late as 1888, the words of administration in the missal appeared to envisage communion under both kinds.

The practice of giving holy communion to infants was abolished by Pope Benedict XIV (1740-1758).

The words of administration at the communion of the people are the same as those used by the priest at his own communion.

The choir in the meanwhile sings *Yakhobz al haya:*[220] "O bread of life, food of souls and pledge of heaven. Thou art the Son of man, Son of the merciful God. If the angels

---

[218] Canon 2.

[219] *ita* Gabriel Siouni, † 1648; Abraham of Hekel, † 1664.

[220] The hymn is not ancient, and consequently it is not found in Syriac. It appears, possibly for the first time, in the *diaconicon* printed in 1736 in Rome. The ancient Syriac hymn sung during the communion of the people, that figured in the first edition of the *diaconicon* (1596) and in part also in more recent editions, has fallen into disuse.

are standing with awe and fear in the presence of thy magnificence, how can we, humble sinners, receive thee in our sinful hearts," etc.

Then the priest gives a blessing and says the following prayer: [221] "Thy servants and thy adorers, mayest thou give them life, and mayest thou sign them, O our Lord and our God, by thy cross, triumphant over evil and all its powers, to thee be glory for ever."

The deacon responds: "Raise thy glory, O God, above the heavens and over the whole earth."

Signing the right side of the corporal with the paten, the priest says: "The Church says, [222] holy, holy, holy art thou, O Lord; blessed be he who hath given me his body and his blood to purify me."

The deacon responds: [223] "Alleluia, alleluia, to him be glory, who gave us his body and life-giving blood, so that through them we might be reconciled."

Moving the chalice three times to the left of the corporal, the priest continues: "May thy holy one [224] supplicate thee for us, in the day of judgment, before the throne, which shall be surrounded with fear and grandeur."

Deacon: "Alleluia, alleluia, to him be glory, from whom the Church and her sons drink and tell forth their praise."

The sacred ministers now say together: "I am the bread of life said our Lord, everyone who eateth me in faith shall inherit life. Behold the cup, which our Lord mingled over the head of the tree (†): draw near, mortals, and drink from it for the remission of sins. Brethren, receive the body of the

---

[221] Not in the Syrian rite. A veil at one time hid the altar at the communion of the celebrant, and was removed at the beginning of this prayer.
[222] Not in the Syrian rite.
[223] Not in the Syrian book.
[224] *P. M. S.*, "mystery."

Son, exclaims the Church, drink his blood in faith and sing of his glory."

The priest, holding the paten, says: "Receive, O Lord, in thy goodness the oblation of thy adorers, and in thy clemency have mercy, O Lord, on the souls of the faithful departed."

The deacon answers: "Behold the sacrifice which has been offered, and behold the souls commemorated through it. May there be rest for the dead for whom it has been offered."

The dialogue between the priest and the deacon still continues.

Priest: "By this sacrifice which the living offer for the dead."

Deacon: "May he who called Lazarus and the widow's young son sprinkle the dew of his mercy upon the members of the dead."

Priest: "Pardon our soul its offences and blot out its sins. Grant, O Lord, that the name of him for whom we offer this sacrifice may be written with that of Abraham, of Isaac, and of Israel the just."

Priest (holding the chalice and paten): "O heavenly King, accept the offering of thy servants, and grant that their names may be written in the heavenly Jerusalem."

Deacon: "In the heavenly Jerusalem and in the Church on earth, may there be a good memorial [225] for them on the altar in heaven."

Priest: "O lamb of God, O shepherd who didst die for thy flock, grant in thy mercy peace to the faithful departed."

Deacon: "My soul is athirst for thy body. I fear to

[225] The first edition of the missal (1592) had the words: "Make a memorial of those that love thee."

approach it, for my sins terrify me. Through thy love, O Lord, may they be remitted."

Priest: "May thy body and thy blood, which we have carried, be to us the road, the bridge and the passage by which we may cross without fear from darkness to light."

Priest and deacon (*P. M. S.*): "Joy be to the inhabitants on high, and good hope to those below, through this victim, which the living offer up for the dead."

The priest then makes a cross with the holy vessels on the altar stone, and, turning to the people with the chalice in his left hand and the paten in his right, holds his arms crosswise and blesses them (the bell is rung).

The form used at the blessing is not found in the Syrian rite: "Again we glorify thee, O Lord, and we offer praises to thee, because thou hast given us thy body for our food, and thy blood for our drink. O merciful one, who lovest men, have mercy on us."

The priest now genuflects and consumes the blessed sacrament, as he says: "By thy living and vivifying blood, may my sins be forgiven and my offences blotted out, O Word of God, who didst come for our salvation."

It would seem that the above ceremony was first introduced into the missal of 1716.

At the first ablution, the priest says: "May the Lord and his elect, angels and saints, be appeased by this offering which we have made this day. May the Lord grant peace and eternal rest to all the faithful departed, and in particular to him, for whom this sacrifice was offered this day."

The deacon recites the psalm [226] of communion and also "And to thee it belongeth glory, O God."

---

[226] Psalm XXXIII, *Benedicam Dominum*, or psalm CXXXIII, *Ecce nunc benedicite*.

At the second ablution, the fingers of the right and left hands are washed separately.

The priest says for the right hand: "My fingers sound thy praises and my mouth sings thy glories. By the nails that pierced thy hands and thy feet, by the lance which opened thy side, pardon me my sins and offences."

For the left hand: "Guard me from all evil, and let thy right hand preserve me from all the works of iniquity, and keep me for ever and ever."

Then, consuming the wine and water, he continues: "They shall be inebriated with the plenty of thy house, and thou shalt make them to drink of the torrents of thy delights, for in thee is the source of life."

Finally, the priest wipes the chalice, as he says: "Blot out, O Lord, in thy mercy [227] all my sins, and pardon in thy clemency all the offences which I have committed in thy presence. O King, Christ our Saviour, whose holy mysteries I have celebrated, render me worthy to serve thee with joy in thy heavenly kingdom, together with the saints and the just, who have loved thee, now and for ever and ever."

A post-communion prayer [228] is now said aloud by the priest in Arabic (with arms extended): "We supplicate thee, O Christ, our God, and we beseech thee to grant that thy body which we have eaten and thy blood which we have drunk may be for our salvation and the pardon of the sins of all the faithful, living and dead; and we will make glory to ascend to thee, now and for ever and ever. (People) Amen."

This is followed by "Peace be with you all" and the customary response: "And with thy spirit."

---

[227] *P. M. S.*, " by the sponge of thy love; cf. Byzantine μοῦσα.
[228] Cf. prayer at the second ablution in the Roman rite.

Then a prayer of inclination is recited aloud in Arabic: "Stretch forth, O Lord, the right hand of thy power; remove all offence from thy Church; preserve thy flock from all that is injurious, and we will make glory and thanksgiving to ascend to thee; to thy blessed Father and to thy Holy Spirit, now and for ever and ever. (People) Amen."

A second Arabic prayer [229] follows, which is said over the people in a loud voice, by way of commendation: "O Lord, bless us all; preserve us all; protect us, help us, and show us the way of life and salvation. May thy mercy and thy goodness descend upon us all; guard our brethren, both those who are far away and those who are near. As for those who have associated with us in this sacrifice, whether by word or deed, may the Lord God, who deigned to accept the sacrifices of the just in olden times, of Abraham, Isaac and Jacob, accept also their sacrifices, their vows, their alms, their contributions; and may he grant peace and repose to their dead, and true hope to the living; through the prayers of the mother of life, Mary, Mother of God, and through the prayers of all the saints." (Assistant): [230] "Amen."

The dismissal by the priest has been described by Donald Attwater [231] as a "pleasantly domestic form": "My brethren and my friends, whom we have recommended to the goodness and mercy of the holy and glorious Trinity, you have been delivered by the glorious cross; whether you are separated from us or present with us, living or dead: go in peace with the provisions and the blessings which we have

---

[229] These two Arabic prayers are not found in the Syrian rite.

[230] *P. M. S.*, People: "Amen." The rubrics give "Amen" as the response but general practice, has introduced: "to thee (or to our Lady) the most noble greeting. *La Messa Siro-Maronita* (Rome, 1946), p. 99, n. 53.

[231] Catholic Eastern Churches, p. 194.

obtained at the altar of the Lord who pardons: may God preserve you from the corruption and the entrance of sin. We beseech the help of your prayers, O our father and our brethren, for ever and ever. Amen."

The choir chants a hymn which begins: "Alleluia, alleluia. Be graciously mindful, O Lord, of our departed fathers and brethren. Vouchsafe to record their names in the book of life, in the heavenly Jerusalem, the dwelling of the blessed."

The blessing [232] is given with the hand-cross: "May the blessing † of our Lord Jesus Christ descend from heaven, and dwell in me and in you; pardon your sins; blot out your offences; grant peace to the souls of your dead; and write your names in the book of his heavenly kingdom. May God save you from the condemnation and the shame of the day of the just and strict judgment, † Father, † Son, and Holy † Ghost, glory be to thee, for ever and ever. Amen."

At a solemn liturgy, a prayer of invocation for the blessing of God follows, together with the chanting of psalm CXVI [233] and a hymn [234] of praise.

The glories of Rome are extolled in the hymn: "By the prayers of Simon Peter, Rome was made the royal city, and she shall not be shaken."

A bishop recites the prayer of invocation from the footpace of the altar facing west, [235] holding the hand-cross and attended by candle bearers.

The liturgy is concluded with the Lord's prayer said by

[232] *P. M. S.*, before the blessing, has a further prayer. A bishop or chorepiscopus gives a triple blessing.

[233] *Laudate Dominum omnes gentes.*

[234] Not in the Syriac book.

[235] Cf. Last gospel in the Armenian rite.

the people, but at a "low Mass" the Leonine prayers are now recited in Arabic.

The rubrics would seem to require the priest to unvest at the altar, but, even in a pontifical liturgy, this is often done in the sacristy.

The priest in the meanwhile says the following prayers:

a) "I have eaten thy sacred body; let not the fire devour me; I have touched it with my eyes: [236] let my looks perceive thy mercies. I have not been in this world a stranger to thy mysteries: let me not be separated from thee. Place me not with the goats at thy left hand, but make me worthy to praise thee at thy right."

b) I carry thee as my nourishment on the journey, O Son of God, and in my hunger I nourish myself with thee, O Saviour of the world. The fire ceases to burn in my body when I feel the perfume of thy body and blood. Thy baptism is for me as a vessel which cannot be submerged, and I

---

[236] A reference to the ancient custom of placing the sacred mysteries to the eyes and lips. Narsai in the *Exposition of the mysteries* (Homil.XVII, A) says: "He (the priest) receives in his hands the adorable body of the Lord of all; and he embraces and *kisses* it with love and affection." In another place (vol. I, p. 319), the same writer says: "the lips which have shouted praise and *kissed* the mystery of the medicine of life are shouting phrases of blasphemy."

The custom is mentioned by St. Cyril of Jerusalem (Catech. XXIII, 21, 22) of touching the eyes with the consecrated particle, and, after the reception of the chalice, of moistening the hand at the lips and touching the eyes, brow and other senses.

St. Aphraates (Homil. IX, 10) also says: "Let thy lips beware of dissension with which thou *kissest* the King's Son"

A similar custom was once observed in the West. Beleth (*De divin. offic.*, c. 48) records the practice, enjoined in some Roman missals of the 12th century, of kissing the host before reciting the prayer of the *pax* (*Domine Jesu Christi*). Durandus (*Ration.*, L. III, c. 53) mentions the same practice, which seems to have spread to most of the churches of France, and to have been retained until the 16th century. Paris observed the custom until 1615, and Meaux as late as 1642.

use it to pass from the place of despair to the abode of life."

c) "O God, I beseech thee to grant me the grace of thy Holy Spirit, which thou didst accord to thy chaste apostles, in the holy cenacle of Sion and on the blessed Mount of Olives: grant that I may not lose it, neither in this world nor in the next, for thou art the source of all good and of every perfect gift. O light of lights, [237] O creator of the ages, [238] we offer to thee adoration and glory, now and always, for ever and ever. Amen."

The first two strophes have been attributed to St. Ephrem, [239] for, although only a fragment is found in his works, the subject matter is knitted together so as to form a single whole.

When the priest has unvested, he kisses the altar, and addresses to it a last and touching farewell: "Remain in peace, O holy altar; in peace I will return to thee. May the sacrifice which I have taken from thee be for the remission of my sins and the pardon of my offences; may it assist me to keep myself before the throne of Christ, without spot or shame. I know not if I shall return again to offer upon you another Sacrifice. Glory be to the Father and to the Son and to the Holy Ghost, one God, who is the beginning and end of all things."

Then, if he wishes, the priest may offer incense for the dead: "May it be pleasing, O holy and glorious Trinity, through this sweet-smelling incense, which my feebleness offers for the rest and remission of thy servant (handmaid), and for the souls of our fathers, our brethren, our relatives, of all who have done good to us, and for the souls of all our

---

[237] *P. M. S.,* " Light of men."
[238] *Ibid.,* " world."
[239] T. III, p. 355.

faithful departed, in the name of the Father and of the Son and of the Holy Ghost. Amen."

The custom of distributing blessed bread at the end of the liturgy is mentioned in the Maronite missal of 1592, but it has fallen into desuetude.

Other Anaphoras

In the last five editions of the liturgy, the number of anaphoras [240] has been reduced to eight, with the rite of the Presanctified for Good Friday.

The missal of 1635 had fourteen anaphoras, including St. John Chrysostom, St. Basil, St. Cyril, St. Denys, St. John of Harran († 1165), and Marutha of Tagrith (Maypherkat). This Marutha has been identified [241] with the saint of that name (December 4), who occupied the see of Antioch some time before 420.

The present service-book contains the following anaphoras: 1) Anaphora according to the Order of the Holy Catholic and Roman Church, the Mother of all the Churches. 2) St. Peter, the Head of all the Apostles. 3) Twelve Apostles. 4) St. James, the Apostle and Brother of the Lord. 5) Saint John, the Apostle and Evangelist. 6) St. Mark, the Evangelist. 7) St. Xystus, Pope of Rome. 8) St. John surnamed Maro, Patriarch of Antioch.

The normal anaphora, as we have seen, is that which professes to be taken from the *Roman Church;* while those

[240] Bickell (*Conspectus rei Syrorum litterariae*, Munster, 1875, pp. 65-68) for the Maronites and Jacobites enumerates 65 anaphoras; P. A. Raes (*Introductio in Anaphorarum Syriacarum*. Edit., Roma, 1939, pp. xi-xiv) 70 anaphoras; and Brightman (*Liturgies Eastern and Western*, I, 1896, p. lvii) 64 anaphoras that have been published.

[241] Stephen DUAIHI, *De Orthodoxis Anaphorarum Auctoribus*, chap. II.

of *St. James* and *St. John* have been considered in the preceding chapter.

St. Peter, the Head of all the Apostles, is the title given to the second anaphora in the missal, although it is obvious that its author can have had little connection with the first bishop of Antioch. Renaudot [242] gives two distinct liturgies under this name, but, as the late Syrian patriarch [243] pointed out, the learned Jesuit never seemed to perceive that the second prayer of the first anaphora becomes the first prayer in the second.

Some of the prayers in the second anaphora have been borrowed from a composition attributed to the Monophysite Peter the Dyer.

The liturgy which is used to-day is substantially the second of those given by Renaudot, although there have been considerable alterations and additions in the various editions of the missal. This anaphora of St. Peter begins with the words: "To thee and before thee, O Lord, we bend the necks of our souls and bodies, so that we may receive blessing and help from thee in our weakness."

The ancient "book of life" is recalled after the peace, when the celebrant remembers the passion of our Lord, the blessed Virgin, St. John Baptist, the Church, patriarchs, prophets, ... kings, hierarchy, those who have asked our prayers and, finally, the faithful departed and benefactors.

At one time, the Maronites used another anaphora ascribed to St. Peter, which was described as that of the Apostles or the "Strengthening" anaphora (*Charar*). The last named title was derived from the first word of the first prayer of the veil, "*Strengthen,* Lord, in our hearts."

[242] *Op. cit.,* t. II, pp. 145-154; 155-162.
[243] RAHMANI, *op. cit.,* chap. II, p. 297, n. 1.

The anaphora was the last in order of sequence in the missal of 1592; while later books have used it for the liturgy of the presanctified, with two prayers substituted for the post-sanctus.

In more recent times, however, this interesting anaphora, which bears a striking resemblance to the East Syrian liturgy of Addai and Mari, has fallen into desuetude. Manuscripts of the "Strengthening" anaphora, probably dating from the 13th century, are preserved in the Vatican, as well as in the libraries of the Maronite archbishop of Aleppo and the Syrian Catholic patriarch.

Twelve Apostles. Some manuscripts have ascribed the authorship of this anaphora to St. Luke, possibly because the text of the words of the consecration of the chalice have been taken from his gospel, but the claim is valueless.

What is of interest is the remarkable similarity between this eucharistic prayer and one found in the liturgy of St. John Chrysostom: "O God, merciful and holy, who hast prepared a holy and spiritual table for us, by thy only Son, our Lord, God and Saviour Jesus Christ." The wording, except for a tendency to abbreviation and a certain freedom in translation, is almost identical; while the style, both in the choice of words and in the ease of expression, points to a compiler who lived not later than the 7th or 8th century, at a time when Syriac literature flourished.

Two very ancient manuscripts of the anaphora are preserved in the British Museum.

Internal evidence points to great antiquity for the liturgy, and James of Edessa was apparently quoting from it when he wrote that St. John Chrysostom had said that our Lord "has drunk of his blood that he has given his disciples to drink."

The Syrian celebrant, when he invokes the Holy Spirit,

is directed to bow profoundly, a ceremony anticipated by James of Edessa, whereas St. Ephrem speaks of the priest prostrating himself on the ground. In this anaphora, the prayer of the invocation of the Holy Spirit indicates the more primitive posture: "Lord, we pray thee in prostrating ourselves on the ground before thy face."

As a further proof of antiquity, the liturgy of the Twelve Apostles has retained the recitation of only two prayers at the commemoration of the living and the dead, although, from at least the time of James of Edessa, the normal Syrian rite, in imitation of the Byzantines, had divided the prayers and mementoes into six.

A comparison with the Te igitur of the Roman canon has been seen in the prayer following the diptychs for the Church and her rulers: "That is why we offer thee, O God, for thy Church," as they both express causality.

The commemoration of our Lady and the saints: "Grant us a share in the prayers of thy elect, make us worthy to reach their estate, and give us in thy company the enjoyment of thy kingdom" may be examined in relation to the *communicantes et venerantes*.

On several occasions, St. John Chrysostom refers in his homilies to the Syriac liturgy rather than to that of Constantinople which bears his name. Examples of this may be found in the 82nd *Homily on St. Matthew* and the 36th *on the 1st Epistle to the Corinthians*.

St. Mark. Mar Ephrem Rahmani [244] says that the anaphora begins with the words: "Almighty Lord, true and holy love," whereas Renaudot [245] gives: "O God the Father, who didst send thy beloved Son for our salvation."

---

[244] *Les Liturgies Orientales et Occidentales*, chap. II, 4, p. 296.
[245] *Liturgiarum Orientalium Collectio*, t. II, p. 176.

St. Xystus, Pope of Rome. This anaphora—"O calm, peace and love eternal—,which was appended to the *ordo generalis* in the Syrian rite prior to the publication of the missal in 1922, stands seventh in the service-book of the Maronites.

The ascribed authorship is fictitious, and Rahmani [246] considers it to be the work of a certain Aaron, who has not yet been identified with any certainty.

The position between the initial dialogue and the consecration is occupied by a doxology: [247] "Glory be to the Father and to the Son and to the Holy Ghost: adorable and glorious mystery, in which there is no division: now and always, for ever."

John Maro. [248] The last anaphora in the missal, beginning with the words: "O God, generous and merciful, who hast prepared a holy and spiritual banquet for us through thy only-begotten Son our Lord Jesus Christ," is a compilation borrowed from several liturgies. The first three prayers have been taken from the anaphora of the Twelve Apostles, and the fourth from James of Sarugh. It has been said of the alleged authorship: "not only is it uncertain, but it has been proved by the strongest arguments to be entirely false."

Brightman says that the anaphora was in the missal of 1716, and it has found a place in the later service-books. It would appear, however, to have been missing from the manuscripts used by Renaudot, since it has not been transcribed *in extenso* by him.

Until at least the 15th century, a liturgy of the *Presanc-*

---

[246] Op. cit., p. 303, n. 1: "*Dans notre ms. son nom est écrit Xyste, qui est le patriarche Aron.*"

[247] RENAUDOT, *op. cit.*, t. II, p. 135.

[248] The authorship of John Maro was maintained by Stephen Duaihi.

tified [249] was celebrated on the Lenten ferias, and we have already seen how an anaphora of St. Peter was used for this rite.

Present day usage confines the Presanctified to Good Friday, when it is offered after the Roman manner. This restriction already existed in the missal of 1716, and the council of the Lebanon (1736) enacted two decrees [250] on the subject.

---

[249] H. W. CODRINGTON, *Syrian Liturgies of the Presanctified. Journal of Theological Studies,* IV, 1902-3.

[250] a) *Excipimus feriam sextam majoris hebdomadae, in qua nulli liceat missam celebrare, sed tantum dicatur in ecclesiis cathedralibus, patriarchalibus, regularium, missa praesanctificatorum, quemadmodum in missali praescribitur;* b) *Praesanctificatorum missa, quae toto jejunii quadragesimalis tempore (sabbato et dominicis exceptis) olim a nostris fiebat et nunc etiam fit a Graecis .... a majoribus nostris ad solam feriam sextam in parasceve, sicut et in sancta Romana ecclesia, restricta est.*

BIBLIOGRAPHY

1. *Bullarium Maronitarum* complectens Bullas, Brevia, Epistolas, Constitutiones aliaque documentis a Romanis Pontificibus ad Patriarchas Antiochenos Syro-Maronitarum. Tobias ANAISSI. Romae: Max Bretschneider. 1911.

2. *The Golden Book of Eastern Saints.* Donald ATTWATER. The Bruce Publishing Company, Milwaukee. 1938.

3. *The Language of Christ.* Place of the Syrian Maronites in History. Peter F. SFEIR. Buffalo, N .Y. 1929.

4. *La Liturgie de l'Eglise Maronite. La Semaine des Liturgies Catholiques.* Conférence donnée par Emmanuel PHARÈS. A l'occasion du seizième centenaire du Concile de Nicée célébré à Paris du 13 au 20 décembre, 1925.

5. *The Liturgy of the Maronites.* Donald ATTWATER. *Orate Fratres.* July & September, 1942.

6. *Maron.* H. LERCLERCQ. *Dictionnaire d'Archéologie Chrétienne et de Liturgie.* T. X, col. 2188-2202.

7. *Maronite (Eglise).* P. DIB. *Dictionnaire de Théologie Catholique.* Vol. X (1928), col. 1-142.

8. *Les Maronites au Liban et en Amérique.* Allocution par Mgr. Alfred BAUDRILLART, le dimanche, 4 mai 1924, dans l'Eglise maronite de N.-D. du Liban à Paris.

9. *The Maronite Liturgy or The Holy Sacrifice in the Syriac-Maronite Rite.* Translated by Joseph P. GORAYEB. Canisius High School, Buffalo, New York.

10. *Modo facile di seguire la Messa Siro-Maronita.* Pont. Istit. Orient. Stud. Roma, 1943.

11. *La Messa Siro-Maronita* annotata: cenno storico sui Maroniti. Pietro SFAIR, Segretario Generale dell'Ottavario. Roma, 1946.

12. *Missa Syro-Maronitica* quam ex lingua Syriaca in idioma Latinum traduxit cum commentario praevio MAXIMILIANUS, PRINCEPS SAXONIAE. Sumptibus et Typis Friderici Pustet. 1907.

13. *Palestine Exploration Fund. Bliss.* Quarterly Statement for 1892. *Maronites.* London: Society's Office, 24 Hanover Square, W.

14. *La Sainte Messe selon le Rite Maronite.* Traduite et expli-

quée. Eglise Maronite de Notre-Dame du Liban. 17 Rue d'Ulm, Paris.

15. *The Syrian Maronite Mass in English*. Peter F. SFEIR. Detroit, Michigan. 1935.

ACKNOWLEDGEMENTS

1. Joseph Rahmé, Chorepiscopus.
3. Fr. Joseph Chehwan, Antonian Aleppine monk.
3. Fr. Joseph el-Khazan, Antonian Aleppine monk, Rome.
4. Mgr. Peter Sfair, Chorepiscopus.

CHAPTER IV

SYRO-MALANKARA RITE

Recent developments in South India have necessitated a chapter on the Syro-Malankara rite, for, although the remote origins are found in the section devoted to Malabar, and the present rite is West Syrian and described in another chapter, the importance of the new group makes a separate notice imperative.

The Christians of Malabar, who in the 16th century, under Portuguese influence, were brought into direct relation with the Holy See, had previously come within the orbit of the Nestorian church. Whether or not they had been infected with the heresy is discussed elsewhere, but they had adopted the East Syrian liturgy.

In 1653, a number of the Malabarese, led by Archdeacon Thomas Palakomatta (Parambil), seceded from the Church and founded a schismatic body. The leader had received a sort of commission by the imposition of the hands of twelve priests, but for some reason the Nestorian patriarch declined to give him episcopal consecration. The Jacobite patriarch was next appealed to, and although he sent Mar Gregory, bishop of Jerusalem, to Malabar there was again no transmission of orders. First steps, however, were taken in reintroducing oriental usages, and in 1665 Antiochene vestments, leavened bread and the Julian calendar were restored. Twenty years later, Mar John, another Jacobite visitor, prohibited the liturgy on fast days, and also genuflections and statues, while in the following year (1686) the Syro-Antiochene rules [1] in regard to fasts and feasts were accepted in Malabar.

The theological position of the schismatics seems to have been very uncertain. In 1704, Thomas IV wrote to Pope Clement XI, assuring him that the conduct of the Jesuits had been the sole cause of the schism, and asking for union with the Apostolic See, if the pope would permit the Syro-Chaldaic rite and nominate him as bishop. Not obtaining any satisfaction from Rome, Thomas wrote five years later (1709) to the Jacobite patriarch, requesting that a "patriarch" and a metropolitan might be appointed for his church. As no answer was received to this letter, Thomas applied again in 1720, in which he acknowledged the Jacobite patriarch as his "head," and referred to himself as the "gate of all India." There was again no reply. His successor, Thomas V, was no more successful in obtaining a valid hierarchy for Malabar. In 1730, Thomas admitted that the Jacobite patriarch of Antioch was his superior, but as he had received no answer to his request he hoped that the Dutch might be able to provide a bishop. Mar John, a Jacobite prelate, came to Malabar in 1747, but beyond destroying some venerated statues and collecting a large sum of money nothing was effected. In the following year (1748), Thomas V wrote to Rome, and assured the pope that if they could retain the use of fermented bread his church would return to unity. Three Jacobite bishops were sent by

---

[1] There seems to have been no general observance of these rules, and it has been only since the visit of the patriarch in 1876 that feasts have been everywhere restricted to Jacobite observances. In the calendar of a breviary, written in Chaldaic characters in 1734 by a Jacobite deacon, we find many feasts that were introduced by the synod of Diamper, and Corpus Christi is indicated as a day of obligation.

the patriarch to Malabar in 1751, and Mar John was recalled.

It was not, however, until 1772 that the dissident church of Malabar obtained a valid hierarchy, and a Jacobite bishop consecrated Thomas VI as Mar Dionysius I.

There may have been good reasons why Rome was unable to accede to the two requests for union, but on the other hand it is possible that political influence prevented any real consideration of the case. The dissidents seem to have been very reasonable in their demands, and to have suffered from few anti-Catholic prejudices.

The change in rite was a very gradual process, and the schismatic church of Malabar continued to use the Latinised Chaldean liturgy, although Mar Basil in 1685 had brought the Antiochene liturgy of St. James. Mar Ivanios informed the writer that the Jacobite service books have been in use since the 17th century, but a more generally accepted view, which finds expression in a pamphlet [2] published in 1924 to commemorate the restoration of the Catholic Malabarese hierarchy, shows the change of liturgy to have taken place in the 19th century. Up to 1840, sacraments and sacramentals were administered in either the Jacobite or the latinised Chaldean rite, and it was the visit of Mar Cyril in 1846 that brought about the systematic adoption of the Antiochene liturgy, although it was not before 1875, when the patriarch came to Malabar, that the last vestiges of the East Syrian rite disappeared. In 1864, the Malabar liturgy [3] had already included the anaphoras of St. James, St. Peter, the Twelve Apostles, Mar Dionysius, St. Xystus and Mar Ivanios, with a common order. To-day, there are many old Jacobite priests

[2] *A Brief Sketch of the History of the St. Thomas Christians.* Fr. Bernard of St. Thomas, T. O. C. D. Trichinopoly, 1924.
[3] G. B. HOWARD, *The Christians of St. Thomas and their Liturgies,* pp. 222-326.

who still remember their forbears administering baptism and other sacraments according to the Syro-Chaldaic ritual (Roman), translated by the Portuguese and in use after the synod of Diamper. The change of characters from East to West Syrian was a very slow process, and many words are still pronounced in a Syro-Chaldaic way. Malayalam is now increasingly used in the liturgy and other ecclesiastical ceremonies.

Mar Gregory not only conferred the episcopate upon the sixth Thomas, but he also consecrated Mar Cyril, whom Dionysius speedily exiled. Cyril took refuge in British territory at Anjur (Tholyur), where his successors still govern a small church, which is Syrian in rite, but subject to no one. Dionysius, having obtained episcopal orders, seems to have ignored Antioch and its patriarch, and in 1799, with some of his priests and laity, he made his submission [4] to the Holy See, acknowledging the synod of Diamper. After six months, however, the bishop returned to schism, and, some years later, came under the influence of the Anglican Church Missionary Society. Dionysius now attempted to Protestantise his church, encouraging clerical marriage, and a successor, Dionysius III (1818-1825), set an example by taking a wife himself.

Mar Dionysius IV (1825-1846) reacted against Protestant interference, and appealed for help to the Jacobite patriarch, who sent Mar Athanasius to Malabar. In 1836, a local synod prohibited *communicatio in sacris* with Anglicans, and, in the following year, 6,000 native Christians who had been contaminated by the English missionaries formed another

---

[4] According to tradition, Mar Dionysius accepted azyme bread as the sole change in rite. *De Fontibus Juris Ecclesiastici Syro-Malankarensium.* P. a S. Joseph. Ser. II, Fasc. VIII, p. 61, n. 3.

schism, arrogating to themselves the title of "St. Thomas Christians." The Jacobite patriarch, Peter Ignatius XXIII, came to Malabar in 1875, when he consecrated six bishops, establishing eparchies at Quilon, Kottayam, Thumpamam, Angamale, Niranam, Kandanat and Cochin. At the same time also, the tonsure [5] was abolished in favour of a small tight fitting black cap.

The history of the Malabar Jacobites in the 18th and 19th centuries is not edifying, and there was a wearisome succession of squabbles, lawsuits and sub-schisms. [6] In 1905, a schism took place within the Jacobite body itself, arising from a dispute between the patriarch, Abdullah Sattuf, and the metropolitan of Malabar, Dionysius V, when the former was on a visit to India. The immediate cause of the quarrel concerned church property, but the real point at issue was more fundamental, namely whether the Jacobite church in Malabar should continue as a province of the patriarchate of Antioch or be independent under a katholikos.

The two parties still exist, with a roughly computed membership of 100,000 in the patriarch's church (*patriarchistae*) and 200,000 in the metropolitan's church (*metropolistae*).

In 1913, the latter introduced the title of katholikos, which was suppressed in 1931, but restored three years later.

The bishops of the *metropolistae* wear rings. [7]

---

[5] The " St. Thomas Christians" have kept the tonsure introduced by the synod of Diamper.

[6] About the year 1890, two apostate Latin priests—Francis Xavier Julius Alvarez and Joseph Renatus Vilatte—were consecrated bishops in Malabar, and were permitted to retain their rite.

[7] The archdeacon, who after the schism of 1653 assumed pseudo-episcopal powers, had adopted the use of a ring.

In recent [8] times this body has been manifestly stirred by the Spirit of God, and from it the Catholic Syro-Malankara church has sprung. Fr. George (Givergis) Panikerveetil, rector of the principal Jacobite seminary, founded in 1919, at a place [9] he named Bethany, a religious brotherhood ("of the Imitation of Christ") for missionary and educational work, which was followed by a similar institute for women, for whom no provision had been made in the Jacobite church.

In place of an endless succession of dissensions and law suits, Fr. George infused a spirit of true religion. The rule of the brotherhood was a synthesis of the regulations of St. Basil, St. Benedict and St. Francis of Assisi, taking from east and west alike what was serviceable to India. The habit of the religious is the yellow gown (*sanyasin*) of the Hindu holy man, with a wooden cross about the neck and a black close-fitting cap. The cap for the professed has seven crosses on its upper side. The women wear a white or black habit, with the cross and a black veil for the professed.

The primary work of the brotherhood is prayer and contemplation.

The monastery is known as an *ashram*, and the superior is called *reesh*, "governor." All this splendid material [10] for the extension of the kingdom of Christ was put at the disposal of the Catholic church by the conversion of the superior, and in 1934 there were 6 priests, 10 brothers and 7 aspirants; while 17 sisters conducted educational work.

---

[8] From 1868 there has been a tendency for the Jacobite church to get nearer to Rome, and the metropolitan Dionysius IV was secretly a Catholic.

[9] Tiruvella, Travancore.

[10] At the time of the conversion of Mar Ivanios, many of the brothers and all the sisters became Catholics.

The reception into the Church of Fr. George, who had become in 1925 Mar John (Ivanios), bishop of Bethany, brought into being the Catholic Malankara [11] group, and it is therefore necessary to say something of the circumstances attending the conversion. At a synod of the bishops of the *metropolistae*, held in November 1925 to consider the necessary measures for the spiritual regeneration of their church, Mar Ivanios moved: "it being the will of God that the schisms of Christendom should be healed and the unity of the Church and the true faith restored, practical steps should be taken to explore avenues for healing the schism in Malabar." The bishops had already come to realise that the only centre of unity for the Church of Christ is the papacy, and that the ecclesiastical books [12] of the Jacobites bear ample witness to the supremacy of Peter in that church. The synod unanimously supported the proposal, and passed a resolution "authorising Bishop Mar Ivanios to open correspondence with the church of Rome with a view to exploring the avenues for ending the schism so far as it concerned Malabar."

The synod put forward the following considerations:

1. The Papacy as the centre of unity for the visible Church of Christ on earth, and the supremacy of the pope as the successor of St. Peter, Prince of the Apostles.

2. The preservation of the ancient rites and usages of the Jacobite Syrian church of Malabar.

3. The retention on the part of the Holy See of the re-uniting bishops in their office and jurisdiction.

On the basis of this questionnaire, Mar Ivanios submitted

---

[11] Malankara is the native name for Malabar.

[12] "There are four patriarchs just as there are four quarters of the world; and the head of all these (is) that of Rome." BAR HEBRAEUS, *Nomocanon*, VII, 1.

a memorandum to Rome. The Holy See, [13] in answer to the enquiry, gave an assurance that the pure Syrian rite of Antioch would be maintained, and that, having verified the validity of the baptism, ordination and consecration of the bishops concerned, they would be allowed to retain their respective offices and jurisdiction. Mar Ivanios, who in 1928 had been made metropolitan, and Mar Theophilus (Kalapurakal), a Bethany brother who had been consecrated bishop of Tiruvella, were alone in their acceptance of the pope's paternal invitation. The "bishops [14] were to depend immediately from the Holy See, without any dependence on the Syrian patriarchate of Antioch."

The conversion of the two bishops on September 20, 1930, was followed by that of the brothers and sisters of the " Imitation of Christ," two *rambans* (solitaries, who were also bishops designate), several of the secular clergy and about a thousand of the laity, including the octogenarian parents of Mar Ivanios.

The priests and religious had given up all their material possessions, and they had much to endure from the hostility and petty persecution of their former coreligionists.

A profession of faith, made in 1931 by Mar Theophilus, said: "Communion with the Roman pontiff is a certain sign that one is a member of the true Church. To be separated from the Roman pontiff is schism."

Jacobite Suddites [15] who become Catholics are normally to be under the jurisdiction of the Suddite bishop of Kot-

---

[13] A letter of the Apostolic Delegate (September 14, 1930) to the convert bishops said: "*che verrà conservato il rito siro puro, antiocheno e che non si confonderanno quindi coi siro-malabaresi, il cui rito è di origine siro-caldaica.*"

[14] *S. Congr. Orient.* Apost. Deleg. of the E. Indies, Pr. No. 2035-30.

[15] Secretary of the Oriental Congregation, November 25, 1931.

tayam, a Syro-Malabarese, although they are to retain the Syro-Antiochene rite.

Mar Ivanios in a letter (1931) to the Jacobite patriarch of Antioch, Mar Elias III Shagr, reminded him that the ferial office of his church proclaimed the supremacy of Peter:

1. "Moses was the head of the Old Testament and Simon of the New. These two are alike one to the other, and God dwells in them. Moses received the tables of the Law and Simon received the keys of the kingdom. Moses built the temporary tabernacle and Simon built the church. Glory be to thee, O Lord, from the Old and New Testaments. Alleluia. May their prayers help us."

2. "The church answered and said: Upon that rock of Simon, the head of the disciples, I am built, and I fear not. The waves and storms beat upon me, but dismayed me not; and the accursed Nestorius made war upon me and fell."

The apostolic constitution *Magnum nobis* (February, 13, 1932) created Mar Ivanios titular bishop of Phasis and Mar Theophilus titular bishop of Aradus. Later in the same year (June 11, 1932), another constitution, *Christo pastorum Principi,* erected the province of Trivandrum with a suffragan see at Tiruvella, confirming the two prelates as metropolitan and bishop respectively. The constitution was executed on March 12, 1933, and a former cinema theatre at Trivandrum became the cathedral church of the blessed Mother of God; while the episcopal church of Tiruvella was that of St. John the Evangelist.

In order to distinguish the rite of these new converts from that of the Syro-Malabarese, the official title is *Syro-Malankarenses ritus antiocheni.*

In 1934, the Jacobites who had returned to Catholic unity were reckoned at about 19,000, but by 1937 the numbers had increased to 36,000. Two more dissident bishops have been reconciled, Mar Severios, metropolitan of Niranam (1937), and Mar Dioscoros Thoma of Kanara (1939), while in 1946 Mar Simon Karott, chorepiscopus of the church of Kandanat, was received into the Church.

Missionary work is carried on, not only among the dissidents, but also with the Hindu *nadars* and depressed classes.

There are 59 priests, [16] most of whom are married, with 27 monks and and 17 nuns. For the future, [17] candidates for the priesthood must pledge themselves to celibacy, but those priests who have wives may continue in their ministry, and deacons who are already married can be promoted to the priesthood.

The catholic authorities in respect to the *bigami* [18] are less "strict" than the Jacobites. These *bigami* are priests who after the reception of the priesthood have contracted a second marriage, and have since become reconciled to the Catholic Church. The Jacobites forbid a second marriage after ordination, and in many cases those who have thus violated the canons joined themselves to the sect of the Mar Thomas Christians, returning later to the Jacobite church, although they were *ipso facto* suspended from the celebration of Mass. When, however, they become Catholics, the Church has permitted them to say Mass and to exercise their other priestly functions.

The outdoor dress of the clergy is a white or black

[16] By 1946, the number of clergy had risen to 98, with more than 50,000 faithhful. Stephen RAHHAL, *Some Notes on the West Syrians.* *Eastern Churches Quarterly* (July-September, 1946), p. 380.

[17] S. Orientalis Congregatio, 4 Julii 1930, Ap. Delegation of East Indies, Prot. No. 2035-30.

[18] *Fontes Juris Canonici Syro-Malankarensium. Fonti.* Serie II. Fasc. IX (Typ. Pol. Vat., 1940), chap. IX, p. 100, No. 1.

wide-sleeved gown, with a black girdle and a round flat cap.

In the archeparchy of Trivandrum, a *periodeuta* ("visitor") has been appointed, with the right to wear a ring, but the office does not exist among the Jacobites of Malabar.

A candidate for the first minor order is expected to present a letter in which the consent of the parishoners is expressed.

A layman designed to serve a priest at Mass receives an imposition of hands.

It is now customary for a priest to wear a beard. Beards were proscribed by the synod of Diamper, but it is not known when the prohibition came to be disregarded.

The Western mitre is worn with the *masnaphtho* by dissidents and Catholics alike.

Vestments may be of any colour, with the exception of black.

Malayalam is largely used in the celebration of Mass, and some priests, [19] at least among the Jacobites, recite the words of consecration in that language.

Some of the dissidents think that the epiclesis effects the consecration, while others frankly do not know when this takes place. There are, moreover, many anaphoras [20] (*plures anaphorae*) in which the words of consecration are not given at all, and celebrants use them without scruple.

As we have seen, the Holy See [21] ordered the continued use of the Syrian liturgy by the new converts, but the *filioque*

---

[19] Placidus A S. JOSEPH, *De Fontibus Juris Ecclesiastici Syro-Malankarensium, commentarius historico-canonicus* (1937), p. 103.

[20] *Ibid.*, p. 103, No. 2.

[21] Thus, the Sacred Congregation for the Oriental Church wrote: "*Ciò posto e considerato che nei libri liturgici Antiocheni che sono in uso presso i Giacobiti suddetti la voce* Filioque *già si trova, tale parola nella liturgia verrà recitata; nelle preghiere volgari invece si potrà continuare nella presente consuetudine.*" *Ibid.*, p. 84.

was to be inserted in the creed at Mass, although at other times it might be omitted.

At first, the Syro-Malankara group used, with a few local variations in the text, either the missal published in 1843 at Rome or that authorised by the Syrian patriarch in 1922 and produced at Sharfeh. The variations were submitted to the Sacred Congregation for the Oriental Rite, and a *Missale Syro-Malankarense*, edited by Mar Ivanios, appeared in 1934. Three years later (1937), an *Ordo precum Catholicorum Syro-Malankarensium* was published. The rite is practically identical with that used in the Syrian patriarchate of Antioch. It is therefore singularly free from latinisation, and several things that were introduced by Mar Ephrem Rahmani, the late patriarch, have been incorporated into this rite. Thus, the liturgy of the Presanctified [22] or "signing of the chalice," no longer in use among the Jacobites, may be celebrated on the week days of Lent and Good Friday. The anaphora of St. James is said on feasts of our Lady, in addition to those days when it is used in the Syrian patriarchate. There is no necessity that an altar should be "fasting," and bination is permitted in cases of urgency. Concelebration, as in the Byzantine rite, is unknown, but three or five priests may celebrate at the same time, each on a separate altar, consecrating his own bread and wine. In a Mass "of three priests" all should have the same intention. Four candles and at least two cantors are required [23] at a solemn liturgy. The eucharistic bread is no longer baked daily. It is leavened, but not thick, and sometimes marked with twelve crosses. Some particles are consecrated separately, as in the Latin rite, and the blessed sacrament is

---

[22] Mar Ivanios, 1936.
[23] Mar THEOPHILUS, *Leges Eccl.*, p. 9, 11.

reserved for the sick and for adoration in a pyx in the tabernacle. In 1931, the bishops ordered the water [24] in the chalice not to be more than a quarter of the wine, but the missal of 1934 only says that "a little water (*kalil maia*) should be added to the wine."

In a calendar authorised by Mar Ivanios, the following days of obligation [25] were prescribed: Circumcision (January 1); Epiphany (January 6); Annunciation (March 25); Corpus Christi; St. Metrophanes, bishop of Constantinople (June 4); St. Peter and St. Paul (June 29); St. Thomas (July 3); Transfiguration (August 6); Assumption (August 15); Exaltation of the Cross (September 14); Immaculate Conception (December 8); Christmas (December 25). This list was emended in 1937 in the *Ordo precum Catholicorum Syro-Malankarensium*, with the approbation of the metropolitan: St. Metrophanes, Transfiguration, and Exaltation of the Cross were omitted, but the Purification (February 2); Good Friday and Ascension were added. The Gregorian calendar is observed.

The rules in regard to fasting have not been changed, but the abstinence is slightly altered. Mar Ivanios (1936) ordered the following fasts: [26] Nativity (25 days); Nineveh (3 days); Lent (50 days); Apostles (15 days); Assumption (15 days). The fast of the 8 days before the Nativity of our Lady (September 8) is not of obligation, but, said the metropolitan (1936), "it is kept in a special way by virgins."

---

[24] Bar Hebraeus (*Nomocanon*, IV, I) prescribed a equal quantity of wine and water.

[25] The Jacobites have a similar number of days of obligation: twelve.

[26] The days of fasting and abstinence ordered by the synod of Diamper were observed by the Jacobites until 1686, and long after the schism the dissidents had the blessing of ashes at the beginning of Lent.

The text of the Syro-Malankara liturgy, as we have seen, remains substantially unaltered, and the clause added to the trisagion by Peter the Dyer has been retained, in spite of its rejection by the Syrians and Maronites alike. The insertion of the word "Christ" before "who was crucified for us" ensures the orthodoxy of the phrase.

A little table, on which there is a cross and two candles, is used at the gospel and again when the sacred mysteries are brought down to the people at the time of communion. It would seem that the communicants adopt the Indian posture of kneeling, with the body resting on the heels.

The new missal has enjoined the practice of placing the paten *in front of* the chalice at the prothesis, a custom referred to by John of Harran [27] († 1165), whereas the more general usage, described by Denys bar-Salibi († 1171), places the paten and chalice to the right and left respectively.

The sacraments are administered according to the Syrian books.

Funeral feasts, known as *chata*, [28] are observed in both of the oriental rites in Malabar.

Mar Ivanios has introduced into the churches of his jurisdiction statues, the rosary, Sacred Heart devotions, stations of the cross and benediction with the blessed sacrament. Benediction consists of an excerpt from the end of the Syrian liturgy, in which the priest invites the faithful to unite with him in offering worship to the Holy Trinity through the sacred humanity of our Lord in the blessed sacrament. A hymn and a blessing with the Holy Things has been added:

"Holy art thou, O Father, who created us by thy mercy;
Holy art thou, O Son, who redeemed us by thy cross;

[27] Canon 4.
[28] These feasts are also called by the Sanscrit word *sradha*.

Holy art thou, O Holy Spirit, who sanctified us by thy works.

Have mercy on us. Alleluia.

Glory to the Father, who sent forth his Son for our salvation.

Glory to the Son, who suffered and died and gave us life;

Glory to the Holy Spirit, who begins and perfects the mysteries for our salvation.

O holy and exalted Trinity, have mercy on us. Alleluia.

Holy, holy, holy art thou, O Lord, lifted up in majesty,

Who magnified the memory of the Mother of God and of the apostles and saints.

Have mercy on our faithful departed, our dear ones. Alleluia."

BIBLIOGRAPHY

1. *Fontes Juris Canonici Syro-Malankarensium.* PLACIDUS A S. JOSEPH. Fonti. Serie II, fascicolo IX. Typis Polyglottis Vaticanis. 1940.

2. *De Fontibus Juris Ecclesiastici Syro-Malankarensium.* Commentarius Historico-Canonicus. PLACIDUS A S. JOSEPH. Fonti. Serie II, fascicolo VIII. Typis Polyglottis Vaticanis. 1937.

3. *The Malabar Reunion. Ivanios. Pax,* No 114. Prinknash Priory. 1931.

ACKNOWLEDGEMENTS

1. Mar Ivanios, Archbishop Metropolitan of Trivandrum.

Priest of the Syro-Malankara rite, South India

Coptic (dissident) deacons and subdeacon, Cathedral of St. Mark, Cairo

Coptic (dissident) deacons, Luxor,
Upper Egypt

Monophysite priest in festal vestments, Cathedral of St. Mark, Cairo

Monophysite priest in outdoor dress,
Cairo

CHAPTER V

COPTIC RITE

The second patriarchal see of Christendom in the course of centuries evolved the national rite of Egypt, [1] to which the name "Coptic" has been attached.

Alexandria was founded in B. C. 331 by Alexander the Great, to replace the small town of Racondah (Rakhotis), and the Ptolemies made it the intellectual and commercial metropolis of the world. A Catholic Copt, [2] who has served in the diplomatic service of his country, described Egypt as "the Queen of high antiquity," which by the labour of its people and the fertility of the soil became the granary of Rome. Alexandria, however, despite its intimate Latin connections remained a fundamentally Greek city.

Various theories [3] have been put forward as to the derivation of the term "Coptic," but it probably comes from the Arabic form (*Ḳibṭ, Ḳibṭi*) of the Greek word for "Egypt" (Αἰγύπτος) or "Egyptian" (αἰγύπτιος), which had been taken from *Ha-ka-ptah* ("Houses of Ptah"), the ancient religious name for Memphis. The loss of the first syllable (a)

---

[1] Coptic, *Khemi.*

[2] Sesostris Sidarouss Pasha, Egyptian minister in the United States, in a lecture given on May 27, 1931, to the Society of St. John Chysostom in London.

[3] From the town of Coptos in the Thebaid; or from the Greek κόπτειν, "to cut," in allusion to the well-nigh universal practice of ricumcision.

is in accordance with Arabic philology. The old Semitic name for the country was *Misraim*, from which the Arabs have derived *Misr*.

The Copts themselves trace their ancestry back to the days of the Pharoahs, when the Egyptians were the "first legislators of the world" and the architects of such remarkable constructions as the pyramids and the sphinx.

The Coptic language shows a marked resemblance to the hieroglyphics of ancient days; while the physical features of the modern Copts often exhibit a striking similarity to those portrayed in the old statues and wall-paintings.

History

Tradition ascribes Alexandria to be the scene of the missionary labours of St. Mark, and a church in that city, although less than ninety years old in its present form, claims to occupy the site of his preaching.

There is, however, no trace of the tradition in Clement of Alexandria († ab. 215), Origen (185-ab. 253) or Dionysius of Alexandria († 265), so that it does not appear to have been in circulation in the middle of the 3rd century. It is first stated by Eusebius [4] (ab. 260-ab. 340) and the *Apostolic Constitutions*, and confirmed by Epiphanius of Salamis (end of 4th century) and St. Jerome († 420). Eusebius does little more than report a popular tradition: "they say (φασιν) that Mark was the first who brought the gospel to Egypt." The *Apostolic Constitutions* [5] state that Annianus, the first bishop of Alexandria, was ordained by the evangelist Mark, the second bishop, Abilios, by Luke who was also an evangel-

---

[4] *Hist. Eccles.*, II, 16.
[5] VIII, 46.

ist. In the apochryphal "Acts of the Apostles" we find an account of the "Martyrdom of St. Mark" in which it is related that he was appointed to preach in Egypt, Libya and Marmarica, and exercised his ministry in Rakhotis (Alexandria), where his first convert was a shoe-maker named Abilios.

The apochryphal "Acts" also relate that St. Bartholomew [6] was sent to preach in the Oasis (of Behnesa) in the borders of Upper Egypt, from whence he passed into the land of the Berbers, to Libya and Cyrenaica.

The Roman Martyrology under April 25 gives the following reference: "At Alexandria the anniversary of Blessed Mark the Evangelist. He was the disciple and interpreter of Peter the Apostle; at Rome the brethren asked him to write a Gospel. This he did, and having finished it he went into Egypt. First of all he preached Christ at Alexandria and formed a Church there; later on he was arrested for Christianity, bound with cords, and grievously tortured by being dragged over rocks; after this he was kept in prison, and there he was strengthened first by a visit of an angel and later by an apparition of our Lord. He was called to the kingdom of heaven in the eighth year of the reign of Nero. Likewise at Alexandria, of St. Anianus, [7] Bishop, a disciple of St. Mark and his successor in the bishopric. He rested in the Lord, renowned for his virtues."

The story of St. Mark's martyrdom cannot be traced back earlier than the 4th century, and there is more than one version of it. Thus, we read that on the 29th *Barmoudeh*, 62

[6] Commemorated in the Coptic *Synaxarion* on the 1 *Tout* (August 29), with a second feast, the commemoration of his preaching in the Oasis, on the 19 *Hator* (November 15).
[7] Commemorated by the Copts as the second bishop of Alexandria on the 20 *Hator* (November 16).

(April 24), at Easter, as the saint was celebrating the liturgy at Alexandria in a church which was being built at a place called *Bucolia* ("Pasture of the Cattle"), the mob rushed upon him, tied him with ropes and dragged him through the streets. On the following day, the saint died in excruciating torture, but when the pagans were about to burn his body an earthquake caused them to scatter, thus affording an opportunity for him to receive Christian burial. Tradition affirms that the body of St. Mark was translated to Venice in 829, disappearing after the fire of 976, but that it was in 1094 miraculously recovered. Relics, however, are not wanting at the scene of the saint's apostolic labours, and the cathedral church of the dissidents at Alexandria has preserved the alleged right arm, encased in what appears to be a blue velvet bolster, which is kept on the north side of the sanctuary. The Monophysite patriarch at his consecration is blessed with the relic. The head of St. Mark is said to lie some thirteen metres below the relic of the arm.

At a fairly early date, Christianity spread out amongst the native population of the Nile valley, but we have no serious history of the Church in Egypt before the time of the patriarch Demetrius (189-231), when it was a flourishing community sharing in the cultural life of the country.

Persecutions by the Roman emperors figure very prominently in Coptic literature, and the development of the cult of the martyrs occupied an important place in the history of the Church at an early date. The constancy of the Egyptian Christians has been attested by Origen in his *Exhortation to the Martyrs* and also by the letters of St. Dionysius the Great (246-ab. 264); while their fortitude in the time of Diocletian introduced a new reckoning of time, the "Era of the Martyrs," which dates from the 1st *Tout* of the common year 284. Thus, 1946 becomes 1662 of the Martyrs' Era.

The first series of authentic martyrdoms dates from the edict of Decius in 250, but the main body of Egyptian martyrs belongs to the time of the persecution carried out by Diocletian and his colleague Maximian.

Gnosticism was strong in Egypt, and the struggle against it may have been largely responsible for the formation of the first Christian university, the *Didascalion* or Catechetical School, founded by Pantaenus († ab. 200) at Alexandria. The School fostered such giants of theological learning as Clement of Alexandria († ab. 215), Origen († ab. 253), the Isapostolic Athanasius († 373), and St. Cyril († 444), but, as Dr. Adrian Fortescue[8] points out, this Neo-Platonic academy was never considered quite safe from the point of view of orthodoxy. The 5th general council[9] (553) declared Origen to be a heretic, while Pope Benedict XIV in the bull *Postquam intelleximus* (1748) refused to Clement the honours of a saint, because of the suspicion of want of orthodoxy[10] in his works.

Egyptian Christianity, before all else, was the mother of monasticism, which represented a living and moving power in reviving and sustaining the religious life of the people.

A remark of Sozomen[11] suggests that the first hermits in the desert were persons who fled for safety there during the persecutions. In some cases the solitaries seem to have inhabited the tombs of Upper Egypt. Monastic life proper dates from the persecution under Decius (249-251), but the first ascetic who made his permanent abode in the desert is believed to have been Paul of Thebes († 340).

---

[8] *The Orthodox Eastern Church*, chap. I, p. 12.
[9] Canon 11 of the second council of Constantinople.
[10] *Opera sin minus erronea, saltem suspecta.*
[11] *Hist. Eccles.*, X, 12.

Early monastic life, apart from solitaries and hermits, may be divided into three phases:

a) *Bohairic monasticism* in Lower Egypt, especially associated with Nitria [12] and Scetis, where the ideal was patriarchal, based on the type of the family. To this monastic group belongs St. Antony († 356), who embraced the religious life about the year 305. The colony in Scetis was founded by St. Macarius the Great († before 390) and his companions, several of whom had been under the influence of St. Antony. The proximity to Alexandria caused the houses of this region to take a very leading part in the history of the Coptic church.

b) *Syrian monasticism,* passing through St. Hilarion into Palestine, and from thence to Syria and Mesopotamia. The tone of these communities was more severe, multiplying austerities and formulating more elaborate discipline and organisation

c) *Sahidic monasticism* of Upper Egypt, with its headquarters in the Theban desert, where in 318 St. Pachomius († ab. 346) founded Tabennisi. The ideal of this group was that of a soldier in a great and highly organised army, with minute subdivision of labour. This monastic life later produced St. Shenout (Shenudah), the reformer and writer, who was the "only character of literary eminence in the history of the Coptic church" [13] after the schism.

From the 4th century onwards the number of monks in the country was prodigious, and by the 5th and 6th centuries their fame had "gone out into all lands." "Scetis [14] became

---

[12] Nitria applies more properly to the north part of the valley, and Scetis to the south, but both names are used to designate the whole country.

[13] De Lacy O'Leary, *The Saints of Egypt,* IV, p. 26.

[14] De Lacy O'Leary, *op. cit.,* IV, 27.

the focus of the monastic movement which spread out from Egypt to every part of Christendom." Travellers, also, came from countries as far distant as Spain and Ireland in order to visit the monasteries, and an Irish guide book for visitors to the Holy Land of Scetis is still preserved in the *Bibliothèque Nationale* in Paris. The earliest description of monastic life in Egypt was written in 390 by Ammonius.[15] Among the pilgrims to the desert houses, we may mention St. Paula († 404), St. Melania († 410), St. Jerome († 420), St. John Cassian († ab. 433), and Palladius [16] († before 431). Rufinus,[17] visiting Egypt so early as 273, says that in the region about Arsinoe he found 10,000 monks, and that the land "so swarmed with monks that their chants and hymns by day and night made the whole country one church of God." In the following century, we read [18] that "the Patriarch Cyril had a standing army of some 5,000 monks in Nitria alone." "With all due allowance for oriental weakness in arithmetic," as Butler puts it, the wonder is that the nation was not extinguished by universal celibacy.

Pope Leo XIII recalled these past glories of the church of Egypt in an apostolic letter to the Coptic nation, which was written on July 11, 1895, under the title of *Unitas Christiana:* "From the dawn of Christianity the Roman and Alexandrine churches have been united by the bonds of the

[15] Bollandist *Acta* for May 16.
[16] The *Historia Lausiaca*, written about 420, is an eye-witness account of Egyptian monasticism at the closing years of the 4th century (chiefly of the Greek speaking communities).
[17] BUTLER, *Ancient Coptic Churches of Egypt,* vol. I, chap. VIII, pp. 341-342.
[18] BUTCHER, *Story of the Church of Egypt,* vol. I, chap. XXIII, p. 273.

most notable and closest kinship. [19]   The Prince of the
Apostles himself entrusted to St. Mark, his disciple and
interpreter, the foundation and rule of the Alexandrine
church, whose name was to become illustrious on many
grounds. No one is ignorant of the majestic dignity with
which men distinguished for their holiness and learning
filled this see—among them Dionysius, Peter the Martyr,
Athanasius and Cyril, who, according to the testimony of St.
Celestine I, "were always the invincible defenders of Catholic

---

[19] In the following liturgical points, Egypt agreed with the West
rather than with Constantinople:

a) Rome and Alexandria both had " popes," and their jurisdiction
was more centralised than that of the other patriarchs.

b) Egypt and Rome had the same length of Lent.

c) " The Lord be with (you) all" and not " Peace be to (you) all."

d) Prayers preceded by a bidding by the priest, and a short proclamation by the deacon, e. g. prayer of thanksgiving or the first prayer
of the morning; proem of the fraction, followed by " Pray ye" and the
prayer of the fraction before the Lord's prayer; and the " three great
solemn prayers." Cf. solemn prayers on Good Friday in the Roman rite.

e) In the Greek litanies at the beginning of the liturgy of the
faithful, the Copts have the counterpart of *Flectamus genua*, although
these are omitted by the Catholics.

f) Cf. Preface of Coptic St. Mark with the Roman *Vere dignum*.

g) In St. Mark, the great intercession is in the preface, and in the
Roman rite the diptychs for the living are in the first part of the canon,
but the two more or less agree, as against eastern usage.

h) Now in Coptic St. Mark there are two prayers for consecration,
the one immediately before the words of institution, the other the
epiclesis, but the first, a " diluted" epiclesis, corresponds in place with
the Roman *Quam oblationem*.

i) Coptic, " For this is my body .... For this is my blood;" cf. Roman, *Hoc est enim corpus .... Hic est enim calix sanguinis*.

j) The Coptic anaphora ends with the response of the people: " As
it was and is and shall be for generations of generations and for all the
ages of ages. Amen." The formula is as early as Serapion; cf. *Sicut
erat in principio*, etc.

H. W. CODRINGTON, *Eastern Churches Quarterly*, October, 1940.

This affinity must be of early date, for the schism dates from the dogma" and whose perfect harmony with the Roman Pontiff and religious submission to his authority are witnessed to in history by numberless facts. There was also under the shadow of the Chair of St. Mark a school of consummate learning, universally renowned, that showed forth what aid can be afforded in the exposition and defence of divine truth by human sciences when handled with judgement and wisdom. But the greatest glory of your Church is to have been the first to furnish examples of the highest virtue. The most remote posterity will hold in remembrance the men who, through St. Antony's admirable institution, made the solitudes of Egypt the dwelling place of evangelical perfection."

Monophysism

In spite, however, of this background of holiness and spiritual learning, almost the whole of the Alexandrine church in the 5th century fell into the Monophysite schism—the heresy [20] that there is only one nature in Jesus Christ, his humanity being entirely absorbed in his divinity, and his body not of one substance with ours. On the theological side, an excessive and even perverted devotion to St. Cyril forced the Egyptian church along the path of heresy, although other causes were at work which probably had a greater influence. Butcher in his *Story of the Church of Egypt* has thus explained the causes of the schism: "To them (the

5th century, and Palestinian influence on Egyptian formulae is already apparent in the 4th. Edmund BISHOP, *Journal of Theological Studies,* XIV, pp. 27 seq.

Cf. also the prayer for the offerers in the intercession of Coptic St. Mark with the Roman *Supra quae* and *Supplices,* especially as the words "into thy vastnesses in heaven" should read: "unto thy majesty in the heavens."

[20] Greek, μονή φύσις "one nature."

Egyptians after the excommunication of Dioscorus) it was
a question of national freedom, and the doctrinal question a
mere difference of expression, except in so far as the formula
which their own pope (Dioscorus) had sanctioned became to
them a national watchword .... It became a point of honour,
as a true patriot, to reject the decrees of the council of Chalcedon." A point of view held to-day by many of the clergy.
National sentiment was hostile to the Greek foreigner and
his imperial church, while the spiritual and, even, temporal
power of the patriarch of Alexandria was conducive to the
formation of a national church. The ignorance of the clergy
and the predominance of the monastic body that was wholeheartedly attached to the patriarch without showing much
intelligent discrimination helped to further the schism. A
succession of rival patriarchs was maintained for about a
hundred years, but Dioscorus [21] (444-451), the twenty-fifth
successor of St. Mark, is looked upon as the true founder
of Monophysism in Egypt, although the present dissident
hierarchy claims its spiritual descent from Peter III (567-
570). In the reign of the emperor Justinian (518-527) the
country became a "cave of Adullam" for Monophysite nota-
bilities from Syria and elsewhere.

The Coming of the Arabs

The Persians ruled in Egypt from 616-628, but in December 639 the country was overrun by the Arabs. It is said
that the conquest under 'Amr was facilitated by the Copts
themselves, who, hating the Greek imperial authorities, wel-
comed the Mohammedan invasion.

[21] Dioscorus was banished by the emperor Marcian to Gangres in
Paphlagonia for refusing to accept the decrees of the council of Chalcedon.
He died in 455.

The dissidents certainly gained possession of a number of orthodox churches, but they were required to pay a poll tax of two gold pieces per head, with exemption for monks, women, old people, and children under the age of sixteen. The Monophysite patriarch, Benjamin, was recalled from his hiding place of the past ten years, and Al-Mecaukes, the former governor, who was said to have helped the invaders, was permitted to continue in office in Alexandria under the khalif. The capital had fallen in 641, but the conqueror fixed his place of residence at Fustat, "the camp" where his army lay.

From the 7th century, the condition of the Coptic church and people makes sad reading, with sporadic but fierce persecutions and many apostasies. Under the circumstances little or no progress could be made either intellectually or materially.

The Fatamid khalifs (Shi'ah Moslems) governed Egypt from 969-1171, and Al-Mu'izz (953-975) built Cairo [22] to serve as his capital. The Copts under Al'Aziz (975-996) passed through a time of toleration and even prosperity. Most of the civil service was in Christian hands, and the Coptic patriarch was generally reckoned to be the wealthiest person in Egypt. The patriarch Ephraim (977-980) became a favourite at the court, and the church of St. Mercurius (Abu-Saifain) was rebuilt, while several of the Fatimid khalifs retired to Coptic monasteries for a country holiday, and were entertained right royally.

Good fortune, however, was shortlived, and with the accession of the mad Al-Hakim [23] (996-1021) so great a

---

[22] *Al-Kahirah,* "the Victorious."
[23] "Father of the two swords."

persecution [24] was launched against the Christians that church services practically ceased; more than 1,030 churches were destroyed. Those who lost their lives for their faith under Moslem rule were termed "New Martyrs."

The patriarch Christodulos (1047-1077) published a code of thirty-one canons, which still holds a high place in Coptic canon law. Great efforts were made to eradicate simony, always a besetting sin among the Copts. The same code, also, enacted that holy communion, if possible, should be given to an infant immediately after baptism.

The seat of the patriarchate was moved about this time [25] from Alexandria to Cairo, and the patriarchal consecration began to be held at the two places alternately, although the actual enthronement was retained in the city of St. Mark.

The successor of Christodulos, Cyril II (1078-1092), also enriched Coptic canon law, and he is said to have determined the patriarchal vesture, blue silk for ordinary wear and red silk embroidered with gold for festal occasions. New canons were passed by two patriarchs in the 12th century, Macarius II (1103-1129) and Gabriel II ibn Tarik [26] (1132-1145). The last named, on the day of his enthronement in

[24] "The wonder is rather that any Copts at all kept the faith during these hideous centuries. When the last day comes, weightier than their theological errors will count the glorious wounds they bore for Him under the blood-stained banner of Islam." Adrian FORTESCUE, *Lesser Eastern Churches*, chap. VII, p. 251; chap. VIII, 2, p. 227.

[25] De Lacy O'Leary (*op. cit.*, IV, 27) says that "about 551 the patriarchal see was transferred from Alexandria to Scetis and remained there until it was removed to Cairo about 970, though certain official acts of the patriarch, such as the consecration of the chrism on Maundy Thursday, and other pontifical functions, were still performed at the monastery of *Abu Maqar* in Scetis."

[26] 30 canons were drawn up by Gabriel II. Canon 25 enjoined that the liturgy should not be celebrated otherwise than according to the accepted order.

the monastery of St. Macarius, gave rise to a small controversy by adding to the confession of faith in the real presence made before communion the words: "he united it with his divinity." Michael V [27] (1145-1146), who succeeded him, was the very antithesis of his predecessor, since he was an illiterate monk who could neither read nor write, and had to learn by heart the text of the Mass and ritual. He performed several ordinations however. At the end of six months, he was poisoned by the monks he had tried to reform. In the second half of the century, in the patriarchate of John V (1146-1164), an important controversy took place in regard to sacramental confession.

Most of the eastern liturgies in some way connect incense with the public confession of sin, prayers for forgiveness rising up to God like the smoke. Thus, with the idea of hallowing and purifying the holy place, incense, in preparation for the solemn act, is used at the beginning of the Mass. This connection between the offering of incense and the confession of sin is very clear in the Coptic liturgy, and in the 12th century an attempt was made to substitute a general avowal of sin on the part of the faithful at the time of the censing at the beginning of Mass for sacramental confession. The "absolution [28] to the Son" was thus considered to give absolution to all those present.

Others, on the plea that it was an era of persecution, lit censers in their own homes for the private reading of the lessons from the Morning Office of incense, and then con-

[27] *Dictionnaire de Théologie Catholique*, t. X, col. 2256.
[28] In the dissident church, the absolution to the Son is given after a sacramental confession has been made *and* the penance performed, by way of a final reconciliation.
It is the sacramental form for penance among the Catholic Copts. *Dict. de Théol. Cath.*, t. X, col. 2287.

fessed before them. The patriarch supported those who wished to abolish the sacrament, and excommunicated a priest named Mark Ibn al-Kanbar, who had defended the teaching of the Church.

Appeal was made to the Jacobite patriarch of Antioch, Michael I (1166-1199), a rare occurrence for a patriarch of lower rank to be consulted. The answer was ambiguous, but, although it was on the whole unfavourable to Mark, little more seems to have been heard of the abuse. About the same time, also, a controversy arose as to whether circumcision should take place before or after baptism. The question was finally settled by enjoining circumcision on the 8th day after birth, and the deferring of the rite until after baptism was condemned as a return to the Old Law.

The relations of the Copts with the crusaders (1219-1249) were chiefly in the nature of acrimonious polemics, and they had never forgiven the Latins for expelling them from the holy places of Palestine, and for putting obstacles in their way for making pilgrimages to Jerusalem. Nicholas I, however, the Byzantine patriarch of Alexandria, wrote submissive letters to two popes—Innocent III (1210) and Honorius III (1223). In the second, he called Honorius "our lord and spiritual father" and spoke of him as "by divine grace chief pontiff of the holy Roman Church and universal bishop."

The Latin patriarchs of Alexandria date from the capture of Damietta in 1219, but they were never more than titular. Saladin, despite his reputation for chivalry, adopted repressive measures against the Copts. Bells, exterior crosses and outside processions were prohibited; while he ordered the churches to be painted black, and attempted to forbid the singing of the ecclesiastical chant.

Cyril III ibn Laqlaq (1235-1243), although suspected of simony, held a reforming synod during his patriarchate, and edited the *Book of Instruction for Beginners*. The same patriarch also is said to have at one time shown a desire for union with Rome. He had a dispute with the Jacobite patriarch of Antioch, who had consecrated a Coptic bishop [29] in Jerusalem.

Further repressive measures came into force against the Copts, who were compelled to wear black clothes. The colour was later changed to dark blue, which in consequence has become the distinctive colour for members of the national church.

The Copts are sometimes known as the "People of the Girdle," [30] a name which is also given to the Syrian Jacobites. The term probably originated in an early Moslem decree which forced the Christians in Egypt to wear a girdle as a mark of humiliation. The order was given by the Khalif Mutawakkil, a century and a half before the days of Al Hakim. Butler [31] has suggested that the name was given first by the Venetians.

In the 13th century, the bishop of Sandafah achieved the unenviable notoriety of embracing Islam.

In 1250, the Sunni Moslems, descendents of Saladin, were replaced by the Mamluk [32] or "Slave" dynasty, but a change of rulers brought little alleviation to the Copts.

Churches were pillaged and destroyed in the 14th century, and for one year there were no religious services in Egypt.

[29] The office exists to-day.
[30] Arabic, *Ahl-almantal kah*. Some have derived the name from the symbolical linen girdle given in baptism.
[31] *Ancient Coptic Churches of Egypt*, vol. II, chap. IV, p. 104.
[32] Arabic, *mamlūk*, "slave."

It was, however, in this century of misery and desolation that Abu'l Barakat (1273-1363) produced the encyclopedia of the Coptic church—*The Lamp of the darkness and exposition (full of light) of the service (liturgical)*. A manuscript of the work, copied about 1363, is preserved in Paris, and another at Upsala (1546, but reproducing a manuscript of 1357).

In 1362, the patriarch Niphon seems to have written to Blessed Urban V (1362-1370) with a view to union with Rome, but without result.

The streets of Cairo in 1389 witnessed a novel procession, composed of apostates, wishing to reaffirm their allegiance to Christ. They were all put to death.

In the time of the Burgi sultans (1390-1517), the country was in a state of anarchy, but the patriarch Gabriel V (1409-1427) reformed the liturgical books, and wrote an explanation of the Coptic rite.

The Coptic Church and Rome

His successor, John XI (1427-1453), seems to have shown some desire for union with the Catholic Church, and John, [33] abbot of St. Antony, who also represented the king of Abyssinia, was sent as Coptic legate to the council of Florence (1442). The delegate addressed Pope Eugenius IV as "God on earth" and "vicar of Christ," [34] and signed the *Decretum*

---

[33] ANDREW, *Incontro ai fratelli separati di Oriente*, p. 210.

[34] *Pulvis sum et cinis coram te, Deo in terris. Es namque Deus in terris et Christus et ejus vicarius; es Petri successor et pater, caput et doctor ecclesiae universalis, cui datae sunt claves claudendi, et paradisum cuicumque voluerit, reserandi. Tu princeps regum et maximus es magistrorum.* MANSI, t. XXXI, col. 1732.

pro Jacobitis, but its decrees were never promulgated in Egypt, and the union was still-born.

In the patriarchate of Gabriel VII (1525-1568), Pope Pius IV (1561) sent two Jesuits, Christopher Rodriguez and John Baptist Eliano, to negotiate in regard to the submission of the Coptic church. The question was resumed in 1582 by the patriarch John XIV (1574-1589), who summoned a council of bishops at Babylon [35] to hear the legates and consider their proposals. The deliberations were stormy, but the personal influence of the patriarch prevailed on the council to draw up decrees in conformity with the suggestions of the Catholic delegates. The agreement, however, was never signed, as the patriarch died suddenly in the night. The Moslems arrested the legates as foreign spies, and threw them into a dungeon. A ransom of 5,000 pieces of gold was paid by the Copts, which the pope in due course repaid.

An attempt at reunion by the patriarch Gabriel VIII (1590-1610) in 1549 was no more successful, although letters [36] of submission were sent to Pope Clement VIII. In 1630, a Capuchin mission was established at Cairo which did not prosper, and at the end of 1633 Father Agathangelo of Vendôme was sent there to take charge. He was joined by Father Cassian of Nantes and two others. Their first success was among the Syrian Jacobites of the Nile delta. Then, getting into personal touch with the Coptic bishops, Matthew, their patriarch, opened all the dissident churches to Father Agathangelo, who, using powers granted by Rome, said Mass, preached and catechized therein, and reconciled a number of Copts. Later, since the Coptic bishops were

---

[35] Babylon is often erroneously called Old Cairo.

[36] Butcher (*Story of the Church of Egypt,* vol. II, chap. XXXIII, p. 251) maintains that there was no submission on the part of the patriarch, but that oriental courtesy deceived the pope.

chosen from the monks, Agathangelo and Cassian, accompanied by the Syrian bishop, visited the monastery of St. Macarius in the Nitrian desert. In 1636, Father Agathangelo went to the monastery of St. Antony in the Lower Thebaid, where he stayed for four months, conducting doctrinal discussions and giving spiritual conferences. Two out of the fifteen monks were reconciled to the Church. There were, however, no Catholic churches of the Coptic rite for reconciled dissidents to attend, and priests were allowed to celebrate the liturgy in, and lay-people to frequent, the schismatic churches. Later, the Congregation of Propaganda declared the practice to be irregular, but it would seem that a spirited remonstrance on the part of Father Agathangelo to the cardinal prefect must have borne fruit, as we find the custom followed at Cairo by his successors. The prospect of the reconciliation of the Coptic church was, however, wrecked by the evil conduct of the Latins resident in Egypt, and of the consul of France in particular. Agathangelo and Cassian in 1637 left in despair for Ethiopia, where in the following year they were both martyred. Thus ended ingloriously the attempts at corporate reunion, which at one time seemed to have had a real chance of success.

Catholic Missions in Egypt

In 1675 the Friars Minor of the Observance were given charge of a prefecture apostolic (in adjutorium Coptorum) in Upper Egypt, and the Jesuits came to Cairo. There were nine Catholic missions south of Cairo in 1731—Antinoe, Assiut, Abu Tige, Sedfeh, Akhmin, Girgeh, Luxor, Assuan, and at Deyr in Nubia. In that year, Pope Clement XII (1730-1740) sent directions to the superiors of those places instructing them to send Coptic children to be educated in Rome.

Twelve students arrived at the Propaganda College in 1738, among whom was Abul Kher Bichara, who died the same year in the odour of sanctity. The same pope also wrote to the patriarch John XVII with a view to union, but without success.

Little indeed was achieved until 1741, when Pope Benedict XIV (1740-1758) appointed Amba Athanasius, the convert Coptic bishop of Jerusalem to govern the faithful of his rite,—"I have seen the affliction of my people in Egypt, and I have heard their cry." [37] The new pastor, fearing imprisonment or worse at the hands of the dissident patriarch, continued to live in Palestine, and made Justus Maraghi his vicar general in Egypt. About the same time, the learned Raphael Tukhi († 1787), a native of Girgeh, was editing and publishing the Coptic liturgical books in Rome, becoming successively titular bishop of Acante and Arsinoe. The successors of Amba Athanasius as vicars apostolic, John Faragi (1781) and Matthew Righet (1788-1822), although receiving the titles of Hysopolis and Utina respectively, were never consecrated, apparently because there was no Catholic bishop in Egypt, although in the time of Faragi Antony Flaifel, [38] bishop of Girgeh, renounced Monophysism and made a Catholic profession of faith.

In 1815, Ghali, Catholic secretary of Mohammed Ali, made an attempt to reconcile the Coptic church to Rome, but through the intrigues of a bishop the negotiations fell through. Maximus Joed was nominated Coptic Catholic bishop in 1824, with the title of his predecessor, Utina. He received consecration at the hands of Ignatius V Kattan, Melkite patriarch of Antioch. In 1824 also, Pope Leo XII,

---

[37] Exod., III, 7.
[38] The convert bishop was persecuted by the dissidents and fled to Rome, where in 1807 he died.

understanding that it was the wish of the Khedive Mohammed Ali, reestablished, by the apostolic letter *Petrus Apostolorum princeps* (August 15, 1824), the Coptic Catholic
patriarchate, but it was not put into effect until the close of
the century. It is said that this was due to the opposition of
Abraham Cashoor, who had been consecrated as archbishop
of Memphis by the pope himself, and was living in Rome at
the time. On the death of Maximos Joed (August 30, 1831),
Theodore Abukarim (1832-1854) succeeded as titular bishop
of Alia, and was nominated in 1840 delegate and visitor
apostolic to Abyssinia. In 1854, Pope Pius IX appointed
Athanasius Khuzam (1854-1864) as titular bishop of Maronia
and administrator of the Catholic Copts. He was succeeded
by Aghapios Bishai (1866-1887), bishop of Cariopolis, who
represented his church at the Vatican Council (1870). Disputes caused his recall to Rome in or soon after 1878, and
until 1895 the Copts were governed by an apostolic visitor,
who was neither a Copt nor a bishop.

An invitation was accorded to the bishops of the national
church to attend the Vatican council, and Mgr. Ciurcia, the
apostolic delegate to Egypt, was charged to hand them the
papal letter, *Divinae providentiae*. The bishop of Cairo, to
whom it was first given, expressed astonishment that it had
not been written by the pope personally, and that it did not
even bear the pontifical seal. The delegate, realising that to
an oriental the seal affords the sole proof of the authenticity
of a document, admitted the reasonableness of his complaint.
On the arrival of the patriarch, a formal invitation in the
name of the pope was given to attend the council. The patriarch, while thanking the delegate, made it quite clear that
he was unwilling to accept, adding that, in regard to the
letter, if it had been written in an imperative tone he did
not even wish to see it, but that if it was couched in friendly

terms he would read it. The delegate thereupon gave the
patriarch a Latin copy of the letter with a printed translation,
bound in a rich cover ornamented with gold characters.
Somewhat mollified by its tone, the patriarch abandoned his
haughty attitude and discussed theological points of difference. At the end of the interview, the delegate asked
leave to call again, saying: "How shall we ever be able to
understand each other, if we never see one another!" The
patriarch replied by alluding to the very few occasions on
which Copts and Latins meet. In his letter to the pope, the
delegate said that it would have been much better if a
special letter had been sent to each patriarch, signed with a
coloured seal, and that the text of the council of Florence,
contained in the papal document, could not have much interest for the Copts.

Up to 1893, the Coptic clergy and the Franciscans had
separate districts, both of which were under Austrian protection, but in that year the Franciscans ceded ten churches,
for the most part in Upper Egypt, to the Catholics of the
oriental rite.

A few years later, the patriarch opted for his rite to become a national community, although the churches until
1914 remained under Austrian protection.

The Catholic patriarchate of Alexandria was effectively
reestablished on November 26, 1895, by the apostolic letter
Christi Domini. In the March of that year, Amba Cyril II
Makarios had been consecrated bishop with the title of
administrator, and in a consistory held on June 19, 1899,
he was officially proclaimed "Patriarch of Alexandria and of
all the Preaching of St. Mark," and two suffragans (Minieh
and Thebes) were assigned to him. Certain difficulties,
however, compelled Amba Makarios in 1908 to resign and,
four year later, he lapsed into schism, although before his

death in 1922 at Beirut he was happily restored to communion with the Catholic church. The patriarchate has since remained in abeyance, and the bishop of Minieh (Hermopolis Major), Amba Maximos Sedfaui, became apostolic administrator. In November 1926, this office devolved upon Amba Mark Khuzam, the present bishop of Thebes (Tahta).

Present Condition of the Dissidents

At the time of the Moslem invasion, the Copts are said to have numbered six million, with from two to three hundred thousand members of the Byzantine rite, who represented the Greek functionaries and imperial garrison. Centuries of persecution with resultant apostasy has, however, so depleted the numbers of the national church that they now hardly reach a total of nine hundred thousand. [39] Ignorance among the clergy is widespread and simony has been a besetting sin, but there are encouraging signs of revival on the part of the better educated laity, although this has led to opposition from the more conservative bishops. The present dispute dates from 1883, when the reforming party forced the Egyptian government to authorise the formation of a Coptic national body, to be known as the *Maglis Milli*, which should have the right to supervise church affairs. The patriarch, Cyril V (1874-1927), a prelate of the old school, actively opposed this limitation to his authority, and in 1892 retired to a monastery. In the following year, however, he returned to Cairo, where he remained until his death on August 7, 1927. "I have no reason to doubt," wrote

[39] Amba Mark Khuzam (*Missions des Coptes Catholiques en Egypte*, p. 1) says that at the beginning of the 19th century there were no more than 100,000 Copts, whereas they had at one time numbered 13 millions. He gives the present total as 989,000.

Fr. Adrian Fortescue,[40] "that his holiness is a pious and zealous prelate, but he will not see strangers. When you go to his palace (next to the Coptic patriarchal church in the Darb alwaṣāh at Cairo) he sends you his blessing by a secretary." This was certainly not the experience of the writer, who, as an Anglican clergyman (May 20, 1924), was most graciously received by the "Most holy Pope and Patriarch of the great city Alexandria, of Abyssinia, Nubia, the Pentapolis and of all the country evangelised by Saint Mark."[41] The patriarch, who was shrivelled and bowed with age,[42] spoke through an interpreter, and gave to each of the party, not only the customary refreshment, but also a gold medal commemorating his golden jubilee as patriarch. His blessing, also, was given personally, not through a secretary.

On the death of Cyril V, the *Maglis Milli* elected Hanna Salama, the reformist bishop of Khartum, as his successor. This was a universally popular choice, especially to the Ethiopians, although the translation of a bishop to another see was contrary to Coptic canon law. The Egyptian government, however, had no desire to see the reforming party in power, and the election was never confirmed.

Numberless intrigues followed, until the acting patriarch and former auxiliary, Amba John, bishop of Alexandria, was chosen by nominees of the government. The former election was declared invalid, and Amba John was consecrated pa-

---

[40] *Lesser Eastern Churches*, part II, chap. VIII, p. 259, n. 2.

[41] The jurisdiction of the patriarch was defined by canon 6 of the council of Nicea (325). The Sunday *Theotokion* (*Psali*, in section VII) speaks of the patriarch as "Father of fathers, Shepherd of shepherds, High Priest of our high priests."

[42] Rumour alleged that the patriarch was 130 years old. This was certainly an exaggeration, but it was known that he was at least 94.

triarch as John XIX on December 16, 1928. Thus, for the second time, Coptic canon law was set aside.

Although of the traditionalist party, the new patriarch had promised certain measures of reform, but his subsequent policy showed little that was progressive. All his appointments were of the reactionary type, and efforts were made to get rid of the democratic *Magliss Milli*. Amba John had also a wholesome fear of contact with Protestants, and his students were forbidden to attend English universities or to receive instruction from Anglicans.

On his death, canon law was again broken, and on February 4, 1944, Amba Makarios, archbishop of Assiut, was elected patriarch († August 1945). The present holder of the title, Amba Jussab II, who had been archbishop of Girgeh, was appointed on May 13, 1946.

The Coptic Christians are intensely national, and they have identified themselves with the independence of Egypt. In the parliamentary delegation to London in 1930, which demanded freedom for the country, there were two Mohammedans and two Copts, while of the six Egyptian representatives put forward in 1936 for the negotiations in regard to the treaty of independence two were Copts.

The Copts are rich and influential beyond their numerical strength, and in the ministry of Nahhas Pasha (1936) they were represented by the Minister of foreign affairs and the Minister of finance.

Under King Faud, the Egyptian ambassador at Washington was a Catholic Copt, while two Catholics were among his counsellors.

The present situation is not so favourable to the Copts, and there seems a certain recrudescence of Mohammedan fanaticism.

The Hierarchy

The ordination of the dissident patriarch requires twelve bishops, which seemingly is a relic of the ancient Alexandrine *presbyterium* of twelve members, of whom the writers of the early centuries speak.

It seems probable that Alexandria until the era of persecution was the only see in Egypt, just as there was one heathen high priest and one prefect.

Before 700, the patriarchal election was always held at Alexandria; until about 1000 generally at Cairo; then alternately at Alexandria and Cairo; and, finally, always at Cairo.

The enthronement still takes place at Alexandria, followed by a formal proclamation in the monastery of St. Macarius. [43]

The lots are drawn by a child. If the patriarch, or indeed any bishop elect, has not already received the order of *kommos* (*hegumenos*), which, as with the Byzantines, is conferred by a special rite, he must obtain this before he proceeds to consecration.

As we have seen, the rule forbidding the election of a translated bishop is sometimes waived, and there are several cases [44] in history of a patriarch who was not a monk.

If, however, a secular is elected patriarch he must first be invested with the "angelic raiment."

A sense of unworthiness, combined with a dread of responsibility, has sometimes necessitated the bringing of a patriarch in chains to be consecrated.

[43] On rare occasions the patriarch has been also elected in the monastery. It is required of a patriarch that he should know all the liturgy by heart.

[44] e. g. 609, Andronicus, deacon of Alexandria; ab. 663, Agathon, and his successors John and Isaac; 775, John; 977, Ephraim; 1002, Zacharias; 1131, Gabriel, deacon of Abu Sefein; 1163, Mark.

The senior bishop lays his hand on the head of the patriarchal candidate in silence, after which all the bishops impose their hands, while the ordination prayer is recited.

This prayer is an expanded form of that found in the *Apostolic Tradition* [45] of Hippolytus (early 3rd century) for the consecration of a bishop.

When the patriarch is proclaimed, the people cry out "ἄξιος".

The gospel-book is then laid on his head, and he is vested, while the other bishops remove their crowns.

The title "*amba,*" [46] which is given to saints and bishops, seems to be generally reserved by the Monophysites for the patriarch.

The Copts use the term "metropolitan" in a purely honorific sense, and only for the bishops of Damietta (12th century) and Jerusalem (beginning of the 13th century).

There were at one time 100 dioceses, but by the end of the 16th century the number had fallen to 10. To-day there are 15 (13 in Egypt; 1 in the Sudan; and 1 at Jerusalem).

The majority of the bishops [47] live with the patriarch, and form his court. The bishop of Jerusalem (*Al-Kuds*) lives at Jaffa, but an altar is reserved for the Copts against the wall of the Holy Sepulchre itself, while a modern church and monastery have been erected by the traditional site of the ninth station of the cross. Since 1897, the abbots of the four important monasteries of Moharag (province of Assiut), St. Antony (a monk of the house was formerly chosen as patriarch), St. Paul (desert of Arabia) and Baramus (desert

[45] Pp. 4-6, edited by Gregory Dix. London, 1937.
[46] Greek, ἀββᾶς ;Syriac, *abba;* Arabic *abū,* often contracted into *bū,* "father."
[47] The *theotokion* for Sunday calls the bishop: "the tongue of sweet scent, the chosen vessel, the good shepherd and chosen one."

of Nitria) have been consecrated bishops. The bishops of
Lower Egypt (north), by an agreement made in 1240 between
the patriarch Cyril Ibn Laqlaq and ten bishops, have had
precedence over the bishops of Upper Egypt (south). Four
reasons have been adduced for the greater importance of
the northern prelates. 1) Tradition has shown that it was
always a bishop of the north who ordained the patriarch, and
in acts of synods it is the bishops of Lower Egypt who sign
first. 2) Our Lord was first in the north of the country, and
only later in the south. 3) St. Mark preached the gospel
at Alexandria. 4) In the north is the desert of Scetis and the
monastery of St. Macarius, where the chrism is consecrated
and the patriarch is proclaimed before his enthronement.
This last reason would not have any further value to-day.

The patriarch, in the consecration ceremony, lays his
hand upon the head of the episcopal candidate, while the
bishops place their hands upon the shoulder.

Abbots, as we have seen, receive a form of ordination,
and also archpriests [48] and archdeacons. [49] The last named
acts as vicar general of the bishop, and wears an iron
pectoral cross.

Priests [50] are required to be at least thirty years old,
although ordination at twenty has not been infrequent, while
deacons [51] are sometimes mere youths of twelve or thirteen,
and even younger. The number of dissident priests

[48] Archpriests receive the honorific title of *kummos;* Greek,
ἡγούμενος; Coptic, *hygomenos.*
[49] *Ra'is shamamish.*
[50] *Kess, kassis.*
[51] The liturgy should not be celebrated without the assistance of a
deacon, but a church is not permitted to have more than seven deacons.
In practice, however, large churches sometimes have as many as twelve
"supernumerary" deacons, occupying the stalls outside the screen (e. g.
St. Mark's cathedral, Cairo).

is estimated at about a thousand, with six hundred churches. There is a seminary in Cairo. The ordination to the priesthood and the diaconate has a second imposition of hands towards the end of the liturgy, with the accompanying words: "Receive the Holy Spirit for the Church of N."

An imposition of hands on the temples is enjoined for the ordination of lectors and subdeacons, but at the present day minor orders appear to have fallen into desuetude in the national church. There was, however, a small boy of six, the grandson of the celebrant, who as "little deacon" was assisting at the liturgy (May 21, 1924) in the church of Abu Sergeh, Old Cairo.

The deacon at ordination receives a spoon, and the "little deacon"[52] a lighted candle. The reader[53] of the lessons in the Monophysite church is an important person, in view of the fact that there are priests who are unable to read the liturgy, and recite it by rote.

With the patriarchate in abeyance, the Catholic hierarchy is composed of two bishops, Minieh[54] and Thebes (Tahta), appointed directly by the Holy See.

Priests, since the synod of 1898, have been bound to celibacy, but the Holy See, especially in the case of converts from Monophysism, sometimes grants dispensations. Thus, in 1928, three married clerics were advanced to the priesthood, on the understanding that the permission was not to be taken as a precedent.

In respect to ecclesiastical training, so long ago as 1637 Pope Urban VIII in the brief *Altitudo divinae* confirmed

---

[52] Greek, ὑποδιάκονος; Coptic, *ypodiakōn;* Arabic, *abūdīyākun.*

[53] Greek, ἀναγνώστης; Coptic, *anagnóstēs;* Arabic, *karīanjīlī; anāgnust.*

[54] George Baraka was consecrated bishop of Minieh in 1938 († December 9, 1946).

two burses for Coptic students in the College of *Propaganda fide,* which had been founded by Cardinal Antonio Barberini. The Holy Office in 1757 permitted Copts to be ordained with the Byzantine rite in the church of the Greek College, Rome.

A "great" seminary of St. Leo the Great was founded in 1899 at Tahta, which was reorganised in 1920; while the "little" seminary, conducted by the Jesuits in Cairo from 1879 till 1907, was reopened in 1927. Both of these seminaries [55] are now directed by the Coptic secular clergy, and the junior students study under Jesuit professors at a neighbouring college. Other aspirants to the priesthood go to the College of St. Joseph, Beirut, where in 1930 there were three students, or to the College of Propaganda, Rome.

There are about 68 churches [56] or chapels, served by 66 priests (1931). [57]

In 1937, there were only 52 Coptic Catholic schools—40 in the diocese of Tahta and 12 in Minieh.

The African Missionaries of Lyons administer three districts in Lower Egypt under the jurisdiction of the Latin vicar apostolic of the Nile Delta. Permission was given in 1921 for priests of the congregation to adopt the Coptic rite, and two have availed themselves of the privilege. In 1934, there were 1,000 Coptic Catholics in this area, in the proportion of 1 Catholic to 120 dissidents.

---

[55] In 1938, the seminary at Tahta had 9 students with 3 professors, while the "little" seminary at Cairo had 50 students.

[56] 11 in the patriarchal diocese; 12 in Minieh; 40 in Tahta.

[57] In 1937, there were 36 priests in the diocese of Tahta; 14 in Minieh; and 17 in the patriarchal diocese.

The clergy for the most part live heroic lives in circumstances of grinding poverty.

The Friars Minor [58] have begun to form subjects of the Coptic rite in their college at Assiut.

In 1898, the Mariamettes of Syria came to work in Egypt, first at Minieh and then at Mallaoui and Tahta. They were recalled to Syria in 1911, and Propaganda authorised the Coptic members of the congregation to found a new order for Egypt, under the patronage of the Sacred Heart. The congregation was established in 1913, and their constitutions were approved for seven years by the Sacred Congregation for the Oriental Church in 1934. The sisters have four schools—Tahta, Sohag (Upper Egypt), Heliopolis and Cairo (Faggala)—with 31 religious.

In 1929, an Arabic apologetic review—Al-Salah—was started for the Catholic Copts.

Western influence is less noticeable in Upper than in Lower Egypt, where the churches are for the most part furnished in bad Latin taste.

There has been a steady flow of converts, and the present apostolic administrator in an address given in 1943 to Mgr. (now Cardinal) Spellman, archbishop of New York, at the Coptic Catholic patriarchate in Cairo said that the Catholic Copts have multiplied five times in sixty years, and that they now number 50,000. In 1895 they were said to be not more than 5,000, and in 1934 41,316. The reconciliations in 1936 were estimated at 1,522, which is about the annual number of conversions in England and Wales.

Monasticism

We have seen the growth of monasticism in Egypt, and the very large number of religious houses, but only seven monasteries are still inhabited by monks (100-150 in all),

[58] The first Franciscan Copt was ordained in Cairo in Nov. 1939.

and there has been no revival as yet among the Catholics of the rite.

Four of the monasteries are in the Wadi Natrun, the famous district of Scetis (Nitria), where the settlement owes its foundation [59] to St. Macarius the Great († ab. 390). A community was settled here in 340, and by 356 the place was crowded.

Deir Makarios is named after its founder; Deir Baramus, a corruption of "of the Romans," was probably built in 383-4 in honour of St. Maximus and St. Domitian, "the Roman Saints;" Deir es-Suryan or monastery of the Syrians, [60] founded in the time of the patriarch Joseph (830-849); and Deir Bishai, [61] where since the time of the patriarch Joseph the bodies [62] of St. Bishai, St. Paul of Tamwah and St. Ephrem the Syrian have rested in a wooden shrine set against the east wall of the entrance of the main *haikal*. There are two monasteries in the Arabian desert, not far from the Red Sea—Deir Antonios and Deir Bulos, near to which are the respective caves of St. Antony and Saint Paul of Thebes. Finally, the dissidents have a monastery at Moharag near Manfalut, in Upper Egypt, with about 40 monks, which is the largest and richest of the existing houses.

The Monophysites have three convents for women. One

[59] St. Macarius "popularised" the settlement, but the actual founder seems to have been St. Amoun (ab. 275-ab. 337), who is commemorated in the Greek Church on October 4, but who has been forgotten by the Copts.

[60] Syrian monks were numerous in Scetis. A group from Tagrit came to Wadi Natrun.

[61] An Arabic corruption of the Coptic *Isa*, which probably stands for Isaias.

[62] They were removed here from Antinoe.

of these, Deir al Banat or convent of the Maidens, is near the church of Abu Sefein in Old Cairo.[63]

The monastic habit [64] consists of a brown woollen tunic, black mantle with long sleeves, and a cincture of leather. The turban, which is streaked with blue and white, is not removed in church, and a small band [65] of black serge (askim), two fingers in width, falls from the turban to the neck, serving as a distinctive badge of the monastic state. The wearing of the askim entails 300 daily prostrations, as well as additional fasting and mortification.

The monks, during the long duration of the offices, lean upon a T shaped staff. The novitiate lasts three years.

The monks, except in Lent, take their meals alone.

Theology

The marked resemblance in matters of faith between the dissident Copts and the Catholic Church so impressed Vansleb of Erfurt († 1679), a Lutheran under the patronage of the grand duke of Saxony, who had been sent to Egypt to study Coptic liturgical manuscripts, that he not only became a Catholic, but also a Dominican friar.

Some writers have said that Monophysism in the Coptic church is only material, but the authorised cate-

[63] Butler (op. cit., vol. I, chap. III, p. 128, n. 15) refers also to two convents in new Cairo.

[64] Vansleb (Nouvelle Relation d'un Voyage fait en Egypte, Paris, 1698) mentions seven articles of monastic clothing: Shirt of white wool; tunic of brown wool; black serge overall with wide sleeves; small close-fitting hood of black serge; girdle of leather; mantle of black stuff with white lining, seldom used except on journeys; and askim or "angelic habit."

[65] Possibly a relic of the monastic hood. Peyron identifies the askim with the monastic girdle. The word is probably derived from $\sigma\chi\hat{\eta}\mu\alpha$, "shape."

chism [66] of the dissidents, in use to-day,—*The Blossoming of the Beginner in the study of Religion*—clearly teaches the error of Severus [67] of Antioch, that our Lord "became one person, one only distinct substance, one only nature, with one will and one operation."

On the other hand, a booklet, [68] written by the priest of the church of Abu Sergeh, Old Cairo, says: "The controversy is only a matter of wording. No doubt the belief of the Coptic church is the correct and true one. There are many verses in the ritual books of the Coptic church which indicate that divinity did not absorb humanity, which is made one with this divinity, without mixture, confusion or alteration, and that Jesus Christ is one in two: the holy divinity and the undefiled humanity."

Fr. Shenouda Hanna, also, a priest of the church of El-Moallaka ("Hanging Church"), Old Cairo, clearly expressed to the writer (December 1944) the orthodox doctrine in regard to the person of Christ, although he denounced the council of Chalcedon, which had defined the doctrine. It would seem therefore that rejection of Chalcedon is made a question of Coptic nationalism, and that the dogmatic issue has fallen into the background.

Protestant schools, both English and American, have been responsible for many Copts [69] losing their faith, and the patriarch Cyril IV (1854-1862), who was an alumnus of

---

[66] *Tanwir almubtada' in fi ta' lim ad-din.* Hegumenos Filuthā 'us. New edition. At press of Tufik at Cairo, 1629 (1912), p. 29.

[67] The dissidents, on the 2nd of the month *Paopi* (28 September-27 October), observe a feast in commemoration of the coming of Severus of Antioch to Egypt.

[68] *Short Note on the History of St. Sargius (sic) Church. The Oldest Church in Egypt.* George Bistavros. M. Thomas Press, Cairo, pp. 3-4.

[69] Ab. 30,000.

the Church Missionary Society, imbued with the iconoclasm of his teachers, destroyed many holy pictures.

No liturgy, save that of the daughter church of Ethiopia, has such a definite profession of faith in the real presence as that made by the celebrant in the Coptic rite before holy communion.

Devotion to our Lady is very marked, with 32 feasts in her honour, and an office known as the *Theotokia*, [70] of which there is a special one for each day of the week, although it is now only used in the month *Khihak* (December 10-January 9).

Opposition to the Catholic Church has sometimes caused a denial of truths which have been taught in the past, and a dissident priest in speaking of the blessed Virgin said that he certainly believed the Mother of God to be free from all stain of *original* sin, but that he did not believe in the Immaculate Conception, for that is what the Uniates say!

The Copts have not retained the explicit teaching of St. Athanasius and St. Cyril in regard to the *filioque*, [71] and it is difficult to determine from their formulas the relation existing between the Son and the Holy Spirit. In the middle ages, theologians, [72] in condemning the Latin addition to the creed, have seemed to deny the doctrine that it expresses.

Purgatory and prayers for the dead are clearly taught by the Copts, but foolish fables, apparently borrowed from the religion of ancient Egypt, have become connected with the state after death.

---

[70] The *Theotokion* is generally neglected by the Catholics, although it is sung in some villages of Upper Egypt at least every Saturday of the month *Khihak*. Elsewhere, only on Christmas night before the solemn liturgy.

[71] *Dict. de Théol. Cath.*, t. X, col. 2276-2277.

[72] Severus of Aschmunain (end of the 10th century) denied the doctrine.

The dissidents are vague in respect to the canon of Scripture, and they have admitted the Epistle of Barnabas, "Shepherd" of Hermas, letter of Clement of Rome, and various Clementine and apochryphal writings.

St. Peter, in virtue of divine institution, is called in Coptic literature the "head of the apostles. John Ibn Saba [73] said that "the Church is built on the rock of the faith which is Peter, the head of all the apostles;" while Abu'l Barakat, [74] without denying the primacy of Peter, understands the "Thou art Peter" to be the *faith* of the apostle.

The *Synaxarion* commemorates St. Celestine (422-432) on the same day as St. Cyril, 3 *Abib* (June 27); St. Clement of Rome, 29 *Hator* (November 25); St. Fabian, 11 *Amshir* (February 5); Liberius, 9 *Babeh* (October 6); and St. Sylvester, 7 *Tubeh* (January 2).

The patriarch of Alexandria is the supreme authority for the Copts, whose rôle is to preserve the established order, the tradition of the fathers. Doctrinal progress stopped at Ephesus and Dioscorus.

Coptic Writers

Coptic writers in the main have been unimportant, but all their works were essentially theological.

The only prominent original writer in Coptic literature is St. Shenudah (ab. 333-ab. 466), founder of the "White Monastery" and a religious leader of Upper Egypt, as a monastic and ecclesiastical reformer. He wrote vigorously against the uncritical acceptance of any unnamed human

[73] *Precious Pearl*, chap. XXXIII, p. 704; GORDILLO, *Compendium Theologiae Orientalis*, chap. IX, art. IV, p. 261.

[74] *Lamp in the Darkness*, chap. II, edit. VILLECOURT-TISSERANT, *loc. cit.*, pp. 709, 726.

remains as sacred relics. Some of his writings are still read as liturgical lessons. St. Shenudah assisted at the councils of Ephesus (431) and Chalcedon (451).

Severus (Abu'l Baschr Ibn al-Muqaffa), bishop of Aschmunain at the end of the 10th century, was the author of the *History of the Patriarchs of Alexandria* (down to Philotheos, 976-999).

Peter, bishop of Malig (end of the 12th century), wrote the *Book of Sects,* a polemical work attacking all those who were not Copts, and he may also have compiled the *Synaxarion.*

In the 13th century there were three famous brothers [75] Awlad al 'Assal, namely: Abu'l Farag ibn 'Assal, who wrote an exegesis of the gospels; Assafi Abu'l Fadail ibn al 'Assal (1234), the author of a collection of canons, a *Shorter tract on the Trinity and Unity,* and the *Book of Controversies;* and Abu Ishaq ibn al 'Assal, whose chief work was a *Collection of the Foundations of Religion.*

About the same time lived Abu'l Khair ibn at-Tayib, the author of the *Illumination of Minds,* a work directed against the Jews and Moslems.

The ecclesiastical encyclopedia, known as the *Lamp in the Darkness,* was edited by the most celebrated of all the Coptic theologians, Abu'l Barakat ibn Kabar († ab. 1323).

Finally, reference must be made to the 14th century writer, Yahya ibn Abi Zakarya, who is commonly known as Ibn Sabba, and who was the author of the *Precious Pearl,* [76] a theological-canonical-liturgical *summa.*

By the 15th century, centuries of persecution and isolation had produced a state of intellectual stagnation and even

[75] GORDILLO, *Compendium Theologiae Orientalis,* cap. IX, art. IV, p. 256.
[76] *Jauharat an-nafisah.*

decadence, although the patriarch Gabriel V (1401-1418) was responsible for a ritual that codified the rules for the administration of the sacraments, the celebration of the liturgy, and the taking of the monastic habit.

A few comparatively unimportant theological writers are found in the 19th century.

Coptic Egypt and Ireland

The Copts, before the Moslem conquest had reduced them to a condition of slavery, were great travellers.

A colony of Egyptians [77] settled at Lerins, [78] and it is said that "the Egyptian plan was followed at Glastonbury."

Ireland appears to have been the country most affected by Egypt, as Coptic asceticism [79] had an especial attraction for the Celtic temperament. Thus, one of the commonest names for townlands and parishes in the country is Disert or Desert [80] (Desertum), a solitary place where an anchorite took up his abode. The Irish monasteries usually had such a desert or solitude connected with them, especially in the dioceses of Connor and Down.

Warren [81] speaks of seven Coptic monks who were buried at Disert Ulidh in Ulster, and we find their names invoked in the Litany [82] of Oengus: "*Morfesseor do manchaib*

---

[77] LEDWICH, *Antiquities of Ireland*, 2nd edition, pp. 88-89.

[78] An abbey situated about three miles from the coast of Provence, which was founded in the 5th century by St. Honoratus.

[79] BAÜMER, *Histoire du Bréviaire*, vol. I, chap. VI, p. 235.

[80] STOKES and LAWLOR, *Ireland and the Celtic Church*, 7th edition, lecture IX, pp. 178-179. London, S. P. C. K., 1928.

[81] *Liturgy and Ritual of the Celtic Church*, p. 56.

[82] *Irish Litanies*. Henry Bradshaw Society, vol. LXII. *Litany of the Irish Saints*, II, pp. 64-65.

Egipt (e) in Disiurt Uilaig" (Seven monks of Egypt in Disert Uilaig).

These Irish litanies, which were the product of private devotion, are of great antiquity, although the earliest manuscript attestation does not go beyond the 12th century. The second litany, in which this invocation to the Coptic monks occurs, has been commonly attributed to Oengus [83] "the Culdee," the author of the well-known *Félire* or festal calendar. No author's name, however, is found in any of the manuscripts of the litany; and the attribution of it to Oengus seems to have originated with Colgan, [84] who has been blindly followed by later writers.

Irish monks also are known to have visited Egypt, and we read of Dicuil, [85] who probably came from Clonmacnois, travelling to the pyramids on his way to Palestine. He was the author of *Liber de Mensura orbis terrae* (ab. 825).

Dom Henri Leclercq [86] has justly observed that the claim of Irish monasticism to be directly derived from Egypt is lacking in all proof, but there is nevertheless a certain similarity in the grouping together of several small churches, one of which is a monastery, within a *cashel* or fortified enclosure.

Interlacing, the most characteristic motif of Celtic ornamentation, [87] often introduces designs which resemble those found in the Coptic churches of Old Cairo.

Both countries also made use of a metal case [88] to enclose

[83] *Irish Litanies.* H. B. S., vol. LXII, Introduction, p. xx.
[84] *Acta Sanct. Hib.*, p. 539.
[85] *Ireland and the Celtic Church*, lecture XI, pp. 214-216.
[86] *Dict. d'Archéol. Chrét. et de Lit.*, fasc. LXXIV, col. 1479.
[87] Good examples of this interlacing may be seen on many of the old crosses and in the manuscripts.
[88] WARREN, *op. cit.*, p. 21; BUTLER, *op. cit.*, II, 61.

the book of the gospels, which the Irish called *cumhdachs;*
while St. Patrick's bell, [89] dating from the 5th century, appears to have been made in imitation of the Coptic bells.
Waggon-vaulted roofs [90] in Irish churches may well have
been suggested by those of ancient Egypt. Finally, attention
may be drawn to the *Saltair Na Rann,* [91] which is simply an
Irish 11th or 12th century edition of the *Book of Adam and
Eve,* [92] composed in the 5th or 6th century in Egypt, and
known in no other European country save Ireland.

Coptic Churches

The patriarch Theonas (282-300) is said to have been
the first to build churches and worship openly.

The first Christian churches in Egypt were the great
halls of the pagan temples, [93] but the desert monasteries
soon developed a style of their own, and the Egyptians were
early inventors of the dome. [94]

The basilican plan of church is rare, and the best example extant is probably the Jewish synagogue [95] in old Cairo,
which up to the end of the 9th century had been the Coptic
church of St. Michael. In the majority of cases the architec-

[89] W. GAMBLE, *Irish Antiquities and Archaeology,* p. 62; BUTLER
op. cit., II, 81.
[90] BUTLER, *op. cit.,* I, 14.
[91] Published in the *Anecdota Oxoniensia* by Whitley STOKES (Clarendon Press, 1882).
[92] Published in English in London by S. C. MALAN (1882).
[93] The apse and altar of the Coptic church in the great temple of
Luxor are still to be seen.
[94] The dome is said to have been used in the granaries of Egypt long
before the Christian era.
[95] Eutychius claims this to be the last church in Orthodox hands
(until ab. 725). It was sold to the Jews in ab. 880 by the patriarch
Michael.

ture of the churches is of a mixed type, half-basilican and half-Byzantine.

Only one example of a completely cruciform church is mentioned by Butler, [96] and the dome is almost, if not quite, universal. There are often three domes over the three eastern altars.

Persecution accounts for the absence of windows other than small skylights, and the early disuse of the three western doors.

"An Egyptian church," says Butler, [97] " has neither outline nor exterior architecture." It is usually surrounded by houses, which seem piled at random about it, for the Coptic rayah [98] had no wish to attract the attention of their Mohammedan oppressors.

At the same time also the surrounding buildings often served as a monastery, when Egypt was still par excellence the land of religious.

In many instances small churches were grouped about the main building, much as we find in Ireland [99] in the early days of monasticism.

Old Cairo has many ancient Coptic churches and a museum of old ecclesiastical art.

The underground church of El-Athra (the Virgin) in the Haret el-Zuelah dates from the 10th century, and some archaeologists believe that it goes back to the 5th or 6th.

The famous church of Abu Sefein (St. Mercury), in the

---

[96] Ḳadîsah Burbârah, Cairo. Coptic Churches of Egypt, vol. I, p. 22.
[97] Ibid., p. 12.
[98] Turkish, "cattle."
[99] In Ireland, there were several small churches close together, but no large church, and the monastic settlement was enclosed in a cashel or "ring-wall." The connections between Coptic Egypt and Ireland have been noted elsewhere.

immediate vicinity, is said to have been founded in 927, and to have been rebuilt about fifty years later. The church seems to have been the seat of the patriarch in the 14th and 15th centuries.

Abu Girgis (St. George), better known as El-Moallaka or "the Hanging church," on account of its unique position suspended between two bastions of the old Roman fortress of Babylon, is a domeless double aisled basilica, without transepts. It was founded in the 4th century, and from 617-822 served as the cathedral church of the bishops of Cairo. In 1039 the patriarch Christodulus removed his seat from Alexandria to this church, and in the 12th century all the patriarchs were consecrated here.

Abu Sergeh for some considerable time laid claim to be the cathedral church, and great rivalry existed between the two churches.

El-Moallaka has a much venerated picture of our Lady on the south side of the nave, and an 11th century ambo, [100] similar in design to those in the basilicas at Rome.

The church of Abu Sergeh, dedicated to St. Sergius and St. Bacchus, [101] probably dates from the 8th century, with a crypt of the 6th, but there is no foundation for the legend that the latter marks the site of the resting place of the Holy Family.

In the 18th century, the seat of the patriarch was moved from old Cairo to the *Hârat-ar-Rûm*, and after the French invasion to the present site in the Azbikiâh quarter of Cairo.

---

[100] Greek, ἄμβων; Coptic, *anbal;* Arabic, *anbān.*

[101] The name of St. Bacchus has been suppressed. The feast is observed on the 4 *Babeh* (October 1) and 10 *Babeh* (October 10). The first of these commemorates the death of St. Bacchus. The Coptic church observes also the festival of the Egyptian martyr, St. Sergius of Atripe, on the 13 *Amshir* (February 7).

The patriarchal church of St. Mark in *Darb alwaṣāh* (Cairo) was first erected in 1790, but the present building is modern.

Catholic Coptic churches are for the most part small and insignificant, showing signs of great poverty and often little more than mud-walled halls. The pro-cathedral of the Holy Family at Cairo is a rotunda of eleven square metres, while that of Minieh (Holy Family) has about ten. Both of these churches are hardly distinguishable from those of the Latin rite, but the chapel in the patriarchate is more faithful to tradition, with a screen and the blessed sacrament reserved in a pyx in the form of a dove. The pro-cathedral of the Immaculate Conception at Tahta, which is said to be the first Catholic church in the Delta since the schism, has been planned according to traditional usages, but it is unfinished from lack of funds. Twenty churches were built between the years 1927 and 1937, but of these 13 are neither plastered nor paved, and lack furniture. In country churches the blessed sacrament [102] is rarely reserved. The church at Heliopolis is a fine building, but its interior arrangements are purely Latin, although it is said that the priest is hampered in returning to Coptic usages by a congregation who are averse to change.

As in the case of other churches subject to Mohammedan rule, bells were forbidden (850), and a wooden board or metal plate struck with a hammer was substituted. This latter device was in 1352 also prohibited. A few bells in the desert monasteries and other isolated places have survived.

[102] KHUZAM, *Missions des Coptes Catholiques en Egypte* (Cairo, 1937), p. 12.

Interior Arrangements and Church Ornaments

The narthex, which is seldom used, sometimes has a tank [103] for the Epiphany water, and there may be also a smaller tank for ablutions, such as one finds in the courtyard of a mosque.

In former times, the "triforium" was often reserved for women, but to-day the side aisles or a part of the central nave, shut off by a screen of open lattice work, normally serves the purpose.

Many of the modern Coptic churches suffer from "Byzantinization," but that at Heliopolis [104] has a traditional screen, in place of the " iconostasis" that one finds in the patriarchal church, Cairo, and the church of St. Mark at Alexandria. [105]

The Coptic screen is a solid wall of wood, carved and inlaid with mother of pearl set in geometrical patterns, and sometimes surmounted by holy pictures, or it may take the form of a wooden lattice. The screen is pierced by one or three openings, closed by curtains [106] marked with a cross, which the pious Copt kisses after prostrating himself.

The rule [107] for the laity to remove their shoes before entering the sanctuary [108] is not universally observed. The east end of the church often terminates in three apses, [109]

---

[103] Butler (op. cit., II, chap. IX, pp. 347-8) says that prior to the Arab conquest there were no tanks in the churches, as the ceremony was performed outside.

[104] The church (Monophysite) has also two fine ambones.

[105] The screen is surmounted by " Rood, Mary and John" (not in relief), illuminated by electric light.

[106] Greek, καταπέτασμα; Coptic, katapetasma; Arabic, hijāb, sitārah.

[107] The church of Abu Sergeh in Old Cairo was the only place in which the writer was asked to conform to this rule.

[108] Coptic, erphei; Arabic, haikal, " temple."

[109] Modern churches are usually rectangular.

each with an altar. The side chapels are used for the liturgy
on the feast of the saint to whom the chapel is dedicated.

Seats are ranged round the central apse, with the bishop's
throne in the centre, and on each of the steps leading up to
the throne a specific order of the ministry is conferred. This
arrangement of curving steps with a bench and a throne at
the top is styled a "tribune." The niche in the apse is re-
miniscent of the *mihrab* in a mosque, and there is often an
ever-burning lamp in it.

The high altar [110] and sometimes the side altars have a
ciborium or baldachino in the form of a cupola, which,
according to the rubrics, should have a veil [111] suspended
from the columns, behind which the celebrant is directed to
recite the "prayer of the veil." The altar is a large isolated
cube of stone, built round with bricks and hollowed out
underneath, with an opening towards the east that formerly
contained relics. The wooden *mensa,* [112] which is consecrated separately, lies in a sunken space on the altar, and the
whole is covered with a silk or cotton cloth of any colour,
brocaded or embroidered. A second cloth is used at the
time of the liturgy. An altar cross is not specified as an
ornament requisite for the Monophysite liturgy, but the
hand-cross, used in blessing the people, normally lies on the
altar. Two candles are ordered, but some churches have
four [113] or even more.

The gospel-book that rests on the altar and is carried in
procession is often nailed up in a costly metal cover, while

[110] Greek, τράπεζα; Coptic, *trapeza;* Arabic, *mā'idah.*
[111] There is no instance of the curtains remaining, but in the church
of Abu Sefein, Old Cairo, the beams and rings are *in situ.* The erection
of the screen probably did away with the need of curtains.
[112] Coptic, *lax, nakis;* Arabic, *lauḥ.*
[113] e. g. Abu Sergeh, Old Cairo.

a more ordinary and inexpensive copy is used for the reading
of the lessons. The carrying of the *textus* in procession is
alluded to in the time of the patriarch Ephraim (ab. 980),
and again at the institution of Macarius (ab. 1100).

During the liturgy, the chalice stands in a painted cubical
box or "ark," called the *tote*, [114] which has a round aperture
in the top, corresponding to the mouth of the chalice which
rests within, and is flush with the top of the box. The aperture is covered with one of the small mats [115] that lie on the
altar, and the paten is placed on the top. The larger veil
for the oblations is called the *prosfarin*. [116]

The anonymous Syriac author of the *Explanation of the
Mass* refers to eight pieces of "stuff" on the Coptic altar,
two for the covering of the altar vessels after consecration,
and six for the use of the communicants after holy communion.

The celebrant during the liturgy has two of these cloths
stretched on his hands, and the people are blessed with the
right-hand cloth. The vessels and the sacred species are
handled with them, and also the cruets by the deacon.

In consequence of Moslem spoliation, the Copts in the
8th century were forced to use glass chalices and wooden
patens. [117] The Catholic synod of Alexandria (1898) direct-

---

[114] Also, Coptic, *thronos nte pipotērion, pitote;* Arabic, *cursī alcās,*
" stand for the chalice."

[115] Coptic, *thom,* " plate;" Arabic, *ṭabak, ḥaṣīrah.*

[116] Greek, πρόσφορα; Arabic, *lafāfah, ibrūsfārin.*

Janin (*Eglises Orientales et les Rites Orientaux,* chap. XVII, p. 574)
calls the three or four small veils *lafā'if,* " small bands," and the large
veil, *al-ghita,* " cover," or *al-abrausfarin* (πρόσφορα). Butler (*op. cit.,*
t. II, p. 48) says that in the desert monasteries the *lafāfah* is used for
waving over the sacred gifts.

[117] The church of Abu Sergeh, Old Cairo (May, 1924), used a glass
paten, and a large earthenware amphora for a water cruet.

ed that both paten [118] and chalice [119] must be consecrated
with chrism by a bishop. The Monophysites use an asterisk, [120] which has two metal bars with the half hoops crossed
and rivetted in the centre.

The Catholic Copts traditionally give holy communion by means of a spoon, [121] but, without any direction
from Rome, communion in one kind has become very general.

Liturgical fans, [122] embossed with a representation of the
cherubim, are no longer used in the liturgy, although they
are sometimes carried in processions. The *Lamp* speaks of
priests and deacons in attendance on the bishop "waving fans
after the manner of the wings of the cherubim."

A lectern [123] and a large candlestick usually stand in the
sanctuary (*haikal*); while the censer often hangs either from
the candlestick or the ciborium. The censer [124] is of the
ordinary oriental type, adorned with bells.

About the year 420, the patriarch St. Cyril is said to
have been the "first to set up figures in the churches of
Alexandria and in the land of Egypt." These "figures" were
distemper paintings or frescoes, with which the churches

[118] Greek, δίσκος; Coptic, *diskos*.
[119] Greek, ποτήριον; Coptic, *potērion*.
[120] Arabic, *kubbah*, "dome."
[121] Coptic, *kokliarion, mystēr, mysthēri*.
A spoon was used at Abu Sergeh (May 21, 1924) to give communion
to the "little deacon."
[122] Greek, ριπίδιον; Coptic, *ripidion, ripistērion, cheroubim*; Arabic, *mirwahah*.
Butler (*op. cit.*, vol. II, p. 48) saw a rude axe-shaped fan of woven
rushes to wave over the sacred gifts at the church of Anba Shenudah,
Old Cairo.
[123] The lower part of the lectern often has a cupboard for books.
[124] *Shourē*.

were adorned until the Moslem profanations [125] in the 9th
and 10th centuries. The churches of old Cairo and elsewhere
have preserved some remains of these frescoes, but pictures
or icons have long since taken their place, which in recent
years have been Byzantine in style. Coptic art generally has
a certain large leaven of Byzantine influence.

The icon, however, has never assumed the importance
accorded to it in the Orthodox church, and in 1851 the patriarch, thinking that too much reverence was being paid to
them, ordered the pictures to be brought from all quarters,
and made a grand bonfire of them!

"There is not the smallest evidence," writes Butler, [126]
"that the Copts at any period sanctioned the use of statues
or sculptured images for the adornment of their religious
buildings, and there is decided evidence to the contrary."

This categorical statement, however, seems to be falsified
by an Arabic manuscript [127] of the 11th century (ab. 1028),
translated by Quatremère, [128] and quoted by Butcher: [129]
"The church of St. Mena [130] is a vast building, decorated
with statues and pictures of great beauty .... The marble

---

[125] Usâma ben Zaid " broke the crosses, rubbed off the pictures,
broke up all the images," and ab. 860 Theophilus " ordered all pictures
to be effaced from the churches, so that not a picture remained in any
one church." In December 1944, the Moslem guide in the temple of
Karnak indicated the fresco of a Coptic saint on a pillar, in a part of the
building which had served as a church, by throwing a stone and damaging
the painting.

[126] *Op. cit.*, vol. II, p. 84.

[127] Al Bukri was the author of the manuscript.

[128] Etienne QUATREMÈRE, *Recherches critiques et historiques sur la
langue et la littérature de l'Egypte.* Paris, 1808.

[129] *Story of the Church of Egypt,* vol. I, part 2, chap. V, p. 409.

[130] Mari Mena in the Mareotis, a church long since destroyed.
St. Menas was at one time the patron saint of Lower Egypt.

statue of a man [131] stands upright with one foot on each
camel .... In the same church are statues of John, Zacharias
and Jesus carved in a great marble pillar .... Also there is a
statue of the Virgin Mary behind two curtains, and statues
of the prophets."

Reliquaries, taking the form of velvet "bolsters," are
sometimes placed under the pictures.

Ostrich eggs, suspended from the roof or door of the
sanctuary, are said to symbolise the virtue of faith, as it is
commonly believed that an ostrich hatches her eggs by gazing
at them. Thus, the *Precious Pearl* [132] says: "Ostriches have
this peculiarity, that the females do not cover their eggs to
hatch them, but the incubation is produced simply by the
constant gazing of the male and female on the eggs until
they are hatched. But if the ostrich turns away from the egg
for a moment it is spoilt and no longer becomes a living
being. So also is it with a Christian, who during prayer
should fix his whole attention on God, for fear of losing its
fruits." A more prosaic reason for the hanging of eggs is
to prevent mice from climbing down the cords to get at the
oil in the many hanging lamps.

Coronae, supporting many candles or lamps, often hang
from the roof of the church.

The buildings of the national church, no less than those
of the Catholics, often show signs of extreme poverty, but
the Monophysite churches sometimes witness also to great
negligence and lack of decency. Thus, the sacristy table in
the church of St. Mark, Alexandria (May 1924), with its
heaped up pile of vestments, cloths, etc., had all the ap-

[131] " The man with one foot one each camel is probably St. Menas
himself, who is said to have had his body brought to this spot by a
camel, which refused to proceed any further with its burden.
[132] Chap. LV.

Coptic Catholic priest

Coptic Catholic Church, Heliopolis, Egypt

Coptic church of El-Moallaka,
Old Cairo

Interior of the church of El-
Moallaka, Old Cairo

pearance of a rummage sale after the contents of the stall
have been well picked over; while the altar of the Coptic
church in Port Said seemed to be a dumping ground for
empty boxes, books, linen and the sacred vessels. A similar
state of affairs was recorded by Butler [133] who, writing in
1884 of the church of Anba Shenudah, Old Cairo, says: on
the high altar was a "tumbled disarray of vestments, candle-
sticks, altar-casket, etc."; in the south-aisle chapel, "torn
books, dirty vestments, etc."; and the north-aisle chapel altar
was "covered with a mass of old Coptic books, piled together
and crusted with dust." The natural "virtues" of order
and cleanliness, however, seem to be gaining ground, and
in 1945 the churches of Old Cairo showed a very marked
improvement in respect to their maintenance.

Reservation of the Blessed Sacrament

The Catholic Copts reserve the blessed sacrament in a
tabernacle on the altar, *more romano*, but the Monophysites
have long since abandoned the practice of reservation.

If, however, after the ablutions a particle of the sacred
bread is found unconsumed, and no one is fasting, the priest
is directed to wrap it in a veil, and place it between two
candles in the eastern niche, where a priest is to watch by
it until the liturgy of the following day.

Reservation was certainly practised at one time in the
Coptic church. The *Synaxarion* [134] quotes a legend about
St. Biouka and St. Tayaban, two 5th century priests of
Tounah in the diocese of Tanda, who are commemorated on
June 25 (1 Abib): "The sacrament reserved for the sick was
kept in a chest: one day a serpent entered this chest and

---

[133] *Op. cit.*, vol. I, chap. III, pp. 141-142.
[134] De Lacy O'LEARY, *The Saints of Egypt*, p. 106.

devoured the sacrament. The two brothers killed the serpent and then considered: "Must we eat the reptile?" Whilst they were in doubt an angel appeared and told them that they must do so. They ate the serpent and died."

Reservation in the Coptic church is referred to in two Arabic manuscripts, [135] describing a controversy between the Coptic patriarch Alexander John, and a Jew and a Melkite. The title records that the dispute took place in the reign of 'Abd-el-Aziz, king of Egypt, who constructed the nilometer of Helwan.

It is sometimes said that the Copts, by reason of the thickness of the eucharistic bread and the carelessness of the baking, would be unable to reserve the sacred species without the bread becoming mouldy and hard as a stone. This indeed was one of the reasons put forward by the patriarch Christodulus in the 11th century, when he forbade the monks of St. Macarius to reserve from Palm Sunday to Holy Thursday. The patriarch protested that the custom was contrary to the law of the Church, but until a treatise had been written on the subject the monks continued the practice, asking whether Christodulus was better than his predecessor, who had allowed it.

In the following century, Michael of Damietta, in a treatise on the customs of the Copts, justified the absence of the reserved sacrament by an appeal to Scripture.

The author of the *Lamp in the Darkness* (ab. 1320) says: "Consume all that is left and do not carry the *oblata* from one place to another, since none of the Passover was suffered to remain over, and what was left had to be burnt with fire .... Nothing at the institution of the Eucharist was kept for the

---

[135] Bibliothèque Nationale, Paris.

second day, neither was it carried [136] about .... And our fathers ordered this rule of conduct to be kept. And we have persevered in it until to-day according to the teaching of Mark. And there is no difference between the offering of Thursday (Holy) and the daily offering, because they all are the body and blood of our Lord Jesus Christ. To him be glory for ever. Amen."

Butler, [137] commenting on the absence of reservation, mentions the legend of the snake who ate the sacred species, but giving as a more probable reason the "compactness of Coptic communities, which made it easy to find a priest at hand to consecrate in case of sickness." In 1924, the headmaster of the school at St. Mark's cathedral in Cairo explained to the writer that there was no reservation in the Coptic church as none of the manna was kept until the next day, and a fresh supply appeared daily.

Liturgical Language

The language of the liturgy is Coptic, but with many Greek words and written in Greek characters of a beautiful uncial form. The Egyptians on the introduction of Christianity accepted the religious terminology of their teachers, with the result that the Coptic rite has retained more Greek words and expressions than many other liturgies.

It is uncertain when the church of Egypt changed her liturgical [138] language from Greek to Coptic. Certain indica-

[136] Cf. "For, also, the Lord did not order the bread, which he gave to his disciples and said to them, 'take and eat,' to be carried about, nor yet to be kept until the morrow." Origin. *In Hom. V in Levit.*

[137] *Op. cit.*, vol. II, p. 42.

[138] Long after the Arab conquest Greek continued to be the language used in public business, and we read of a governor named Abdallah (705-709), who tried to enforce the use of Arabic on such occasions, but for some time both were used side by side.

tions have pointed to the end of the 3rd century. St. Pachomius († ab. 346) about the year 300 is said to have translated the psalms into the language of the people, and Palladius, [139] who lived from 368 till some time before the council of Ephesus (431), spoke of the religious services conducted by the hermits, which were unlikely to be celebrated in Greek. Those who have maintained this view have put forward the case of St. Antony († 356 at the age of 105), who while attending the liturgy was weaned from the world by hearing the call [140] of our Lord to perfection: "If thou wilt be perfect, go sell what thou hast, and give to the poor, and thou shalt have treasure in heaven: and come, follow me." It is argued that St. Antony was no scholar, and that consequently he must have heard the gospel read in Coptic. This is certainly possible, but it is more likely that reference is made here to the homily [141] after and on the gospel, which would be given in the vernacular. In support of this, the author [142] of an Arabic note upon a Coptic manuscript says that before the Arab conquest the lessons were read in Greek, but explained in Coptic.

It seems probable that the liturgy was early translated into the Sahidic or Theban dialect, but that the Hellenized Egyptians of Lower Egypt only felt the need of a national liturgical text after the completion of the Monophysite schism.

Three classes of Coptic manuscripts exist: a) bilingual Greek-Coptic, which, although changed with the Arab conquest, did not disappear entirely till the 10th century;

[139] *Paradise of the Fathers.*
[140] St. Matth., XIX, 21.
[141] Dom Prosper GUÉRANGER, *Institutions Liturgiques*, I. III, p. 69-70.
[142] BUTLER, *op. cit.*, vol. II, chap. VI, p. 251.

b) Coptic alone; *c*) bilingual Copto-Arabic, which date from the 13th century, or even earlier, till to-day.

The first Coptic manuscripts were written in demotic not Greek characters, and the patriarch Shenudah [143] (859-881) is said to have established the Coptic way of writing sacred letters still in use. Many phrases, ritual notes and rubrics in the liturgy have been retained in Greek, together with short formulas, which were too well known to have required translation, while *Kyrie eleison* has been kept in its original wording. Such explanatory words as "the deacon says" and "silently" [144] have also remained in Greek, although transcribed in Coptic characters.

Vansleb is said to have conversed in 1672 with the last man who spoke Coptic as his mother tongue, and the people generally had given up the use of the language a century earlier. It is doubtful how much reliance can be placed on this assertion, and we know that soon after the 9th century Coptic theology was written almost exclusively in Arabic. Thus Severus of Aschmunain, who at the end of the 10th century compiled a list of the patriarchs of Alexandria from Coptic and Greek manuscripts in the monastery of St. Macarius, says in the preface that he made the translation in Arabic, because Arabic was everywhere spoken, and most people were ignorant of Greek and Coptic alike. About 850, however, we find the patriarch Joseph addressing the assembly at his trial in Coptic, and being understood even by the Moslems. "It [145] would seem that there was a renascence of Coptic in the 10th century, closely allied with a reassertion of nationalism on the part of the Coptic community, a polit-

[143] MALAN, *History of the Copts*, p. 84.
[144] Greek, μυστικῶς; Coptic, *ĕsychia.*
[145] De Lacy O'LEARY, *The Saints of Egypt*, II, p. 10.

ical development with which a language revival often is associated."

It has been said that from the 10th century Coptic was no longer understood in Lower Egypt, and from the 12th century in the Thebaid, and certainly the constitutions of the patriarch Gabriel II (ab. 1140) ordered the bishops to explain the creed and the Lord's prayer to the people in Arabic. The monasteries of the Wadi Natrun appear to have retained the use of the old language, and there is a fair amount of educational material surviving which shows that those who entered Scetis or other Coptic-speaking communities had to learn Coptic, as it was no longer their mother tongue.

Almakrizy, writing in the early 15th century, says that the monks of the monasteries near Assiut speak the Sahidic dialect, and that the women and children of Upper Egypt talk scarcely anything else. In the 14th century, the Coptic service books had begun to have Arabic translations, usually side by side with Coptic.

A remarkable revival of interest in the language followed the discovery of Champollion the younger, that Coptic bears a striking resemblance to the hieroglyphics of ancient Egypt. "The Coptic language to-day," says Butler, [146] "is no doubt virtually the same tongue that was spoken by the builders of the pyramids: and it still retains many words scarcely changed from that epoch." And again, [147] "the romance of language could go no further than to join the speech of Pharoah and the writing of Homer in the service book of an Egyptian Christian."

Other theories, however, as to the origin of Coptic have been current, such as a fusion of Lybian-Egyptian and Ara-

[146] *Op. cit.*, vol. II, chap. VI, p. 248.
[147] *Op. cit.*, p. 247.

bic-Egyptian; while others again have maintained that it is an artificial tongue, and not really ancient.

The Coptic and Greek alphabets are identical, with seven additional characters borrowed from the demotic by the Copts to express sounds or a combination of sounds unknown to the Greeks.

The 11th century grammarian, Athanasius of Qos in Upper Egypt, mentions three dialects-Sahidic or Theban in Upper Egypt; Bohairic or Memphitic in Lower Egypt; and Bashmuric in Middle Egypt or the Fayyum. De Lacy O'Leary [148] includes no less than five:

a) Akhmimic, which provides the earliest literary material, remains of which continue as late as the 4th and 5th centuries.

b) Sub-Akhmimic, a variant of the Akhmimic.

c) Sahidic [149] or *Theban,* which seems at first to have been a local dialect of Athribis near Akhmim, the *locus* of the White Monastery (Deir el-Abiad), founded by St. Shenudah (7 *Abib,* 1 July) in 385. It came into use as a literary medium by Shanudah, and was then the favourite dialect of monastic writers. The use of Sahidic spread from Assiut to the Delta, holding its own from the 5th to the 9th century, and under the influence of the Pachomian monasteries it became the literary language of the Coptic church in pre-Islamic times.

d) Fayyumic, the dialect of the Fayyum, west of the Nile valley about Wasta, and so only a little south of Lower Egypt.

e) Bohairic or *Memphitic,* the dialect of Bohaireh or the "Region of the Lake" (?Mariut), a name now applied to the

---

[148] *Op. cit.,* II, p. 10.
[149] Arabic, *Essa'id,* " the high."

north-west province of the Delta, and particularly in the
Nitrian valley.   In the monasteries of Scetis the Coptic
liturgies developed and became standardised, a development
with which the use of Bohairic for literary composition was
very closely connected.   Under ecclesiastical influence Bohairic replaced Sahidic as the literary language of the Copts
in the 9th century.

The modern study of Coptic dates from the *Podromus
Coptus* of Kircher, published in 1636, and some 80 years
later a Coptic grammer was produced by Blumberg.   In
1778, Tukhi edited an Arabic and Latin treatise entitled
Rudimenta Linguae Copticae, while the first scientific grammar [150] of the three dialects appeared in 1830.   Few Copts
to-day understand very much about their liturgical language,
and some even maintain that *Kyrie eleison* and other Greek
phrases are really Coptic.   A brilliant exception is found in
Gabriel Labib, a rich merchant of Cairo, who in the 19th
century edited the liturgical books of the rite, and endeavoured to revive the language among the people.   Some of
these books are printed in Coptic and Arabic in parallel
columns, while the rubrics are often in Arabic only.   To-day,
some Copts appear to desire a revival of their old language,
and in December 1944 the writer heard two blind men
from the choir of St. Mark's cathedral (Cairo) speaking in
Coptic.

Music and Musical Instruments

In 1927, thanks to the studies of Professor Ernest
Nicolandsmith, the western world was given a rich musical
treasure hitherto undreamed of,—music that had never been

---

[150] Edited by Tattam.

committed to writing, but had been handed down through generations of singers, many of whom were blind.

Close investigation had led the Professor to come to the conclusion that Coptic music is not Arabic, Turkish or even Greek, but that it is a lineal descendent of the temple-music heard in the Egypt of the Pharaohs. The Copts repudiated the pagan theological terminology, but borrowed such things as the tonsure; [151] while several Coptic hymns, still bearing the name of ancient Egyptian cities that perished long ago, were probably sung in the vanished temples.

Hymns are rubricated *echos Adam, Job* or *Batos*, and, in Arabic, simply *Adam (sic) aiyub* or *watus*, the tones being named apparently from some typical hymns. The Coptic chant abounds, even more than most eastern music, in long wailing neums, and the liturgy in consequence is long. There are, as in the Byzantine rite, eight tones. [152] Organs are not used, but cymbals, triangles, hand-bells and, occasionally, the flute (*mizmar*) accompany the singing.

Liturgical Books

The liturgical books for the Catholics were first printed in the 18th century at Rome by Raphael Tukhi.

In 1736, a missal was published in Coptic and Arabic,— *Book of the three Anaphoras, namely, those of St. Basil, St. Gregory the Theologian, and St. Cyril, with the other holy prayers, containing the Evening and Morning Incense, with the proprium temporis thereto; the Liturgy including the three Anaphoras; Prayers before and after meals; Blessing of the water and the Ordo Renovationis Calicis.*

---

[151] The ancient Egyptians had a saying: "White linen and a tonsure will not make a follower of Isis."

[152] Arabic, *lahn, tariq, tariqah.*

Assemani [153] in 1754 reprinted the Ordo *Communis* and "St. Basil," with the rubrics in Latin. This Catholic missal differs but little from the manuscripts of the 13th century in the Vatican library, beyond the insertions of the filioque and the name of the pope, and the removal of the names of Monophysites. The English translation of the Coptic liturgy, made by John, Marquess of Bute (1908), is based on this missal.

In 1746, the *Book of the Theotokia and Katataxis* (doxology) *of the month Choiac (Khihak)*, offices in honour of our Lady and the saints, was published, and, four years later (1750), a *Book of the seven prayers of the day and of the night*.

The *Book containing all the holy prayers* or Pontifical was produced in two volumes in 1761-2; and in the following year the *Book of the Service of the Holy Mysteries* or Ritual.

A new edition of the Missal, with a slightly different arrangement, and called the *Euchologion of the Alexandrine Church*, [154] was published in 1898 in Cairo, which was followed four years later by a further edition.

Mgr. Makarios (1898-1906), under whose guidance the missal was produced, was also responsible for new editions of the Ritual and Office.

Abu'l Barakat, the author of the *Lamp*, enumerates eight liturgical books in use in the Coptic church.

a) The *Book of the Egyptian Easter* [155] (Pasch), attributed to the patriarch Gabriel Ibn Tarik (1131-1145), and containing the Office of Holy Week. A Catholic edition [156]

---

[153] *Missale Alexandrinum*, part II, 1-90, in *Codex liturgicus*, VII.
[154] Cairo, Catholic Press of St. Mark, Era of the Martyrs, 1614.
[155] *Kitab il Pasca*.
[156] Cairo, Catholic Press of St. Mark.

was printed in 1899 under the title of *Book of the Holy Pasch according to the rite of the Alexandrine Church*.

b) The *Antiphoner*, [157] which has also been ascribed to the patriarch Gabriel, consists of two (alternative) hymns for each day of the year, celebrating the saints of the day. The hymns are in Coptic, but in respect to the material they are based on the Arabic Synaxary.

c) The *Synaxary* [158] or Martyrology, compiled in Arabic on the lines of the Greek synaxary, contains for every day of the year abridged summaries of homilies on the lives of the saints. These homilies are read in the office and sometimes also in the liturgy, in place of the Acts of the Apostles. Peter Al-Gamil, bishop of Malig (12th-13th century), may have been the compiler, but he was more probably Michael, bishop of Athrib and Malig (about the beginning of the 15th century).

d) The *Pontifical*, which is called by Abu'l Barakat the *Books of Priestly Offices*, combines the pontifical and ritual of the Latin church.

e) The *Euchologion* [159] is the missal for the priest's part of the liturgy.

f) The *Psalmody* contains the odes, *theotokia*, [160] and doxology. The odes are the four canticles from the Old Testament; *theotokia*, as the name indicates, is an office of our Lady, first composed for the Coptic month of Mary (*Choiac, Khihak*) in preparation for the feast of Christmas,

---

[157] *Difnari, andifnâri.*

[158] *Synaxar, sinaksâr.*

[159] *Hulaki, ḳûlâgî.*

[160] The series of *troparia* and *theotokia* are taken from the Greek *Horologion*, and were included in the Coptic offices some time before the schism.

but now very generally neglected; doxology are hymns in honour of the saints.

g) The *Egbiyah* (*Egbieh*) or breviary. The divine office, which is recited by the Catholics in Arabic, was revised by Amba Khuzam, and reprinted at Cairo in 1930.

h) The *Lectionary*[161] has lessons from the apostle (epistles of St. Paul), *catholicon* (7 catholic epistles), and the *praxis* (Acts of the Apostles), in addition to some psalms and the gospels for all the offices and liturgies of the year. The arrangement of the book is attributed to Gabriel II Ibn Tarik, to whom the choir-books generally have been ascribed.

Calendar

The ecclesiastical calendar has an unusual method of reckoning, the Era of the Martyrs,[162] or Era of Diocletian, dating from August 29,284. The Greek historian Malakas claims the second title to be the original, named in commemoration of the clemency of Diocletian in sparing the lives of the Alexandrines after the capture of the city. The ferocity of the persecution against the Christians, however, caused the name of the era to be changed in the 11th century. The use of the era began in the 6th century, but it was not adopted in the Coptic church until the 8th century. The Julian calendar is sometimes followed by the dissidents, but in civil affairs the date is reckoned by the *Higrah* or by the Gregorian calendar.

The Catholics of Lower Egypt use the Gregorian computation of Easter, whereas those of Upper Egypt, at least

---

[161] Greek, καταμέρος; Coptic, *kataméros*; Arabic, *koṭmarus*.
[162] Arabic, *Sanat ash-Shahada*.

until recently, follow the reckoning of the patriarch Demetrius († 231).

The Coptic months have preserved the names that were
used in ancient Egypt, with a slight change of orthography.
The year is divided into three divisions in relation to the
river Nile and the crops—Inundation, Sowing, Harvest.

It has 12 months of 30 days, with a little month of 5 (6 in
leap year) complementary days, which was adopted in 1792
by the French revolutionaries.

The ecclesiastical year begins in the month *Tout*, on a
day approximately equivalent to September 10.

There are 14 feasts of our Lord, of which the 7 greater
are the Annunciation [163] (29 *Barmahat*, March 25); Christmas [164] (29 *Kihak*, December 25); Baptism [165] of our Lord
or Epiphany (11 *Tubeh*, January 6); Feast of Olives or Palm
Sunday; Easter; Ascension; and Pentecost. On the feast
of the Baptism of our Lord (*Al-Gitas*), water is blessed in
the river, sea or a tank in the narthex of the church.
This blessing is repeated on the "Supper of the New Covenant" or Maundy Thursday, and on the feast of St. Peter
and St. Paul, while on each of these days there is a *mandatum* in every church. A symbolical burial of the cross, after
the manner of the Byzantine rite, takes place on "Great
Friday" (Good Friday). The 7 lesser feasts of our Lord are
the Circumcision (6 *Tubeh*, January 1); Miracle of Cana in
Galilee (13 *Tubeh*, January 8); Presentation in the Temple

---

[163] The earliest Coptic calendar commemorates St. Gabriel on
December 18, but this is probably the feast of the Annunciation, and only
secondly and accidentally refers to St. Gabriel. Kellner. *Heortology*,
part II, chap. II, p. 332.

[164] 28 *Kihak* in leap year, when the feast is prolonged for two days.

[165] The earliest Coptic calendar referred to the Epiphany as *Dies
Baptismi Sanctificati*, and a later one as *Immersio Domini*. *Ibid.*, Part II,
chap. I, p. 168.

(8 *Amshir,* February 2); Maundy Thursday; Sunday of St. Thomas (first Sunday after Easter); Entry into Egypt (24 *Bashons,* May 1); and Transfiguration (13 *Mesore,* August 6).

A second feast[166] of the Holy Family seems to be observed on November (*Hator*) 6, commemorating the "Flight of the Holy Family from Mehsa Koskuam in Upper Egypt."

The Copts have a great devotion to our Lady, and no less than 32 days are kept in her honour, including a memorial on the 21st of each month. The three major feasts of the blessed Virgin are days of obligation—Nativity (10 *Tout,* September 7); Presentation in the Temple (3 *Khihak,* November 29); and the Assumption (16 *Mesore,* August 9).

When, as is often the case, two days in the year are observed for the same feast, the second is almost invariably taken from the Byzantine or Syrian calendar. Thus, the Coptic synaxary records the following feasts of our Lady: Conception or "Annunciation of the birth of the blessed Virgin Mary," 7 *Mesore* (July 31), and a second feast[167] on the 3 *Khikak* (December 9); Nativity, 1 *Bashons* (April 26) and 10 *Tout* (September 7); and Assumption, 21 *Tubeh* (January 16), which is commemorated as the "Blessed Virgin Mary rested in the Lord," and 16 *Mesore* (August 9), which is the "Ascension" or Assumption proper.

The Catholics[168] observe the January feast as a commemoration of the consecration of the first church dedicated under the patronage of our Lady.

The Gallican feast of the *Depositio* or *Adsumptio,* which

---

[166] Not in the *Synaxarion.*
[167] Not in the *Synaxarion,* but found in some ancient manuscripts.
[168] *Incontro ai Fratelli Separati di Oriente* (Rome, 1945), p. 383.

was kept on January 18 (15th of the Kalends of February), may possibly have had Egyptian affinities. [169]

The 6th century Coptic calendar of Oxyrynchus commemorates January 16 as the "Day of Mary."

June 16 (21 *Baounah*) is observed as the feast of the Dedication [170] of the church of the Sovereign Lady at Atrib, a memorial that has passed to the Syrian rite.

Vansleb [171] includes among the feasts of our Lady the giving of the pontifical habit to St. Dekesius, which, as we have shown in the next chapter, is an oriental form of the legend of St. Ildephonsus of Toledo.

St. Mercurius, an important figure in the Coptic church, is kept on *Epip* 25.

Other commemorations include the Primacy [172] of Peter the Apostle (8 *Mesore*, August 1); St. Antony the Great, Star of the Desert (22 *Tubeh*, January 17); St. Michael [173] the Archangel, together with prayer for the Rising of the Nile (12 *Baounah*, June 6); St. Peter and St. Paul (5 *Abib*, June 29), when, in addition to the *mandatum*, grapes and wine are blessed; Four Incorporeal animals [174] (8 *Hator*, November 4); and the Twenty-four Elders sitting around the throne of God (24 *Hator*, November 20).

[169] H. W. CODRINGTON, *Egypt and the West.* *Eastern Churches Quarterly.* No. 10, vol. V, p. 286. April-June, 1944.

[170] Not in the *Synaxarion.*

[171] *Histoire de l'Eglise d'Alexandrie* (1677). Not in the *Synaxarion.*

[172] Not in the *Synaxarion.*

[173] An early Coptic calendar commemorates St. Michael no less than six times – April 7, June 6, August 5, September 9, November 8, December 8. H. KELLNER, *Heortology*, part II, chap. II, p. 331. The *Synaxarion* has four memorials of St. John Baptist: February 24 (30 *Amshir*); September 23 (26 *Tout*); August 30 (2 *Tout*); and May 27 (2 *Baounah*).

[174] The symbols of the four evangelists. Ezech. I, 5-12; Apoc. IV, 6-8.

The Copts keep two feasts in honour of the Holy Cross, March 6 (10 *Barmahat*) and September 13 (16 *Tout*). The second commemoration includes the consecration of the church of the Resurrection in Jerusalem, and the manifestation of the cross by Heraclius. The major celebration lasts for three days, ending with a memorial of Porphyrius, bishop of Gaza (395-420), of whom his biographer, Mark the Deacon, says: "Unto him was committed the safe-keeping of the precious wood of the cross." Formerly on this day, the patriarch threw a silver cross into the Nile at Old Cairo, near to the spot where the level of the river had been measured, and men dived to recover it. The custom is obsolete, but in some churches a cross is still thrown into a basin of water. The death of St. Helen is observed on May 4 (*Bashons*), and there is an entry in Ludolf's Ethiopic calendar: "*Helena reperit crucem.*"

The first mention of St. Joseph in a calendar would seem to be in the Coptic church, where, under the date July 20 (26 *Abib*), a calendar of the 8th century has the entry "the Carpenter Joseph," and a synaxary, probably dating from the 9th century, has a similar commemoration.

The feasts of saints are observed for the most part by simple memorials, and the majority of them are Egyptians and martyrs. As De Lacy O'Leary [175] points out, "the majority of the passions of the martyrs connected with the persecution of Diocletian seem to be of the same period and to be the work of the same authors.... All follow the same model with only a few trifling differences in detail. In some cases the martyr was put to death several times in succession and raised to life after each until the last when he is suffered to rest in peace because "he was quite fatigued with dying."

[175] *The Saints of Egypt*, III, p. 19.

And again, [176] "When the people wanted to hear the life
and suffering of their martyr they ordered a ready made
biography from a wholesale furnisher of martyrs' lives at
Alexandria, where such biographies were produced under
Greek influences." St. Shenudah († ab. 466) shows villagers
inventing patron saints and erecting shrines for bones
discovered and assumed to be martyrs, and the identification
of remains as those of martyrs was generally made after
alleged visions.

Many Monophysites, also, are honoured in the calendar
of the dissidents, whose claim to sanctity appears to lie in
little more than their opposition to the council of Chalcedon
(451).

Thus, we find commemorated: Barsuma, "father of
Syrian monks" (9 *Amshir*, February 3); Daniel, hegumenos
of St. Macarius, who was driven from his monastery for
refusing to accept the tome of St. Leo (8 *Bashons*, May 3);
Dioscorus, first Monophysite patriarch of Alexandria (7
Tout, September 4); Severus of Antioch, leading opponent
of the council of Chalcedon, (14 *Amshir*, February 8; 2
Babeh, September 29); Timothy *Aelurus* (the Cat), 26th
patriarch of Alexandria, who excommunicated all Egyptian
clergy who accepted the decrees of Chalcedon (7 *Mesore*,
July 31).

In addition to the five Roman popes, there is a further
borrowing from the calendar of the West on November 10
(14 *Hator*), when the Copts commemorate Martin, bishop
of Tarakya, who has been identified with St. Martin of
Tours.

The Catholics have nine holy days of obligation, in-

[176] *The Saints of Egypt*, p. 14.

cluding Corpus Christi, and the Coptic church and people in 1898 were dedicated to the Sacred Heart.

Many Latin devotional practices have been adopted, and not always in accordance with the best liturgical principles. Thus, in a church in Cairo in 1924 the writer found the rosary recited in French by a boys' school during Mass, without even the excuse of it being the month of October!

The Coptic church has retained the old liturgical vigil ($\pi\alpha\rho\acute{\alpha}\mu o\nu\alpha\iota$) on the night before a great feast, although the custom of thus passing the night from Saturday to Sunday has fallen into desuetude.

Lent begins on the Monday of "Sexagesima," 52 days before Easter, and a strict fast is observed until noon, with abstinence from drink and tobacco. Saturdays [177] and Sundays are excluded from the fast, although milk foods, oil, wine and fish are forbidden on these days. Catholics are accorded certain dispensations, but many priests do not make use of them for fear of causing scandal to the dissidents or new converts.

Holy Week is known as the "fast of the crucifixion," when a single meal, [178] consisting of bread and salt, is taken "when the stars appear."

The Lent of the Apostles [179] (Lent of Pentecost) begins 13 days before the feast of St. Peter and St. Paul, but Catholics, according to the district in which they live, observe from 3 to 13 days.

Advent or the Lent of Christmas varies for the individual in duration, and the clergy fast 43 days, while the laity only

---

[177] *Dict. de Théol. Cath.*, t. X, col. 2296.

[178] Canon 22 of Hippolytus.

[179] According to Coptic canonists, the fast follows the length of the interval between Christmas and Lent. *Dict. de Théol. Cath.*, t. X, col. 2297.

23 – Catholics 16 or 41, according to the place in which they live. This fast is said to have been instituted by the patriarch Christodulus [180] (1047-1077), in imitation of the blessed Virgin, who, according to the Copts, "fasted from the seventh and a half month of her pregnancy until childbirth, by reason of the fear that she had of St. Joseph."

The Lents of the Apostles and Christmas permit the use of oil and fish, but they are forbidden in the 13 days' fast before the Assumption. [181] The 3 days' fast of Nineveh is kept about a fortnight before great Lent (47 days), but the fast of Heraclius now coincides with the first week of Lent. This last named fast is said to have originated in a promise made to the emperor Heraclius (610-641), that if he would massacre all the Jews in Jerusalem the Christians would fast for his benefit until the end of the world. The emperor acceded to their suggestion!

Wednesdays and Fridays, except at Christmastide and Easter, are days of abstinence, and the vigil of the Epiphany, even for Catholics, is a fast.

The Copts comply with the Mosaic law, not only in the matter of circumcision, [182] but also in regard to the prohibition of unclean animals, blood and things strangled.

The sign of the cross is made with one finger from left to right, and four reasons are put forward for the use of this method:

a) God ordered the sprinkling of the blood of the victims to be made with one finger.

---

[180] *Ibid.*

[181] 15 days. *Ibid.*

[182] Two patriarchs in the 12th century—Macarius II and Gabriel II—condemned the practice of circumcision immediately after baptism.

b) Our Lord said in the gospel: [183] "If I with the finger of God cast out devils." He did not say "fingers."

c) One finger indicates the unity of the essence of the Trinity, and the single φύσις resulting from the hypostatic union.

d) St. Mark taught this method of making the sign of the cross to his disciples.

Eucharistic Bread and Wine

The Coptic rite requires the use of leavened bread in the liturgy, but with the unauthorised extension of communion under one kind the faithful often receive the host under the form of azymes from the tabernacle. The synod [184] of Alexandria (1898), however, directs that Coptic priests travelling in Catholic districts, where azyme bread is customary, must not consecrate with it.

The same synod [185] also forbade the dissident practice of adding a little salt to the bread.

Coptic tradition, enforced by a canon of St. Basil (106) and St. Athanasius, requires the bread to be baked on the morning of the liturgy. The patriarch Christodulos (1047-1077), possibly on account of persecution, enjoins the faithful to prepare the *oblata* in their own homes, but Cyril III ibn Laqlaq (1235-1243) says that this should be done in the furnace of the church. In regard to this, the Catholic synod [186] (Alexandria) forbade the making of the eucharistic bread by non-Catholics, and ordered it to be prepared in a sacred place, not in the houses of the laity, by an official of

---

[183] St. Luke XI, 20.
[184] HANSSENS, *Instit. Lit. de Rit. Orient.*, t. II, part I, p. 125.
[185] *Ibid.*, p. 122.
[186] *Ibid.*, p. 210.

the church, who, during the baking, should recite psalms and canticles. The thicker bread, which serves for solemn feasts, must be baked on the day of the liturgy, but this is not necessary in the case of the bread for the daily Mass.

Each leavened cake or *korban* (3½ × 3 ins) has a Greek inscription [187] in Coptic lettering round the edge: " ἅγιος ὁ θεός, ἅγιος ἰσχυρός, ἅγιος ἀθάνατος." The bread is divided into 12 little squares, with a larger square in the centre, each marked with a cross. The small squares [188] symbolise the apostles, and that in the middle, [189] which is detached at the commixture and placed in the chalice, is called the *isbodikon* [190] and represents our Lord. The stone and plaster moulds now in the museum at Cairo show that the breads were at one time much larger, and the surface of the mould is divided into two or three dozen divisions for the communicants.

A canon (99) of St. Basil gave a mystical meaning to the number of the breads prepared by the deacon for the communion of the people. Thus, if three breads were used, it symbolised the Holy Trinity, and if one, the divinity of our Lord.

The *Lamp* directs that the altar should be prepared by the priest [191] himself, and several loaves are to be brought to him that he may select one. This is then rubbed back

---

[187] ἅγιος, ἅγιος, ἅγιος, κύριος. *Dict. de Théol. Cath.*, t. X, col. 2295.

[188] Arabic, *alḥamal*, "lamb."

[189] The middle square is larger than the others, and contains four smaller parts. The synod of Alexandria (1898) confirmed for the use of the Catholic Copts the traditional form of the eucharistic bread.

[190] This is the "lamb" of the Byzantine rite. Greek St. Gregory, δεσποτικόν (sc. σῶμα); Greek St. Basil, σπουδικόν; Coptic, *spoudikon, isbodikon, isbadikon;* Arabic, *isbādyaḳūn.* The word is never used of the unconsecrated particle.

[191] A bishop does not prepare the altar.

and front with a moist hand, kissed, and laid on the altar, while the others serve for the *antidoron*. This custom is not observed by the Catholics.

The Copts, in the dark days of Islamic persecution, were forbidden to ferment wine, and the practice therefore grew up of using unfermented wine in the liturgy.

To-day, some Monophysite churches in Upper Egypt appear to use date juice, which is invalid matter. Fermented raisin juice, however, *is* wine, and consequently valid.

The proportion of water to the wine in the chalice was said by Farag Allah of Akhmin [192] (14th century?) to be from one-third to one-tenth water. The Catholic synod of Alexandria (1898) directed *modicissima aqua* to be mixed with the wine.

Vestments

The vestments[193] were enumerated by patriarch Gabriel II ibn Tarik (1131-1146). Except for a kind of amice, they correspond to those of the Byzantine rite. They may be of any colour and almost any material. Poor churches sometimes affect cheap calicoes with sprawling flowers printed all over them, while richer districts use silk, satin or velvet embroidered with gold and silver. White vestments with pink and red designs is a favourite colour scheme. Catholics in some respects tend to imitate the modern western style.

The one distinctive Coptic vestment, worn by dissident bishops, archdeacons and priests alike, is a kind of amice or turban. This is a long band of white material, embroidered

[192] RENAUDOT, *op. cit.*, t. I, p. 178; HANSSENS, *op. cit.*, t. II, part I, p. 249.
[193] Coptic, *tistolē nieratikon, hbōs ethouab nte nouēb;* Arabic, *badlāt almukaddasah, alcahnūtyah.*

with two crosses, which is arranged round the head like a
hood, hanging back and front over the right shoulder, and
worn in the liturgy until the "preface." The *tailasān*, [194] as
it is normally called by the Copts, is not worn by the Catholics, and Propaganda [195] ordered the priests of the rite to
celebrate the holy mysteries with uncovered heads, except
for serious health reasons, when they must apply for dispensations from the Apostolic See. That worn on feasts by
the dissident clergy at St. Mark's Cathedral, Cairo, and
Heliopolis has the appearance of a Latin mitre with a broad
tail down the back. A bishop of the national church on Good
Friday and in the presence of the patriarch, when he does
not wear a crown, has a special *ṭailasān* of coloured silk,
embroidered with texts.

The *stikharion* [196] is worn by all the ministers of the
sanctuary, but Catholic priests often wear the Western alb
of crochet work variety, and modern Catholic usage permits
the assistants to wear lace cottas or even ordinary clothes.

The girdle, [197] which is often discarded by the dissidents,
is a belt of coloured silk or velvet, fastened by a clasp.

When a stole [198] is worn by the "little deacon" it is
passed across the breast, under the arms, crossed on the

---

[194] Coptic, *palin, ballin* (pallium), *kidaris, logion* (Greek, λογεῖον, "breastplate;" cf. rational of judgment of the Jewish priest, Exod. XXVIII, 22 seq.), *efouti, ephout* (ephod, Exod. XXVIII, 4 seq.); Arabic, *ballīn, shamlah, ṭailasān*.

Attwater (*Dissident Eastern Churches*, p. 248) considers that historically the *ṭailasēn* is the same as the fanon worn by the pope, and as
the veil or hood of Eastern bishops and monks.

[195] Prop. Congr., 15-11-1790, No. 9.

[196] Coptic, *stoicharion* (στοιχάριον), *stychari, poterion* (ποδήρης), *shento, marppa, mappa*; Arabic, *tuniyah*.

[197] Coptic, *zounarion* (ζωνάριον), *zunarion*; Arabic, *mintaḳah, zinnār*.

[198] Coptic, *orarion* (ὡράριον), *shordion*; Arabic, *batrashīl*.

back, drawn over the shoulders, and the ends tucked through the band in front, [199] thus producing the appearance of an H in front and an X at the back.

The prohibition of the council of Laodicea (363 or 370) in regard to the wearing of stoles by subdeacons does not seem to have affected the church of Alexandria, and the pontifical [200] edited by Tukhi has a rubric for the investiture of a subdeacon with the *orarion* at ordination.

The deacon has the stole under the right arm, with the ends thrown over the left shoulder; while the priest wears his stole in the Byzantine way, but over the girdle.

"Cuffs" [201] or "sleeves" are longer than those in the Byzantine rite, but they have been very generally discarded by the dissidents, except at the ordination of priests, bishops and the patriarch. They are, however, worn by the Catholic Copts.

Many writers seem very confused in respect to the Coptic vestments, and Renaudot identifies the "cuffs" with the Latin maniple; Neale [202] says that "the chasuble is named *tilsan* by the Copts;" while Butler, [203] who criticises these errors, persists in calling the *stikharion* a "dalmatic," and writes as though the cope-like vestment was the equivalent of the Latin cope instead of the chasuble.

The Coptic chasuble [204] takes the *form* of a western cope

---

[199] Cf. Byzantine deacon at the time of communion, when it is crossed again in front.

[200] DENZINGER, *Rit. Or.*, II, 6.

[201] Coptic, *kamasion;* Arabic, *cumm* (plural, *cummān*); *kamān.* Cf. Metal bracelets or cuffs of silk, worn in 6th century Gaul. WARREN, *op. cit.*, p. 117.

[202] *Eastern Church*. Gen. Introd., I, 309.

[203] "The vestment is what we call a dalmatic," *op. cit.*, vol. II, p. 101.

[204] Coptic, *felonion* (Greek, φαιλόνιον), *kouklion, amforion*, Arabic, *burnus.*

without a hood, and shows an evolution of the Byzantine vestment, with a broad band at the top not cut through, although the two sides are fastened together by a clasp.

Monophysite priests, especially in small churches, often celebrate the liturgy in *kidaris*, stole and alb only. One of the clergy of the church of Abu Sergeh, Old Cairo, told the writer that it was at the discretion of the celebrant to discard the *burnus*.

The omophorion, [205] worn by Catholic and dissident [206] prelates alike, is of white silk and sewn together in the form of a broad Y. In form, it resembles the Roman rather than the Byzantine pallium, although the shape may very well be early Greek.

The first mention of the pallium in the East comes from the patriarchate of Alexandria (ab. 385), and in the 6th century it was the custom for a new patriarch to take the pallium of St. Mark from the neck of his dead predecessor as part of a solemn rite.

The Roman mitre, ring and pectoral cross are now used by Catholic bishops, but, although the western crozier is occasionally seen, the eastern form of staff, [207] terminating in two twined serpents, is the more usual. In the centre between the retorted heads is a small round boss surmonted by a cross; while a silk veil—often green in colour—is fastened near the top of the staff. The snake-headed wand [208] was a familiar sight in ancient Egypt.

---

[205] Coptic, *omoforion* (Greek, ὠμοφόριον), *pallin;* Arabic, *ballin* (Greek, παλλίον).

[206] Butler (*op. cit.,* vol. II, chap. IV, p. 156) says that the omophorrion is no longer worn by the Monophysite bishops, but only by the patriarch.

[207] Greek, δικανίκιον; Coptic, *shvōt;* Arabic, *'akāz.*

[208] Cf. *Lituus* or "augur's wand" of classical times; herald's wand (σκῆπτρον, ῥάβδος) of Hermes; *caduceus* of the Latin Mercury.

A cap (*cidaris*) for priests adorned with small crosses
was mentioned by a bishop of Akhmim in the 12th century,
but it is now only worn by Monophysite deacons. [209] Three
small boys, who acted as deacons in the liturgy at Luxor
(December 1945), wore gilt crowns surmounted by crosses.

Bishops of the national church have a bronze cross and
a crown [210] of silver gilt. The episcopal crown and staff may
only be used by a bishop in his own diocese, and never in the
presence of the patriarch.

The patriarch Cyril V had a crown presented to him by
the king of Abyssinia, which in its three bands of ornament
round the high metal cap showed an accidental resemblance
to the papal tiara.

The outdoor dress of the clergy consists of a wide-sleeved
rason over a cassock. Monophysite priests wear a black or
dark blue tight fitting turban, and the Catholics a black
cylinder hat, about six inches high and growing wider at
the top.

The patriarch, except for a pectoral cross, is indistinguishable in his dress from a simple monk.

History of the Rite

The early history of the liturgy of Alexandria was considerably augmented by the fortunate discovery of the Russian
liturgist Dmitrievsky, who in 1895 in the monastery of
Laura, Mount Athos, discovered an 11th century manuscript
of the Greek euchologion of Serapion.

Serapion († ab. 360) had been bishop of Thmuis and the
correspondent of St. Athanasius. A close study of the document points to a Syrian origin, but adopted and modified

---

[209] BUTLER, *op. cit.*, vol. II, chap. IV, pp. 209-210.
[210] Coptic, *mētra* (μίτρα), *klam, tschrēpi;* Arabic, *tāj.*

about the middle of the 4th century as a local variant of the Alexandrine rite.

There are, however, writes Gregory Dix, [211] "strong indications that this extant form is only a revision of an older Egyptian prayer, whose outline can be established in some points by comparison with eucharistic passages in 3rd century Egyptian writers."

The liturgy has the two normal divisions—liturgy of the catechumens and liturgy of the faithful—but what are especially valuable are the intercessions and the anaphora. Here we have what is probably a full set of the original form of the intercession, a series of short prayers for "all sorts and conditions of men," traces of which may be found in the intercession of the liturgy of St. Mark. Serapion has, moreover, a rubric, [212] that extreme rarity in the earliest liturgical books, directing the prayers to be said *before* the prayer of oblation, which, as Edmund Bishop, [213] points out was the original place of the intercession. The short prayer for the dead and the diptychs for them come abruptly in the middle of a prayer for the communicating congregation after the epiclesis, but they are an interpolation and not in accordance with the tradition of the Alexandrine patriarchate. Whence then is this novelty derived? From what church has it been borrowed?

The Holy Sepulchre at Jerusalem, says Bishop, [214] has become the starting-point for a new religious development in Christianity, and an important pilgrimage centre. What then

[211] *Shape of the Liturgy*, chap. VII, p. 162.
[212] Πρὸ τῆς εὐχῆς τοῦ προσφόρου.
[213] Notes and Studies. Liturgical Comments and Memoranda. VIII., p. 27. *The Journal of Theological Studies.* Vol. XIV. Oxford, Clarendon Press, 1913.
[214] *Ibid.*, pp. 36-39.

is more likely than that Jerusalem was the source of inspiration to Serapion. The presence of a clause of intercession for the dead at the close of the consecration prayer and a prescription of the recital of particular names are an imitation of what the person responsible for this clause had seen and observed at Jerusalem.

The anaphora of Serapion is probably the earliest to be called the "prayer of oblation."

In the middle of the thanksgiving, a little after the *sanctus*, the celebrant brusquely interrupts the theme to address an invocation to God on behalf of the Catholic Church. This invocation [215] is borrowed from the Didache (1st century). Another point to notice is that the epiclesis, which follows the institution, is 'addressed to the Word, not to the Holy Spirit.

The prayer which begins: "For thou art he who art over all principality and power and virtue," and ends with the *sanctus* is found almost word for word in the liturgy of St. Mark. The epiclesis, also, is said immediately in both liturgies, has similar expressions, and is bound to the words of institution.

The *Testament of the Lord (Testamentum Domini)*, dating from the 4th-5th century, is of the same Egyptian type.[216] The anaphora found in place of the original in the Arabo-Coptic version, and existing in a manuscript of the patriarch Cosmas (901), has many similarities with the Greek and Coptic St. Mark.

---

[215] "As elements of bread, scattered on the mountains have been reunited into a single whole, even so may thy Church reassemble from the ends of the earth in thy kingdom."

[216] The *Testament of the Lord* seems to have been originally a Syriac form of Hippolytus. It has left its mark on the Ethiopic liturgy (*qv.*).

In 1897, a manuscript of the 7th or 8th century, but incorporating a much older text (ab. 400), was discovered in the ruins of the monastery of St. Apollonius at Deir Balizeh near Assiut in Upper Egypt. The *sanctus* in the fragment was not followed by the *benedictus;* while the epiclesis was *before* the words of institution, although it is possible that a second epiclesis came in the usual position, and the extant manuscript ends immediately before this. The chief value of this liturgical fragment lies in its witness to the liturgies of St. Mark and St. Gregory. Thus, one passage begins almost verbatim from "St. Gregory;" while it ends with words found in "St. Mark." Other Coptic fragments, also, of the 7th and 8th centuries, and now in the Vatican library, agree in part with "St. Cyril" ("St. Mark"), and at the same time embody some of the eucharistic prayer of St. Gregory.

The first Alexandrine liturgy [217] was in all probability Greek "St. Mark," which dates back to at least the 5th century, with much that is more primitive. The Papyrus of Strassburg, which has six fragments of the great intercession, is said to be of the 3rd-4th century.

Three manuscripts of the liturgy are still extant, although they are not of earlier date than the 12th century, when the schism of the Copts had led the orthodox into considerable "Byzantinisation," and by the 13th century they themselves had given up the use of "St. Mark."

The Copts have three anaphoras, [218] and the pro-anaphoral liturgy is a Coptic variant of the Greek "St. Mark."

Several other anaphoras were at one time in use, at least in some parts of Egypt, and Vansleb mentions no less than twelve, taken from Coptic writers. Manuscripts also exist

---

[217] Greek, πρόσφορα ; Coptic, *prosfora;* Arabic, *kurbān.*
[218] Coptic, *anafora, agiasmos;* Arabic, *ḳuddās.*

containing extracts of different anaphoras [219] in the Sahidic
dialect. St. Cyril, the Coptic successor of Greek "St. Mark,"
has been thus described by the author of the *Lamp*: "the
Liturgy of St. Mark which Cyril perfected for the great
fast and month of *Khihak*."

This anaphora is used by the Catholic Copts, according
to Mgr. Gubran, vicar patriarchal in Alexandria, only once
in the year, the Friday [220] before Palm Sunday. It would
seem, however, that the dissidents have it on the feasts of
St. Cyril and St. Mark, and at the consecration of a bishop.
The *Catholic Encyclopedia*, [221] seemingly quoting from the
Lamp, says that the liturgy of St. Cyril is used in "the month
of Chosiac (Advent) and Lent."

"St. Gregory Nazianzen, [222] which, like "St. Basil,"
exists in Greek in an altered form, is used at the evening
liturgy on the vigils of Christmas, Epiphany and Easter, when
it normally begins at nine or nine-thirty, and is timed to
finish on the stroke of midnight. This anaphora is addressed
throughout to God the Son, [223] apparently inspired by the
definitions of the first council of Nicea (325). "St. Basil,"
the normal liturgy with both Catholics and dissidents, is a
rearrangement of the Byzantine anaphora, altered to fit into
the Egyptian liturgical scheme.

The chief difference between the Syrian and Egyptian
type of liturgy is the position of the intercession prayers and
the diptychs, which the former has after the epiclesis, and the

[219] e. g. St. Matthew, St. James, St. John of Bosra.
[220] This is supported by Bute. *The Coptic Morning Service*,
pref. p. VII.
[221] Art. *Egypt*, vol. V, p. 361.
[222] The liturgies of St. Gregory and St. Basil have both been
subjected to Syrian influences.
[223] Cf. Maronite anaphora.

latter as an interruption in the eucharistic prayer, between the dialogue and the preface.

Renaudot [224] affirms that the Copts once had a liturgy of the presanctified, although no trace of it exists to-day.

Concelebration [225] with two assistant priests was envisaged in the *Lamp* as of normal occurrence, but the Catholic synod of Alexandria (1898) restricted its use to solemn liturgies on great feasts.

The same synod also spoke of the twofold method of celebrating the liturgy—the simple or "low Mass" and the solemn.

"The ordinary minister of the sacrifice," says the synod, "is the deacon; if the deacon is not present, his place may be taken by one of the inferior ministers; and if there is no cleric, a layman may assist, provided he is a Catholic, respectable (*probus*) and not twice married (*bigamus*)."

The dissidents to-day seldom offer the holy Sacrifice more frequently than Sundays, feasts and special occasions. The church of St. Mark, Alexandria, and probably others also celebrate the liturgy on Wednesdays and Fridays, as well as every day in Lent (with a sermon).

In the time of Socrates (5th century), the synaxis on Wednesdays and Fridays at Alexandria was restricted, as at Rome, to the lessons, a homily and prayers, whereas Jerusalem and Antioch had the liturgy.

The *Synaxarion* on the 5th *Barmahat* (March 1) commemorates Peter the Presbyter, who was accustomed to offer morning incense and celebrate the liturgy every day.

Frequent communion for many centuries was the custom

[224] *Lit. Orient. Collect.*, t. I, pp. 321-322.
[225] Arabic, *alcāhin, alsharīc;* the *Lamp* uses *hadīm.*

in the Coptic church, and all who assisted at the liturgy received the blessed sacrament.

The *Synaxarion* for the 19th *Khihak* (December 15) mentions John, bishop of Nikedjoou (el-Bolos), who in the time of Amba Daniel († ab. 570) was much troubled by heretics, some of whom were accustomed to communicate twenty times a day!

Michael of Damietta (12th century) spoke of frequent communion as a practice which distinguished the Copts from the members of other churches, orthodox or heretical. In the same century, Peter of Malig writes that the Melkites reproached the Copts with showing by frequent communion a lack of respect to the holy Sacrament. In this complaint, however, they were not altogether wrong, as it was the period in which the abandonment of sacramental confession had become general.

To-day, in Monophysite churches, hardly anyone, except children, approach the holy mysteries. It is only in Lent and on some great feasts that the communicants are more numerous.

It is required of those who wish to receive holy communion that they fast from the evening before, avoid during the day all contact with Jews, infidels or Mohammedans, refrain from spitting on the ground, smoking, and making on that day any prostration or *metanoia,* as the day of communion is a day of triumph and happiness, and not of humiliation and sadness. Infants receive holy communion by the priest placing his finger, which has been dipped in the chalice, in the mouth of each.

The people, when there is no choir, sing the chants and make the responses, and the liturgy has a marked social character, with the celebrant acting as the delegate of the Christian community.

The rite has been described as an "uninterrupted dialogue between priest and people," and at the time of the consecration the connection is so vital and sustained that they may literally be said to "hang on one another's words."

The anaphora of St. Basil, which is the normal liturgy of the Copts, is given here after the *ordo communis*.

The liturgy of St. Basil appeared first in Greek, and its order agrees rather with the Syrian liturgy of St. James [226] than with the Alexandrine St. Cyril.

There is an epiclesis after both offertory and anamnesis; while the intercessions and diptychs instead of interrupting the "preface" are connected with the invocation.

One of the prayers of the peace ("O great [and] everlasting God, who didst create man in corruption") seems to have been borrowed from the Syrian liturgy of St. Basil, another from the Syrian St. Athanasius, while the third is derived from St. James.

The prayer of the veil is also taken from St. James.

Churches, which have screens, have their curtains drawn back during the liturgy, so that the altar is always visible, although Le Brun, commenting on the prayer of the veil, says: "It would seem that in this place the curtain was drawn to hide the sacrifice, and that the priest was there, as in the holy of holies, beyond the sight of the people."

The rubric in the liturgy of the Monophysites which requires the celebrant to wash his feet before entering the sanctuary now seems to be interpreted by the putting on of a special pair of slippers.

The liturgy appears to have been developed and standardised in the patriarchate of Gabriel II Ibn Tarik (1131-1145).

---

[226] Cf. the liturgy of St. Gregory.

Office of Morning Incense

The tradition of the church, says the author of the *Lamp in the Darkness,* demands that the liturgy should be celebrated after an office, and preferably the prayer of the hour which precedes it, following the time of the ecclesiastical year. The prayer of the Morning Incense is joined to the office, and for this, if the liturgy is to follow, the celebrant is fully vested.

In the church of Abu Sergeh, Old Cairo, the Morning Incense is offered daily, with the priest fasting.

Incense is of great importance to all Eastern Christians, but especially to the Copts, who are greatly concerned with the quality of the incense, of which there are four kinds. [227]

a) *Sandarus* (from Java or Sumatra), whose smell is penetrating and which does not leave any residue, is said never to have been offered to idols. *b*) *Luban,* the incense offered by the Magi to our Lord. *c*) Incense made with the wood of Indian aloes, and alleged to have the property of chasing away impure spirits and of upsetting the evil designs of sorcerers. *d*) *Maia,* incense of an unknown quality.

The office of the Morning Incense (a similar office takes place in the evening) includes the Lord's prayer, prayer of thanksgiving, hymn, intercessions, second hymn, creed, gospel, intercessions, and prayer of absolution to the Son.

When the liturgy is celebrated without this office, it is customary [228] to prefix at least the opening part.

The priest goes up to the altar (carrying the chalice and paten, if they are not already there, which he places on the

[227] *Dict. de Théol. Cath.,* t. X, col. 2301.
[228] BUTE, *The Coptic Morning Service for the Lord's Day,* p. 46, n. 1.

altar), kisses it, and signs himself, saying: "In the name, etc.," and so on till the Lord's prayer.

The last words of the Lord's prayer are sung by the cantor, after which they begin the "Alleluia" very slowly.

Meanwhile the priest says inaudibly what is sung and said by the choir, and after the Lord's prayer (without saying "Alleluia") begins at once the prayer of preparation.

The Liturgy with the Anaphora of St. Basil

The liturgy of the Monophysites begins with a clashing of cymbals.

The Catholic celebrant goes fully vested to the altar, where he uncovers the sacred vessels, and places the three veils on the right side. He opens the missal, which is on his left, signs himself, and says: "In the name of the Father and of the Son and of the Holy Ghost. Amen."

He kisses the altar, and continues: "We worship thee, O Christ, with thy holy Father and the Holy Ghost, for thou hast come to redeem us (he blesses the people). Have mercy on us, Almighty God, most holy Trinity, O Lord, God of hosts, have mercy on us, for in our trials and distress we have no helper but thee. Make us all worthy to speak to thee in thankfulness."

The priest then joins with the people in the "Our Father," which ends with the words: "through Christ Jesus our Lord."

Thus ends the abbreviated form of the office of Morning Incense, and the celebrant, silently and with hands extended, recites the prayer of preparation: [229]

---

[229] Prayer of the iconostasis. "A prayer of the Patriarch Severus for the preparation of the holy altar of the Lord." BRIGHTMAN, *op. cit.*, p. 144.

"Lord, who knoweth the hearts of all, who is holy, and who resteth amid the saints, who alone is without sin, and who is mighty to forgive sin; thou, O Lord, knowest my unworthiness and my unfitness and my unmeetness, that I should draw near unto this thy holy ministry; and I have no boldness to draw near, and to open my mouth before thy holy glory; but according to the multitude of thy tender mercies, pardon me a sinner, and grant unto me that I may find grace and mercy in this hour; and send me strength from on high, [230] that I may begin, [231] and may be made fit, and may finish thy holy ministry according to thy pleasure, according to the good pleasure of thy will, for a sweet savour of incense. Even so, O our Lord. Be thou with us, take thou part with us in this thing: bless us: for thou art the forgiveness of our sins, the light of our souls, our life, and our strength and our confidence. Thou art he unto whom we ascribe praise, glory and worship, the Father and the Son and the Holy Ghost, now, and ever, and unto the ages of all ages. Amen."

This is followed immediately, and still inaudibly, with the prayer [232] after the preparation of the altar: "Thou, O Lord, hast taught us this great mystery of salvation; thou hast called us, thy holy and unworthy servants, to be ministers of thine altar. Do thou, O our Lord, make us meet, in the power of thy Holy Spirit, to finish this service; so that

[230] Bute (op. cit., p. 47) says: "here he uncovers the chalice, and arranges it upon the altar, together with the paten and the spoon, continuing meanwhile."

[231] It has been suggested that the expressions "may begin," "may be made fit," and "may finish" have reference to the three essential parts of the Mass,—oblation, consecration, communion.

[232] Brightman (op. cit., p. 144) adds the words "to the Father." Jacob Muijser, in the Dutch translation (p. 16), speaks of the prayer as "preparatory to the offering."

without falling into condemnation before thy great glory, we may offer up unto thee a sacrifice of praise, glory, and great beauty, in thy sanctuary. O God, who givest grace, who sends forth salvation, who workest all in all, grant, O Lord, that our sacrifice may be accepted before thee, for my sins, and for the ignorances of thy people; for, behold, it is holy, according to the gift of thy Holy Spirit, in Christ Jesus our Lord (the priest joins his hands and kisses the altar). Through whom becometh thee glory, and honour, and power, and worship, with him, and the Holy Ghost, the life-giver, of one substance with thee, now, and ever, and unto the ages of the ages. Amen."

The priest then kisses the altar and, turning to the west, chooses the bread for the oblation from among several loaves which are presented to him by the minister.

He prepares the bread, kisses it, and lays it upon the altar; then he examines the wine and smells it or causes it to be tasted, in order to be sure of its fitness.

At the right side of the altar, the priest now washes his hands, as he says parts of the 50th and 25th psalms: "Thou shalt sprinkle me with hyssop, and I shall be clean: thou shalt wash me, and I shall be whiter than snow. Thou shalt make me hear of joy and gladness: that the bones which thou hast broken may rejoice. I will wash my hands in innocency, O Lord: and so will I go to thine altar. That I may show the voice of thanksgiving: and tell of all thy wondrous works."

Then, "rubbing [233] the bread above and below," to test the soundness of the loaf and to remove loose particles, the celebrant places it on the veil, and offers it to God, saying: "Grant, O Lord, that our sacrifice may be accepted in thy

---

[233] Arabic, *massah alḥamal.*

sig^lt, for my sins, and for the ignorances of thy people, and let it be sanctified by the gift of thy Holy Spirit, in Christ Jesus our Lord, through whom becometh thee glory, and honour, and power, and worship, with him, and the Holy Spirit, the life-giver, of one substance with thee, now, and ever, and unto ages of ages. Amen."

A short prayer is added, in which the priest directs his intention for the particular liturgy. Several of these prayers are found in the missal. For the dead: "Remember, O Lord, thy servant N., and grant him a place of rest and refreshment and repose in the dwelling of thy saints, in the bosom of our fathers Abraham, Isaac and Jacob, in blessed paradise."

For the sick: "Remember, O Lord, thy servant N., and keep him by an angel of peace and make him whole."

At a solemn liturgy, the priest now takes the bread ("lamb") in a veil and, holding it up to the level of his head, makes a procession round the altar, in what is known as the "circuit [234] of the lamb," preceded by a minister carrying the cruet of wine in a veil, and another minister bearing a lighted taper.

The ceremony is found in Greek St. Mark, but, as in the Byzantine liturgy, its position is after the dismissal of the catechumens.

The priest in the meanwhile says: "Glory and honour unto honour and glory unto the all-holy Trinity, the Father, the Son, and the Holy Spirit. Peace and edification unto the one only holy Catholic Apostolic Church of God. Amen. Remember them, O Lord, who have brought these gifts unto thee, and them for whom they have been brought, and them by whom they have been brought: give unto them all a

---

[234] Arabic, *dūrat alḥamal*.

recompense from the heavens. Remember, O Lord, all who have bidden us to remember them in our prayers and supplications. May the Lord remember them in his heavenly kingdom."

The choir (people), who at the prayer of preparation began to sing "Alleluia," protract this until the commencement of the procession, when they continue with a hymn.

On fast days, the following, with an accompaniment of cymbals, is sung: "Alleluia. The thought of man shall praise thee, and the rest of (his) thought shall keep holiday before thee. Alleluia."

In Lent and the fast of Nineveh: "Alleluia. I will ascend to the altar of God, who rejoices at my youth. With the harp shall I glorify thee, O God, my God. Alleluia. Think, O Lord, of David and all his meekness. Alleluia."

On the remaining days: [235] "Alleluia. This is the day which the Lord hath made; let us rejoice and be glad in it. O Lord, thou wilt save us. O Lord, thou wilt guide our ways. Blessed be he that cometh in the name of the Lord. Alleluia."

At the conclusion of the procession, the priest ascends to the altar, where at the left side he blesses the bread and wine three times.

If there are concelebrating priests, the chief celebrant says to them: "Do ye bless."

The bread is held close to the vessel of wine, which the deacon still carries, and the priest says:

"In the name of the Father and of the Son and of the Holy Ghost. Amen. Blessed be † God the Father Almighty, Amen (Answer: "Amen"). Blessed be † his only-begotten Son, Jesus Christ our Lord. Amen (Answer: "Amen").

---

[235] BUTE, op. cit., p. 49, Paschal time.

Blessed be † the Holy Ghost the Comforter. Amen (Answer: "Amen")."

The priest puts bread on the paten, and continues inaudibly: "Glory and honour unto honour and glory unto the all-holy Trinity, the Father, the Son and the Holy Ghost."

Then, pouring wine into the chalice and adding a little water, he offers it to God with the same prayer [236] as for the bread: "Grant, O Lord, that our sacrifice may be accepted in thy sight, for my sins, and for the ignorances of thy people, and let it be sanctified by the gift of thy Holy Spirit, in Christ Jesus our Lord." [237]

The deacon, in the meanwhile, recites aloud: "Amen, amen, amen. One holy Father: one holy Son: one Holy Ghost. Amen. Blessed be the Lord God unto all ages. Amen. O all ye nations, bless the Lord. Let all peoples bless him. For his mercy is confirmed towards us, and the truth of the Lord endureth for ever. Amen. Alleluia."

The paten and chalice are covered with their respective veils; while a third and larger veil is placed over the two vessels. The people respond: "Glory be to the Father and to the Son and to the Holy Ghost, both now, and ever, and unto the ages of the ages. Amen." [238]

The priest, turning to the people, blesses them with the hand-cross, as he says in Greek: "Peace be with you all," and the deacon [239] or other minister answers: "And with thy spirit."

[236] The dissidents do not repeat the prayer.
[237] The doxology is not given in either place in the Dutch translation.
[238] Bute (op. cit., p. 52) adds " Alleluia."
[239] Bute (Ibid.), " people."

Enarxis

The prayer of thanksgiving of St. Mark, which begins the enarxis, has passed into the liturgy from the office, and not vice versa. It is also said in the prayer of the morning incense, and forms the chief part of the enarxis in Greek St. Mark and the Ethiopic liturgy.

The enarxis, which is generally related in structure to the divine office, appears in Byzantine literature of the 9th century, and its existence in the Coptic rite is no doubt a trace of Greek influence.

The priest recites the prayer aloud: "Let us give thanks unto the beneficent and merciful God, the Father of our Lord and God and Saviour Jesus Christ. For he hath protected us, he hath succoured us, he hath preserved us, he hath purchased us unto himself, he hath spared us, he hath helped us, he hath brought us unto this hour. Let us then pray him that he, the Almighty Lord our God, will keep us in all peace this holy day, and all the days of our life. (Deacon in Greek) Pray ye. (People in Greek) Lord have mercy. (Priest continues) O Lord and Master, Almighty God, Father of our Lord and God and Saviour Jesus Christ. We give thee thanks upon all things, and for all things, and in all things. For thou hast protected us, thou hast succoured us, thou hast preserved us, thou hast purchased us unto thyself, thou hast spared us, thou hast helped us, thou hast brought us unto this hour. (Deacon) Pray that God will have mercy upon us, will pity us, will hear us, will help us, will receive the prayers and supplications of his saints on our behalf, unto our good at all times, will forgive our sins, will make us worthy to receive, through the communion of his holy blessed mysteries, the remission of our sins. (People in Greek) Lord have mercy. (Priest continues) Wherefore we pray and entreat thy goodness, O thou lover of men. Grant unto us to pass this holy day and all the days of our life in all peace and (in) thy fear. All envy, all temptation, all the work of Satan, the counsel of wicked men, the insurrection of enemies that are hidden, or are manifest—do thou take away (he crosses himself) from us (he makes a cross over his left shoulder) and from all thy people (he makes a cross over his right shoulder) and from this holy table (he makes a cross over the altar). But such things as be meet for us, as such things as be useful unto us, do thou cause to be ministered unto us. For thou art he who hast given unto us the power to tread upon serpents and scorpions, and upon all the power of the enemy. [240]   (Priest continues inaudibly) And lead us not into temptation, but deliver us from evil, through the grace, and mercy, and love toward men, of thine only-begotten Son, our Lord and God and Saviour Jesus Christ, through whom are due unto thee, and the Holy Ghost, the life-giver, who is of one substance with thee, glory and honour and power and worship, now and ever and unto the ages of all ages. Amen."

The choir (people), by way of an acclamation, sings: "Saved indeed and (so be it) with thy spirit."

The prayer [241] of St. Mark over the offerings immediately follows (silently): "O Lord and Master, Jesus Christ, the only-begotten and eternal Son and Word of God the Father, who art of one substance with him and with the Holy Ghost; thou art the living bread which came down from heaven, and hast made thyself a lamb without spot for the life of the world. We pray and beseech thy goodness, O thou lover of

---

[240] Bute (op. cit., p. 55, n. 1) says that, in spite of the rubric, it is the "invariable practice for the choir to begin answering at this point."

[241] Note the formula of epiclesis for the conversion of the oblations *before* the recital of institution.

men, (he points to the bread) cause thy face to shine upon this bread, (he points to the chalice) and upon this cup, which we have set upon this thine holy table, bless † them, sanctify † them, hallow † and change them, (he points again to the bread) that this bread may become indeed thine holy body, (points again to the chalice) and the mingled wine and water which is in this cup, may become indeed thine own honourable blood; that they be unto us all, help and healing and health for our souls, [242] and our bodies, and our spirits. For thou art our God, and unto thee, with thy good Father and the Holy Ghost, the life-giver and of one substance with thee, are due glory and power, now and ever and unto the ages of all ages. Amen."

This prayer, although it does not name the Holy Spirit as the consecrating agent, has certain similarities with the eastern form of epiclesis. Le Brun, commenting on it, said: "The Copts show by this prayer that they put bread and wine upon the altar for no other purpose than that they may be changed into the body and blood of Jesus Christ, but they do not pretend that the change is made by this preparatory prayer. They fully believe that this does not take place until the words of Jesus Christ"—"This is my body...—have been said, and the Holy Spirit invoked."

The bread and the wine are now covered with their veils, as a symbol [243] of the wrapping in linen of the body of our Lord in the tomb; while the third and larger veil represents the stone rolled before the door of the sepulchre.

Then, kneeling, rising, and kissing the altar, the priest

[242] The threefold division in man is often expressed in the Coptic liturgy.
[243] The symbolism, as is so often the case, is probably a pious gloss on practical actions.

goes round it, beginning by the south, and gives thanks for
his call to this office; while the deacon does likewise.

They both now leave the sanctuary, and the priest pro-
nounces the prayer of absolution to the Son [244] inaudibly over
those present, standing between the choir and the sanctuary,
with the faithful kneeling.

The missal has a long rubric (in Arabic only), entering
into the most minute details and mystic applications of
the ceremonies.

Among other things, the priest and deacon, in accordance
with certain popular ideas, are enjoined to put their left
feet first in leaving the sanctuary.

If there is an assistant priest [245] the rubric directs that
he should say the prayer of absolution.

This prayer, which asks pardon for the priests, ministers
and congregation, has been already referred to in the controversy regarding confession:

"O Lord and Master, Jesus Christ, the only-begotten
Son and Word of God the Father, who by his saving and
life-giving sufferings hath broken all the chains of our sins,
who hath breathed into the face of his saintly disciples and
holy apostles, saying unto them. Receive the Holy Ghost,
whose sins ye remit, they are remitted unto them, and whose
sins ye retain, they are retained unto them. Thou also now,
O our Lord, by thine holy apostles hast given grace unto them
who for the time do discharge the office of the priesthood
in thine holy Church, that they may remit sins upon earth,
should bind and should loose all the bonds of iniquity; we
now pray and entreat thy goodness, O thou lover of men,

---

[244] The prayer of absolution to the Father occurs towards the end
of the liturgy.

[245] "He that is foremost among the priests shall read it, if he be
present." BRIGHTMAN, op. cit., p. 148.

for thy servants, my fathers and my brethren, and mine own
weakness, who are now bowing down their heads before
thine holy glory; grant unto them and grant unto us thy
mercy, and loose all the chains of our sins, if we have anywise
sinned against thee knowingly or unknowingly, or through
fear, in word, or in deed, or by cowardice, do thou, O Lord,
as a merciful God who lovest man, who knowest man's
weakness, grant unto us remission of our sins † (he signs
himself with a cross), bless us † (he signs the ministers),
purify us, absolve us † (he signs the people) and absolve all
thy people (here he prays for whom he pleases), fill us with
thy fear, and lead us unto thine holy and good will, for thou
art our God, and unto thee with thy good Father and the
Holy Ghost, the giver of life, who is of one substance with
thee, are due glory and honour and power, now and ever
and unto the ages of ages. Amen.

"May thy servants who serve thee this day (he makes the
sign of the cross towards each, as he mentions them; those
not present are omitted), † my father the priest, † my
fathers the priests, † and the deacon, † and the assistants, †
and all the people, † and mine own weakness, may they be
absolved from the mouth of the all-holy Trinity, the Father
and the Son and the Holy Ghost; and from the mouth of the
one only holy Catholic Apostolic Church; and from the
mouths of the twelve apostles; and from the mouth of the
ecstatic (exalted) St. Mark, the apostle and evangelist and
martyr; and of the holy Athanasius, (who was) like unto an
apostle; and of the golden-mouthed John; and of the holy
Cyril; and of the holy Gregory; and of the holy Basil; and
from the mouths of the 318 fathers who were gathered
together at Nicea; and of the 150 fathers at Constantinople;
and of the 200 fathers at Ephesus; and of the 630 fathers at
Chalcedon; and from the mouth of our fathers the bishops

who are united together in the orthodox faith; and from the
mouth of our most holy father, Pope N., the chief priest; and
from the mouth of our honourable father Amba N., the head
of the bishops; and from the mouth of his fellow servant
Bishop Amba N.; and from the mouth of mine own abjec-
tion, for blessed and full of glory is thine holy name, O
Father, Son and Holy Ghost, now and ever and unto the
ages of all ages. Amen."

The prayer said by the dissidents, given by Renaudot [246]
and Brightman, [247] differs from the Catholic text, as immediately after the mention of St. Mark occur the words:
"as also of the holy patriarch Severus, and of our holy
teacher Dioscorus." All allusion to St. Athanasius is omitted
by Renaudot, St. Basil is named before St. Gregory, and
there is no reference to Chalcedon; while the names in the
diptychs are changed.

The Liturgy of the Catechumens

The priest kisses the threshold of the sanctuary, enters,
kisses the altar, and puts incense into the censer.

Then the choir or people sing the following anthems:
"This is the censer of pure gold, holding sweet spices, in the
hands of Aaron the priest, offering up incense upon the
altar. The censer of gold is the Virgin; her sweet cloud is
our Saviour; she hath borne him; he hath saved us; may
he forgive us our sins. Thou art the censer of pure gold,
holding live coals of blessed fire."

The priest in the meanwhile says inaudibly the prayer of

[246] Op. cit., t. I, p. 4.
[247] Op. cit., p. 149.

incense: [248] "The mighty eternal God, without beginning, and without end, mighty in his works, who is in all places, and with all beings.

"Be with us also, O our Lord, in this hour, and stand in the midst of us all. Purify our hearts and sanctify our souls, cleanse us from all sin which we have committed, willingly or unwillingly. And grant us to offer up before thee reasonable oblations and sacrifices of praise."

Still silently, the deacon adds: "Pray concerning the sacrifice which we are offering. Lord, have mercy." The low voice, however, is obviously a corruption, as the diaconal answer is a bidding. "Lord, have mercy" is not in the text, although it is added by the Catholics.

The priest now continues: "And spiritual incense. May they enter in within the veil, into the holy place of thy holy ones. And we pray thee, O our Lord.

Remember, O Lord, the peace of the one holy Catholic and Apostolic, Orthodox Church of God.

(Deacon) Pray for the peace of the one holy Catholic and Apostolic, Orthodox Church of God.

(Priest kisses the altar at the south corner) Which is from one end of the world unto the other. Remember, O Lord, our Patriarch, the honourable Father, the Pontiff, the Pope, Amba N., and his fellow-servant, the Bishop Amba N.

(Deacon) Pray for our Pontiff, the Pope, Amba N., and our holy Father the Bishop, Amba N., and for our orthodox bishops. Lord have mercy.

(Priest, with a deacon, walks round the altar, kissing it at each corner) Preserve him in safety unto us for many years and peaceful times. Remember, O Lord, our congrega-

[248] Butler (op. cit., vol. II, chap. VII, p. 284) says that the priest holds the censer during the prayer of incense, then "waves it over the elements," and walks round the altar.

tions. Bless them. (Deacon) Pray for this holy church and our congregations.

(Priest, as he returns to the front of the altar). Grant that they may be unto us without hindrance, without disturbance; that we may hold them according to thy holy and blessed will, houses of prayer, houses of holiness, houses of blessing. Grant them unto us, O Lord, and unto thy servants who shall come after us for ever."

The deacon leaves the sanctuary, and the priest before the altar says: "Arise, O Lord God, let all thine enemies be scattered; let all them that hate thy holy name flee before thy face."

Meanwhile the priest goes round again, and at the east side continues: "And let thy people be blessed a thousand-thousand fold and ten-thousand-ten-thousand fold; may they do thy will. Through the grace and mercies and love towards man of thine only-begotten Son, our Lord and our God and our Saviour Jesus Christ."

The priest goes round a third time, saying: "Through whom are due unto thee, with himself and the Holy Ghost, the life-giver, (who is) of one substance with thee, glory and honour, and power and worship, now and ever and to the ages of all ages. Amen." Having arrived before the altar again, the priest kisses it, and leaves the sanctuary.

In dissident churches, [249] the choir sings: "We adore thee, O Christ, and thy good Father, and the Holy Ghost. Behold, thou hast come, thou hast saved us." This is said only by the priest in the Catholic rite. Bute [250] says that the

---

[249] "*non a choro canitur sed a sacerdote recitatur.*" *Comparatio ritus Coptici Catholici cum ritu Coptico Jacobitico.* HANSSENS, *Instit. Liturg. de Ritibus Orient.*, t. II, part. I cap. X, p. 394.

[250] *Op. cit.*, p. 64. Hanssens (*ibid*), however, says that in Catholic churches, after "*Adoramus te, O Christe,*" said by the priest: "*Omissis*

priest censes the altar thrice, saying the first time: "We adore thee, O Christ, and thy good Father, and the Holy Ghost. Behold, thou hast come, thou hast saved us."

The second time: "Before the angels will I sing praise unto thee, and will worship toward thy holy temple."

The third time: "As for me, I will enter into thine house, in the multitude of thy mercies, and will worship toward thy holy temple. Then the picture of our Lady is three times censed, as he says: "Hail to thee, Mary, the fair dove, which hath borne for us God the Word. We give thee salutation with the angel Gabriel, saying, Hail, thou that art full of grace; the Lord is with thee.

Hail to thee, O Virgin, the very and true Queen; hail, glory of our race. Thou hast borne for us Emmanuel.

We pray thee, remember us, O thou our faithful advocate with our Lord Jesus Christ, that he may forgive us our sins."

The celebrant now censes the other pictures once each, and then the priests. [251]

Catholics celebrate "low Mass" without incense; while the Monophysites, when the full complement of assistants is wanting, sometimes suspend the censer from a side beam of the ciborium, and, at the times required, the priest puts on incense and gives the thurible a swing. [252]

The liturgy has four lessons, three of which are recited

---

ceteris omnibus precibus, diaconus ante lectionem epistolae statim proclamat."

[251] Bute (*op. cit.*, p. 65, n. 1) says that the missal has several phrases of a complimentary kind, with which the priest greets the clergy of different grades as he censes them. Thus, in the case of a priest, he says: "I ask for a blessing upon thee, my father the priest; remember thou me."

[252] This was done in the church of Abu Sergeh, Old Cairo (May 22, 1924).

outside the sanctuary, although the catholic epistle is some-times omitted.

The lessons [253] are read in both Coptic and Arabic, but this is often done by laymen.

Contrary to Syrian and Byzantine usages, no anthem precedes the epistle.

The deacon, before reading the lesson from St. Paul, says: "Paul, the servant of our Lord Jesus Christ, called to be an apostle, who was separated unto the Gospel of God."

At the conclusion [254] of the lesson: "For grace (be) with you, and peace therewith. Amen, so be it."

The priest, while the epistle of St. Paul is being read in Coptic, censes the choir, as he says: "The blessing of Paul the Apostle of Jesus Christ: may his holy blessings be upon us. Amen."

Then leaving the choir, he goes throughout the church censing the congregation, with the thurible in his left hand and his right hand placed on the heads of the people, as he says: "Jesus Christ, the same yesterday, to-day, and for ever, in one person, let us worship him, let us glorify him."

Catholics [255] omit this prayer, and also that which the Monophysites say when the priest has returned to the altar, and is offering incense "on behalf of the people": [256] God, who received the confession of the thief upon the honourable cross, receive the confession of thy people, and forgive all their sins, for the sake of thy holy name which hath been

---

[253] The Coptic epistle is often read facing east, and the Arabic epistle facing west.

[254] In the liturgy of the Monophysites, the conclusion is said by the people. HANSSENS, *op. cit.*, p. 394.

[255] *Ibid.*

[256] Renaudot (*op. cit.*, t. I, p. 185) says that this prayer is not found in the most ancient manuscripts, although it was referred to by Michael of Damietta (ab. 1171).

called upon us. According unto thy mercy, O Lord, and not according unto our sins."

While the lesson [257] is being read in Arabic, the priest says inaudibly the prayer of St. Paul: "O God of knowledge and giver of wisdom, who bringest to light the hidden things of darkness, and givest the word unto them that preach the gospel with great power, who of thy goodness didst call Paul, who was sometime a persecutor, to be a chosen vessel, and wast pleased in him, that he should become a chosen apostle and preacher of the gospel of thy kingdom, O Christ our God. Thee also do we now entreat, O thou good and that lovest man. Graciously grant unto us and unto all thy people a mind without wandering and a clear understanding, that we may learn and understand how profitable are thy holy teachings, which are now come unto us by him; and even as he was made like unto thee, the leader unto life, so make us to be like unto him in deed and doctrine, that we may glorify thy holy name and ever glory in thy cross. And thou art he unto whom we ascribe praise and glory and worship, the Father and the Son and the Holy Ghost, now and ever and unto the ages of all ages. Amen."

The reader before beginning the catholic epistle in Coptic says: "(The lesson from the) Catholic (Epistle) of N., my beloved (brethren)," and, at its conclusion, the people answer: [258] "Love not the world, neither the things which are in the world; the world passeth away and the lust thereof; he that doeth the will of God abideth for ever. Amen."

The lesson is then read in Arabic, during which the

---

[257] In practice, the lesson is often read only in Arabic.

[258] BUTE, op. cit., p. 67. The Dutch translation of the Catholic rite (p. 26) says the "deacon."

priest [259] says inaudibly the prayer of the catholic epistle:
"O Lord God, who hast revealed unto us through thine holy
apostles the mystery of the gospel of the glory of thy Christ,
and hast given unto them, according to the power of the
infinite gift of thy grace, that they should proclaim among
all nations the glad news of the unsearchable riches of thy
mercy. We pray thee, O our Lord, make us worthy to have
a share and lot with them. Graciously grant unto us always
a share in their footsteps, and to imitate their wrestling,
and to have communion with them in the sweat which they
had for godliness' sake.   Keep thou thine holy church,
which thou didst found through them, and bless the lambs
of thy flock, and make to increase this vine, which thy right
hand hath planted; through Christ Jesus our Lord, through
whom are due unto thee glory and honour and power and
worship, with him and the Holy Ghost, the life-giver, (who
is) of one substance with thee, now and ever and unto the
ages of all ages. Amen."

When the catholic epistle is finished in Arabic, the choir
sings: "God taketh away the sins of the people through the
burnt offering and the sweet savour of incense. (Even he)
who offered up an acceptable sacrifice upon the cross for
the salvation of our race. (Here is inserted a passage varying
according to the day) Blessed in truth art thou, with thy
good Father, and the Holy Ghost; thou hast come; thou hast
saved us: and have mercy upon us."

Then is read the lesson from the Acts of the Apostles,
which is prefaced by the reader: "Acts of our fathers the
apostles: their holy blessings be with us."

[259] A common, though corrupt, practice is for the priest to say the
prayer of the catholic epistle immediately after that of St. Paul, and
then to go and sit down until the reading of the catholic epistle in Arabic
is over. BUTE, *op. cit.*, p. 68, n. 1.

When it is finished in Coptic, the people answer: "The word of the Lord shall endure, and shall be multiplied, and shall wax mighty, and shall be confirmed in the holy church of God. Amen."

Then it is read in Arabic, and the reader repeats the same phrases before and after it, as he has done in Coptic.

As soon as the lesson from the catholic epistle is finished in Arabic, the priest, standing at the altar, puts incense into the thurible and says inaudibly the prayer of the Acts:

"O God, who didst accept the sacrifice of Abraham, and didst prepare for him a lamb in place of Isaac, even so accept now at our hand, O our Lord, this sacrifice of incense, and send down upon us in return thine abundant mercy, and make us pure from all pollution of sin, and make us worthy to minister in holiness and righteousness before thy goodness, all the days of our life. Remember, O Lord, the peace of thine one only holy Catholic and Apostolic Church."

The deacon says: "Pray for the peace of the one only Catholic and Apostolic Church of God."

The priest, kissing the altar at the south side, continues: "Which is from one end of the world unto the other. Remember, O Lord, our Patriarch, the honourable Father, the Pontiff, the Pope, Amba N."

The deacon responds: "Pray for our Pontiff, the Pope, Amba N. Lord, have mercy."

Then the priest and the deacon (server) go round the altar, with the former at each corner kissing the hand-cross, as he says: "Preserve him in safety unto us for many years and peaceful times. Remember, O Lord, our congregation. Bless them."

Again the deacon gives a bidding: "Pray for this holy church and (for) our congregation."

The priest, as he returns before the altar, continues:

"Grant that they may be unto us without hindrance, without disturbance; that we may hold them according to thine holy and blessed will, houses of prayer, houses of holiness, houses of blessing. Grant them unto us, O Lord, and unto thy servants who shall come after us, for ever."

The deacon then leaves the sanctuary, and the priest, before the altar, says: "Arise, O Lord, let all thine enemies be scattered; let all them that hate thine holy name flee before thy face."

Once again going round the altar, the priest says at the east side: "And let thy people be blessed a thousand-thousand fold and ten-thousand-ten-thousand fold; may they do thy will. Through the grace and mercies and love toward man of thine only-begotten Son, our Lord and God and Saviour Jesus Christ."

Making the circuit yet a third time, he says: "Through whom are due unto thee, with himself, and the Holy Ghost, the life-giver (who is) of one substance with thee, glory and honour and power and worship, now and ever and to the ages of all ages. Amen."

The priest again kisses the altar, and leaves the sanctuary. Then he censes the altar thrice, saying, the first time: "We adore thee, O Christ, and thy good Father, and the Holy Ghost. Behold, thou hast come, thou hast saved us."

The second time: "Before the angels will I sing praise unto thee, and will worship toward thy holy temple."

And the third time: "As for me, I will enter into thine house, in the multitude of thy mercies, and will worship toward thine holy temple."

The picture of our Lady is censed three times, as the priest says: "Hail to thee, Mary, the fair dove, which hath borne for us God the Word. We give thee salutation with the Angel Gabriel, saying, Hail, thou that art full of grace; the Lord is with thee.

"Hail to thee, O Virgin, the very and true Queen; hail, glory of our race. Thou hast borne for us Emmanuel.

"We pray thee, remember us, O thou our faithful advocate with our Lord Jesus Christ, that he may forgive us our sins."

He censes the other pictures once each, and then the priests. When the priest censes the choir, he says: "The blessing of our teachers (lords and fathers) the apostles, of our father Peter and our master Paul, and the rest of the disciples; may their holy blessings be upon us. Amen."

He leaves the choir, and goes throughout the church censing the congregation, as he says: "Jesus Christ, the same yesterday, to-day, and for ever, in one person,—let us worship him, let us glorify him."

This he repeats again and again, while he is outside the choir.

The priest returns to the altar, where he offers incense "on behalf of the people," saying inaudibly: "God, who received the confession of the thief upon the honourable cross, receive the confession of thy people, and forgive all their sins, for the sake of thy holy name which hath been called upon us. According unto thy mercy, O Lord, and not according unto our sins." [260]

During these processions and censings, the choir sings: "Blessed in truth art thou, with thy good Father, and the Holy Ghost; thou hast come; thou hast saved us: and have mercy upon us."

The lesson from the Acts is thus prefaced: "Acts of our Fathers the Apostles: their holy blessings be with us," and

---

[260] The priest sometimes goes and sits down till after the trisagion.

concluded: "The word of the Lord shall endure, and shall be multiplied, and shall wax mighty, and shall be confirmed in the holy Church of God. Amen."

The trisagion [261] is sung three times by the priest and people alternately, but the Catholics [262] have omitted the insertions, as well as the doxology and the repetition of the invocation: "have mercy on us."

The translation in the Catholic liturgy given by Fr. Muij-ser [263]: "Holy God, holy Mighty, holy Immortal, have mercy on us. Glory be to the Father, etc."

The synod of Alexandria (1898), following the regulation of the Syrian synod of Sharfeh (1888), prohibited any additions to the trisagion, as it considered that the insertions served to promote the heresy of physical Theopaschism, [264] although they had been for long recited in an orthodox sense.

The Monophysites have a form of the trisagion peculiar to Egypt, with the following interpolations: "who wast born of the Virgin;" "who wast crucified for us;" "who didst rise from the dead and ascend to the heavens."

Coptic commentators [265] rarely mention the singing of the trisagion, and there appears to be no document that throws light on its history in the Egyptian rites.

In Eastertide, the *agios* is preceded by a procession, accompanied by cross and candles, and an icon of the risen Christ.

At the conclusion of the trisagion, the priest blesses the people with the hand-cross: "Peace be with you," and the deacon responds: "And with thy spirit."

[261] Arabic, *ajūs althalathah.*

[262] HANSSENS, *op. cit.,* t. II , part. I, p. 394.

[263] *Op. cit.,* p. 27.

[264] Theologians to-day tend to consider that the accusations were without foundation.

[265] HANSSENS, *op. cit.,* t. III, part II, p. 151.

Then, taking the censer and giving the cross to the deacon, the priest chants the prayer before the gospel: "O Lord and Master, Jesus Christ our God, who hath spoken unto his saintly disciples and holy apostles, saying: 'many prophets and righteous men have desired to see the things which ye see, and have not seen them, and to hear the things which ye hear, and have not heard them, but blessed are your eyes, for they see, and your ears, for they hear. May we be made worthy to hear and to do (what is written in) thy holy gospels, through the prayers of thy saints.'"

(Deacon) "Pray concerning the holy gospel."

(People) "Lord have mercy."

(Priest continues) "And remember also, O Lord, all those who have bidden us to remember them in our prayers and supplications which we offer up unto thee, O Lord our God. Give rest to those who have fallen on sleep before (us): heal those that are sick. For indeed thou art the life of us all, and the salvation of us all, and the hope of us all, and the healing of us all, and the resurrection of us all. And unto thee we ascribe the glory and the honour and the worship, with thy good Father and the Holy Ghost, the life-giver, who is of one substance with thee: now and ever and unto ages of all ages. Amen."

The deacon now recites a variable verse from the psalms, and says: "From the psalms of David, the singer and prophet, his blessing be with us. Amen," and, at the conclusion, psalm CXVI with "Alleluia." At a solemn liturgy, the priest censes the book of the gospels, [266] as he says inaudibly: "Worship the gospel of Jesus Christ. O Lord pour on us through the intercession of the prophet and singer David, forgive us our sins."

---

[266] Bute (*op. cit.*, p. 76) says that the altar is first censed.

Then, going up to the altar, the priest again puts on incense and, accompanied by the deacon who carries the open book of the gospels, he processes three times round the altar, censing the book. During the procession, the priest says secretly the Song of Simeon, [267] while the people sing: "Let me with respect listen to thy mercies, for I place my hope in thee. Let me see thy way, so that I may walk in it, for upon thee, O Lord, have I put my hope. God be merciful unto us and bless us and make his face to shine upon us and be gracious unto us."

This "little entrance" recalls the spreading of the gospel throughout the world; while the placing of the book on the altar before the reading of the lesson signifies that "the words which shall be read out of it have gone forth from the mouth of Jesus Christ."

The deacon now gives the warning: "Stand ye with fear of God. Let us hear the holy gospel," but its repetition [268] in Arabic immediately before the gospel is omitted in the Catholic rite, as also is the formula [269] after the lesson: "Glory be unto our God unto the ages of all ages. Amen," and the singing of "an hundred years" by the people.

The priest and deacon, after the diaconal monition, leave the sanctuary, and the priest censes the book, as he again says: "Worship the gospel of Jesus Christ, the Son of the living God; the glory be unto him for ever."

Then he takes the book, and gives it to the other priests to kiss, saying "Worship the gospel" etc. The celebrant kisses the book himself.

Censing the gospel-book, the priest chants: "Blessed is he that cometh in the name of the Lord."

[267] St. Luke II, 29-32.
[268] BUTE, op. cit., p. 77.
[269] Ibid., p. 78.

The deacon responds: "Bless, O Lord, the reading from the holy gospel according to N.," and the people say: "Glory be to thee, O Lord."

Priest (at a solemn liturgy): "The Lord and God and Saviour and King of us all, Jesus Christ, the Son of the living God; unto him be the glory for ever."

At the beginning [270] of the lesson, the celebrant again turns to his assistants and censes them, as he recites appropriate formulas.

The gospel [271] is sung by the senior officiant, although there is little doubt that it was at one time recited by the deacon. [272]

The gospel is sung facing the people, and even at a "low Mass" [273] an assistant holds a lighted candle.

It is customary for the men to wear the tarbush during the liturgy, but it is removed at the gospel and consecration.

The Arabic gospel is recited from the doorway of the screen, but the Catholic rite [274] makes no mention of the recitation in two languages.

The author of the *Lamp* says that the deacon reads the gospel facing east, the priest standing with the censer at the

---

[270] HANSSENS, *op. cit.*, chap. X, p. 394.

[271] Coptic, *evangelion* ($\epsilon\dot{\upsilon}\alpha\gamma\gamma\acute{\epsilon}\lambda\iota o\nu$); Arabic, *anjîl*.

[272] RENAUDOT (*op. cit.*, t. I, p. 7) says: "*dat autem Evangelium legendum Diacono, si probe illud legere sciat, sin minus, leget illud ipse Sacerdos.*"

[273] At a "low Mass," the gospel is read from the footpace of the altar.

[274] "*Nulla est mentio binae singularum lectionum recitationis.*" HANSSENS, *op. cit.*, p. 395.

The reading of the gospel in the Monophysite church is thus described by Butler (*op. cit.*, vol. II chap. VII, p. 286): an assistant priest sings the gospel in Coptic facing east, while the celebrant stands in front of him, censing the book continually. A deacon with a lighted taper stands on either side, and a candle burns also by the side of the lectern.

corner of the altar or near the veil of the sanctuary; while the patriarch or bishop recites it facing west at the door of the sanctuary. The same directory prohibits the kissing of the gospel-book on Maundy Thursday and Holy Saturday; while on the first of these days the lessons from the catholic epistle and the Acts are omitted.

"After the reading of the gospel," says a rubric in the Monophysite missal (1902), "the priest will hold the gospel-book on his arms, and the priests according to their dignity will draw near to kiss it."

The priest, at the conclusion of the gospel, blesses the people with the book.

Then the prayer [275] after the gospel is said: "O thou that art long-suffering, abundant in mercy and true. Receive our prayers and supplications, receive our petitions and repentance and confession upon thy holy stainless altar in heaven; may we be made worthy to hear thy holy gospels, and may we keep thy precepts and commandments, and bring forth fruit therein, a hundred-fold and sixty-fold and thirty-fold. Remember, O Lord, such of thy people as are sick; thou hast visited them in mercy and pity; do thou heal them. Remember, O Lord, our fathers and brethren who are journeying; do thou bring them back to their homes in peace and safety.

(At the time of sowing) Remember, O Lord, the sowings, the herbs and the plants of the fields, may they grow and multiply.

(At the time of harvest) Remember, O Lord, the atmospheric changes of the air and the fruits of the earth; do thou bless them.

---

[275] HANSSENS, *op. cit*, p. 395. Bute (*op. cit.*, p. 79-80), n. 2) gives the prayer, but says that he was assured that this prayer and that of the veil were never said.

(At the time of the rising of the Nile) Remember, O Lord, the waters of the river; bless them, bring them up to their right measure.

Remember, O Lord, the safety of men and beasts; do thou save them all. Remember, O Lord, the safety of this thine holy place, and of all places; do thou save them from all evil.

Remember, O Lord, the Christ-loving (*sic*) servant, the king of our land; do thou keep him in peace, and truth and power. Remember, O Lord, those who are in bondage; do thou save them all. Remember, O Lord, those who suffer under afflictions and necessities; do thou save them from all their sufferings. Remember, O Lord, our fathers and our brethren who have fallen on sleep, who have gone to rest in the orthodox faith; do thou give rest to all their souls.

Remember, O Lord, those who have brought unto thee these gifts, and them for whom they have been brought, and them by whom they have been brought; do thou give unto them all the recompense from the heavens. Remember, O Lord, the catechumens; do thou have mercy upon them; do thou strengthen them in faith in thy name; do thou take from their hearts all trace of idolatry; do thou strengthen in their hearts thy law, thy fear, thy precepts, thy truths, thy holy commandments; do thou grant unto them a firm knowledge of the words where in they are instructed; and at the appointed time may they be worthy of the washing of the new birth for the remission of their sins. Do thou prepare them for a temple of thine Holy Spirit." [276]

---

[276] BRIGHTMAN (*op. cit.*, p. 158) and BUTE (*op. cit.*, p. 80, both give a doxological ending.

The Liturgy of the Faithful

The liturgy of the faithful begins with the prayer of the "Iconostasis of St. James," also called the prayer of the veil or the epiclesis.

The second name recalls the rubric of the *Testamentum Domini:* "While he (bishop) offers the oblation the veil of the door should be spread out."

The rubric directs that the priest should say the prayer inaudibly, standing bowed down beside the door of the sanctuary, immediately before entering it for the last time.

"O God, who in thine unspeakable love towards mankind didst send thine only-begotten Son into the world, that he might bring the lost sheep home unto thee. We pray thee, O King, thrust us not behind (thee; when) we offer this awful and unbloody sacrifice. For we put no trust in our righteousness, but in thy mercy, whereby thou hast given life unto our race. We pray and entreat thy goodness, O thou lover of men, that this mystery which thou hast appointed unto us for salvation may not be for condemnation unto us or unto any of thy people, but unto the washing away of our sins and the forgiveness of our negligences, and unto the glory and honour of thy holy name, O Father, Son and Holy Ghost, now and ever and unto the ages of all ages. Amen."

The people (choir) now sing: "Blessed be the Father and the Son and the Holy Ghost; the perfect Trinity, we worship him, we glorify him."

Then the priest kisses the threshold of the sanctuary and the altar, and, half turning to the faithful, gives them a blessing: "The Lord [277] be with you," to which the people respond: "And with thy spirit."

---

[277] Bute (*op. cit.*, p. 80): " Peace be unto all."

The Greek litanies, which follow in the rite of the dissidents, are omitted in the Catholic [278] liturgy, together with "Lord have mercy" after the subsequent commemoration of the pope. [279]

The prayer of St. Mark for the peace of the Church, the first of the "three great prayers" ($\alpha\acute{i}\gamma'$), is said in the following form: "(Priest) 'Again let us pray to God Almighty, the Father of our Lord and God and Saviour Jesus Christ. We pray and beseech thy goodness, O thou lover of men, remember the peace of the one, only, holy, Catholic Apostolic Church of God."

(Deacon) "Pray for the peace of the one, only, Catholic Apostolic Church of God."

(People) "Have mercy upon us."

(Priest) "This peace extends from one end of the world to the other. All nations and every field do thou bless them. Grant unto all our hearts the peace which is from heaven, but give also the peace of this life. Adorn with thy grace the king, the armies, the rulers, the counsellors, the people, our neighbours, our coming in, and our going out. Adorn them all with peace, O King of peace, grant us thy peace. For thou hast given us all things. Possess us unto thyself, O God, for we know no other save thee. We call upon thine holy name. May our souls live by thy Holy Spirit, and let not the death of sin get the dominion over thy servants, nor over any of thy people."

(People) "Lord have mercy."

Prayer is now said for the "spiritual shepherds," pope, patriarch, bishop and priests:

(Priest) "Again let us pray to God Almighty, the Father

---

[278] HANSSENS, *op. cit.*, chap. X, p. 395.
[279] In the Catholic liturgy, the pope is named before the patriarch.

of our Lord and God and Saviour Jesus Christ. We pray and beseech thy goodness, O thou lover of men. Lord, remember our most holy Father, the high priest, Pope N., and our very reverend father the Patriarch, head of the bishops, Amba N., and his assistant in spiritual functions Bishop Amba N."

(Deacon) "Pray for the high priest Pope N., and the first of our priests, the father and patriarch Amba N., the head of the bishops of the great city of Alexandria, and for our orthodox bishops."

The response of the people: "Lord have mercy on us," although given by Bute [280] and Jacob Muijser, [281] is said by Hanssens [282] to be omitted in the Catholic rite.

(Priest) "Preserve him in safety unto us for many years and peaceful times. Finishing that holy office of the pontificate which thou hast entrusted unto him from thyself, according to thy holy and blessed will. Rightly dividing the word of truth. Ruling thy people in holiness and truth. With all the orthodox bishops and the priests and the deacons, and all the fulness of thy one only Catholic Apostolic Church. Grant unto them and unto us peace and salvation in every place. The prayers which they offer up unto thee for us and for all thy people do thou receive, and also ours for them. (he puts incense into the censer, holding the thurible in his right hand). Receive them upon thy reasonable altar in heaven for a sweet savour of incense. And all their enemies visible and invisible do thou crush speedily and bring down under their feet. But them do thou preserve in thy holy church, in peace and righteousness."

"Lord have mercy on us," answered by the people, is

[280] *Op. cit.*, p. 83.
[281] *Het Heilig Offer in den Koptischen Ritus*, p. 33, 1928.
[282] *Op. cit.*, chap. X, p. 395.

not said in the Catholic rite, [283] neither is the commemoration "of those who have offered," with all the subsequent prayers and a further *kyrie*.

It would seem, however, that they are recited in the Morning Office of Incense, when the liturgy is to follow. Here, the priest immediately says the prayer for the congregation, called the prayer of St Mark: "Again let us pray to God Almighty, the Father of our Lord and God and Saviour Jesus Christ. We pray and beseech thy goodness, O thou lover of men. Lord, remember our congregations. Bless † them."

(Deacon) "Pray for this holy church and for our congregations." The *kyrie* of the people is again omitted in the Catholic rite.

(Priest) "Grant, O Lord, that they be unto us without trouble or hindrance that we may hold them according to thy holy and blessed will." (the priest three times censes the altar and the oblations.) "A house of prayer" (he stretches his hand over the altar eastward, holding the veil).

"A house of holiness" (he stretches his hands westward).

"And a house of blessing" (he stretches his hands northward).

"Grant them unto us, O Lord, and the same unto thy servants who shall be after us for ever" (he stretches his hands southward, making the sign of the cross).

The celebrant, turning to the east, incenses the priests, as he says: "Arise, O Lord, let all thine enemies be scattered. Let all that hate thy holy name flee before thy face."

Then, turning to the west, he incenses the people: "But let thy people be blessed a thousand-thousand fold and ten-thousand-ten-thousand fold, may they all do thy will.

---

[283] HANSSENS, *Ibid.*

Through the grace and mercies and love towards men of thine only-begotten Son, our Lord and God and Saviour Jesus Christ (he offers incense [284] thrice towards the altar). Through whom are due unto thee, with himself and the Holy Ghost, the life-giver, (who is) of one substance with thee, glory and honour and power and worship, now and ever and to the ages of all ages. Amen."

Before the recitation of the creed, the deacon says in Greek: "In the wisdom of God let us attend. In righteousness," but the threefold *kyrie* and also the monition of the priest ("In truth") are omitted in the Catholic rite.

The creed, which has the conciliar "we," is repeated in Arabic by the people with uplifted hands, and in honour of the Egyptian martyrs the two final clauses are chanted.

The *filioque* has been inserted by the Catholics; while the dissidents also omit "God of God."

The whole creed, according to the *Lamp,* is not recited on either the Thursday of Alliance (Maundy Thursday) or the Saturday of Joy (Holy Saturday). On the second of these days, a pause after the words "and was buried" is enjoined.

The priest in the Catholic rite now washes his hands in silence, but the Monophysite priest says: "Wash me; I shall be whiter than snow. Make me to hear of joy and gladness; the bones that are broken will rejoice. I will wash mine hands in innocency, and I will go round about thine altar, O Lord, that I may hear the sound of praise."

Then, making the sign of the cross over the people, he says: "Peace be unto all," and the people respond: "And with thy spirit."

[284] BUTE, *op. cit.,* p. 88.

The two hymns sung at the kiss of peace by the people are recited in the Catholic rite by the deacon.

One of these hymns is as follows: "Come unto us to-day, O Christ the King, enlighten us through thy supreme Godhead. Send down upon us the abundant graces of thine Holy Spirit the Comforter."

The priest says the prayer of the kiss, called of St. Basil: "O great and everlasting God, who didst create man in incorruption, and by the life-giving manifestation of thine only-begotten Son our Lord and God and Saviour Jesus Christ, didst destroy that death which by the envy of the devil hath entered into the world. And hast filled the whole world with peace from heaven. For which the host of angels doth glorify thee, saying, glory to God in the highest, and peace on earth, and good will towards men."

Two further prayers are recited by the Catholic celebrant, one of which, known as the prayer of St. James, is found in the Syrian liturgy: "O God of all and Lord, account these our unworthy selves worthy of this salvation, O thou lover of men, that pure of all guile and all hypocrisy we may greet one another with a kiss holy and divine, being united with the bond of love and peace: through our Lord God and Saviour Jesus Christ thine only Son our Lord, through whom and with whom to thee is fitting glory and honour and dominion with thy Spirit all-holy and good and adorable and life-giving and consubstantial with thee now and ever and world without end."

The deacon says: "Pray for perfect peace and love and the holy kisses of the apostles," to which he adds [285] "Lord have mercy upon us."

Then the priest continues: "In thy good will, O God,

---

[285] HANSSENS, *op. cit.*, p. 395.

fill our hearts with thy peace. And cleanse us from every stain and every guile and every hypocrisy and every iniquity. And the remembrance of injuries, which bringeth death. Make us all meet, O King, to greet one another with a holy kiss that we may share therein without reprobation unto judgment from thine immortal and heavenly gift through Christ Jesus our Lord."

The priest embraces the deacon, and the kiss [286] of peace is passed among the people by touching each other's hands, and then kissing their own.

In the time of the *Lamp*, however, it was the custom for the men to embrace the men and the women the women.

The alternative hymn, recited by the deacon, is as follows: "Greet one another with a holy kiss, purify your hearts from all evil and be ready to receive the gift of God, in order to participate in the mysteries and the forgiveness of sins and thereby obtain the mercy according to his immense mercifulness."

The deacon then continues: "We worship thee, O Christ, with thy holy Father and the Holy Ghost, for thou hast come to redeem us. Lord, have mercy; Lord, have mercy; Lord, have mercy; have mercy upon us. O Jesus Christ, Son of God, hear us and have mercy upon us."

Anaphora

Here begins the anaphora of St. Basil.

The priest, uncovering the oblations, slowly waves the great veil above his head, and then places it on the right side of the altar.

In the meanwhile, the deacon says: "Offer, offer, offer

---

[286] Coptic, *aspasmos* (ἀσπασμός); Arabic, *ṣulḥ*.

in order, stand ye with trembling, look eastward. Let us attend; (it is) a mercy of peace, a sacrifice of praise."

The people respond: "A mercy of peace, a sacrifice of praise."

Then, turning to the people, the priest blesses them with the chalice veil: "The Lord † be with you all," to which the response is given: "And with thy spirit."

It may be noted that this Pauline [287] salutation is found in the *Apostolic Canons* and the *Testament of the Lord*, but not in the Jerusalem, Antiochene and Byzantine rites, as James of Edessa in the Commentary on the Liturgy of St. James has pointed out.

The priest now turns to the assistants and blesses them: "Lift † up your hearts;" and the people answer: "Let us have them (lifted up) unto the Lord."

He blesses the people: "Let us give thanks † unto the Lord," receiving the reply: "It is meet and right."

The ritual of the patriarch Gabriel II (1131-1146) enjoins the celebrant at "Lift up your hearts" to sign himself, the deacons, the assistants and the people.

The priest continues: "Meet and right, meet and right, meet and right, for verily it is just, meet and right. Who is the Lord, the Lord God of righteousness. Who is before the worlds, and is King for ever. Who is in the highest, and who beholdeth the things that are lowly, who hath created the heaven and the earth and the sea, and all things that are in them. Father of our Lord and God and Saviour Jesus Christ. Who hast created all things by him, the things which are seen and the things which are not seen. Who sitteth upon the throne of his glory. Whom all the holy powers do worship."

[287] II. Thess., III, 16.

The deacon then gives the monition: [288] "Ye that be sitting, arise," and the priest says: "Around whom do stand the angels and the archangels, principalities, powers, thrones, dominations and mights."

Again the celebrant is interrupted by a diaconal monition: "Look eastward," and then he continues: "For round about thee do stand the cherubim full of eyes, and the seraphim with six wings. They sing without ceasing, with unfailing voices, and they cry unto thee."

A responsary, of which there are five in the missal, is now generally sung by the people, but, as Fr. Hanssens [289] says, the celebrant seems to take no part in it.

The most usual form is as follows: "Rejoice, O thou heaven; shout aloud, O earth. The cherubim have spread their wings. They cry aloud three times, according to the type of the Trinity."

The deacon says: "Come near this table, O God, saying to thee with the angels and archangels: Holy, holy, holy is the Lord. Alleluia. Glory be to the Father and to the Son and to the Holy Ghost. Both now and ever and unto the ages of the ages. Amen."

The people respond: "The cherubim worship him and the seraphim glorify him and hosts rejoice with threefold praise. The cherubim and seraphim shout aloud, they cry, saying: Holy, holy, holy is the Lord of Sabaoth, heaven and earth are full of thy holy glory."

Then the priest, taking the hand-cross and the chalice veil, [290] blesses himself, the assistants and the people, as he says a prayer after the form of a Gallican *vere sanctus*.

---

[288] Coptic, *prosfonêsis*; Greek, προσφώνησις.

[289] *Op. cit.*, p. 396.

[290] Butler (*op. cit.*, vol. II, p. 288) says: "Now the lesser veil or red *ṭabak* is removed from the chalice; and the priest, taking it in his

The fall and redemption of man are reviewed, while
the atoning work of our Lord is a paraphrase of the creed:

"Holy, holy, holy, of a truth, is the Lord our God, who
formed us and created us and placed us in the garden of
delight. When we broke thy commandment through the
guile of the devil, we fell from eternal life, and were cast
forth out of the garden of delight. Thou didst not leave
us for ever, but didst visit us continually by thy holy
prophets. And in the end of days, when we were sitting
in darkness and in the shadow of death, thou hast enlightened us, through thine only-begotten Son, our Lord
and God and Saviour Jesus Christ, who of the Holy Ghost
and of the Virgin Mary (People: "Amen") took flesh and
was made man, and taught us the paths of salvation. He
gave unto us the grace of the birth from on high, of water
and spirit. He made us unto himself a people united. He
sanctified us by thine Holy Spirit. He loved his own who
are in the world, he gave himself up for our salvation unto
the death which reigned over us, whereby we were bound
on account of our sins. He descended into hell from the
cross (People: "Amen, I believe"). He rose again from the
dead upon the third day. He ascended up into the heavens:
he sat down at thy right hand, O Father. He hath appointed
a day of retribution wherein he will appear to judge the
world in righteousness. And he will give unto every man
according to his works" (People: "According to thy mercy,
O Lord, and not according to our sins").

The censer is now held for him by the deacon, and the

right hand, holds also the green *tabak* in his left, and raises his arms.
And in like manner he takes many more little mats, which are upon the
altar, and holds them with outspread arms, during the commemoration
of the redemption."

priest, putting incense into it, hold his hands for some moments in the smoke, as he says: [291] "And he hath instituted for us this great mystery of godliness."

During the consecration at a solemn liturgy, lights are held and the censer is swung, but there does not seem to be any bell.

The Copts only tardily and under anti-catholic Greek influence concerned themselves with the moment when the transubstantiation operates.

The multiplicity [292] of epicleses in the Egyptian liturgies so far from contradicting the Catholic doctrine on the form of the sacrament rather supports it.

The patriarch Matthew IV (1660-1675) sent to the French ambassador at Constantinople a profession of faith in which he said: "Jesus Christ makes his body by his word in saying by the mouth of the priest: This is my body."

On Holy Thursday, also, the Copts read the homily of St John Chrysostom on the treason of Judas, in which the great doctor explicitly attributes the consecration to the words of Christ.

Now, however, the dissidents are at pains to assert that the change is effected by the epiclesis *after* the words of institution.

The priest, extending his hands over the oblations, says: "For when he was determined to give himself up to death for the life of the world" (People: "We believe, we believe, that it is so indeed. Amen").

Then, taking the bread into his hands, he continues in

---

[291] Cf. *Apostolic Constitutions*, VIII, 12: "This mystery of the New Testament; take eat" etc.; Gallican rite: "This is the chalice of my blood, the mystery of faith, which is shed for the remission of sins."

[292] ARNAULD, *Perpétuité de la foi touchant l'eucharistie.* Edit. Migne, t. II, col. 1265.

a loud voice: "He took bread into his holy, spotless, pure, blessed and life-giving hands."

Again the people express their faith in the real presence: "I believe. It is so indeed. We believe [293] and we confess and we glorify."

Looking up to heaven, he proceeds: "He looked up to heaven, to thee, O God, who art his Father, and Lord of all," and, holding the bread in his left hand, he says: "He †gave thanks" (People: "Amen"). "He † blessed it" (People: "Amen"). "He † sanctified it" (People in Greek: "Amen"; and then: "Amen, amen, amen. We believe and we confess and we glorify").

The priest then breaks the bread into three parts, but without separating them, as he says: "He break it, and gave it to his saintly disciples and holy apostles, saying: Take, eat ye all of it. For this is my body, which shall be broken for you, and for many, to be given for the remission of sins (he places the host on the paten, and genuflects, [294] but without any elevation). Do this in remembrance of me." (People: "We believe thus is it indeed. Amen").

After this, the Catholic celebrant holds his thumbs and forefingers joined, except when he has to touch the host, until after the ablutions.

Uncovering the chalice, the priest touches the lip of it with the joined thumb and forefinger of his right hand, saying: "In like manner also after supper he mingled the cup with wine and water. "He † gave thanks" (People: "Amen"). "He † blessed it" (People: "Amen"). "He † sanctified it" (People in Greek: "Amen"; and then: "Amen,

---

[293] This conclusion is said only by the Catholics. HANSSENS, op. cit., p. 396.
[294] The dissidents make a profound bow.

amen, amen. Again we believe and we confess and we glorify").

A second time, the priest touches the lip of the chalice, and says: "He tasted, [295] he gave it also to his saintly disciples and holy apostles, saying (he moves the chalice in form of a cross): Take, drink ye all of it. For this is my blood of the New Testament, which shall be shed for you and for many, to be given for the remission of sins. Do this in remembrance of me" (he covers the chalice, and genuflects).

The people again affirm their belief: "Amen. Thus we believe it indeed to be. Amen."

With these repeated affirmations on the part of the faithful, it is difficult to understand how the Copts can deny that the change in the elements takes place at the recital of the words of institution.

The *Lamp* is very explicit in associating the deacon with the chalice, forbidding anyone who has not used the censer and assisted in the liturgy to touch it; while a canon of the patriarch Gabriel II (1131-1146) said that priests have no need to raise the chalice, since this is the especial duty of deacons.

Pointing to the sacred host, the priest says: "For as often as ye eat of this bread (and pointing to the chalice) and drink of this cup, ye do show forth my death, ye do confess my resurrection, ye do make memorial of me until I come."

The deacon [296] responds: "Amen, amen, amen. We show forth thy death, O Lord, and we confess thine holy resurrection and ascension. We praise thee; we bless thee;

---

[295] Cf. St. John Chrysostom, *Homil.* LXXXII; Syrian Liturgy of the Twelve Apostles. RENAUDOT, *op. cit.*, t. II, p. 171.

[296] Bute (*op. cit.*, p. 102) says " people."

we give thee thanks, O Lord, and entreat of thee, O our God."

The priest in the meanwhile continues the anamnesis silently: "We make memorial of his holy passion, and of his resurrection from the dead, and of his ascension into the heavens, and of his session at thy right hand, O Father. And of his second coming which shall be from heaven, terrible and full of glory. We offer unto thee these thy gifts of thy gifts. (he concludes aloud) Of all, and for all, and in all."

The deacon then says: "Worship God in fear and trembling," and the people answer: "We praise thee; we bless thee; we serve thee; we worship thee."

Lifting up his hands and leaning over the altar, the priest inaudibly begins the epiclesis: [297] "And we beseech thee, O Christ our God, [298] we, thy sinful and unworthy servants, and worship thee, by the pleasure of thy goodness, that thine Holy Spirit may come upon us and upon these gifts here present, and may purify them unto us, (he continues aloud) and may make them manifest as a sanctification of thy saints."

The deacon gives the monition: "Let us attend. Amen," and the people rise to their feet.

Then the priest thrice makes the sign of the cross over the host, saying: "And make this † bread the holy body (People: "I believe") of our Lord † and God and Saviour Jesus Christ. It is given for the remission of sins † and eternal life unto them who shall take thereof, even of our Lord and God and Saviour Jesus Christ" (People: "Amen").

Thrice, also, he signs the chalice, as he says: "And this

[297] Coptic epiklēsis (ἐπίκλησις); Arabic, sirr ḥalūl ilrūḥ al ḳuds.
[298] It may be noted that the prayer is not addressed to the third person of the Holy Trinity.

cup † the glorious blood of the New Testament (Deacon: [299] "I believe") of our Lord † and God and Saviour Jesus Christ. It is given for the remission † of sins and eternal life unto them who shall take thereof (Deacon: [300] "Amen. O Lord have mercy upon us"). Make us all worthy, O our master, to take of thy holy body and blood unto the sanctification of our souls and our bodies and our spirits, that we may be one body and one spirit, and have part and lot with all the saints who have ever pleased thee. [301] Remember, O Lord, thine one, only, holy, Catholic and Apostolic Church."

The deacon repeats the intercession in the form of a bidding: "Pray for the one, only, Catholic, Orthodox and Apostolic Church." People: "Lord, have mercy upon us."

The priest continues with a prayer for the hierarchy: "This Church which thou hast purchased unto thyself with the glorious blood of thy Christ. Keep her in peace, with all the orthodox bishops who are in her. And first remember, O Lord, the Supreme Pontiff, Pope N.; and our reverend and blessed father, the head of the bishops, the Patriarch N.; and his assistant in spiritual matters, Amba N.

The people, [302] joining in the petition, say: "Pray for our Supreme Pontiff, Pope N.; and the first of our priests and father, the Patriarch Amba N., the head of the bishops of the great city of Alexandria; and our other orthodox bishops."

Deacon: [303] "Lord, have mercy upon us."

---

[299] Bute (*op. cit.*, p. 105), "People."

[300] Bute (*op. cit.*, p. 106), "People: Amen. Lord have mercy" (three times).

[301] It would seem that the epiclesis is modelled upon the Byzantine liturgy of St. Basil.

[302] Bute (*Ibid.*, p. 107), "Deacon."

[303] Bute (*Ibid.*), "People."

The priest continues: "And them that with them rightly divide the bread [304] of truth. Grant them (long) unto thine holy Church, that they may feed thy flock in peace. Remember, O Lord, the abbots and the orthodox priests and deacons."

People: [305] "Pray for the priests and deacons and subdeacons, and for the seven orders in the Church of God."

Deacon: [306] "O God the Father Almighty, have mercy upon us."

Priest: " And all ministers, and all thy faithful people that are in virginity and holiness. Lord, in thy mercy, remember us all."

At a solemn liturgy, a short litany [306] for the ills and needs of the church is now said by the priest, and to each petition the people respond: "Lord, have mercy upon us."

"We beg thee, O Christ our God."

"Strengthen the foundations of the Church."

"Plant the one true charity in our hearts."

"Spread the true faith."

"Make even for us the way of godliness."

"Guide the pastors in the right way and strengthen their flocks in the faith."

"Give splendour to the clergy."

"Give recollection to the religious."

"Give purity to the virgins."

"Give a happy life to the married people."

"Give mercy to the penitents."

"Give generosity to the rich."

"Give humility to the virtuous."

"Give help to the poor."

---

[304] "Word," BUTE, op. cit., p. 107.
[305] Bute (p. 108) reverses people and deacon.
[306] Not in Bute.

"Strengthen the old in days and stand by the young."

"For the unbelievers in thee."

"Make the disunion of Christians to cease."

"Drive away the pride of the teachers of error."

"And reckon us all in the number of the godly of thy one true Church."

The intercession then continues: "Remember, O Lord, the safety of this thine holy place, and of all places of our orthodox fathers."

The people [307] respond: "Pray for the safety of the world, and of this city, and of all cities, and lands, and islands, and monasteries," and the deacon says: "Have mercy on us."

The priest continues: "And them who dwell in them in the faith of God."

Fr. Hanssens [308] says that the prayers for the atmospheric changes are omitted in the Catholic rite, but Fr. Muijser [309] gives the following prayers as said to-day in that liturgy.

a) Prayer for the time of sowing, from 11 *Babeh* (October) to 11 *Tubeh* (January):

Priest: "Bless, O God, the seed, the herbs and the plants of the fields this year."

Deacon: "Ask that the seeds, the herbs and the plants of the fields be blessed this year by our Lord Jesus Christ, so that they grow, multiply and bear much fruit, and that he may have mercy on the creation of his hands and forgive us our sins."

People: "Lord, have mercy upon us."

---

[307] Bute (p. 108) reverses people and deacon.

[308] *Op. cit.*, p. 396.

[309] *Op. cit.*, pp. 44-45.

b) Prayer for the fruits of the earth, from 12 *Tubeh* (January) to 11 *Baounah* (June):

Priest: "O Lord, be graciously pleased to give us this year the atmospheric changes of the air and the fruits of the earth; do thou bless them."

Deacon: "Pray for the atmospheric changes of the air, and for the fruits of the earth, and for the trees and the vineyards, [310] and for every fruitful tree in all the world. That Christ our God will bless them, and bring them to perfection in peace without hardship, and will forgive us our sins."

People: "Lord, have mercy upon us."

c) Prayer for the waters of the Nile, from 12 *Baounah* (June) to 11 *Babeh* (October):

Priest: "Bless, O Lord, this year the waters of the rivers."

Deacon: "Ask that the rise of the waters be blessed by Christ, our God, and make them rise considerably, so as to beautify the face of the earth; give nourishment to us, thy people, and ensure the well-being of the cattle, and forgive us our sins."

People: "Lord, have mercy upon us."

The concluding prayer in this section of the liturgy is a prayer for the gifts of nature: "Bring them up according to their measure, according to thy goodness. Make thou the face of the earth to rejoice, let her furrows overflow, and her fruits be abundantly multiplied. Make ready her seed-time and harvest, and govern our life as is best for us. Bless the crown of the year with thy goodness. For the sake of the poor of thy people, for the sake of the widow,

[310] Vineyards have not been cultivated in Egypt since the 10th century.

and the orphan, and the stranger, and the wanderer, and for the sake of us all, who hope in thee, and who entreat thy holy name. Behold the eyes of us all hope in thee, that thou wilt give them their meat in its good season. Deal with us after thy goodness, O thou who givest meat unto all flesh. Fill our hearts with joy and gladness. That we may have sufficiency in all things at all times, and that we may have abound in every good thing (People: "Lord, have mercy upon us."). Remember, O Lord, them who have brought these gifts unto thee, and them for whom they have been brought, and them by whom they have been brought. Give unto them all a recompense from the heavens."

Deacon: "Pray over these holy and awful gifts and sacrifices, and them that bring them."

People: "Lord, have mercy upon us."

This is followed by the commemoration of the saints, said by the priest: "Moreover, O Lord, it is a commandment of thine only-begotten Son, that we should take part in the commemoration of thy saints. Be pleased, O Lord, to have in remembrance all the saints who have pleased thee since the beginning of the world. Our holy fathers the patriarchs, prophets, apostles, preachers, evangelists, martyrs, confessors, and all the spirits of the just made perfect in the faith; and chiefly she that is full of glory, that is a virgin unto all time, holy Mary, the holy Mother of God; and the forerunner of Christ, the blessed John the Baptizer; holy Stephen, protodeacon and first martyr; the ecstatic evangelist Mark, the holy apostle and martyr; the holy patriarchs, the equal of the apostles Athanasius, Cyril, Basil and Gregory; our great and good father Amba Antony (the hermit), and the righteous Paul (of Thebes), and Macarius (the priest) and the other Macarius, and of St N., whose feast we keep to-day, and all the choir of the saints. O Lord, have mercy on us all together by their prayers and supplications, and deliver us for the sake of thy holy name which is called upon us."

On great feasts, the priest says an alternative commemoration of the saints, including the names of many Egyptians: "And our fathers the holy patriarchs Dionysius, Maximus, Peter the Martyr, Cyril, Athanasius the equal of the apostles, John Chrysostom, Basil, Gregory the Wonderworker, Gregory the Theologian, Gregory the Armenian, and our great and blessed father Antony, the blessed Amba Paul (of Thebes), our father Amba Macarius (the priest) and Amba Macarius, our father Amba Bischoï the perfect and strong man of God, St. Moses (the Abyssinian), St. Isidore the priest and our father Pachomius, the father of monastic life, and Theodore his pupil, Amba John the Short, and our father Abu Nafar, and Serapion the bishop, Saints Paphnutius and Apsadius and Alynikus, and their children the martyrs, and all the multitude of thy saints."

As a preface to the diptychs [311] of the dead, the deacon says: "Let those who read publish the names of our fathers the patriarchs, who have fallen on sleep, may the Lord give rest to the souls of them all, and forgive us our sins."

The priest continues inaudibly: "Remember also, O Lord, all them who have fallen asleep, who are gone to rest in the priesthood and in every order of the laity. Be graciously pleased to give rest to all their souls in the bosom of our holy fathers Abraham and Isaac and Jacob. Feed them in a green pasture, beside the still waters, in the garden of delight, the place whence soreheartedness and sorrow and sighing have fled away, in the light of thy saints."

[311] Coptic, *diptichon, touptikon;* Arabic, *tarhīm.*

Then, taking the veil [312] that covered the chalice [313] in his right hand, the priest half turns to the people, as he blesses them and says: "God have mercy upon us and bless † us, cause his face to shine upon us, and have mercy upon us. O Lord, save thy people, bless thine inheritance, sustain them, lift them up for ever, exalt the horn of the orthodox Christians through the power of the life-giving cross, and through the blessing of the feast of this day, N., through the prayers and supplications which our Lady, the Lady of us all, the holy Mother of God, holy Mary, doth at all times make for us all, and the prayers and supplications of the three luminous and holy heavenly spirits, Saints Michael and Gabriel and Raphael, and of the four incorporeal living creatures [314] and of the four and twenty elders [315] and of all the choirs of angels and heavenly hosts; and through the pleading of the patriarchs and prophets, apostles, martyrs and bearers of the cross, of holy maidens and all the righteous and just, of the blessed N. (saint of the day), and of the angel of this holy sacrifice and through the blessing of the Mother of God, holy Mary, ever virgin, (if it be a Sunday) and the blessing of the day of the Lord, our good Redeemer. May their blessing † and power and grace and help be with us for ever. Amen. So be it." The blessing is given towards the people with the veil.

[312] Before taking the veil, Bute (*op. cit.*, p. 113) says that the priest " puts incense into the censer, and prays for the dead as he pleases."

[313] Muijser (*op. cit.*, p. 48). Bute (*op. cit.*, p. 113), however, says " the veil, which was on the *paten.*"

Butler (*op. cit.*, vol. II, pp. 289-290) writes: " at the time of the intercession the cover of the elements is changed; and for a saffron-coloured veil with which they were vested before then, another of deep crimson with a white border is substituted."

[314] Ezechiel I, 5-14.

[315] Apocalypse IV, 4.

Deacon: "We commemorate the great Amba Antony (the Hermit) and the blessed Amba Paul (of Thebes) and Amba Macarius and Amba John the Short and Amba Bischoï and Amba Isidore and Amba Pachomius, Amba Paphnutius and all who have rightly taught the words of truth, right-believing bishops, priests, deacons, ministers and lay folk, both these and all orthodox Christians." [316]

People: "Glory to thee, O Lord. *Kyrie eleison* (thrice). Grant them eternal rest. Amen."

Here the priest, in memory of the dead, puts incense [317] into the censer, and says: "Give, O Lord, to the souls thou hast taken, rest in paradise, that place of light, in the heavenly Jerusalem for ever. And we who are still pilgrims here keep in thy faith, giving us thy peace even unto the end and leading us into thy kingdom."

People: "As it was and is and shall be for ever and ever. Amen."

The priest continues: "That as in this, so in all things thy holy name may be glorified, blessed and praised, together with thy beloved Son Jesus Christ and the Holy Spirit. [318] Peace be with you all."

People: "And with thy spirit."

Priest: "Let us again give thanks to Almighty God, Father of our Lord and God and Saviour Jesus Christ. He hath made us worthy now to stand in this holy place, to lift up our hands and minister to his holy name. Let us beseech him to make us worthy even of communion and participation in his divine and everlasting mysteries. Amen."

---

[316] In the Catholic rite, the names of deceased prelates are mentioned here.

[317] Cf. Byzantine rite.

[318] Cf. conclusion of the Roman canon.

This prayer, which is known as the preface of the fraction, is followed by the elevation.

The priest [319] takes the host in his right hand, and says:

"The holy body."

Then, raising it above the chalice, he continues: "and the precious blood of his anointed, the Almighty Lord, our God."

The deacon responds: "Amen, amen. Pray ye," and the people make a profession of faith: [320] "We worship thy holy body and precious blood. *Kyrie, eleison.*" [321]

The priest then says: "Peace be with you," and the people reply "And with thy spirit."

Afterwards the prayer of the fraction [322] follows, and the missal gives a choice of six such prayers, including one added by the Catholics in recent years for feasts of our Lady.

The priest, who recites the prayer aloud, takes the host, [323] breaks off a third part, and from that third a small particle.

He then replaces the whole on the paten.

---

[319] Brightman (*op. cit.*, pp. 180-181) gives the following rubrics for the Monophysite rite: "He shall take the pure body in his left hand, and shall put his right finger upon it, saying ... Then he shall dip his finger in the blood, and make a sign on the blood, saying ... Then he shall sign the body twice with the blood, above and below, saying ... "

[320] Priest and people kneel and adore the blessed sacrament. MUIJSER, *op. cit.*, p. 50.

[321] The Catholic rite omits *Kyrie eleison.* HANSSENS, *op. cit.*, p. 396.

[322] Coptic, *fōsh;* Arabic, *ḳismah.*

[323] Butler (*op. cit.*, vol. II, p. 290) says that the priest breaks the housel into five portions, which he arranges on the paten in the form of a cross, leaving the *isbodikon* unbroken in the centre; and the smaller portions are again broken up into little pieces (" pearls").

The prayer[324] most commonly used is the one given here, which is also much the shortest: "O Lord and master, our God, who giveth light to the world, who hath crowned us with his faith, who giveth unto us before we ask. Grant that we may bring forth acceptable fruits, so that we may confidently say to thee: our Father who art in heaven."

The Lord's prayer[325] is now said in Arabic by the people, with uplifted hands, but in a different form from

[324] The following prayer is said on some feasts: "Behold, Emmanuel, our God, the lamb of God, that taketh away the sin of the whole world, is with us this day upon this table. When he raiseth his voice upon his throne, then all the hosts of heaven stand before him. The angels sing hymns with voices of benediction, the archangels fall down and worship his great and invisible (so called because the proper vowels of the Tetragrammaton are unwritten and unknown) name. The four immaterial living creatures praise him with the song of the thrice-holy. The four-and-twenty elders arise from their thrones —having four-and-twenty crowns of gold upon their heads, having four-and-twenty phials of gold in their hands, filled with the prayers of the saints—they offer them in oblation before him who liveth for ever. The holy hundred-and-forty-four-thousand virgins without spot, who have washed their robes in the blood of the lamb, praise the Lord, saying: Holy, holy, holy, amen alleluia. Holy is God the Father almighty, amen, alleluia. Holy is the only-begotten Son Jesus Christ our Lord, amen, alleluia. Holy is the Holy Ghost the Comforter, amen, alleluia. Holy and full of glory is the holy Mother of God, the holy Virgin Mary, amen, alleluia. Holy and full of glory is this sacrifice, pierced for the life of the whole world, amen, alleluia. Of this our good Saviour hath openly spoken, saying: my body is meat indeed, and my blood is drink indeed; he that eateth my body and drinketh my blood, dwelleth in me and I in him. Grant that with a pure heart and pure lips and enlightened soul and face not ashamed and faith unfeigned and pure conscience and full patience and firm hope, we may dare with boldness without fear to supplicate thee, O our holy Father who art in the heavens, and to say: Our Father who art in heaven."

[325] Thus, the Copts, say: "Give us this day the morrow's bread," which seems to contradict the teaching of our Lord—"Be not therefore solicitous for to-morrow" (St. Matth. VI, 34). The mistake, however, is very ancient, appearing in two translations—Sahidic and Bohairic—of

that recorded by St. Matthew [326] and, as in the Syrian rite, with the addition of the ascription.

In the meanwhile, the priest says silently: "Also we pray thee, O good Father, who lovest goodness, lead us not into temptation, nor let any iniquity get the dominion over us, but deliver us from unseemly deeds and desires, their sight and their feel: curb the tempter and drive him far from us. Rebuke the evil which springs within ourselves, keep far away all which leads us to sin, and deliver us through thine holy power, (aloud as an ekphonesis) [327] through Christ Jesus our Lord."

The prayer of inclination of St. Mark, which is also said inaudibly with an ekphonesis, is preceded by the diaconal monition: [328] "Bow down your heads before the Lord," and the response of the people: "Before thee, O Lord."

"Full and abounding hath been the grace of his goodness to usward, thine only-begotten Son our Lord and God and Saviour Jesus Christ. We have confessed his saving passion, we have told of his death, we have believed in his resurrection, the mystery is accomplished. We give thee thanks, O Lord God Almighty, for that great hath been thy mercy towards us, to prepare for those things whereon the angels desire to gaze. We pray and entreat thy goodness, O thou lover of man, that since thou hast sanctified us, thou wouldest join us unto thyself through the communion of thine holy mysteries, that we may become full of thy Holy Spirit and strong in the right faith, full also of the desire of thy true

the New Testament, as well as in the apocryphal gospel to the Hebrews. Some Greek scholars have seen the cause of the error in reading ἐπουσόν "the bread of to-morrow" for ἐπιούσιον, supersubstantial bread, which nourishes or sustains strength.

[326] St. Matthew VI, II.

[327] Coptic, ōsh ebol; Arabic, yaṣrukh.

[328] Cf. Ordo Romanus VI; Mozarabic rite; rite of Lyons.

love, and may speak of thy glory at all times, (aloud) through Christ Jesus our Lord."

The deacon gives another monition: "Let us wait on God with fear," and the priest gives his blessing: "Peace be with you."

Then, the people having responded: "And with thy spirit," the priest recites inaudibly the prayer of absolution [329] to the Father: "O Lord and Master, Almighty God, healer of our souls and our bodies and our spirits, thou art he who hast spoken unto our father Peter, by the mouth of thine only-begotten Son, our Lord and God and Saviour Jesus Christ, saying: thou art Peter; upon this rock I will build my Church; and the gates of hell shall not prevail against it; and I will give unto thee the keys of the kingdom of heaven; whatsoever thou shalt bind on earth shall be bound in heaven, and whatsoever thou shalt loose on earth shall be loosed in heaven. Therefore, O Lord, let thy servants, my father and my brethren and my own unworthy self, be loosed by my mouth, through thine holy, good and man-loving Spirit. O God, who takest away the sin of the world, be ready to accept the repentance of thy servants for a light of the understanding and forgiveness of sins. For thou art a God, compassionate and merciful; thou art long-suffering; great and true is thy mercy. If we have sinned against thee either by word or by deed, spare us, forgive us, in thy goodness and love to man. O God, absolve us and absolve all thy people."

The dissident priest now takes the little veil in his right hand, and, half turned towards the people, he first com-

---

[329] This prayer is a feature unique to this rite. Cf. absolution to the Son before the censing at the beginning of the liturgy.

memorates the living at will, and then says inaudibly a long
formula: "Remember, O Lord, thy servants" etc.

Catholics, however, only say the prayer annexed to the
formula: "Deliver us and deliver all thy people, from
all sin, and from all curse, and from all denial, and from
every false oath, and from all evil dealing with the heretics
and the heathen. O our Lord,[330] be pleased to grant unto
us a mind and strength and reason, to escape any evil thing
of the enemy, and grant unto us ever to do all such things
as be pleasing to thy holy will. Write our names next to
those of all the saints in heaven (he uncovers the chalice and
continues aloud) in Christ Jesus our Lord."

The deacon then says: "We are saved indeed by thy
spirit. With fear of God let us give heed," and the people
three times respond: *Kyrie, eleison.*

The priest raises the particle of the host (*isbodikon*),
reserved for the communion of the celebrant and assistant
clergy, to the level of his head, as he says in Greek: "This
is the holy thing for the holy," and the people kneel in
adoration.

Then, making a cross with the particle over the chalice,
he continues: "Blessed be the Lord Jesus Christ the Son
of God. He hath hallowed this offering by his Holy Spirit."

The people answer: "Amen. There is one Father, one
Son and one Holy Ghost. Amen."

The priest dips the particle into the chalice, saying:
"Peace be with you." and the people respond: "And with
thy spirit."

The sign of the cross is made with the intincted host[331]

---

[330] Muijser (*op. cit.*, p. 52) begins the prayer here, substituting
"King" for "Lord."

[331] Coptic, *rasam*, "consignation." Bute (*op. cit.*, p. 123) says that
the priest here "touches the rest of the sacred host with the particle."

over the chalice, and the celebrant says in Greek: "This is truly the holy body and the precious blood of Jesus Christ, the Son of God. Amen." (People: "Amen").

A cross also is made with the particle *inside* the chalice, while the priest continues: "This is truly the holy and precious body and blood of Jesus Christ, the Son of God. Amen." (People: "Amen").

Finally, he lets the small particle fall into the chalice, as he says in Greek: "This is truly the body and blood of Emmanuel our God. Amen." (People: "Amen: I believe").

The first part of this magnificent confession of faith in the real presence, which both priest and people make before receiving holy communion, is said in Greek. It is therefore more ancient than that which follows in Coptic. According Renaudot it is made in Greek, Coptic and Arabic.

The later confession [332] of faith, which has given rise to two controversies in the Egyptian church, has been unjustly suspected of Monophysism, but it is said to-day by the Catholics.

The first controversy [333] was brought about by the introduction of the words: "He made it one with his Godhead," which the patriarch Gabriel II ibn Tarik (1132-1145) inserted on the day of his enthronement in the monastery of St. Macarius. The monks protested, and only accepted the expression when there was added: "without mingling, without confusion and without alteration."

The second controversy occurred in the patriarchate of John V (1146-1147), when the monks of the laura of St. Justus qualified the word "body" with the adjective "life-

---

[332] Coptic, *omologia*.
[333] *Dict. de Théol. Cath.*, t. X, col. 2282-2283.

giving." The bishops, however, agreed to retain the interpolation as expressive of the truth.

This confession of faith is as follows: "Amen, amen, amen. I believe, I believe, I believe and confess till my last breath that this is the life-giving body which thine only-begotten Son, our Lord and God and Saviour Jesus Christ (he holds up the paten to the level of his head), took from our Lady, the mistress and queen of all, the holy sinless Virgin Mary, Mother of God. He made it one with his Godhead, without mingling, without confusion and without alteration. He witnessed a good confession before Pontius Pilate. He gave it for us upon the holy tree of the cross by his own will, in very truth for us all. I believe that his divinity was not separated from his manhood for one moment, for the twinkling of an eye. He gave his body for the forgiveness of our sins, and for eternal life to them that partake of it. I believe, I believe, I believe that this is in very truth that body."

The deacon (people) now says: "Amen, amen, amen. I believe, I believe, I believe that this is it in very deed. Amen. Pray for us and for all Christians who have bidden us to remember them. Peace and the love of God [334] be with you. Sing!"

In the meanwhile, the priest moves the paten crosswise and replaces it on the altar, thrice kissing the holy table, and saying inaudibly: "All glory and all honour and all worship are eternally due unto the Holy Trinity, Father and Son and Holy Ghost, now and ever and unto the ages of all ages. Amen."

Then the deacon, accompanied by the singer who plays

[334] Bute (*op. cit.*, p. 125) gives: "Jesus Christ."

on the cymbals, chants psalm CL, with "Alleluia"[335] as an antiphon.

On some days of the year a hymn is sung, and in Lent the following is chanted: "Made partakers of the body and blood of God's only-begotten, let us give thanks unto him. Glory be to the Father and to the Son and to the Holy Ghost. Made partakers of the body and blood of God's only-begotten, let us give thanks unto him. Now and ever and unto the ages of ages. This is the body and blood of God's only-begotten; made partakers thereof, let us give thanks unto him; let us sing with the angels and the armies on high and the choir of the saints, who cry aloud, who proclaim, saying, Alleluia."

The priest, during the singing of the psalm or hymn, strikes his breast, and continues inaudibly: "O God, grant us remission and forgiveness of our sins, which we have committed willingly and which we have committed unwillingly; which we have committed knowingly and which we have committed unknowingly. O Lord forgive us our sins (repeated thrice).

A prayer preparatory to the reception of holy communion follows: "Lead us unto life, O eternal King, Word of God, the Father of our Lord and God and Saviour Jesus Christ. O thou, the very bread which hath come down from heaven, the giver of life unto them who receive thereof, make us worthy without condemnation to partake of thy holy body and of thy honourable blood. May our participation of thy holy mysteries unite us unto thee for ever, since thou hast blessed us. Thou art the Son of God, unto thee with him

[335] In Bute (op. cit., p. 126), each verse of the psalm is farced with "Alleluia."

and the Holy Ghost, the life-giver, be glory for ever. Amen."

Another preparatory prayer may be said, but that which is recited by the Monophysites inaudibly in Arabic ("O Lord Jesu Christ") [336] is not in the Catholic liturgy. [337]

The alternative prayer is as follows: "O our King, make us all worthy to partake of thine holy body and thine honourable blood, to the sanctification of our souls and our bodies and for the forgiveness of our sins and transgressions, that we may become one body and one spirit with thee. Glory be to thee, with thy holy Father and the Holy Ghost, for ever. Amen."

The priest now turns to the people, and, raising the paten above his head, he blesses them with the holy sacrament, as he says in Greek: "This is the holy thing for the holy." Then he continues: [338] Blessed is the Lord Jesus Christ, the Son of God. He hath hallowed it by his Holy Spirit."

The people respond with a loud voice: "Blessed is he who cometh in the name of the Lord. This is the holy thing for the holy. This is the lamb of God who taketh away the sins of the world. Blessed is he who cometh in the name of the Lord."

The priest, kissing the host, receives it in holy communion, [339] saying: "(This is) the body and blood of Emmanuel our God. It is so in very truth. Amen." "(This is) the body of Emmanuel our God. It is so in very truth. Amen."

---

[336] BUTE, op. cit., pp. 128-129.

[337] HANSSENS, op. cit., p. 396.

[338] Jacob MUIJSER, Het Heilig offer in den Koptischen Ritus. (Nijmegen-Utrecht, 1928), p. 55.

[339] Coptic, tschi, jin-tschi; Arabic, tanâwul.

He signs himself with the chalice, and receives the precious blood, saying: "(This is) the blood of Emmanuel our God. It is so in very truth. Amen."

The deacon receives communion standing, but in the Catholic rite the people, without any prescription from the Holy See, normally receive kneeling and in one kind. It is said that more traditional usages exist in some churches of Upper Egypt, where communion is given under two kinds in a spoon.

As in the Roman rite, the Catholic priest turns to the people with the paten or ciborium, as he says three times: "Lord, I am not worthy that thou shouldst come under my roof, but speak the word only and my soul shall be healed."

Among the Monophysites, it seems to be the custom [340] for the men to drink of the chalice, and the women to receive an intincted particle.

As we have seen, there is no longer reservation in Monophysite churches, and those in danger of death may have the liturgy celebrated for them at any hour of the day or night, receiving communion with the species of bread, on which two crosses have been made with the precious blood. The blessed sacrament is taken from the altar to the sick room.

During the communion of the people, the deacon [341] stands behind the altar facing west, which is a relic of the precautionary measures undertaken against a possible Melkite raid. [342]

An assistant accompanies the celebrant, and the faithful

---

[340] In a liturgy celebrated at the church of Abu Sergeh, Old Cairo (May 21, 1924), the "little deacon" received the blessed sacrament four times in a spoon, alternately with the priest, his grandfather.

[341] This is the custom in the churches of the dissidents.

[342] i. e. the Orthodox of the Byzantine patriarchate of Alexandria.

sing [343]—without ceasing:—"Blessed is he who cometh in the name of the Lord."

It is the Monophysite custom for the men to enter the *haikal,* and the women to receive communion in their own seats.

The priest says to each communicant: "This is in very truth the holy body and blood of Emmanuel our God," and the recipient answers: "Amen." [344]

The communicant holds a "mat" or veil, and wipes his lips with it, while he is then enjoined out of respect to drink a little water, "the water of the covering of the communion."

According to Vansleb, it was customary to eat lupins immediately after communion, as a precaution against certain Sabaeans, who frequented Coptic churches, but to whom any fruit grown on an angular stalk was an abomination.

When the communion is finished, the deacon gives a monition in Greek: "Pray for those who truly receive these holy, honourable and heavenly mysteries," and the people respond: *"Kyrie, eleison."*

The priest finishes the chalice, wipes the inside with his finger, and licks his finger. Then he washes out the chalice with water, and drinks it. The paten is cleansed also with water, and the rinsings are drunk by the deacon. Sometimes the deacon [345] puts the spoon several times to his lips, eyes and forehead.

The priest continues with the prayer of thanksgiving: "Our mouth is filled with gladness and our tongue with

---

[343] "*het volk zingt, zonder ophouden.*" MUIJSER, *op. cit.,* p. 55.
[344] "Amen: I believe." BRIGHTMAN, *op. cit.,* p. 186.
[345] Cf. "Further, touching with thy hands the moisture remaining on thy lips, sanctify both thine eyes and thy forehead and the other organs of sense." ST. CYRIL, *Catech. Mystag.,* XXII.

joy, for that we have been made partakers of thine immortal mysteries, O Lord. For those things, which eye hath not seen nor ear heard neither hath it entered into the heart of man, thou, O God, hast prepared for them that love thy holy name, and thou hast revealed them unto babes of thy holy church. Even so, Father, for so it seemed good in thy sight; for thou art merciful and unto thee, O Father, together with the Son and the Holy Ghost, we ascribe glory and honour and worship, now and ever and unto the ages of all ages. Amen."

The prayer of inclination, [346] which follows, is preceded by a bidding from the deacon in Greek: "Bow down your heads before the Lord." The priest continues: "Live, O Lord, in the hearts of thy servants who keep thy commandments, who for ever invoke thy holy name, and who bow down before thee. Live amongst them and succour them in all good works. Drive out of their hearts all evil and earthly thoughts. Give to them holy thoughts, so that they may live next to God, and may always consider thy holy commandments, by the grace of our Lord and God and Saviour Jesus Christ, thine only Son, through whom thou comest and with whom and the holy and life-giving Spirit be all glory and honour and power and virtue, for now and for all time, for ever and ever. Amen."

In the Catholic rite, [347] the people at the conclusion of the prayer do not answer thrice "*Kyrie, eleison.*"

Then, turning to the people, the priest, [348] with outstretched hands, gives the final blessing.

---

[346] Coptic, *Jebs-Jof*; Arabic, *khuḍū'*.

[347] HANSSENS, *op. cit.*, p. 397.

[348] The priest comes before the screen, in those churches where they exist.

The very long form [349] used by the dissidents, beginning
"O all-holy Trinity," is considerably curtailed by the Catholics, who say: "O Lord, save thy people, bless thine
inheritance, govern them and lift them up for ever; and
keep them in right faith and in glory and honour all the
days of their life. And establish them in the love which
is above all things, and the peace which passeth all understanding. Through the prayers and supplications which
our Lady, the Lady of us all, the holy Mother of God, holy
Mary doth make for us, and of the blessed *N.* (whose feast
is commemorated), and all the heavenly choir and holy
host." [350]

In the Catholic rite, the diaconal formula of dismissal:
"Pray for the peace of the one only holy Catholic Apostolic
Church," etc. is not said, but the priest continues: "O
Christ, King of peace, our God, grant us thy peace and make
thy peace to rest upon us, for thine are the power and glory
and the blessing and the might for ever. Amen. Make us
truly in thankfulness to say: Our Father, who art in heaven."

The people, with loud voice and hands outstretched,
recite together the Lord's prayer, and the priest, holding the
hand-cross, gives the blessing in Arabic: "May the almighty and merciful God, Father, Son and Holy Ghost, bless
† you, by the intercession of St. *N.* (whose feast is commemorated). Amen. Go in peace."

Then the priest sprinkles the altar and the people with
holy water, scattering it in all directions, and distributes the
blessed bread, [351] unless it has been already handed round

---

[349] BUTE, *op. cit.,* pp. 132-133, n. 2.
[350] The dissidents have a long list of saints. BUTE, *op. cit.,* p. 133.
n. 2.
[351] Arabic, *baracah.*

Coptic eucharistic bread

Icon of the Flight into Egypt, Church of
Abu Sergeh, Old Cairo (17th century)

Cistercians of the Ethiopic rite
Abbey of Valviciolo, Sermoneta

Students of the Ethiopian
Pontifical College, Vatican City

by an assistant. Sometimes the priest passes his hand, [352] wet with holy water, down his own face and those of the faithful, symbolising the application of the blessing given or invoked.

The deacon, at the conclusion of the blessing by the priest, says: "The grace of our Lord and God and Saviour Jesus Christ be with you all," and the people respond: "Amen. So be it. A hundred years." [353]

The *Lamp* enjoins that on Maundy Thursday, in place of the dismissal, three lessons (Isaias; Psalms; St. John) shall be chanted to the funeral tone.

The priest then returns to the altar, which he kisses before retiring to the sacristy. He recites on his way psalm XLVI (XLVII), *Omnes gentes, plaudite.*

Anaphora of St. Gregory Nazianzen

The *Anaphora of St. Gregory Nazianzen*, as we have seen, is used three times in the year. It is addressed throughout to our Lord, and translated from Greek. [354] It is Antiochene in structure.

The version given here is a translation of Renaudot. [355]

Priest: "The love of God the Father and the grace of his only-begotten Son, our Lord and God and Saviour Jesus Christ, and the fellowship and gift of the Holy Spirit be with you all."

People: "And with thy spirit."

---

[352] Arabic, *massaḥ wajh*, "wipe the face."

[353] "A hundred years" denotes an infinity of time.

[354] The anaphora, though composed when Greek was still used in Egypt, is not of great antiquity.

[355] *Op. cit.*, t. I, pp. 27-34.

Priest: "Let us lift up our hearts."

People: "We lift them up unto the Lord."

Priest: "Let us give thanks unto the Lord."

People: "It is meet and right."

Priest: "It is meet and right, meet and right. It is indeed meet and right to praise thee, to bless thee, to worship thee, to glorify thee, the only true God, lover of mankind, ineffable, invisible, infinite, without beginning, eternal, without time, immeasurable, immutable, incomprehensible, maker of all things, deliverer of all. Who dost forgive all our iniquites and healest all our infirmities, who redeemest our life from corruption and crownest us with mercy and loving kindness. Angels praise thee, archangels adore thee, principalities hymn thee, dominions hail thee, authorities proclaim thy glory, and thrones raise acclamation to thee. Around thee stand thousands of thousands, and ten-thousand-times-ten-thousand offer thee service. The invisible powers celebrate thee, the visible adore thee, all doing thy will, O Master."

Deacon: "Ye who are sitting, stand up."

Priest: "O great I am, Lord God, very Lord of very God, who hast shown to us the light of the Father, who hast vouchsafed to us true knowledge of the Holy Spirit: who hast displayed to us this great mystery of life, who hast instituted for men the choirs of incorporeal beings and hast committed to us who are on earth the seraphic hymn: receive, together with those of the invisible choir, even our voices. Unite us with the celestial powers. May we also speak with them, having cast aside all unseemly thoughts, and may we cry aloud those things which they proclaim with voices that are never silent, and may we with unresting mouths hymn thy greatness."

Deacon: "Look to the East."

Priest: "For the seraphim encircle thee, each having six wings and with twain they cover their faces, and with twain they cover their feet, and with twain they do fly, and they cry aloud, the one to the other, the triumphal hymn of our salvation, with clear and joyous voices, celebrating, singing, shouting, glorifying, crying aloud and saying."

Deacon: "Let us attend."

People: "Holy, holy, holy, Lord God of hosts. Full is the heaven and earth of thy holy glory."

Priest: "Holy, holy art thou, O Lord, and all-holy. Surpassing is the light of thine essence, unutterable is the power of thy wisdom; words may not measure the ocean of thy loving kindness towards men. Thou didst make me man, as lover of men; not that thou didst need ny service, but rather that I had need of thy governance. Thou broughtest me forth out of nothing, in mercy and loving kindness; thou didst set the heavens to be my covering and establish the earth for me to tread. For me thou didst rein in the sea; for me thou didst create the nature of animals; thou didst put all things under my feet, nor didst thou omit any kindness toward me."

People: "Lord, have mercy."

Priest: "Thou didst fashion me and lay thy hand upon me, and didst inscribe in me the image of thy power, and place in me the gift of reason. Thou didst open paradise for my delight; thou didst commit to me the precepts of thy knowledge; thou didst show to me the tree of life;[356] thou didst make known to me the sting of death lest I should eat of it. Thou didst forbid to me the fruit of one tree, from which alone thou didst command that I should not eat: I ate; I set at naught the law; I neglected thy command

[356] Cf. St. Basil.

through my own self-will, and I snatched for myself the sentence of death."

People: *"Kyrie, eleison."*

Priest: "Thou, O Lord, for me didst bear the punishment and as the good Shepherd thou didst run to the wanderer. As a true Father, thou didst sympathise with me when I fell, and didst win me back to life with every remedy. Thou thyself didst send to me the prophets, for me when sick thou gavest the law to be my helper, and thou thyself didst minister healing to my transgressions. Thou didst arise as a light to the wanderers: thou who art always present, didst sojourn with the ignorant, and didst enter the Virgin's womb. Being infinite God, thou didst not esteem it a prize to be equal with God, but didst empty thyself and take upon thee the form of a servant. Thou didst bless my nature in thee; and for my sake didst fulfil the law, and give me an example how I might rise from my fall. Thou didst give remission to those whom hell detained and didst abolish the curse of the law; thou didst destroy sin in the flesh and didst make known to me the majesty of thy power; thou didst restore sight to the blind, thou didst raise the dead from their graves, thou didst restore nature by a word; thou didst show to me the dispensation of thy clemency; thou didst endure the violence of wicked men, didst give thy back to the scourge, thy cheeks to be smitten, and for my sake didst not turn away thy face from shame and spitting."

People: *"Kyrie, eleison."*

Priest: "Thou didst come as a sheep to the slaughter, and didst display thy solicitude for me even to the cross; thou didst bury my sin in thy sepulchre, and didst elevate to the heavens my firstfruits: thou didst signify to me the approach of thine advent, in which thou shalt come again to judge the living and the dead, and to render to everyone according to his works." [357]

People: "According to thy mercy, O Lord, and not according to our sins."

Priest: "Of this my freedom I offer to thee the symbols, and ascribe to thy words [358] that which is accomplished, for thou art he who didst commit to me this mystic participation of thy flesh in bread and wine."

People: "We believe."

Priest: "For in the same night in which thou didst deliver thyself up of thine own power, taking bread in thy holy, immaculate and unspotted hands, (People: "We believe that it is so"), thou didst look up to heaven to thine own Father, our God and the God of all. Thou didst give thanks (People: "Amen"), bless (People: "Amen"), sanctify (People: "Amen") and break, and gavest to thy holy disciples and apostles, saying: Take, eat ye all of it, this is my body which is broken for you and for many, and is given for the remission of sins: do this for my memorial."

People: "It is so in very truth. Amen."

Priest: "Likewise, after supper, thou didst take the cup and didst mix it with the fruit of the vine and water; thou didst give thanks (People: "Amen"), bless (People: "Amen"), sanctify (People: "Amen"), taste and gavest to thy holy disciples and apostles, saying: Drink ye all of it: this is my blood of the New Testament which is shed for you and given for many for the remission of sins. Do this for my memorial."

People: "It is also so in very truth. Amen."

Priest: "For as often as ye eat this bread and drink this

[357] Cf. St. Basil.
[358] The words of institution seem to be considered as effecting the consecration.

cup ye proclaim my death and confess my resurrection and make memorial of me until I come."

People: "We proclaim thy death, O Lord, and thy holy resurrection, and we confess thy ascension; we praise thee, we give thanks to thee, and we pray thee, O Lord our God."

Priest: "Therefore, O Lord, mindful of thy descent upon earth, and thy life-giving death, thy three days' burial and thy resurrection from the dead, thy ascension into heaven, and session on the right hand of the Father, and thy coming from the heavens—thy terrible and glorious second coming. We offer to thee thine own of thine own gifts, in relation to all, through all, and in all."

Deacon: "Worship God with fear and trembling."

Priest: "Do thou therefore, O Lord, with thine own voice, change these gifts lying before thee: thyself being present, accomplish this mystic liturgy; do thou thyself preserve for us the memorial of thine adoration and worship. Send down thy Holy Spirit, that, coming with his holy, good and glorious presence, he may sanctify and change these precious and holy gifts lying before thee into the very body and blood of our salvation. And that he may make this bread to become the holy body of thee our Lord and God and Saviour, the King of all of us, Jesus Christ, for the remission of sins and for eternal life to those communicating from it. And again this cup, thy precious blood of the New Testament of our Lord and God and Saviour and King of all of us, Jesus Christ, for the remission of sins and for life eternal to those communicating from it." [359] (People: "Amen").

Here follow the intercessions.

Priest: "For thou art our God, full of pity, not wishing

---

[359] Cf. Anaphora of St. Basil.

the death of a sinner, but rather that he may be converted and live. O God, visit us in thy salvation, deal with us according to thy kindness, who dost more than we ask or think, that in this, as in all things, thy holy honourable and blessed name may be glorified, extolled, praised, blessed and honoured, together with thy good Father and the Holy Spirit. Peace be with all."

The Anaphora of St. Cyril (St. Mark)

The oldest and most distinctive anaphora, *St. Cyril* (*St. Mark*), is now used on a single day in the year.

Some expressions in the prayers point to a time when the Roman persecutions were still a reality; while a reading from the gospel of St. John, [360] although found in two Egyptian manuscripts, is unknown in any extant Greek codex. It has therefore been assumed that, since the passage in question dropped out before the 4th century, the prayer in which it is found must have been composed not later than that time.

As we have seen, the Liturgy of St. Cyril claims to be that of St. Mark "perfected," although the earliest Coptic manuscript, now in the Vatican library, dates from 1288.

Among the features of the anaphora, the position of the great prayer of intercession and the diptychs may be noted, interrupting the preface and preceding the *sanctus*. A peculiarity already existing in the 5th century, and commented on by James of Edessa in the 7th.

The same writer also mentioned the Alexandrine salutation before the preface, which is simpler and less complicated than that found in the Antiochene rites.

---

[360] St. John XX, 22, 23.

The anaphora has two epicleses, the one before [361] the consecration, as in Serapion, and the other, which has probably been borrowed from the Byzantine rite, after the recital of the words of institution.

Four prayers in the liturgy would seem to have been taken from the Syrian anaphora of John of Bostra, — the prayer of the veil; the prayer before receiving communion; and the third and fourth prayers after communion; while the prayer of the peace is also found in the Syrian anaphora of Severus.

The translation of the Liturgy of St. Cyril is taken from Renaudot. [362]

Priest: "The Lord be with you."

People: "And with thy spirit."

Priest: "Lift up your hearts."

People: "We lift them up unto the Lord."

Priest: "Let us give thanks to the Lord."

People: "It is meet and right."

Priest: "It is meet and right, for thou truly art worthy, right and holy, becoming and necessary for our souls, our bodies and our spirits, O eternal Master, Lord God, Father Almighty, at all times and in all places of thy dominion, to praise thee, to hymn thee, to bless thee, to serve thee, to adore thee, to give thanks to thee, to glorify thee and confess to thee day and night, with unceasing lips, unsilenced heart and uninterrupted praise. For thou it is who didst create the heavens and the things that are in the heavens, the earth and all that is therein, the seas, rivers, fountains, lakes and whatsoever is within them. Thou didst create

[361] Mar Ephrem Rahmani (*Les Liturgies Orientales et Occidentales,* part III, chap. I, p. 557) has maintained that this was originally the position of the epiclesis in the Roman rite.

[362] *Op. cit.,* t. I. pp. 39-48.

man in thine image and similitude, and thou didst create all things in thy wisdom, in thy true light, thine only-begotten Son, our Lord, our God, our Saviour and our King, Jesus Christ: wherefore we give thanks to thee and we offer to thee and also to thy Son and the Holy Spirit, the holy consubstantial and undivided Trinity, this reasonable sacrifice and this unbloody service, which all peoples offer to thee from the rising of the sun even to its going down, from the north to the south, for thy name, O Lord, is great among all people, and in every place they offer incense to thy holy name and a pure sacrifice, together with this sacrifice and this oblation."

The intercession follows, towards the end of which the deacon gives the monition: "Ye who are sitting, stand up."

Then, after another prayer, the deacon says: "Look to the East," a formula found only in the Alexandrine liturgies.

Priest: "Thou art God, high above all principalities and powers, dignities and authorities, and above every name that can be named, not only in this world, but in that which is to come. Thou art he in whose presence stand thousand-thousands and ten-thousand-times-ten-thousand holy angels and archangels serving thee. Before thee stand thy two most glorious living creatures, [363] six-winged and many-eyed, the seraphim and cherubim; and with twain of their wings they cover their faces because of thine invisible and incomprehensible divinity, and with twain they cover their feet and with twain they do fly.

(He continues with a loud voice). One and all they ever hallow thee, but with all who hallow thee, receive also from

[363] A qualification found in Novatian († ab. 257), *De Trinitate;* Serapion (ab. 380), in the preface of the eucharistic anaphora. *Bishop Serapion's Prayer-Book,* p. 61. John WORDSWORTH, *Early Church Classics.* S. P. C. K., 1910.

us our hallowing †, that with them we may praise thee, saying."

Deacon: "Holy, holy, holy, Lord God of hosts, the heaven and the earth are full of thy holy glory."

Priest: "Truly the heavens and the earth are full of thy holy glory, through thine only-begotten Son, our Lord, our God, our Saviour and King of us all, Jesus Christ. Fill this sacrifice, O Lord, with the blessing which is from thee, by the descent upon it of the Holy Spirit †. [364] Amen. And in blessing, bless †. Amen. And in purifying, purify. Amen. These thy venerable gifts laid out before thee, this bread and this cup. [365] Amen. For thine only-begotten Son, our Lord, our God, our Saviour and King of us all, Jesus Christ, in the same night in which he gave himself up that he might suffer for our sins, before his death which he took upon himself of his own will, for us all (People: "We believe"): taking bread into his holy hands, immaculate, pure, blessed and life-giving, and looking up to heaven to thee, his God and Father and the Lord of us all, he gave thanks (People: "Amen"), and blessed it (People: "Amen"), and sanctified it (People: "Amen"), and broke it and gave to his holy disciples and pure apostles, saying: Take, eat ye all of it: this is my body, which is broken for you and shall be given for many for the remission of sins. [366] Do this for my memorial. (People: "Amen") Likewise also the cup after supper, he mixed with wine and water: and gave thanks. (People: "Amen") And blessed it. (People:

---

[364] Cf. *Quam oblationem* in the Roman rite.

[365] It may be noted that as there is a double oblation, so also is there here a double invocation, first upon the bread and wine, and then upon the body and blood. This would seem a further indication of belief in the words of institution as effecting the consecration.

[366] Cf. SERAPION, *ibid.*, p. 62.

"Amen") And sanctified it. (People: "Amen") And tasted,
and gave to his excellent and holy disciples and apostles,
saying: Take, drink ye all of it: this is my blood of the
New Testament. which is shed for you and shall be given
for many for the remission of sins: Do this for my memorial.
(People: "Amen") For as often as ye shall eat of this bread
and drink of this cup, ye proclaim my death, and confess my
resurrection, and make memorial of me, till I come."

People: "We proclaim thy death, O Lord."

Priest: "Now, O God, Father Almighty, we proclaim
the death of thy only-begotten Son, our Lord, our God,
our Saviour and King of us all, Jesus Christ: and we confess
his holy resurrection and his ascension into heaven, his
session at thy right hand, O Father, and we look for his
second coming, terrible and glorious, when he shall come
from the heavens at the end of this age to judge the world
in righteousness, and shall render to every man according
to his works, whether good or evil."

People: "According to thy mercy, O Lord, and not
according to our sins."

Priest: "Thou art he in the presence of whose glory
we lay out these holy gifts from those things which are thine,
O holy Father."

Deacon: "Worship God with fear."

Priest: "We pray and beseech thy goodness, O lover
of men, not to confound us with eternal confusion, nor
reject us thy servants, nor drive us away from thy presence,
nor say to us: 'I know you not': but grant water to our
heads and a fount of tears to our eyes; that we may bewail
our sins day and night before thee; for we are thy people
and the sheep of thy pasture. Blot out our iniquities and
forgive our offences, which we have committed voluntarily
and involuntarily, knowingly and in ignorance, hidden or

manifest, those which we did not know and those which we have forgotten, and those which thy holy name knoweth. Hear, O Lord, the supplications of thy people; have regard to the sighs of thy servants, and withold not for my sins and the wickedness of my heart, the descent of thy Holy Spirit from thy people."

People: "Have mercy upon us, O God the Father Almighty."

The priest, wrapping his hands in the veil, makes the sign of the cross towards the people, and continues in a loud voice: "For thy people and thy church beseech thee, saying": (a rubric directs that he now looks to the east).

People: "Have mercy upon us, O God the Father Almighty."

Priest: "Have mercy upon us, O God the Father Almighty."

Deacon: "Worship God the Father Almighty."

The priest now says the invocation secretly: "And send down from thy holy heights, and from thine appointed habitation, and from thine infinite bosom, and from the throne of thy glorious kingdom, the Paraclete, thy Holy Spirit, subsisting in thy person, indivisible, changeless, lord and lifegiver, who spake in the law, and by the prophets and apostles; who is everywhere and fills all places nor does any place contain him: who freely and of his own power and not as a servant, according to thy will, worketh purity in those whom he loveth, who is simple in his nature and manifold in his operations: fount of divine gifts; consubstantial with thee, proceeding from thee; partner of the throne of thy glorious kingdom, together with thine only-begotten Son, our Lord, our God, our Saviour and the King of us all, Jesus Christ: send him down upon us thy servants, and upon these thy precious gifts which have been set before thee, upon this bread and upon this cup, that they may be sanctified and changed."

Deacon: "Let us attend."

People: "Amen."

The priest, signing the host three times, says in a loud voice: "And that he may make this bread the body of Christ." (People: "Amen") "And that he may make this cup the precious blood of the New Testament." (People: "Amen") "Even of our Lord, our God, our Saviour and King of us all, Jesus Christ." (People: "Amen") "That they may be to us all, who shall partake of them, of avail for obtaining faith without disputation, love without hypocrisy, perfect patience, firm hope, confidence, protection, healing, joy, and restoration of soul, body and spirit, to the glory of thy holy name; to the blessed fellowship of life eternal and incorruptible, and to the remission of sins."

People: "As it was, and is, and shall be to the generations of generations, and to all ages of ages. Amen."

Priest: "That in this as in all things, thy great, most holy, venerable and blessed name may be glorified, [367] blessed and extolled, with Jesus Christ, thy beloved Son, and the Holy Spirit."

[367] Cf. Liturgy of St. James.

BIBLIOGRAPHY.

1. *Alexandrie (Liturgie)*. H. LECLERCQ, *Dictionnaire d'Archéologie Chrétienne et de Liturgie*. T. I, part. I, col. 1182-1204.

2. *The Ancient Coptic Churches of Egypt*. Alfred J. BUTLER. 2 vols. Oxford: At the Clarendon Press. 1884.

3. *The Catholic Coptic Mission in Egypt:* Cairo: Kawa's Printing Office. 1929.

4. *The Coptic Church of El-Moallaka* and Others at Old Cairo. *Shenouda Hanna*. C. Tsoumas, Cairo. 1944.

5. *The Coptic Morning Service for the Lord's Day*. Translated into English by John, MARQUIS OF BUTE. London: Cope & Fenwick. 1908.

6. *Coptic Offices*. Translated by R. M. WOOLLEY. London: S. P. C. K. New York & Toronto: The Macmillan Co. 1930.

7. *The Daily Office and Theotokia of the Coptic Church*. De Lacy O'LEARY. London: Simpkin, Marshall, Hamilton, Kent & Co. Ltd. 1911.

8. Het *Heilig Offer den Koptischen Ritus volgens den H. Basilius den Groote*. In het Nederlansh vertaald door Pater Jacob MUIJSER van de Societeit der Afrik Missien. Nijmegen - Utrecht. 1928.

9. *Ireland and the Celtic Church*. George T. STOKES. 7th edition, revised by Hugh Jackson LAWLOR. London: S. P. C. K. 1928.

10. *Irish Antiquities and Archeology*. W. GAMBLE. Printed for the Author. The Rectory, Redhills, Co. Cavan.

11. *Irish Litanies*. Text and Translation. Edited from the manuscripts by Charles PLUMMER. Henry Bradshaw Society. Vol. LXII. London. 1925.

12. *Lecture* by his Excellency Sesostris Sidarouss Pasha, Egyptian Minister in the United States, to the Society of St. John Chrysostom. Wednesday, May 27, 1931.

13. The *Liturgy of the Copts*. Donald ATTWATER. *Orate Fratres*. April & May 1942.

14. *Missions des Coptes Catholiques en Egypte*. Marc KHOUZAM. Albertiri, le Caire. 1937.

15. *Monophysite (Eglise Copte)*. M. JUGIE. *Dictionnaire de Théologie Catholique*. T. X, col. 2251-2306.

16. *Les Observances Liturgiques et la Discipline du Jeûne dans l'Eglise Copte* d'après *La Lampe des Ténèbres d'Abû'l Barakāt ibn Kubr.* Extrait du *Muséon.* T. XXXVI, XXXVII, XXXVIII (1923-1925). Dom Louis VILLECOURT. Louvain. J.-B. Istas, 1925.

17. *The Saints of Egypt.* De Lacy O'LEARY. London: S. P. C. K. 1937.

18. *The Story of the Church of Egypt.* E. L. BUTCHER. 2 vols. London: Smith, Elder & Co. 1897.

ACKNOWLEDGEMENTS.

1. His Excellency Sesostris Sidarouss Pasha, late Minister of the Royal Egyptian Legation, Washington, D. C.

2. Fr. Edmund O'Callaghan, O. D. C.

3. Fr. Malek, Professor of the Seminary of Tahta, Upper Egypt.

4. Fr. George Bistavros, Priest of Abu Sergeh, Old Cairo.

5. Fr. Shenouda Hanna, Priest of El-Moallaka, Old Cairo.

6. Clergy of the Coptic Cathedral of St. Mark, Cairo.

CHAPTER VI.

ETHIOPIC RITE

Abyssinia, the home of the Ethiopic rite, resembles in contour a vast fortress towering above the plains of eastern Africa.

The rite is used from Eritrea on the shores of the Red Sea to British East Africa, and Somaliland to the Sudan.

Divided into Tigré, Amhara, Shoa and Galla lands, the whole country is known as Abyssinia, although the term [1] is rejected by the inhabitants, on the ground that it is derived from the Arabic *ḥabaše* (Ethiopic, *ḥabaš*), a word signifying "mixed things" or "mixed races" The people resent the implication of "mongrel," but it has passed into Geez (*ḥabaš*), and *hawace* [2] or "mixed," a Semitic word, is found in Tigré and Tigrinya. Mohammed wrote of the *negassi* or king of the Hebechi, who reigned at Axum.

The natives themselves speak of their country as Ethiopia (Ityōpyā) or Kus. The first name appears to be derived from the Greek αἴθω ("I burn") and ὄψ ("face"), thus implying the "land of the scorched faces" or "coloured man's land," although it has been sometimes thought that the Greeks learnt the word from the Egyptians. So early as

---

[1] The term has been rejected since the 7th century.
[2] Cf. Oromono, *makada*, "mixture."

the twelfth dynasty, the Ethiopians were known as *Ksh* or *Kshi,* and one form of the word, with the prefix *aleph,* would thus be *Ekoshi.* [3]   Another theory as to origin suggests the Arabic *atyab,*[4] "spices" or "perfumes," while the Arabo-Sabean word *atyub* has a similar meaning.

St. Athanasius, St. Epiphanius and other writers, both ecclesiastical and profane, speak of the Ethiopians as Axumites, [5] a name derived from the spiritual capital of the country.

Ethiopia, however, has not always implied the same geographical area, and when its inhabitants are referred to in the Septuagint, [6] the descendents of Kûs (Cush), the son of Cham, are mentioned. The natives themselves claim Nubia as the cradle of the people of the Nile valley, although it is evident from writing on old monuments that their civilisation and culture were derived from Egypt.

Ethiopia under the rule of the Pharaohs from time to time asserted her independence, but with the destruction of Napata, the capital, by the Roman legionaries the old country disappears.

Later, with the history of modern Nubia, a new civilisation came into being. The heart of this state lay in the kingdom of Axum (Tigré), which had been founded by refugees from Sabean (Semitic) tribes, who had been engaged in the gold and spice trade between Arabia and the Roman Empire. Their descendents, mingled with an aboriginal race (Shangalā), are still found in the country.

Thus, the earliest blood was negro, mixed in prehistoric times by a Hamitic (Gallas) strain, akin to the ancient Egyp-

---

[3] Coptic, *eshoosh, eshôsh, ethosh.*
[4] Plural of *tib.*
[5] LE BRUN, *Explication de la Messe,* t. IV, p. 227.
[6] Genesis X, 6.

tians. This was later followed by a Semitic element, which probably came from Arabia, and succeeded in becoming the predominant culture. Amharic when spoken sounds like a rough Arabic dialect. Geez, [7] the ancient tongue, is now purely hieratic.

Of the three vernacular languages, Tigré is spoken in the mountains of the north; Tigrinya around Axum; and Amharic by the court, government and official classes.

Polytheism is said to have been introduced into the country at the same time as the civilisation of the Ptolemies, taking the form of a cult of snakes, birds and divinities of the waters (*Zar*), although inscriptions discovered at Axum and Adulis seem to point to a Chaldean or Syrian origin.

History

The tradition that the royal house of Ethiopia is descended from King Solomon, although recorded in the Fethé-Neghest, [8] is of no great antiquity. The legend records that the Queen of Sheba (Makeda) came from Ethiopia, and that Menelik, her son by Solomon, was the ancestor of the old dynasty. Thus, the king of Ethiopia styles himself "King of the kings of Ethiopia, Lion of the tribe of Judah."

Three legends exist in regard to the introduction of Christianity into the country: *a*) Ethiopia was miraculously converted at the time of the baptism of our Lord; *b*) St. Matthew, [9] about the year 30, preached the gospel and suffer-

---

[7] *Lesân ge'z,* "tongue of the freeman."

[8] "The glory of the kings."

[9] *Ita* Origen. The *Roman Martyrology* (September 21) says: "In Ethiopia, the birth to heaven of St. Matthew, apostle and evangelist: preaching in this region he suffered martyrdom there." On May 6, the *Martyrology* has the following entry: "At Salerno, the

ed martyrdom there; and *c*) the first apostle of Ethiopia was the eunuch [10] of Queen Candace, who about the year 35 had been baptised by St. Philip the Deacon. In regard to this third legend, it may be pointed out that Candace was queen of Ethiopia Meroitica, which bordered on Egypt, not of Ethiopia Axumita, and that in the latter country the dynastic laws of the time prohibited the rule of queens.

The Christian faith was probably first brought to the country in the reign of the emperor Constantine by St. Frumentius (ab. 330-340), a supposition corroborated by Rufinus [11] of Aquilea (ab. 345-ab. 410). Frumentius and Aedesius, two young men from Tyre, are said to have been captives at Axum, and later promoted as fuctionaries of the court. When they were given leave to go where they pleased, Aedesius returned to his native town, while Frumentius visited St. Athanasius at Alexandria. Returning to Ethiopia, Frumentius began his apostolate, and succeeded in converting two royal rulers, Abreha and Asbeha. These kings have been canonised (October 1), and a church (Abraha-Atsbaha), cut out of the solid rock, has been dedicated to them at Aïba near Agula (Enderta).

Aedesius, now a priest, also returned to Ethiopia, where he took his share in the conversion of the country.

The church of our Lady in the island of Massawa, which for a time served as a mosque, [12] is said to date from

translation of St. Matthew, apostle and evangelist: his holy body formerly translated from Ethiopia into different provinces was finally brought to this town and laid to rest with great honours, in the church dedicated under his name."

[10] *Act. Apost.*, VIII, 26-40.

[11] " *Terram hanc (Indiam), in qua praedicavit Frumentius, nullo apostolico doctrinae vomere proscissam.*" In later years, John of Nikiou and Marco Polo both referred to Ethiopia as " the Indies."

[12] Sheïk-al-Kamal.

the days of St. Frumentius. This apostle, who became metropolitan of Aksum and primate of Ethiopia, was known after his death (ab. 380) as "the Father of Peace" [13] and "the Illuminator." [14] Sapeto, a Lazarist missionary who came to the country in 1838, maintained that St. Frumentius died at Ibo, although it is commonly said that his remains lie on the top of a high mountain (Edda Abba-Salāma) in the Tambien.

St. Frumentius is honoured by Ethiopia on August 2; by Rome on October 27; and by Constantinople on November 30. The Coptic *Synaxarion* makes no mention of his name.

A sanctuary to his memory was erected at Mai Guagua near Axum, from which the surrounding district has received the name Fremona. This was once a station of the Jesuits, and later, bearing the designation Addi-Abun, became the residence of abuna.

In 365, the emperor Constantius made an unsuccessful attempt to draw the Ethiopian church into Arianism, urging King Azana and his brother Sazana to send away St. Frumentius and to receive the Arian bishop George.

The faith was strengthened and promoted by monks from Upper Egypt, who built churches in Nubia; while in the 5th and 6th centuries Coptic monks effected so much for the benefit of religion that their work has been called a second conversion.

About the year 480, in the reign of King Ameda, the "Nine Saints" [15] appear to have come to Ethiopia. They

---

[13] *Aba salāma*, a title used to-day by abuna.
[14] *Kassatie-kerehan.*
[15] Aragawi, Pantaleon, Garima, Alef, Saham, Afe, Libanos, Adimata, Oz or Guba. Each of the "Nine Roman Saints" has a commemoration in the Catholic liturgy.

are reckoned as secondary apostles of the country, although there has been a certain amount of doubt as to their orthodoxy. Some have said that they were Syrian exiles from imperial persecution, and that they introduced Monophysism into the country. On the other hand, Catholic scholars [16] for the most part maintain that Ethiopia did not fall into heresy till the middle of the 7th century. [17] It is alleged in support of the orthodoxy of the "Nine Saints" that the chronicler speaks of the monks as *Romawsuian*, citizens of the Roman Empire, whereas if they had been Monophysite exiles they would have been styled *Surian* or *Gebtsawian*. However this may be, the church of Ethiopia eventually fell away from orthodoxy, in what has been described [18] as "one of the most excusable and least responsible schisms in church history." Egypt had turned Monophysite, the country from which the Ethiopians derived their religion, and from which they received the apostolic succession. It has been said, also, that Coptic monks were responsible for the first Geez [19] Bible, although this has been disputed, for *haïmanouth* as the word for "faith" would seem to point to a Syrian origin. The Roman martyrology on October 27 commemorates St. Elesban, who in the 6th century ruled Ethiopia as King Caleb [20] (510-558), famous in native literature for his expedition against the Jewish kingdom of Yemen. Caleb in 558 resigned the throne to his son, Ghebra-

---

[16] *Dict. de Théol. Cath.*, t. V, col. 926-927.

[17] It is said by some that a Catholic minority existed till the 13th century.

[18] Adrian FORTESCUE, *Lesser Eastern Churches*, Part III, chap. IX, p. 299.

[19] Idiom of Tigré.

[20] Some writers have maintained that Caleb was, at least materially, a Monophysite, but he is honoured as a saint by the Catholics (May 28).

Meskel (558-584), and, having presented his crown to the Holy Sepulchre, he died as a monk in Jerusalem.

The 6th century is said to have ushered in the golden age of the Ethiopian church, and the numerous monasteries became the centres of ecclesiastical culture and theological discussion. Each of the "Nine Saints" is alleged to have founded a religious house in Tigré; while about the middle of the 6th century Yared, a monk of Debra-Damo and a pupil of St. Pantaleon, taught, in the presence of the king, the principles of liturgical chant, which had been brought to the country by the "Nine Saints." Legend, however, tells of a visit made by Yared to Paradise, from whence he brought back the church music. The melodies of the chant are in three modes—*Geez, Ezel, Ararai*. Yared also edited a compilation of chants for the cycle of the ecclesiastical year, known as the *Mezgheba-Deggoua;* while to him are ascribed the drum, sistrum, clapping of hands and dancing as accompaniments of liturgical worship. Ghebra-Meskel sent his monastic son, Abba Moses, to Jerusalem, where a hospice was founded, and a sanctuary near Nablus (Samaria) was later dedicated to Moses. A distinctive dress—black habit and *qob* (lofty white hat)—is worn by those priests who have been in the Holy Land, much as a green turban may be used by the Mohammedans who have made a pilgrimage to Mecca.

King Ghebra-Meskel was known as a promoter of church building, and the churches of Barekmaha, Behat (in the Choumenaza) and Sabea (Sourrekso), as well as the monasteries of Debra-Damo (Tigré), erected in memory of Abba Aragawi, and Abba Garima near Adowa, date from his reign. The 6th century ruler of this black kingdom may be not unjustly compared with Charlemagne in his active interest in ecclesiastical matters. The king and Yared have

THE RITES OF EASTERN CHRISTENDOM

both been regarded as saints by the Senkessar.[21] This liturgical book, translated at the beginning of the 15th century by Abba Simeon, a monk of St. Antony, is but the synaxary of the Byzantines, compiled by two bishops of Lower Egypt, with the addition of a certain number of Ethiopic saints and, at the end of each commemoration, a short rhymed poem (*salām*).

The emperor Justinian (483-565) is said to have sent, during the reign of Ghebra, some orthodox monks to Ethiopia, which the empress Theodora thought to counter by despatching Monophysite monks from St. Macarius in Upper Egypt. The latter seem to have been speedily sent back to their own country, which, if this is true, supports the contention that the schism was only effected some considerable time after Egypt had fallen away. All the monks were under the austere rules formulated in the Thebaid, and from the 7th to the 10th century the two branches of the religious life were in process of formation.

Nubia[22] seems to have received the Christian faith in the time of Justinian from a Coptic monk of the name of Julian, and consequently to have received its bishops from Egypt. By the 7th century, Nubia had become a powerful Christian state, with the capital at Dongola on the Nile, and, when in the following century the Coptic patriarch, Michael I (743-767), was imprisoned, the country was strong enough to attack Egypt and secure his release. Christianity, however, in the 11th century began to lose ground in Nubia, and, despite a temporary revival, it was finally swept away by Islam about the 15th century. Two

[21] An English translation has been made by Sir E. A. WALLIS BUDGE, *The Book of the Saints of the Ethiopian Church.* 4 vols. Cambridge University Press, 1928.
[22] Northern Sudan, from the southern frontier of Egypt.

hundred years later, the churches still remained, but there were no priests to serve them.

As we have seen, the date of the schism of the Ethiopian church is a matter of doubt, but it is well substantiated that the Coptic patriarch, Benjamin I (620-659), sent one of his monks, Cyril by name, to hold the office of abuna. The definite ruling that abuna must be a Coptic monk is said to date from the reign of Yekuno Amlak (1268-1283), at a time when Takla Haimanot was the moving spirit in the affairs of the country, although it seems probable that the alleged canon [23] of Nicea, making provision for this, was the forged work of an 8th century Coptic patriarch. At times, communication with Egypt was impossible, and in the middle of the 9th century there was no abuna for 80 years. On the strength of the legend that Prester John once lived in Abyssinia, the kings are said to have performed episcopal functions. It is difficult to know exactly what these "functions" entailed, but "Abu Salih [24] expressly tells us that they (the kings) considered themselves invested with the supreme power in the Church as well as in the State, and that on solemn occasions they celebrated the Holy Communion." The quotation, however, does not make it clear whether the king actually celebrated the liturgy or whether he only administered holy communion. The emperor [25] of Byzantium in quality of the Lord's anointed used to enter the sanctuary at certain times to offer incense and to bless the people.

A Jewess of the name of Judith usurped the throne about

[23] Canon 42. Fonti. Testi di Diritto Antichi riguardanti gli Etiopi. Fascic. VI (1932), p. 181.

[24] E. L. BUTCHER, Story of the Church in Egypt, vol. I, part 2, chap. XII, p. 487.

[25] Balsamon; MIGNE, Pat. Graeca, vol. CXXXVII, col. 753.

the year 1000, and her dynasty (*Zâguê*) governed the country until 1268, when a counter-revolution restored the old royal line in the person of Yekuno Amlak. The conquests of Islam disturbed relations with Egypt, but numbers of Copts fled from the persecutions of Hakim (996-1021) and his successors to Ethiopia. In the 11th century, Abuna Severus obtained the headship of the church by bribing the Fatamid khalif and promising to work in the interests of Islam, but the erection of mosques in the country so infuriated the Christian population that he was banished.

The Middle Ages

Little intercourse with Rome was possible during the middle ages, but in 1177 a letter was written, probably by King Keddus [26] Harbé (1150-1182), under the name of "Priest John," to the emperor Frederick Barbarossa, in which he says: "We have learnt that the Pope [27] of Rome, our friend and our brother, bears himself well and that with the good pleasure of God, he interests himself in our people." The same king, also, told an explorer and doctor named Philip that he wished to have an Ethiopian sanctuary in Rome, as well as in Jerusalem. Pope Alexander III is said by some to have given him, in response to his desire, the church of St. Stephen near the basilica of St. Peter, although it is more probable that this was acquired from Eugenius IV after the council of Florence (1439) or even later.

King Lalibela (1182-1220), an outstanding figure in the history of the Ethiopian church, was the reputed builder

---

[26] Chenouda.
[27] Alexander III, 1159-1181.

of eleven churches, into one of which no female may enter. Other churches of the same period are found at Sokota, Aïba, Gherehalta, Amba-Saneiti and Ago-Eddi, the last named built with a triple nave, like the primitive form of Latin basilica. Lalibela, who died on June 12, 1220, and was buried in the holy mountain church of Biete Mariam, is honoured as a saint (June 6) by the dissidents.

The restoration of the old dynasty (1268) was largely the work of a monk, Takla Haimanot,[28] with whom an alliance was made of such far reaching importance that 1268 came to be known as the "Year of the Agreement." By means of this African "Donation of Constantine" monasticism gained immense wealth and prestige, and it is reckoned that about one-third of the whole land came into the possession of the church. The alliance or pragmatic sanction created the abbot of Debra Libanos (Takla Haimanot) and his successors, under the title of *etcheghie,* an assistant to the throne, which, since the office of abuna was often in abeyance, gave him immense power. In addition, the holder of the office was the head of all the religious houses in the country; while all the administrative and judicial powers of the church rested in his hands. It has been said that the privileges and advantages afforded to the clerical estate generated vocations[29] at Debra Libanos by the hundreds and thousands, and it became a historic event, told in detail in the imperial chronicles. In the 16th century, an abbot of the house was a convert from Islam, named Habakkuk, who is claimed as a saint by the dissidents.

The reign of Yekuno Amlak witnessed further contact[30] between Ethiopia and the Catholic church, and the king

---

[28] Not to be confounded with his namesake of the 7th century.
[29] *Dictionnaire de Théologie Catholique,* t. V, col. 937.
[30] *Ibid.,* col. 935.

requested Ignatius (David II), Syrian bishop of Jerusalem, to send a bishop. Ignatius, since 1237, had been reconciled with the Apostolic See, and he had written to Pope Gregory IX (1227-1241): "We have sent from our brothers in Egypt to the Coptic patriarch, Abuna Kerlos... and this patriarch has witnessed also to us the desire to come back to the unity of the Church." In response to the request, Abba Yub [31] (Job) was sent to the country, and he was followed by a number of Dominicans, probably from Armenia, who settled at Debra-Damo on the plateau of Gole-Mekada. The work of the Catholics, however, was short-lived, and the next king, Yagba Tsion (1283), expelled Yub and persecuted those who favoured the cause of unity. The martyrs nevertheless have left their mark on the country, and oratories [32] enshrining their bones still serve as parish churches at Gherehalta, Akran, Tesne and Bareknaha, where they are venerated by the dissidents. These sanctuaries take the form of vast galleries cut in the mountains. The legend of the "Sleeping Saints," [33] also, is connected with this period. The Coptic patriarch, in order to reestablish Monophysism on a firm basis, sent a learned man, Salama II, as abuna. [34] The reign of Yagba Tsion has been described [35] as one of "treason against the state in face of Islam and of persecution against the Church."

Further intercourse with Rome comes from the year 1310, when King Wedem Raad (1298-1313) sent an em-

[31] The altar vessels of Yub are still preserved.

[32] Some writers have computed that the remains date from the first half of the 14th century.

[33] *Tsadhan neouman.*

[34] *Abûna* (" Our father"), the head of the Ethiopian Church.

[35] *Dict. de Théol. Cath.*, t. V, col. 938. In 1449, the king presided over a council at Amhara, and excommunicated those who affirmed that the individual persons of the Trinity are without a human form.

bassy to Avignon to implore the help of Clement V (1305-1314) against the advancing tide of Islam. It is possible that Nicholas IV (1288-1292) corresponded with Ethiopia; while, in 1329, letters were sent by John XXII (1316-1334) to King Amde-Tsion. David I (1381-1410) has been canonised by the dissidents, and his feast is observed on December 23.

Of the 14th century, it has been said: *"Le formalisme supplanta le culte en esprit et en vérité,"* but in the succeeding period a literary revival was cut short about the year 1470, by the Mohammedan invasions. Zara-Jacob, [36] who governed the kingdom from 1434 till 1468, was largely occupied with the spread of religion, but as nearly two centuries later Socinios said of him to Fr. Paez: he "with the best intentions was the evil genius of the Church of Ethiopia; he wished to save it and he lost it." In the harshness of his methods, the king was ably seconded by the etcheghie, Sa'at Amda Sion. The people were ordered to have tattooed on the forehead the names of the "Father, Son and Holy Spirit;" on the right arm, "I renounce the devil and am a servant of Mary, the Mother of the Creator," and on the left arm, "I renounce the impure devil and adore Christ, my God." The refractory were put to torture. Saturday was to be observed as Sunday, and those monks of Debra Libanos who refused to obey the Judaising commands were decapitated. Many monasteries and churches were founded in his reign; and matters of church discipline and worship were regulated. The holy days and fasts were strictly determined, and, in addition to the feasts common to the whole Ethiopian church, Zara-Jacob instituted a further thirty-three. A fierce persecution was carried out

[36] *Ibid.,* t. V, coll. 947-948.

against idolators and dealers in magic, and we find large numbers of pagans on the banks of the river Abay and its tributaries in Choa and Damot submitting to baptism.   The chroniclers assert that in spite of his intense preoccupation with religious matters the king had no less than six wives. His palace, however, was a literary laboratory; while his genius, even more than that of his predecessor, was comparable to Charlemagne.   He extended a warm welcome to the Venetian traveller, Francesco Brancaleone, and attempts were made in his reign to heal the breach with Catholic unity, notwithstanding an official publication which styled the council of Chalcedon an "assembly of dogs." [37]

Two separate deputations attended the council of Florence.   The first, which was sent in common with the Copts and arrived in 1440, had two representatives, Andrew, an Egyptian monk of St. Antony, and Peter, a deacon who acted as delegate for the Ethiopian prior of Jerusalem.   On August 31 of that year, the deputy of the Jacobite patriarch and the ambassador of the king of Abyssinia had an audience with Pope Eugenius IV, in which they humbly acknowledged the primacy of the Apostolic See.   Peter [38] said: "All men who come to your holiness, O blessed father, have much to give thanks for to God, since they see Christ in you."

---

[37] *Mehabere-kelabat.*

[38] "*Salva ceterorum pace, non credimus gentem aliam esse quae maiore fide et reverentia Romanum Pontificem veneretur. Quod quidem ab experientia apud nos notorium dignoscitur, ut reversuri in patriam, applausus exultationesque nostrorum hominum et populi obviam processuri timere cogamur; quia semper hactenus observatum est ut venientium a Romani Pontificis conspectu plebs et omnis sexus atque aetatis multitudo conferta pedes osculari et vestis partem pro reliquiis servandam lacerare contendat; unde intelligi potest quanta sit nostris hominibus Romani Pontificis opinio sanctitatis.*" — MANSI, t. XXXI, col. 1744; *Incontro ai Fratelli Separati di Oriente,* p. 210.

The second deputation was undertaken by the Ethiopian prior of Jerusalem himself, Nicodemus, who on September 2, 1440, declared that "the emperor of Ethiopia has nothing on this earth nearer to his heart than to unite himself to the Roman Church and to throw himself at your sacred feet..." It may be noted that the deputies seem to have come to the council prepared to accede to the decisions of the pope rather than to dispute with him. A special visit was made by the travellers to Rome, in order that they might see the handkerchief of St. Veronica in the basilica of St. Peter. The Coptic and Ethiopian churches by the decree *pro Jacobitis* (February 4, 1441) [39] were reunited to Rome, and Abba Andrew, in the name of them all, made an act of acceptance in Arabic. The union, however, was stillborn, as the Copts followed the Greeks in their repudiation of the decree; while the Ethiopians only learnt of it when its reversal had become an accomplished fact. Abuna had died in 1447 or 1448, and no successor was appointed till 1468, so it is interesting to speculate as to whether the king had hoped to obtain a bishop as a result of his negotiations with Rome. Zara-Jacob was buried in the monastery of Debra-Libanos. His successor, Beede-Mariam (1468-1478), did indeed ask the pope for a Catholic bishop, but he was sent three Franciscans first to reconcile the people, although their arrival in the coutry coincided with the accession of a new king (Eskander, 1478-1495), and they were immediately sent away. Beede-Mariam had an Italian picture of our Lady and child, which was preserved at Atronsé Mariam, much to the disgust of the dissident clergy, but it was destroyed in 1709 by the Gallas. In 1481, an Ethiopian deputation was well received in Rome by Pope Sixtus IV; while about the

[39] 1442, new style.

same time the little church of St. Stephen and its adjacent hospice were probably given for the use of the nation, under the title of *San Stefano dei Mori* or *degli Etiopi* (*Abissini Indiani*).

The Coming of the Portuguese

The first Portuguese expedition to reach Ethiopia was that of Pedro da Covilham, sent in 1487 by King John II, and in 1502 Emmanuel I obtained a bull from Pope Alexander VI bestowing upon the king of Portugal the title of "Lord of the navigation, conquest and trade of Ethiopia, Arabia, Persia and India."

In 1513, Queen Helena, as regent of the youthful king, Lebné-Denghel (1508-1540), invoked the aid of Portugal against the invasions of the Mohammedans. A mission of help, under Rodrigo da Lima, arrived in the country in 1520, and permission [40] was given for the Portuguese to say Mass in the Ethiopian churches. Soon after their arrival, however, the monks of Bisan were so shocked at the seeming irreverence of the westerners that the permission was withdrawn. "They were surprised," says the chronicler, "at our coming into the church with our shoes on, and still more at our spitting in it!" In spite of this, Abuna Mark in 1521 expressed the desire to be united to Rome, and Lebné-Denghel sent a letter to the king of Portugal, in which he said: "I send Padre Francisco Alvarez to the pope [41] with my obedience which is a personal matter for me."

---

[40] The Congregation of the Holy Office in 1704 renewed the permission, at the discretion of the local authorities, for the Latin Mass (with Latin accessories) to be celebrated in special cases on altars in dissident churches. *Congr. del S. Ufficio*, 12.IV.1704.

[41] Clement VII, 1523-1534.

The Ethiopians, on March 7, 1529, received a crushing defeat at Chambra Kouré; while, two years later, the monastery of Debra Libanos and many others were destroyed. The custom of the people to eat their meat raw is said to date from this time, when it was considered unsafe to light fires. The threat of Islam to the independence of the country demanded a Portuguese expeditionary force, and in 1540 Christopher da Gama arrived in Ethiopia. He was killed soon after his coming, but the victory that he achieved ensured the safety of the Christian kingdom.

The Portuguese, John Bermudez, in a book published in 1565, maintained that he himself was nominated abuna (1538) by Mark, at the express wish of the king. Such a proceeding, [42] however, was contrary to normal procedure, and there is no proof of it extant, although Bermudez seems to have gone to Pope Paul III (1534-1548) with the declaration of the king, to the effect that he was desirous of making his submission.

The king (Gladios, 1540-1560) and his allies, on February 21, 1543, defeated and killed Gran, [43] the Moslem leader, at Darasge on Lake Tana. With the country safe from Islam, Gladios returned to his schismatic leanings, showing himself in many ways hostile to Catholicism. In March 1557, a Portuguese bishop, Andrew d'Oviedo, and five Jesuit priests came to the country in the hope of restoring Catholic unity, but their tactless behaviour had the reverse effect. The National Church now appears to have passed through a period of renaissance, religious life was

---

[42] The story is maintained in the *Dictionnaire de Théologie Catholique* (coll. 950-951), which goes on to say that King Gladios withdrew the recognition of his authority from him, and, as a result of his threats, expelled him from the country (1556).

[43] "the left handed," Emir of Harar.

shown, not only in polemics and controversial works, but also in liturgical worship. The clergy became more active, schools reopened, and churches were to an extent restored. At the same time, the antiphonary [44] for all feasts of the year and the ritual [45] for extreme unction and penance made their appearance.

Minas, the successor of Gladios (1560-1564), was even more adverse to the Catholic missions, and forbade, under, severe penalties, any form of proselytism. Oviedo, in revenge, is said to have allied himself with the enemies of the king, even Moslems. St. Ignatius Loyola, realising the harm that was being done in the country in the name of Christ, even if some of the charges were untrue, obtained the consecration at Lisbon of Nuñez de Barreto as "Patriarch of Abyssinia." Opposition, however, detained him at Goa, where in 1562 he died, and the "patriarchate" automatically fell to Oviedo. Sertsé Denghel (1564-1597) was less hostile to Catholicism than his predecessor, but he declined to allow missionaries at court and, at the same time, prohibited proselytism.

Again, Oviedo, with his impetuosity and impatience, entered into active opposition, and, appealing to Portugal for armed forces, said that they "might easily make themselves masters of the sea ports, rescue the other Portuguese, and compel the Ethiopians to submit to the see of Rome." Cardinal Prince Henry, regent for King Sebastian, was, however, not deceived in the situation, and asked the new pope, St. Pius V (1566-1572), to grant permission to Bishop Oviedo to leave Ethiopia and "to proceed to Japan or China, or somewhere else, where he might do more good and make

[44] *Degwa.*
[45] *Maṣâhefâ.*

less noise!" The bishop begged to be allowed to stay in the country, and he died in 1577 at Fremona, [46] a Jesuit settlement between Axum and Adowa. The work of Oviedo was, as we have seen, more of a hindrance than a help, but his courage and constancy were amazing. At Fremona, "his palace was a thatched hut, his diet a thin cake of *tef*..., his other dainties were cabbage or linseed without any other seasoning but salt and water; and even these he was to sow and cultivate himself... In the midst of his sufferings he spared no labour, attending the poor of all sorts, which was the occasion of converting many schismatics... His poverty was such that he was reduced to tear the first white page out of his breviary to write a letter on. Another he afterwards wrote to the pope and, wanting even such a leaf, he cut off the margins of his breviary and sewed them together to write on."

The original Jesuit mission died out, but in 1603 a member of the Society of Jesus came to the country, who has been called the "second apostle of Abyssinia," Fr. Peter Paez. It would seem that he was the antithesis of his predecessor, and *persona grata* with the royal house. Soon after his arrival, Fr. Paez said Mass in Geez and preached in the presence of King Zè-Denghel (1597-1607), who was desirous of becoming a Catholic himself and of having his subjects instructed in the same faith. The Jesuit, however, mindful of the ill-advised zeal of Bishop Oviedo, "advised him to proceed more gently." The king wrote to the pope, asking for "fathers to instruct us that we may be all one heart and one body and establish the faith of Christ which was lost among the Gentiles." Too impatient to wait for the answer from Rome, Zè-Denghel issued decrees on

[46] The original name was Maigoga, "noise of water."

disputed points, such as the observance of Saturday, with the result that a civil war ensued and abuna excommunicated the king for betraying the national religion. Soon afterwards, Zè-Denghel was killed, and Jacob, his successor, only reigned for one year, when he too, together with abuna, met a violent death. Tsegga-Christos,[47] an illegitimate son of Jacob, became a Catholic in 1632 at Jerusalem, but the crown descended to Socinios, a cousin (1607-1632).

The new king [48] was well disposed to Catholicism, but he feared at first to show his hand, although his brother the viceroy, Ras Sela Cristos, had already been reconciled. In the year of his succession, embassies were sent to Pope Paul V (1605-1621) and King Philip III of Spain and Portugal (1598-1621); while, undeterred by the disastrous policy of his predecessor, he sought to obtain a further contingent of Portuguese soldiers, in order that he might convert his country by force. The military expedition was not forthcoming, and the king contented himself with the issue of a proclamation, in which it was stated that "for the future no one should presume to maintain that there was but one nature in Christ, but that all should own two distinct natures, the human and the divine, both united and in the divine person." Abuna Simon excommunicated all those who should hold such a doctrine; while the king retaliated with the threat of decapitation for disobedience to his order and openly advocated union with the Catholic Church. Revolts were continuous from 1618 till 1623, although Socinios persisted in the fatal policy of dragooning his subjects. Thus, Saturday was declared to be a day of

[47] Tsegga-Christos, who visited both the pope and the king of France, died in 1638 at Rugil.

[48] The first position of Socinios may be compared with that of Charles II of England and James, Duke of York, later on in the century.

work, and a general who refused to violate the Sabbath was beaten and publicly degraded; while a monk who maintained that there was only one nature in Christ had his tongue cut out. Early in 1622, the king was publicly reconciled to the Catholic Church, and sent his profession of faith to Rome. In May of the same year, however, Fr. Paez, the hinge upon which the faith in Abyssinia turned, died at Gorgora, and ten years later Catholicism followed him to the grave. Fr. Paez will be remembered not only for the work that he did for the Church, but also as the discoverer of the source of the Blue Nile and the builder of the royal palace at Gorgora.

Alfonso Mendez, also of the Society of Jesus, was consecrated "patriarch" of Ethiopia in February 1623 at Lisbon. Two assistant bishops were also consecrated, although one of them died at Goa before reaching the country. The other two prelates reached Fremona on June 21, 1625. In the following year (February 11, 1626), King Socinios made a further profession of faith and submission to the pope (Urban VIII, 1623-1644), in order that he might "publicly swear obedience to the Holy See, and union of faith with the Catholics." The text of the pronouncement was as follows: "We, Seltan Sagad, by the grace of God ruler of Ethiopia, believe and confess that St. Peter was constituted Prince of the Apostles, head of the Universal Church, our Lord having said to him." 'Thou art Peter and upon this rock I will build my Church and I will give to thee the keys of the kingdom of heaven, and whatsoever thou shalt bind on earth shall be bound in heaven, and whatsoever thou shalt loose on earth shall be loosed in heaven.'" On another occasion he said to him: "Feed my sheep." That moreover the pope of Rome is the true and legitimate successor of St. Peter, that he has the same power, dignity and primacy over all the Catholic Church throughout the world, and that he cannot err in matters of faith, as having that promise of the Son of God in the person of St. Peter: "I have asked for thee that thy faith shall not fail." Therefore, we recognise the Roman Church as the Mother and Mistress of all churches, and with her condemn and anathematise all the heresies which she has condemned and anathematised, notably those of Dioscorus and Eutyches, as they had been specially embedded here, and promise the obedience due to the said Roman Church in the person of our holy Father Pope Urban VIII at present sitting. So God help us and these holy Gospels." The king's sons, Fasilides and Mark, as well as all the public officials were required to take the same oath. This was followed by ecclesiastical reforms [49] in respect to the priesthood, feasts and fasts; while any priest,[50] secular or regular, who should minister without first showing the validity of his ordination and taking the Catholic oath was liable to be put to death, and the same penalty was threatened for those who gave refuge or help to the refractory. The year 1628 may be reckoned the high water mark of Catholicism in the country, at least in respect to the influence that it exerted.

The Jesuits translated the Bible and many works of devotion, and established a printing press. Eleven mission stations were founded, with a "patriarch," bishop and nineteen priests, while the converts were said to number from 100,000 to 130,000. The chief Catholic centres were Fremona (Tigré), Gorgora (Dembia), Quelela (Godjam) and Mai-Guaggua (near Aksum).

Tactless intolerance and inquisitorial violence continued to foment discontent, and the exhumation and throwing out

[49] Among the "reforms" were the translation of the Roman missal into Geez and the adoption of the Latin calendar.
[50] *Dict. de Théol. Cath.*, t. V, col. 958.

of the body of the *etcheghie,* who, according to custom, had been buried under an altar, was the direct cause of a revolt that led eventually to the overthrow of the Catholic religion in Ethiopia. The date of Easter was also a very sore point, but in justice to the Jesuits it must be noted that one of the main grievances of the dissidents was the establishment of monogamy and the abolition of divorce. In 1631, the king, wishing to obtain peace, issued a proclamation of toleration, which infuriated Mendez, although it had expressly forbidden the return of Catholic converts to Monophysism. Concessions were granted, such as the use of Geez in the liturgy, the celebration of some feasts, other than Easter, on the days customary in the Ethiopic church, and the Wednesday fast, in place of Saturday. The time of compromise, however, was past, and the opposition gathered momentum. Worn out by the struggle, Socinios abdicated in 1632 in favour of his son Fasilides (1632-1667), and died on September 17 of the same year. He lived long enough to see the downfall of his cherished hopes, and in June 1632 his son issued the following edict: "Hear, hear, we first gave you this faith believing it was good, but innumerable people have been killed on account of it, among whom were Elos, Gabriel, Tekla Giosgis, Cerica Cristos, and now lately these peasants; for which reasons we restore you the faith of your forefathers. The former priests may return to their churches, put in their tabots, and say Masses, and do you rejoice."

The chronicler has thus described the effect of the proclamation on the people: "The whole camp, as if they had had some great deliverance from the enemy, rang with shouts and acclamations. The monks and clergy who had felt the greatest weight of the fathers' hatred lifted up their thankful voices to heaven. The promiscuous multitude of men and women danced and capered... They brake to

pieces their own and the rosaries of all they met and some
they burnt... others ran about singing for joy... chanting
forth the following lines:

> At length the sheep of Ethiopia freed
> From the bold lions of the West
> Securely in their pastures feed.
> Saints Mark's and Cyril's doctrines have o'ercome
> The follies of the Church of Rome.
> Rejoice, rejoice, sing alleluias all
> No more the Western wolves
> Our Ethiopia shall enthral." [51]

A few days after the edict had been published, "there
was a general circumcision, and then followed a universal
baptism, after their former manner, which being done they
concluded themselves free from the obligation of being tied
to one wife, and publicly declared that for the future they
would marry and re-marry as they pleased." Mendez was
ordered to leave the country, but he asked the king to give
his reasons for such summary dismissal, saying in his
defence: "I granted the ceremonies desired by your father,
except the communion under both kinds which only the
pope himself can dispense. The same also I again offer,
so that you and your subjects will yield obedience to the
Church of Rome as the head of all the churches."

The king replied by discussing the two natures in our
Lord and communion in both kinds, declaring: "These are
the things that gave offence to our people, but they detested
nothing more than the reiteration of baptism, as if we had
been heathens before we had been baptized by the fathers.

---

[51] There is another version of the same popular chant: "Here
now the sheep have escaped from the hyenas of the West, thanks to
the teaching of Mark and of Cyril, columns of the Church of Alexandria. Let us rejoice, let us rejoice and sing alleluia. Ethiopia has
escaped from the hyenas of the West."

They re-ordained our priests and deacons, they burned the wooden chests of our altars, and consecrated others of their own, as if ours had not been consecrated before .... These and other things of the same nature were the true causes that we abandoned the Roman faith, though it was not we who gave it protection but our father .... We command you to hasten to Fremona. These things are offered now too late which might have been easily at first allowed, for now there is no returning to that which the whole nation abhors and detests; for which reason all further colloquies and disputes will be in vain."

The Portuguese laity, if they wished, were allowed to remain in the country, but the Jesuits were expelled. The Ethiopian chronicler, under the year 1635, records: "That year there arrived the patriarch whose name was Rezeq, with the holy ark .... The Frank Alfonson returned into his own country." Mendez himself, after a two years imprisonment by the Turks, died at Goa, but a bishop (Apollinaris de Almeida) and six priests remained in the country and suffered martyrdom.

Possessed of so many virtues, the Catholic missionaries were unhappily devoid of common sense; while their tactlessness and intolerance in regard to non-essentials, combined with an unblushing support of the rapacious "imperialism" of Portuguese politics, lost Abyssinia to the Catholic faith, and at the same time imbuted the minds of the people with a distrust for Europeans. Catholicism was virtually stamped out, and Sehele-Christos, brother of King Socinios, was hanged.

From time to time missionaries [52] returned to the country,

---

[52] Protestant missionaries, notably in 1734, 1830-1850, and 1858, have had no more success than the Catholics, and the common name for them is *tsèrè-Mariam,* "enemy of Mary."

and in 1633 Abyssinia was placed by the Congregation of Propaganda under the Capuchin friars of Cairo, who in 1637 established a mission station.

In the following year, there came Blessed Agathangelo of Vendôme and Blessed Cassian of Nantes, but they were soon captured and hanged at Gondar with the cords of their Franciscan habits. [53] For four nights miraculous lights were reported to be seen above the bodies, and the king in terror ordered them to be buried. Some Catholics, however, took them away by stealth, and their resting-place is to this day unknown. The cause of their beatification was begun in 1665, but was interrupted for two hundred years, until it was taken up again in 1887 by Cardinal Massaia, who had worked for thirty-five years in the country. Finally, on January 7, 1905, the two martyrs were declared blessed by Pope Pius X.

Undeterred by the fate of their religious brethren, three Franciscans attempted to enter the country in 1648, but they were speedily put to death at Suakim, and their heads forwarded to King Fasilides. Two years later, Fr. Antonio d'Andrade, an Ethiopian by birth who had studied at Rome, was named vicar apostolic, but little was achieved and when in 1671 he reached Massawa with two Franciscans they were all immediately executed. A further abortive mission was undertaken in 1698, but it would seem that in 1702 three Franciscans arrived in Gondar, where they reconciled several of the princes. The negus [54] himself wrote to Pope Clement XI (1700-1721) with a promise of submission, while seven young Ethiopians were sent to Rome for education. Unhappily, a palace revolution deposed the king,

---

[53] Apollinaris de Almeida, a Jesuit, suffered in the same year.

[54] *Negus neghesti*, "King of kings," is the title given to the ruler of Ethiopia.

and destroyed any chance of union. It has been thought
that King Yostos (1711-1717) may have been a secret
Catholic.

In the 18th century, further attempts were made to
enter the country. Some French Jesuits were killed at the
beginning of the century, three Capuchins and others were
stoned to death in 1711, Fr. Antony da Rivarolo and two
others were sent into slavery at Socotra in 1725, and Fr.
Ignatius Ballerini was killed in 1797.

King Sahle-Salassie (1816-1849) discussed with the
French representative the similarities between their respective religions, and even contemplated asking the pope
for a bishop. Nothing further, however, was done in the
matter.

About this time, Abuna Cyril († ab. 1828) ordered, on
pain of excommunication, all *tabots* to be made of wood,
while those of marble were to be destroyed, as the former
Jesuit missionaries had used that material.

Ethiopia by the end of the 18th century had become
feudalised, with the country parcelled out among *ras* or
provincial chieftains. Kings reigned at Gondar (1633-1839),
but they did not govern, and civil wars were frequent.

Establishment of the Catholic Church

In 1836, some Ethiopian priests of Adowa sent a letter [55]
to Pope Gregory XVI (1831-1846), in which they styled
him "Vicar of Jesus Christ, seated on the throne of Peter,
Sovereign Pontiff of the Universal Church," and declared:

---

[55] J.-B. COULBEAUX, *Histoire de l'Abyssinie* (Paris 1929), t. II,
chap. XIV, p. 403.

"We should then recognise that the Roman Church is the very Church of Jesus Christ."

Their request was due to the work of the Irish-French traveller Arnauld d'Abbadie d'Arrast, who with his elder brother Antony and the Italian Lazarist Sapeto had arrived at the court of Dejach Oubie, king of Tigré (1830-1855), where they had met with a cordial reception. About a hundred persons were reconciled to the Catholic church, and the converts, in a profession of faith forwarded to the pope, requested that priests might be sent to them.

In 1840, the pope suggested that Theodore, vicar general of the Copts, might send a bishop of his rite to Ethiopia, but there is no evidence that any action was taken.

Fr. Justin de Jacobis from the Italian province of Basilicata (kingdom of Naples) and Fr. Montuori arrived at Adowa in 1839, and a prefecture apostolic was established.

In the province of Amhara, the scene of the former labours of Fr. Paez, it was found that the people still took dust every year from the tombs of the Jesuits, and scattered it to the winds.

Mgr de Jacobis, who had learnt Geez, Tigré and Amharic, was consecrated titular bishop of Nilopolis and vicar apostolic of Abyssinia in 1849 by Mgr. Massaia, vicar apostolic of the Gallas. Permission was given for the missionaries to celebrate Mass according to the Ethiopic rite, whenever it might be deemed expedient.

In 1841, Mgr. de Jacobis led a deputation to Egypt and Rome, when one of the party was the future martyr and *beatus* Gabra Michael. [56] A letter from King Oubie was given to the Coptic patriarch which greatly angered the prelate, as reconciliation with Rome was suggested,

---

[56] *Gabra Mika'el,* " servant of St. Michael."

and permission was asked for the building of Catholic churches. While in Cairo, the patriarch Peter consecrated Aba Andrew as abuna (Salama), an ignorant man who had till recently been a camel driver. Some of the deputation now went on to Rome, where they were received by Pope Gregory XVI.

On their way home they visited Jerusalem, and one of their number, seriously ill at Jaffa, made a profession of Catholic faith.

Gabra Michael, [57] although still a dissident, was convinced of the truth of Catholic christology, and sought to convince his coreligionists of their error. His efforts were not very successful, despite the fact that his former pupil John (Attieh Yohannes) had come to the throne of Gondar. In despair at the dissensions in his church, Gabra Michael was received into the Catholic church at Adowa in 1844 by Fr. Justin de Jacobis, and was ordained priest in 1851, one of the first episcopal acts of his spiritual father. At Guenda-Guende a number of the monks were reconciled, and a college was established at Guala. Here, in 1846, over a dozen Ethiopian priests were received into communion with the Church. Abuna Salama, who had been exiled by King John, stirred up feeling against "the Franks," and banished the two European leaders Mgr. Massaia and Mgr. Justin de Jacobis.

Returning to the country, however, they had an almost startling success. The negus John formally repudiated the heresy and schism of his church, and was followed by many others, both clerics and laymen. In February 1855, the dissident opposition and persecution were redoubled by the

[57] Gabra Michael had been a monk at his native town of Mertola Mariam and later at Gondar, although appalled at the spiritual state of monasticism and of the Ethiopic church generally.

accession to the throne of Cassa, son of the governor of Kowara, who received the name of Theodore II.

Mgr. de Jacobis, in the hope that an exposition of papal supremacy drawn from the *Fethé Neghest* [58] might lessen the hostility of the dissidents, drew attention to the following passage:

"In the same way that the father has authority and jurisdiction over his sons, the bishop over his subjects, and the patriarch over the suffragan bishops, so, in like manner, the patriarch of Rome, in his quality of successor of St. Peter, Prince of the apostles, has authority and sovereign jurisdiction over all the patriarchs in the Universal Church, and over all human society, holding as he does the place of Jesus Christ, and being his vicar upon earth."

In 1854, Gabra Michael, Takla Haymanot and three other Ethiopians were arrested, and brought before Salama at Gondar, where all the clergy with the exception of these five repudiated Catholicism.

Three weeks later, they were confronted with Theodore and the dethroned negus John, who had himself apostasised. Again firm in their faith, the five were incarcerated in a filthy cell, scourged and tortured. At intervals they were brought before Theodore, but nothing could shake their constancy. In March 1855 Theodore went to war with the ruler of Shoa, and Gabra Michael was taken along with the army, in chains. Two months later, he was offered the choice of apostasy or death, but at the request of

---

[58] The Ethiopian civil, criminal and religious code, of which a translation was made in the 16th century from an Egyptian nomocanon. The authority of the emperor in spiritual matters was, however, supreme, and on one occasion Theodore said to Abuna Salama: "I have paid enough for you; you are no different from my other slaves except in the matter of the price that you have cost me." COULBEAUX, *op. cit.*, I, p. 215.

one of the English advisers [59] of the king his life was spared. He was ordered to wear chains for the rest of his life, but on August 28 of that year the martyr, now afflicted with cholera, gave up his soul to God at the foot of a tree by the wayside. [60] Gabra Michael was buried at Berakit, and Rome set her seal upon his heroic sanctity on January 30, 1926, by declaring him to be a *beatus*. The Congregation of Rites on January 25, 1927, conceded and approved an office and Mass in his honour (September 1). The Ethiopic rite observes the feast on October 6 (26 *maskarem*).

Mgr. de Jacobis, after many years of unremitting toil and labour, laid down his life on July 31, 1860, in the desert of Ali-gade.

He left behind him a magnificent native clergy and about 12,000 converts. The Catholic mission, although so late as 1871 two priests were put to death for their faith, has never again been uprooted. On June 25, 1939, the venerable Justin de Jacobis was declared blessed by Pope Pius XII.

Partial toleration of the Catholic religion was granted in 1889, on the accession of Menelik (1889-1913) to the throne.

It is recorded that on one occasion Menelik said to Cardinal Massaia, the venerable vicar apostolic of the Gallas: "You have saints and that is a wonder which neither my priests nor *depteras* (lay teachers) can accomplish."

[59] Walter Chichele Plowden, who was murdered five years later.
[60] The martyr died actually from hardship and exposure: he had recovered from the attack of cholera.

The National Church in Modern Times

King Menelik described his kingdom as "an island of Christianity in a sea of black paganism," although it is estimated that of the eight million inhabitants not more than half are Christians.

Menelik's grandson and heir apostasised [61] to Islam, and, after civil war, the crown was settled upon Princess Zaodito, the daughter of the late king.   In 1930, Hailie Salassie I (Ras Tafari) ascended the throne, bringing with him a very real desire to promote the welfare of his country, combined with a wish to break with the tradition that abuna, the head of the Ethiopian church, must be a Coptic monk.   This regulation, which limits the choice of abuna to a monk from the monastery of St. Antony [62] near the Red Sea, was, as we have seen, probably formulated in the 13th century, and enjoined in the *Fethé Neghest*.

The following reasons have been alleged for making the church of Ethiopia "a humble and backward daughter of the Coptic church":

a) It maintains a link with the outside world; *b*) It prevents disorders, intrigues and rivalry in the country; and *c*) a foreign abuna is more likely to hold an independent position.

No council limits his power, and, in theory, the state alone can control his activities, although on more than one occasion abuna under threats of excommunication has had to give way on some disputed point.   The residence of abuna was moved in 1892 from Gondar to Addis Ababa, but at one time, as guardian of the royal commands, he followed

---

[61] The father of the prince had been a convert from Islam.

[62] The monastery of St. Macarius in Nitria. *Dict. de Théol. Cath.*, t. V, col. 926.

the king on his travels and in his wars, so that he could justly say that "my episcopal see is the back of my mule."

It is generally stated that abuna was the only dissident bishop in the country, but although this has normally been the case there have been examples of assistant bishops, as when King Chenouda [63] attempted to get more than seven bishops consecrated, presumably with the idea of obtaining the twelve necessary for the consecration of abuna. In the time of John IV (1872-1889) also, three bishops [64] were appointed for Tigré, Goggiam and Shoa respectively, although they had no successors.

When, in 1926, Abuna Matthew died, Ras Tafari, voicing popular "progressive" opinion, demanded the independence of the Ethiopian church from Egypt. Negotiations went on for three years, and the office was offered to the bishop of Kaneh, a layman, and four other monks before it was finally accepted by Sidaros ben Antoni, second in command at the Egyptian monastery of St. Antony, who took the name of Qerillos (Cyril). Abuna was consecrated on June 2, 1929, by the Coptic patriarch John XIX, who at the same time consecrated four auxiliary Ethiopian bishops. It was, however, stipulated that none of these assistants should succeed as abuna; while any increase in the number of bishops was expressly forbidden.

In January 1930, the Coptic patriarch, suspicious of the papal mission sent to Addis Ababa in the previous November, paid a short visit to the country, where he consecrated a fifth Ethiopian, in the person of the *etcheghie*. [65]

---

[63] The plan was frustrated by the Coptic patriarch, Gabriel Ibn Tarik (1131-1145), *Dict. de Théol. Cath.*, t. X, col. 2259.

[64] GORDILLO, *Compendium Theologiae Orientalis*, chap. IX, art. V, p. 263, n. 2.

[65] The present *etcheghie* (1946) is Gabre Giorgis.

Under the influence of the Italians, who had conquered the country, the Ethiopian church on November 27, 1937, nominated Abba Abraha, a monk of Gondar, as abuna, together with three other monks as bishops [66]—for Debradamo, Sala Dingai and Axum respectively.

After the return of the emperor during the second world war (1939-1945), Abuna Qerillos was restored.

Early in 1946, the emperor sent a mission [67] to Cairo to persuade the Copts to grant full autonomy to the Ethiopian church. Less than a week after the arrival of the delegates, the Coptic holy synod decided to allow the major requests.

These include the election of an archbishop (*abuna*) from their own clergy, and the formation of a holy synod in Addis Ababa. It is understood that Ethiopia will now have an archbishop, who is bound to the Coptic church only by allegiance to the same patriarch.

Hierarchy

In their list of abunas [68] the dissidents omit the names of those who were reconciled to the Catholic church.

The *etcheghie,* as we have seen, is the abbot of Debra Libanos, and responsible for administrative jurisdiction. He now resides at Addis Ababa.

There are two categories of clergy (*kahenat*).

a) The lay clerics or *depteras,* who interpret and apply the written law of the church, look after the chant, and teach in the schools.

---

[66] *L'Oriente Moderno,* t. XVII (1937), p. 633.

[67] Cairo, February 6; quoted in *The Times,* February 7, 1946.

[68] The position of abuna ("our father") as metropolitan of Ethiopia, and his subjection to the Coptic patriarch, have been already mentioned.

b) The ecclesiastical clerks perform the services, but they are often despised by the *depteras* for their ignorance and lack of culture. Many of the priests are said to be unable to read; while others have little or no knowledge of the liturgical language (Geez).

The dissidents have no seminary, although this is one of the reforms that has been suggested.

Various stories have been current in regard to the ordination of priests, but it is difficult to establish the truth of these alleged scandals. Converts to Catholicism, who are already in orders, are ordained conditionally.

It has been said, for example, that a present of two blocks of salt has been the sole condition necessary to obtain ordination; while hundreds of candidates have been made priests at the same time, so that material contact of hands was out of the question.

The Portuguese Alvarez spoke of little children being admitted to the diaconate, who were too small either to speak or walk, and who could only swallow the host by having water poured down their throats. The same writer also claims to have witnessed an ordination in 1521 in which 2,357 persons were ordained to the priesthood!

In the 18th century, James Bruce [69] speaks of a number of men and children standing at a distance from abuna, not daring to approach. On being asked what they wanted, and replying to be made deacons, abuna made two or three signs of the cross over them with a small iron cross and, blowing on them, said: "Let them be deacons." The same writer also records that "it once happened that almost 3,000 resorting to abuna to be ordained, he being then busy, bid them take what orders they would and go about their business."

---

[69] *Travels to discover the Source of the Nile*, 1790.

Coming to the 19th century, the notorious Abuna Salama (1842-1860) is alleged to have used as a formula of ordination: "Go, son of a dog, be a priest!"

These stories may be of the nature of calumnies invented and embroidered by opponents, but boys who can barely read are still ordained as deacons; while little seems to be required of a priest beyond a knowledge of the Nicene creed and the most essential rites of the liturgy. The clergy marry as deacons "once for eternity." In practice, minor orders are included in the diaconate, although ancient formularies recognise the subdiaconate [70] as a distinctive order.

The Catholic Mission

Catholic life was restored in the country by the erection of a prefecture apostolic in 1839, which ten years later was raised to a vicariate.

The number of these vicariates [71] apostolic by 1937 had risen to four, with the same number of prefectures. [72]

The Latin rite has been exclusively used by the Capuchins in the Galla country of south Abyssinia, and to a great extent in the vicariate of Addis Ababa, although the latter district has 13 secular priests of the Ethiopic rite.

In 1930, an ordinariate of Eastern rite was formed in the Italian colony of Eritrea, and on August 4 of that year Abba Khidane Mariam Kassa was consecrated bishop of the

[70] Nefka diyakon, "half-deacon." Fethé Neghest, p. 90; Testo di Diritto Antichi e Moderni riguardanti gli Etiopi. Fascic. V, Tipografia Vaticana, 1931.

[71] Addis Ababa (1913); Eritrea (1911); Harrar (the Galla, 1846); Jimma (1937).

[72] Dessie (1937); Gondar (1937); Neghelli (1937); Tigré (1839).

titular see of Thibaris in the then Ethiopic church of Santo Stefano in the Vatican City by Cardinal Sincero, secretary of the Sacred Congregation for the Eastern Church.

The faithful of the rite number 27,415 in Eritrea, and 2,422, under the care of the Lazarist vicar apostolic, elsewhere.

There are 89 churches and chapels with 76 native priests, and a seminary at Keren.

In September 1919, a college was opened in Rome for the formation of clergy of the Ethiopic rite, and the church of San Stefano degli Abissini was restored for the use of their liturgy.

The first connection of the Ethiopians with this church has been already mentioned, and it was here that the monk Tasfa Seyon produced the liturgical books [73] of the rite in the 16th century. In a letter to the pope, the Ethiopian liturgist said: "It is only at Rome that I have found the repose of my body and my soul. The repose of the soul is in the orthodox faith of Peter; the repose of the body is in Paul III, the successor of Peter." Tasfa Seyon, after a twelve years residence in Rome, died there in 1550, and his tombstone, together with that of a prior named Mark († 1581), may be seen in the church of San Stefano.

In the time of Innocent XI (1676-1689) the house

[73] There were published, the Geez psalter (1513); New Testament (1548-1549); *Ordo communis* of the liturgy with a Latin translation (1548). — In the 17th century, some Ethiopic priests in Rome, who were shortly leaving for their own country, asked for permission to say Mass in the Latin rite, using the Geez version translated by order of the patriarch Alphonsus Mendez. The Congregation of Propaganda refused to permit this, and ordered the priests to use their own Ethiopic liturgy, as emended under Pope Paul III (1534-1549). *Congr. Prop.*, 29.III.1639; *Testi di Diritto Antichi e Moderni riguardanti gli Etiopi*, Fascic. V (Tip. Pol. Vat., 1931), pp. 211, 213.

adjoining the church was unoccupied save for a chaplain who acted as caretaker, and in 1731 by the brief *Alias postquam* the buildings were given by Clement XII (1730-1740) to the Copts.

Here Raphael Tukhi published the Coptic missal for the use of Catholics of his rite.

From 1782-1816, the church was restored to the clergy of the Roman rite, but in the last named year it was given to an Ethiopian monk, George Galabadda († 1845).

The buildings in 1833 passed to the Calced Trinitarians, but in 1919 they once again served for clergy of an Eastern rite.

A young Ethiopian of Teramni, named Ghebre Mariam Andikiel, had come to Rome for purposes of study in 1916 or 1917, and Pope Benedict XV (1914-1922) conceived the idea of establishing an Ethiopian college. This was done, and the church of San Stefano and the house adjoining formed the beginnings of the new venture.

The Sacred Oriental Congregation placed the college under the direction of the Italian Capuchins, with an Ethiopian, Abba Tekle Mariam Semharay Selam, as spiritual director.

In 1928, a magnificent new building was erected, which two years later (February 12, 1930) by the constitution *Curis ac laboribus* was granted by Pius XI (1922-1939) the title of *Collegio Pontificio Etiopico*. By the terms of the Lateran Treaty (February 11, 1929) the college was now in the Vatican City.

The church of San Stefano, since the erection of the new building, has once again reverted to the Latin rite.

In 1931, there were 14 students in the college, which by 1939 had increased to 27. It is, however, to be greatly deplored that whereas the revision of the Ethiopic rite has been carried out in accordance with the best liturgical traditions, the chapel of the college is indistinguishable from a Latin building. Pictures of St. Frumentius and Blessed Gabra Michael are the only indications that the chapel is one of Ethiopic rite.

Three priests have made their ecclesiastical studies at the Latin patriarchal seminary in Jerusalem. [74]

The majority of the Catholic clergy are celibate, although there is no formal prohibition of married priests.

The Italian conquest of the country (Ethiopia) in 1936 brought about the replacement of the French missionaries by Italian. These in their turn left the country after the emperor, with the aid of British arms, had regained his throne. The present provisional arrangements [75] (March 1946) for the Catholics in Ethiopia are as follows:

Mgr. Kidane Mariam Kassa, ordinary for the Catholics of the Ethiopic rite in Eritrea, is regent of the apostolic delegation [76] at Addis Ababa and administrator of the vicariates of Addis Ababa and Jimma, as well as of the prefectures of Adigrat and Dessie. A priest of the Congregation of the Holy Ghost is vicar delegate of Harar and also vicar for the Latins in Addis Ababa.

Three Canadian Jesuits are in charge of the Tafari Makoonen School at Addis Ababa, a government post to which they are appointed by the emperor.

French Lazarist fathers are at the *procura* of the Lazarists at Addis Ababa and Adigrat. A French Capuchin is in

---

[74] There is a small colony of Ethiopian Catholics at Jerusalem.

[75] The information has been kindly supplied by Mgr. David Mathew, titular archbishop of Apamea, who in 1945 visited Ethiopia as a delegate of the Holy Father.

[76] In 1946, Fr. Theodore Monnens, a Jesuit of the north Belgian province, was appointed regent of the delegation.

charge of the printing press at Diredawa, together with a Canadian Capuchin brother. The Holy Ghost fathers are in charge of the *grand séminaire* at Harar and of the Latin church of St. Sauveur at Addis Ababa. A community of French sisters of charity is coming out to Addis Ababa, and there are Maltese Franciscan nuns in the Harar vicariate.

It is hoped that the supply of European priests will be augmented after the arrival of an apostolic delegate.

Monasticism

The monastic clergy rank higher in the esteem of the people than the seculars, although only a comparatively few monks are ordained.

There are two dissident religious observances in the country, both of which profess to follow the "rule of St. Antony"—Takla-Haimanot and Ewostatewos (Eustathius).

The main difference between them is that the latter has a fraternal régime [77] without an abbot, [78] although the superior of Debra-Bizan [79] near Adowa, the chief house of the "order," takes the first place in the observance.

Takla-Haimanot, with its headquarters at Debra Libanos in the mountainous Salaleh district of Shoa, has the *etcheghie* as abbot general, who formerly lived at Gondar and now at Addis Ababa.

Other important monasteries are at Debra Nequaquad on an island in Lake Haik, Lalibela (an important pilgrim-

---

[77] The monastic government seems very similar to that which prevails in the idiorrythmic houses of Mount Athos (e. g. Vatopedi), where there is a deliberative assembly and two or three elected presidents.

[78] *Mamher, ḳōmōs*; Coptic, *ḳummus*.

[79] *Debra*, "mount."

age centre), Debra Tabor, Debra Zeit, and Addis Alem. A writer, [80] however, has described the Ethiopian monk as a gyrovague, who, from motives of curiosity or love of learning, wanders from house to house and, above all, frequents the castles and courts of the feudal nobility, living but little in community. The monastery of Deir-es-Sultan, near the Holy Sepulchre in Jerusalem, has long been a source of discord between the Ethiopians and Copts. The negus in 1904 broke off relations with the Coptic patriarch, claiming the house on the ground that it was given by St. Helen, mother of the emperor Constantine, to Ethiopia. The Turks promised to see that the monastery was returned, and the Russians were also favourable, but the *status quo* was supported by the English, and in the end Turkey was compelled to do nothing in the matter. Ras Tafari, in his voyage to Europe in 1924, attempted unsucessfully to get possession of Deir-es-Sultan. There is, however, near this disputed property, a mediaeval house formerly belonging to the canons of the Holy Sepulchre, where the Ethiopians have a small monastery and "roof garden," consisting of a number of small "cabins" and enclosing the alleged tree in which Abraham so conveniently found a ram. An Ethiopian monastery exists also at Cairo.

Convents for women follow the same two observances as the men.

The austerities of the religious were a source of wonderment to the Portuguese, and Fr. Francis Alvarez, the scribe of the expedition of 1520, has left on record some of the mortifications practised. Thus, he says, some of them

---

[80] "*Le moine* .... *est vagabond. Pendant que celui-ci vole d'école en école au gré de sa curiosité ou de son amour de l'étude, celui-là court les couvents et surtout les châteaux, la cour et les camps des seigneurs féodaux.*" — E. COULBEAUX, *Dict. de Théol. Cath.*, t. V, col. 966.

ate nothing but herbs and lentils during the whole of Lent. Some slept in water up to their necks every Wednesday and Friday in Lent; others stood upright in a "tabernacle .... made like a box without a covering, much plastered with clay and dung;" while yet others wore "hair shirts within which was an iron girdle four fingers broad .... lined on both edges on the side towards the skin with points the size of those of a saw." Fr. Alvarez also told how the Ethiopians living in the world would not meet their enemies in battle during Lent, because of the "debility and weakness of their bodies, for the fast must on no account be broken." The ordinary diet at this time seems to have been unleavened bread and water.

The dissidents have also hermits, but the cenobites live much to themselves, and have only the morning office in common. The canonical hours were not fixed before the 14th century.

The monastic habit consists of tunic, belt, great cloak and hood, but there is no fixed rule in regard to colour, and but little in respect of the shape or material.

There are three stages in the religious life. In the first, the superior gives the novice a girdle (*quenat*), "that the loins girded with manly courage, as St. John Baptist, he may walk hardily in the strict way of mortification." In the second, he imposes the cassock (there are two grades known as "blessing" and "perfection"); while in the third, he clothes the candidate with a kind of scapular (*askêma*), made of two pieces of stuff and ornamented with twelve crosses, said to represent the *rationale* of the Jewish high priest. In the solemn profession, the monk puts on a lofty white hat, known as the "bonnet of perfection" (*véfe' tsamié qob'*).

When in 1924 Cardinal [81] Lepicier visited Eritrea as apostolic visitor it was recognised that the Ethiopian church suffered from the want of Catholic monks, and it was decided to attempt the formation of Cistercians who would be members of the oriental rite. On September 3, 1930, Pope Pius XI agreed that the abbey of Casamari [82] near Veroli should be permitted to undertake the monastic training of such aspirants. Two Ethiopic priests, who felt the call to the religious life, arrived at the abbey on Christmas eve of the same year; while the first alumni were received on May 19, 1931. The numbers finally rose to 32, and in 1940 it was possible to send 9 monks to open a house at Belesà, about 7 miles from Asmara, where the little church [83] has been dedicated to the Assumption. In this present year (1945) Casamari has one Ethiopian (Dom Jeremiah) who has received the habit and 3 students; while the abbey of Valviciolo near Sermoneta has a priest (Dom Fidele Andikiel), who is solemnly professed, and about 8 monks.

Ethiopia has no "united" nuns living the common life, but the primitive practice of women under vows living in their own homes is found among the Catholics. In 1932 there were reckoned to be about 20 of these sisters in the Latin vicariate of Abyssinia and 78 of the oriental rite in Eritrea.

[81] The apostolic visitor was archbishop of Tarsus, not yet cardinal.

[82] Two previous attempts at restoring Ethiopian monasticism had failed—Trappists in Palestine and Benedictines at Farfa.

[83] An elementary school has been opened, dedicated to Blessed Justin de Jacobis.

Theology

The Monophysism of the dissidents favours the doctrine of Severus [84] of Antioch, and the Ethiopian church did not rank Dioscorus among the saints before the 15th century. The *Senkessar*, under the date of August 23 says: "They anathematise the priest Eutyches, who said that in Christ the divinity was mixed with his humanity."

Two schools of thought existed in the country, the "Sons of Unction" (*Walda-Qeb*) and the "Sons of Grace" (*Walda-sega; Sega-ledj*). Stress is laid on the unction of our Lord rather than on the union of the two natures. One party admits two births in Christ, the eternal generation by which the Word is *Unigenitus Patris*, and the birth through the blessed Virgin, by which he is *Primogenitus Virginis;* while the other admits of a third birth, which took place when the man-God became by unction *Primogenitus omnis creaturae*. This last existed from the moment of union, although it was only manifested at his baptism. The controversy first arose about the year 1654, after the expulsion of the Catholic missionaries, and the entry into the country of Peter Heiling, a German Protestant. Synods, [85] with a view to solving the question, were held in 1654, 1684 and

---

[84] The theory of Severus started from the proposition that all activity, all will and intelligence proceed from the person, as ultimate principle, and on this ground alone asserted the unity of each in Christ. In speaking of one activity, one will, one knowledge in Christ, Severus was reducing Monophysism to pure heresy; for he refused to distinguish between the human faculties of our Lord—activity, will, intellect—and the divine nature itself. John CHAPMAN, *Catholic Encyclopedia*, art. *Monophysites*.

[85] I. GÒRDILLO, *Compendium Theologiae Orientalis*, chap. IX, art. V, p. 268. Lino Lozza (*Unitas*, Dicembre 1946 (Roma), pp. 56-60) has given other dates for the synods.

1707, but it was not before the 19th century that the emperor John IV (1872-1889) in a synod at Axum put an end to the dispute by declaring in favour of the *Tigrenses,* who maintained that unction and union were one and the same thing.

In regard to the doctrine of the Holy Spirit, the *Summa* of the Ethiopic church (*Hâymanotâ Abaw*) explicitly states that the Holy Spirit proceeds from the Father *and the Son,* but in the copy which Mgr. de Jacobis saw in the monastery of Guenda-Guende (Agamie) the word *wawald* ("and the Son") had been erased, without, however, entirely effacing the original lettering.

Devotion to our Lady sometimes degenerates into superstition, and the blessed Virgin is spoken of as dwelling in sacred trees, holy wells and high places; while phraseology is used which seems to imply that our Lady was the mother of the godhead, dying for the sins of the world. At the beginning of the 19th century there was a controversy [86] between the monks of Tigré and those of Debra-Libanos. The former maintained that "to the Mother of God belongs honour and glory; to the Son adoration," whereas the latter said: "to the Mother of God together with the Son belong adoration." The words *wa-la Waldâ* (and to her Son) and *za-mysla Waldâ* (together with her Son) thus became the names of the two conflicting parties. The emperor John IV finally intervened in the dispute, and at the council of Vallo (1878) settled the question in favour of the monks of Tigré.

The Ethiopic [87] is the only Eastern rite with the "Hail Mary" in anything approaching a Western form: "Hail Mary, full of grace, the Lord is with thee; blessed art thou

[86] GORDILLO, *op. cit.,* pp. 269-270.
[87] The Coptic rite in the prayer of the 11th hour has a form of the "Hail Mary."

among women and blessed is the fruit of thy womb. Pray and intercede with thy beloved Son that he may forgive us our sins."

The following passages, taken from the *salâm* in the synaxary for the feast of the Assumption, express the devotion with which the Ethiopians commemorate the mystery, of which they celebrate a monthly commemoration:

a) "I salute the Assumption of thy body which the human heart can never conceive. Doubly surrounded with grace and clothed in a like glory, O Mary, thy flesh was like to a pearl, and death itself was shamed when with wonder it saw thee ascending resplendent through the clouds to heaven."

b) "I salute the Assumption of thy body truly worthy to be praised, which outshines in beauty the splendour of the sun and the glory of the moon.

Except thee, O Virgin and thy first-born Son of joy, there is no one who has loosened the bonds of death and has awakened the dead from *Sheol.*"

c) "I salute the resurrection of thy flesh, twin of the resurrection of Christ, who hid himself alive in thee. Clothe me, o Mary, dove of Ephrata, and shelter me under thy wings in the day of judgment, when the earth will give back those whom she had taken into her keeping."

In Ethiopian art the Son is represented in his Mother's arms, and the representation is called *Medhanié Alem,* "Saviour of the world." The expression "pact of mercy," in reference to the power of Mary in saving a sinner who has recourse to her, is synonymous in Ethiopia with our Lady.

The hymn-book is called the "Praises of Mary" (*Weddase Mâryam*).

The dissidents have no clear idea of purgatory. The

good are said to live until the last judgment in an earthly paradise, while the bad exist in various places, even on the earth.

We have already had occasion to refer to the *Fethé-Neghest* in respect to the primacy of Rome, and in chapter I there is a further reference: "The successor of St. Peter on the seat of Rome is the sovereign pastor and judge over all the churches of Christ;" while the *Senkessar* (August 7) says: "The Apostle Peter was the chief of the apostles and the vicar of our Lord in the town of Rome. He has jurisdiction over all the doctors of the world, over all the patriarchs and over all the bishops." There is a special commemoration on August 13 (7 *nahasé*) in honour of St. Peters' profession[88] of faith, and the martyrology for the day ends with the words: "Hail Peter, made leader of the apostles and of priests throughout the world."

The ambassador[89] of Menelik II on October 8, 1907, said to Pope Pius X: "Thou art exalted in power and greatness, O great apostle! Thou art the son and successor of the apostle Peter and faithful follower in his works. Thou sittest on the glorious and splendid throne of Rome, and with thy teaching dost illuminate Italy and all nations. Thou art the foundation of the Church, the rock of Christian faith, as Jesus Christ our Saviour said in speaking with the Apostle Peter: " Thou art Peter, the rock; and on this rock I will build my Church."

The Russians, towards the latter part of the 19th century, made great efforts to win the Ethiopian church to Eastern Orthodoxy, but each time that the union seemed imminent the king drew back and nothing was effected.

---

[88] St. Matth. XVI, 17-19.
[89] *Incontro ai Fratelli Separati di Oriente*, pp. 210-211.

The canon of Scripture, which was revised in the 14th century, includes the Book of Enoch, *Kufale* or Little Genesis, Book of the Mysteries of Heaven and Earth, Combat of Adam and Eve, and the Ascension of Isaias, although hardly two lists of the books of the Old Testament agree as to their contents.

Theological books include *Faith of the Fathers (Hây-manotâ Abaw), Book of the Mystery* [90] *(Mashafa Meṣtir), Book of the Compilation (Mashafa Hawi), Cyrillis (Qêrlos),* and *Tradition of the Faith (Zênâ hâymânot).* Original works are very rare, and they are of little importance.

The Ethiopian church is ruled by a nomocanon known as the *Fethé Neghest* ("Legislation of the King"), which was translated from the Arabic in the 15th century.

Jewish Rites

It seems improbable that the Ethiopians were originally converted Jews, and the prevalence of Jewish customs may be due to the fact that a backward people surrounded by pagans were inclined to over-emphasise the Old Testament teaching without giving the Christian fulfilment its proper value.

Thus, we find Saturday observed as a second sabbath, and called by the Gallas and Shoas "Little Sunday." The Semitic laws regarding food and unclean meats, such as the "sinew that shrank." pigs, hares and aquatic fowls, are respected; while circumcision is practised on the fourteenth day after birth.

[90] The first known work which was not a translation from Greek, Coptic or Arabic. It was written before 1425 by George Saglensi against a certain Frank touching the Trinity and Incarnation. GORDILLO, *op. cit.,* pp. 265-266.

The Congregation of the Holy Office [91] forbade the observance of Saturday as the Sabbath, the distinction between clean and unclean animals, and the rite of circumcision, for the Catholic Gallas. [92] Circumcision, however, had been already condemned in a letter of Pope Leo X to King David in 1515, and by an instruction of Propaganda to the patriarch Alphonsus Mendez (1637). [93]

The feast of "our holy Fathers Abraham, Isaac and Jacob" is kept as a monthly observance. Tradition maintains that the stone tables of Moses (*Tsellate-Moussie*) and the ark of the covenant (*tabot*) have been preserved at Axum since they were brought to Ethiopia by the Queen of Sheba. Great devotion is paid to them, and they were referred to by Abû Sâlih in the 13th century: "The Abyssinians possess the ark of the covenant, in which are the two tables of stone, inscribed by the finger of God with the commandments which he ordained for the children of Israel. The ark of the covenant is placed upon the altar .... The liturgy is celebrated upon the ark four times in the year within the palace of the king." After much difficulty, the stone tables were seen in 1867 by an Armenian envoy, and it was established that they were not of a date earlier than the 13th or 14th century.

The cathedral at Axum is dedicated in honour of the Tables of Moses (*Tsellate-Moussie*), the Dwelling of Sion (*Edda-Tsion*), and the Dwelling of Mary (*Edda-Mariani*),

[91] *Congr. S. Ufficio*, 20-VI-1866.
[92] The Council of Laodicea (can. 29, ab. 370), which is acknowledged by the Ethiopian church, enacted: "*Non liceat Christianis Judaeorum opera facere et non otientur neque requiescant die Sabbati, sed operent in eodem die. Sed celebretur Eucharistia.*" Tertullian (ab. 200, *Adv. Marcion.*, IV, 12), also, said that the Sabbath has been abolished by Jesus Christ.
[93] *Prop.*, 28-VIII-1637.

and the town is said to have had 500 *debteras*, 500 deacons and 500 priests.

The Ethiopian Christian attaches great importance to the blue cord that he wears round his neck, to which are affixed crosses and other objects. A common form of amulet is a silver or leather casket, inscribed with texts, and blessed by abuna.

Calendar

The Ethiopian church places the year under the especial patronage of an evangelist. Thus, 1901 (September 11, 1908-September 10, 1909) was dedicated to St. Matthew; 1902 (1909-1910) to St. Mark; 1903 (1910-1911) to St. Luke; and 1904 (1911-1912) to St. John.

The era followed is seven years behind the West during the last four months of the year, and eight years during the remaining months. There are 13 months in the year, which in the Julian calendar begins on August 29, and in the Gregorian on September 11.

Easter [94] is reckoned by a system invented by an Egyptian monk named Ammon at the end of the 4th century.

Nearly one-third of the year comprises days on which it is forbidden to work.

The basis of the calendar [95] is Coptic, and the same feast is often celebrated many times in the year. Thus,

---

[94] Propaganda (*Prop. Congr.*, 28-VIII-1637, No. 19), in answer to a query sent by the patriarch Alphonsus Mendez, said that the celebration of Easter according to the ancient calendar might be tolerated.

[95] The *Fethé Neghest* (chap. XIX) indicated seven solemn feasts— Christmas, Baptism, Hosannas, Easter, Ascension, Pentecost, and Tabor (Transfiguration).

except in March, Christmas is commemorated on the 24th or 25th of each month.

The Baptism of our Lord (*Timkat*), corresponding to the Latin Epiphany, is a great feast, when the *tabot* is carried in procession for the annual blessing of the waters, and the people wash themselves and put on a garment, "white without reproach."

The present calendar was largely the work of King Zara-Jacob (1434-1468), who, as we have seen, took the liveliest interest in ecclesiastical affairs.

The Immaculate Conception [96] (*Sensata*) is observed by the Catholics on December 9 (13 *tachsas*), and by the dissidents on July 31 (7 *nahasè*), but in the calendar of the latter we find also December 12 (16 *tachsas*). The Assumption [97] of our Lady, as in the Coptic rite, has two feasts in both the Catholic and dissident calendars—January 16 (21 *ter*) and August 22 (17 *nahasè*). The first commemorates the death (*Erafta*), the second the assumption into heaven (*Felsata*). The tradition that 205 days passed between the events is, however, contrary to the teaching of other churches. The Nativity [98] of the blessed Virgin (*Ledata*) has also two days—April 26 (1 *ghenbot*) [99] and September 7 (10 *maskaram*),—but the Catholics observe only one, September 8 (9 *maskaram*).

---

[96] G. HANSSENS, *Cinque Feste Mariane dei Riti Orientali. Incontro ai Fratelli Separati di Oriente* (Rome, 1945), p. 370.

[97] Ibid., p. 383. Salaville (*Studia Orien. Lit.-Theol.* Append. II, p. 190, Rome, 1940) gives May 9.

[98] *Ibid.*, p. 386.

[99] A feast especially honoured by the women of Ethiopia. 21 *ghenbot* (May 29) is observed as a great festival, the apparition of our Lady in the convent of Metemma. In the following month, 20 *senè*, there is a commemoration of the building of the house of the blessed Virgin in the Holy Land.

The calendar of the dissidents honours our Lady with 32 feasts and St. Gabriel with 2; while St. Michael is commemorated on the 12th day of each month. "Our holy Fathers Abraham, Isaac and Jacob" have also a monthly memorial. The feast of the four animals (*arbata-an'sasa*) of the vision of Ezechiel is the festival of the evangelists.

The royal feast of the Holy Cross [100] (*Maskal-Atsé*) on September 27 was introduced later than the time of Zara-Jacob, on the receipt of a relic of the true cross. St. Thomas is kept on the Tuesday in Easter week, with a second commemoration on October 9, the Preaching of St. Thomas in the Indies.

One of the few Ethiopic manuscripts of the 15th century extant is that of the *Twelve Miracles of St. George*, written by Theodosius, bishop of Jerusalem, which shows the popularity of the cultus of the "Great Martyr." St. John Baptist is kept at the close of the rainy season, and is the day in Ethiopia for the giving and receiving of presents.

The Ethiopic saints are about 40 in number, but only a small proportion are honoured by the Catholics.

Abunas, who so often ranked as unpopular foreigners, seldom appear in the catalogue of saints, although Mauro [101] da Leonessa records Abuna Bartholomew (feast of Axum) on October 14 (11 *techemti*).

The synaxary [102] or book of the saints gives an interesting entry for December 18 (22 *tachsas*): "Salutation to Dekesius, Bishop of Telteya, to whom Mary gave heavenly

[100] *Dict. de Théol. Cath.*, t. V, col. 940.

[101] *Computo per il Calendario Abissino Confrontato col Computo Latino.* Asmara, 1918.

[102] *Book of the Saints of the Ethiopian Church*, vol. II, p. 395 E. A. Wallis Budge. Cambridge University Press, 1928. Salaville (*op. cit.* p. 191) says that "Doksyos" is the name of an alleged patriarch of Alexandria.

apparel, because he wrote the account of the miracle of her Annunciation." The chief commemoration on this day is of St. Gabriel, but there seems little doubt that Dekesius [103] is none other than St. Ildephonsus, bishop of Toledo († 667), who is said to have received a chasuble from our Lady as a reward for writing a defence of her perpetual virginity. The frequent intercourse between Moslem Spain and the Levant sufficiently accounts for the travelling of the legend to Egypt, and from thence to Ethiopia. December 18 was the old Mozarabic feast of the Annunciation, which is now observed as the Expectation of our Lady.

The Ethiopic synaxary (*Senkessar*) has been taken from the Arabic, and a corruption in names is to be expected, as many letters in that script are only differentiated by dots, while the vowels are not usually indicated. The most ancient manuscript of the synaxary extant is of the 15th century.

Pontius Pilate and Procla, [104] his wife, are honoured by the dissidents on June 25. The former on account of his protestation of innocence of the "blood [105] of that just man."

The Monophysites [106] commemorate also Abba Dioscorus, doctor of Alexandria, on September 17 (7 *maskaram*); [107] Severus, patriarch of Antioch, arrives in Egypt

---

[103] VANSLEB, *Histoire de l'Eglise d'Alexandrie*, p. 159 (1677). The theory is discussed by H. W. Codrington in *Egypt and the West*, pp. 287-288. *Eastern Churches Quarterly*. No. 10, vol. V. April-June, 1944.

[104] The Byzantine church commemorates St. Procla on October 27.

[105] S. Matth. XXVII, 24.

[106] The death of Adam and Eve is commemorated on April 14 (6 *miazià*).

[107] Mauro DA LEONESSA, *Computo per il Calendario Abissino*. Asmara, 1918.

on October 12 (2 *techemti, tekemt*); and the Translation of the body of Severus on December 19 (10 *tachsas*).

The Catholic calendar [108] includes St. Frumentius (*Abba Salama*) on August 2 (26 *hamlè*), St. Caleb on May 28 (20 (*ghenbot*), St. Takla Haymanot (ab. 620) on August 20 (14 *nahasè*), and Blessed Gabra-Michael on October 6 (26 *maskaram*).

St. Takla Haymanot has a place in the diptychs of the dead in the liturgy: "Remember, O Lord, the soul of thy servant, our father Takla Haymanot, and all his companions."

The Nine Roman Saints have each a day set apart for their commemoration—Abba Alef on March 20 (11 *meggabit*), Abba Tsahma (Saham) on January 24 (16 *ther*), Abba Aregaoui (Aragawi) on October 22 (14 *tekemt*), Abba Afetsiè (Alef) on May 20 (12 *ghenbot*), Abba Gherima (Garima) on June 24 (17 *senié*), Abba Pantalemon (Pantaleon) on October 16 (5 *tekemt*), Abba Libanos on December 5 (26 *hedar*), Abba Guba on June 6 (29 *ghenbot*), and Abba Yemata (Adimata) on November 2 (23 *tekemt*).

There are about 150 days of fasting in the year, including Wednesdays and Fridays (excluding Paschaltide); Advent (40 days); 3 days of Nineveh before Lent, with 40 fasting days of Lent, Sundays inclusive, and preceded by the fast of Heraclius (55 days in all); Lent of the Apostles (15 days); and Lent of the Assumption (15 days). In great Lent, the single meal is taken at sunset.

The Catholics have modified the rules of fasting.

---

[108] Information given by a student of the *Collegio Pontificio Etiopico*, Vatican City.

Music

The Ethiopic chant is enharmonic, and it is often accompanied by bells, rattles [109] (after the manner of the old sistrum) and big drums. [110]

There are three kinds of modes, known as *Ezli*, *Ararai* and *Gheez* respectively. The last two are very similar and they are often fused together.

The use of these modes in the liturgical year is as follows:

a) *Ezli*: from after September 26 to November 6; from the first Sunday in Advent till the vigil of the season of Lent (*chebelà*); from Easter till June 16; and on all solemnities that fall in the period of *Gheez* (*Ararai*).

b) *Gheez*: from November 7 till the first Sunday in Advent; all Lent till Easter; and from June 17 to September 27.

In the Monophysite church, priests dance before the altar, and sing wild melodies.

Joy is expressed by that shrill howling, which has been referred to by many writers, both classical [111] and modern, and drums throb in double quick time.

There is a dance of the priests on the feasts of the Epiphany (Baptism of our Lord), Easter and the Holy Cross. Two parallel ranks are formed facing one another, with a drummer at each end. Then holding staves [112] in their right hands as symbols of office, they advance and retreat in a stately dance, to the accompaniment of chanting. The

---

[109] *Zenà-zil.*

[110] *Koborò; coe'anatà.*

[111] Cf. Herodotus in Egypt.

[112] *Mekamia*, staves with bifurcated tops, which also serve as crutches during the long services.

drummers follow the movements of the priests, and beat time with remarkable precision. The steps are for the most part light and springy, but there are also heavy punctuating steps, which express joy and an offering of praise to God on behalf of the people.

Church Architecture and Ornaments

There are said to be more than 6,000 churches [113] in the country, with three distinctive types of building. The first resembles that of the ancient basilica, with three naves and only a veil to separate the apse or sanctuary from the rest of the church. Examples of this type may be seen at Debra-Damo and Aïba. The second style retains a quadrangular form, but it has a square or polygonal construction in the centre, separated or isolated by a gallery or passage which goes all round and takes the place of the *kedest* occupied by the communicants. The interior structure, closed by a door, forms the sanctuary (*makedes, magdas*), where the altar, behind a veil, is a kind of closet surmounted by a baldachino.

The third and more modern type, [114] which is borrowed from the rotunda of the Holy Sepulchre, has two rotundas one inside the other. The passage which forms the circle between the two is the *kene mahelet*, reserved for the choir; while the isolated rotunda [115] in the centre is the *kedest*, where behind a veil stands the altar. This is the most common type of church at the present day, probably because of

[113] Gondar, before it was sacked by the Mahdists in 1889, had no less than 42 churches.
[114] The church with an imposing cupola outside the walls of Jerusalem, known as the " Mount of Paradise" (*Debra-Ghennet*) and built by King John IV (1872-1882), is of this type.
[115] Cf. Holy Sepulchre in Jerusalem.

the facility with which it can be constructed. The roof is sometimes of thatch, surmounted by a metal or wooden cross.

Churches built by the Jesuits still exist at Gorgora and Azazo; while at Fremona the church was discrowned and lowered to half its height by Abuna Salama in the reign of Theodore II, in order to remove from the eyes of the people the remembrance of the Catholic mission of the 17th century.

In imitation of the Temple, the church is divided into three parts: *a*) vestibule for the use of the choir; *b*) *kedest*, where holy communion is given to the people; and *c*) sanctuary, [116] reserved for the celebrant and his ministers, where only the king may receive communion. Entrance to the sanctuary is forbidden to the laity, who often assist at the liturgy from outside the church, by means of holes in the wall.

It is a custom of the people not to enter a church unless they have been continent for the previous 24 hours.

The altar is a square or parallelogram, made of wood or stone, which Mgr. de Jacobis has described as "generally of a polished kind of agate (*ebn-bered*), sometimes of a very hard wood as incorruptible as cedar (*wonza*)." Before a church is consecrated the dissidents hide the *tabot* or altar stone and then "discover" it, a custom which may perhaps be traced to the sacred fire [117] miraculously found at the time of the consecration of the second Temple. The word *tabot*,

---

[116] "*Solis ministerio sacro deditis ad altare ingredi, et communicare ibidem liceat.*" Conc. Laodicea, can. 19.

[117] The story of the miraculous discovery of the sacred fire, which is found in 2 Machabees 1, 19-22, was inserted to enhance the dignity of the restored Temple, and to place it on a par with that of Solomon's. There is no mention of this by Jeremias, Ezra or the writer of the Kings or Paralipomenon (*Chronicles*).

as Abba Semharay Selam pointed out to the writer, is a
very confusing word, and it is used to express many different
things. Thus, it may mean the Ark of the Covenant as well
as the Tables of the Law, although Catholics do not use
the term in either of these senses. It is, however, sometimes
confused with *tablīth,* and employed for an altar-stone.
The *mensa* of the Catholics is always of stone, covered with
a silk veil, whereas that of the dissidents is of hard wood,
inscribed with the names of our Lord, the blessed Virgin,
the bishop and others. It is the object of an exaggerated
cult [118] for the Monophysites, tending almost to idolatry,
and the people are said to prostrate themselves in adoration
as it passes in procession, while popular superstition
attributes to it marvellous effects of preservation from plague
and other ills. After the liturgy, the altar-stone is often
placed in a box, which is also called a *tabot*; while the
rubrics use the word for the altar as a whole: "And then
the priest shall compass the tabot [119] with the taper in front
of him." Finally, the dissidents speak of *tabot* for the
models of the Ark of the Covenant, which they reverence
in their churches as symbols of the "original" preserved at
Axum. These they carry in procession down to the water
on the feast of *Timkat* (Epiphany).

Dr. Neale [120] has expressed the belief that the Monophysites reserve the blessed sacrament in the *tabot,* but
there does not seem to be any evidence to support the

[118] *Dict. de Théol. Cath.* T. V, *col.* 967. The *tabot* is spoken of
as the "equivalent of our portable altar," but the processional use of
the *tabot,* to which this exaggerated honour is paid, may well be that
of the "arks."

[119] BRIGHTMAN, *op. cit.,* p. 199.

[120] "simply used for the reservation of the blessed sacrament."
Eastern Church. Gen. Introd., vol. I, p. 186.

statement. Reservation [121] undoubtedly was once practised in Ethiopia, as in the Coptic church of Egypt, but the custom has long since fallen into desuetude, and it is forbidden in the *Fethé Neghest*.

The Catholics of the rite use a tabernacle on the altar.

The altar (*meshwa-ᶜe*) should be furnished with a cross[122] and two candles. [123]

The veil or napkin in which the *oblata* are wrapped and covered is called a *māchfad*, [124] which is evidently a transliteration of the Arabic *miḥfaẓah*, "that in which a thing is kept," and then assimilated to a like-sounding Ethiopic word denoting "tower."

Macdan is the name given to the veil that covers the sacred vessels, and *cedāna'āwed* the covering for the paten. The veil over the chalice has no special name.

The bread is brought to the altar before the prothesis in a round covered box of metal or wickerwork, known as the *masob* [125] or "pot." The prayer [126] over the *masob*, which is said by the dissidents, shows that it was at one time used as the paten: "that they may make therein the

---

[121] "*Non auferant chrisma et oleum sanctum (e loco suo) nisi ad baptizandum et custodiant illud sic ut Corpus et Sanguinem Christi.*" *Parvum Euchologium ex Monasterio Gundegunde*, p. 56; *De Sacramentis secundum ritum Aethiopicum.* Semharay Selam, p. 75.

[122] The Ethiopian church at Jerusalem has "Rood, Mary and John" painted on three upright pieces of wood.

[123] Three lights, at the western angles and the middle of the east side. BRIGHTMAN, *op. cit.*, p. 580.

Propaganda was asked whether at a Catholic Mass it was permissable to have only one candle and one cloth. A reply of *affirmative* was given, with the added permission to celebrate, if necessary, without any candles. *Prop. Congr.* 17-VI-1939, *dub.* 3.

[124] Plural, *māchfadāt*.

[125] Cf. στάμνος, "golden pot that had manna;" Hebrews IX, 4.

[126] BRIGHTMAN, *op. cit.*, p. 198.

holy body of thine only Son in this holy apostolic church."
Fr. Hanssens, [127] comparing the Catholic and Monophysite
liturgies, calls this prayer, a "prayer over the paten."

The paten, known as the *çāchel* [128] or *'āwed,* [129] is
about seven inches in diameter. The chalice is called the
çewa'e.

Eucharistic Bread and Wine

The eucharistic bread is a flat round leavened cake, [130]
stamped with a cross of nine squares, and with four squares
added in the angles of the cross. It is variously designated
ḥᵉbst ("bread"), *ḳu'rbān* ("offering") and "reward of the
dead." The central square is the *asbadikon,* which Ethiopic
transliteration from Arabic has changed into *'āsba dīyāḳōn,*
"reward of the deacon."

All the provinces of Ethiopia have special fields for the
growing of corn destined for the altar.

The eucharistic bread, which must be unbroken and
without blemish, has to be made on the actual day of the
liturgy, and there must be none of the bread left over for
use on another day. [131] It is baked by deacons in a house
near the church, called *bet lechem* or "house of bread."
Large churches normally bake twelve breads, three of
which are selected and brought ceremonially into the church.
There the celebrant chooses one, and the other two are
shared by the priest and his ministers.

[127] *Op. cit.,* t. II, part I, chap. X, p. 399.
[128] Cf. Exodus XXV, 29; πίναξ, Math. XIV, 8.
[129] "Tray."
[130] 4 × ¾ ins.
[131] Cf. *"Offerant (sacerdotes) super altare panem eucharisticum
ipso die factum et non die praecedenti pro die crastino, et ministrent
ipso die. Nihil autem reponatur pro die sequenti. Etenim non licet."*
Can. Apost. (l. III), 30.

The *Fethé Neghest* [132] says: "Let the Eucharist be prepared from that bread which the church has, but if it does not possess any, let it be prepared from the oblation brought by the faithful."

"The offerings of blasphemers, homicides, fornicators and worshippers of idols are to be rejected, because the Lord abhors the sacrifice of the ungodly. Neither can the offering of the excommunicated be accepted. Deacons must daily inscribe the names (living and dead) of the offerers, so that they can be commemorated."

Unleavened bread is used by the dissidents on Holy Thursday, in memory of the Last Supper.

Catholics now normally use unleavened bread at "low Mass", and leavened at a solemn liturgy.

In respect to the species of wine, which is prepared by deacons, the Monophysites often content themselves with steeping some dried grapes (*zibibo*) in a little water, and extracting the juice, but it is difficult to see how this can be valid matter.

When asked for a ruling on this point, Propaganda [133] quoted a decree of the Holy Office, given on July 23, 1706.

The *Fethé Neghest* [134] forbids the use of old wine, and directs the use of limpid and pure wine. More than one-third part water is prohibited by the same nomocanon, and in districts where wine is plentiful the proportion should be one-tenth water.

A banquet or feast (*tezkar*), the lineal descendent of the agape, appears to be a well-nigh universal custom after a funeral. If the family is poor, the feast may be postponed

[132] "On the Eucharist," chap. 13.
[133] *Prop. Congr.* 17-VI-1839, dub. 4.
[134] *Op. cit.*, chap. 13.

for months or even years. King Gladios in his confession of
faith (1555) said that the Ethiopians every Sabbath had an
Oblation or Sacrifice of the Mass *and a banquet,* according
to the precepts of the apostles handed down in the *Didascalia.*

Outdoor Dress and Vestments

The ordinary outdoor dress consists of a long cassock,
with wide sleeves, reaching to the ankles; leather belt;
cloak; hood (*kōb'e*); and either a round black cap or a
white *kalimavkion* (turban).

Deacons should wear a cassock with full sleeves only,
but their present day appearance is scarcely distinguishable
from laymen.

Priests at the sacred offices at one time wore a garment
called the *azf,* which was similar in shape to the toga, but
with rounded corners, and a girdle round the loins.

Deacons and subdeacons also used the *azf,* but prior
to putting it on they covered their shoulders with a coloured linen cloth reaching to the girdle. Sometimes another,
but similar, garment was worn called the *percale;* while
there was a third choice, the *gabi,* which was ornamented
on its lower edge by a red border (*quari*).

The vestments [135] of the Ethiopic rite are derived from
the Coptic church of Egypt, but there has been some doubt
in the past as to which should be worn in the liturgy.
Intercourse with other rites, however, has to some extent
rectified this confusion, especially in the larger and monastic churches.

The missal, except in some fragmentary notes in the

[135] The *Fethé Neghest* (cf. St. Basil, 96) directs that the vestments
should be kept in the house of the "servant of the church" (*chesci
ghebez,* priest-treasurer), or where the books are stored.

margin of a manuscript [136] in the British Museum, gives no directions in regard to the use of the vestments, and no prayers are enjoined at the vesting of the celebrant.

The vestments of the priest comprise first the alb (*ḳamīs*) of white or coloured silk, reaching to the ankles, which in the Catholic rite is often of the inevitable lacy variety.

The *kidaris* of the Copts, which answers to the Latin amice, is called the *hebanie* or *ghelbab*. Some Ethiopians [137] maintain that a white linen cloth, which has been identified with the *ghelbab*, should cover the head or, in the case of the monastic clergy, the hood, whereas others [138] say that the hood is worn without the cloth.

The stole (*mothat*) is of the usual Byzantine pattern.

The girdle (*zenār*), which is of the same colour as the vestments, confines the alb, but not the stole.

Cuffs (*acmām, edjgē*) are worn, similar to those in other oriental rites, although there is a tendency among the dissidents to discard them. Brightman [139] says that there is some confusion in the text in regard to the term *acmām,* where it is used for *ḳamīs.*

The vestment [140] *par excellence* or *cappa* (*ḳābā*) is a kind of cloak with a "hood," hanging from the neck down to below the knees and fastened at the top. Abba Semharay Selam suggests that it originated in the rich garments given to the clergy by the princes and chieftains. In course of

[136] 545.
[137] *Ita* Aleka Wolde Tecle.
[138] *Ita* Abba Ghebre Jesus.
[139] *Op. cit.*, p. 591.
[140] The *Fethé Neghest*, reiterating the prescriptions of Abulides (Hippolytus, can. 37) and St. Basil (96), says that the vestments should be white, and not of different colours, following the practice of our Lord on Mount Tabor, and the angels in their appearances to men.

time the "hood" was separated from the rest of the vestment, which was lengthened to the ankles and opened out,
so that the celebrant could freely move his arms, thus
approximating it to the Byzantine *phelonion*.

Another liturgical vestment, which is also worn by
secular dignitaries, is the *lanka*. This is a kind of *mozzetta*,
almost circular in shape with five points which are cut in
the form of a cross. These cruciform points are said to
symbolise the five wounds of our Lord. The *lanka* is worn
over the *cappa* and is sometimes sewn to it. Some writers
have derived the origin of the *lanka* from the Coptic turban,
a long linen strip, the upper part of which encircles the
temples, the lower part reaching to the loins. Others, however, maintain that it comes from the head-gear of Coptic
abbots, from which a band, marked at the end with a cross,
hangs to the loins.

In recent years, says Abba Semharay Selam, several new
forms of the *cappa* have made their appearance.

The *cappa* of the priest is ornamented in its upper part
with small gold or silver balls. It reaches to the feet, with
two apertures for the arms and short sleeves to the elbow.

The *cappa* of the ministers only extends to the loins,
and it is provided with a collar.

The new fashions were first adopted at the beginning
of the reign of the empress Zaodito (1914-1930), and they
were worn in the churches of St. George and Holy Trinity
at Addis Ababa, as well as in those of the territory under
the rule of Ras Kassa.

The deacon wears a silk alb with wide sleeves, girdle,
collar and *cappa* fastened at the breast.

The ends of the linen collar (*hebanie*), which are sewn
to the *cappa*, stretch to the breast, and are said to give a
suggestion of the Byzantine *orarion*. Some Ethiopians have

Cistercians of the Congregation of
Casamari, Valviciolo
Subprior (Latin rite) and monk
(Ethiopic rite)

Cistercian priest of the Ethiopic
rite
Abbey of Valviciolo, Sermoneta

Church of San Stefano degli Abissini, Vatican City

Reading of the Gospel. Pontifical Liturgy in the Ethiopic rite

Ordination of a priest in the Ethiopic rite

called this collar the *kesela,* which priests place upon their heads; while others have referred to it as the *wegheret,* worn over the shoulders of monastic superiors.

The subdeacon [141] wears a linen alb with wide sleeves, girdle and a shorter form of *cappa,* likewise fastened at the breast.

Deacons acting as subdeacons or priests acting as deacons wear the vestments of their own order, not those of the order that they are representing.

The taperer wears a silk cincture over the alb, which is divided crosswise on the breast, its two ends ornamented with wool and thrown over the back.

The other assistants are similarly vested, save for a different arrangement of the cincture.

A head-covering should be worn only by priests, and neither writers nor manuscripts make any reference to its use by anyone else.

The missal printed at Addis Ababa, however, has the following direction: "The deacon, having put a crown on his head and being vested in cappa with *mozzetta* (*lanka*), shall say: 'If any should suffer from an unclean mind, let him not draw near,' etc." Commenting on this rubric, Abba Semharay Selam says: "such a prescription is an innovation or rather an abuse, that a deacon should wear a *mozzetta* over a *cappa.*"

Crowns are worn by deacons (not by lesser clerics) at Jerusalem, but even there the *mozzetta* is not used.

Zewd, the name given to the crown, seems to suggest a royal diadem, and that worn in Jerusalem was the votive

---

[141] Among the dissidents, minor orders exist in theory, but to-day in practice there are only priests and deacons. *Dict. de Théol. Cath.* t. V, col. 946-947.

offering of princes.   Bishops and abbots wear a handsome
and barbaric triple crown, but the Catholic ordinary of the
Ethiopic rite has a Roman mitre (and crozier).

Abuna enjoys the privilege of having a cloth of gold
umbrella held over him in processions; while umbrellas of
less costly material figure largely in out of door functions.

The T-shaped staff, used to rest on in church by many
Eastern monks, is a token of priestly office in Ethiopia, and
many examples may be seen in the church at Jerusalem.

Finally, we may note the vestments worn in the monastery of Lalibela, which Memer Welde Michael, superior
of the house and overseer of the province of Lasta, described
to Abba Semharay Selam (October 22, 1916).

The priest wears the ordinary vestments.   The deacon
has a *cappa* over the *kamīs* and girdle, while the subdeacon
and other inferior clergy have *kamīs,* girdle and a kind of
stole which hangs down the back.

The synod [142] of Laodicea (ab. 370) is certainly complied
with in the subdeacon not having the same vestments [143]
as the deacon, but for inferior clergy to dress as subdeacons
seems to be a violation of the canon.

There is no liturgical fan in this rite.   The blessing in
the liturgy is given with the hand-cross.

Liturgical Language

The hieratic language is *lesana Ge'ez,* the "tongue of
the free," which according to Salaville [144] was the spoken
language of the country until the 17th century.   The same
author says that it was brought from Yemen in Arabia to

[142] Can. 22.
[143] Cf. *Fethé Neghest.*
[144] *Introduction to the Study of Eastern Liturgies.* Chap. II, p. 39.

Abyssinia in Africa by a group of pre-Christian immigrants. On the other hand, Geez has been thought to have been Christian in origin and to have remained so, as there is no original literature in the language, with the exception of some theological works. It is, however, akin to Sabean. [145] Tigré and Tigrinya, daughter languages of Geez, are said to have originated about the 10th century. The earliest writings in Amharic date from the 14th century, and by the time of the Portuguese missions Geez had been very largely superseded. Thus, we find that the Jesuits always used Amharic in their instructions.

The first European to make a study of Geez was Job Ludolf (1624-1704), a German, who in the 17th century compiled a grammar and dictionary in that language. In the second half of the 19th century the subject was revived by Professor Dillmann of Berlin.

It was probably under Greek influence that Ethiopic writing was changed from right to left. There are 26 characters in the alphabet, 22 of which are similar to Hebrew and Syriac.

The liturgy has three foreign interpolations—*amen, alleluia,* and *Kyrie eleison.*

Many of the clergy, as in the mother church of Egypt, are deplorably ignorant of their liturgical language.

Liturgical Books

The liturgical books of the Monophysites have remained in manuscript, with the exception of a missal [146] recently printed at Addis Ababa (1926).

[145] Cf. Himyaritic inscriptions discovered in southern Arabia, ranging from B. C. 1, 000-A. D. 600.
[146] Maṣḥafa ḳeddāsē.

The earliest extant copy of the complete liturgy dates from the 17th century, although there exist fragmentary anaphoras of the 15th and 16th centuries respectively. The Church Order of King Zara-Jacob (1434-1468) throws some light on a section of the anaphora; while the 64th of the Sahidic ecclesiastical canons has valuable liturgical rubrics.

The dissidents, in addition to the liturgy, have the book of hours, [147] antiphonary [148] and lectionary. [149]

In 1548, Tasfa Seyon produced at Rome the Ethiopic liturgy in Latin, and the *ordo communis* [150] was printed in the New Testament, between the Acts of the Apostles and the Epistle to the Romans. Two anaphoras were included: Our Lord Jesus Christ and the Apostles;—while a third appeared at the end of the book—"the Anaphora of our Lady Mary, which Father Cyriac, pope of the city of Behnsa, composed." The *filioque* was inserted in the creed and the epiclesis was altered.

The Catholic rite was revised in 1890 and again in 1913, [151] when a missal was published at Asmara, with the title: "*Ritus Aethiopici secundum usum Catholicorum ipsum missale seu .... Asmarae, Typographica Catholica.* 1907."

Pope Pius XI ordered a further revision to be made in strict accordance with the best liturgical traditions. Much of the earlier work of this character had been undertaken by the veteran missionary, Fr. John Baptist Coulbeaux (1870-1900—† 1921), who had lived for thirty years in the country.

---

[147] Maṣḥafa Sâ'atât.

[148] Mawâse'et, "answers."

[149] *Sher'ātā geçāwē*. A book similar to that used in the Coptic church, containing the psalms and gospels for vespers, the four lessons and the psalms sung in the liturgy.

[150] *Sher'ātā ḳeddāsē*.

[151] 1907 in the Ethiopic calendar.

In 1937, a special sub-commission of the Congregation for the Oriental Church was formed, but the main task of producing the new missal devolved upon the Premonstratensian canon, Arnold Van Lantschoot, who, after eight years work, completed the impression in 1945. The missal, which is entitled the "Book of the Oblation," was produced by the Vatican Press, and embellished by three fine miniatures, [152] the work of Dom Jerome Leussink, a Benedictine of the Greek College, Rome. The text of the missal (228 pages) is based on old manuscripts [153] and on that of Diredawa. Seventeen anaphoras have been given, in addition to the Ordinary of the Mass and the Anaphora of the Apostles.

The text is integral, and only those corrections which were found to be absolutely indispensable have been made. The formulas of consecration are printed in large type and isolated from their context, but the recitation of the institution is proper to each anaphora. When a passage has had to be supplied, it has been taken from another anaphora. Thus, the institution in the anaphora of James of Sarug, which is pure narrative, and without the words of consecration, has been given that of the Apostles.

In some of the anaphoras which are unmeasureably long, as for example Our Lady (1), St. John the Evangelist, 318 Orthodox and St. Athanasius, passages have been marked which may be recited or omitted at the discretion of the celebrant.

The seventeen anaphoras, supplementary to that of the

[152] The style is purely Ethiopian. a) the Crucifixion; b) a seated figure of our Lord, in the act of blessing; c) our Lady and the Infant Jesus between two angels.

[153] The war prevented the study of all the manuscripts in the libraries of Europe. The two editions of the missal brought out by the dissidents in 1926 were also taken into account, in order to depart as little as possible from their version.

Apostles, are as follows: *a*) Our Lord Jesus Christ; *b*) Mary the Virgin Daughter of God, which Abba Heriacus, bishop of the city of Bahnasa, composed; *c*) Our Lady Mary, the Mother of God, which Abba George composed; *d*) John the Son of Thunder; *e*) James the brother of the Lord; *f*) Our Father Mark the Evangelist, patriarch of Alexandria; *g*) The 318 Orthodox Fathers; *h*) Apostolic Athanasius; *i*) Basil of Caesarea; *j*) Gregory of Nyssa; *k*) Epiphanius of Salamis; *l*) John Chrysostom; *m*) Cyril of Alexandria; *n*) James of Sarug; *o*) Dioscorus of Alexandria; *p*) Gregory the Armenian; and in an appendix *q*) a second anaphora of Cyril of Alexandria.

Before the Ordinary of the Mass, the missal has the "testament" (*kidan*) for the morning and evening; prayers for various occasions and classes of people (*mastabqu'e*); seven formulas (*liton*), one for each day of the week ; prayers for eucharistic accessories; and extracts from the *Fethé Neghest* ("Law of kings") concerning the Eucharist.

The missal properly so called has a Latin translation [154] for the private use of the Congregation for the Oriental Church, and written prior to the corrections found necessary.

The manuscripts [155] in the libraries of Europe all differ in some respect from the present text of the Monophysite liturgy.

The psalter, lessons and office of our Lady had been published for the Catholics in 1926, but the sub-commission of the Congregation for the Oriental Church in 1940 produced a practically definitive edition of the breviary, and the Ethiopic text will, it is hoped, appear shortly. The horology

---

[154] *Liturgia-Etiopi. Allegato I, Testo Latino dell'Ordinario della Messa con l'Anafora degli Apostoli. Allegato II, Testo Latino di 17 Anafore Etiopiche.* Tipografia Poliglotta Vaticana, 1944.

[155] S. A. B. MERCER, *The Ethiopic Liturgy*, p. 158.

corresponds substantially to that of the Byzantines, but it exists in four different recensions, one of which approximates to the Copto-Arabic text.

The most generally used exemplar had been known until then only through a Russian version: the commission compared it with the other recensions and with parallel texts in Coptic, Greek and Syriac, as well as with a Slav translation.

The revision of the ritual has been put off by the commission until a later date. At the present time the Roman ritual is used in Geez, and editions have been published in 1910 and 1924.

Until recently there was neither Ethiopic ritual nor pontifical in the national church, since the ordaining bishop was always a Copt, and consequently used a Coptic book. The ritual [156] of the dissidents was mainly that of the Coptic patriarch Gabriel V (1401-1418), but differed in many respects from that used in practice by the Ethiopians.

Shortly before the outbreak of war between Italy and Ethiopia, when King Hailie Salassie had obtained five bishops from the Coptic patriarch, the ritual of ordinations was translated into Geez for the dissidents.

Among the Catholics, orders were being conferred in Latin after the form of the Roman pontifical, [157] and certain officials, not only approved this, but would have had it extended to all pontifical functions through the introduction of an abridged Roman pontifical translated into Geez.

---

[156] Semharay SELAM, *De SS. Sacramentis secundum ritum Aethiopicum.* Introd., p. 10.

[157] Pope Leo X in 1521 (September 20) sent a copy of the Roman pontifical to Mark, patriarch of Alexandria and metropolitan of Ethiopia. *Testo di Diretto Antichi e Moderni riguardanti gli Etiopi* (Tip. Pol. Vat., 1931), p. 317.

Happily, however, the Eastern Congregation thought other-wise, and in 1931 published a provisional edition of the authentic Ethiopic version, which had been carefully revised under Arnold Van Lantschoot, a Premonstratensian canon and consultor to the Sacred Congregation for the Eastern Church.

This Geez pontifical was used for the first time on Easter Sunday (eastern style) 1940 in the Pontifical Ethiopian College, Rome.

One point of difference between the Roman and Ethiopic ordinations is that in the eastern rite the newly ordained priest does not participate in the ordination Mass.

History of the Rite

The liturgy has received the following names: sanctification, consecration, mystery, oblation, sacrifice, praise, thanksgiving, eucharist and eucharistic sacrifice.

The designation "sanctification" or "hallowing" [158] (*keddāsē*) is also used in two other senses—for the anaphora and for the proclamation of the divine holiness [159] in the *sanctus*.

The Greek word anaphora is never found in Ethiopic, and the usual expression for that part of the liturgy which lies between the *sursum corda* and the epiclesis is the "thanksgiving of the Eucharist" (*'akuatêta querbān*).

The full title of the liturgy, which is not only used to-day, but is found in three manuscripts in the British Museum and two in Berlin, is "the Order of the *Keddāsē*, which is to be said by the presbyter and the deacon and the people, together

---

[158] The new Catholic Ethiopic missal (1945) is called the "Book of the Oblation."

[159] Ἁγασμός. BRIGHTMAN, *op. cit.*, pp. 579, 594.

with everything that is proper at its time, according to the order of our fathers the Egyptians." It would seem that the title was first used between the years 1548 and 1670-5.

Le Brun [160] has suggested that some of the Ethiopic liturgies may be the earliest to have been written. St. Frumentius, he argues, was consecrated *per saltum* and sent to a land where there were no Christians, so that he must have required a liturgy. It may be noted also that the translation made by Ludolf contains no reference to any of the fathers subsequent to the 318 of Nicea, who were personally acquainted with St. Athanasius. Brightman, [161] however, is on safer ground when he says that "the history of liturgical development is too little known to justify even conjecture." [162] Nevertheless, the earliest form of the liturgy extant comes from the *Ethiopic Church Ordinances,* which form a part of the *Ethiopic Statutes of the Apostles,* and constitute a section of the larger *Sinodos.* In the Ordinances, the anaphora is connected with the consecration of a bishop; while historically it has affinity with the *Apostolic Constitutions* (Book VIII). Some features, such as the offertory rubric, opening dialogue and the oblation of oil after the invocation, are derived from Hippolytus. Indeed, the normal anaphora in use, that of the Apostles (*Zahâwâriât*), is an expansion of the *Apostolic Tradition of Hippolytus,* as it is found in the Ethiopic version, which now forms an

---

[160] "*Elles sont peut-être les plus anciennes de toutes celles qui ont été écrites.*" *Explication de la Messe,* t. II, dissert. VIII, art. II, p. 561. Paris, 1726.

[161] *Op. cit.,* p. LXXV.

[162] Salaville (*Introduction to study of Eastern Liturgies,* chap. II, p. 39) says that the translation of the liturgy was probably the work of Egyptian monks in the 5th or 6th century.

integral part of the *Sinodos*, [163] the Ethiopic book of canon law. There is reason to suppose that this Ethiopic version was translated from an Arabic one about the 13th or 14th century. If this is the case, the anaphora of the Apostles [164] must be later still, and probably the Liturgy of St. Mark had previously been in use.

The influence of the *Testament* [165] *of the Lord,* which is a Syriac form of Hippolytus, is seen in the suffrage of the litany immediately preceding the Mass of the catechumens: "For those of our brethren and sisters who lag behind," although "come late" might be a more accurate translation.

It has been maintained by the Armenian, Abu Salik (early 13th century), that the liturgy in Ethiopia, until about the year 480, was written in Greek, and certainly early Abyssinian coins bear a Greek legend.

Until recently, authorities admitted 16 Ethiopic anaphoras, although no manuscript in the British Museum gives more than 14. Abba Tecle Semharay Selam has published a 17th, that of St. Mark, which is a translation of the liturgy of Alexandria.

The majority of the anaphoras seem to have been comparatively late in appearance, and were probably subsequent to the 10th century.

The Catholics used the same 14 anaphoras as the Monophysites, which differ only in some of their names and in

---

[163] The *Sinodos* is largely composed of an Ethiopic translation of the Sahidic Heptateuch.

[164] Gregory DIX. *Treatise on the Apostolic Tradition.* General Introduction, p. XLIX. The anaphora of the Apostles is substantially identical with the Coptic liturgy of St. Cyril.

[165] A Latin form of the *Testament of the Lord* is found in the fragments of a palimpsest manuscript at Verona, which was published in 1900 by Hauler.

certain slight corrections, found necessary by the compilers of the Asmara missal (1913).

The recent missal, published by the Vatican press (1945), has 17 anaphoras, with the fragment of an 18th in the appendix. Thus, for the first time the anaphoras of Our Lady, which Abba George composed, St. James, the brother of our Lord, and St. Mark the Evangelist have been given.

The second anaphora of St. Cyril [166] has been relegated to the appendix, as the one manuscript in which it has been found contains only a fragment.

There are no fixed days for the use of particular anaphoras, but the celebrant chooses that which he considers most appropriate to the day. A similar custom prevails among the dissidents, although a 17th century manuscript [167] gives marginal notes appointing special days for the various anaphoras.

There is no liturgy of the Presanctified in this rite.

The Monophysites consider that four, five or even six assistants should take part in the liturgy, and if there are less than four the service has to be abandoned. Echoing the council [168] of Nicea, the *Fethé Neghest* [169] directs that it is not fitting for a priest to celebrate the holy sacrifice without a deacon, while the same nomocanon speaks of two deacons with *flabella* to prevent flies falling into the chalice.

A form of "low Mass" is found in the Catholic rite.

According to the *Fethé Neghest*, [170] the liturgy should

[166] It has been published in O. LÖFGREN & S. EURINGER, *Die beiden äthiopischen Anaphoren " des heiligen Cyrillus Patriarchen von Alexandrien."* Zeitschrift für Semitistik und verwandte Gebiete, 8 (1932), pp. 230-234; 9 (1933), pp. 44-86.
[167] J. M. HARDEN, *Anaphoras of the Ethiopic Rite*, p. 8.
[168] *Of Various Ecclesiastical Constitutions*, chap. 13.
[169] Chap. 12.
[170] Cf. *Didascalia*, can. 38.

be celebrated every Sunday, Wednesday, Friday and Saturday, and on feasts falling between these days. The same authority, however, directs that a bishop should, if possible, receive holy communion every day, while the *Epistle* [171] *of Peter to Clement,* which the Ethiopic church receives, says: "Do not neglect the holy things of God on all the days of thy life, for the offering of the Mass turns aside temptation."

The normal length of the liturgy is from three to four hours, and frequently begins at a very early hour, [172] which may be a relic of the days of war or persecution. On fasts, however, the liturgy begins at a corresponding time in the afternoon, lest the reception of the sacrament should break the fast.

The invariable *ordo communis* comprises the pre-anaphora, intercessions and postcommunion prayers. It has been ascribed to St. Basil, but from the enarxis it is probably a version of Alexandrine St. Mark.

The normal anaphora, as we have seen, is that of the Apostles.

Liturgy with Anaphora of the Apostles

Before entering the church, the celebrant is directed to wash his hands [173] and his feet.

Then, as he goes to the altar, having said: "In the name of the Father and of the Son and the Holy Ghost, one God," the priest recites the following prayer: "Believing in the Holy Trinity and having recourse to it" etc.

---

[171] Par. 16.

[172] In 1924, the liturgy at Jerusalem began at 4.0 a.m.

[173] At S. Andrea della Valle, the priest washed his hands at the foot of the altar.

Thus, Fr. Hanssens [174] gives the beginning of the Catholic rite.

Two deacons and three servers assisted at the "low Mass" celebrated during the Epiphany octave (1928) at Sant'Andrea della Valle, Rome. A table with two candles stood on either side of the sanctuary, while a further two candles were lit on the altar. The missal, to the left of the centre, was not moved during the liturgy.

The Lord's prayer, hail Mary and creed are added to the above prayer.

Then the priest recites the following psalms: XXIV, XXIX, LX, LXV, CI, CII, CXXIX, and CXXX.

When the priest or deacon has admonished those who are about to receive holy communion, the celebrant says the prayer [175] of penitence "of St. Basil": "Lord, our God and our Creator, who hast made all things through thy Word, and has brought us to this mystery by thy wisdom, who didst form man and madest him to be ruler over all creatures, that he might judge in righteousness and in purity, grant us the wisdom which dwelleth in thy treasures, create in us a clean heart, and forgive us our sins and hallow our souls and make us meet to draw nigh to thy sanctuary, that we may offer to thee an oblation and spiritual sacrifice for the remission of the sin of thy people. O our Lord and our God and our Saviour Jesus Christ, who hast raised us from the earth and lifted us up out of the dust, that thou mightest set us with the angels of thy people, make us worthy of thy holy gospel and of love, and in the greatness of thy loving-kindness hear us, that we may do thy will in this hour, offering to thee an oblation, sweet-smelling and good, and

[174] *Instit. Lit. de Rit. Orien.*, t. II, part I, chap. X, p. 398.
[175] Not in Tasfa Seyon, 1548.

fruit, good and spiritual, that we may be well-pleasing unto
thee in thy loving-kindness and mercy. Accept this spotless
oblation, and send upon us, upon this mystery, the Holy
Spirit; let it be to the glory of thine only Son, our Lord
and Saviour Jesus Christ, world without end. Amen."

At the conclusion of the prayer, the priest turns first
to the east and then to the west, as he makes a memorial of
those who are with him, and afterwards of the pope, bishop,
king, priests, and of all the faithful, both living and dead.

In the rite of the dissidents, [176] the commemorations
are made after the Lord's prayer, inclination and prayer of
penitence, and before the commixture.

The priest in the Catholic rite now says the prayer [177] of
Gregory before the approach to the veil, which begins with
the words: "O Lord our governor, who rulest all things and
knowest the thoughts of men. This prayer is not the same
as that which is given by Brightman, [178] but it is followed by
the "prayer, [179] of John," which is said also by the dissidents,
as a prayer before the altar prior to the entrance of the
celebrant into the sanctuary: "Lord, our God, who sittest
above the angels and the archangels, the lords and the
dominions, the cherubim and the seraphim, who wast before
all creatures; who art exalted above all glory; who liftest up
the dead and lowly from the earth, and exaltest them to
heaven; thou who hast manifested to us a new way for
our salvation, whose mercies are numberless; O good one
and lover of men, who by thy will hast taught us poor ones,

[176] BRIGHTMAN, op. cit., pp. 235-237.
[177] Cf. Coptic rite.
[178] Op. cit., p. 195.
[179] Not in Tasfa Seyon, although it may possibly have been recited
from memory. The rubric in the dissident liturgy says: "And next
he shall go in and worship before the tabot and then he shall say the
prayer of John." BRIGHTMAN, op. cit., p. 196.

thy people, to know the mystery of thy holiness and thine
awful word; praised also be the glory which thou hast ordained for us. Lord, our God, O good one and lover of man,
suffer us to come into thy holy of holies and read thy mysteries as befitteth thy Godhead, with a right faith in thee; do
thou make to shine upon us thy glory, which removeth from
us both the polluting thought and the deed of sin; and send
upon us the Holy Ghost, the consuming fire, which the
fiery ones cannot approach unto, which consumeth the evil
thought and burneth up sins; vouchsafe knowledge to the
eyes of our heart and keep our lips from speaking evil; give
us peace and teach us righteousness; for thou art the holy
garment and the medicine of our sickness in thy wisdom;
and make us to become meet for this thine holy mystery,
and put away from us all evil thoughts and lusts which fight
against our soul, that we may offer to thee a good heavenly
oblation without spot or uncleanness. Through thy great
loving-kindness and mercy and favour may we accomplish
this heavenly mystery which is above all mysteries. To
thee with thy good heavenly Father and the Spirit, the
giver of life, we will raise majesty and honour, world
without end. Amen."

The "prayer of Basil the Antiochene" is then said for
the second time, as the priest [180] opens the repository containing the vestments and sacred vessels.

When these prayers have been said, the celebrant begins
to "vest" the altar, saying both then and afterwards the
same prayers [181] as the dissidents.

[180] HANSSENS, op. cit., p. 398. At the "low Mass" both at S. Andrea della Valle and Santo Stefano in Rome, and also at Valviciolo, the
priest vested before the liturgy in the sacristy, and the altar was already
prepared.
[181] Ibid., p. 398.

Before he "dresseth the *tabot*," the priest bows "before the *tabot* once and once to the presbyters and to the deacons once."

Then the priest puts on the sacred vestments.

The rubric: "And then let him put on the *akman* and tie it with the *zenar*" has been changed in the Catholic rite: [182]

"Then, let him put on the *epimanikia* and gird himself with the cincture."

During the vesting at the altar, the priest says the Lord's prayer, and bows three times.

The missal of Asmara has added certain prescriptions, directing that the priest must not celebrate without lighted candles; while he must see that the bread is intact and that the wine has been correctly made.

The first prayer, said at the vesting of the altar, is found almost *verbatim* in Coptic St. Cyril and Coptic St. Basil: "Lord who knoweth the hearts of each and all, who dwelleth in the holy place, who is without sin and alone able to forgive sin: whereas thou knowest, O Lord, that I am not pure for this thine holy service and that I have not the countenance wherewith to draw nigh and to open my mouth before thine holy glory: yet according to the multitude of thy mercy forgive me my sin, for I am a sinner: grant me to find grace and mercy in this hour and send me thy power from on high that I may be made worthy and may accomplish thine holy service according to thy will and thy good pleasure, and that this incense also may be a sweet-smelling savour.

(In the Catholic rite, [183] the priest puts incense into

---

[182] *Ibid.*, p. 399.
[183] HANSSENS, *op. cit.*, p. 398.

the censer) And do thou also, O our Lord, be with us and bless us: for thou art the absolver of our sin and the light of our souls and our life and our strength and our hope and our refuge and to thee we send up unto the highest thanksgiving and honour and worship, to the Father and the Son and the Holy Ghost, at all times both now and evar and world without end."

This is followed by a "prayer after he hath prepared the altar, of the Father:" "O God who hast taught us this great mystery for our salvation, thou who hast called us thy lowly servants, although we be unworthy, to be ministers unto thine holy altar; do thou, O our master, make us meet in the power of the Holy Ghost to accomplish this mystery to the end that without falling into judgment in the presence of thy great glory we may present unto thee a sacrifice of praise and glory and great comeliness in thy sanctuary. O Lord, giver of redemption and sender of grace, who workest all in all, grant us, Lord, that our gift be accepted in thy sight. Yea, Lord our God, we pray thee and beseech thee that thou wilt not forsake thy people by reason of their sin and especially not by reason of my foolishness: for holy is thine holy place according to the gift of the Holy Ghost: in Jesus Christ our Lord, to whom with and the Holy Ghost the life-giver, who is coequal with thee, are fitting honour and glory and power, both now and ever and world without end. Amen."

Then, in the "prayer [184] after the withdrawal of the

---

[184] *La Santa Messa in rito Alessandrino-Etiopico* (pp. 5, 6), which is the merest sketch of the liturgy, says that this prayer is said after the entrance of the oblations, the choir having sung the anthem: " Salutations to thee, our mother, holy Church whose foundations are adorned with precious stone of topaz." This is followed in the same brochure by the following admonition from the deacon: " If anyone

veil," the priest continues: "How awful is this day and how marvellous this hour wherein the Holy Ghost will come down and overshadow this oblation and hallow it. In quietness and in fear and trembling stand ye up and pray that the peace of God be with me and with all of you."

The celebrant, at the entrance of the sanctuary, now washes his hands, but does not dry them, and, "Alleluia" [185] having been sung, he recites a prayer of approach: "Truly I enter thy house in the multitude of thy mercy" etc.

The above prayers and ceremonies are found in the Asmara missal and also in that recently published by the Vatican press, but in practice they are sometimes omitted, as they are not considered an integral part of the liturgy.

At "low Mass," [186] it is customary to go straight from the sacristy to the altar, and proceed at once with the offertory.

The service of the prothesis is longer than in the Coptic rite, although it ends in both liturgies with psalm CXVI and the doxology.

As we have seen, the "prayer [187] over the masob" was

of the faithful should enter the church during Mass and hear the holy Scriptures and not persevere to the end of the prayers and of the Mass, and not go to holy communion, let him be expelled from the church, for he has violated the divine law and has been esteemed of no worth to stand before the presence of a celestial king, a king of the body and of the soul. As the apostles and their canons have taught us."

[185] From Easter until Pentecost, the people sing three times: "Alleluia, Joseph and Nicodemus wrapped in a winding sheet Jesus, who miraculously rose from the dead."

[186] At San Stefano (Rome), the priest, before beginning the offertory, placed his head against the altar. At S. Andrea, the celebrant carried Latin vessels, and a bell was rung before the offertory.

[187] BRIGHTMAN, op. cit., p. 198.

not said in the Asmara missal, [188] but when the paten was oiïerea the following formula was recited, which Mercer [189] gives under the rubric "Then he shall gc around with the eucharistic host:"

"Remember those who bring near to thee this oblation, and let it be brought for the sake of those whom he, who is in heaven, has purchased, and especially for thy work which is found with thee in this hour. Accept it for thyself, like as thou didst accept the offering of righteous Abel and the oblation of our father Abraham, and also the widow's mite; in like manner receive the salutations of the many and of the few, of the hidden and of the manifest, and fill their homes with all thy goodness, wherever thy holy name is recorded on earth. Remember them, O Lord, in thy heavenly kingdom, and leave me not here for ever and ever. Amen."

In the Monophysite rite, the priest, "making the sign over the bread," says in Greek: "Εὐλόγιος Ἰησοῦς Χριστός, Son of the living God, ἁγίασμα τῶν πνευμάτων ἅγιος in truth. Amen."

The Catholics [190] substituted the following prayer: "I have sought thy face, O Lord, thy face will I seek. Do not turn thy face from me; do not turn aside from thy servant in thine anger; be to me a helper, do not despise me, O God my Saviour."

Then the bread is blessed, as the priest says: "Christ our very God, sign with thy right hand † and bless with

[188] HANSSENS, *Instit. Lit. de Rit. Orien.*, t. II, part I, chap. X, p. 399.

[189] *Op. cit.*, p. 303. The new missal (1945) has a similar prayer, which is said by the priest as he goes round the altar with the *oblata*. Pietros HAILÙ, *La Messa Etiopica, detta " degli Apostoli"* (Roma, 1946), p. 6.

[190] HANSSENS, *Ibid.*

thine hand † and hallow † with thy power and give virtue to this bread; let it be for the remission of the sins of thy people. Amen."

During the recitation of this prayer, the priest "with his wet hand shall rub the bread over and under and he shall sign over it a second time."

The rubbing [191] of the bread is to test the soundness of the loaf, and to remove loose particles.

The new Catholic missal (1945) would seem to have somewhat changed this. The prayer "Remember those who bring near to thee" is again said at the circuit of the altar, and at its conclusion the people say: "Thou art the *masob* ('pot') of pure gold, wherein is hidden the manna, the bread which cometh down from heaven and giveth life unto all the world."

The prayer [192] over the *masob* is said when the repository in which the body and blood of our Lord are kept for communicating the faithful is blessed:

"Our God, Lord, our God who said unto Moses, his servant and prophet, in mount Sinai, make me a choice vessel and set it in the tabernacle; now also, Lord our God Almighty, stretch forth thine holy right hand upon the *masob*, and fill it with power and virtue, and the grace of the Holy Ghost and thy glory, that they may make therein the body of thine only holy Son in this holy apostolic Church; for thine is the glory, with thine only Son and the Holy Ghost, both now and ever and world without end. Amen."

The *masob* itself, in which the bread is brought from the "house of bread," is blessed with the sign of the cross,

---

[191] *Mazmaza ku'rbāna.*
[192] BRIGHTMAN, *op. cit.,* p. 198; MERCER, *op. cit.,* p. 304.

as the priest says: "In the name of the Father and of the Son and of the Holy Ghost, one God."

At a "low Mass," the bread is placed at once on the altar, and covered with the *māchfad,* but in a solemn liturgy the deacon receives the bread in the veil, as he says:

"Like as Joseph and Nicodemus wrapped thee in linen clothing and spices, and thou wast well pleased in them, in like manner be well pleased in us."

The priest, taking the bread, then continues: "The hallowing and the thanksgiving and the exaltation, be it accepted of God the Father, for the remission of sin. Power and blessing and light, hallowing and the holy be in this holy apostolic church. Amen."

A rubric [193] directs the priest to "compass the *tabot* (altar) with the taper in front of him and the deacon shall compass it thrice holding the chalice."

The Italian translation [194] of the rite gives the following particulars: the subdeacon offers three breads to the priest, who chooses one and blesses it, as he says: "Bless, O Lord Jesus Christ, Son of the living God." Then, covering the bread with the *māchfad,* he (the priest) processes round the altar, preceded by an acolyte with a candle and followed by the deacon carrying an ampulla of wine.

The following prayer, said by the priest as he walks round the altar, is found also in the Maronite and Chaldean rites: "Lord our God, who didst accept the offering of Abel in the wilderness and of Noe within the ark (*tabot*) and of Abraham on the mountain top and of Elias on the top of Carmel and of David in the threshing floor of Ornan the

---

[193] BRIGHTMAN, *op. cit.,* p. 189.
[194] *La Santa Messa in rito Alessandrino-Etiopico* (Rome, 1938), p. 6. Pietros Hailù (*op. cit.,* p. 7) says that the subdeacon carries the candle.

Jebusite and the widow's mite in the sanctuary: accept likewise the oblation and offering of thy servant N., which he has brought unto thy holy name and let it be the redemption of his sins: recompense him with a godly recompense in this world and in that which is to come, both now and ever and world without end."

The deacon responds: "The Lord seeth me."

The priest, placing the bread on the paten, continues: "Lord our God, good and life-giving, who didst spread forth thy holy hands on the tree of the cross: place thine holy hand on this paten which is filled with good things, whereon they that love thy name have prepared the sustenance of a thousand years. Now, our God, bless with thine hand and hallow and cleanse this paten which is filled with live coal, even thine own holy body, which we have presented on thine holy altar in this holy apostolic church: for thine is the glory, with thy good heavenly Father and the Holy Ghost the lifegiver, both now and ever and world without end."

A rubric in the Monophysite liturgy now directs the deacon to pour the blood (*sic*) into the chalice.

In the Catholic rite, the word has been altered to "wine," and it is the priest, not the deacon, who is required to do this. The Monophysite custom was borrowed from Egypt, and the Lamp directs that the deacon prepares the chalice alone.

Water [195] is added to the wine in the customary way,

---

[195] The Italian translation of the rite (Rome, 1938), p. 7, expressly mentions water: the deacon, after the bread has been placed on the paten, carries the wine a second time round the altar, reciting psalm. XXII. Then, at the right side of the altar, he gives the wine to the assistant priest, who pours in the wine *and water*, as the celebrant says the "second prayer of the nuptials over the chalice." The deacon goes three times round the altar. HAILÙ, *op. cit.*, p. 8.

although neither the Catholic (Asmara) nor the dissident missal make any mention of it.

The priest says the prayer over the chalice: "Lord our God, Jesus Christ ἀληθινός, in truth our God who was made man, whose godhead was not severed from his manhood, who of his own good pleasure did pour out his blood for the sake of his creatures: now our God, place thine holy hand on this cup, hallow it and cleanse it that this may become thy precious blood, for life and for remission of sin unto every one that shall drink thereof believingly. Glory be to thine heavenly Father and to the Holy Ghost the life-giver, both now and ever and world without end."

This is followed by a "second prayer of the nuptials over the chalice," which owes its name to the reference to the marriage of Cana in Galilee:

"Christ our very God, who wentest to the marriage feast when they called thee in Cana of Galilee, and didst bless them, and didst make the water wine: do thou in like manner unto this wine which is set before thee: bless † it and hallow † it and cleanse † it: let it become the joy and the life of our soul and our body. At all times may the Father and the Son and the Holy Ghost be with us. Fill it with the wine of rejoicing for good, for life and for salvation and for the remission of sin, for understanding and for healing and for counsel of the Holy Ghost, both now and ever and world without end. Purity and sweetness and blessing be to them that drink of thy blood precious ἀληθινός true."

In the missal of Tasfa Seyon, the prayer is called the "prayer at the mixture of the water with the wine," but it has been placed after the prayer of offering.

The "prayer over the cross-spoon" [196] is for the bless-

---

[196] *Ḳasīs zayetrādā'e.* The handle of the spoon ends in a cross.

ing of the spoon (*'erfa maskal*) in which the faithful are
communicated with the chalice: "Lord our God, who didst
make thy servant Isaias meet to behold the seraph, when
with the tongs in his hand he took therewith a live coal from
off the altar and laid it on his mouth: now, O Lord
Father almighty, place thine holy hand upon the cross-spoon,
for the administering of the holy body and blood of thine
only Son our Lord and our God and our Saviour Jesus
Christ: bless now and hallow and cleanse this cross-spoon,
and give it power and glory, as thou gavest to the tongs of
the seraph: for thine is the glory and the dominion, with
thine only Son our Lord Jesus Christ and the Holy Ghost,
both now and ever and world without end. Amen."

The priest then makes the sign of the cross over the
bread, as he says: "Blessed be the Lord almighty. (People:
"Amen") And blessed be the only Son our Lord Jesus Christ.
(People: "Amen"). And blessed be the Holy Ghost the
Paraclete." (People: "Amen").

"And he shall say over the chalice also in like manner."
This rubric is followed immediately in the liturgy [197] of
the dissidents by another rubric and prayer, but it is evident
that at one time the prayer "Lord our God, who didst accept
the offering of Abel" was repeated here. The new Catholic missal (1945) has restored the second recitation of the
prayer.

"Again he shall say over both" (i. e. the bread and
wine): "Glory and honour are unto the Holy Trinity,
the Father and the Son and the Holy Ghost coequal Trinity,
both now and ever and world without end."

The priest turns and, taking the hand of the assistant
priest, says: "Remember me, my father presbyter," to which

[197] BRIGHTMAN, *op. cit.*, p. 201, l. 5.

the response is made: "The Lord keep thy priesthood and accept thy oblation."

Then, with his face towards the east and his hand outstretched, the priest continues in a loud voice:

"One God is the holy Father, one God is the holy Son, one God is the Holy Ghost," and the people answer: "The Holy Ghost." The Italian translation [198] of the rite says that the people respond: "Truly the Father is holy, truly the Son is holy, truly the Spirit is holy."

The preparatory section of the liturgy is concluded by the recitation of psalm CXVI [199] by the priest and people alternately.

These prayers must be of later date than the 5th century, as they are not found in the Alexandrine St. Mark.

Enarxis

The Ethiopic enarxis, which is longer than that in the Coptic rite, begins with the monition of the deacon: "Stand up for prayer."

The people respond in Greek: "Lord have mercy on us."

Then, when the priest has said: "Peace be unto you all" ("The Lord be with you all"), and the people have answered: "And with thy spirit," the celebrant recites the prayer of thanksgiving. The Catholic liturgy ascribes this prayer to St. Basil. The Coptic rite calls it "of St. Mark."

It is found in all known Ethiopic manuscripts, as well as in Tasfa Seyon, Greek St. Mark, Coptic St. Cyril and Coptic St. Basil:

"We give thanks unto the doer of good unto us, the

---

[198] *La Messa in rito Alessandrino-Etiopico* (Rome, 1938), p. 7.
[199] Psalm CL. *Ibid.*, p. 7.

merciful God, the Father of our Lord and our God and our
Saviour Jesus Christ: for he hath covered us and succoured
us, he hath kept us and brought us nigh and received us
unto himself and undertaken our defence and strengthened
us and brought us unto this hour. Let us therefore pray him
the almighty, our Lord God, keep us in this holy day all
the days of our life in all peace."

Deacon: Pray ye."

Priest: "Lord, Lord God almighty, Father of our Lord
and our God and our Saviour Jesus Christ, we render thee
thanks upon every thing, for every thing and in every thing,
for that thou hast covered us and succoured us, hast kept
us and brought us nigh and received us unto thyself and
undertaken our defence and strengthened us and brought
us unto this hour."

Then the deacon says: "Entreat ye and beseech, that
the Lord have mercy upon us and compassionate us, and
receive prayer and supplication from his saints in our behalf,
according to what is expedient at all times. May he make
us meet to partake of the communion of the blessed mystery,
and remit unto us our sins."

Deacon: "Kyrie, eleison." [200]

The priest continues: "For this cause we pray and
entreat of thy goodness, O lover of man, grant us to fulfil
this holy day all the days of our life, and in all peace along
with thy fear. All envy and all trial, and all the working
of Satan and the counsel of evil men, and the influence of
the adversary secret and open (*he shall bless himself once*),
remove O Lord, (be) far from me and far from all thy people
(*he shall bless the people*), and from this holy place of thine

[200] "The people shall say *Kyrie eleison* thrice." Missal of Tasfa
Seyon.

(*he shall bless the altar once*); all good things that are expedient and excellent command them for us, for thou art he who hath given us power to tread upon scorpions and serpents, and upon all the power of the enemy. Lead us not into temptation, but deliver us and rescue us from all evil; in the grace and loving-kindness of the lover of man, of thine only Son our Lord and our God and our Saviour Jesus Christ, through whom to thee with him and the Holy Ghost, the lifegiver, are fitting glory and honour and might, now and ever and world without end. Amen."

The deacon again gives the monition: "Stand up for prayer," and the people respond: "Lord have mercy on us."

The priest says: "Peace be unto you all," [201] and the people answer: "And with thy spirit."

The prayer of the oblation of the apostles follows:

"And again let us beseech the almighty Lord, the Father of our Lord and Saviour Jesus Christ, on behalf of those who bring an offering within the one holy catholic church, an oblation, firstfruits, tithes, a thanksgiving, a memorial, whether much or little, in secret or openly, and of those who wish to give and have not wherewith to give, that he may accept their ready mind, that he vouchsafe the heavenly kingdom, who hath power unto every deed of blessing, even the Lord our God."

Then the deacon says: "Pray for them that bring an offering," and the people respond: "Accept the offering of the brethren, accept the offering of the sisters, and ours also accept, our offering and our oblation."

The assistant priest now repeats the prayer of the oblation of the apostles.

---

[201] "The Lord be with you all." *La Santa Messa in rito Alessandrino Etiopico*, p. 7.

The monitions, etc. are again recited before the prayer of the mystery, a prayer which Dr. Mercer[202] cites as the "prayer of the anaphora:"[203]

"O my master, Jesus Christ, co-eternal pure Word of the Father, and Word of the Holy Ghost the life-giver: thou art the bread of life which camest down from heaven and didst foretell that thou wouldst be the lamb without spot for the life of the world: and now also we pray and beseech of thine excellent goodness, O lover of man, make thy face to shine upon this bread (pointing),[204] and upon this cup (pointing), which we have set upon this spiritual altar (tabot) of thine: bless † the bread, and hallow † the cup, and cleanse them both †, and change this bread (pointing); let it become thy pure body, and what is mingled with this cup (pointing), let it be thy precious blood offered for us all, and let it be the healing and salvation of our soul and our body and our spirit. Thou art the king of us all, Christ our God, and to thee we send up praise and worship, and to thy good Father and to the Holy Ghost the lifegiver, who is co-equal with thee, both now and ever and world without end. Amen."

The deacon in the Catholic rite[205] now says: "The commandment of our fathers the apostles: let none keep in his heart rancour or revenge or envy or hatred towards his neighbour. Worship the Lord in fear." The people respond: "Before thee, Lord, we worship and thee we glorify."

---

[202] *Op. cit.*, pp. 313-314.

[203] The prayer is found in all Ethiopic manuscripts, Tasfa Seyon, Coptic St. Cyril and Coptic St. Basil.

[204] *emārē*, i. e. by way of making the application of the spoken formula.

[205] HANSSENS, *op. cit.*, p. 399.

The priest says the "prayer of burial," [206] while he covers the bread and wine with a veil: [207]

"The wrapping of the bread in linen, and our placing it upon the blessed paten, is like to the sepulchre and thy resting in it three days and three nights; so make our hands like the hands of Joseph and Nicodemus, who wrapped the body in linen clothes and placed it there, with the repose and the glory of the Father and the Son and the Holy Ghost, both now and ever and world without end. Amen."

The priest and the deacon then make a reverence to the altar, while the Catholic priest, omitting the "prayer of St. Basil, [208] which is said in the rite of the dissidents, says the "absolution [209] of the Son:"

"O Lord, Lord Jesus Christ, the only Son, the Word of the Lord the Father, who hast broken off from us the bond of our sins through thy life-giving and saving sufferings, who didst breathe upon the face of thine holy disciples and pure ministers, saying to them, "Receive the Holy Ghost: whatsoever men's sins ye remit they are remitted unto them, and whatsoever sins ye retain they are retained:" thou therefore now, O Lord, hast vouchsafed unto thy pure ministers that do the priest's office at all times in thy holy church, that they should remit sin on earth, should bind and loose every bond of iniquity. Now again, we pray

---

[206] Not in Brightman.

[207] Note the general Eastern impression that the covering of the offering with a veil symbolises the burial of our Lord. The Italian pamphlet (p. 8) says that the priest, after he has said the first prayer of the offertory, covers the bread with a small veil, the chalice with a second veil, and, finally, the bread and the chalice with a larger veil.

[208] HANSSENS, op. cit., p. 400.

[209] The absolution in the Monophysite rite is said by the assistant priest, and this would seem to be the current Catholic usage. La Santa Messa in rito Alessandrino-Etiopico, p. 8.

and entreat of thy goodness, O lover of man, on behalf of these thy servants, my fathers and my brothers and my sisters, and of me thy sinful and feeble servant, and of them that bow their heads before thine holy altar: make plain for us the way of thy mercy, break and sever every bond of our sins, whether we have trespassed against thee wittingly or unwittingly, or in deceit, whether in deed or in word, or through faintheartedness, for thou knowest the feebleness of man. O good lover of man and Lord of all creation, grant us the forgiveness of our sins, bless us and purify us and free us and set us loose, and loose all thy people (here he shall mention those lately departed), and fill us with the fear of thy name and stablish us to do thine holy will, O good one; for thou art our God and our Saviour, and to thee is fitting the glory and the praise with thy good heavenly Father and the Holy Ghost the life-giver, who is co-equal with thee, both now and ever and world without end."

The second part of the absolution, with a prayer for the remission of the sins of all those present, "out of the mouth of" the holy Trinity, the fathers of the first general councils, and of the saints, is not said by Catholics. [210]

The enarxis is concluded by a diaconal litany [211] for all sorts and conditions of men, the people responding "Kyrie, eleison" to each petition.

The litany is very similar in the Catholic and Monophysite rites, but the Catholics omit the petitions for rain, the fruits of the earth, etc.

[210] HANSSENS, op. cit., p. 400. It is, however, in the new Catholic missal (HAILÙ, op. cit., p. 16).

[211] Not found in Tasfa Seyon or the Coptic rite; cf. Testament of the Lord.

Liturgy of the Catechumens

The liturgy of the catechumens begins with the blessing of incense [212] and the following prayer:

"I pray and beseech thee, O Lord God, as thou wast well pleased with the offering of Abel thy beloved and the oblation of Enoch and of Noe and the incense of Aaron and Samuel and Zacharias: in like manner accept from us this incense as a sweet-smelling savour for the remission of our sins and forgive all thy people their trespasses: for thou art merciful and to thee glory is fitting, with thine only Son and the Holy Ghost, both now and ever and world without end. Amen."

Then, "casting the incense," the priest says: "Blessed be the Lord, the almighty Father," and the people respond: "Amen."

The assistant priest, if he is present, continues: "And blessed be the only Son our Lord Jesus Christ, who was made man of Mary, the holy Virgin, for our salvation." (People: "Amen").

The celebrant now takes up the prayer: "And blessed be the Holy Ghost, the Paraclete, who strengtheneth us all (People: "Amen"). Glory and honour be to the Holy Ghost, both now and ever and world without end. Amen. I will offer unto thee incense with rams: all thy garments smell of myrrh, aloes and cassia: let my prayer be set forth in thy sight as the incense. Yet again we offer unto thee this incense for the remission of my sins and the trespass of thy people. For blessed and full of glory is thy holy

---

[212] The celebrant blesses five grains of incense, three of which he puts into the censer. Of the other two, one is kept for the reading of the gospel and the other for the moment of consecration. *La Santa Messa in rito Alessandrino-Etiopico* (Rome, 1938), p. 8.

name, Father and Son and Holy Ghost, both now and ever
and world without end. Amen. Praises of the angels singing
in the highest. Alleluia to the Father: alleluia to the Son:
alleluia to the Holy Ghost. Worship we the Father: worship
we the Son: worship we the Holy Ghost, three in one and
one in three."

The priest then says the "prayer of the incense:"[213] "O
God,[214] the first and the last, who hath neither beginning
nor end, who is great in his counsel and mighty in his work
and righteous in his purpose and strong in his might, who
is and is to be in all things: be with us in this hour and
stand in the midst of us all and purify our hearts and
sanctify our souls and our flesh and wash us from all our
sins, which we have done wittingly or unwittingly: grant
us to offer before thee a reasonable oblation and an oblation
of blessing, the which thou wilt make to enter in within
the inner chamber of the veil, the holy of holies, the dwelling
place (and here he shall compass the *tabot* three times,
saying). We pray thee, O Lord, and beseech thee that thou
remember the one holy apostolic church, which reacheth
from one end of the world to the other."

The deacon responds: "Pray for the peace of the church,
one holy apostolic, orthodox in the Lord."

Then, when the people have answered *"Kyrie eleison,"*
the priest prays for the hierarchy and faithful: "Remember,
O Lord, the honoured father our pope N. and all orthodox
bishops, presbyters and deacons. (And if the pope or the

---

[213] Cf. Coptic rite.

[214] Mercer (*op. cit.*, p. 321) precedes the above prayer with the
following: "Accept of me my prayer, that the incense in thy presence,
gift of the Father, present of the Son, communion of the Holy Ghost,
even now may ascend to thee; and praise to our Lady Mary Mother
of God, lover of the prophets and true apostles and martyrs and
fathers of old, be with me and with all of you."

bishop be entered into rest he shall say) Rest, O Lord, the
soul of our father N. and make him to dwell in the kingdom
of heaven with the righteous: seat for us on his throne a
good shepherd, and let us not be like a flock having no
shepherd and let not the ravenous wolf make havoc of us,
nor alien folk that are contrary to us reproach us."

The deacon shall say: "Pray for our blessed pope N.
and for all orthodox bishops, presbyters and deacons."

The priest continues: "Remember, Lord, our congregation, bless them and make them to be neither separated
nor estranged: make them a house of prayer, a house of
purity and a house of blessing: vouchsafe it, Lord, unto us
thy servants and to them all that shall come after us, unto
eternal days vouchsafe it."

The deacon shall say: "Pray for our congregation which
is the keeping of us all."

The priest proceeds: "Arise, Lord my God, and let
thine enemies be scattered, and let all those who hate thy
holy and blessed name flee before thee, but let thy people
who do thy will be blessed with blessings, thousand-thousands and ten-thousand-times-ten-thousand; through thine
only Son, through whom to thee with him and with the
Holy Ghost be glory and dominion, both now and ever
and world without end. Amen."

Then the deacon says: "Stand up for prayer," and the
people respond: "Lord have mercy on us."

"On every great day, and on the first day of the week,
on the feast of Mary and on the feast of the Son," the
priest and the people recite the following: [215]

Priest, standing before the altar: "We worship thee,

---

[215] Brightman (op. cit., p. 211) gives a larger share of the prayer
to the people.

Christ, with thy good heavenly Father and thine Holy Spirit, the life-giver, for thou didst come and save us" (three times).

While this is being said, the priest censes the altar three times.

People: "The Father and the Son and the Holy Ghost, three in one." Priest: "Peace be unto thee, holy church, dwelling place of the godhead. Pray for us, Virgin Mary, parent of God."

The image (picture) of our Lady is censed three times.

The priest then says: "Thou art," and the people continue: "the golden censer which didst bear the live coal of fire. Blessed is he who receiveth out of the sanctuary him that forgiveth sin and blotteth out error, who is God's Word who was made man of thee, who offered himself to his Father for incense and an acceptable offering. [216] We worship thee, Christ, with thy good heavenly Father and thine Holy Spirit the life-giver, for thou didst come and save us."

In the Catholic rite, the priest [217] now goes to each of the doors of the church, as he says: "Glory [218] and honour to the Holy Trinity, the Father and the Son and the Holy Ghost, both now and ever and world without end. Amen."

Then, returning to the door of the sanctuary, the bishop (if he is present) is censed three times and the priests once each. At the censing of the bishop, the celebrant says: "Remember, O Lord, our father abba (and again the same), preserve him to us for many years and days of peace (a

---

[216] Cf. Coptic rite.

[217] HANSSENS, op. cit., p. 400.

[218] This doxology must have been originally the hymn of the little entrance; cf. hymn of Justinian: "They sing the only begotten Son and Word" in Greek St. Mark.

third time he shall say), let him trample our enemy under
his feet, and let him intercede for us to the Lord, that he
may cleanse us from our sins."

At the censing of the priest: "I pray thee, O my father
presbyter, remember me in thy prayer, this is my holiness,
accept it."

"After this he shall lay hands upon the deacons and say
the blessing of Paul, then he shall stretch his hand over the
people:" "The Lord bless."

This is followed by the customary monitions and salutations, with which the enarxis was begun.

Four lessons,[219] as in the Coptic rite, are read at a
solemn liturgy, two at the Catholic "low Mass."

The assistant priest says the prayer[220] before the epistle
of St. Paul: "Lord of knowledge and declarer of wisdom,
who hast revealed to us what was hidden in the depth of
darkness, giver of a word of gladness to them that proclaim
the greatness of thy power: thou it was that after thy great
goodness didst call Paul who was before a persecutor and
didst make him a chosen vessel and wast well pleased with
him that he should become an apostle and a preacher of the
gospel of thy kingdom, a summoner thereunto, O Christ our
God. Thou art a lover of man, O good one: vouchsafe us
a mind without distraction and a pure understanding that
departeth not from thee, that we may both perceive and
know how great is thine holy teaching which is now read
to us out of him: and as he was like unto thee, O prince
of life, so make us also meet to be like unto him in deed
and in faith, and to praise thine holy name and glory in thy
precious cross at all times: for thine is the kingdom, the

---

[219] *Menbāb.*
[220] The prayer in the Coptic rite is said after the lesson.

might, the majesty and the sovereignty, the honour and the glory, world without end. Amen."

The deacon, as he goes to read the lesson, says: "Everyone that loveth not our Lord and our God and our Saviour Jesus Christ and believeth not in his birth of Mary the holy Virgin, in the twofold ark of the Holy Ghost, until his coming again, as saith Paul, let him be anathema."

The epistle of Paul is read *in plano* facing the people, and at its conclusion the deacon [221] adds: "May the epistle of Paul be to us pure and sincere, and clean and well pleasing to the Lord" etc.

Then the priest again goes round to each of the doors of the church, as he repeats the same doxology [222] as before.

He censes the deacons and the faithful, and returns to the sanctuary, where the following formula is recited as the altar is incensed: "O Lord our God, who of old didst make the wall of Jericho to fall down by the hand of Joshua thy servant: in like sort now make the wall of the sin of these thy servants and thine handmaids to fall down by the hand of me thy servant."

Then the priest, alternately with the people, recites the praises [223] of the blessed Virgin in the "hail Mary."

Priest: "Hail, O Mary, full of grace."

People: "The Lord is with thee."

Priest: "Blessed art thou among women."

---

[221] HANSSENS, *op. cit.*, p. 400.

[222] *Ibid.* The Catholic rite omits certain other formularies found in the Monophysite liturgy. Cf. BRIGHTMAN, *op. cit.*, p. 213, l. 4-11.

[223] In the Monophysite rite, the praises of the blessed Virgin are said after the trisagion. BRIGHTMAN, *op. cit.*, p. 218.

The Italian translation of the rite (*La Santa Messa in rito Alessandrino-Etiopico*, p. 10) gives a similar position, which may very well represent current Catholic usage in modification of the Asmara missal (1913).

People: "And blessed is the fruit of thy womb."

Priest: "Pray and intercede for us with thy beloved Son."

People: "That he forgive us our sins."

The altar is again censed, as the priest says:

"O accepter of penitence and remitter of sin, Jesus Christ, remit my sin and the sin of all thy people: accept the penitence of these thy servants and thine handmaids, and make the light of thy grace to shine upon them for thine holy name's sake by which we are called: through whom to thee with him and the Holy Ghost be glory and dominion, both now and ever and world without end. Amen."

"The deacon entering after the reading of Paul shall say: The blessing of the Father and the bounty of the Son and the gift of the Holy Ghost who came down upon the apostles in the upper room of holy Sion, in like sort come down and be multiplied upon us. Amen."

The people respond: "Holy apostle Paul, goodly messenger, healer of the sick, thou hast received the crown: pray and intercede for us: cause our souls to be saved, in the multitude of his loving kindness and his mercy for his holy name's sake."

Before the reading of the catholic epistle, the customary monitions and salutations are again said; while the priest recites the prayer, which in the Coptic rite is found at the beginning of the censing in this part of the liturgy:

"O eternal God, the first and the last, who hath neither beginning nor end, he that is great in his counsel and mighty in his work and wise in his purpose, who is in all things: we pray thee, Lord, and beseech thee that thou be with us in this hour: make thy face to shine upon us and abide with us in the midst of us: purify our hearts and sanctify our souls and remit our sin which we have done with our will or without our will: make us, Lord, to offer unto thee a pure oblation, a reasonable offering and spiritual incense: let it enter into the holy temple of thine holiness: through thine only Son our Lord, through whom to thee with him and with the Holy Ghost be glory and dominion, both now and ever and world without end. Amen."

The subdeacon before the lesson says: "The word from the epistle of *N.*, disciple and apostle of our Lord Jesus Christ. His prayer and his blessing be with us. Amen," and at its conclusion: "May this epistle of the Holy Ghost, which came forth from the mouth of Peter (if it be his epistle), the rock of truth, be purity and tribute, light and exaltation. His blessing be with us for ever and ever. Amen."

The people respond: "Holy consubstantial Trinity, preserve our congregation for thine holy elect disciples' sake: comfort us in thy loving-kindness for thine holy name's sake."

The same monitions and salutations precede the third lesson (Acts of the Apostles).

The prayer said by the priest is in the Coptic rite the prayer of the catholic epistle:

"O Lord our God, thou it was that didst reveal to thine holy apostles the mystery of the glorious gospel of thy Messiah, and didst give them the great and immeasurable gift that is of thy grace, and didst send them to proclaim in all the ends of the world the inscrutable riches of thy grace through thy mercy: we pray thee also and beseech thee, our Lord and our God, that thou wouldest make us meet for an inheritance and a portion with them, that we may walk in their ways and follow in their footsteps: and vouchsafe us at all times to imitate them, and to continue in their love and to have fellowship with them in their labour in godliness: and do thou keep thine holy church which thou hast founded by their means (he shall bless himself), and bless the sheep of thy flock (he shall bless), thy people, and increase this vine (he shall bless the oblation), which thou hast planted by thy holy right hand (he shall bless the priesthood), through Jesus Christ our Lord, through whom to thee with him and with the Holy Ghost be glory and dominion, both now and ever and world without end. Amen."

The lesson from the Acts [224] of the Apostles is read by the assistant priest, who first says: "A pure fountain which is from the pure fountains of the law, which is the history of the acts of the pure apostles. The blessing of their prayer be with us. Amen."

Then, when he has finished the lesson, he continues: "Full and great and exalted is the word of the Lord, and it hath increased in his holy church, and many are the people who believe in our Lord Jesus Christ, to whom be glory world without end. Amen."

The people respond: "Holy, holy, holy art thou, God the Father almighty; holy, holy, holy art thou, only Son, who art the living Word of the Father; holy, holy, holy art thou, Holy Ghost, who knowest all things."

The priest, as he offers incense, [225] says: "Glory and honour [226] be to the Holy Trinity, the Father and the Son and the Holy Ghost, both now and ever and world without end. Amen."

Then, "standing before the altar," he recites the prayer, which in the Coptic rite is the prayer of the Acts of the Apostles:

[224] *Gebra ḥawāryāt.*
[225] *Mā'eṭant;* cf. Hebrews IX, 4.
[226] Cf. "Glory be" in the Mozarabic rite. The *sanctus* without "hosanna" is another point of similarity between the two rites.

"Lord our God, who didst accept the sacrifice of our father Abraham, and in the stead of Isaac didst prepare and send down to him a ram for his ransom: even so, O our Lord, accept from us our oblation and this savour of our incense, and send unto us from on high, in recompense thereof, the riches of thy loving-kindness and thy mercy, that we may become pure from all ill savour of our sins; and make us meet to minister before thy glorious purity, O lover of man, in righteousness and purity all the days of our life, in joy and in rejoicing."

The priest, "compassing the *tabot* (altar) three times," recites the same prayers for the hierarchy as he said after the "prayer of the incense."

These are followed by praises of our Lady: "Hail, O thou of whom we ask salvation, O holy praiseful ever-virgin parent of God, Mother of Christ: offer up our prayer on high to thy beloved Son that he forgive us our sins. Hail, O thou who barest for us the very light of righteousness, even Christ our God. O virgin pure, plead for us unto our Lord, that he show mercy unto our souls and forgive us our sins. Hail, O virgin pure, Mary, holy parent of God, very pleader for the race of mankind, plead for us before Christ thy Son, that he vouchsafe us remission of our sins. Hail, O virgin pure, very queen: hail, O pride of our kind: hail, O thou that barest for us Emmanuel. We pray thee that thou remember us, O very mediatrix, before our Lord Jesus Christ, that he forgive us our sins."

In Eastertide, the following chant is sung (thrice), as the celebrant processes three times round the altar: "He who raised himself at his resurrection is Christ: he hath raised the dead from death, and triumphed in death over those who were in the grave, and hath given them a life of eternal rest."

At other times, the priests go outside the veil, where they chant: "This is the time of blessing, this is the time of choice incense, the time of the praise of our Saviour, lover of man, Christ. The incense is Mary: the incense is he who was in her womb which is fragrant: the incense is he whom she bare: he came and saved us, the fragrant ointment, Jesus Christ. O come let us worship him and keep his commandements that he forgive us our sins.

To Michael was given mercy, and glad tidings to Gabriel and a heavenly gift to Mary the Virgin. To David was given understanding, and wisdom to Solomon and an horn of oil to Samuel, for he was the anointer of kings. To our father Peter were given the keys, and virginity to John and apostleship to our father Paul, for he was the light of the church.

The fragrant ointment is Mary: for he that was in her womb, who is more fragrant than all incense, came and was made flesh of her. In Mary virgin pure the Father was well-pleased and he decked her for a tabernacle for the habitation of his well-beloved Son.

To Moses was given the law, and the priesthood to Aaron: to Zacharias the priest was given the choice incense. They made the tabernacle of the testimony according to the word of the Lord and Aaron the priest in the midst thereof made the choice incense to go up.

The seraphim worship him and the cherubim glorify him: they cry saying: Holy, holy, holy is the Lord among the thousands and praised among the tens of thousands.

Thou art the incense, O our Saviour, for thou didst come and save us. Have mercy upon us O Lord."

While this hymn is sung, the second deacon carries the book of the gospels from the sanctuary, preceded by an acolyte with a lighted taper.

The trisagion [227] is chanted by the priest in the tone of *araray,* [228] in a special form:

"Holy God, holy mighty, holy living immortal, who was born of Mary the holy Virgin, have mercy on us, O Lord.

Holy God, holy mighty, holy living immortal, who was baptized in Jordan and was hung on the tree of the cross, have mercy on us, O Lord.

Holy God, holy mighty, holy living immortal, who rose from the dead the third day, ascended with glory into heaven, and sat down at the right hand of the Father, shall come again with glory to judge the living and the dead, have mercy on us, O Lord.

Glory be to the Father, glory be to the Son, glory be to the Holy Ghost, both now and ever and world without end. Amen and amen; so be it, so be it."

In the Catholic rite, [229] the trisagion is said without interpolations: "Holy God, holy mighty, holy living immortal, have mercy on us" (three times).

"And after finishing this they shall say: O Holy Trinity, pity us: O Holy Trinity, spare us: O Holy Trinity, have mercy on us."

Then, when the priest and his ministers have left the sanctuary, and stand before the veil, the celebrant gives his blessing to each of the priests, and says: "Glory and honour to the Holy Trinity, the Father and the Son and the Holy Ghost, now and ever and world without end."

The deacon in the Catholic rite [230] chants "Alleluia," but this is omitted by the dissidents.

---

[227] Cf. pseudo-Germanus, *Expositio Missae.*
[228] The name given to one of the three modes of the chant.
[229] *La Santa Messa Alessandrino-Etiopico* (Rome, 1938), p. 10.
[230] HANSSENS, *op. cit.,* p. 401.

The gospel section of the liturgy begins with the customary monitions and salutations.

Tasfa Seyon, St. Mark and Coptic St. Cyril have a
simpler form at the gospel, but Coptic St. Basil approximates more closely to the Ethiopic liturgy.

The priest, as in the Coptic rite, now says a prayer
addressed to our Lord: "Lord, Lord Jesus Christ our God,
who saidst to thine holy disciples and pure apostles, many
prophets and righteous men have desired to see the things
which ye see, and have not seen them, and have desired to
hear the things which ye hear, and have not heard them,
and blessed are your eyes that have seen and your ears that
have heard: like them do thou make us also meet to hear
and to do the word of thine holy gospel through the prayer
of the saints."

The deacon gives the monition: "Pray on account of
the holy gospel," and the priest continues: "Remember
again, Lord, them that have bidden us to remember them in
the time of our prayer and our supplication wherewith we
make request of thee, O Lord our God. Give rest to them
that have fallen asleep before us: heal speedily them that
are sick: for thou art the life of us all and the hope of us
all and the deliverer of us all and the raiser up of us all,
and to thee we send thanksgiving unto highest heaven, world
without end."

In the Catholic rite [231] the deacon proclaims: "Alleluia.
Stand up and hearken to the holy gospel, the message of
our Lord and Saviour Jesus Christ."

This was said later by the dissidents, after "Blessed be
the Lord the Father," etc., but as the Italian translation [232]

---

[231] HANSSENS, op. cit., p. 401.
[232] La Santa Messa Alessandrino-Etiopico (Rome, 1938), p. 11.

of the Catholic rite gives the same position it would seem
that current Catholic and Monophysite usage is the same.

The rubric in the Asmara missal preceding the next
prayer does not enjoin the putting of incense into the thurible, but directs the celebrant, as he recites the prayer, to
give a blessing [233] towards the four extremities or four
corners (? of the church):

"And the Lord most high bless us all †, and sanctify
us with all spiritual blessing †, and make our entry into
his holy church † to be joined with (the entry of) his holy
angels, who chant unto him with fear and with trembling †,
and glorify him at all times and all hours, world without
end."

A second prayer is said by the priest, with his face
turned towards the book of the gospels:

"Lord, our God and our Saviour, lover of mankind,
thou didst send them to propagate thy holiness and to announce thy purity in all ends of the world, that they may
proclaim the gospel of thy kingdom, and heal all sickness
and misery among thy people, and tell to them the hidden
secret which is from of old: now, O Lord, our God and our
King, send upon us thy light and thy righteousness, and
illuminate the eyes of our hearts and our understanding, and
make us meet to hear with fortitude the word of thy holy
gospel; not only that we may hear, but that we may also do;
that thou mayest hear us, that we may bear good fruit, for
one thirty-fold and sixty-fold and an hundred, for the sins
of us thy people, who pray for the kingdom of heaven."
A rubric [234] now enjoins that "the priest shall compass the

[233] At "low Mass," the priest blesses towards the four points of
the compass.
[234] The Italian brochure (p. 11) says that the priest puts the
fourth grain of incense into the censer, with the addition of other

tabot (altar) once with the taper before him and the gospel
behind him, and, making the sign of the cross with the
censer towards the gospel, he shall say: "Blessed be the
Lord the Father almighty."

(Assistant, turning to the people: "Give thanks unto
the Father").

"And blessed be the only Son, our Lord Jesus Christ."
(Assistant: "Give thanks to the Son").

"And blessed be the Holy Ghost the Paraclete."
(Assistant: "Give thanks unto the Holy Ghost").

The priest gives the salutation: [235] "The Lord be with
you all," and the people answer: "And with thy spirit."

Then, in response to "the holy gospel which *N.* preached,
the word of the Son of God," the people say: "Glory be to
thee, Christ, my Lord and my God, at all times. Sing [236]
we merrily unto God our strength: make a cheerful noise
unto the God of Jacob. Take the psalm, bring hither the
tabret: the merry harp with the lute."

"And the people shall kiss the gospel by their several
ranks, when he shall read the gospel."

The assistant, holding the gospel before the cross, says
in a low voice: "O far from anger and abundant in mercy,
and righteous indeed, receive our prayer and our humility
and our penitence, and our confession towards thy *tabot* and
thine holy altar, heavenly, stainless and spotless; make us
meet to hear the word of thine holy gospel, and to keep thy
commandments and thy testimony. Bless us that we may

incense, and three times incenses the book of the gospels, which is held
open by the priest assistant.

[235] MERCER, *op. cit.*, p. 338. The salutation and its response are
not given in Brightman.

[236] In Lent: " In the gospel thou hast shown us the way and in
the prophets thou hast comforted us. O thou who hast brought us
nigh unto thyself, glory be to thee."

bear fruit, for one thirthy-fold and sixty-fold and an hundred-fold."

An intercessory litany for all sorts and conditions has been added to the prayer, and, although the present form is older than the 13th century, it is evident that the first part was, as it is now, a preparation for the gospel; while the memorials, as in the Coptic rite, originally came after the lesson.

Thus, we find the final intercession is a prayer for the catechumens: "Remember, Lord, the catechumens of thy people, and teach them and stablish them in the right faith; banish from their heart all remains of idolatry; stablish in their heart thy law and the fear of thee, thy commandment and thy righteousness and thine ordinance; grant them to know the certainty of thy word wherein they have been instructed; and when they have been instructed, make them all meet for the new birth and for the remission of their sin, and prepare them to be a *tabot* for thine Holy Ghost; through the grace and loving-kindness of thine only Son, lover of man, our Lord and our Saviour Jesus Christ, through whom to thee with him and with the holy life-giver, who is coequal with them, both now and ever and world without end.   Amen."

The assistant priest [237] says: "Praise be to thee," and the priest who reads the gospel: "Εὐλογιός (sic) Χριστός".

"While finding the place which he shall read he shall say: "Bless †, O Lord, the reading of the gospel of N., the disciple and apostle of our Lord Jesus Christ, the Son of the living God: through whom to thee be glory continually, world without end.   Amen."

The gospel [238] is read by the priest *in plano* facing east,

---

[237] MERCER, *op. cit.*, p. 340.   Not given by Brightman.
[238] Wangēl.

with a deacon [239] on either side holding a lighted candle.

Before the reading of the gospel, if it is from St. John, a special formula of blessing is given: "Bless, Lord, through the Gospel of John, the disciple and apostle of our Lord Jesus Christ, the Son of the living God; to him be glory continually, world without end. Amen."

At the conclusion, the priest kisses the book, and adds a verse "distinguishing the several gospels:"

Matthew's: "Heaven and earth shall pass away, but my words shall not pass away, said the Lord to his disciples."

Marks: "He who hath ears to hear, let him hear."

Luke's: "It is easier for heaven and earth to pass than for one tittle of the law and the prophets to fail, said the Lord to his disciples."

John's: "He who believeth on the Son hath everlasting life."

The people [240] shall say at each gospel in tone as follows:

Matthew's: "We believe in the very Father, and we believe in the very Son, and we believe in the very Holy Ghost."

Mark's: "They, the cherubim and seraphim, offer up glory to him saying, Holy, holy, holy art thou, Lord, the Father and the Son and the Holy Ghost."

Luke's: "Who is like unto thee, O Lord, among the gods? Thou it is who doest wonders; thou didst show thy power unto thy people, and didst save thy people with thine arm; thou wentest into hades and broughtest up thence those who were in captivity, and didst desire us again to

---

[239] At "low Mass," one assistant with a taper. The Italian brochure (p. 12) says that the book of the gospels is held by the deacon, while the celebrant holds in his left hand the cross.

[240] "Priest," MERCER, op. cit., p. 340.

be set free, for thou didst come and save us. For this cause we glorify thee, saying, blessed art thou, our Lord Jesus Christ, for thou didst come and save us."

John's: "In the beginning was the Word; the Word was the Word of God; the Word was made flesh and dwelt among us and we beheld his glory as of the only-begotten of his Father; the living Word of the Father and the life-giving Word, the Word of God, rose again and his flesh was not corrupted."

A rubric in the Coptic liturgy seems to imply that a sermon was preached in the Ethiopic rite after the gospel, but this has long since been discontinued, although the *Fethé Neghest* directs that the bishop or, in his absence, the priest is to explain the gospel to the people.

The dismissal of the catechumens,[241] which follows, is found in Alexandrine St. Mark after the salutation at the great entrance. This is probably a late introduction, although the short form in the two rites indicates a close relationship.

Deacon: "Go forth ye catechumens."

A secret prayer "of St. Basil," [242] which in the Monophysite rite more often precedes the absolution to the Son, is sometimes said before the liturgy of the faithful:

"Lord our God, who by reason of thine unspeakable love towards mankind, didst sent thine only Son into the world to bring back unto thee the lost sheep; we beseech thee, O our master, turn us not back as we draw nigh to this awful sacrifice, without defilement and trusting not in our own righteousness but on thy mercy wherewith thou hast loved our race; we pray and beseech of thy goodness,

---

[241] *Ne'ūs crestīyān,* "young Christian."
[242] *Liturgia-Etiopi. Allegato* I (Tip. Pol. Vat., 1944), pp. 41-42; MERCER, *op. cit.,* p. 341.

O lover of man, that this mystery, when thou hast prepared it for our salvation, be not to us thy servants and all thy people for condemnation, but that it may be profitable for the blotting out of our transgression and the forgiveness of our negligence. Glory and honour be to thine holy name, both now and ever and world without end. Amen."

Liturgy of the Faithful

The liturgy of the faithful begins with the customary monitions and salutations, after which the priest says:

"Again let us beseech the almighty Lord, the Father of our Lord and Saviour Jesus Christ. We ask and entreat thy goodness, O lover of man. Remember, O Lord, the peace of the Church, holy, one, apostolic, which reacheth from one end of the world to the other."

Then the deacon gives the monition:

"Pray for the peace of the one, holy, apostolic Church, orthodox in the Lord."

The first of the three solemn prayers follows:

"Do thou bless † all the people and all the flocks; the peace that is from heaven do thou send into the hearts of us all, and the peace of our life vouchsafe us therein. Vouchsafe peace to our king, N., to his palace and to his armies, and to his princes and to his nobles, and to the multitude of our neighbours at home and abroad; adorn them with all peace. O king of peace, give us peace for thou hast given us all things; possess us, O Lord, and requite us, for beside thee we know none other; we make mention of thy holy name and call upon it, that our soul may live through the Holy Ghost, and that the death of sin may not have dominion over us thy servants and all thy people."

The people answer: "Kyrie, eleison." and the deacon

gives the monition: "Stand up for prayer." This is followed by "Lord have mercy on us," said by the people.

The salutation of the priest and its response are omitted in the Catholic rite.

Prayer is again made for the hierarchy.

The priest says: "And again let us beseech the almighty Lord, the Father of the Lord and our Saviour Jesus Christ, for the blessed Pope N., that he truly preserve him to us for many years and in peaceful days to fulfil the office of the priesthood which thou hast committed unto him. The Lord our God who is rich in grace vouchsafe it."

The deacon then gives the bidding: "Pray for our Pope N., and for the blessed bishop amba N., and all orthodox bishops, presbyters and deacons."

The priest continues: "Lord our God, who art almighty, we pray and beseech thee for our blessed bishop amba N., that thou truly preserve him for many years in peaceful days fulfilling the office of the priesthood which thou hast committed unto him, with all orthodox bishops, presbyters and deacons, and with all the entire congregation of the one holy catholic Church: and the prayer also which he shall make on our behalf and on behalf of all thy people do thou accept: open to him the treasure-house of thy blessing. Furthermore vouchsafe him abundantly the grace of the Holy Ghost: pour upon him from heaven thy blessing that he may bless thy people: and all his enemies visible and invisible do thou subdue and bruise under his feet shortly: but himself do thou still preserve unto us, unto thine holy church, in thy priesthood: through thine only Son through whom to thee with him and with the Holy Ghost be glory and dominion, both now and ever and world without end. Amen."

The monitions and salutations are repeated.

The priest says: "And again let us beseech the almighty

Lord, the Father of the Lord and our Saviour Jesus Christ; we pray and implore of thy goodness, O lover of man; remember, O Lord, our congregation; bless † thou them."

The deacon gives the bidding: "Pray for this holy church and our congregation therein," and the priest continues: "and make them to be to thee without hindrance and without intermission, doing thy holy and blessed will: a house of prayer, a house of purity, and a house of blessing, vouchsafe, Lord, unto us thy servants, and to them that shall come after us unto eternal days vouchsafe it. (and the priest [243] shall cense the altar, saying) Arise, O Lord my God, and let thine enemies be scattered, and let all them that hate thine holy and blessed name flee before thee: (while speaking he shall sign with the censer over the people and bow three times) but let thy people be blessed with blessings a thousand-thousand and ten-thousand-times-ten-thousand: through the grace and loving-kindness of the lover of man, thine only Son our Lord and our God and our Saviour Jesus Christ, through whom to thee with him and with the Holy Ghost be glory and dominion, both now and ever and world without end. Amen."

Then the deacon shall say: "Speak we all in the wisdom of the Lord. Answer ye the prayer of faith."

The people respond with the creed: "We believe in one God, the Lord, the Father almighty, maker of the heavens and the earth, the visible and the invisible. And we believe in one Lord Jesus Christ, the only Son of the Father, who was with him before the world was created, light of light, God of very God, begotten not made, equal with the Father in his godhead; by whom all things were made, but without him was not anything made, neither in heaven nor in earth,

---

[243] "Assistant, MERCER, op. cit., p. 345.

who for us men and for our salvation came down from
heaven, and was incarnate of the Holy Ghost and of Mary,
of the holy virgin: he was made man and was crucified for
us in the days of Pontius Pilate, he suffered and died and
was buried, and rose again from the dead the third day, as
it is written in the holy scriptures: he ascended with glory
into the heavens and sat down on the right hand of his
Father: he shall come again with glory to judge the living
and the dead, and of his kingdom there shall be no end.
And we believe in the Holy Ghost, the Lord, the giver of
life, who proceedeth from the Father and the Son: [244] we
worship and glorify him with the Father and the Son, who
spake by the prophets. And we believe in one holy Church,
catholic apostolic, and we believe in one baptism for the
remission of sin, and look for the resurrection of the dead,
and the life to come world without end. Amen."

The earliest eucharistic creed extant in Ethiopic dates
only from the 17th century, but the form in the missal of
Tasfa Seyon represents a manuscript of the 16th century
or even earlier.

At the end of the creed, the priest [245] removes the
covering of the paten, and washes [246] his hands.

Then he sprinkles water with the moisture of his hand,
turning his face to the people, as he says: "If there be any
who is pure let him receive of the host, and whoso is not
pure let him not receive, that he be not consumed in the

---

[244] *Filioque* is only said in the Catholic rite, but in the new missal
(1945) it has been put in parentheses, with the note that it may be
omitted at the discretion of the celebrant.

[245] The assistant priest removes the covering. MERCER, *op. cit.*,
p. 346.

[246] The *lavabo* is probably a later addition to the liturgy, and it
is not found in this position in either the Coptic rite or the missal
of Tasfa Seyon.

fire of the godhead, whoso hath revenge in his heart and whoso hath an alien mind by reason of unchastity. I am pure from the blood of you all and from your sacrilege against the body and blood of Christ: I have nought to do with your reception thereof; I am pure of your error, and your sin will return upon your own head, if ye receive not in purity."

In the Catholic rite, the deacon at a solemn liturgy adds the following warning, which, as Fr. Hanssens [247] says, "does not err on the side of too much indulgence:"

"If there be any amongst us who despises this command of the priest, or who jeers or presumes to speak falsely and have a depraved mind; let him know that he would provoke Christ to anger, and that there would come upon him anger for blessing, and as a result the fires of hell would overtake him from the Lord."

The celebrant continues: "O my Lord and my God, maker of order and giver of peace and love, drive away from me every thought of evil, revenge and hatred, and all evil concupiscence of the body; apportion me with thy holy servants, join me to those who are pleasing to thee in their life, in the time of love and peace; for thou who didst come down from heaven, wilt give peace to all those of thy people who listen and understand; that they may praise thee, for to thee be praise for ever and ever. Amen."

The customary monitions and salutations are followed by the "prayer of the kiss, of Basil:" [248] "Lord great eternal, who formedst man incorrupt, thou didst abolish death, that came at first into the world through envy of satan, by the advent of thy living Son our Lord and our God and our

---

[247] *Op. cit.*, p. 402.
[248] "Prayer for perfect peace," missal of Tasfa Seyon.

Saviour Jesus Christ, who didst fill all the earth with thy peace which is from heaven, wherein the armies of heaven glorify thee, saying, glory to God in heaven, and on earth peace, his goodwill towards men."

Then, when the people have said "in like manner," the priest says the "prayer of the peace" or "salutation:" "O Lord, in thy goodwill fill our hearts, and purify us from all filthiness and lasciviousness, and from all revenge and envy, and from all wrongdoing, and from the remembrance of ill which clothes with death. Make us all meet to salute one another with a holy kiss."

The deacon gives the monition: "Pray for perfect peace and love. Salute one another with a holy kiss," and the people [249] respond: "Christ our God, make us meet to salute one another with a holy kiss."

The priest continues: "and to partake without condemnation of thine holy, immortal, heavenly gift; through Jesus Christ our Lord, through whom to thee with him and with the Holy Ghost be glory and dominion, both now and ever and world without end. Amen."

The pax [250] (amchā), at least in the Catholic rite, is conveyed by means of bows. Thus, at Sant'Andrea della Valle (Rome, 1928), in response to the deacon's exhortation, the priest bowed to the deacons, who in turn bowed to each other, the choir and the people. At a "low Mass," the priest bows to the server.

[249] Priest, La Santa Messa in rito Alessandrino-Etiopico, p. 13.
[250] A rubric directs that priests are to salute priests, deacons deacons, men men and women women. La Santa Messa etc., p. 13.

Anaphora of our holy fathers the Apostles

The dialogue preceding the anaphora in the Monophysite rite is variable, but in the missal of Asmara it is constant both in form and position.

Western in origin, these opening salutations seem to have been originally prefixed to the Greek prayer, suggesting Rome in the days of Callixtus and Hippolytus (3rd Century).

Priest: "The Lord [251] be with you all" (He blesses [252] himself).

People: "And with thy spirit."

Priest: "Lift up your hearts" (He blesses the ministers).

People: "We lift them up unto the Lord our God."

Priest: "Give ye thanks unto our God" (He blesses the people).

People: "It is right; it is meet."

The dissidents reverse the last two versicles and responses.

The Catholic [253] rite directs that during the dialogue the priest should twice bless the people, and then sign himself; whereas a rubric [254] in the Monophysite liturgy says: "And then he shall bless once towards the people and once towards the height."

The beginning [255] of the "Keddāsē [256] of the Apostles" strikes the keynote of the eucharistic prayer. In the

---

[251] Cf. Coptic rite.

[252] Liturgia-Etiopi. Allegato I (Tip. Pol. Vat., 1944), p. 47.

[253] HANSSENS, op. cit., p. 402.

[254] MERCER, op. cit., p. 349.

[255] Cf. Apostolic Tradition; prayer in the Ethiopic rite, cf. Testament of the Lord.

[256] " Ἁγιάξειν," " sanctify," " hallow," " consecrate."

Apostolic Constitutions, the simple words have been concealed in a mass of verbiage; while other liturgies have lost the position of the words.

There is no rubric in the Catholic rite to indicate the tone of voice in which the prayers of the anaphora are to be said.

The priest says: "We give [257] thee thanks, O Lord, in thy beloved Son, the Lord Jesus, whom in the last days thou didst send unto us, thy Son, the Saviour and Redeemer, the angel of thy counsel, who is the Word from thee, and through whom thou madest all things by thy will."

The deacon then begins the great intercession, in which he recalls the hierarchy, and asks for the prayers of the saints.

The opening clause is chanted: "For the sake of our blessed and supreme pontiff *abba N.,* and for the blessed pontiff *abba N.*"

Then in a low voice he continues, invoking holy Mary the Mother of God, our holy fathers Zacharias the priest and John Baptist, and all apostles, evangelists and martyrs, Simon Peter and Andrew, James and John, Philip and Bartholomew, Thomas and Matthew, Thaddeus and Nathaniel, and James the son of Alphaeus and brother of our Lord, bishop of Jerusalem; Paul and Matthias, Mark and Luke, Stephen the protomartyr, Timothy, Silas and Barnabas, Titus Philemon and Clement, and all the seventy-two disciples, five hundred companions, and three hundred and eighteen Orthodox.

"May the prayers of them all come unto us and with them do thou visit us."

The above seems to be the order of saints in the Cath-

[257] Cf. *Ethiopic Church Ordinances.*

olic [258] liturgy, but in that of the dissidents [259] our Lady [260] is commemorated *after* Stephen, Zacharias, John Baptist and the evangelists.

The last two memorials in the first part of the intercession are said aloud in the Catholic rite: "And remember thou the catholic apostolic Church in peace, which was made by the precious blood of Christ. Remember thou the pope, all patriarchs, metropolitans, bishops, presbyters and deacons, and all Christian people."

The assistant presbyter [261] continues the "prayer of benediction:" "O holy Trinity, Father and Son and Holy Ghost, bless thou † thy people, christians beloved, with blessings heavenly and earthly, and send upon us the grace of the Holy Ghost, and make the doors of thine holy church open unto us in mercy and in faithfulness. Perfect unto us the faith of the Trinity unto our last breath. O my master, Jesus Christ, visit the sick of thy people: heal them. And guide our fathers and our brethren who have gone forth and are travelling abroad: bring them back to their dwelling-place in peace and health. † Bless the airs of heaven and the rains and the fruits of the earth of this year according to thy grace, and make joy and gladness perpetual on the face of the earth, and stablish for us thy peace. Turn the hearts of mighty kings to deal kindly with us always. † Give favour to the elders of the church that are gathered in thine holy church, to all, to each by their several names, in the presence of powerful kings: lift them up. Rest the

[258] *Liturgia-Etiopi. Allegato* I (Tip. Pol. Vat., 1944), p. 48.

[259] BRIGHTMAN, *op. cit.*, p. 228; MERCER, *op. cit.*, p. 350.

[260] Cf. prayer of the priest in the intercession of the Syrian anaphora of St. James. BRIGHTMAN, *op. cit.*, p. 93.

[261] BRIGHTMAN, *op. cit.*, p. 229; "The assistant shall go around, the priest shall say," MERCER, *op. cit.*, p. 351.

souls of our fathers and our brothers and our sisters that have fallen asleep and gained their rest in the faith of Christ; rest them.

And bless † them that occupy themselves with the incense and the oblation and the wine and the oil and the chrism and the veils and the books of the lessons and the vessels of the sanctuary, that Christ our God may bring them to the heavenly Jerusalem. And all them that are assembled with us to entreat for mercy: Christ our God be propitious unto them: and all them that give alms before thine awful throne, receive them.

Lift up every straitened soul, them that are bound with chains, and them that are in exile and captivity, and them that are held in bitter bondage; our God, deliver them in the greatness of thy mercy. And all them that have entrusted it to us to remember them: Christ our God, remember them in thine heavenly kingdom. O Lord, save thy people and bless † thine heritage: govern them and lift them up for ever and ever, and keep them in the right faith, in glory and honour all the days of their life, and endue them with love that is exalted above all understanding and above all wisdom."

The second series of commemorations [262] of saints is omitted in the Catholic rite, [263] and in its stead the second deacon (subdeacon) recites a short memorial of the orders in the Church, while the priest has his face turned towards the people: "Have mercy on them, O Lord, and be propitious to our bishops, presbyters and deacons, and all thy Christian people."

---

[262] BRIGHTMAN, op. cit., p. 230.
[263] HANSSENS, op. cit., p. 402; MERCER (op. cit., p. 352) also omits the list of saints, and gives the short memorial, but as said by the priest.

Then, twice blessing the people, the priest turns to the altar and continues the anaphora:

"And for these and for them all, rest their souls and be propitious unto them. Thou who sendest thy Son from heaven into the bosom of the Virgin."

The deacon proclaims: "Ye that sit, stand up," and the priest says: "He was carried in the womb, was made flesh, and his birth was revealed of the Holy Ghost. Unto thee, before whom stand thousand-thousands and ten-thousand-times-ten-thousand, and the holy angels and archangels, and thine honourable creatures that have six wings, the seraphim and the cherubim."

Deacon: "Look to the east."

Priest: "with two of their wings they cover their face, with two of their wings they cover their feet, and with two of their wings they fly from end to end of the world."

Deacon: "Give we heed."

Priest: "Continually therefore as they all hallow thee and praise, with all them that hallow thee and praise thee, receive our hallow also which we utter unto thee: Holy, holy, holy Lord of sabaoth; the heavens and the earth are *wholly* [264] full of the holiness of thy glory."

It would seem that the original liturgy did not have a *sanctus*, and it has been awkwardly inserted here, although as early as the days of St. Irenaeus [265] († ab. 202) it was probably used in Christian worship.

A bell was rung at the *sanctus* in the liturgy celebrated in Sant'Andrea della Valle, but not in the "low Mass" at San Stefano.

---

[264] "Wholly" has been omitted in the Catholic rite. *Liturgia-Etiopi. Allegato* I (Tip. Pol. Vat., 1944), p. 51.

[265] *Demonstration of the Apostolic Preaching*, chap. X.

The deacon gives the monition: "Answer ye," and the people reply: "Holy, holy, holy Lord of Sabaoth: the heavens and the earth are wholly full of the holiness of thy glory."

In regard to the word "wholly," the following explanation has been given by Harden: [266] "It seems to me likely that originally the opening words only of the *sanctus* were written, followed by the adjective 'complete' or 'full' in the sense of 'etc.' Afterwards when the full form came to be written, this adjective would be retained under the erroneous impression that it formed part of the wording. From the liturgy the word has even found its way into the text of the Ethiopic Bible in some MSS. in Isaias IX."

The priest, before the *post-sanctus* prayer, signs himself, the people and the ministers.

He then says: "Truly the heavens and earth are full of the holiness of thy glory, in our Lord and our God and our Saviour Jesus Christ thine only Son. He came and was born of the Virgin, that he might fulfil thy will and make a people for thee."

The people respond: "Remember us, O Lord, in thy kingdom; remember us, O Lord, O master, in thy kingdom; remember us, O Lord, in thy kingdom as thou rememberest the thief on the right when thou wast on the tree of the holy cross."

The assistant priest in the meanwhile is directed to put incense (the 5th grain with a little other incense) into the thurible and to cense the offerings, while the celebrant places his hands [267] in the smoke, and spreads them over the *oblata*, as he continues: "He stretched out his hands to the

---

[266] *The Anaphoras of the Ethiopic liturgy*, pp. 50, 51.
[267] In the missal of Tasfa Seyon; cf. Maronite rite.

passion, suffering to save the sufferers that trust in him; who was delivered of his own will to the passion, that he might abolish death and burst the bond of Satan and trample on *Sheol* and lead forth our saints, establishing a covenant which shall make known his resurrection."

Then, when the celebrant begins the narrative of the institution, the deacon [268] exclaims: "Lift up your hands, ye presbyters."

The priest proceeds: "In the same night in which they betrayed him he took bread [269] in his holy hands which were without spot and blessed."

The people respond: "We believe that this is true, we believe," and the priest continues: "He looked up to heaven toward thee, his Father †, he gave thanks †, he blessed †, and brake (and then he shall break the bread into five parts, but not separating) and gave it to his disciples and said to them, Take, eat, this is my body (pointing and bowing profoundly) which is broken for you for the forgiveness of sins."

In the Catholic rite, a bell is rung, and the people [270] answer: "Amen, amen, amen: we believe and confess: we praise thee, our Lord and our God. This is true: we believe."

The celebrant (Catholic), as in the Roman rite, keeps his fingers joined until the ablutions.

The priest, for the consecration of the chalice, says: "And likewise † also the cup, giving thanks †, he blessed

---

[268] HANSSENS, *op. cit.*, p. 402.

[269] "Here he elevateth." HARDEN, *op. cit.*, p. 35.

[270] The response is made also in the liturgy of the dissidents, where the people are directed to "adore with their faces to the ground." Thus, the consecration is considered to have already taken place. At a "low Mass," the server replies after each consecration with a single "Amen."

it †, and hallowed it, and gave it to his disciples, and said unto them, Take drink this is my blood (Pointing and bowing profoundly), which is shed for you for the remission of sin."

The same response [271] as before is made by the people, but the dissidents only say the threefold "Amen."

The Monophysites have a slightly different formula of consecration, which has given rise to much controversy:

"Take eat: (pointing) this *bread* (he shall bow himself) is my body (pointing), [272] which is broken for you for the forgiveness of sin."

"Take drink: (pointing) this *cup* is my blood (pointing), which is shed for you and for many (shaking the cup while he points at the cross)."

Writers [273] have affirmed that the words of consecration as used by the dissidents are invalid, but the late spiritual director of the Pontifical College, Abba Tecle Semharay Selam, has written a monograph [274] on the subject, in which he maintains that the dissident form was an accidental insertion arising from unintentional error. Thus, he says, the words in question are not to be found in the Ethiopic versions of either St. Mark or St. James, nor yet in the *Sinodos* (*Apostolic Constitutions*), from which the anaphora of the Apostles was derived.

They are equally wanting in the *Testament of the Lord*, the source for the anaphora of our Lord, which holds second place in the missal.

---

[271] HANSSENS, *op. cit.* p. 403.
[272] "While he shall break it with a spear." MERCER, *op. cit.*, p. 354.
[273] Tellezius, Ludolf.
[274] *De Indumenis sacris ritus Aethiopici. De Verbis Consecrationis apud Aethiopes.* Rome, 1930.

A Paris manuscript of the anaphora of our Lady has "This bread my body: This is my blood," which shows clearly that here, at least, the word "bread" was mistakenly written for "is."

The anaphora of St. John Chrysostom, in nearly all extant Ethiopic manuscripts, has the *ipsissima verba* of Holy Scripture.

Finally, it may be noted that the correct form appears in some codices of the anaphora of St. John the Evangelist.

Evidence indeed is forthcoming that the change in the words of consecration was a gradual and haphazard process. Thus, if we take the anaphora of St. John from the manuscripts in the *Bibliothèque Nationale*, Paris, we find that numbers 72 and 76 give the correct form; 67 the correct form for the bread and "This chalice my blood" for the wine; while in 74 both forms show additional wording.

The printed Monophysite missal, [275] published at Addis Ababa in 1926 (1918), gives the accurate form of the words of institution.

Abba Kidane Mariam, the restorer of the purity of the liturgy in the province of Beghiemeder, affirmed that by received tradition the words "This is my body: This is my blood" are always consecratory, and Ethiopic professors are accustomed to explain the words in Amharic by saying: "This is my body which to-morrow will be crucified: This is my blood which to-morrow will be poured out upon the cross."

The formula used by the dissidents, says Abba Selam, thus expresses no more than the connotation of the species already consecrated.

[275] p. 123.

The anamnesis, which follows the consecration, shows an early liturgical form: [276] "And as often as ye do this, make ye memorial of me."

The people respond: "We show thy death, O Lord, and thine holy resurrection: we believe thine ascension: [277] we praise thee and confess thee: we supplicate thee and confess thee, O Lord our God."

It is doubtful whether the anaphora of Hippolytus had an epiclesis, and no manuscript of the *Sinodos* offers any suggestion.

The present text of the liturgy of the Apostles, which is based on the *Sinodos*, has patched up the passage; while the sense of the epiclesis [278] in the Catholic [279] rite has been changed: "Now also, Lord, remembering his death and resurrection, we confess thee and offer unto thee this *holy* bread (pointing) and this *precious* cup (pointing), giving thanks unto thee: and thereby thou hast made us meet to stand before thee and to do thee priestly service. (then secretly and with head bowed): We pray thee, Lord, and beseech thee that thou wouldest send *upon us* the Holy Spirit and power *in the communion* of this bread (pointing) and cup (pointing and then chanted). And *grant* that it may become (*evadat*) [280] for our salvation the body ††† and

[276] Cf. St. Justin Martyr, *Dialogue* XL; St. Irenaeus, *Contra Haer.* XXIX, 15.

[277] "and thy coming again." Tasfa Seyon.—MERCER, *op. cit.,* p. 355.

[278] The epiclesis in the dissident rite has the following form: "that thou wouldest send the Holy Ghost and power upon this bread, and over this cup, that he my make it the body and blood of our Lord and our Saviour Jesus Christ for ever and ever."

[279] HANSSENS, *op. cit.,* p. 403. The words in italics show the chief alterations and additions in the Asmara missal.

[280] *facias. Lit.-Eth., op. cit.,* p. 53.

blood ††† of our Lord *God* and Saviour Jesus Christ for ever and ever."

This is the form of epiclesis given by Fr. Hanssens, but the Italian translation [281] of the Catholic rite has a different text:

"We pray thee, O Lord, and we beseech thee because thou hast sent thy Holy Spirit upon this bread (pointing), and this chalice (pointing), because with his power thou hast transformed it into the body ††† and the blood ††† of our Lord God and Redeemer Jesus Christ," for ever and ever."

The people respond: "Amen. Lord, have mercy on us. Lord, have mercy on us. Lord, be propitious unto us."

The priest, without, as in the Monophysite rite, signing the body with the blood, continues: "Give it together unto all them that take of it, that it be unto them for sanctification and for fulfilling with the Holy Spirit, and for confirming true faith, that they may hallow and praise thee and thy beloved Son Jesus Christ world without end."

The new missal (1945) says that the priest signs the body with his thumb intincted in the precious blood.

Then the deacon says: "With all the heart we beseech the Lord our God, that he vouchsafes unto us the good communion of the Holy Spirit."

The people answer: "As it was, is, and shall be unto generations of generations world without end."

---

[281] *La Santa Messa in rito Alessandrino-Etiopico* (Rome, 1938), p. 15. The same translation has also a different anamnesis (p. 15): "Now, O Lord, mindful of his death and resurrection, we offer to thee this bread (pointing), and this chalice (pointing), giving thanks for having deigned to be present before thee and for having served as a priest."

These alterations from the Asmara missal (1913) represent current modifications in the rite in accordance with the new missal.

The priest divides [282] the bread into 13 (parts), and says alternately with the people:

"Grant us to be united in thine Holy Spirit, and heal us by the *presphora*, that we may live in thee for ever, world without end. (People: "Amen. Grant us"). Blessed be the name of the Lord and blessed be he that cometh in the name of the Lord, and let the name of his glory be blessed. So be it: so be it. Send the grace of the Holy Spirit upon us."

"The people shall say in like manner." [283]

Then the customary monition and salutation with their respective responses are said, and the priest begins the prayer [284] of the fraction: [285]

"I adore thee, O Lord my God, almighty, eternal, who sittest above the cherubim and seraphim, and who givest rest unto the world, who hast shown to us the hidden

---

[282] *Liturgia-Etiopi. Allegato* I (Tip. Pol. Vat., 1944), p. 54. The parts of the host are arranged in the form of a cross.

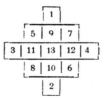

[283] BRIGHTMAN, *op. cit.*, p. 234.

[284] MERCER, *op cit.*, p. 356. A slightly different version of this prayer is given in *Liturgia-Etiopi. Alleg.* I (Tip. Pol. Vat., 1944), pp. 54-55.

The prayer of the fraction in Brightman (*op. cit.*, p. 234) and Harden (*op. cit.*, p. 38) is as follows: "And again we beseech the almighty Lord, the Father of our Lord and Saviour Jesus Christ, to grant us to take with blessing of this holy mystery, to grant us confirmation and not to condemn any of us, but to make meet all that partake of the reception of the holy mystery of the body and blood of Christ, the almighty Lord our God."

[285] Fetāte.

mystery on the tree of the cross; for who is a God merciful and holy like thee? Who art powerful and givest to thy apostles who minister to thee a sweet savour, thou, O our Lord and our God and our Saviour Jesus Christ, the almighty Lord our God."

During this prayer, the priest, by reason of the consignation and commixture, divides the host into two unequal parts.

This was the direction in the missal of Asmara, but it is not done in the Monophysite liturgy, and it is doubtful whether the dissidents make the fraction here.

In response to the diaconal "Pray ye," the people recite the Lord's prayer, with the ascription "for thine is the kingdom," etc.

Brightman, [286] Mercer [287] and the *Liturgia-Etiopi* [288] give three different prayers by way of an embolism.

The version in the last named is as follows:

"O Lord, who sittest above the cherubim, and regardest thy people and thine heritage, bless thy servants, thy handmaids and their children; whosoever comes and partakes from thy wonderful table with a pure conscience, for the remission of sins, make him a partaker of that union which is from the Holy Spirit, for the salvation of soul and body, to the kingdom of heaven and inheritance for grace and good will. Through thine only-begotten Son, in whom to thee with him and the Holy Spirit be glory and dominion, now and always and for ever and ever."

The people respond three times: "According to thy mercy, O our God, and not according to our sins."

[286] *Op. cit.*, pp. 234-235. Harden (*Anaphoras of the Ethiopic Liturgy*, p. 38) has a variation of this prayer.

[287] *Op. cit.*, pp. 356-357.

[288] p. 55.

Then [289] the priest assistant, subdeacon and all the people say or sing alternately:

"The hosts of the angels of the Saviour of the world stand before the Saviour of the world and encompass the Saviour of the world, even the body and blood of the Saviour of the world. And let us come before the Saviour of the world. In the faith of him give we thanks to Christ." [290]

The "inclination" follows.

Subdeacon: "Open [291] the doors, ye leaders" (*principes*).

Deacon: "Standing, bow down your head the while."

The priest continues with the "prayer of the imposition of the hand:"

"Lord eternal, who knowest what is hidden and what is manifest, before thee thy people have bowed down their heads and unto thee have subdued the hardness of heart and flesh: behold from heaven thy dwelling-place: bless them, men and women: incline thine ear to them and hearken unto their prayer: stablish them with the strength of thy right hand, protect and succour them from evil affliction: be a guardian both to our body and to our soul, and increase to them, both men and women, thy faith and the fear of thy name, through thine only Son, world without end."

The deacon gives the monition: "Worship the Lord with fear," and the people respond: "Before thee, Lord, we worship and thee we glorify."

This is followed by the "prayer of penitence of St.

---

[289] *La Messa in rito Alessandrino-Etiopico* (Rome, 1938), p. 16, gives it after the "prayer of the imposition of the hand." In the new missal the hymn follows the embolism.

[290] "In the faith of him the apostles followed his footsteps." *Liturgia-Etiopi*, p. 56. This last phrase is variable. HAILÙ, *op. cit.*, p. 50.

[291] *Liturgia-Etiopi*, p. 56.

Basil:" "Lord almighty, it is thou that healest our soul and our body and our spirit, because thou saidst by the word of thine only Son our Lord and our God and our Saviour Jesus Christ, which thou spakest unto our father Peter: Thou art a rock and upon this rock I will build mine holy church, and the gates of hell shall not prevail against it: and unto thee I will give the keys of the kingdom: what thou hast bound on earth shall be loosed in heaven: let all thy servants and thy handmaids, according to their several names, be loosed and absolved, whether they have wrought wittingly or unwittingly: keep them, Lord, and defend them, thy servants and thy handmaids, my fathers and my brethren, and moreover loose my humility, me thy sinful and guilty servant: and let them be loosed and set free out of the mouth of the Holy Ghost and out of the mouth of me also thy sinful and guilty servant. O merciful and lover of man, Lord our God, that takest away the sin of the world, receive the penitence of these thy servants and thy hand-maids, and make to arise upon them the light of everlasting life, and forgive them, Lord, their sins: for thou art good and a lover of man. O Lord our God, long suffering and plenteous in mercy and righteous, forgive me and all thy servants and thy handmaids, and deliver them from all transgression and curse: if we have transgressed against thee, Lord, whether in our word or in our deed or in our thought, pardon and forgive, be propitious and remit, for thou art good and a lover of man. O Lord forgive me and all thy people: loose them."

"Then the priest shall turn towards the people, and sign three times, and shall make mention of them that are with him."

After a short commemoration of the hierarchy and the orders in the church, as well as of all faithful Christians, the priest prays for the king and makes mention of the dead:

"Remember, Lord, and loose all them that are asleep and resting in the right faith and lay their souls in the bosom of Abraham, Isaac and Jacob."

"And us also deliver from every transgression and curse and from all apostasy and from all error and from all anathema and from all perjury and from mingling with heresy and pollution. Give us, Lord, wisdom and strength of understanding and prudence and knowledge, that we may depart and flee for evermore from every work of Satan, the tempter: give us, Lord, to do thy will and thy good pleasure at all times, and write our names in the book of life in the kingdom of heaven with all saints and martyrs: through Jesus Christ our Lord, through whom to thee with him and with the Holy Ghost be glory and dominion, both now and ever and world without end. Amen."

The deacon now gives the monition: "Give we heed," and the priest, bowing profoundly and elevating [292] the sacred gifts, chants: "Holiness [293] to the holies."

In the Catholic rite, a bell [294] is rung. The people [295] respond: "One is the holy Father, one is the holy Son, one is the Holy Spirit."

The priest, taking the central square of the host or

---

[292] It is doubtful whether the Monophysites have an elevation here.

[293] i. e. "holy things." The Ethiopic word is frequently used in this second sense. The phrase is the equivalent of *Sancta sanctis*.

[294] Renaudot (*Hist. Pat. Alex.*, p. 282) says that the bishops who accompanied George, the son of the king of Nubia, on his mission to Egypt, used to ring bells at the elevation of the host, adding that the practice was in conformity with the early usage of the church. This was ab. 850.

[295] "Assistant priest." HARDEN, *op. cit.*, p. 42; BRIGHTMAN, *op. cit.*, p. 237.

'*āsba dīyākōn* (*asbadikon*), and signing the blood, gives the salutation: "The Lord be with you all."

Then, when the people have answered: "And with thy spirit," the priest shall say: [296] "Lord Christ, have mercy on us," "with a loud voice three times, in a low voice three times, five each, and the people also shall say likewise."

The consignation with the intincted bread is deferred until after the profession of faith, but a rubric in the Asmara missal [297] orders a kind of preliminary consignation to be carried out here: "And then the priest takes the '*āsba dīyākon* and signs the blood with it and lays it down."

Then the deacon says: "Ye that are in penitence bow down your head," and the priest continues: "Unto them that are in penitence, thy people, have mercy upon them after thy great goodness and according to the multitude of thy mercy blot out their transgression: guard them and keep them: redeem in peace their souls. Cutting short their former conversation, join them with thy holy church: through the grace and might of thine only Son, our Lord and our Saviour Jesus Christ, through whom to thee with him and with the Holy Ghost be glory and dominion, both now and ever and world without end. Amen."

For the last time in the liturgy, the customary monitions and salutations are recited.

The priest, holding the *asbadikon*, then says: "This is the body, holy, true, of our Lord and our God and our Saviour Jesus Christ, which is given for life and for salvation and for remission of sin unto them that partake of it in faith, Amen. (People: "Amen").

"This is the blood, precious, true, of our Lord and our

---

[296] The Italian translation (p. 16) says: "*Qui segue 41 volte: Signore, abbi pietà di noi.*"

[297] HANSSENS, *op. cit.*, p. 403.

God and Saviour Jesus Christ, which is given for life and for salvation and for remission of sin unto them that receive of it in faith. Amen.

"For this is the body and blood of Emmanuel, our very God. Amen. I believe, I believe, I believe and confess unto the last breath that this is the body and blood of our Lord and our God and our Saviour Jesus Christ, which he took of the lady of us all, the holy and pure Virgin Mary, and made it one with his godhead without mixture or confusion, without division or alteration: and he verily confessed with a good testimony in the days of Pontius Pilate, and he gave it up for our sake on the tree of his cross, of his own sole will for the life of us all. Amen. I believe, I believe, I believe and confess that his godhead was not divided from his manhood, not for an hour nor for the twinkling of an eye, but he gave it up for our sake, for life and for salvation and for remission of sin unto them that partake of it in faith. Amen. I believe, I believe, I believe that this is true. Amen.

"This is he to whom are fitting all honour and glory and adoration, to the holy Trinity, the Father and the Son and the Holy Ghost, coequal at all times, both now and ever and world without end."

In the Catholic [298] rite, this profession of faith contains the principal consignation, [299] when the priest takes the 'āsba dīyāḳōn, on which a cross is marked, into his hand and intincts it in the chalice with the tips of his fingers.

He moistens the holy bread with the blood and signs the body and blood with a cross. Then he makes a cross on either side of the consecrated bread, and also on the smaller particle.

[298] HANSSENS, *op. cit.*, pp. 403-404.
[299] *Ataba*, " to sign."

Finally, the priest signs the chalice separately, as he says: "Blessed be the Lord God for ever. Amen."

The particle is now put into the chalice, and the following prayer is said: "Behold, thy Son, the sacrifice that is well-pleasing unto thee, and through this pardon me, because for my sake thy Son died. Behold the pure blood that was poured out for my sake upon Golgotha, and let it cry aloud in my stead: receive my petition for the sake of it. By reason of my sin thy beloved received the spear and the nails: he suffered that he might be well-pleasing unto thee. After that I was saved, Satan returned and pierced me through with his darts. Grant me thy mercy, for he that summoneth to judgment is mighty and with the burden of sin he hath slain me. Avenge me of the crafty one that is insatiable for my life. Thou, Lord, King and Saviour, bind up my wound. I will believe aright until the going forth of my last breath, that this is the body and blood of Emmanuel our very God, which he took of the lady of us all, holy Mary."

Before receiving holy communion, a threefold profession of faith is thus made by the priest, expressing belief in a) the true manhood of our Lord; b) the doctrine that the Godhead was not divided from the manhood; and c) that the bread and wine have truly become the body and blood of Christ.

The next prayer [300] is said by all: "O Lord, Lord, it in nowise beseemeth thee to come under the roof of my polluted house, for I have provoked thee and stirred thee to anger

[300] This prayer in the Monophysite rite is said by the priest before the preceding prayer and the consignation. BRIGHTMAN, *op. cit.*, p. 239. The Italian translation of the Catholic rite (p. 16) says that the prayer of absolution is said by the second assistant (*assistente secondo*), who adds: "let us recite seven times: Wash me from my iniquity and cleanse me from my sin."

and have done evil in thy sight and have polluted my soul
and my body, and I have no good deed at all. But for the
sake of thy being made and thy becoming man for my salvation, for the sake of thy precious cross and thy life-giving
death and resurrection on the third day, I pray thee and
beseech thee that thou wouldest purge me from all guilt
and curse and sin: and when I have received thy holy mystery let it not be unto me for judgment nor for condemnation,
but have mercy upon me and be propitious unto me in the
abundance of thy mercy and grant me remission for my sin
and life for my soul: through the petition of our Lady Mary
and of John Baptist, and for the sake of all the saints and
martyrs, world without end."

The following order in the reception of holy communion [301] is enjoined: bishops, priests, deacons, and the
remainder of the faithful according to their position and
rank, with the women last.   Newly baptized infants are
given communion immediately after the priests.

Before the order of communion, the celebrant recites the
following prayer: "O my Lord Jesus Christ, let not this thy
mystery bring guilt upon me: rather let it be for the purifying of my soul and body."

If there is no bishop present, the celebrant, after kissing
the host, communicates himself, and then administers to the
assistant priest in both kinds.

The priests and deacons are given the host by the celebrant, and the consecrated wine in a spoon by the assistant
priest.

The celebrant says to each communicant: "The bread
of life which came down from heaven, the body of Christ,"
and the recipient answers: "Amen, in truth, we believe."

[301] *Sūtāfē*.

The communicant places his hand over his mouth until the eucharistic species is consumed, as he prays [302] "with fear and trembling:"—"Fill my mouth with thy praise, my heart with joy and my soul with gladness who have received the divine mystery that was with it in communion. The Holy Ghost came down upon it when the Lord's priest did consecrate in the great mystery."

In administering the chalice, the deacon or assistant priest says to each one: " This is the chalice of life that came down from heaven: this is the blood of Christ," and the communicant answers: "Amen, in truth we believe, amen and amen."

The deacon, when he receives the chalice from the assistant priest, says: "I will receive the cup of salvation" etc.

When the priests and deacons have communicated, the deacon adds: "Pray ye for us and for all Christians that bid us make mention of them in the eucharist, and in the love of Christ praise ye and sing."

While the faithful are receiving communion outside the sanctuary, the priests, singly or two together, sing [303] continuously either a hymn of praise ("Precious is the praise of the psalm") or psalm CL.

The celebrant, as he goes to administer the host, says:

"Those whom thou hast called, Lord, and whom thou hast sanctified make partakers in thy calling, and keep them from evil in thine eternal kingdom in Christ: through whom to thee with him and with the Holy Ghost be glory and dominion, both now and ever and world without end."

[302] In the Monophysite rite, the prayer is said "while he receiveth the blood." BRIGHTMAN, op. cit., p. 241.

[303] " Et tunc cantent sacerdotes: " Magnificentia haec" in laudem psalmi 150. Et non intermittant, sed singuli vel bini psallent.—Liturgia-Etiopi. Allegato I (Tip. Pol. Vat., 1944), p. 62.

Then he signs once over the paten, and, unless the hymn known as the "incense [304] of perfuming" is sung, all the people say:

"Holy, holy, holy Trinity unspeakable, grant me that I receive unto life the body and blood without condemnation. Grant me that I bring forth fruit that shall be well-pleasing unto thee, to the end that I may appear in thy glory and live unto thee doing thy will, with confession calling upon thee, Father, and calling upon thy kingdom; hallowed, Lord, be thy name with us: for mighty art thou, praised and glorious, and thine is the glory world without end."

This chant is not found in any other liturgy, but it may be compared with a passage in the *Testament of the Lord*.

The celebrant, deacon and assistant priest, in giving communion to the people, use the above respective formulas.

After the reception of the host, the faithful say: "Amen," and after the chalice: "Amen, amen."

The foregoing account [305] is taken from the Catholic rite, but there appears to be some diversity in practice, with a certain freedom in the manner of reception.

Communion [306] in one kind had been one of the outstanding objections to the union with Rome in the 17th century. The Ethiopians in the time of King Fasilides (1632-1667) made the following protest: "We have no peace with

---

[304] *Etana mogar, incensum suffitus.*

[305] HANSSENS, *op. cit.*, pp. 404-405.

[306] In answer to a doubt expressed to Propaganda by the missionaries (*Prop. Congr.* 28-VIII-1637), the cardinal prefect in a letter to the patriarch Alphonsus Mendez more or less shelved the question, and replied: "*pro nunc silentio rem hujusmodi praeteriri* (September 12, 1637). The strong line rightly taken on this matter by the council of Trent (Sess. XXI, c. 2), in view of the teaching of Western heretics, certainly influenced the authorities against the traditional Ethiopian custom. *Testi di Diritto Antichi e Moderni riguardanti gli Etiopi. Fascic.* V (Tip. Pol. Vat., 1939), pp. 139, 141.

the Romans, neither have the Romans peace with us, O Jesus Christ (Word) incarnate, because thy blood [307] has separated us like the blackness of a drawn line."

All the Vicars apostolic, from Blessed Justin de Jacobis (1838-1860) to Mgr. Crouzet (1888-1894), sanctioned the traditional custom of the Ethiopic rite, communion in both kinds, although a little before the arrival of Mgr. Crouzet it had been the practice of priests celebrating on an altar where the blessed sacrament was reserved in the Latin rite to give azyme hosts in holy communion. The new vicar apostolic permitted this practice before and after the liturgy, but ordered communion under both kinds *in* the Mass. His successors, however, would seem to have encouraged the Latin discipline, and in 1920 a book was published in which it was laid down that in a solemn liturgy [308] communion should be given to the people under both kinds, but in a daily said Mass under the species of bread only, although on great solemnities, such as Easter, those who desired it might receive in the traditional manner, even at a low Mass. The publication of the book caused much dissatisfaction and all the priests of the province of Acheleguzai refused to receive it. At the present time, however, the above ruling has become the norm in the Catholic Ethiopic rite, and Dom Fidele Andikiel, a Cistercian of the rite, informed the

---

[307] i. e. the reception of thy blood.

[308] In the Epiphany Octave (1928) at Sant'Andrea della Valle, Rome, at a solemn liturgy, communion was received standing, with two deacons bearing tapers on either side of the priest. The bread was leavened, but round and white resembling azyme. The precious blood was given in a spoon, the communicant holding a purificator. In 1947 on the feast of the Epiphany in the College of *Propaganda fide* and during the Octave at S. Andrea della Valle (Rome) holy communion was given in a similar manner at " low Mass," with the deacon administering the chalice.

writer (1945) that with the exception of one church in Eritrea and the College in the Vatican City communion in one kind is always given at a low Mass.

Among the dissidents, as we have seen, the reception of holy communion is very infrequent. The obligation is not prescribed by any ecclesiastical law, except immediately after baptism on account of the literal interpretation of the gospel, [309] and the consequent fear of dying without having received the body and blood of Christ. Custom also demands communion on the attainment of the age of reason. It has been said [310] that the neglect of communion in the life of the average Ethiopian has been largely responsible for the frequency of crime and polygamy in the country. One of the requirements for holy communion is to refrain from spitting for three days before and three days after the approach to the holy table.

It is customary [311] for the non-Catholic celebrant to break the host for the communicants in a large paten (sahâl), which two deacons hold before him on a tray covered with a cloth.

Communion [312] of the sick can be given in two ways: a) The concelebrating priests, after the communion of the people, go immediately to the sick man's house, taking communion in both kinds, saying nothing, but with attendants to clear the way. In the house, communion is given in the

---

[309] "Nisi manducaveritis carnem filii hominis, et biberitis ejus sanguinem, non habebitis vitam in vobis." Joann. VI, 54.

[310] Dict. de Théol. Cath., t. V, col. 945. At the time of the Portuguese conquest communion was more frequent, and Fr. Jerome Lobo says: "Spesso pure si comunicano, ma non si confessano ogni volta.

[311] Ibid.

[312] Semharay SELAM, De Sacramentis secundum ritum Aethiopicum, p. 76.

customary manner or saying: "Holy, [313] holy, holy Trinity unspeakable" etc., or psalm XLVI. Then the clergy return to the church and finish the liturgy.

b) When the thanksgiving has been said, the celebrant puts a particle into the chalice and takes it to the sick man, saying nothing. Communion is given as above, and on his return to the church the celebrant cleanses the vessels and finishes the liturgy. The ceremonies and prayers for the communion of the sick are the same as those in church, unless the sick man is given communion by intinction, when the formula is the same as for newly baptized children.

When communion in the liturgy has been administered, the priest says: "O my Lord and my God, Jesus Christ, behold I have received thy pure body and thy precious blood for the forgiveness of my sins and for the remission of my error besides, and, O lover of man, fill my mouth with praise, for thou art praised; for our salvation is in this thy name for ever and ever. [314]

Then drinking a little water, [315] the priest continues: "I pray thee, O Lord and my God, good shepherd who lovest thy flock, and didst give thy life for thy sheep." etc.

The thanksgiving [316] which follows may be compared with the "prayer of the laying on of hands" in the anaphora of Serapion. [317]

[313] *V Missale Aethiopicum.*
[314] A second prayer ("Glory to thee, my Lord and God," etc.) is sometimes said. *Liturgia-Etiopi,* Alleg. I, p. 63.
[315] This is the custom in the Catholic rite. HANSSENS, *op. cit.,* p. 405.
[316] A variation of these prayers is given in *Liturgia-Etiopi* (Tip. Pol. Vat.), Alleg. I, pp. 64-65.
[317] After the offering of oils and waters. John Wordsworth. *Bishop Serapion's Prayer Book,* pp. 67-68. London: S. P. C. K. 1910.

The deacon says: "Let us give thanks unto the Lord, after taking part of his holy things. That what we have received may be to us medicine for the soul's life, let us ask and entreat, while we praise the Lord our God. We have received of his holy body: this is the blood of Christ: and let us give thanks unto him that maketh us meet to communicate in the precious and holy mystery."

The thanksgiving is continued in a dialogue [318] between priest and people:

Priest: "I will magnify thee, O God my king, and I will praise thy name for ever and ever."

People: "Our Father who art in heaven, lead us not into temptation."

Priest: "Every day will I give thanks unto thee and praise thy name for ever and ever."

People: "Our Father who art in heaven, lead us not into temptation."

Priest: "My mouth shall speak the praise of the Lord, and let all flesh give thanks unto his holy name for ever and ever."

People: "Our Father who art in heaven, lead us not into temptation."

The prayer [319] "to the pilot of the soul" in the Liturgy of the Apostles is found verbatim in the ordinances of Zara-Jacob and in the Anaphora of our Lord; while a prayer is so named in all the other anaphoras, with the exception of that of our Lady.

---

[318] Current Catholic usage seems to insert two further diaconal interpolations: "We have taken of his body and of his blood;" "We should give thanks in order that we may be sharers of the great and holy mystery." *La Santa Messa in rito Alessandrino-Etiopico* (Rome, 1938), pp. 17-18.

[319] Cf. *Ethiopic Church Order;* Syriac *Testament of the Lord.*

"Pilot of the soul, guide of the righteous, and glory of the saints. Grant us, O Lord, eyes of knowledge ever to see thee and ears also to hearken to thy word alone. When our souls have been fulfilled with thy grace, create in us pure hearts, O Lord, that we may ever understand thy greatness, who art good and a lover of men. O our God, be gracious to our souls, and grant unto us thy humble servants who have received thy body and thy blood, a pure and steadfast mind, for thine is the kingdom, O Lord, blessed and glorious, Father and Son and Holy Spirit, now and ever and world without end."

The people [320] respond: "Alleluia, alleluia, our Father who art in heaven, lead us not, Lord, into temptation."

The priest then says: "And again we beseech thee, Lord almighty, Father of the Lord and our Saviour Jesus Christ: we give thee thanks for that thou hast granted us to take of thine holy mystery. Let it not be unto guilt or unto judgment, but unto renewing of soul and body and spirit: through thine only Son through whom to thee with him and with the Holy Ghost be glory and dominion, both now and ever and world without end. Amen."

The Catholic missal (Asmara) directs that the ablutions be taken after the thanksgiving, but in the liturgy at Sant'Andrea della Valle (Rome, 1928) the vessels [321] were cleansed in the Roman place and after the Roman manner.

When the purification is finished, the priest says: "Thy [322] holy incorruptible mystery which thou hast given to us has been perfectly completed, O Lord, which is with thee

---

[320] HANSSENS, op. cit., p. 405. Mercer (op. cit., p. 368) gives a longer form, and directs it to be said by the priest.
[321] The vessels were covered with a veil, and taken after the liturgy by a priest to the sacristy.
[322] HANSSENS, op. cit., p. 405; Ltturgia-Etiopi, alleg. I, p. 66.

strength and salvation, a memorial of thy death, and we have seen the mystery of thy holy resurrection. Make us heirs of life, and guard us in this hour and at all times; because thou art a glorious King over all men, the Ruler, our Lord and our Saviour, Jesus Christ, our God; we offer and send up to thee thanksgiving and magnificence together with thy good celestial Father and thy life-giving Holy Spirit, for ever and ever. Amen."

The deacon then adds: "To our thanksgiving, let us pray that the Lord may inscribe our prayer in the book of life, and that our eternal God may be mindful of us in the place of the rest of the saints in his own light. For those of our fathers, brethren and sisters who come later, let us pray that the Lord may bestow upon them zeal and perfect diligence, and may avert from them the bond of this world, and may give them liberty and charity, faith and good hope by reason of the body and blood of the living Son of God. Amen and amen; so be it, so be it."

The "prayer [323] of the imposition of the hand" follows, a prayer found almost *verbatim* in the ordinances of Zara-Jacob:

"Lord eternal, light of life unquenchable, look upon thy servants and thine handmaids, and sow in their hearts the fear of thy name, and give them in blessing to bear fruit unto that which in thine own name hath been given unto them, even thy body and thy blood. And let thine hand be upon them that have bowed their heads before thee, thy people, men and women, adults and children, virgins and monks, widows and orphans. And us also here protect and succour and strengthen with the strength of thine archangels: from every evil work turn us away, in every good work

---

[323] *Anbero ed,* " blessing," " prayer of blessing."

join us in Christ: through whom to thee with him and with the Holy Ghost be glory and dominion, both now and ever and world without end. Amen."

In the Catholic rite, the assistant priest now says a long prayer, [324] in which the intercession of many saints, including Egyptians and Ethiopians, is asked:

"And keep them in the right faith, in glory and honour all the days of their life, and endue them with love and peace, which is exalted above all understanding and above all wisdom.

By the intercession and by the supplication which the lady of us all, the holy Mother of God and the immaculate Mary, maketh on our behalf, and by the four luminaries, Michael and Gabriel, Raphael and Uriel, and by the four incorporeal creatures, and the twenty-four priests of heaven, and our holy fathers of exalted memory, the chief of the fathers, Isaac, and Jacob and St. John Baptist, and by the one hundred and forty-four thousand babes, and our fathers, the elders, the apostles, the seventy-two disciples, and St. Mark the Evangelist, apostles and martyrs, the three hundred and eighteen Orthodox who were at Nicea, the one hundred and fifty bishops in the province of Constantinople, the two hundred Ephesians, holy children, St. Stephen, the head of deacons and first martyr, St. George and St. Theodore the Illuminator, and St. Mercury and St. Mennas and St. Auwetos, and St. Mermehnām and St. Kirkōs, and St. Theodore and St. Manādelēwōs, and St. Claudius and St. Philotheus, and St. Basilides, and St. Victor, and St. Abli and St. Esderos, and holy abba Nob, virgin and singular martyr, Eleazar, the warrior, and all the martyrs, and the

---

[324] HANSSENS, *ibid.* The prayer, which is not given by Brightman, has been taken from Mercer (*op. cit.* pp. 369-370), but the list of saints in the Catholic liturgy is curtailed. It is not given by Hailù (*op. cit.*).

chief of the fathers, the elect father of Abib and righteous father Antony and our holy fathers the three Macarii and our father abba John Heḍīr, and our father abba Besōi and our father abba John Kamā, and righteous abba Būl, and our father abba Pachomius, and our father abba Barsūmā, and our father abba Sinōdā, and our father St. Arsenius, and St. Theodore, son of Pachomius, and our father abba Agtōn, and our father Palmān, our father abba Kīrōs, and our fathers abba Sanael, Gedmāwī, and our Roman fathers, Maximus and Demetrius, the strong, and holy abba Moses the black, forty-nine martyrs and all those who wear the cross, righteous and warriors, martyrs and the elect, angels and the angel of this blessed day; their blessing, and the intercessions of their long-suffering and the grace of their help, world without end. Amen."

Then the priest begins the blessing of the dismissal with the following prayer: "O peaceful king of peace, Jesus Christ thy peace, give us and confirm unto us our meekness, and forgive us our sins and make us worthy that we may go out and come into our homes in peace."

The deacon gives the monition: "Bow down your heads before the Lord our God, that by the hand of the acting priest he may bless us."

The people respond: "Amen. The Lord bless us and pardon us."

The priest, blessing the people with the sign of the cross, says: "O Lord save thy people and bless † thine heritage, govern them and lift them up for ever, and keep thine holy Church which thou hast purchased and ransomed with the precious blood of thine only Son, our Lord and our God and our Saviour Jesus Christ, which thou hast called (to be) a congregation for kings and for princes, for a pure generation and for a holy people."

Then, standing at the door of the sanctuary, he adds:
"Ye who are come, and ye who are gone away, and ye who
have prayed in this holy church, who have fed upon the
blessed body and precious blood of our Lord Jesus Christ,
which is medicine for your sins which ye have committed
wittingly or unwittingly, in charity which is transitory have
mercy upon you, and in the future be ye crucified in this
his body, the body divine, and in this his blood, the blood
of law; and the oblation of Jesus Christ the Son of the God
of Sabaoth, begotten of Mary, immaculate in virginity, pure
for ever and ever."

When the priest [325] has finished the cleansing of the
paten and chalice, he blesses with his hand the whole
company of the faithful, after which he blesses each order
separately, from the priests down to the women.

The people in the meanwhile sing a chant.

The deacon [326] says: "Go in peace," and the celebrant
again gives the salutation: "The Lord be with you all."

The people respond: "And with thy spirit," and the
priest continues: "The Lord bless us his servants in peace.
Be it unto us for forgiveness that we have received thy body
and blood. Suffer us by the Spirit to tread on all the power
of the enemy. The blessing of thy holy hand which is full
of mercy, even that we all hope for. Remove from us every
work of evil; unite to us every work of good. Blessed be
he who hath given us his holy body and precious blood.
Grace have we received and life have we found by the
power of the cross of Jesus Christ. To thee, O Lord, do

[325] HANSSENS, op. cit., p. 406.
[326] In the Monophysite rite, the deacon says "Go in peace" *after*
the final prayer. BRIGHTMAN, op. cit., p. 244. This seems also to be
the usage in the Catholic rite. *La Santa Messa in rito Alessandrino-Etiopico*, p. 19. Fr. Hailù (op. cit., p. 63), however, gives it before the prayer.

we give thanks, after taking of the grace which is from the Holy Ghost."

At a solemn liturgy, blessed bread [327] is distributed by the assistant priest, and the following prayer is said: "O Lord our God and our Creator, who givest good and food to all flesh, thou art he that giveth blessing to thy servants that fear thy holy name: stretch forth thine holy right hand to-day also in this hour, and bless † this bread upon mine hand, and let thy blessing and thy goodness be upon it, and let it be now to everyone that taketh of it salvation and medicine to the soul, strength and power to the flesh: the food that thou hast given us for thanksgiving is thine and that we may praise thy kingdom, Holy Trinity, O Father and Son and Holy Ghost. O Lord, let thy blessing be upon this bread and upon him that giveth and upon him that taketh of it and upon them that minister it in thy fear. Glory be to the Father and to the Son and to the Holy Ghost, both now and ever and world without end."

A final prayer "May the most high Lord bless us [three times]; and may he show us his face," etc. is given in *Liturgia-Etiopi*. [328]

Alternative Anaphoras [329]

As we have seen, the Ethiopic rite had fourteen anaphoras, which were used by Catholics and dissidents alike, and that the new missal, published by the Vatican press in 1945, added a further three anaphoras.

Thus the fourth is now the Anaphora of our Lady Mary,

---

[327] *Baracat, aulōgyā.*

[328] p. 69.

[329] The description of the anaphoras is taken from HARDEN, *The Anaphoras of the Ethiopic Liturgy*, pp. 19-26.

the Mother of God, which Abba George composed. The sixth is the Anaphora of James the brother of the Lord, and the seventh the Anaphora of our father Mark the evangelist, patriarch of Alexandria.

The missal of Asmara (1913) had one fixed form for the words of institution and the epiclesis, which was used in all the anaphoras, but the new book has reverted to the traditional practice of each anaphora having its own.

The following order is taken from the missal of Asmara, but the missal recently published in Rome (1945) has nearly the same order with the three additional anaphoras [330] cited above:

a) "Of our Fathers, the Holy Apostles." The normal liturgy, which has been already described.

b) "Of our Lord and God." An anaphora that follows a farced and expanded version of Hippolytus, as it is found in the *Testament* [331] of our Lord. The Ethiopic version is generally bound up with the *Sinodos*.

In one manuscript, [332] the anaphora is called " The Book of the Covenant which our Lord Jesus Christ spake to his apostles before his ascension after his resurrection from the dead."

After an exhortation by the deacon ("Let your hearts be in heaven"), the people respond, and the deacon gives a long series of monitions, which end with "Lift up your hearts" and a kind of invitation ("Let us draw nigh to the salvation of life," etc.).

Then, in reply to the priest, the people answer: "It is

---

[330] The 4th, 6th and 7th anaphoras in the new missal are described after those found in the Asmara missal.

[331] διαθήκη, more correctly " will" or " testament." It often stands also for " covenant", in addition to the word συνθήκη.

[332] Monophysite. *Orient.* 545.

meet and right," and the deacon [333] exclaims: "That which is holy among the holy;" while the people recite: "Holy, holy, holy," etc.

The words of institution are unusual, and for the consecration of the chalice the formula [334] changes into the second person.

c) "*Of our Lady, Mary the Virgin,*" which has the title: "The Eucharistic Thanksgiving of our Lady the holy Virgin Mary, Mother of God, which Abba Cyriacos, [335] bishop of the city of Behnesa, composed."

"This is in some respects the strangest of all," says Harden, [336] although "the order of parts does not differ from the normal," except in the omission of the oblation and the "pilot of the soul." Cyriacos promises to set forth Mary's praises *with brevity,* but he can hardly be said to carry out this intention.

After an ascription of holiness to the Trinity, the first part of this section is in praise of the Virgin, who is seen as typified in the lives of Old Testament characters, and also as the source of all Christian graces.

Then follows a discussion concerning the nature of the deity, and a defence of the doctrine of the Trinity against the Jews and Moslems.

This leads up to the "prayer of faith," after which there is a return to a consideration of the wonderful nature of the Virgin and her child-bearing, ending with the words:

---

[333] HANSSENS, *op. cit.,* p. 338, " Priest;" HARDEN *op. cit.,* p. 62.

[334] Cf. James of Sarug.

[335] *Heriacus* in the Latin translation (Tip. Pol. Vat., 1944) made in preparation for the new missal. Certain passages in this anaphora may be omitted at the discretion of the celebrant (Vatican missal, 1945).

[336] *Op. cit.,* p. 20.

"now will we praise the Son by saying, Holy, holy, holy, etc."

The reference to Islam is a mark of lateness of origin, as is also the mention of incense after the *sanctus*.

The monitions of the deacon are not given before the anaphora, but before communion.

Between the anamnesis and the epiclesis, some manuscripts have inserted the rubric: "Here the deacon rejoiceth," which means literally makes a "hissing" or "chuckling" noise.

d) "Of John, Son of Thunder." The parts of this anaphora are normal, although in a different order.

The *sanctus* is early, and the intercession deferred until immediately before the words of institution.

The commemoration of the incarnation, life, passion, death and burial which follows the *sanctus* is of considerable length.

The diaconal monition ("Look to the East") is succeeded by worship addressed to our Lord under many extravagant titles, with further references to the gospel miracles.

The anaphora has two oblations. The first comes after "Ye who sit, arise" and before the intercession; while the second is in the normal place, but includes an unusual reference to the saints of the Old and New Testaments, along with whom it is offered.

e) "Of three hundred and eighteen Orthodox" [337] (Fathers of Nicea). The order of the parts is quite exceptional.

The monitions of the deacon are not in their customary order, and a new one has been inserted at the end of the first part of the anaphora: "Upward be your thoughts."

---

[337] Certain passages in the Anaphoras of St. John and the 318 Orthodox may be omitted in the new Catholic missal at the discretion of the celebrant.

The *sanctus* and the "answer ye" of the deacon are both omitted.

The intercession precedes the institution, and is separated from it by a commemoration of the incarnation, works and preaching of our Lord.

The anaphora show signs of a late authorship. Thus, part of the preface is borrowed from St. John Chrysostom; the allusion in the preface to the "great sea where fire and water are mingled together" seems a late touch; as also does the curious passage in which our Lord is said to have "answered his disciples concerning his essence."

Later in the anaphora, there is a strange reference to the cry to Adam and all his sons, when our Lord was in the tomb.

f) *"Of Athanasius."* [338]   This anaphora has obvious tokens of very late origin.

Though it bears the name of Athanasius, it is better described in its opening words: "the Keddase of the holy Christian Sabbath."

The sabbath is glorified throughout the anaphora, and is finally personified, so that it is asked to "pray for us and plead for us with the Lord our God."

The lengthening of the deacon's exclamations ("Ye who sit, arise in the fear of God;" "Let us look to the east in the fear of God") also suggests lateness of origin; while the style everywhere is forced and rhetorical.

The order of the various parts follows in the main the normal anaphora, but the intercession does not come at the beginning, and is deferred until after the *sanctus*.

There is no oblation in the usual place, although as in

---

[338] Certain passages in this Anaphora may be omitted in the new Catholic missal at the discretion of the celebrant.

Coptic St. Cyril there is a formula of oblation before the institution.

The diaconal monition: "Answer ye" is omitted, and the anamnesis is also wanting.

g) "*Of St. Basil.*" The order in this anaphora is altogether the same as in Coptic St. Basil, but the Catholics formerly changed the words of institution to those common throughout the Ethiopic rite.

h) "*Of Gregory of Nyssa*" or "*the Brother of Basil.*"

The Monophysites speak of the anaphora of "St. Gregory of Alexandria."

Here also are late features. The deacon's exclamation: "Let us attend" has been lengthened to "Let us attend to the beauty of the glory of God."

The intercession comes after the institution, though the anaphora begins with a proclamation by the deacon asking for the prayers of the people.

The most evident sign of lateness is the insertion after the institution of the five-fold "cycle" of hosanna.

There appears to be a double epiclesis, the first preceding the institution, and the second following the intercession.

The parts omitted are the *sanctus* (although it is implied in "Answer ye"), oblation, Lord's prayer, and inclination.

i) "*Of Epiphanius.*" The only noteworthy feature in this anaphora is the number of omissions, although it must not be inferred from this that they are therefore omitted in the liturgy, as the missing parts would be supplied from the anaphora of the Apostles.

The omission of the *sanctus* with the diaconal "Answer ye" is remarkable, and is only found in one other anaphora. [339]

[339] Of 318 Orthodox.

The oblation and "Pray ye" introducing the Lord's prayer are also missing from the text.

The passage of the epiclesis [340] is similar to that in the anaphora of the Apostles.

j) "*Of John Chrysostom.*" The anaphora begins with an exclamation of the deacon, which carries on the thought of the *Sursum Corda.*

The opening section of the preface is of considerable length, speaking of the eternity of the divine essence, and of God's goodness to man as shown in the incarnation.

The order of the parts is normal save for two exceptions, the commemoration of the passion follows, not precedes, the institution; while all expression of oblation is wanting.

Diaconal warnings against unworthy reception occur before the Lord's prayer.

The only omission is the final "imposition of the hand."

k) "*Of Cyril, Patriarch of Alexandria.*" The *sanctus* is after the first section of the thanksgiving, and it is followed by the commemoration of the incarnation, passion, etc.

The intercession comes immediately before the institution, being itself preceded by a form of oblation.

The anamnesis is wanting, as also are the diaconal "Let us attend" and the "imposition of the hand."

The reference to "Melos, the sword of fire" is a mark of lateness of origin, as are the passages which immediately precede and follow the exclamatory "Pray ye."

This anaphora and also St. Gregory of Nyssa have a certain connection with St. Basil, as after the "pilot of the soul" they both refer the celebrant for the whole or part of the concluding portion of the liturgy to that anaphora.

---

[340] Gregory DIX, *Treatise on the Apostolic Tradition.* Introduction, p. L.

l) "Of Dionysius, Patriarch of Great Alexandria."

The Monophysites name this anaphora after the heretical patriarch Dioscorus. The new missal has discarded the name "Dionysius," for which there is no justification, and speaks of "the Anaphora with which the book of Oblation is ended."

m) "Of Mount Olivet and Mount Epagomenus." This anaphora is ascribed by the Monophysites to James of Sarug.

Harden [341] considers this liturgy to be the most interesting of all. There are certainly indications of late origin, but it was composed by someone who could enter into the spirit of the ancient formulas.

The parts run on normal lines, and no feature is wanting except the diaconal "Answer ye" after the *sanctus*, which may be an accidental omission, and the anamnesis.

In the rite used by the dissidents, the narrative [342] of the institution is of the nature of a prayer, in which our Lord is asked to sanctify the bread and wine. This possibly may suggest an early date, although the long passage about the four evangelists, inserted before the institution, seems to be a mark of late origin; as also is the obscure reference to "Melos, the terrifying sword of fire;" the passage about three blasts of the trumpet; and the reference to the blessed Virgin. [343]

The exclamation of the deacon—"Be it in heaven"—, which follows the institution, asks that the bread and wine may be the body and blood of Christ in heaven.

[341] *Op cit.*, p. 24.

[342] As we have seen, the new Catholic missal (1945) has borrowed the words of institution from the Anaphora of the Apostles.

[343] The blessed Virgin is described as " our Lady and the glory of our race," to which are added the words: " Thou didst say unto her, who so maketh memorial of thee, and calleth on thy name, shall live in life eternal." HARDEN, *op. cit.*, p. 125.

The anamnesis is wanting.

n) "*Of Gregory the Armenian.*" This is one of the shortest and probably also one of the earliest anaphoras.

The reference in the first section of the thanksgiving to making the sign of the cross may easily be a later addition.

The various parts of the anaphora, so far as they are present, follow one another in the normal order, except that the intercession immediately precedes and is closely joined to the institution.

This institution is not unlike that in the anaphora of Serapion. Here, we find the words "In the same night in which he was betrayed" following almost immediately after "Look to the East," although there is a long passage, including the intercession, between them and the actual words of institution.

"Let us attend" and the "imposition of the hand" are not found in the anaphora, while, except in a very rudimentary form, there is no commemoration of the passion.

In the Monophysite rite, the epiclesis also is wanting.

Three Anaphoras added to the Missal

a) "*Of our Lady Mary, Mother of God, composed by Abba George.*" This second anaphora of our Lady has been placed fourth in the new Catholic missal (1945).

The devotion to our Lady expressed in it points to late authorship, and after the *sanctus* Mary is hailed as the counterpart of the leading figures in the Old and New Testaments.

There is an invocation to the blessed Virgin in the epiclesis: "And now therefore, O Virgin, intercede with thy Son, that he may visit our community, and bless our congregation, and sanctify our souls and bodies."

The "imposition of the hand" is wanting.

b) "*Of James the Brother of the Lord.*" The sixth anaphora in the missal is normal in all its parts, although inordinately long.

The Monophysite book in the institution has the words: "he mingled blood and wine with water."

c) "*Of our Father Mark the Evangelist, Patriarch of Alexandria.*" The seventh anaphora is also normal in all its parts.

The institution says: "he received the chalice mixed with wine and water."

The *second Anaphora of St. Cyril,* which is found in the appendix of the Latin translation made for the new missal, has expressions and words which are either faulty or obscure, while it is wanting in the prayer of the fraction, Lord's prayer, embolism, inclination, pilot of the soul, and imposition of the hand.

BIBLIOGRAPHY

1. *Abyssinia and its Apostle*. Lady HERBERT. London: Burns, Oates & Co.

2. *Africa's Last Empire*. Through Abyssinia to Lake Tana and the Country of the Falesha. Hermann NORDEN. London: H. F. & G. Witherby.

3. *The Anaphoras of the Ethiopic Liturgy*. J. M. HARDEN. London: S. P. C. K. New York & Toronto: The Macmillan Co. 1928.

4. *The Treatise on the Apostolic Tradition of St. Hippolytus of Rome*. Edited by Gregory Dix. London: S. P. C. K. 1937.

5. *Computo per il Calendario Abissino Confrontato col Computo Latino*. Mauro DA LEONESSA, Cappuccino. Asmara: Tipografia Francescana (Missione Cattolica). 1918.

6. *The Ethiopic Liturgy*. Its Sources, Development and Present Form. Samuel A. B. MERCER. The Young Churchman Company. London: A. B. Mowbray & Co. 1915.

7. *Ethiopie*. H. LERCLERCQ, *Dictionnaire d'Archéologie Chrétienne et de Liturgie*. T. V., col. 584-624.

8. *Ethiopie (Eglise d')*. E. COULBEAUX. *Dictionnaire de Théologie Catholique*. T. V, col. 922-969. Paris: Letouzey. 1913.

9. *George of Lydda*. The Patron Saint of England. A Study of the Cultus of St. George in Ethiopia. E. A. WALLIS BUDGE. London: Luzac & Co. 1930.

10. *Histoire Politique et Religieuse d'Abyssinie*. Depuis les temps les plus reculés jusqu'à l'avènement de Menelick II. J. B. COULBEAUX. T. I, II, III. Editeur: Geuthner. Paris. 1929.

11. *De Indumentis sacris ritus Aethiopici. De Verbis Consecrationis apud Aethiopes*. Abba Tecle Mariam SEMHARAY SELAM. Romae ex Schola Typographica, Pio X. 1930.

12. An *Introduction to Ethiopic Christian Literature*. J. M. HARDEN. London: S. P. C. K. New York & Toronto: The Macmillan Co. 1926.

13. *Liturgia-Etiopi*. Revisione e Ristampa del "Messale Etiopico." Plenaria Seconda. Allegato I. *Testo Latino dell'Ordinario*

della Messa con l'Anafora degli Apostoli. Tipografia Poliglotta Vaticana, 1944.

14. *Liturgia-Etiopi.* Revisione e Ristampa del "Messale Etiopico." Plenaria Seconda. Allegato II. *Testo Latino di 17 Anafore Etiopiche.* Tipografia Poliglotta Vaticana. 1944.

15. *La Messa Etiopica detta "degli Apostoli."* A. Pietros HAILÙ. Roma: Via Pompeo Magno 21. 1946.

16. Il *Monachismo Cattolico in Etiopia.* Abate D. Angelo SAVASTANO. A. Macioce e Pisani - Isola del Liri. 1943.

17. *The Primitive Consecration Prayer.* W. H. FRERE. Alcuin Club. Prayer Book Revision Pamphlets. VIII. London: A. R. Mowbray & Co.

18. *The Romance of the Portuguese in Abyssinia.* Charles F. Rey. H. F. & G. Witherby.

19. Book of the *Saints of the Ethiopian Church.* E. A. WALLIS BUDGE. 4 vols. Cambridge University Press. 1928.

20. *De SS. Sacramentis secundum ritum Aethiopicum.* Abba Tecle Mariam SEMHARAY SELAM. Romae ex Schola Typographica Pio X. 1931.

21. *Modo facile di seguire la Santa Messa in Rito Alessandrino-Etiopico.* Roma: Assoc. Catt. It. "Pro Oriente Cristiano." 1938.

22. *Testi di Diritto Antichi e Moderni riguardanti gli Etiopi.* Mauro DA LEONESSA. Fonti. Fascicolo V. Codificazione Canonica Orientale. Tipografia Poliglotta Vaticana. 1931.

23. *Testi di Diritto Antichi Riguardanti gli Etiopi.* Fonti. Fascicolo VI. Codificazione Canonica Orientale. Tipografia Poliglotta Vaticana. 1932.

24. *Vers la Lumière. Le Bienheureux Abba Ghebre-Michel.* Prêtre de la Mission, martyrisé en Ethiopie. J. B. COULBEAUX 2ᵉ édition. Paris: Librairie René Haton.

ACKNOWLEDGEMENTS

1. Mgr. David Mathew, titular Archbishop of Apamea and Apostolic Delegate to Africa.

2. Mgr. Giuseppe Moioli, *Minutante* of the Special Commission for the Liturgy in the Sacred Congregation for the Oriental Church.

3. Abba Tecle Mariam Semharay Selam, late Spiritual Director of the Collegio Pontificio Etiopico, Vatican City.

4. Fr. Camillo da Torino, O. F. M. Cap., late Rector of the Collegio Pontificio Etiopico, Vatican City.

5. Fr. Donato da Welle, O. F. M. Cap., formerly of the Collegio Pontificio Etiopico, Vatican City.

6. Dom Fidele Andikiel, S. Ord. Cist. (Ethiopic rite), Badia di Valviciolo, Sermoneta.

7. Fr. Giovanni M. Hanssens, S. J., Professor of the Gregorian University, Rome, and Consultor of the Sacred Congregation for the Oriental Church.

INDEX OF NAMES AND PLACES

George, Arian bishop, 501.
Germanus of Constantinople, St, 217-218.
Ghali, 355.
Ghazir, 244.
Ghebra-Meskel, king of Ethiopia, 502-504.
Glabas, Isidore, 33.
Gladios, king of Ethiopia, 513-514, 558.
Glai, Gabriel, 225-226.
Glastonbury, 373.
Gondar, 522, 523, 526, 528, 536.
Gordillo, Maurice, 33.
Gorgora, 517.
Gouraud, general, 237.
Gran, 513.
Gregory the Great (Dialogus), St. 24, 79, 105.
Gregory IX, Pope, 69-70, 508.
Gregory XIII, Pope, 44, 227, 274.
Gregory XV, Pope, 44.
Gregory XVI, Pope, 46, 523, 525.
Gregory bar Hebraeus, 66, 67, 70, 81-82, 93, 96, 99, 104, 106, 118, 121, 125, 204, 224.
Gregory of Nareg, 30.
Gregory of Nyssa, St, 21-22.
Gregory of Tours, St., 91.
Gregory III, Jacobite patriarch, 72, 73.
Gregory, Mar, Jacobite bishop of Jerusalem, 321.
Gregory, Mar, Jacobite bishop in Malabar, 324.
Grottaferrata, 54.
Gryphon, 225.
Guala, 525.
Gubran, Mgr, Coptic patriarchal vicar, 414.
Guenda-Guende, 525, 541.

Guéranger, Dom Prosper, 4, 18, 20, 38-39, 40.

Habbakuk, 507.
Habib Abu Raita, Jacobite theologian, 218.
Habib, John, Maronite archbishop, 241.
Hajudorog, 14, 16.
Hanna, Shenoudah, 369.
Hanssens, Fr. John, 448, 454, 462, 556, 573, 613, 625.
Harbé, Keddus, king of Ethiopia, 506.
Harden, J. M., 620, 648.
d'Hautpoult, General de Beaufort, 236.
Heiling, Peter, 540.
Helen, St, 537.
Helena, queen of Ethiopia, 512.
Heliopolis, 378, 379.
Henry I, king of Cyprus, 43.
Henry, prince of Portugal, 514.
Heraclius, emperor, 213, 214, 216, 403.
Heras, convent of, 242.
Hilarion, St, 342.
Hindîyé, Idjaine, see Aggemi, Anna.
Hindo, Mgr Paul, 119.
Hippolytus, 3, 4, 362, 615.
Hobaich, Joseph, 234-235, 242.
Honorius I, Pope, 214-215, 216.
Honorius III, Pope, 43, 350.
Hormisdas, Pope, 147, 212.

Ibo, 501.
Ignatius, St, of Antioch, 62.
Ignatius Loyola, St, 514.
Ignatius III, patriarch of Antioch, 70.
Ignatius V, patriarch of Antioch, 70, 82.

INDEX OF THE FIRST VOLUME

ILLUSTRATIONS